W9-AQF-525

PROGRAMMING LANGUAGES

McGraw-Hill Computer Science Series

Ahuja: Design and Analysis of Computer Communication Networks
Barbacci and Siewiorek: The Design and Analysis of Instruction Set Processors
Ceri and Pelagatti: Distributed Databases: Principles and Systems
Debry: Communicating with Display Terminals
Donovan: Systems Programming
Filman and Friedman: Coordinated Computing: Tools and Techniques for Distributed Software
Givone: Introduction to Switching Circuit Theory
Goodman and Hedetniemi: Introduction to the Design and Analysis of Algorithms
Katzan: Microprogramming Primer
Keller: A First Course in Computer Programming Using Pascal
Kohavi: Switching and Finite Automata Theory
Liu: Elements of Discrete Mathematics
Liu: Introduction to Combinatorial Mathematics
MacEwen: Introduction to Computer Systems: Using the PDP-11 and Pascal
Madnick and Donovan: Operating Systems
Manna: Mathematical Theory of Computation
Newman and Sproull: Principles of Interactive Computer Graphics
Payne: Introduction to Simulation: Programming Techniques and Methods of Analysis
Révész: Introduction to Formal Languages
Rice: Matrix Computations and Mathematical Software
Salton and McGill: Introduction to Modern Information Retrieval
Shooman: Software Engineering: Design, Reliability, and Management
Tremblay and Bunt: An Introduction to Computer Science: An Algorithmic Approach
Tremblay and Bunt: An Introduction to Computer Science: An Algorithmic Approach, Short Edition
Tremblay and Manohar: Discrete Mathematical Structures with Applications to Computer Science
Tremblay and Sorenson: An Introduction to Data Structures with Applications
Tremblay and Sorenson: The Theory and Practice of Compiler Writing
Tucker: Programming Languages
Wiederhold: Database Design
Wulf, Levin, and Harbison: Hydra/C.mmp: An Experimental Computer System

McGraw-Hill Series in Computer Organization and Architecture

Bell and Newell: Computer Structures: Readings and Examples
Cavanagh: Digital Computer Arithmetic: Design and Implementation
Gear: Computer Organization and Programming: With an Emphasis on Personal Computers
Hamacher, Vranesic, and Zaky: Computer Organization
Hayes: Computer Architecture and Organization
Hayes: Digital System Design and Microprocessors
Hwang and Briggs: Computer Architecture and Parallel Processing
Kogge: The Architecture of Pipelined Computers
Siewiorek, Bell, and Newell: Computer Structures: Principles and Examples
Stone: Introduction to Computer Organization and Data Structures
Stone and Siewiorek: Introduction to Computer Organization and Data Structures: PDP-11 Edition

PROGRAMMING LANGUAGES

SECOND EDITION

Allen B. Tucker, Jr.
Colgate University

McGraw-Hill Publishing Company
New York St. Louis San Francisco Auckland Bogotá
Caracas Hamburg Lisbon London Madrid Mexico Milan
Montreal New Delhi Oklahoma City Paris San Juan
São Paulo Singapore Sydney Tokyo Toronto

This book was set in Times Roman by Publishers Phototype International, Inc.
The editors were Eric M. Munson, Kaye Pace, Ellen W. MacElree, and Susan Hazlett;
the production supervisor was Charles Hess.
New drawings were done by J & R Services, Inc.

PROGRAMMING LANGUAGES

5 6 7 8 9 0 BRBBRB 89

ISBN 0-07-065416-6

Library of Congress Cataloging in Publication Data

Tucker, Allen B.
Programming languages.

(McGraw-Hill computer science series)
Includes bibliographies and index.
1. Programming languages (Electronic computers)
I. Title. II. Series.
QA76.7.T8 1986 001.64'24 84-28941
ISBN 0-07-065416-6

To Maida

CONTENTS

PREFACE

Since publication of the first edition of this text in 1977, dramatic changes have taken place in the field of programming languages. The study of programming languages has changed as well. In this revision, we hope to have captured both the spirit and the substance of these changes.

This edition has two major parts. One part contains a systematic study of eleven major programming languages (Ada, APL, C, COBOL, FORTRAN, LISP, Modula-2, Pascal, PL/I, PROLOG, and SNOBOL) in five distinct programming application areas (scientific, data processing, text processing, artificial intelligence, and systems programming). The second part covers three topical areas (syntax, semantics, and pragmatics) in programming language design and implementation. The two parts are interwoven as shown in the table of contents.

This organization provides a text for a one-semester programming languages course with several alternative approaches, depending upon the students' prior background and the objectives of the course. My own experience is that *three* of the ten language chapters can be covered in one semester, along with the three language design chapters (6, 10, and 15). The major variances from one semester to the next, and from one school to the next, will be in the particular choice of languages covered.

The three language groupings suggested by the chapter ordering (2–5, 7–9, and 11–14) suggest that *one* language from each group be chosen. The first group contains traditional languages: Pascal, FORTRAN, COBOL, and PL/I. The student will already know one of these and should expect to gain a working familiarity with one other. The second group represents a more specialized and stylistically diverse collection: SNOBOL, APL, and LISP. The third group represents more contemporary language concepts and trends: PROLOG, C, Ada and Modula-2.

Our method of developing a working knowledge of three *diverse* languages in one semester relies on the use of "case study" problems, which are representatives of five different areas of programming applications.

Case study	Problem	Application area
1	Matrix inversion	Scientific
2	Employee file maintenance	Data processing
3	Text formatter	Text processing
4	Missionaries and cannibals	Artificial intelligence
5	Job scheduler	Systems programming

These are fully described in Appendixes A–E.

After a thorough introduction to a particular language, each chapter ends with a fully developed program, which exercises that language with one or two of the above case study problems. Students are encouraged to apply their knowledge by developing solutions to short exercises and other case study problems, including one that they design themselves.

To aid readers in exercising these programs, a 5 1/4-inch diskette, compatible with IBM PC DOS or Microsoft (MS) DOS, containing complete ASCII listings of the example and case study programs in this book, is available along with an Instructor's Manual. The latter also contains instructions on how to run the programs on a microcomputer (IBM PC or similar micro) or a VAX, and answers to selected exercises throughout the book. Of course, the student is expected to obtain access to the various compilers as appropriate to his or her particular language interests and the requirements of the course. We have run the case study programs on an IBM PC. We have also used the Digital VAX and the IBM mainframe to run several of the case study programs. To obtain copies of this diskette and Instructor's Manuals, contact your local McGraw-Hill representative.

The three language design chapters are placed at appropriate intervals in the text, rather than grouped all together. The motivation here is that this material can be covered in lectures while students are completing a case study problem in the laboratory. End-of-chapter exercises in these chapters do not require laboratory work and can be more regularly managed.

Also included in this organization is a common format for the ten language chapters. This encourages more direct comparisons to be made and, together with the common case study programs, provides a consistent framework for language comparisons to be made. Our basis for language comparison is substantially revised from the one used in the first edition. It is more straightforward and has the following nine criteria.

1 Expressivity	**6** Portability
2 Well-definedness	**7** Efficiency
3 Data types and structures	**8** Pedagogy
4 Modularity	**9** Generality
5 Input-output facilities	

Each language chapter concludes with an evaluation of that language, using the case study program and these criteria as a basis. The final chapter includes a section that compares the ten languages, in application areas where comparisons are valid, using these criteria again.

In addition to containing extensive new material on language design, this second edition differs from the first in other significant ways. New language chapters are added for the artificial intelligence (LISP and PROLOG) and systems programming (C, Ada, and Modula-2) application areas, and two new case studies are added appropriately. The treatment of scientific programming is also enhanced by the addition of Pascal (replacing ALGOL) and APL chapters. The overall effect of these changes is, it is hoped, a more balanced treatment of programming languages across a wider spectrum of applications and programming styles.

This text is intended for use in a senior-graduate level course in programming languages, such as CS-8 in the "ACM Curriculum 78" guidelines. The topics covered in that course outline are covered here in the following way.

ACM CS-8 topic	Section in this text
A Language definition structure	Chapters 1 and 6
B Data types and structures	Sections 2-1 and 2-3 of each language chapter
C Control structures and data flow	Sections 2-5 and 2-7 of each language chapter
D Run-time considerations	Chapters 10 and 15
E Interpretive languages	Chapters 1, 7, 8, and 9
F Lexical analysis and parsing	Chapter 6

In a one-semester course, the topics may be taken in this order or else in the order that they appear in the text. By nature of the text's organization, the individual language chapters can, in fact, be taken in any order.

ACKNOWLEDGMENTS

A textbook of this size and breadth cannot be done without the help and advice of several persons. Colleagues Scott Deerwester and Sergei and Irene Nirenburg deserve thanks for their critical reviews of selected language chapters. Colgate senior Steve Stuart deserves credit for running various case study programs on different compilers, resolving discrepancies, and collecting the execution times needed for language evaluation.

My appreciation also extends to Colgate University for its unusually strong support of computer science, to the MacArthur Foundation for the resources required for preparing this manuscript, to the Colgate Computer Center, and to Syracuse and Clarkson Universities for providing timely access to IBM mainframe computers. The following readers also deserve credit for their critiques of earlier versions of this manuscript: Richard Allen, Richard Andree, Moshe Augenstein, John Beidler, John Johnson, Edward Miranda and Susan Rulon. Of course, any remaining inadequacies in this book are the responsibility of the author.

My family deserves the most credit for their contributions, both tangible and intangible, to this book's development. My wife, Maida, spent hours typing countless pages of prose during the early months of this revision; months when the result was nearly out of sight. She and our children, Jenny and Brian, are the best friends a person could have; I am truly thankful for their constant support and encouragement.

Allen B. Tucker, Jr.

CHAPTER 1

A PERSPECTIVE

The study of programming languages conjoins three different interests: that of the professional programmer, that of the language designer, and that of the language implementer. Moreover, all three of these interests work within the constraints and capabilities provided by a computer organization and the fundamental limitations of computability itself.

The term ''the programmer'' is an amorphous one, in the sense that it camouflages important distinctions among different levels and applications of programming. Clearly the programmer who attends a 12-week COBOL course and then enters the data processing field is different from the programmer who writes a Pascal compiler, or the programmer who designs an artificial intelligence experiment in LISP, or the programmer who combines FORTRAN subroutines to solve a complex engineering problem, or the programmer who develops a multiprocessor operating system in Ada. In this study, we will try to clarify these distinctions by discussing different programming languages in the context of each different application area.

The ''language designer'' is also a somewhat nebulous term. Some languages (like APL and LISP) were designed by a single person with a unique concept, while others (like FORTRAN and COBOL) are the product of several years' development by language design committees.

The ''language implementer'' is that person or group which develops a compiler or interpreter for a language on a particular machine or machine species. Most often, the primary compiler for language Y on machine X is developed by the corporation that manufactures machine X. For example, there are several FORTRAN compilers in use; one developed by IBM for an IBM machine, one developed by DEC for a DEC machine, one by CDC for a CDC machine, and so forth. Software companies also develop compilers, and so do university research groups. For instance, the University of Waterloo develops compilers for FORTRAN and Pascal that are useful in a student programming environment because of their superior diagnostics and compile speed.

There is also a great deal shared among programmers, language designers, and language implementers. Each must understand the needs and constraints that govern the other two activities. By definition, a good language designer *must be* a good programmer. In many instances the designer of a language is also its primary implementer. Needless to say, no effective implementation of a language can be developed unless the implementer has unusual programming and software engineering skills.

1-1 PROGRAMMING LANGUAGES—AN OVERVIEW

There are at least two major ways in which programming languages can be viewed, or classified: by their level and by their principal applications. Moreover, these views are tempered by the historical evolution through which languages drift. Moreover, there are four distinct levels of programming languages, as we see in Figure 1-1.

The "declarative languages" are the most like English in their expressive power and functionality, and thus are the highest level in comparison with the others. They are fundamentally *command* languages, dominated by statements which express "what to do" rather than "how to do it." Examples include statistical languages like SAS and SPSS and database retrieval languages like NATURAL and IMS. These languages are developed with the idea that skilled professionals can more quickly assimilate such a language and use it in their work, without the need for programmers or programming skills.

The "high-level" languages are the most widely used programming languages. Although not fundamentally declarative, these languages allow algorithms to be expressed in a level and style of writing which is easily read and understood by other programmers. Moreover, high-level languages usually have the characteristics of "portability." That is, they are implemented on several machines, so that a program

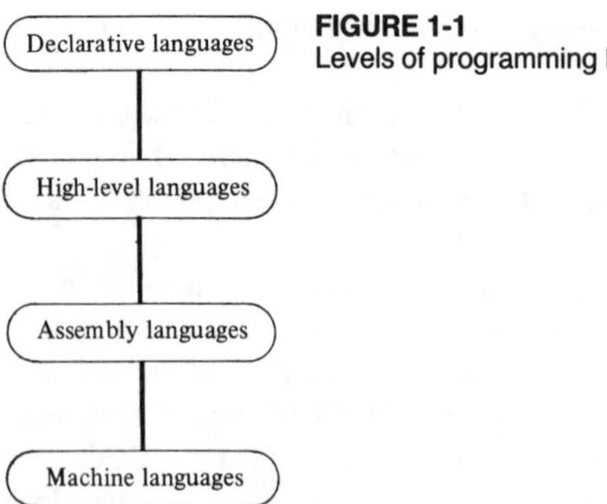

FIGURE 1-1
Levels of programming languages.

may be easily ''ported'' (transferred) from one machine to another without substantial revision. In this sense, they are called ''machine independent.'' Examples of high-level languages are Pascal, APL, and FORTRAN (for scientific applications), COBOL (for data processing applications), SNOBOL (for text processing applications), LISP and PROLOG (for artificial intelligence applications), C and Ada (for systems programming applications), and PL/I (for general-purpose applications). In this book, we confine our study to these types of languages, their design, and their applications.

The ''assembly languages'' and the ''machine languages'' are machine dependent. Each machine species, such as Digital's VAX, has its own distinct machine language and associated assembly language. The assembly language is simply a symbolic representation form for its associated machine language, allowing less tedious programming than the latter. However, a mastery of the underlying machine architecture is necessary for effective programming in either of these language levels.

The following three equivalent program segments expose the basic distinctions between high-level, assembly, and machine languages:

Pascal	Assembly language	Machine language
Z:=W+X*Y	L 3,X	41 3 0C1A4
	M 2,Y	3A 2 0C1A8
	A 3,W	1A 3 0C1A0
	ST 3,Z	50 3 0C1A4

As this example shows, the *lower* the level of language, the *closer* it is to complete comprehension by a particular machine species and the *further* it is from comprehension by an ordinary human. There is also a close kinship (1 to 1 correspondence) between assembly language statements and their encoded machine language forms. The main difference here is that symbols (X, Y, Z, A for ''add,'' M for ''multiply'') are used in assembly language programming, while numeric codes (0C1A4, etc.) are required for comprehension by the machine.

Programming in a high-level language or an assembly language therefore requires some sort of interface with the machine language at the time the program is to be run. In Figure 1-2*a* to 1-2*c*, we exhibit the three most common such interfaces: an ''assembler,'' a ''compiler,'' and an ''interpreter.''

As shown, the assembler interface and the compiler interface each translates the program into an equivalent program in the ''host'' machine's language X as a *separate* step prior to execution. The interpreter, on the other hand, directly executes instructions in the high-level language Y, without a prior processing step.

Compilation is a far more machine-efficient process, in general, than interpretation for most common machine species. This occurs mainly because statements within ''loops'' must be reinterpreted each time they are executed by an interpreter. With a compiler, each statement is interpreted and then translated into machine language, only *once*.

Some languages are mainly interpreted languages, like APL, PROLOG, and LISP.

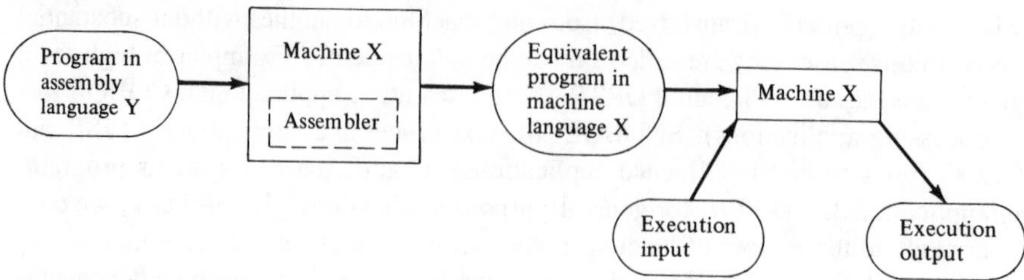

FIGURE 1-2*a*
The assembler interface.

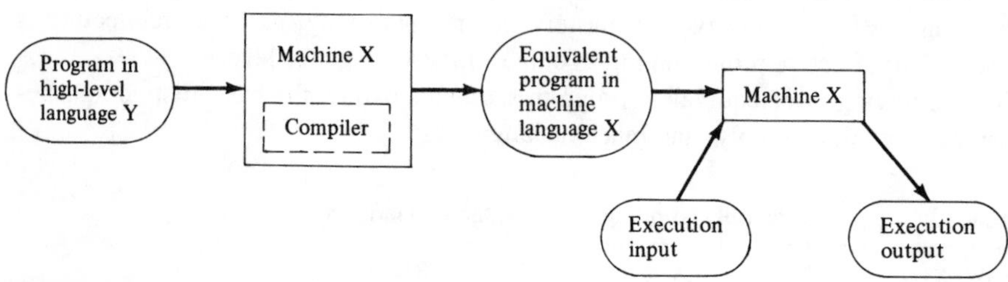

FIGURE 1-2*b*
The compiler interface.

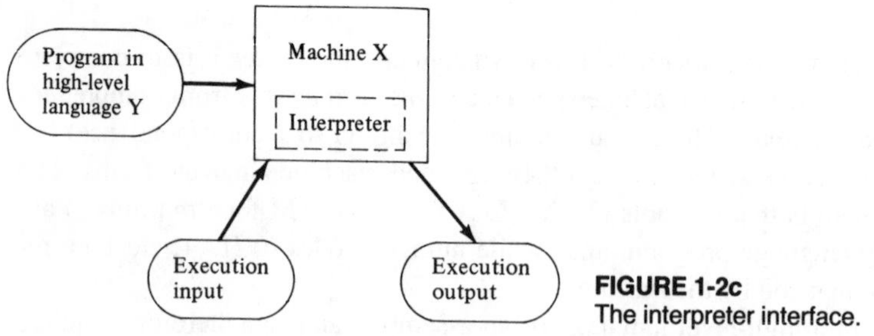

FIGURE 1-2c
The interpreter interface.

The rest of the languages in this book—Pascal, FORTRAN, COBOL, PL/I, SNOBOL, C, Ada, and Modula-2—are usually compiled languages. In some cases, a compiler will be alternately available for an interpreted language (such as LISP), and conversely (such as Bell Laboratories' SNOBOL4 interpreter).

Interpretation is often preferable to compilation in experimental or educational programming environments, where each new run of a program involves a change in the program text itself. The quality of diagnostic and debugging support for interpreted languages is generally better than that of compiled languages, since error messages are tied directly to statements in the original program text.

Moreover, the efficiency advantage that is traditionally enjoyed by compiled languages over interpreted ones may soon be eliminated, due to the evolution of machines whose languages are high-level languages themselves! An example of this is the new LISP machines which have been recently designed by the Symbolics and Xerox Corporations.

1-2 HISTORICAL PERSPECTIVE FOR PROGRAMMING LANGUAGES

The programmer, designer, and implementer of a programming language must understand the historical evolution of languages in order to appreciate why different features are present. For instance, "younger" languages discourage (or prohibit) the use of GO TO statements as inferior control mechanisms, and that is correct in the context of current philosophies of software engineering and structured programming.

But there was a time when the GO TO, combined with the IF, was the *only* available control structure, the programmer had nothing like a WHILE construct or an IF - THEN - ELSE to choose from. Thus, when viewing a language like FORTRAN, which has deep roots in the history of programming languages, one should not shudder upon seeing the old GO TO statement within its repertoire.

More important, history allows us to see the evolution of *families* of programming languages, to see the influence of evolving *computer architectures* and *applications* on language design, and to avoid future design mistakes by learning the lessons of the past. Figure 1-3 is a brief diagram summarizing some of the important high-level language design trends made over the past three decades.

This figure represents only a small sample of all the programming languages. There are well over 100 different programming languages in use today, with names as diverse as AMBIT, BASEBALL, LOGO, and MAD. Many are dialects of the ones shown in Figure 1-3. The ones covered in this text are chosen because of their strong influence and heavy use among programmers, as well as their distinctive design and implementation characteristics. Collectively, they cover most of the important issues that confront the language designer and most of the applications that confront the programmer. For readers who are interested in a broader historical survey of programming languages, we recommend the proceedings of a recent (1981) conference on this topic, edited by Richard Wexelblat.[1]

Figure 1-3 also contains lines connecting various languages. The solid lines depict direct ancestry, while the dashed lines depict strong influence. For instance, we see that FORTRAN I is a direct ancestor of FORTRAN II, while all of FORTRAN, COBOL, ALGOL 60, LISP, SNOBOL, and assembly languages influenced the design of PL/I.

Also several languages in this figure are prefixed by the letters ANS. This means that the American National Standards Institute has adopted that version of the language as a national standard. Once a language is so standardized, the machines which implement that language must conform to all of the standard's specifications, thus encouraging maximum portability of programs from one machine to another. A federal policy not to purchase any machine that does not conform to the standard version of any language that it supports, tends to put "teeth" into the standardization process, since the government is by far the largest single purchaser of computers in the nation.

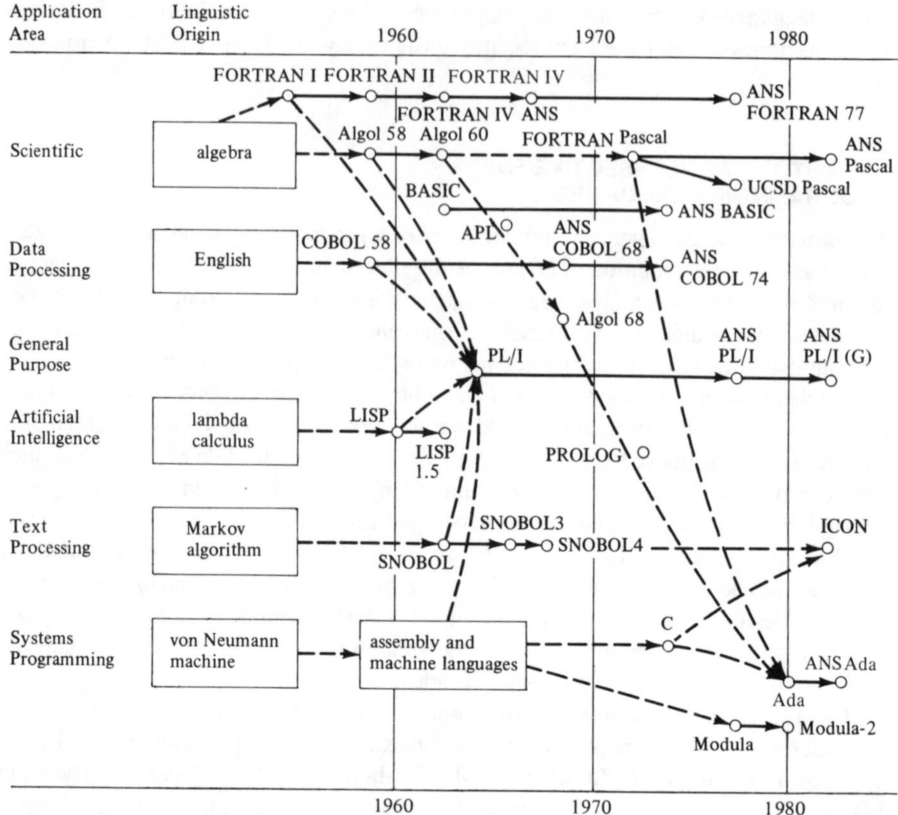

FIGURE 1-3
Historical perspectives for several programming languages.

Finally, Figure 1-3 shows several pre-1960 influences on programming language design. Ordinary algebraic notation, for instance, strongly influenced the design of FORTRAN and ALGOL. On the other hand, English influenced the development of COBOL. Church's lambda calculus[2] provides the foundation for the functional notation of LISP, while the Markov algorithm[3] motivates the pattern-matching style of SNOBOL. The von Neumann computer architecture,[4] which evolved out of the earlier Turing machine,[5] is the basic model for most computer designs of the last three decades. These machines not only influenced the early languages but also provided the operational framework within which systems programming evolved. A more direct discussion of these early models is not permitted by the objectives of this text. However, it is important to point them out here because of their fundamental influence in the evolution of early programming languages on the one hand, and their status at the heart of computability theory on the other.

More to the point, any *algorithm* that can be described in English can be equivalently written as a Turing machine (von Neumann machine), a Markov algorithm, or a recursive function. This assertion, known widely as "Church's Thesis," allows us to write algorithms in a variety of different programming styles (languages) without sacrificing any measure of generality, or programming "power," in the transition.

1-3 APPLICATIONS OF PROGRAMMING LANGUAGES

As Figure 1-3 shows, different programming languages tend to be developed for different *application areas:* principally "scientific," "data processing," "artificial intelligence," "text processing," and "systems programming" applications. In this section, we briefly characterize each of these application areas so that the reader has a clear idea of their main interests and their differences.

Scientific applications can be characterized as those which predominantly manipulate numbers and arrays of numbers, using mathematical and statistical principles as a basis for the algorithms. These algorithms encompass such problems as statistical significance tests, linear programming, regression analysis, and numerical approximations for the solution of differential and integral equations.

Often the amount of data in such problems is relatively small (on the order of a few hundred numbers) and its structure is relatively simple (a one- or two-dimensional array). Yet some scientific problems encounter a *vast* amount of data (as would be retrieved from a satellite or a radar device) and immediately face a problem of "data reduction" before any meaningful and feasible analysis can take place.

The mathematical complexity of scientific problems is also a significant characteristic. Programmers must be well versed in the mathematical principles underlying the algorithms in order to properly diagnose problems or make refinements. Moreover, unstable algorithms—ones whose results may become inaccurate for certain input data values—must be properly handled.

Finally, scientific problems usually require significantly more of a computer's central processor than its input-output devices. That is, most of the computing time will be consumed with arithmetic calculations as opposed to input-output operations; this is often known as "compute bound."

In these fundamental ways, the scientific programming area differs from the other areas described below. Case Study 1, described in Appendix A, exemplifies scientific applications and will be used in later chapters to illustrate and compare the scientific programming features of Pascal, FORTRAN, and APL.

Data processing applications can be characterized as those programming problems whose predominant interest is the creation, maintenance, extraction, and summarization of data in records and files. Normally, data processing is found at the heart of an organizations's management support, and includes the payroll, accounting, billing, inventory, production, and sales data processing functions. The volume of data found in these files is generally large—typically several thousand records per file and several hundred characters of information per record.

By contrast, the amount of arithmetic calculation or other manipulation of data in an individual record is relatively low. A typical data processing program spends most of its computing time doing input-output operations: passing through the records of a file to locate and/or update some of the information on a regular (daily, weekly, or monthly) basis. Thus, the "scarce" resource in a typical data processing task is more likely to be a tape drive or disk space, rather than the central processor.

By their nature, most of the classical data processing applications are "batch" rather than "interactive." That is, they can be scheduled on a regular, predictable basis, and their computer requirements are generally known in advance. For instance, a company's weekly payroll goes through the same basic processing cycle each week, and each of its steps is thus easily scheduled.

There are many exceptions, of course, to this generalization. Organizations have found increasingly that interactive, rather than batch, computing is imperative for certain of their data processing functions. One classical example is the order-entry function, which must respond immediately to each customer's telephone inquiry for its product, whether it be a seat on an airplane flight or a set of spark plugs for a particular automobile engine.

Data processing applications must usually be more concerned with "data integrity" than other areas. Mainly, this involves not only the question of accuracy and reliability but also the question of data security. Data processing programs must at least protect the files from becoming contaminated by inaccurate data. Moreover, they must ensure that sensitive data be accessible only to those who need to have access to it, and no others.

Case Study 2 is an example of a data processing application. It is implemented in the COBOL and PL/I chapters of this book, to illustrate their respective support for data processing programming.

Text processing applications are characterized as those whose principal activity involves the manipulation of natural language text, rather than numbers, as their data. The evolution of modern word processing technology relies principally on text processing algorithms to perform the various formatting and other functions that the typist uses during manuscript preparation. For example, the text for this book was prepared using word processing software on a microcomputer.

Usually the text in such an application is in English, although recent advances in word processing show multilingual capabilities in the form of alternative keyboards and alphabets, as diverse as Arabic and Japanese. Text processing algorithms are distinct from others in the kind of programming challenges they present. This will be apparent in the solutions for Case Study 3, which is a text processing problem. We shall illustrate this problem using the SNOBOL and C languages, since they have strong text processing capabilities.

Artificial intelligence applications are characterized as those programs which are designed principally to emulate intelligent behavior. They include game-playing algorithms such as chess, natural language understanding programs, computer vision, robotics, and "expert systems." In the latter, the computer is programmed to play the role of an expert, such as a medical diagnostician, in carrying out one of his or her tasks (such as diagnosing a disease from a given set of symptoms).

Until recently, artificial intelligence (or AI) has confined its work to the research laboratory, where various pilot experiments modeled different kinds of interesting intelligent behavior. Now, however, many of these experiments have been brought into practical domains, and their effects are shown in such diverse areas as automobile production lines and the monitoring of complex instruments.

Our AI application is given as Case Study 4, and is illustrated in the LISP and PROLOG chapters. LISP has long been the predominant AI programming language, while PROLOG is a newer language designed on the principle of "logic programming."

Systems programming applications involve developing those programs that interface the computer system (the hardware) with the programmer and the operator. These programs include compilers, assemblers, interpreters, input-output routines, program management facilities, and schedulers for utilizing and serving the various resources that comprise the computer system.

Two characteristics that usually distinguish systems programming from other types are (1) the requirement to deal effectively with unpredictable events, or "exceptions" (such as an I/O error), and (2) the need to coordinate the activities of various asynchronously executing programs, or tasks. Typical operating systems support, for example, the simultaneous activity of several independent programs (or on-line users) which, for the most part, have no need for interaction with each other. In the infrequent event that they *do* interact (or conflict in their use of the same file simultaneously), the system must respond gracefully and manage the interaction (or resolve the conflict).

Traditionally, most systems programming has been done with assembly languages. Recently, however, a strong effort has been made to break that trend, and we shall see the results of that effort when we study the languages Ada and Modula-2. We will use them in solving Case Study 5, which is a systems programming application.

Many programming problems do not fall neatly into one or another of these five application areas. For example, the need to effectively apply "database" techniques originated in the data processing area, but now this need is shared by many scientific and artificial intelligence applications that store large volumes of data (e.g., "census data" or "world knowledge data") in an effective way. Boundaries are also fuzzy between artificial intelligence and text processing, as illustrated by such applications as natural language translation. In order for natural language translation to be effective, the program must, at least marginally, be able to understand the text to be translated. Thus, the need for AI in addition to text processing for this problem is apparent.

Nevertheless, we distinguish these five application areas throughout the book because they tend to reasonably represent well-defined and well-developed programming "domains." Moreover, the programming languages used in each of these areas are quite different; we shall see that the needs of different application areas tend to foster different language choices. The five case study problems, their application areas, and the language chapters where they are solved, are thus summarized in Figure 1-4.

In this scheme, each case study is designed to exercise various languages' strengths and expose their weaknesses in that application area which it represents. Moreover, the language pairings for each case study will provide a basis for many interesting and important comparisons. For example, the FORTRAN and APL programs for Case Study 1 will permit a comparison of these two languages for scientific programming.

FIGURE 1-4
THE CASE STUDY PROBLEMS AND THEIR ILLUSTRATIONS

Case study	Application area	Languages (chapters) where illustrated
1 Matrix inversion	Scientific	Pascal (2), FORTRAN (3), APL (8)
2 Employee file maintenance	Data processing	COBOL (4), PL/I (5)
3 Text formatter	Text processing	SNOBOL (7), C (12)
4 Missionaries and cannibals	Artificial intelligence	LISP (9), PROLOG (11)
5 Job scheduler	Systems programming	Ada (13), Modula-2 (14)

Although the titles of the different case studies tend to portray their substance, a complete description of each one is given in Appendixes A through E, respectively. The reader should become familiar with these case study descriptions before reviewing the corresponding programs in the language chapters themselves.

1-4 PROGRAMMING LANGUAGE EVALUATION

A major purpose of this text is to describe and to apply effective criteria for evaluating and comparing programming languages. This area has received only occasional attention until recently, when an extensive set of language evaluation criteria were developed during the Ada design process.[6] There, the criteria were used as a common basis upon which several existing languages could be evaluated as candidates to satisfy the Defense Department's common high-order language requirements. Among the languages considered were Pascal, JOVIAL, and PL/I. As a result of this evaluation, *none* of the languages were found to meet the requirements, and thus the Department of Defense initiated the design of an entirely new language. The result was Ada, and a complete review of this language appears in Chapter 13.

However, the complete set of requirements that were used in the Defense Department's language evaluations are unsuitable as a tool for our use; they are very long, detailed, and cumbersome to work with. Our goal here is rather to define a reasonably small list of characteristics that one generally looks for in a programming language. Each single characteristic should be clearly understood, and all characteristics taken together should define what it is that makes a language "good" in a fairly precise sense. These characteristics also include the different points of view of the programmer, the language designer, and the language implementer. A complete list of the characteristics, which we identify as *criteria* for language evaluation and comparison, is given in Figure 1-5, and they are individually discussed and illustrated in the ensuing paragraphs.

Although these criteria are not exhaustive in their detail, they are sufficiently broad to permit meaningful language evaluation and comparison to be made. That is, if a language is viewed as "excellent" in all (or most) of the nine criteria listed in Figure 1-5, it is likely to be a superior programming language.

By "expressivity," we mean the ability of a language to clearly reflect the meaning intended by the algorithm designer (the programmer). Thus, an "expressive" language permits an utterance to be compactly stated, and encourages the use of statement forms associated with structured programming (usually "while" loops and "if-then-else" statements). Moreover, an expressive language embodies notations which are consistent with those that are commonly used in the field for which the language was designed. Thus, a mathematician using FORTRAN should expect to find its algebraic expressions to be consistent with those used in conventional algebra. Finally, an expressive language is one whose symbols are uniformly used; the meaning of a symbol should not vary unreasonably from one instance in a program to another.

To illustrate, consider the following equivalent statements, from four different languages, which express the calculation of a sum and its subsequent assignment:

```
C = A + B
C := A + B
(SETQ C (+ A B))
ADD A, B GIVING C
```

(The reader may recognize one or more of these statements.) In the first two, the operators (assignment and +) are "infixed" as they are in ordinary algebra, while in the third the operators are "prefixed" and the statement is fully parenthesized. The fourth example bears a resemblance to English in its style and is less compact than the others. Finally, only the symbols = and := distinguish the first example from the second. In the second language, the symbol = is reserved exclusively for use as a comparison operator (as in "**if** A = B **then** . . ."), and thus the unique symbol := distinguishes assignment from comparison. This distinction is handled differently in the first language. Thus, even the relatively simple problem of choosing symbols to denote operations has a direct influence on a language's expressivity.

FIGURE 1-5
NINE CRITERIA FOR LANGUAGE EVALUATION AND COMPARISON

1 Expressivity
2 Well-definedness
3 Data types and structures
4 Modularity
5 Input-output facilities
6 Portability
7 Efficiency
8 Pedagogy
9 Generality

By "well-definedness," we mean that the language's syntax and semantics are free of ambiguity, are internally consistent, and complete. Thus, the implementer of a well-defined language should have, within its definition, a complete specification of all the language's expressive forms and their meanings. The programmer, by the same virtue, should be able to predict exactly the behavior of each expression *before* it is actually executed. Thus, well-defined languages encourage portability and provability.

For example, early versions of some languages were not particularly well defined. FORTRAN, for instance, allowed "DO loops" like the following:

```
DO 10 I = 1
```

to be parsed as an assignment statement, since spaces were not significant and variables (like DO10I) did not have to be declared. More recent versions of FORTRAN have eliminated most of these problems, due to the evolution of formal language description methods and language standardization procedures.

By "data types and structures," we mean the ability for a language to support a variety of data values (integers, reals, strings, pointers, etc.) and nonelementary collections of these. The latter include arrays and records primarily, but do not exclude such dynamic data structures as linked lists, queues, stacks, and trees.

"Modularity" has two aspects: the language's support for subprogramming and the language's extensibility in the sense of allowing programmer-defined operators and data types. By subprogramming, we mean the ability to define independent procedures and functions (subprograms), and communicate via parameters or global variables with the invoking program. Most languages are strong in this latter regard, while few are extensible in the sense described above. In this book, the chapters on Pascal and Ada will illustrate language extensibility.

In evaluating a language's "input-output facilities," we are looking at its support for sequential, indexed, and random access files, as well as its support for database and information retrieval functions. Files generally reside on secondary (direct access or magnetic tape) storage, as opposed to data structures, which generally reside in primary memory. A file is usually too large for all of its records to fit within the memory at once, and thus different programming strategies apply to files than to data structures.

A language which has "portability" is one which is implemented on a variety of computers. That is, its design is relatively "machine independent." Languages which have ANS standard versions are generally more portable than others (but there are exceptions). Also, languages which are well defined tend to be more portable than others. Thus, it is not surprising to find ANS FORTRAN (1977) or ANS COBOL (1974) supported on almost all mainframes because they are standardized. Concurrently, it is not surprising to find LISP or C implemented on a variety of machines because they are well defined, even though they are not standardized.

On the other hand, BASIC is a less portable language than these. Although BASIC is implemented on almost every machine imaginable, each implementation reflects a slightly different *dialect*. For instance, some dialects support one collection of graphics functions, some support another, and some support none at all! Thus, when trying to ''port'' a BASIC program from one machine to another, the programmer must be both aware of the different dialects and willing to rewrite portions of the program accordingly. A truly portable language would not have such dialects, and thus a program can be run on different machines without any changes whatsoever.

An ''efficient'' language is one which permits fast compilation and execution on the machines where it is implemented. Traditionally, FORTRAN and COBOL have been relatively efficient languages in their respective application areas, while PL/I has been an inefficient language by comparison. Our case study programs will illustrate these differences.

As noted above, compilers are generally more efficient than interpreters. For instance, a LISP program which is compiled will execute many times faster than the same program running under an interpreter. Using an interpreter, however, has other advantages during program development. In this case, machine efficiency takes secondary importance to the programmer's own time to complete the program.

Some languages have better ''pedagogy'' than others. That is, they are intrinsically easier to teach and to learn; they have better textbooks; they are implemented in a better program development environment; they are widely known and used by the best programmers in an application area. Some languages, like BASIC and Pascal, were designed *especially* as pedagogical tools. Today, BASIC enjoys preeminence in elementary and high schools that teach programming, while Pascal enjoys the same in university computer science curricula.

''Generality,'' the last of our nine language evaluation criteria, means that a language is useful in a *wide range* of programming applications. For instance, APL has been used in mathematical applications involving matrix algebra and in business applications as well. The most general of all current languages is probably PL/I. It was intentionally designed as a ''general-purpose language,'' and its sheer size attests to that. We shall see in Chapter 5 some of the advantages and disadvantages that one inherits when using a general-purpose language like PL/I. Most other languages are designed for a narrower purpose and audience.

Thus, these nine criteria will allow us to evaluate each language in this text by a uniform scale. Admittedly, they are not all as quantifiable and conclusive as the efficiency criterion, which can be measured in nanoseconds. Yet they provide a substantially more probing basis than ''Well, I use language X because I've *always* used it'' provides. Although we are not expecting here to change many minds about what programming languages are the best, we will hopefully encourage readers to be reasonably circumspect and analytical about making good language choices.

1-5 PROGRAMMING LANGUAGE DESIGN

Many of the language evaluation criteria presented above reflect the interests of the programmer, while others reflect those of the designer. Programming language design comprises (and compromises) knowledge from many fields, especially computer architecture, formal languages, automata theory, and linguistics. Because the study of programming languages is undertaken by those who will participate in the design of future languages, we pay special attention to the basic principles of language design in this text. Placed selectively among the individual language chapters are three "language design" chapters, as follows:

Chapter 6. Language Design: Syntax
Chapter 10. Language Design: Semantics
Chapter 15. Language Design: Pragmatics

The "syntax" of most programming languages permits fairly rigorous or "formal" definition. That is, a brief mathematical expression can be used to characterize which statements are syntactically valid and which are not. This formalism greatly eases the task of the implementer, whose compiler or interpreter must syntactically analyze the text of the program before it can be run. Issues in syntax include its formal description device, the language's character set, the elimination of ambiguity in the language, parsing, lexical analysis, and the influence of syntax on programming style and vice versa. These issues are developed and illustrated in Chapter 6.

"Semantics," on the other hand, deals with the meaning of the various syntactic forms in a program and the selection of suitable machine representation for them. Issues important to language semantics include binding, coercion, implementation of different data types and structures, dynamic storage allocation, run-time diagnostics, exception handling, scope, separately compiled procedures, input-output, and code optimization. These issues are developed in Chapter 10.

"Pragmatics" of programming language design constitute the discussion in Chapter 15. Here, we consider additional issues in implementation and programming style which tend to influence contemporary language features. Such issues in implementation include the management of concurrency, optimization, programming environments, and diagnostics. Programming style issues include such philosophies as "logic programming," "object programming," "data abstraction," "functional programming," "software engineering," the relationships among them, and their relationships to the languages presented in the various chapters of this text.

Chapter 15 concludes with a broad assessment of programming languages, from the different viewpoints of the programmer, the designer, and the implementer. Here, we also comparatively evaluate the several languages that are studied in earlier chapters. That comparison uses as a basis the nine criteria introduced here, combined with our case study implementations in the various languages. The results are interesting and, in most cases, not surprising. But since they are based on relatively concrete and evenhanded experience, these results may be more reliable then those which our intuition alone might provide. Moreover, the methodology of language evaluation used here can be reapplied to other languages beyond these, and in an equally evenhanded way.

EXERCISES

1 With which of the languages to be covered in this book are you already familiar? Among the five application areas described in section 1-3, which one(s) most closely describes your programming experience? With which of the case study problems can you most readily identify?

2 Read one of the case studies for the application area with which you are most familiar. Using your favorite language, implement it.
3 Using your program in Exercise 3, together with your general knowledge of that language, make a brief evaluation of the language using the criteria outlined in section 1-4. For each criterion, rate your language as "excellent," "good," "fair," or "poor." For some criteria, your experience may not be sufficient to draw a conclusion; in this event say "unknown" and thus defer your conclusion to a later time.
4 Describe an additional problem (call it "Case Study 0") and use the same style and precision shown in the descriptions of Case Studies 1 to 5. That problem should represent an actual programming task in your application area. Save that description for use whenever exercises in subsequent chapters call for an implementation of Case Study 0.
5 To contrast the quality of language definitions over time, locate the definition of an early version of FORTRAN and compare its style with that of the ANS FORTRAN 77 standard.
6 "Sigplan" is the ACM Special Interest Group for Programming Languages, and it publishes a monthly newsletter and informal journal called *Sigplan Notices*. Obtain a recent issue of *Sigplan Notices* and identify a current topic in language design. Also, find a new language and try to determine from the presentation what its application area is, what historical roots it has, and what machines implement it.
7 Recent trends indicate far greater activity in the development and implementation of programming languages for microprocessors than for mainframes and minicomputers. Why is this happening? What are the potential advantages and disadvantages presented by this trend?
8 Briefly define and give a Pascal (or other language that you know) example or counterexample for each of the following evaluation criteria: expressivity, pedagogy, portability, generality, data types and structures, input-output facilities.
9 Within what constraints can the efficiency of two languages be meaningfully compared? In what different ways can efficiency be measured?
10 Obtain and read the STEELMAN requirements for language evaluation.[6] In what ways are they similar with our nine criteria? How do they differ?

REFERENCES

1 Richard L. Wexelblat, ed., *History of Programming Languages,* Academic Press, New York, 1981.
2 Alonzo Church, *The Calculi of Lambda Conversion,* Princeton University Press, Princeton, NJ, 1941.
3 A. A. Markov, "Theory of Algorithms," *Trudy Mathematicheskogo Instituta imeni V.A. Steklova* 42 (1954); (English translation—Jerusalem: Israel Program for Scientific Translations, 1961.)
4 A. W. Burks, H. H. Goldstine, and J. von Neumann, "Preliminary Discussion of the Logical Design of an Electronic Computing Instrument," *U.S. Army Ordinance Department Report,* 1946.
5 A. M. Turing, "On Computable Numbers, with an Application to the Entscheidungsproblem," *Proc London Mathematical Society* 2 (42): 230–265 and 43: 544–546 (1936).
6 "STEELMAN: Requirements for High Order Computer Programming Languages," Department of Defense, Washington, D.C., 1978.

CHAPTER 2

PASCAL: HEIR TO THE ALGOL TRADITION

2-1 INTRODUCTION TO PASCAL

Pascal was designed in the early 1970s as a language for teaching principles of computer science and algorithm design. It is a true descendent of ALGOL (*Algo*rithmic *L*anguage), which served the decade of the 1960s in the same way. Pascal is found as the main teaching vehicle in most computer science textbooks. It is also moderately used as a practical programming language in mathematical, data processing, and artificial intelligence applications. As ALGOL inspired much in programming language design and implementation during the 1960s, so Pascal has in the 1970s and 1980s. Newer languages like Ada and Modula-2 are extensions and generalizations of the Pascal style.

2-1.1 Brief History of Pascal

The history of Pascal would be incomplete without first tracing the history of ALGOL, from which Pascal has itself evolved. The history of ALGOL began in 1958, when a committee of representatives from GAMM (a European organization of computer scientists) and ACM (its U.S. counterpart) met in Zurich and produced a preliminary report on an "International Algebraic Language,"[1] or IAL. This later became known as "ALGOL 58," attracted much interest, and was implemented on a variety of computers.

European and U.S. representatives met again in Paris in 1960 to consider a completely new version of this language, and that version became known as "ALGOL 60." In 1962, at a meeting in Rome, the representatives revised and clarified the ALGOL 60 definition, and thus issued the "Revised Report on the Algorithmic Language ALGOL

CHAPTER 13

ADA

13-1 INTRODUCTION TO ADA

The Ada programming language was designed out of a collaborative effort sponsored by the Department of Defense (DOD), and including contributions from industry, academia, and the international community. Its primary purpose is to provide a high-level language in which systems programming problems can be expressed, developed, and maintained. Ada has special provisions for managing concurrent events in a real-time environment, developing application-specific packages, and defining generic operators and procedures.

Because of this power, Ada is considered by some to be a general-purpose language. On the other hand, this same power adds to the complexity of Ada's implementations, and current compilers are not yet ideally suited for widespread use in a productive or academic programming environment.

13-1.1 Brief History of Ada

In the early 1970s, the DOD identified a serious problem of rising software costs for ''embedded'' computer systems; that is, systems which are embedded in various military vehicles. A major cause of this problem was the absence of a single suitable programming language and programming environment for developing and maintaining this software. The applications fall into the general area of ''systems programming'' as we have defined it, and most such programs in the early 1970s had been written in the assembly language of a particular machine. Thus, their portability as well as their maintainability was seriously limited.

In 1975, the DOD formed a High Order Language Working Group, whose charge was to (1) identify a complete set of requirements for DOD languages, (2) evaluate the suitability of selected existing languages on the basis of these requirements, and (3) make a recommendation that the DOD either adopt one or more existing languages or sponsor the design of a new one.

The first requirements document, called STRAWMAN, was issued and widely circulated for review and comment in 1975.[1] Subsequent refinements were made to these requirements over the next four years, called successively WOODENMAN (1975), TINMAN (1976), IRONMAN (1977), and STEELMAN (1978) to suggest that the requirements had become more and more firmly defined.

During the period 1976–1977, extensive evaluation of twenty-three existing languages (including SIMULA, ALGOL, JOVIAL, Pascal, FORTRAN, COBOL, and PL/I, but surprisingly excluding C) was made, on the basis of the TINMAN requirements. The final report concluded that none of the twenty-three languages evaluated was a suitable candidate, and that a new language should be developed from an "appropriate base" language.[2] Candidate base languages were determined to be Pascal, ALGOL, and PL/I.

In 1977, the design of the new language was initiated in a competitive framework, and four of the competitors were selected later that year to develop detailed language designs. These four designs, labeled BLUE, YELLOW, RED, and GREEN (to encourage anonymity), were extensively evaluated in 1978, and two were selected for further refinement before the final choice was made. Final evaluation took place in 1979, and the GREEN design, proposed by Honeywell-Bull, was selected as the new DOD high-order language for programming embedded systems. The language was dubbed "Ada" in recognition of Augusta Ada Byron, daughter of the poet Lord Byron. She is considered by some to be the world's first programmer, since she worked with Charles Babbage during the early nineteenth century on machines which became forerunners of the modern stored program computer.

Since 1979, efforts have been directed at developing a standard document and implementations for Ada. The first such document was published in 1980,[3] and the final version, called *Reference Manual for the Ada Programming Language*,[4] was approved in early 1983 as a military standard. We shall use this document as our basis for discussion of Ada throughout this chapter.

13-1.2 Implementations and Variations of Ada

At this writing, full Ada implementations are just beginning to gain wide circulation. They are available on the following machines.

Amdahl	470
Data General	Nova
Digital	VAX
IBM	4341
Motorola	68000

Some of these implementations are, at the present time, quite inefficient and/or consumptive of machine resources. However, this situation should improve as more experience with Ada implementation is gained. Also, a subset Ada compiler, called JANUS, is now available for the IBM PC.

13-1.3 Major Applications of Ada

As designed, Ada is intended for use as a systems programming language, particularly in areas where real-time control of asynchronous events is necessary. However, many feel that Ada is truly a general-purpose language, and ultimately may be just as suitable for programming systems which are "embedded in banks" as well as those which are embedded in military vehicles.

At the present time it is too early to tell how widespread Ada use will become. It certainly has the potential, as we shall see, for graceful extension into a wide variety of programming domains. However, the current state of Ada implementations, combined with the limited number of people who have truly mastered Ada's novel facilities, means it is too early to predict the overall impact of Ada in the various programming domains.

13-2 WRITING ADA PROGRAMS

An Ada program is an instance of a so-called "compilation unit," which also may be a "subprogram" or a "package." In its simplest form, a program comprises a "context clause" and a "procedure," which in turn contains "declarations" (for variables, files, arrays, etc.) and a series of statements enclosed within **begin** and **end**. **Begin** and **end** themselves are "reserved words" in Ada, and thus cannot be used as variable names or for any other purpose in individual programs. A complete list of Ada reserved words is given in section 13-2.2.

Below is a simple Ada program which computes and displays the average of an indeterminate number of input numbers. For instance, if the input were 85.5, 87.5, 89.5, and 91.5 the result displayed would be 88.5. The program uses the variable X to hold a single input number and the variable N to determine the number of input numbers in the process. The variables SUM and AV connote the numbers' sum and average, respectively.

```
with TEXT_IO;
procedure AVERAGER is
    use TEXT_IO; use INTEGER_IO; use FLOAT_IO;

-- This program computes the average AV of N input
-- numbers X.

    X, SUM, AV: FLOAT;
    N: INTEGER;
begin
    N:=0; SUM:=0.0;
    PUT ("enter a series of numbers"); NEW_LINE;
    GET (X);
    loop
        N:=N+1;
        SUM:=SUM+X;
        GET (X);
    end loop;
exception
    when END_ERROR =>
        AV:=SUM/FLOAT(N);
        PUT (N, 5); PUT (" numbers were given"); NEW_LINE;
        PUT (AV); PUT (" is their average"); NEW_LINE;
end AVERAGER;
```

The different types of statements in this program will be explained later. Generally, we see that the semicolon is used to terminate statements and **begin** . . . **end** and **loop** . . . **end loop** are used to group statements. Thus, the statements following **loop** in this program are treated as a group to be repeated until the end of the input (END_ERROR) occurs. The general format of an Ada program is freely determined by the programmer. The style of indenting shown here is a fairly conventional one that facilitates program readability.

Note also that comments in an Ada program may be inserted anywhere, provided that they are preceded by a double-dash (– –). Finally, we see that program names, variable names, and other identifiers use the uppercase alphabet. Lowercase letters can also be used, but their use does not create distinct names. That is the variable named X and the variable named x are one and the same. The Ada definition adopts this convention in the interest of promoting maximum program portability.

13-2.1 Elementary Data Types and Values

Ada's "scalar data types" are numbers, which may be FLOAT or INTEGER, and "enumeration types," which may be BOOLEAN, CHARACTER, or some other explicitly defined enumeration of values.

An INTEGER is written as a sequence of decimal digits (0, . . . , 9), optionally preceded by a sign (+ or –). Also, an underscore may be inserted within the number to improve its readability (much like a comma in ordinary usage). A "FLOAT number" is written as either an INTEGER, a decimal fraction, an exponent part, or some combination of these. The "exponent part" consists of the symbol E followed by an integer, denoting multiplication by that integer power of 10. Thus, for example, the FLOAT number –5.33E–4 consists of the integer –5, the decimal fraction .33, and the exponent part E–4, and is equivalent to the number –0.000533. Of course, the number –0.000533 is also a legitimate FLOAT and represents the same value as –5.33E–4. Additional examples of Ada number representations are given below:

Number	INTEGER representation	FLOAT representation
0	0	0.0
4,375	4375	4375.0
	4_375	4_375.0
0.5		0.5
–1	–1	–1.0
22.55		22.55
		0.2255E2

The standard Ada INTEGER type is guaranteed to support a range of values from –32768 to 32767, and some implementations may support wider and/or narrower ranges as well (called LONG_INTEGER and SHORT_INTEGER, respectively).

Moreover, the program may define additional types based on INTEGER by using a so-called "**range** constraint" in a type declaration. For example, the declaration

type OCTAL_DIGIT **is range** 0..7;

defines a new type which would be appropriate for verifying that a value comprises octal digits.

The standard Ada FLOAT type also has a range which is implementation dependent. Typically, this may be between -10^{75} and $+10^{75}$, and the precision may be six or seven significant decimal digits. However, like the INTEGER type, the FLOAT type may be selected as LONG_FLOAT or SHORT_FLOAT on some implementations. Moreover, it may be modified by a range constraint and an accuracy constraint. For instance, if we want to confine our FLOAT numbers to the range $\pm 10^5$, with three significant digits of accuracy, we may define our own variation using a type declaration of the form:

type MYFLOAT **is digits** 3 **range** −1E5..1E5;

Another variation of FLOAT is the so-called "fixed-point type," in which the *accuracy* of the internal representation of values is guaranteed. This is called the **delta** of the type. To illustrate, suppose we want to represent numbers in the range $\pm 10^5$ with four-decimal-digit accuracy. That is, we want all numbers of this type to be of the form ±ddddd.dddd (where each d is a decimal digit). This can be specified by the following form of type declaration:

type MYFIXED **is delta** 0.0001 **range** −1E5..1E5;

The fixed-point type appears to be an effective device for allowing packed decimal machine representations to be accommodated by Ada, and thus the data processing applications are not ignored.

The numeric types have alternative representations in other-than-decimal bases. For instance, the decimal number 255 has a binary representation in Ada as 2#11111111# and a hexadecimal representation as 16#FF#. The mantissa of a REAL value can also be represented this way.

The BOOLEAN data values are TRUE and FALSE. They are used primarily in the evaluation of conditional expressions which appear in **if** statements and **while** statements.

The CHARACTER data type provides the basis for string processing in Ada. A "CHARACTER data value" may be any single ASCII graphic character enclosed in apostrophes, as in the following examples:

'A'   '7'   ' '   '+'   '$'   'a'

The ninety-five ASCII graphic characters are summarized below.

A B C . . . Z
a b c . . . z
0 1 2 . . . 9
“ # ’ ( ) * + , − . / : ; < = > _ | &
! $? @ [\ ] ` { } ~ ↑ % blank

A “string” in Ada is a series of zero or more characters enclosed in quotes, as shown in the following examples:

“SALES SUMMARY REPORT”
“5/15/83”
“May 15, 1983”
“ “ “ “

The last example here illustrates that the quote itself may be embedded within a string if it is typed twice. The *length* of a string is its constituent number of characters (excluding duplicates of the quote).

A final kind of enumeration type in Ada is formed by writing a list of “enumeration literals” enclosed in parentheses. The following are three examples of this specification:

type SUIT **is** (club, diamond, heart, spade);
type DIRECTION **is** (N, S, E, W);
type DAY_OF_WEEK **is** (Mon, Tue, Wed, Thu, Fri, Sat, Sun);

The first would be appropriate for a variable that keeps track of the suits in a bridge game. The second would be useful for recording wind direction, and the third would be helpful in a scheduling program. The basic idea behind enumeration types is to provide the programmer with a means for declaring variables using values that fit the application directly, rather than some awkward codification of INTEGER values instead.

In general, an “enumeration literal” may also be a character value or an integer value as well as the kinds of literals shown above. When such an enumeration type is defined, an *ordering* is implicitly defined as well among its constituent values, in accordance with the order in which they appear in the type declaration itself.

The ’’constant declaration” is a device that can be used at the beginning of an Ada program to identify a numerical value by name. It has the following form:

identifier: **constant** := value;

For instance, if we wanted to define a very small number, say 10^{-5}, as “epsilon” in a mathematical computation, we could write:

epsilon: **constant** := 1E−5;

This allows us to use the word "epsilon" as a synonym for 10^{-5} wherever it is needed throughout the program. The advantage of this occurs when we want to *change* the value of epsilon (to, say, 10^{-8}). To accomplish that, we would need to change only this single declaration rather than every instance of its use.

13-2.2 Names, Variables, and Declarations

An Ada variable is a name which is associated with a value during execution of the program. The value of a variable may be changed by the program as execution proceeds. A variable name is called an "identifier," which formally is defined as follows:

> An *identifier* is a sequence of one or more letters (a–z, A–Z) and/or digits (0–9), the first of which must be a letter. Optionally, underscores may be embedded within an identifier to improve readability.

All variables used in an Ada program *must* be declared. A variable's declaration has the following general form:

```
identifier list : type;
```

Here, "type" may be one of INTEGER, FLOAT, BOOLEAN, CHARACTER, or any enumeration type, and "identifier list" denotes a list of those variable names, separated by commas, whose values are to be of the designated type. For instance, the foregoing sample program had in it the following type declarations:

```
X, SUM, AV: FLOAT;
N: INTEGER;
```

which declare that the three variables X, SUM, and AV will each contain a FLOAT value, while the variable N will contain an INTEGER.

A variable may be initialized at the time that it is declared, by affixing an assignment symbol (:=) and an appropriate initial value after it. For instance, we may initialize the value of variable N to zero here rewriting its declaration as follows:

```
N: INTEGER := 0;
```

When a variable's value is not so initialized, that value is undefined at the outset of program execution.

Finally, Ada identifiers must not be identical with any of the language's *reserved words*. A full list of the Ada reserved words is given in Figure 13-1.

13-2.3 Arrays and Other Data Structures

The two internal data structures provided by Ada are "arrays" and "records." Arrays are usually associated with mathematical and list processing, while records are associated with files and dynamic storage structures.

FIGURE 13-1
ADA RESERVED WORDS

abort	**abs**	**accept**	**access**	**all**
and	**array**	**at**	**begin**	**body**
case	**constant**	**declare**	**delay**	**delta**
digits	**do**	**else**	**end**	**entry**
exception	**exit**	**for**	**function**	**generic**
goto	**if**	**in**	**is**	**limited**
loop	**mod**	**new**	**not**	**null**
of	**or**	**others**	**out**	**package**
pragma	**private**	**procedure**	**raise**	**range**
record	**rem**	**renames**	**return**	**reverse**
select	**separate**	**subtype**	**task**	**terminate**
then	**type**	**use**	**when**	**while**
with	**xor**			

An array type is declared with the following kind of type declaration:

type identifier **is array** (size) **of** element-type;

Here, ‘‘element-type’’ denotes the type of all values stored in the array, ‘‘identifier’’ names the type, and ‘‘size’’ is a (list of) range(s) defining the subscript range in each of the array's dimensions. Once the array type is defined, array variables which have this type may be declared.

For example, suppose we want to define an array A of one dimension and five INTEGER entries, and an array B of two dimensions with five rows and four columns of FLOAT entries, as shown in Figure 13-2. Then we would declare appropriate types as follows:

type LIST **is array** (1..5) **of** INTEGER;
type TABLE **is array** (1..5, 1..4) **of** REAL;

Following this, the arrays A and B themselves can be declared in the usual way:

A: LIST;
B: TABLE;

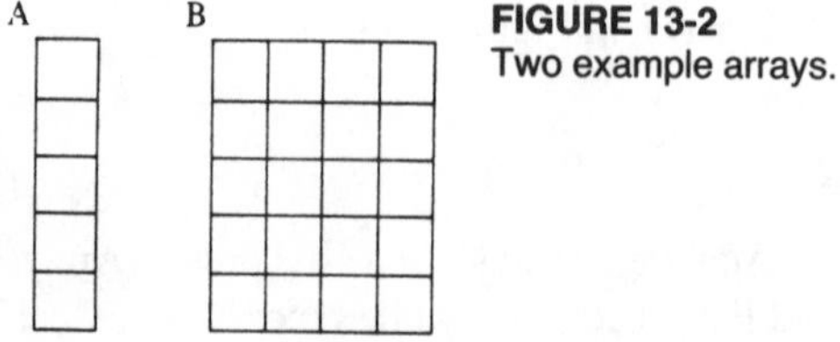

FIGURE 13-2
Two example arrays.

Now, to reference a single entry in an array, we write an ''indexed component,'' which is the array name itself followed by the subscripts of the entry desired. For A above, we can reference any of the first, second, . . . , or fifth entries by writing the indexed component A(1), A(2), . . . , or A(5), respectively. In a similar fashion, we can reference a single entry in B by identifying its row number and its column number in an indexed component. For instance, the entry in the second row and third column of B is referenced by writing B(2,3). The integers within parentheses, ( ), of an indexed component are known as ''subscripts'' or ''indexes.''

An array ''slice'' may also be specified, which is a contiguous sequence of entries within the array, not necessarily beginning with the first. For instance, a slice consisting of the middle three elements of A (defined above) may be defined as A(2..4).

There is one predefined array type in Ada, known as STRING, which can be used immediately in the declaration of a variable as follows:

```
identifier: STRING (1..length);
```

Here, the variable named ''identifier'' may contain any STRING value of ''length'' characters or fewer. For instance, the declaration

```
NAME: STRING(1..20);
```

declares NAME as a twenty-character string variable. Individual characters within NAME may be accessed by using an appropriate indexed variable, such as NAME(1), NAME(2), and so forth.

The ''record'' is Ada's vehicle for defining an entry in a file or a linked list. Such an entry is typically composed of varying types of elements. An example record is shown in Figure 13-3. Here, we see a record composed of a name, a social security number, a gross pay amount, and an address. Each of these ''components'' in the record has a different type; the name is a twenty-five-character string, the social security number is an integer (which may alternatively be defined as a nine-character string), the gross pay is a decimal number, and the address is a forty-character string.

Alternatively, a record can be described as a tree to display its structure and name its nodes, as shown in Figure 13-4.

A record in Ada is viewed as a new data type, and thus is defined by a type declaration, as follows:

```
type identifier is
  record
    identifier: type;
    identifier: type;
    :
    identifier: type;
  end record;
```

ALLENƀB.ƀTUCKERƀƀƀƀƀƀƀƀƀƀ
275407437
25400.00
1800ƀBULLƀRUN,ƀALEXANDRIA,ƀVA.ƀ22200ƀƀƀƀ

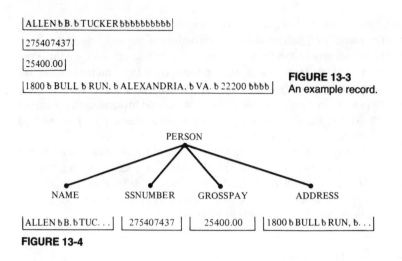

FIGURE 13-3
An example record.

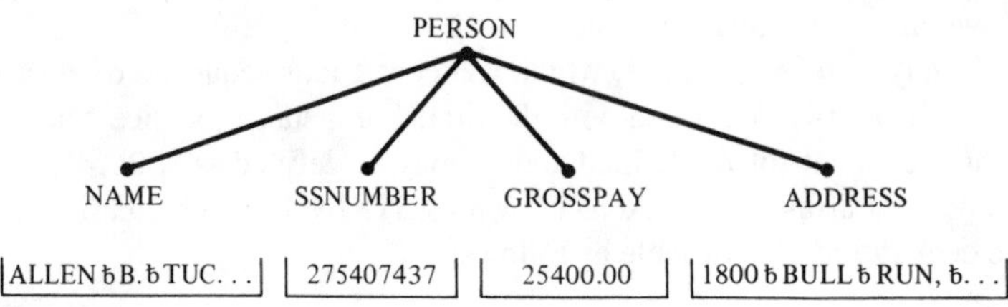

FIGURE 13-4

Here, the first "identifier" names the record type as a whole, while the others name and assign types to each of its constituent components. Thus, the above example record structure is characterized in the following type declaration:

```
type CURRENCY is delta 0.01 range 0.00..99999.99;
type PERSON is
  record
    NAME: STRING (1..25);
    SSNUMBER: STRING (1..9);
    GROSSPAY: CURRENCY;
    ADDRESS: STRING (1..40);
  end record;
```

Note here the new type CURRENCY which guarantees two-digit accuracy for decimal numbers which represent dollars and cents values. Having defined the new type PERSON, we can proceed to declare variables with this type, as in the variable PER below;

```
PER: PERSON;
```

To reference an *entire record* within an Ada program, only the name of a variable declared with that record type needs to be given. For example, the name PER references collectively all four components of a PERSON record. On the other hand, to reference a *single component* of a record, we "qualify" the variable by following it with a dot (.) and the corresponding component's name. For example, to reference a PERSON record's NAME we say:

```
PER.NAME
```

Initialization of Arrays and Records A variable which is an array or a record may have initial values assigned at the time of declaration. This occurs when the declaration contains an assignment symbol (:=) followed by a (list of) value(s) to be assigned to the constituent elements. For example, the array A declared above may be simultaneously initialized to zeros by altering its declaration in the following way:

```
A: LIST := (0,0,0,0,0);
```

Attributes All of the standard types defined for Ada have associated "attributes," which allow the program to obtain basic information about variables, arrays, structures, and other objects of the given type. A brief list of the more significant attributes which are predefined for the standard types is given below.

Type	Attribute	Meaning
INTEGER CHARACTER enumeration	FIRST LAST	The FIRST or LAST data value defined for the implementation of the given type, according to its ordering.
array	FIRST FIRST(*n*) LAST LAST(*n*)	The FIRST or LAST subscript value in its first (*n*th) dimension.
INTEGER FLOAT enumeration CHARACTER	SIZE	The number of bits to store a value of the given type.
INTEGER CHARACTER enumeration	PRED SUCC	The PREDecessor or SUCCessor of a value of the given type, accoridng to its ordering.
FLOAT	DIGITS EPSILON EMAX	The number of decimal DIGITS in the mantissa, the difference between 1.0 and the next successive FLOAT value, and the largest possible exponent value for the implementation.

Any of these attributes for a value of an appropriate type may be referenced in the following way:

```
type'attribute
```

For instance, to learn the number of bits used to store INTEGER values for the implementation, we write:

```
INTEGER'SIZE
```

13-2.4 Basic Statements

The following is a list of the basic statements in Ada, and a general description of their respective uses.

Statement	Purpose
Assignment statement	To perform a series of arithmetic operations (addition, subtraction, etc.) or logical operations (comparison, negation, etc.) and "assign" the final result as the new value of a variable.
Block statement	To delimit the scope of a declaration or an exception handler.
Procedure call statement **Return** statement	To invoke a procedure (subprogram) and return control from it.
Goto statement	To transfer control to a statement which is not next in line.
If statement **Case** statement	To select a statement for execution depending on whether or not a particular condition is TRUE.
Loop statement **Exit** statement	To control the iterative execution of a sequence of statements.
Raise statement Exception handler	To control execution in the event that an exception occurs.
Delay statement **Select** statement **Entry** call statement **Accept** statement **Abort** statement **Terminate** statement	To control execution of asynchronous tasks.

The assignment and block statements will be discussed in this section. The **procedure** call and **return** statements, together with the procedure declaration, will be discussed in section 13-2.7. The **goto**, **case**, **if**, **loop**, and **exit** statements are discussed in section 13-2.5. The **raise** statement and exception handlers will be discussed in sections 13-2.5 and 13-2.6. The remaining statements in this list are related to the control of asynchronous tasks, and will be discussed in section 13-2.8.

The "block statement" is Ada's device for grouping several statements so that the scope of declarations and exception handlers can be localized. It has the following form:

```
identifier:
   declare
      declarations
   begin
      statements
   end identifier;
```

Here, "identifier" serves to name the block, and the reserved word **declare** marks the beginning of the declarations whose scopes are to be localized to the "statements" which are enclosed within **begin** and **end**. The identifier itself is optional, as is the declaration part.

The "assignment statement" has the following basic form:

variable := expression;

Here, "variable" denotes the name of a variable or array reference, and "expression" denotes a calculation, reference, or constant which will give a value. Examples of assignment statements are given in the averaging program such as the following:

N := N+ 1;

The type of value designated by the expression on the right of the assignment operator (:=) must agree with that of the variable on the left. That may be any INTEGER, FLOAT, CHAR, BOOLEAN, enumeration, array, record, or programmer-defined type, but it must agree. In this sense, Ada is said to be a "strongly typed" language.

In the case of any array or record assignment, the number of values in the expression on the right must be identical with the size of the array (or slice) specified on the left. Here, the expression must be an "aggregate," which is a series of values enclosed in parentheses and to be assigned to the constituent entries of the array or record.

A scalar expression, in its simplest form, is called a "primary," which may be either a number, a string, a (simple or subscripted) variable, a function call, or an expression enclosed in parentheses. For instance, the number 0 which appears in the assignment statement N := 0; in our example program, is a primary. The value and type resulting from evaluation of a primary are determined by the nature of the primary itself.

An expression may also be a series of primaries, separated by operators from the following list:

Operator	Meaning
**	exponentiation
* / **mod rem**	multiplication, division, integer modulus, integer remainder
+ − **abs not**	unary plus, minus, absolute value, negation
+ − &	addition, subtraction, one-dimensional array concatenation
= /= < <= > >= **in not in**	equal, not equal, less, less or equal, greater, greater or equal, membership, nonmembership
and or xor	logical "and," "or," exclusive "or"

As examples, the first two expressions below appear on the right-hand sides of assignment statements in the example program.

N + 1
SUM/N
3 + B * (C − D)

The first expression denotes addition of two values. The second denotes division of two values. The third is a series of three primaries; the first two are separated by "+," while the second and third are separated by "∗." The third primary is itself an expression C − D, enclosed in parentheses.

In the above list, the operators are grouped in descending order of precedence, and within each group operators of the same precedence are always evaluated from left to right. Moreover, each operator has strict requirements with respect to the types of operands it can handle and the type of result which it will deliver. Moreover, the type of result delivered by an expression must be compatible with that of the variable on the left of the assignment symbol. That is, Ada is a strongly typed language. However, we shall see in section 13-2.7 how "overloading" of operators may be used to extend the uses of these symbols to other types of operands than the ones given here.

The value and type resulting from evaluation of an expression depends upon the value and type of each primary it contains, according to the following restrictions:

	Operand type(s) required		
Operator	**Left**	**Right**	**Result type**
**	INTEGER	INTEGER >= 0	INTEGER
	FLOAT	INTEGER	FLOAT
* /	INTEGER	INTEGER	INTEGER
	FLOAT	FLOAT	FLOAT
mod rem	INTEGER	INTEGER	INTEGER
unary + − **abs**		numeric	numeric
not		BOOLEAN	BOOLEAN
		BOOLEAN array	same array type
+ −	numeric	numeric	numeric
&	array	array	same array type
= /=	any	any	BOOLEAN
< > <= >=	any scalar	any scalar	BOOLEAN
in not in	scalar	range	BOOLEAN
and or xor	BOOLEAN	BOOLEAN	BOOLEAN
	BOOLEAN array	BOOLEAN array	same array type

In this table, operators whose operands are marked "numeric" will take INTEGER or FLOAT, and deliver a FLOAT result only if at least one of its operands is FLOAT. Operands marked "range" refer to enumeration types, INTEGERs, or CHARACTERs, for which an ordering exists among the constituents.

What does all this mean? It means that if we write

3 + B ∗ C

the product of B and C is computed first, and that result is added to 3. Moreover, it means that *both* B and C must be INTEGER or else both must be FLOAT; otherwise an error will result. On the other hand, to multiply the sum of 3 and B by C, we would override the precedence of "∗" over "+" by using parentheses as follows:

(3 + B) ∗ C

Moreover, we must be sure here that the sum 3 + B has the same type as C (INTEGER or FLOAT).

Reconsidering the third expression listed above, we can now number the operators according to the order in which they will be executed:

```
3 + B * (C - D)
  ↑   ↑    ↑
 (3) (2)  (1)
```

Note that if we had not parenthesized C − D the implied order would have been as follows:

```
3 + B * C - D
  ↑   ↑   ↑
 (2) (1) (3)
```

The result of evaluating the above expression will be a FLOAT value if either D is FLOAT or both B and C are FLOAT. Otherwise it will be INTEGER. Assuming that B, C, and D have INTEGER values 3, 1, and 5, respectively, the original expression's result will be −9, computed as follows:

$$
\begin{aligned}
& 3 + B * (C - D) \\
= & \ 3 + 3 * (1 - 5) \\
= & \ 3 + 3 * (-4) \\
= & \ 3 + (-12) \\
= & \ -9
\end{aligned}
$$

Some of the expressions defined above give BOOLEAN results, and are used primarily in **if**, **case**, and **loop** statements. For example, the expression

H <= 5

gives the result TRUE or FALSE respectively, as the current value of the variable H is less than or equal to 5 or not. The following expression

H <= 5 **and** H > 0

takes advantage of the fact that the relational operators have higher precedence than the conjunction operator **and**. Thus, the test is to see whether the value of H is less than or equal to 5 and greater than 0.

Parentheses may be used here as well to override the predefined precedence. As an example, the following BOOLEAN expression

a **or** b **and** c

has the value TRUE or FALSE, respectively, as the following statement is or is not TRUE:

Both (a **or** b) is TRUE
and c is TRUE

This occurs because **and** and **or** have *equal* precedence in Ada, and are therefore evaluated from left to right! However, if we add parentheses and write

a **or** (b **and** c)

then we have said:

Either a is TRUE
or both b **and** c are TRUE

Sometimes it is useful to test whether or not a scalar variable's value is in a particular range. This can be done using the **in** and **not in** operators. For example, if we have defined the type OCTAL_DIGIT as any of the digits 0 through 7, we may test the value of an INTEGER variable, for example I, to see whether or not it has an octal digit as its value by either of the following expressions:

I **in** OCTAL_DIGIT
I **in** 0..7

and the result will be the BOOLEAN value TRUE or FALSE.

13-2.5 Control Structures

In this section, the Ada statements that control the structure of program execution are presented and illustrated.

Goto Statements The basic form of the **goto** statement is the following:

goto label;

Here, ''label'' denotes the label of some other statement in the program, and can be an identifier which is placed before some other statement and surrounded there by the delimiters ⟨⟨ and ⟩⟩. Moreover, Ada restricts the use of **goto** statements so that they cannot cause transfer into or out of the current block, loop, procedure, or other form which defines a level of execution control. **Goto** statements are generally not preferred, since in most cases a better control structure can be achieved without them.

When executed, the **goto** statement serves to interrupt the normal (textual) sequence of statement execution by transferring control to the statement having the indicated label. For instance, the **goto** statement:

```
goto loop;
```

causes the statement labeled "⟨⟨loop⟩⟩" to be the next one executed, rather than the statement following this one.

Conditional Statements The form of the conditional statement may be any of the following:

1 **if** B **then**
   S_1
end if;
2 **if** B **then**
   S_1
else
   S_2
end if;
3 **if** B **then**
   S_1
elsif B **then**
   S_2
end if;

Here, B denotes any expression whose result is BOOLEAN, while S_1 and S_2 denote any sequence of statements. A conditional statement of form 1 is executed in two steps. First, the expression B is evaluated. Second, if the result is TRUE, then the sequence of statements S_1 is executed. Otherwise, S_1 is skipped.

Form 2 is executed also in two steps. As before, the BOOLEAN expression is first evaluated. Second, either S_1 or S_2 is executed (and the other one is skipped) depending on whether or not the result of evaluating B is TRUE or FALSE, respectively.

Form 3 shows the beginning of a nest of **if** statements, and in fact any number of **elsif**'s may be so nested. Moreover, the last **elsif** in the nest may optionally be followed by an **else** clause, as in form 2. Execution of form 3 proceeds as expected, with each expression B evaluated in turn until the first one delivering the result TRUE is reached, in which its corresponding sequence of statements is executed, and all other such sequences are skipped.

Form 1 of the conditional statement is illustrated in the following example:

```
if A < B then
   A := A + 1;
   B := B - 1;
end if;
```

Here, the BOOLEAN expression is A < B, while the sequence of statements S_1 is the pair A := A + 1; B := B − 1;.

For a more practical example, consider writing an Ada program segment to solve for the real roots x of the quadratic equation

$$ax^2 + bx + c = 0 \qquad (\text{for } a \neq 0)$$

where a, b, and c are FLOAT and given. The number of roots and their values can be determined by first computing the discriminant d from a, b, and c, as follows:

$$d = b^2 - 4ac$$

If $d < 0$ then there are no real roots. If $d = 0$, then there is one real root x_1, given by the calculation $-b/(2a)$. If $d > 0$, then there are two roots, x_1 and x_2, given by the following calculations:

$$x_1 = \frac{-b + \sqrt{d}}{2a}$$

$$x_2 = \frac{-b - \sqrt{d}}{2a}$$

The Ada program segment to compute the number of roots, say NROOTS, and their values X1 and X2, given the coefficients A, B, and C, can be written as follows:

```
D := B ** 2 - 4.0 * A * C;
if D < 0
then NROOTS := 0;
elsif D = 0 then
   NROOTS := 1;
   X1 := -B/(2 * A);
else
   NROOTS := 2;
   X1 := (-B + SQRT (D))/(2 * A);
   X2 := (-B - SQRT (D))/(2 * A);
end if;
```

The "conditional statement" in this example is a combination of form 3 and form 2. The notation SQRT (D) is a call to an assumed predefined function which calculates the square root of D. This will be further discussed in section 13-2.7.

The Case Statement The "**case** statement" provides selection of one from a series of alternative statements, depending on the value of an expression. It has the following form:

```
case e is
   when v1  => S1
   when v2  => S2
   ⋮
   when vn  => Sn
   when others => T
end case;
```

Here, e denotes an expression, v1, . . . , vn denote lists of alternate values that e can have, and each of S1, . . . , Sn and T denotes the corresponding series of statements to be executed for each value. The **others** alternative is optional, and indicates an action T to be taken in the event that e has none of the values v1, . . . ,vn.

For example, suppose we want to take one of four different actions depending on whether the current wind direction DIR is N, S, E, or W, respectively. This can be specified in a **case** statement as follows:

```
case DIR in
   when N => ACTION_1;
   when S => ACTION_2;
   when E => ACTION_3;
   when W => ACTION_4;
end case;
```

Thus, the **case** is equivalent to a nest of **if** statements. The above example can be given equivalently as:

```
if DIR = N then ACTION_1;
elsif DIR = S then ACTION_2;
elsif DIR = E then ACTION_3;
elsif DIR = W then ACTION_4;
end if;
```

which is substantially more tedious to write.

In general, any of the values v1, . . . ,vn may designate a series of alternatives (separated by |) or else a range. For instance, in the above example we may specify ACTION_1 when DIR is N or E by saying "**when** N | E => ACTION_1;".

The **case** and other statements often raise an alternative in which the sequence of statements to be executed is empty. Ada provides the "**null** statement," written simply as

```
null;
```

for this purpose. When a **null** statement is executed, nothing happens, but exit from a complex control structure is often smoother when it is used.

Loop Statements and Iteration Much of programming concerns the proper specification of iterative loops. Ada provides several forms of the **loop** statement for this purpose.

A "controlled loop" may be described as the repeated execution of a sequence of statements until a certain specified condition becomes TRUE. Many such loops are "counter controlled" loops, in which a control variable is initialized and tested and incremented each time the sequence of statements is executed. When the variable is incremented beyond a specific limit, the loop's execution terminates. This is pictured in two different forms in Figure 13-5. In the figure, i denotes the control variable and m_1, m_2, and m_3 denote arithmetic expressions which are the initial value, the limit, and the increment value for the control variable, respectively.

Flowchart (*b*) can be written equivalently as an Ada **loop** statement as follows:

```
for i in m1..m2
  loop
    sequence of statements
  end loop;
```

FIGURE 13-5
Two forms of iterative loops.

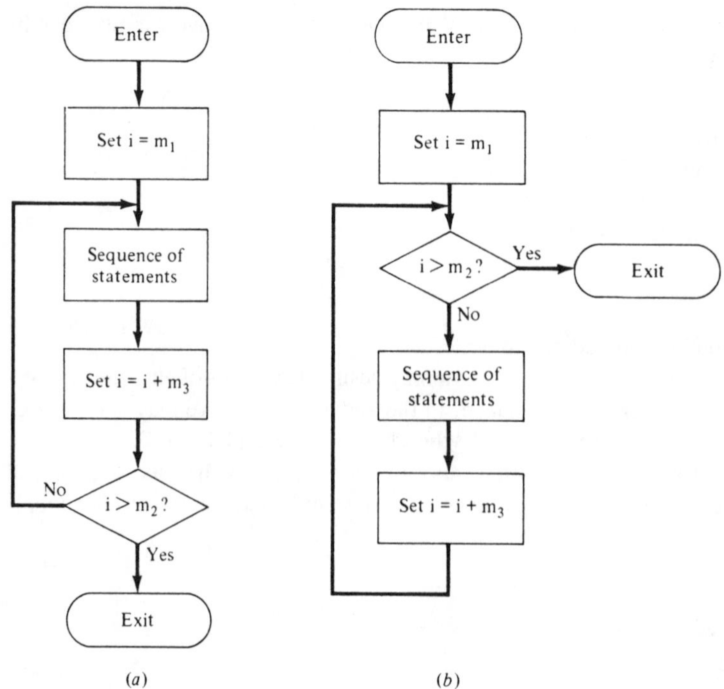

For instance, the following loop denotes a summation in SUM of the integers from 1 to 10:

```
for I in 1..10
   loop
      SUM := SUM + I;
   end loop;
```

assuming that SUM is initially 0.

Two other points should be noted when using **loop** statements. First, the increment value need not be positive. For instance, the SUM may be computed in reverse order in the example above simply by rewriting the **for** statement as follows:

```
for I in reverse 1..10
   loop
      SUM := SUM + I;
   end loop;
```

When the step value is negative, the test for exit in flowchart (*b*) changes its sense as shown in Figure 13-6.

Finally, the value of the loop-control variable upon normal exit from the loop is undefined. Note that this differs from the flowchart version, which suggests otherwise.

The **while** form of the **loop** statement is used for controlling loops which are repeated for an indeterminate number of times. It has the following form:

```
while B
   loop
      sequence of statements
   end loop;
```

Here, B denotes any expression delivering a BOOLEAN result. The semantics of this form is shown in Figure 13-7.

One common use of this form occurs in a simple linear search, where we are looking for an instance of X in the array A of N elements:

```
I := 1;
while X /= A(I) and I <= N
   loop
      I := I + 1;
   end loop;
if I > N then
   NOT_FOUND_ACTION;
else
   FOUND_ACTION;
end if;
```

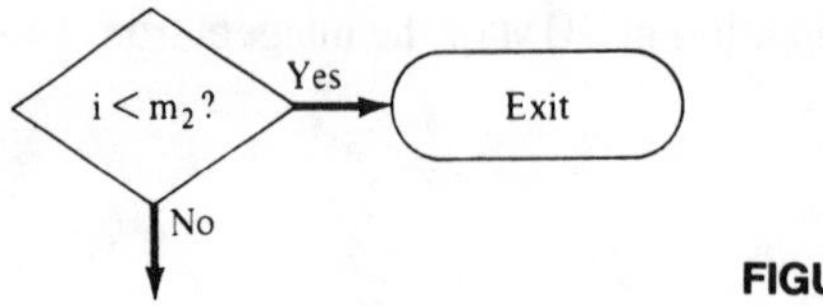

FIGURE 13-6

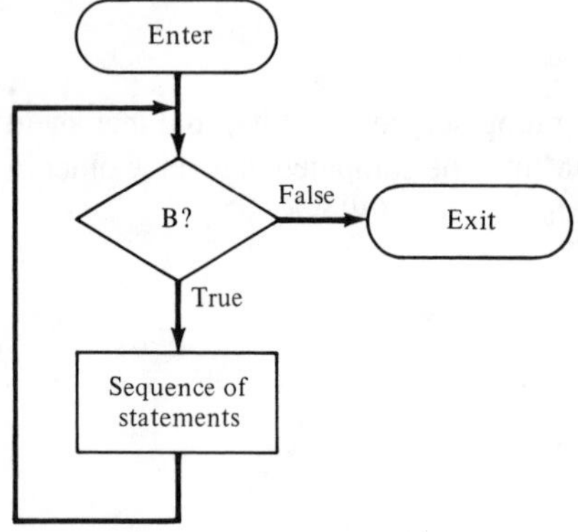

FIGURE 13-7

Another use for this form occurs in numerical analysis, where a sequence of approximations is computed until a specific convergence condition is satisfied. For example, suppose we are developing an approximation to $\sqrt{A}$ by Newton's method. There the next approximation, Y, is computed from the previous one, X, by the formula

$$Y = 0.5(X + A/X)$$

This is repeated until the absolute value of the difference between two successive approximations is sufficiently small, say less than 0.0001. The following loop will exit when that condition occurs:

```
Y := 0.5 * (X - A/X);
while abs (Y - X) > = 0.0001
  loop
    X := Y;
    Y := 0.5 * (X - A/X);
  end loop;
```

The **exit** statement provides a graceful means of leaving a loop before its condition for completion has been met. This is a frequently needed device, and its use often obviates the need to insert a **goto** statement and a label to accomplish the same end. It is written in one of the following two ways:

```
exit;
exit when B;
```

where B designates any expression which delivers a BOOLEAN result. When this statement is reached (and B is TRUE), the innermost loop in which it is enclosed will be terminated prematurely.

A loop may be nested completely within another loop, as illustrated by the following "matrix multiplication" example:

```
for I in 1..M
  loop
    for J in 1..P
      loop
        C(I,J) := 0;
        for K in 1..N
          loop
            C(I,J) := C(I,J) + A(I,K) * B(K,J);
          end loop;
      end loop;
  end loop;
```

Here, the $m \times n$ matrix A and the n × p matrix B are multiplied, with their product being stored in the m × p matrix C. The *ij*th element of C is computed as follows:

$$C_{ij} = \sum_{k=1}^{n} A_{ik}B_{kj} \qquad \text{for } i = 1, \ldots, m \text{ and } j = 1, \ldots, p$$

Exceptions and Their Uses An "exception" in Ada is a condition that marks an unusual, or unexpected event during program execution, and some special action must be taken when such an event occurs. The notion of an exception most closely parallels that of a "condition" in PL/I, as we shall see, and thus is not a novel idea in language design.

The following exceptions are predefined in Ada, with their meanings summarized on the right:

Exception	Meaning
CONSTRAINT_ERROR	Array subscript or enumeration type variable is out of range, and so forth.
NUMERIC_ERROR	Numeric operator cannot deliver a prescribed result within the desired accuracy.
PROGRAM_ERROR	Procedure call or task activation cannot be initiated.
STORAGE_ERROR	A task's dynamic storage has been exceeded, or insufficient storage is available to activate the program or called subprogram.
TASKING_ERROR	An intertask communication error has occurred.

Additional exceptions are predefined for Ada's standard input-output package, such as END_ERROR, and we shall explore these in section 13-2.6.

Moreover, additional exceptions may be declared within the program itself, in the following way:

identifier: **exception**;

Here, "identifier" names the exception. For instance, if we want to associate a distinct exception named NO_SOLUTIONS with the situation that no solutions exist for the quadratic equation example discussed above, we simply define it:

NO_SOLUTIONS: **exception**;

Once we have defined such an exception, we are committed to identify situations within the program where it can occur, and then "raise" the exception accordingly, using a "**raise** statement," which has the following form.

raise exception;

For instance, in our quadratic equation solver, we should raise our newly defined exception as follows:

```
if D < 0 then
   raise NO_SOLUTIONS;
elsif . . .
```

Predefined exceptions are automatically raised by the system whenever their corresponding situations arise. No **raise** statement is needed for them.

Finally, we may prescribe a responsive action which will be taken whenever an exception, either program-defined or predefined, is raised. That action is prescribed using a so-called "exception handler," which has one of the following forms:

1 **when** exception =>
    sequence of statements
2 **when others** =>
    sequence of statements

Here, "exception" names the exception, and "sequence of statements" describes the action to be taken whenever that exception is raised. Form 2 is used as an umbrella, to say that *any* other exception which can be raised will result in the same responsive action given by "sequence of statements."

All exception handlers are grouped just before the **end** of a procedure or block, and preceded by the reserved word **exception**, as shown.

```
begin
  procedure body
exception
  exception handler(s)
end;
```

An example appears in the sample program at the beginning of the chapter, in which a single exception handler appears for the END_ERROR exception.

13-2.6 Input-Output Conventions

Input-output is provided in Ada by way of three predefined "packages," called TEXT_IO, SEQUENTIAL_IO, and DIRECT_IO. TEXT_IO contains support for input and output of ASCII files, normally at the terminal keyboard and screen. SEQUENTIAL_IO and DIRECT_IO support input-output of files in auxiliary storage. Additional input-output packages may be defined by the programmer to extend or complement the facilities provided by these basic packages.

A "package" in Ada is a notion which encompasses more than just input and output. Briefly, a package contains an entire collection of type declarations, objects (variables and structures), and subprograms, which are commonly shared by some particular application, such as input-output. Programmers can also define packages, and we shall return to this idea in section 13-2.7.

When a program wishes to use procedures in any of these packages, an appropriate "**with** clause" must be prefixed to the program. This has the following form:

```
with package name list;
```

Here, "package name list" specifies the input-output package(s) to be used by the program. An example of this clause appears in the sample program at the beginning of the chapter, as follows:

```
with TEXT_IO;
```

Once the program is so linked to an input-output package, it may reference any of the procedures and other names defined within that package.

Text Input-Output For TEXT_IO, the following are among the predefined procedures and other objects:

- A default input file named IN_FILE, with predefined line length and page length.
- A default output file named OUT_FILE, with predefined line length and page length.

• A current column number, line number, and page number, from which (to which) input (output) is being transferred.

• The following procedures and functions for text input:

GET(v); GET(f,v);	To retrieve input from the current default input file (or file named f), and store the result in variable named v. Current column, line, and page numbers are adjusted accordingly.
SET_COL(e); SET_LINE (e);	To set the current column or line number to the value of expression e. Optionally, a file named f may be added as a first parameter (as in GET above).
SKIP_LINE(e); SKIP_PAGE;	To skip forward a number of lines given by expression e. When e is omitted, a skip to the next line or page occurs.
COL LINE PAGE	Functions to inquire about the current value of the column, line, and page number. A parameter f may be added to designate the file name.
END_OF_FILE END_OF_PAGE	Functions to tell whether or not end of file or end of page has been reached. A parameter f may be added to specify a file name.

• The following procedures and functions for text output:

PUT(e); PUT(f,e);	To transfer the value of expression e to the current default output file (or file f). Current column, line, and page numbers are adjusted accordingly.
SET_COL(e); SET_LINE(e);	Same as for text input.
NEW_LINE(e); NEW_PAGE;	Like SKIP_LINE and SKIP_PAGE for text input.
COL LINE PAGE	Same as for text input.

• The following input-output exceptions:

STATUS_ERROR	Attempting to read or write from a file that is not open.
MODE_ERROR	Attempting to read from an output file, or write to an input file.
NAME_ERROR	Attempting to access a file that does not exist.
USE_ERROR	Attempting to create a file on a device that cannot accommodate it, such as input from a printer.
DEVICE_ERROR	A physical device malfunction prevents the input-output operation from being completed.
END_ERROR	Attempt to read past the end of the file.
DATA_ERROR	The data value cannot be converted to the type required by the variable in a GET.
LAYOUT_ERROR	Attempting to SET_COL or SET_LINE past the limit for line length or page length.

The GET and PUT procedures themselves operate on their respective files as stream input, automatically converting values to or from their internal representations. They are referenced using the qualifier TEXT_IO, in the following way. The statement

```
TEXT_IO.GET (X);
```

causes the next value in the input stream to be read and stored in the variable X, after conversion to the type of X. The statement

```
TEXT_IO.PUT(X);
```

transfers the current value of X to the output stream, after converting it to its standard ASCII representation.

The qualifier TEXT_IO can be dropped from these procedure calls if the program is headed with the additional "**use** statement":

```
use TEXT_IO;
```

That is, now we can say simply GET(X); and PUT(X); whenever we want an input-output operation to be performed in the text file. An example of this is given in the sample program at the beginning of the chapter.

Input and output data values can themselves be formatted if the default formatting conventions are not desired. Format items which can be used are summarized below:

Format item	Meaning
WIDTH	The number of positions in the text representation of a value.
BASE	The numeric base in which the text representation will be displayed.
FORE	The number of positions to the left of the decimal point for a FLOAT number.
AFT	The number of positions to the right of the decimal point.

These can be explicitly specified within a GET or PUT procedure call in the following way:

```
format item => value
```

For example, if we wanted to display the numeric value of X as a ten-position field, with three digits to the right of the decimal point, we would write:

```
PUT ( X, WIDTH => 10, AFT => 3);
```

The BOOLEAN predefined function ''END_OF_FILE'' will become TRUE whenever a GET passes the end of the input file. Otherwise, it is FALSE. Thus, the familiar loop structure:

```
GET (X);
while not END_OF_FILE
  loop
    :
    GET (X);
  end loop;
```

provides for handling the data one value at a time, as long as END_OF_FILE remains FALSE. In our sample program at the beginning of the chapter, this form could have been used in place of the **exception** handler for END_ERROR.

Sequential and Direct Input-Output An Ada file is a collection of elements of the same type, called its ELEMENT_TYPE, and has an associated FILE_MODE which may be either IN_FILE, OUT_FILE, or INOUT_FILE. The latter applies to direct input-output only. A file is first declared in a program by ''instantiating'' either the SEQUENTIAL_IO package or the DIRECT_IO package with the file's particular ELEMENT_TYPE. The process of instantiation applies to so-called ''generics,'' which are Ada's rendition of macros, and will be further discussed in section 13-2.7. This instantiation takes one of the following forms:

```
package file-type is new SEQUENTIAL_IO
  (ELEMENT_TYPE => type);
package file-type is new DIRECT_IO
  (ELEMENT_TYPE => type);
```

Here, ''file-type'' is the type for which the file will be declared, and ''type'' is the type of its typical record, or entry. The latter is typically a structure type, such as PERSON defined in section 13-2.3.

Following the establishment of a file type, we may define one or more files with this type, in the same way that we declare simple variables.

```
file-name: file-type.FILE_TYPE;
```

Here, ''file-name'' serves to name the file for the program and ''file-type'' must agree with that type given in the corresponding **package** instantiation described above.

To illustrate, suppose we want to declare a file named EMPLOYEES, to be sequentially processed, containing records of type PERSON (as defined in section 13-2.3). The following are needed:

```
package EMP_FILE is new SEQUENTIAL_IO
  (ELEMENT_TYPE => PERSON);
EMPLOYEES: EMP_FILE. FILE_TYPE;
```

To open a file for input, we use the "OPEN statement," which has the following form:

```
OPEN (FILE => file-name,
      MODE => IN_FILE,
      NAME => system-name,
      FORM => properties);
```

Here, "file-name" is the name by which the file is declared in the program, while "system-name" is a string which identifies the external name by which the file is known to the system. "Properties" is also a string which designates system dependent properties for the file. The FORM specification can be omitted. Moreover, when the FILE, MODE, and NAME specifications are given in the above order, they may be written in the following abbreviated way:

```
OPEN (file-name, IN_FILE, system-name);
```

For example, either one of the following statements

```
OPEN (FILE => EMPLOYEES, MODE => IN_FILE,
   NAME => "SYS. EMPFILE");
OPEN (EMPLOYEES, IN_FILE, "SYS. EMPFILE");
```

opens the EMPLOYEES file for input processing.

Similarly, the "CREATE statement" initializes and prepares for a new output file. It has the same form as the OPEN statement, except that its MODE is specified as OUT_FILE rather than IN_FILE. For instance,

```
CREATE (EMPLOYEES, OUT_FILE,"SYS.EMPFILE");
```

opens the EMPFILE for output, assuming that the file does not already exist in the system.

To transfer the next sequential record from an IN_FILE to a variable of type ELEMENT_TYPE, the following "READ statement" is used:

```
READ (FILE => file-name, ITEM => element);
```

More briefly, this may be written as:

```
READ (file-name, element);
```

The "WRITE statement" transfers a record to an OUT_FILE, and has one of the following forms:

```
WRITE (FILE => file-name, ITEM => element);
WRITE (file-name, element);
```

Thus, if we are processing the input file EMPLOYEES, we would use the following statement to retrieve an individual record, assuming the variable PER is declared with type PERSON (as discussed in section 13-2.3):

```
READ (EMPLOYEES, PER);
```

The functions "END_OF_FILE(file-name)" and "IS_OPEN(file-name)" can also be used to inquire about the status of a file. Moreover, the functions "MODE(file-name)," "NAME(file-name)," and "FORM(file-name)," return the current mode, external name, and form string for the given file to retrieve individual records. Finally, the eight exceptions which were summarized for TEXT_IO above are also applicable to sequential files as well.

To illustrate, the following loop displays a list of the names of all employees in the EMPLOYEES file:

```
OPEN (EMPLOYEES, IN_FILE, "SYS.EMPFILE");
READ (EMPLOYEES, PER);
while not END_OF_FILE(EMPLOYEES)
  loop
    PUT (PER.NAME); NEW_LINE;
    READ (EMPLOYEES, PER);
  end loop;
```

On the other hand, to process a file for output, we use a single CREATE statement, followed by a series of WRITE statements which transfer individual records to the file. Thus, the following code will save in a separate file called NAMES the names (only) of all records in the EMPLOYEES file:

```
OPEN (EMPLOYEES, IN_FILE, "SYS. EMPFILE");
CREATE (NAMES, OUT_FILE, "SYS. NAMFILE");
READ (EMPLOYEES, PER);
while not END_OF_FILE(EMPLOYEES)
  loop
    WRITE (NAMES, PER.NAME);
    READ (EMPLOYEES, PER);
  end loop;
```

Here, we assume that the file NAMES has been appropriately declared.

When a program is finished processing a file, the "CLOSE statement" may be used to disconnect it from the program. It has the form

```
CLOSE (file-name);
```

Alternatively, the ''DELETE statement'' closes a file and also deletes it from the system. This is useful for a file which is used only temporarily by the program. It has the following form:

DELETE (file-name);

Omission of a CLOSE or DELETE statement for a file defers file closing until the program finishes execution.

DIRECT_IO is an alternative to SEQUENTIAL_IO when the elements (records) in a file are to be processed in a nonsequential order, or else when records are to be both read and written to the file during the same run of the program. All the statements described above for sequential file processing are used for direct file processing as well, with minor additions to allow specification of a relative record number when transferring a record to or from the file. This record number is known as the record's ''index,'' and each record in the file is numbered serially beginning with 1. To read a record with a particular index number from a direct file, the READ statement is given in the following form:

READ (file-name, element, index);

The WRITE statement is similarly modified for direct files:

WRITE (file-name, element, index);

An auxiliary procedure, SET_INDEX, may be used to position the current value of a file's index to a new value, as follows:

SET_INDEX (file-name, value);

The corresponding function ''INDEX(file-name)'' is used to retrieve the current value of a direct file's index.

13-2.7 Subprograms, Functions, and Libraries

Ada's subprogramming facilities are extensive. Not only are the conventional forms of procedures and functions provided, but also the notions of operator ''overloading,'' generics, packages, and tasks are added. Briefly, operator overloading allows the program to override or extend the types of operands and the effects of the different operators which are used in expressions (as presented in section 13-2.4).

The notion of a package allows one to combine several related procedures, functions, and data declarations as a single unit. Generics allow such packages, or individual procedures and functions, to be defined for a wide variety of different types of parameters, and then ''instantiated'' each time they are needed for a particular type. Tasks provide facilities for asynchronous programming, or managing parallel events.

These will be described in section 13-2.8, while all the other subprogramming features of Ada will be discussed in this section.

Certain functions are of such widespread importance in programming applications that they are provided as ''standard functions'' in Ada. We have seen some of them in the previous section during the discussion of input-output facilities. Moreover, all the mathematical, relational, and other operators given in section 13-2.3 are also classified as predefined functions.

Defining and Invoking Functions When the Ada predefined functions do not provide the kind of computation desired, the programmer may define a new function by way of a ''function declaration'' and a ''function body.'' It can then be invoked using a ''function call,'' in the same way that the predefined functions are invoked.

A function must always deliver a single value as a result. The type (FLOAT, INTEGER, BOOLEAN, CHARACTER, enumeration) of that result is identified on the first line of the declaration, whose general form is as follows:

function identifier (formal parameters) **return** type;

Here, ''identifier'' names the function, ''formal parameters'' describes the names, types, and usage of the function's parameters, and ''type'' denotes the type of the result returned by the function.

The function body is an extension of the function declaration, in that it appends a definition of the algorithm which defines the function to the declaration itself. The function body has the following form:

```
function identifier (formal parameters) return type is
   declarations
begin
   statements
   exception handlers
end identifier;
```

Separation of the function declaration from the function body allows for modular design, in that the body may be defined and compiled separately from the function declaration itself.

Each one of the formal parameters for a function may supply input to it (designated as an **in** parameter), hold output from it (an **out** parameter), or both (an **in out** parameter). **In** corresponds to call by value, **out** corresponds to call by reference, and **in out** corresponds to call by value-result, as defined in Chapter 10. The form of each formal parameter in a function declaration or body is as follows:

identifier : mode type

Here, ''identifier'' names the parameter, ''mode'' is either **in**, **out**, or **in out** (**in** is assumed by default when mode is omitted here), and ''type'' gives the parameter's type.

To illustrate, let's define a function which computes the factorial of an integer N.

The one parameter, N, is an INTEGER, and the result will also be an INTEGER. When writing the function body, we treat N as if it were an ordinary INTEGER variable whose factorial we are computing. The function declaration and body can thus be written as follows:

```
function FACTORIAL (N: INTEGER) return INTEGER;
function FACTORIAL (N: INTEGER) return INTEGER is
  I, F: INTEGER;
begin
  F := 1;
  for I in 2..N loop
    F := F * I;
  end loop;
  return F;
end FACTORIAL;
```

As a final note, the **return** statement is used to return control from the function body to the invoking program. It has the following general form:

return expression;

Here, "expression" must be the same type as that given in the function's declaration.

As mentioned, a function may be invoked only by execution of a function call within an expression. The function call takes the following general form:

name (actual parameters)

Here, "name" denotes the name of the function to be invoked and "actual parameters" denotes a list of expressions, separated by commas. These actual parameters define the particular values with which the formal parameters will be associated during execution of the body. Therefore, there must be exactly as many actual parameters in the function designator as there are formal parameters in the function declaration. Furthermore, a left-right, one-to-one correspondence is assumed between the actual and formal parameters as they are listed.

An invocation of the function involves the following steps. First, each formal parameter of mode **in** or **in out** is assigned the current value of its corresponding actual parameter. Each formal parameter of mode **out** is associated with the address of its corresponding actual parameter. Second, the body is executed. Third, upon reaching a **return** statement, each **in out** parameter's resulting value is assigned to its corresponding actual parameter. Fourth, control is returned to the expression which contained the function call. The result returned is the value of the expression in the **return** statement.

To illustrate, suppose we want to compute the binomial coefficients

$$a_i = \frac{N!}{i!\,(N - i)!} \qquad \text{for } i = 0, 1, \ldots, N$$

for the familiar polynomial:

$$(x + y)^N = a_N x^N + a_{N-1} x^{N-1} y + \cdots + a_i x^i y^{N-i} + \cdots + a_0 y^N$$

We can write the following program which reads N and displays the desired sequence of coefficients A, assuming that the FACTORIAL function is in a library of functions called MATH_FUNCTIONS.

```
with TEXT_IO, MATH_FUNCTIONS; use TEXT_IO, MATH_FUNCTIONS;
procedure COEFFICIENTS is
  N, A, I: INTEGER;
begin
  GET (N);
  for I in 0..N loop
    A := FACTORIAL(N)/(FACTORIAL(I) * FACTORIAL(N - I));
    PUT (I); PUT (A); NEW_LINE;
  end loop;
end COEFFICIENTS;
```

Writing and Invoking Procedures Often a subprogram is required which will compute a number of results rather than just one, or else compute a result which is an **array** rather than a simple variable. For these situations, the function is not appropriate, and a *procedure* is needed instead. It differs from the function in the following ways:

1 Its name is not associated with any of the results it delivers.
2 Each one of the results it delivers (in addition to each one of the "inputs" it requires) is identified with an **out** formal parameter.
3 Its body therefore contains statements which assign to each of those **out** parameters its designated result, in lieu of assigning a result to the procedure name itself.

The procedure declaration and body are otherwise the same as the function declaration and body, with the omission of the type suffix in its heading, as shown:

```
procedure identifier (formal parameters);
procedure identifier (formal parameters) is
  declarations
begin
  statements
  exception handlers
end identifier;
```

A procedure call statement has the following general form:

```
identifier (actual parameters);
```

Here, "identifier" identifies the procedure being invoked, while "actual parameters" denotes a list of expressions and variables which, respectively, designate value passed to the procedure body and results received from the procedure body at the time of invocation.

The formal-actual parameter correspondence is the same as described above for functions and function designators, except that the actual parameters which correspond to **out** and **in out** parameters must be variables. Those must be prepared to hold *output from* the procedure. To illustrate, suppose we redeclare the factorial function as a procedure with the parameter F added to designate the resulting factorial.

```
procedure FACTORIAL (N: INTEGER; F: out INTEGER);
procedure FACTORIAL (N: INTEGER; F: out INTEGER) is
  I: INTEGER;
begin
  F := 1 ;
  for I in 2 . . N loop
    F := F * I;
  end loop;
  return;
end FACTORIAL;
```

Note here that the **return** statement, which is used to return control to the calling program, has with it no expression since the resulting value(s) are returned through the parameters themselves.

Now the main program which computes the binomial coefficients can be rewritten as follows to make use of this procedure FACTORIAL:

```
with TEXT_IO, MATH_FUNCTIONS; use TEXT_IO, MATH_FUNCTIONS;
procedure COEFFICIENTS is
  N, NFACT, N1, N2, I, A: INTEGER;
begin
  GET (N);
  FACTORIAL (N,NFACT);
  for I in 0..N loop
    FACTORIAL (I, N1);
    FACTORIAL (N - I, N2);
    A := NFACT/(N1 * N 2);
    PUT (I); PUT (A); NEW_LINE;
  end loop;
end COEFFICIENTS;
```

Here, the new variables NFACT, N1, and N2, are used to hold intermediate results delivered by the varying parameters. Below is another example in which a procedure computes and returns more than one value. It also illustrates one way by which an array containing an arbitrary number of elements can be accommodated as a formal parameter. We will name the procedure MMM. Its task is to compute the mean, maximum value, and the minimum value in an N-element array A of FLOAT values.

```
procedure MMM (A: array(INTEGER range <>) of FLOAT;
    MEAN, MAX, MIN: out FLOAT);
procedure MMM (A: array(INTEGER range <>) of FLOAT;
    MEAN, MAX, MIN: out FLOAT) is
  I: INTEGER;
begin
  MEAN := A'FIRST; MAX := A'FIRST; MIN:= A'FIRST;
  for I in A'FIRST + 1..A'LAST loop
    MEAN := MEAN + A(I);
    if MAX < A(I) then
      MAX := A(I);
    elsif MIN > A(I) then
      MIN := A(I);
    end if;
  end loop;
  MEAN := MEAN/(A'LAST - A'FIRST + 1)
end MMM;
```

Note here that **out** parameters MEAN, MAX, and MIN will hold the results. Note finally that the predefined array attributes FIRST and LAST are used to discover within the procedure the actual size of the array A.

The following main program uses MMM as it reads ten values into FLOAT array X, computes their mean, maximum, and minimum, and prints the results:

```
with TEXT_IO, MATH_FUNCTIONS; use TEXT_IO, MATH_FUNCTIONS;
procedure STATISTICS is
  X: array (1..10) of FLOAT;
  XBAR, XMAX, XMIN: FLOAT;
begin
  GET(X);
  MMM (X, XBAR, XMAX, XMIN);
  PUT ("mean ="); PUT (XBAR); NEW_LINE;
  PUT ("minimum ="); PUT (XMIN); NEW_LINE;
  PUT ("maximum ="); PUT (XMAX);
end STATISTICS;
```

Note here that in the procedure call, each actual parameter X, XBAR, XMAX, and XMIN agrees in its type with that of its corresponding formal parameter A, MEAN, MAX, and MIN, respectively.

Operator Overloading The predefined operators (+, −, *, etc.) are applicable only to certain combinations of types in their operands. For instance, the operator +

applies only to scalar operands of type INTEGER or FLOAT. If we want, however, to extend the utility of + as an operator, we may "overload" it by defining an additional function named "+", defining new types for its operands, and declaring a body which reflects the new meaning we wish to attach to it.

Thus, for example, we may want the operator + to apply to operands of type COMPLEX, which is declared as follows:

```
type COMPLEX is record
   REALPART: FLOAT;
   IMAGPART: FLOAT;
end record;
```

Then we may declare the function "+" as follows:

```
function "+" (X, Y: COMPLEX) return COMPLEX;
function "+" (X, Y: COMPLEX) return COMPLEX is
   SUM: COMPLEX;
begin
   SUM.REALPART := X.REALPART + Y.REALPART;
   SUM. IMAGPART := X.IMAGPART + Y.IMAGPART;
   return SUM;
end "+";
```

Now whenever we use the operator + within a program for which this function is defined, and the operands are both of type COMPLEX, this definition will come into effect and the COMPLEX SUM will result. Since the operator + is predefined in the language as an infix operator with a particular priority, that usage is preserved when the operands are COMPLEX as well as when they are numeric. That is, the operator + is *always* used as an infix operator, and its priority with respect to the other operators is not changed.

Packages Still more useful in Ada is the ability to collect several related procedures, functions, type declarations, and exceptions into a single unit called a "package." Some packages, such as TEXT_IO, are predefined in the language and can be immediately used by a program by simply attaching a **with** clause to the program. Other packages can be defined by the programmer and separately compiled for later use. One can easily conceive, for instance, of a database package, a string processing package, a list processing package, or a statistical package like SPSS (Statistical Package for the Social Sciences) for development and wide distribution as a utility for diverse groups of programmers.

The mechanism for defining a package is similar in structure to that for defining a procedure or function; a package specification and a separate package body are both needed. The "specification part" contains just the "visible" parts of its constituent procedures and functions (their declarations), while "the package body" contains the constituent procedure and function bodies. For example, suppose we want to develop a package of arithmetic operations for COMPLEX numbers. The specification part would be as follows:

```
package COMPLEX_ARITHMETIC is
   type COMPLEX is record
      REALPART: FLOAT;
      IMAGPART: FLOAT;
   end record;
   function "+" (X, Y: COMPLEX) return COMPLEX;
   function "-" (X, Y: COMPLEX) return COMPLEX;
   function "*" (X, Y: COMPLEX) return COMPLEX;
   function "/" (X, Y: COMPLEX) return COMPLEX;
   function abs(X: COMPLEX) return COMPLEX;
end COMPLEX_ARITHMETIC;
```

The package body can then be written by writing the respective bodies of the functions, and enclosing them within **package body** and **end**. For instance, the beginnings of our COMPLEX_ARITHMETIC package body would look like this:

```
package body COMPLEX_ARITHMETIC is
   function "+" (X, Y: COMPLEX) return COMPLEX is
      SUM: COMPLEX;
   begin
      SUM.REALPART := X.REALPART + Y.REALPART;
      SUM.IMAGPART := X.IMAGPART + Y.IMAGPART;
      return SUM;
   end "+";
   function "-" (X, Y: COMPLEX) return COMPLEX is
   ⋮
end COMPLEX_ARITHMETIC;
```

Now, any program that needs any of the functions of COMPLEX_ARITHMETIC may be augumented by the prefix

```
with COMPLEX_ARITHMETIC;
```

and all of the functions defined therein are immediately accessible to the program.

Generics Many times, we have a program that needs a package or subprogram, but the particular type of parameters or results is slightly different in the declaration than that which the program needs. For example, we wrote a procedure above which computes the mean, max, and min value in an arbitrarily large array of FLOAT values. Suppose we have a program that needs this procedure, but our array is of type INTEGER rather than FLOAT. To enable this, the procedure must be rewritten so that it can be used for *either* an INTEGER *or* a FLOAT array. This rewriting will make the procedure MMM into a ''generic'' procedure. The notion of generics in Ada is derived from that of macros in conventional assembly languages.

To make a procedure or function generic, we must first check that its algorithm is equally applicable to all the types which we allow for its parameters. Then we augment the declaration and body as follows:

```
generic type ANYTYPE is private;
procedure MMM (A: array(INTEGER range <>) of ANYTYPE;
     MEAN, MAX, MIN: out ANYTYPE);
procedure MMM (A: array (INTEGER range <>) of ANYTYPE;
     MEAN, MAX, MIN: out ANYTYPE) is
   I, N: INTEGER;
begin
   ⋮
end MMM;
```

Now, when we want to use the procedure MMM in a program with an INTEGER array whose max, min, and mean values are sought, we must define a so-called ''instantiation'' of that procedure as follows:

```
procedure INT_MMM is new MMM(ANYTYPE=> INTEGER);
```

In doing this, we are asking for a copy of the procedure MMM in which every instance of the generic type ANYTYPE is replaced by the particular type INTEGER. The reader can see that this replacement will yield the desired instantiation.

On the other hand, if we wanted to use the procedure in a program with a FLOAT array, another instantiation can be defined:

```
procedure FLOAT_MMM is new MMM(FLOAT);
```

In general, as many instantiations of procedure MMM can be so generated as there are array types for which its algorithm is appropriate. Thus, an instantiation of a generic procedure is like an expansion of a conventional macro.

Once the procedure is instantiated, it may be called by its instantiated name. In the above example, for instance, we may call the procedure INT_MMM when we want to apply it to an INTEGER array, and the procedure FLOAT_MMM can be called when we want to apply it to a FLOAT array.

Generic functions and packages can also be defined using the same conventions as for procedures. In fact, whenever we use the standard input-output package SEQUENTIAL_IO or DIRECT_IO, we must instantiate it for the particular record type which applies to the file that we are accessing. That is, these packages are themselves generic.

13-2.8 Additional Features

Ada has three additional features which are significant enough to treat in detail here. These are the notion of "**pragmas**," the list processing facilities, and the facilities for controlling asynchronous processes, or "tasks."

Pragmas A **pragma** is another name for a compiler option, in which the programmer may specify nonstandard activities for the compiler to perform while processing the program. In Ada, **pragmas** are predefined in the language, so that any implementation must support them (in addition to others, as appropriate). A list of the predefined **pragmas** in Ada is given below.

Pragma	Use
CONTROLLED	Limits the garbage collection activities of the automatic storage allocation procedures.
ELABORATE	Controls the elaboration of library units.
INLINE	Expands the code of a procedure call in line.
INTERFACE	Allows subprograms in other languages to be interfaced with Ada programs.
LIST	Controls the listing generated by the compilation.
MEMORY_SIZE	Allocates memory for the compilation.
OPTIMIZE	Specifies time or space as the principal criterion for optimization.
PACK	Minimizes storage for record types.
PAGE	The program text which follows should start on a new page.
PRIORITY	Sets the priority of a task within a multitasking program.
STORAGE_UNIT	Establishes the number of bits per storage unit.
SUPPRESS	Suppresses a particular kind of compile-time check.
SYSTEM_NAME	Names the system on which the compilation is taking place.

List Processing Ada "list processing" facilities provide for dynamic maintenance of linked lists, arrays, stacks, and queues needed for many kinds of systems programming problems. To support this, a so-called "**access** type" must be declared in the program, in the following way:

type pointer-type **is access** record-type;

Here, "pointer-type" is a type which may be used in the subsequent declaration of pointer variables, and "record-type" is the name of an associated record which will be dynamically allocated by the program, and which will be referenced by pointer variables of type "pointer-type." For instance, if we wish to create a linked list of fifteen-character NAMEs, a typical NODE would be defined as follows:

```
type NODE is record
    NAME: STRING(15);
    FPTR: PTR;
  end record;
type PTR is access NODE;
```

Here, the node has two parts, one for the NAME itself, and one for the pointer (FPTR) that will link this node forward to the next one in the list. Thus, a NODE in a linked list is identified by variables of type PTR, and consists of two parts, a NAME and a FPTR, which in turn is of type PTR.

The special value **null** is the designation that a pointer points nowhere, and is indicated graphically as follows:

Assuming the above **type** declarations, we may declare variables HEAD, P, and Q of type PTR in the usual way.

```
HEAD, P, Q: PTR;
```

The standard operator **new** is provided in Ada to allow an individual node to be created and a pointer variable to point to it. The general form of this is as follows:

```
pointer-variable := new record-type;
```

Here, ''pointer-variable'' may be any variable declared with an access type of the indicated ''record-type.'' Continuing our example, the statement:

```
P := new NODE;
```

will create a node and set the variable P to point to it as shown:

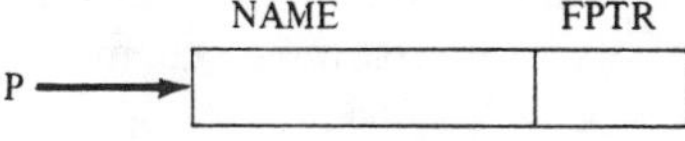

Note that no *value* is stored in the node as a result of this statement; only the node is created.

A pointer variable may be set to point to the same node as another by using a simple assignment statement. For instance, to make Q point to the same node as P, we simply say

```
Q := P;
```

Combining these ideas into a functional example, consider the following Ada program which develops a linked list from a series of fifteen-character names given as input, as shown in Figures 13-8 and 13-9.

```
with TEXT_IO; use TEXT_IO;
procedure LISTER is
   type NODE is record
         NAME: STRING(15);
         FPTR: PTR;
      end record;
   type PTR is access NODE;
   P, Q, HEAD: PTR;
begin
   P := new NODE;
   HEAD := P;
   Q := null;
   GET (P=>NAME);
   while not END_OF_FILE loop
      Q := P;
      P := new NODE;
      Q => FPTR := P;
      GET (P => NAME);
   end loop;
   if Q /= null then
      Q => FPTR := null;
   else
      HEAD := null;
   end if;
end LISTER;
```

The first statement causes a single node to be created, as shown in Figure 13-10. The next three statements set HEAD to point to this node, Q to **null**, and the first NAME in the input data to be read and stored in this node. Thus, after the first three statements

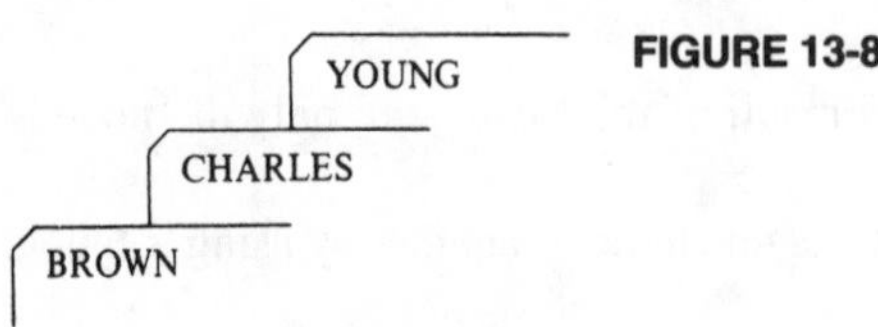

FIGURE 13-8

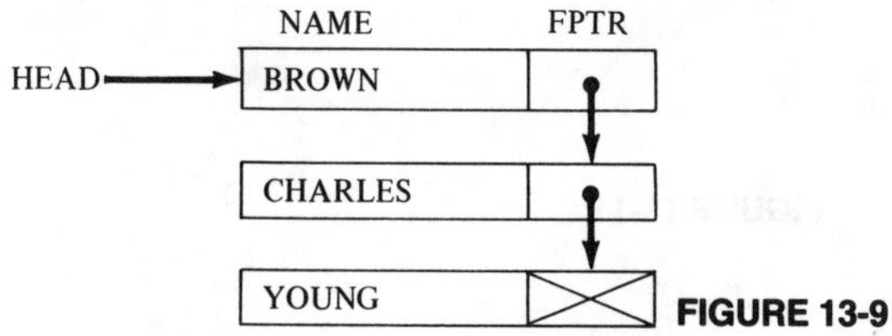

FIGURE 13-9

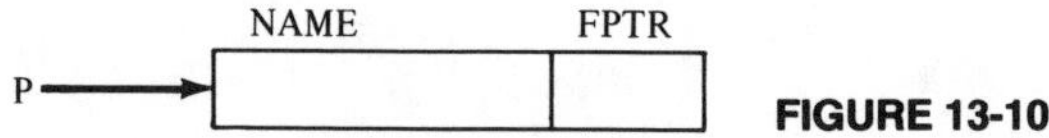

FIGURE 13-10

within the **while** loop are executed, the list is partially constructed as shown in Figure 13-11.

Note that each time through this loop, a *new* node is prepared for receiving the next input name just before the statement "GET (P=>NAME);" is reached. Thus, upon end of input the situation is as shown in Figure 13-12, with an extra node that will not be utilized. The last statement in the program sets the last node's FPTR to **null** (if there is one).

Tasks The specification and control of asynchronous processing in Ada is realized by its facilities for task definition and activation. Like procedures and packages, tasks have two parts: a specification and a body. The "**task** specification" identifies the particular procedures, or "entry points," which can be asynchronously activated by a program, while the "**task** body" defines the algorithms contained within these entry points and the conditions under which they may be activated. Thus, the **task** specification and body have the following forms:

```
task identifier is
   entry name (formal parameters);
   entry name (formal parameters);
   :
end identifier;
task body identifier is
   declarations
begin
   statements
   exception handlers
end identifier;
```

Here, "identifier" identifies the task, while the "names" give the names of the entry points which may be activated by a calling program. Optionally, each of the entry

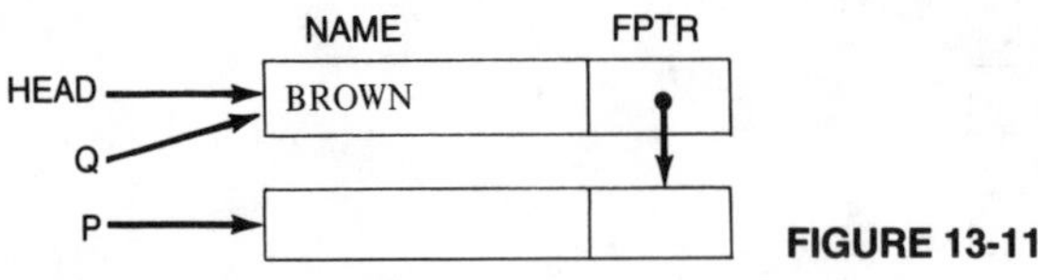

FIGURE 13-11

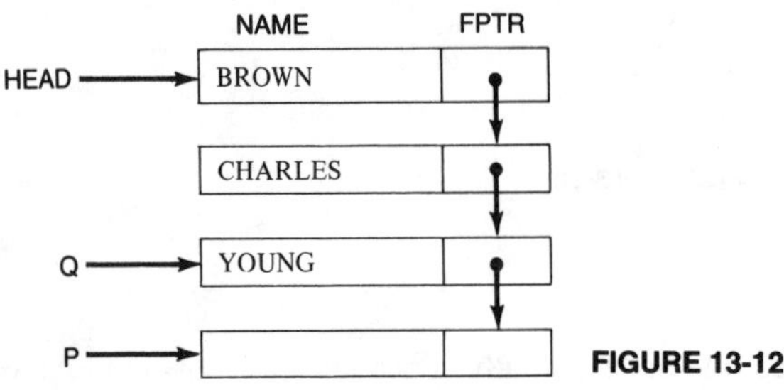

FIGURE 13-12

points may have ''formal parameters,'' just as if they were ordinary procedures. The ''statements'' of a task body must contain one statement of the form:

accept name (formal parameters)
  statements
end name;

for each of the **entry** ''names'' listed in the task specification. This statement defines the action to be taken when ''name'' is called from a calling program.

If a task body is completely embedded within another program or procedure, activation of the latter automatically and asynchronously activates *all* of the task's entries at the beginning of that program's execution. Moreover, termination of that program does not occur until *all* of the active task entries are terminated.

In a more general setting, individual task entries may be selectively activated by way of an ''entry call'' statement, which has the same form as a procedure call. Here, the task is assumed *not* to be embedded within the calling procedure, but moreover to be compiled separately from it. In this setting, a task may be activated when a so-called ''rendezvous'' occurs and task synchronization takes place. Synchronization takes place in either of the two following situations:

1 The calling program reaches an entry call statement before the task reaches its corresponding **accept** statement, in which case the former waits for the latter event to occur.

2 The task reaches its **accept** statement before the calling program reaches its corresponding entry call, in which the task itself waits for this event to occur.

To illustrate these notions, consider the problem of a single buffer, in which two kinds of events can take place:

a A value is placed in the buffer.
b A value is taken from the buffer.

The buffer can hold only one value at a time, so that neither event can occur twice in a row (before the other event occurs), and event "**a**" must occur first. However, the timing in which a value is prepared to enter the buffer is undetermined. The following task definition characterizes this situation:

```
task BUFFER_IO is
   entry INSERT (I: in INTEGER);
   entry TAKE (I: out INTEGER);
end BUFFER_IO;
task body BUFFER_IO is
   IS_FULL: BOOLEAN := FALSE;
   BUFFER: INTEGER;
begin
   loop
      select
         when IS_FULL =>
            accept TAKE (I: out INTEGER) do;
               I := BUFFER;
               IS_FULL := FALSE;
            end TAKE;
      or when not IS_FULL =>
            accept INSERT (I: in INTEGER) do;
               BUFFER := I;
               IS_FULL := TRUE;
            end INSERT;
      end select;
   end loop;
end BUFFER_IO;
```

Here, we see a new form of statement, the "**select** statement," which serves to define conditions under which asynchronous actions may be initiated. The BOOLEAN variable IS_FULL is maintained by these entries, as an INTEGER is placed in or taken out of the BUFFER, accordingly. The **select** statement says, in effect, to permit activation of each of its entries **when** the prescribed condition becomes true. The infinite **loop** surrounding these actions indicates continuous repetition of the tests, as long as the procedure calling the task remains active.

The calling procedure(s) for this task are themselves mutually asynchronous; one or more may be attempting to send values to the buffer and others may be wanting to retrieve values from it. There is only one buffer, however, and when more than one request occurs, duplicate requests are placed in a waiting queue until they can be satisfied. To insert a value into the buffer, a calling procedure gives a call statement:

```
INSERT (value);
```

To retrieve a value from the buffer, a calling procedure gives the following call statement:

TAKE (value);

Such calling procedures are not in any way synchronized with each other, or knowledgeable about each other's existence. All synchronization of INSERT and TAKE requests is managed by the BUFFER_IO task itself. We shall give a more substantial example of asynchronous processing in the next section.

13-3 APPLICATIONS OF ADA

Now that the reader has a working knowledge of Ada, we present and discuss an Ada solution to Case Study 5—Job Scheduler. This discussion will exhibit various concepts of Ada as it is used in systems programming applications.

Following that we will discuss implementation dependent issues for Ada. We conclude this chapter with an overall evaluation of Ada, using this case study and the evaluation criteria discussed in Chapter 1.

13-3.1 Ada Case Study Implementation

Case Study 5—Job Scheduler is defined as an Ada **task** named JOBSCHEDULER in which three principal activities are taking place asynchronously. These are: insertion of

```
task JOBSCHEDULER is
     entry NEWJOB (JOBNO, JOBSIZE: in INTEGER);
     entry ACTIVATE;
     entry DEACTIVATE (JOBNO: in INTEGER);
end JOBSCHEDULER;
```

FIGURE 13-13

```
task body JOBSCHEDULER is

     HIMEM: constant INTEGER := 2000;

     type JOBQUEUE;
     type JQLINK is access JOBQUEUE;
     type JOBQUEUE is record
               JOBNO: INTEGER;
               JOBSIZE: INTEGER;
               PREVIOUSJOB: JQLINK;
               NEXTJOB: JQLINK;
          end record;
     HEAD, TAIL, P: JQLINK;

     type ASL;
     type ASLINK is access ASL;
     type ASL is record
               JOBNO: INTEGER;
               STARTADDRESS: INTEGER;
               BLOCKSIZE: INTEGER;
               NEXTBLOCK: ASLINK;
          end record;
     ASLHEAD, I, J, K: ASLINK;
     QREADY, ASLREADY: BOOLEAN;
```

FIGURE 13-14

a new job into the queue (**entry** NEWJOB), activation of the next job from the queue in storage (**entry** ACTIVATE), and deactivation of a terminated job from storage (**entry** DEACTIVATE). A fourth principal activity, COMPACTIFY, is called by ACTIVATE in situations where storage cannot be allocated because of fragmentation. The principal variables shared and used by these procedures are given in the **task** specification for JOBSCHEDULER shown in Figure 13-13.

Here, we see that the job queue is represented as a linked list, with HEAD pointing to the next job in the queue ready for scheduling. The lists of active storage blocks (ACTIVE) and available storage blocks (ASL) are defined as arrays of MAXBLOCKS entries, representing an upper bound on the number of jobs that can be active (blocks that can be available) at one time. Each block in this list contains a job identification (JOBNO), a starting address (STARTADDRESS), and a size (BLOCKSIZE), each given as an integer representing thousands of bytes. That is, a value 2000 means 2000k bytes, or 2 megabytes.

Two BOOLEAN variables are maintained by these procedures, and are called QREADY and ASLREADY. QREADY is TRUE whenever the queue contains at least one job, and is thus set by **entry** NEWJOB or ACTIVATE. ASLREADY is TRUE

FIGURE 13-15

```
procedure COMPACTIFY is
     TEMPSIZE: INTEGER;
     I, J, K: ASLINK;
     -- This procedure regroups the jobs in ASL, so that
     -- they are contiguous, and all blocks of available
     -- space are compressed into one contiguous block.
     -- It then signals either ASLempty or ASLready,
     -- depending on whether that new block is large enough
     -- to accommodate the job at the head of the queue.
begin
     I:=ASLHEAD;
     while I.NEXTBLOCK /= null loop
        J:=I.NEXTBLOCK;
        if I.JOBNO=0 then      --available block; look for
                               --combining with the next one
           if J.JOBNO=0 then
              I.BLOCKSIZE:=I.BLOCKSIZE+J.BLOCKSIZE;
              I.NEXTBLOCK:=J.NEXTBLOCK;
              J:=null;
           else         -- move available block downward
              I.JOBNO:=J.JOBNO;
              TEMPSIZE:=I.BLOCKSIZE;
              I.BLOCKSIZE:=J.BLOCKSIZE;
              J.JOBNO:=0;
              J.STARTADDRESS:=I.STARTADDRESS+I.BLOCKSIZE;
              J.BLOCKSIZE:=TEMPSIZE;
           end if;
        end if;
        I:=J;
     end loop;
          -- Now check to see if the available block is
          -- adequate to accommodate the next job in the
          -- queue.
     if I.BLOCKSIZE>=HEAD.JOBSIZE then
        ASLREADY:=TRUE;
     else
        ASLREADY:=FALSE;
     end if;
end COMPACTIFY;
```

```
begin
     HEAD:=null; TAIL:=null;     -- initialize the lists
     ASLHEAD:=new ASL;
     ASLHEAD.JOBNO:=0;
     ASLHEAD.STARTADDRESS:=0;
     ASLHEAD.BLOCKSIZE:=HIMEM;
     ASLHEAD.NEXTBLOCK:=null;
     QREADY:=FALSE;
     ASLREADY:=TRUE;

  loop                         -- repeat the cycle

     select

         accept NEWJOB (JOBNO, JOBSIZE: INTEGER) do
             -- This procedure adds a new job to the queue,
             -- accommodating the case where the queue is
             -- initially empty.  The signal Qready is sent in
             -- either case.
          P:=new JOBQUEUE;
          P.JOBNO:=JOBNO;
          P.JOBSIZE:=JOBSIZE;
          P.PREVIOUSJOB:=null;
          if TAIL=null then                -- queue is empty
               HEAD:=P;
               TAIL:=P;
               P.NEXTJOB:=null;
          else TAIL.PREVIOUSJOB:=P;        -- insert at tail
               P.NEXTJOB:=TAIL;
               TAIL:=P;
          end if;
          QREADY:=TRUE;       -- indicate that queue has new entry
        end NEWJOB;
```

FIGURE 13-16

whenever there is a block in the available space list which will accommodate the storage needs of the next job in the queue. It is thus set by ACTIVATE, DEACTIVATE, and COMPACTIFY.

The implementation of this task is described in Figures 13-14 through 13-17, where the bodies of the principal procedures are shown. Sufficient commentary is provided so that their logic should be clear.

This case study was compiled on the Ada implementation shown in Figure 13-18, but not run. This happened because the Ada implementation available to the author does not yet support asynchronous processes.

13-3.2 Implementation Dependent Extensions of Ada

The Ada standard is defined in such a way that discourages implementations from varying from the exact specifications of the language. Because of Ada's several extensibility features—mainly the provision for packages and libraries—many feel that implementation dependent extensions are not necessary.

However, many textbooks on Ada have begun to embody their own packages of utility procedures and functions, such as for string processing, numerical mathematics, and

```
      or when QREADY and ASLREADY =>
         accept ACTIVATE do

            -- This procedure removes the next job from the HEAD of
            -- the job queue and allocates a block of storage for
            -- it, provided that both the queue has at least one
            -- job in it (QREADY) and there is space to accommodate
            -- it (ASLREADY).

            I:=ASLHEAD;       -- search ASL for the place to insert
            while I /= null loop
               if I.JOBNO=0 AND I.BLOCKSIZE>=HEAD.JOBSIZE then
                  I.JOBNO:=HEAD.JOBNO;
                  if I.BLOCKSIZE>HEAD.JOBSIZE then
                     J := new ASL; -- add a block for the remaining
                              -- available space out of this block
                     J.JOBNO:=0;
                     J.STARTADDRESS:=I.STARTADDRESS+I.BLOCKSIZE;
                     J.BLOCKSIZE:=I.BLOCKSIZE-HEAD.JOBSIZE;
                     J.NEXTBLOCK:=I.NEXTBLOCK;
                     I.BLOCKSIZE:=HEAD.JOBSIZE;
                     I.NEXTBLOCK:=J;
                  end if;
                  P:=HEAD;       -- found block; delete HEAD node
                  HEAD:=HEAD.PREVIOUSJOB;
                  P:=null;
                  if HEAD=null then QREADY:=FALSE; end if;
                  I:=null;
               else I:=I.NEXTBLOCK;
               end if;
               I:=I.NEXTBLOCK;
            end loop;
            ASLREADY:=FALSE;      -- no adequate block found
            COMPACTIFY;           -- try to recover for next cycle
         end ACTIVATE;

      or accept DEACTIVATE (JOBNO: INTEGER) do
            -- This procedure deletes an active job from the ASL
            I:=ASLHEAD;
            while I /= null loop
               if I.JOBNO = JOBNO then
                  I.JOBNO:=0;
                  I:=null;
               else I:=I.NEXTBLOCK;
               end if;
            end loop;
         end DEACTIVATE;

      end select;

    end loop;

end JOBSCHEDULER;
```

FIGURE 13-17

FIGURE 13-18
EFFICIENCY OF ADA CASE STUDY 5 PROGRAM

Implementation	Compile speed	Execution speed
1 Digital VAX-750/UNIX Ada	21.3 sec	na

database processing. It is too early in Ada's life, at this writing, to project the nature and impact of different implementations upon its eventual application domains.

13-3.3 Overall Evaluation of Ada

From our case study experience, we evaluate Ada using the nine criteria of Chapter 1 as follows:

1 Expressivity	Good
2 Well-definedness	Good
3 Data types and structures	Good
4 Modularity	Excellent
5 Input-output facilities	Good
6 Portability	Good
7 Efficiency	Fair
8 Pedagogy	Good
9 Generality	Excellent

Ada's main strengths, "modularity" and "generality," come from its strong support of packages and generics combined with its variety of built-in functional support. In this writer's opinion, Ada will eventually find substantial applications outside of the systems programming area.

Ada's main weakness at the present time is the absence of truly efficient and widely available compilers. One user reported at a recent conference that it took a full minute to compile a ten-line program. Our own experience has not been that bad, but it hasn't been nearly as good as for Pascal and other similar languages either. If efficient, economical, and widespread implementations can be realized, Ada seems to have all the necessary ingredients to play a major role in programming for the foreseeable future.

EXERCISES

1 Let x, y, and z be FLOAT variables, and let i, j, and k be INTEGER variables. Assume that they have the following values:

$$x = 2.5 \qquad i = 1$$
$$y = -10 \qquad j = -5$$
$$z = 8 \qquad k = 12$$

Compute the result delivered by evaluating each of the following arithmetic expressions:

(a) x + y ∗ z **(e)** i − 1
(b) (x + y) ∗ z **(f)** i **mod** j ∗ k
(c) (x + y)/z − 3 **(g)** i/j ∗ k
(d) x + y/(z − 3) **(h)** 4 ∗ i + k / j

2 Suppose we have a 5 × 5 **array** A of FLOAT values. The "Trace" of A is defined as the sum of its diagonal elements. For instance, if A's elements are the following,

3	2	−1	9	0
0	1	5	6	7
2	4	6	8	7
−9	2	3	7	10
−1	−2	−3	−4	−5

then its Trace is 3 + 1 + 6 + 7 + (−5) = 12.

(a) Write a declaration for A.

(b) Write an input statement which will store these values in A, assuming they are typed row by row as input lines.

(c) Write a **for** loop which will compute the Trace of A.

(d) Write another **for** loop which will leave the maximum value from A in the FLOAT variable named "Amaxim," and leave that value's row and column numbers in the INTEGER variables named "Arow" and "Acol."

3 Write a function named Trace which will compute the Trace of any nxn FLOAT **array** A.

4 Rewrite the function of Exercise 3 as a procedure.

5 If your installation has a different Ada compiler than the ones used here, adapt our Ada Case Study 5 implementation to run under that compiler. How difficult was that adaptation? What features does your Ada system have that make the program easier to write? More difficult?

6 Implement Case Study 3—Text Formatter in Ada. Evaluate Ada as a text processing language from this experience.

7 Implement Case Study 0 (which you defined at the end of Chapter 1) in Ada. Evaluate Ada's performance and suitability for this application.

8 Consider implementing Case Study 2—Employee File Maintenance in Ada. What are Ada's strengths for data processing applications such as this? What are its weaknesses?

9 Recalling the **task** example given in section 13-2.8, how should it be altered to accommodate a buffer of size N (N ≤ 20), rather than of size 1.

10. Write an Ada procedure that will sort its three parameters into ascending sequence, assuming they are all INTEGERs.

11 Write a procedure which, given an array A of integers, counts the number of positive entries (NPOS), the number of negative entries (NNEG), and the number of zero entries (NZERO) that it contains.

12 Compare Ada's exception handlers with PL/I's on-units. In what ways do they differ, if at all?

13 Ada's design was mandated to be an extension from an "appropriate base language." From your experience, what would you guess is the base language, and why?

14 Ada has incorporated many of its features from older languages. For each of the following Ada features, identify the language(s) from which it came and what it was originally called.

(a) enumeration types
(b) subprograms
(c) generics
(d) tasks
(e) variant records
(f) pragmas
(g) exception handlers
(h) packages

15 Division in Ada (/) is defined only if *both* operands are INTEGER or both operands are FLOAT. Show how overloading can be used to loosen this restriction so that the operands may be mixed (one INTEGER and the other FLOAT).

16 Trace execution of the BUFFER program in section 13-2.8, given the following sequence of calls to INSERT and TAKE coming from various sources.

INSERT(1)
TAKE(X)
TAKE(X)
INSERT(2)
INSERT(3)
INSERT(4)
INSERT(5)
TAKE(X)
INSERT(6)
INSERT(7)
TAKE(X)
TAKE(X)
INSERT(8)
TAKE(X)

17 What is the difference between an ''overloaded operator'' and a ''generic function'' in Ada? Don't they accomplish the same thing? Explain.

REFERENCES

1 *Requirements for High Order Programming Languages, STRAWMAN,* Department of Defense, Washington, D.C., 1975.

2 W. A. Whitaker, ''The U.S. Department of Defense Common High Order Language Effort,'' *Sigplan Notices* (February 1978).

3 *Ada Programming Language*, Department of Defense, Report MIS-STD-1815, Washington D.C., 1980.

4 *Reference Manual for the Ada Programming Language,* Department of Defense, MIL-STD-1815, Washington, D.C., January 1983.

CHAPTER **14**

MODULA-2

14-1 INTRODUCTION TO MODULA-2

Modula-2 is not only the last programming language covered in this book, but is also a direct descendant of the first, Pascal. A recent addition to the family of systems programming languages, Modula-2 embodies many of the principles of Pascal—especially its strong typing and syntactic style. Yet, Modula-2 contains powerful extensions—especially its "module" concept (which permits independent compilation and convenient program libraries) and its provisions for asynchronous processing. In spite of its power, Modula-2 has efficient implementations and, along with C and Ada, must be considered a prominent candidate for future systems programming applications.

14-1.1 Brief History of Modula-2

In 1977, a project to design an integrated hardware-software computer system began at the Institute for Informatik in Zurich, under the direction of Niklaus Wirth. The computer system which evolved was called Lilith,[1] and the programming language Modula[2] was designed to support the systems programming requirements of Lilith's software development.

The design of Modula was strongly influenced by Pascal, as well as a variety of criticisms of Pascal that had arisen out of its first several years of use. Moreover, Modula was influenced by the special needs of systems programming, especially the need for independent compilation of procedures and the need to control asynchronous processes.

Modula-2 emerged in 1979 as a refinement of Modula, and its current version[3] is implemented on the Lilith as well as other machines. Many feel that Modula-2 not only solves Pascal's problems, but also serves as an exemplary language for systems programming, efficient software development, and effective utilization of machine resources.

14-1.2 Implementations and Variations of Modula-2

The first implementation of Modula-2 appeared on the Digital PDP-11 in 1979. Currently, it is available on the following machines:

Digital PDP-11, VAX
IBM PC
Lilith minicomputer

Additional implementations will surely emerge as experience is gained with Modula-2.

14-1.3 Major Applications of Modula-2

The major problems in standard Pascal were identified by various language designers as follows:

- Arrays, and array parameters, are fixed in size.
- Strings are not well implemented.
- No static variables are permitted.
- No separate compilation of procedures is provided.
- The ordering among type, procedure, constant, and variable declarations is too strict.
- Boolean expression evaluation is not clearly defined.
- The case statement has no "otherwise" clause.
- Input-output is severely limited and extensions cannot be written in Pascal itself.
- Type checking is always strictly enforced.

Some Pascal implementations (notably UCSD Pascal) solve many of these problems in different ways, but no uniform and systematic solution appeared until Modula-2 was designed.

In addition to solving these problems, Modula-2 offers several facilities which support systems programming.

- A collection of standard library modules for input-output, concurrency, string processing, and storage management
- Facilities for defining additional modules
- Separate compilation of subprograms and modules
- Asynchronous processing
- Low-level machine access, octal and hexadecimal types
- Efficient and compact compilation and execution

Because of its present youthfulness, Modula-2's future impact on the systems programming community is difficult to predict at this time. Moreover, its applicability to uses outside of systems programming is also difficult to predict.

14-2 WRITING MODULA-2 PROGRAMS

A Modula-2 program is called a "module," and consists of a series of so-called "import lists" and "declarations," followed by a series of statements enclosed within **BEGIN** and **END**. **BEGIN** and **END** themselves are "reserved words" in Modula-2, and thus cannot be used as variable names or for any other purpose in individual programs. A complete list of Modula-2 reserved words is given in section 14-2.2.

Below is a simple Modula-2 program which computes and displays the average of an indeterminate number of input numbers. For instance, if the input were 85.5, 87.5, 89.5, and 91.5, the result displayed would be 88.5. The program uses the variable X to hold a single input number and the variable n to determine the number of input numbers in the process. The variables Sum and Av connote the numbers' sum and average, respectively.

```
MODULE Averager;
     FROM RealInOut IMPORT ReadReal, Done, WriteReal;
     FROM InOut IMPORT WriteInt, WriteString, WriteLn;

(* This program computes the average AV of N input numbers X *)

     VAR X, Sum, Av: REAL;
         n: INTEGER;
BEGIN
     n:=0; Sum:=0.0;
     WriteString("Enter a series of numbers:"); WriteLn;
     ReadReal(X); WriteLn;
     WHILE Done DO
         n:=n+1;
         Sum:=Sum+X;
         ReadReal(X); WriteLn
     END;
     Av := Sum / FLOAT(n);
     WriteLn; WriteInt(n,10);    WriteString(" numbers were given");
     WriteLn; WriteReal(Av,10); WriteString(" is their average")
END Averager.
```

The different types of statements in this program will be explained later. Generally, we see that the semicolon is used to separate statements, while **BEGIN . . . END** and **DO . . . END** are used to group statements. Thus, the statements following "**WHILE** Done **DO**" are treated as a group to be repeated as long as an input value is successfully read (Done).

The format of a Modula-2 program is freely determined by the programmer. The style of indenting shown here is a fairly conventional one that facilitates program readability. Note that comments in a Modula-2 program may be inserted anywhere, provided that they are enclosed within the delimiters (* and *). Finally, we see that the full upper- and lowercase alphabet (A–Z and a–z) can be used in defining variables and other elements in Modula-2 programs.

14-2.1 Elementary Data Types and Values

The basic Modula-2 data types are numbers, which may be INTEGER, CARDINAL, or REAL; logical values, which are called BOOLEAN; and single ASCII characters, which are called CHAR.

An INTEGER number is a sequence of decimal digits (0, . . . , 9), which may be preceded by a sign (+ or −), and whose value must be between system-defined values MaxInt and MinInt. A CARDINAL number is an integer between 0 and MaxCardInt (system-defined), inclusive.

A REAL number is either an INTEGER, a decimal fraction, an exponent part, or some combination of these. The exponent part consists of the symbol E followed by an integer, denoting multiplication by that integer power of 10. Thus, for example, the REAL number −5.33E−4 consists of the integer −5, the decimal fraction .33, and the exponent part E−4, and is equivalent to the number −0.000533. Of course, the number −0.000533 is also a legitimate REAL and represents the same value as −5.33E−4. Additional examples of Modula-2 number representations are given below:

Number	INTEGER value	CARDINAL value	REAL value
0	0	0	0.0
12	12	12	12.0
−1	−1	na	−1.0
22.55	na	na	22.55 0.2255E2

Each number has several equivalent REAL representations. The range of valid INTEGER and REAL numbers depends upon the implementation. For example, the computer can have a 32-bit word size and thus accommodates INTEGERs from -2^{31} to $+2^{31}-1$ and REALs with a magnitude from 10^{75} down to 10^{-75} and a precision of six to seven decimal digits. Numbers may also be written in hexadecimal or octal notation, in which they carry the suffix H or C, respectively, and are composed only of hexadecimal or octal digits.

The BOOLEAN data values are TRUE and FALSE. They are used primarily in the evaluation of conditional expressions which appear in **IF** statements and **WHILE** statements.

The CHAR data type provides the basis for string processing in Modula-2. A CHAR data value is a single character (a letter, digit, or special character) enclosed in quotes, as in the following examples:

'A'   '7'   ' '   '+'   '$'   'a'

The set of characters available as CHAR values depends on the implementation. Usually, this is the ASCII set, as described in Chapter 10.

A "string" in Modula-2 is a series of characters enclosed in single or double quotes, as shown in the following examples:

'SALES SUMMARY REPORT'
"5/15/83"
"May 15, '83"

Although Modula-2 does not directly support string variables or string processing functions, some implementations support strings in a way similar to that of UCSD Pascal. We shall examine this later in the chapter.

Two additional data type classifications in Modula-2 are the "enumeration type" and the "subrange type." These provide a building block for the programmer to define additional basic classes of data beyond those that are provided by the language.

An enumeration type is just a list of identifiers, or names, enclosed in parentheses. The following are three examples of enumeration types:

(club, diamond, heart, spade)
(N, S, E, W)
(Mon, Tue, Wed, Thu, Fri, Sat, Sun)

The first would be appropriate for a variable that keeps track of the suits in a bridge game. The second would be useful for recording wind direction, and the third would perhaps be helpful in a calendar print program.

The subrange type also allows the programmer to define new data types from old ones. It permits the definition of a contiguous range of integers, such as 1 to 10, as the only values that a variable can assume. It is written as a pair of integers or characters, enclosed in brackets, [], and separated by two dots (. .). Thus, the subrange type [1 . . 10] denotes the integers from 1 to 10. This data type is particularly useful for automatically ensuring that an array's *sub*script is within the proper *range:* hence the name "subrange."

Enumeration and subrange types are defined at the beginning of a Modula-2 program by way of the "type declaration," which has the following form:

TYPE identifier = type;
        identifier = type;
        ⋮

Here, "identifier" may be any name that is appropriate to the newly defined type, and "type" may be either a scalar or a subrange type as described above. Thus, the following type declarations can be made:

```
TYPE Digit = [0. .9];
     Day = (Mon, Tue, Wed, Thu, Fri, Sat, Sun);
     Suit = (club, diamond, heart, spade);
     Direction = (N, S, E, W);
```

The "constant declaration" is another device that can be used at the beginning of a Modula-2 program to identify a numerical value by name. It has the following form:

```
CONST identifier = value;
```

For instance, if we wanted to define a very small number, say 10^{-5}, as "epsilon" in a mathematical computation, we could write:

```
CONST epsilon = 1.0 E-5;
```

This allows us to use the word "epsilon" as a synonym for 10^{-5} wherever it is needed throughout the program.

14-2.2 Names, Variables, and Declarations

A Modula-2 variable is a name which is associated with a value during execution of the program. The value of a variable may be changed by the program as execution proceeds. A variable name is called an "identifier," which formally is defined as follows:

> An *identifier* is a sequence of one or more letters (a–z, A–Z) and/or digits (0–9), the first of which must be a letter.

All variables used in a Modula-2 program *must* be declared by a variable declaration, which appears near the beginning of the program and has the following general form:

```
VAR identifier list: type;
    identifier list: type;
    ⋮
```

Here, "type" may be one of INTEGER, CARDINAL, REAL, BOOLEAN, CHAR, or any scalar or subrange type, and "identifier list" denotes a list of those variable names, separated by commas, whose values are to be of the designated type. For instance, the foregoing sample program had in it the following type declaration:

```
VAR X, Sum, Av: REAL;
    n: INTEGER;
```

which declares the three variables X, Sum, and Av will each contain a REAL value, while the variable n will contain an INTEGER.

Unlike other languages, variables' values so declared cannot be initialized here, nor can they be assumed to automatically be assigned an initial value by the system. The values of all variables in a Modula-2 program are initially *undefined*. Finally, Modula-2 identifiers must not be identical with any of the language's *reserved words*. A full list of the Modula-2 reserved words is given in Figure 14-1.

14-2.3 Arrays and Other Data Structures

The three internal data structures provided by Modula-2 are "arrays," "records," and "sets." Arrays are usually associated with mathematical and list processing, records are associated with files and dynamic data structures, and sets are a relatively novel data type that have diverse uses as we shall see.

An array is declared via an "array declaration," which has the following form:

VAR identifier: **ARRAY** size **OF** type;

Here, "type" denotes the type of all values stored in the array, "identifier" names the array, and "size" is a (list of) subrange(s) defining the subscript range in each of the array's dimensions. For example, suppose we want to define an array A of one dimension and five INTEGER entries, and an array B of two dimensions with five rows and four columns of REAL entries, as shown in Figure 14-2. Then we would declare A and B as follows:

```
VAR A: ARRAY [1..5] OF INTEGER;
    B: ARRAY [1..5], [1..4] OF REAL;
```

Now, to reference a single entry in an array, we write an "indexed variable." For A above, we can reference any of the first, second, . . . , or fifth series by writing the indexed variable A[1], A[2], . . . , or A[5], respectively. In a similar fashion, we can reference a single entry in B by identifying its row number and its column number in an

FIGURE 14-1
MODULA-2 RESERVED WORDS

AND	ARRAY	BEGIN	BY	CASE
CONST	DEFINITION	DIV	DO	ELSE
ELSIF	END	EXIT	EXPORT	FOR
FROM	IF	IMPLEMENTATION		IMPORT
IN	LOOP	MOD	MODULE	NOT
OF	OR	POINTER	PROCEDURE	QUALIFIED
RECORD	REPEAT	RETURN	SET	THEN
TO	TYPE	UNTIL	VAR	WHILE
WITH				

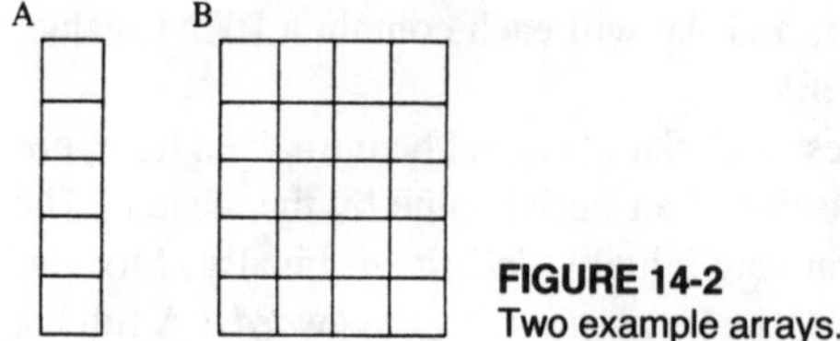

FIGURE 14-2
Two example arrays.

indexed variable. For instance, the entry in the second row and third column of B is referenced by writing B[2,3]. The integers within the brackets of an indexed variable are known as "subscripts" or "indexes."

The "record" is Modula-2's vehicle for defining an entry in a file or a linked list. Such an entry is typically composed of varying types of elements. An example record is shown in Figure 14-3. Here, we see a record comprising a name, a social security number, a gross pay amount, and an address. Each of these "fields" in the record has a different type; the name is a twenty-five-character string, the social security number is an integer (which may alternatively be defined as a nine-character string), the gross pay is a decimal number, and the address is a forty-character string.

Alternatively, a record can be described as a tree to display its structure and name its nodes, as shown in Figure 14-4. A record in Modula-2 is viewed as a new data type, and thus is defined by a type declaration, as follows:

```
TYPE identifier = RECORD
                     identifier: type;
                     identifier: type;
                     :
                     identifier: type
                  END
```

|ALLEN ƀ B. ƀ TUCKER ƀƀƀƀƀƀƀƀƀƀ|

|275407437|

|25400.00|

|1800 ƀ BULL ƀ RUN, ƀ ALEXANDRIA, ƀ VA. ƀ 22200 ƀƀƀƀ|

FIGURE 14-3
An example record.

FIGURE 14-4

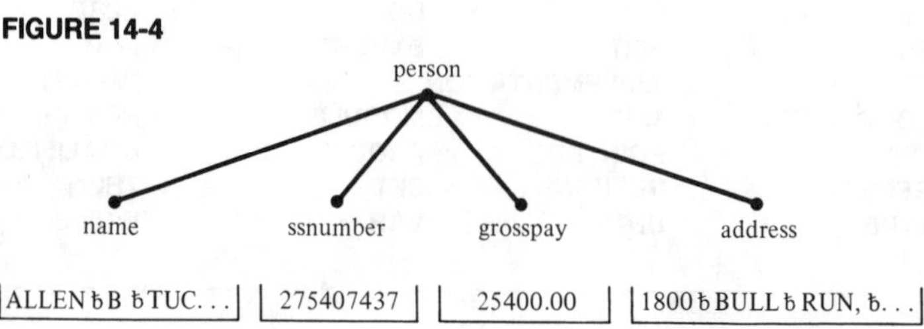

Here, the first ''identifier'' names the record as a whole, while the others name and assign types with each of its constituent fields. Thus, the above example record structure is characterized in the following type declaration:

```
TYPE person = RECORD
                name: ARRAY [1..25] OF CHAR;
                ssnumber: ARRAY [1..9] OF CHAR;
                grosspay: REAL;
                address: ARRAY [1..40] OF CHAR
              END
```

Having defined the new type ''person,'' we can proceed to declare variables with this type, as in the variable PER below:

```
VAR PER: person;
```

Alternately, we can give the **RECORD** description for the variable PER directly when we declare it as follows:

```
VAR PER: RECORD
           name: ARRAY [1..25] OF CHAR;
           ⋮
         END
```

To reference an *entire record* within a Modula-2 program, only the name of a variable declared with that record type needs to be given. For example, the name PER references collectively all four fields of a ''person'' record. On the other hand, to reference a *single field* of a record, we ''qualify'' the variable by following it with a dot (.) and the corresponding field name. For example, to reference a ''person'' record's name field we say

```
PER.name
```

To reference the address, we say

```
PER.address
```

and so forth.

This notation can sometimes be abbreviated by the use of the ''with statement'' in the program, which has the following form:

WITH record variable **DO** statements **END**

Here, the ''record variable'' is named once, and then all references to fields within that record variable can be made *without* the prefixed qualifier.

A final data structure in Modula-2 is the **SET**. A set is a finite collection of elements which share the same (scalar) type. A set variable is declared in the following way:

VAR identifier: **SET OF** type

Here, "identifier" names the set variable, while "type" may be any of the standard types (REAL, INTEGER, CARDINAL, BOOLEAN, or CHAR) or programmer defined types (enumeration or subrange). Thus, for example, if we have

```
TYPE digits = [0..9];
     days = (Mon, Tue, Wed, Thu, Fri, Sat, Sun);
```

then we can declare the following variables:

```
VAR weekend: SET OF days;
    odds: SET OF digits;
    vowels: SET OF CHAR;
```

Correspondingly, a "set value" is just a list of values of its constituent type, separated by commas and enclosed in brackets. Thus, the following set values are appropriate to the set variables weekend, odds, and vowels declared above, respectively:

```
weekend [Sat, Sun]
odds [1, 3, 5, 7, 9]
vowels ['a', 'e', 'i', 'o', 'u']
```

In the following section, we shall see how set variables' values may be assigned and manipulated, using operations that are common to set algebra.

14-2.4 Basic Statements

Modula-2 declarations, whose purpose is to define the variables, arrays, and other data structures, play a passive role in a program. Statements, on the other hand, are executable and thus describe the active aspect of the program. The following page shows a list of the Modula-2 statements and a general description of their purpose.

The assignment statement will be discussed in this section. The procedure call and **RETURN** statements, together with the procedure declaration, will be discussed in sections 14-2.6 and 14-2.7. The rest are control statements, and will be discussed in section 14-2.5. The statements themselves in a Modula-2 program are *separated* by semicolons (;). The reader should note that the semicolon is a statement separator and not a statement terminator, as it is in other languages. It is also worth noting here that Modula-2 has no "go to" statement, which is found in nearly all other languages.

Statement	Purpose
Assignment statement	To perform a series of arithmetic operations (addition, subtraction, etc.) or logical operations (comparison, negation, etc.) and "assign" the final result as the new value of a variable or array element.
Procedure call statement **RETURN** statement	To control procedure invocation and return.
IF statement **CASE** statement	To select a statement for execution depending on whether or not a particular condition is TRUE.
FOR statement **REPEAT** statement **WHILE** statement **LOOP** statement **EXIT** statement	To control the repeated execution of a sequence of statements.

The Assignment Statement The "assignment statement" has the following basic form:

variable := expression

Here, "variable" denotes the name of a variable or array reference, and "expression" denotes a calculation, reference, or constant which will give a value. Examples of assignment statements are given in the averaging program such as the following:

```
n := n + 1
```

The type of value designated by the expression on the right of the assignment operator (:=) must be compatible with that of the variable on the left. In this sense, Modula-2 is a "strongly typed" language.

Expressions can be "arithmetic expressions" delivering REAL, INTEGER, CARDINAL, or subrange results, "Boolean expressions" delivering BOOLEAN results, or "set expressions" delivering **SET** results. The simplest form of arithmetic expression is called a "factor," which may be either a number, a (simple or subscripted) variable, a function procedure designator, or an arithmetic expression enclosed in parentheses. For instance, the number 0 which appears in the assignment statement n := 0 in our example program, is a factor.

An arithmetic expression may be either a factor or a series of factors, each separated from the next by one of the arithmetic operators shown on the next page. Note there that Modula-2 provides *no* exponentiation operator, as most languages do.

The value and type resulting from evaluation of an arithmetic expression depends upon the value and type of each primary it contains, combined with Modula-2's prec-

Arithmetic operator	**Meaning**
+	Addition
−	Subtraction
*	Multiplication
/	Division
DIV	Integer division
MOD	Integer remainder

edence rules for defining the order in which a series of two or more arithmetic operations are carried out.

Operator	**Precedence**
+ −	1
* / **DIV** **MOD**	2

The sequence in which operations are carried out are generally in descending order of precedence (starting with all operations of precedence 2) and then from left to right (when there are two or more operators of the same precedence). The type of the result of evaluating an arithmetic expression will be INTEGER when all its primaries are integer; otherwise the result will have REAL type (but see point 1 below). All operators carry their usual meanings, with the following exceptions and clarifications:

1 The result of "a/b" is REAL, and the types of a and b must be REAL.

2 The result of "a **DIV** b" is INTEGER, and a and b must themselves be INTEGER, CARDINAL, or SUBRANGE. The result is the quotient obtained from truncation of a/b.

3 The result of "a **MOD** b" is INTEGER; a and b must themselves be INTEGER, CARDINAL, or SUBRANGE. The result is the integer remainder obtained from a/b.

Considering, for example, the expression below, we can number the operators according to the order in which they will be executed:

```
3 + B * (C - D)
  ↑   ↑    ↑
 (3) (2)  (1)
```

Note that if we had not parenthesized C − D, the implied order would have been as follows:

```
3 + B * C - D
  ↑   ↑   ↑
 (2) (1) (3)
```

The result of evaluating this expression will be a REAL value if B and C are REAL. Otherwise, it will be INTEGER.

Assuming that B, C, and D have INTEGER values 3, 1, and 5, respectively, the first expression's result will be -9, computed as follows:

$$\begin{aligned} & 3 + B * (C - D) \\ = {} & 3 + 3 * (1 - 5) \\ = {} & 3 + 3 * (-4) \\ = {} & 3 + (-12) \\ = {} & -9 \end{aligned}$$

Boolean expressions are formed using arithmetic expressions, Boolean values, relational operators, logical operators, and parentheses. The simplest form of Boolean expression is the "Boolean factor." It can be (1) a Boolean value (TRUE or FALSE), (2) a variable of type BOOLEAN, (3) a function call (see section 14-2.7), (4) a "relation," or (5) a Boolean expression enclosed in parentheses. A relation is a pair of arithmetic expressions, say a and b, separated by one of the following relational operators:

Relational operator	Meaning of "a operator b"
<	a is less than b
<=	a is not greater than b
=	a is equal to b
>=	a is not less than b
>	a is greater than b
#	a is not equal to b

The result of evaluating a Boolean factor is TRUE or FALSE, accordingly, as (1) the Boolean value is TRUE or FALSE, (2) the value of the BOOLEAN variable is TRUE or FALSE, (3) the value returned by the function designator is TRUE or FALSE, (4) the indicated relation between the values of the two arithmetic expressions is satisfied or not, (5) the value of the Boolean expression within the parentheses is TRUE or FALSE, respectively.

For instance, the factor

$$h <= 5$$

gives the result TRUE or FALSE, respectively, as the current value of the variable h is less than or equal to 5 or not.

Another kind of Boolean factor can be formed using the operator **IN**, denoting set membership. If a is an element, and S is a **SET** containing the same type of values as a, then "a **IN** S" denotes a test to see whether a is a member of the set S.

A Boolean expression can be either a Boolean primary or a series of Boolean primaries, each possibly preceded by the logical operator **NOT**, and each separated from the next by one of the logical operators **AND** (also written as &) and **OR**. For instance, the following are Boolean expressions:

(h <= 5) **AND** (h > 0)
a **OR** b **OR** c

In the first, the test is to see whether the value of h is less than or equal to 5 and greater than 0. The second is a test to see whether at least one of a, b, and c is TRUE or not.

The evaluation of a Boolean expression yields a BOOLEAN result, and depends on the current value of each Boolean factor in the expression, the definition of the logical operators, and Modula-2's precedence rules for defining the order in which two or more (relational or logical) operators are applied in an expression. The logical operator **NOT** has higher precedence than *, /, **DIV**, **MOD**, and **AND**; while **OR** has equal precedence with + and −. The relational operators <, >, <=, >=, =, #, and **IN** have lower precedence than the rest, and are equal in precedence among themselves.

"Set expressions" are formed using some of the operators described above, but with sets or set variables as operands. These operators and their meaning for set operands S and T are summarized below.

Set operator	Result	Meaning
=	BOOLEAN	S equals T
#	BOOLEAN	S is not equal T
<=	BOOLEAN	S is subset of T
+	**SET**	S union T
−	**SET**	S difference T
*	**SET**	S intersect T
/	**SET**	symmetric difference

For example, suppose the set variable S, T, and U have the following values:

S [Mon, Wed, Fri]
T [Mon, Tue, Wed]
U [Mon]

Then the following expressions have values shown on the right:

Sat **IN** S	FALSE
S + T	[Mon, Tue, Wed, Fri]
S * T	[Mon, Wed]
S − T	[Fri]
S = T	FALSE
U <= S	TRUE
U # S	TRUE

14-2.5 Control Structures

In this section, the Modula-2 statements that control the structure of program execution are presented and illustrated.

IF Statements The form of the "**IF** statement" may be one of the following:

1 **IF** B **THEN**
  S_1
END

2 **IF** B **THEN**
  S_1
ELSE
  S_2
END

3 **IF** B **THEN**
  S_1
ELSIF B **THEN**
  S_2
END

Here, B denotes any Boolean expression, while S_1 and S_2 denote any sequences of statements. A conditional statement of form 1 is executed in two steps. First, the Boolean expression B is evaluated. Second, if the result is TRUE, then the sequence of statements S_1 is executed. Otherwise, S_1 is not executed.

Form 2 is executed also in two steps. As before, the Boolean expression is first evaluated. Second, either S_1 or S_2 is executed (and the other one is not executed) depending on whether the result of evaluating B is TRUE or FALSE, respectively.

Form 3 allows the possibility of nesting **IF** statements, in which the sequence S_1 is executed if the first B is TRUE, and then the sequence S_2 is executed if the second B is TRUE. Any number of **ELSIF**'s can be so nested, and moreover, a single final **ELSE** may be added in form 3 to account for the case in which none of the B's is TRUE.

Form 1 of the conditional statement is illustrated in the following example:

```
IF a < b THEN
  a := a + 1;
  b := b - 1
END
```

Here, the Boolean expression is "a < b", while the sequence S_1 is "a := a + 1; b := b − 1".

For a more practical example, consider writing a Modula-2 program segment to solve for the real roots x of the quadratic equation

$$ax^2 + bx + c = 0 \qquad (\text{for } a \neq 0)$$

where a, b, and c are REAL and given.

The number of roots and their values can be determined by first computing the discriminant d from a, b, and c as follows:

$$d = b^2 - 4ac$$

If $d < 0$ then there are no real roots. If $d = 0$, then there is one real root x_1, given by the calculation $-b/(2a)$. If $d > 0$, then there are two roots, x_1 and x_2, given by the following calculations:

$$x_1 = \frac{-b + \sqrt{d}}{2a}$$

$$x_2 = \frac{-b - \sqrt{d}}{2a}$$

The Modula-2 program segment to compute the number of roots, say NROOTS, and their values x1 and x2, given the coefficients a, b, and c, can be written as follows:

```
d := b * b - 4 * a * c;
IF d < 0
THEN
   NROOTS := 0
ELSIF d = 0 THEN
   NROOTS := 1;
   x1 := -b/(2 * a)
ELSE
   NROOTS := 2;
   x1 := (-b + SQRT (d))/(2 * a);
   x2 := (-b - SQRT(d))/(2 * a)
END
```

The **IF** statement in this example combines form 2 and form 3. The notation SQRT (d) is a function reference, denoting the calculation of the square root of d, and assumed to be available to the program through an external library.

FOR Statements and Iterative Loops Much of programming concerns the proper specification of iterative loops where the number of steps is counted. Modula-2 provides several forms of the **FOR** statement as an aid to specifying such loops.

A controlled loop may be described as the repeated execution of a sequence of statements until a certain specified condition becomes TRUE. Many such loops are "counter controlled" loops, in which a control variable is initialized and then tested and incremented each time the sequence of statements is executed. When the variable is incremented beyond a specific limit, the loop's execution terminates. This is pictured in two different forms in the flowcharts in Figure 14-5. In the figure, i denotes the con-

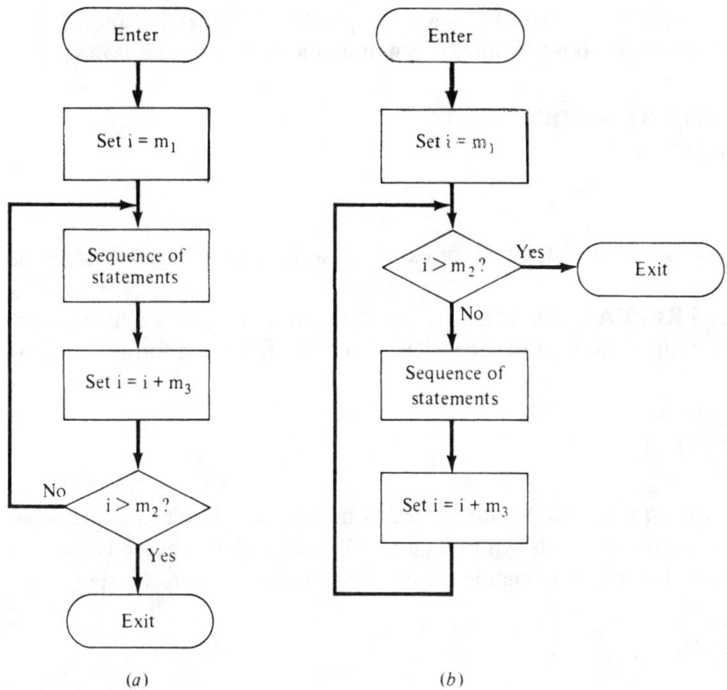

FIGURE 14-5
Two forms of iterative loops.

trol variable and m_1, m_2, and m_3 denote arithmetic expressions which are the initial value, the limit, and the increment value for the control variable, respectively.

Flowchart (*b*) can be written equivalently as a Modula-2 **FOR** statement as follows:

```
FOR i := m1 TO m2 DO
   [sequence of statements]
END
```

For instance, the following loop denotes summation in SUM of the integers from 1 to 10:

```
FOR i := 1 TO 10 DO
   SUM := SUM + i
END
```

assuming that SUM is initially 0.

Two other points should be noted when using **FOR** loops. First, the increment value in a **FOR** statement need not be positive. For instance, the SUM may be computed in reverse order in the example above simply by rewriting the statement as follows:

```
FOR i := 10 TO 1 BY -1 DO
  SUM := SUM + i
END
```

When the step value is negative, the test for exit in flowchart (*b*) changes its sense as shown in Figure 14-6.

The **WHILE** and **REPEAT** statements are used for controlling loops which are repeated for an indeterminate number of times. They have the following forms:

```
WHILE B DO S END
REPEAT S UNTIL B
```

Here, S denotes any sequence of statements and B denotes any Boolean expression. The semantics of these forms are shown in Figures 14-7*a* and 14-7*b*, respectively.

One common use of this form occurs in the example program, where we see:

```
WHILE Done DO
  ⋮
END
```

Further discussion of the special BOOLEAN variable "Done" is given in section 14-2.6.

Another use for these forms occurs in numerical analysis, where a sequence of approximations is computed until a specific convergence condition is satisfied. For example, suppose we are developing an approximation to $\sqrt{A}$ by Newton's method. There the next approximation, Y, is computed from the previous one, X, by the formula:

$$Y = 0.5\,(X + A/X)$$

This is repeated until the absolute value of the difference between two successive approximations is sufficiently small, say less than 0.0001. The following loop will exit when that condition occurs:

```
Y := 0.5 * (X - A/X);
WHILE ABS (Y - X)>= 0.0001 DO
  X := Y;
  Y := 0.5 * (X - A/X)
END
```

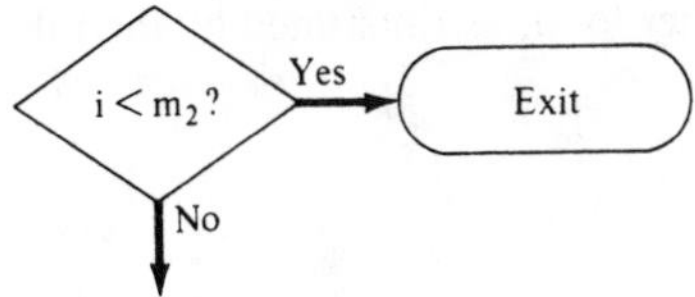

FIGURE 14-6

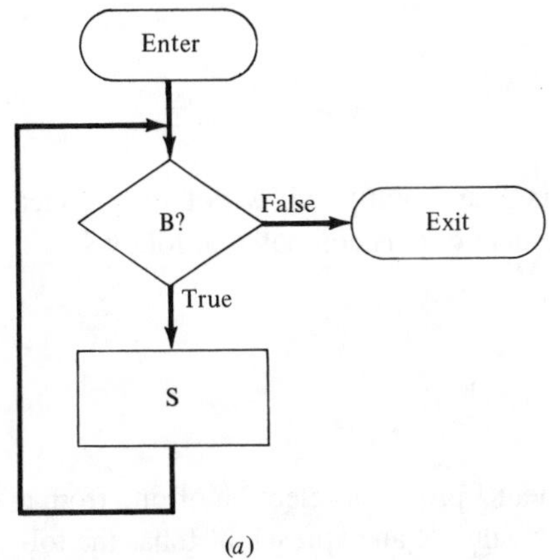

(a)

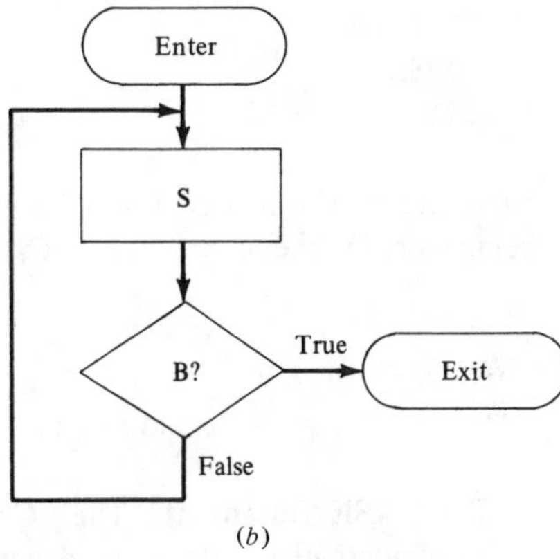

(b)

FIGURE 14-7

Here, ABS (Y − X) denotes the function reference "absolute value of (Y − X)." Alternatively, this loop can be specified by the **REPEAT** statement:

```
REPEAT
  X := Y;
  Y := 0.5 * (X - A/X)
UNTIL ABS (Y - X) < 0.0001
```

The most general form of loop is given by the "LOOP statement," which has the following form:

LOOP S **END**

where S denotes any sequence of statements. A companion to this form is the "**EXIT** statement," which, when executed, forces exit from the innermost loop in which it is embedded. The **EXIT** statement, in fact, can be used in any loop controlled by **FOR**, **WHILE**, or **REPEAT** as well. Failure to provide an **EXIT** statement within a **LOOP** statement will cause an infinite loop to be defined.

Before we leave this section, it is necessary to make an additional point about loops.

That is, a loop may be nested completely within another loop, as illustrated by the following *matrix multiplication* example:

```
FOR i := 1 TO m DO
  FOR j := 1 TO p DO
    C [i, j] := 0;
    FOR k := 1 TO n DO
      C[i, j] := C[i, j] + A[i, k] * B[k, j]
    END
  END
END
```

Here, the $m \times n$ matrix A and the $n \times p$ matrix B are multiplied, with their product being stored in the $m \times p$ matrix C. The ijth element of C is computed at follows:

$$C_{ij} = \sum_{k=1}^{n} A_{ik}B_{kj} \qquad \text{for } i = 1, \ldots, m \text{ and } j = 1, \ldots, p$$

The CASE Statement The "**CASE** statement" provides selection of one from a series of alternative statements, depending on the value of an expression. It has the following form:

```
CASE e OF
  v1: S1 |
  v2: S2 |
  :
  vn: Sn
  ELSE T
END
```

Here, e denotes an expression, v1, . . ., vn denote lists of alternate values that e can have, and each of S1, . . . , Sn denotes the corresponding sequence of statements to be executed for each value. The **ELSE** part is optional, and when included indicates an action T to be taken when e has none of the values v.

For example, suppose we want to take one of four different actions depending on whether the current wind direction DIR is N, S, E, or W respectively. This can be specified in a **CASE** statement as follows:

```
CASE DIR OF
  N: (* action 1 *) |
  S: (* action 2 *) |
  E: (* action 3 *) |
  W: (* action 4 *)
END
```

14-2.6 Input-Output Conventions

Although not explicitly defined within the Modula-2 language, input-output facilities are provided through the so-called "standard modules" named InOut and RealInOut. A "module" can be viewed as a device for packaging collections of related procedures, functions, and data declarations. Some modules are predefined (called "standard") and are thus provided with the implementation, while others may be written by the programmer. We shall discuss the latter subject in the next section. Here, we shall confine our attention to the modules InOut and RealInOut.

InOut contains two standard text files, or streams, one named "in" for terminal input, and the other named "out" for terminal output. Additional "nontext" files may reside on an auxiliary storage device, such as a disk or a tape. These types of files must be accessed by routines outside of those provided by InOut. Moreover, their use is too implementation dependent to be discussed further in this section.

"Text files" are a special class of file in which data is viewed as a continuous stream of display characters. A text file's data are divided into lines of text, with each line terminated by control characters (typically a carriage return called EOL and a line feed). Moreover, the "standard" Boolean variable Done is also provided. Done remains TRUE as long as the file "in" is not at the end of its data, when Done then becomes FALSE.

Input and output from the standard text files are performed via the following procedures. Here, the notation c stands for any CHAR, i any INTEGER, s any STRING, and x any REAL variable or expression, whichever is appropriate. The parameter n denotes the number of output positions to assign to the value.

Input	**Output**
Read(c)	Write(c)
ReadString(s)	WriteString(s)
ReadInt(i)	WriteInt(i, n)
ReadReal(x)	WriteReal(x, n)

Also, the procedure WriteLn produces a carriage return in the file "out."

The data input and output is otherwise taken as a continuous *stream* of values, and each successive read (or write) operation will proceed to the next successive value (or position) in the stream. For example, consider the following series of three input lines.

```
-14
  8   3
 12
```

If we have an integer variable named I then the following read statements:

```
ReadInt(I);
ReadInt(I);
ReadInt(I)
```

will leave the values of I successively as −14, 8, and 3, respectively.

To redirect input and output away from the screen and toward a disk or tape (sequential) file, the OpenInput and OpenOutput procedures are used. Specifically, the statements

OpenInput (s)

and OpenOutput (s)

identify by the string s the system name of the file to which all subsequent stream input or output will be transferred. Conversely, the statements

CloseInput

and CloseOutput

effectively redirect stream input and output back to the terminal screen. During the time when input or output has been so redirected, the actual transfer of input or output values is still governed by the same read and write statements that are summarized above.

14-2.7 Subprograms, Functions, and Libraries

Most practical programming tasks are large enough to justify segmenting the program into a number of functional units, all linked together by a "main" program which controls the sequence in which these units will be executed. The other advantage of program segmentation is that it permits the reuse of code without rewriting and debugging each time it is needed.

Modula-2 provides two different kinds of facilities which enable such segmentation. The first kind, called "procedures," is fairly conventional. The second kind, called "modules," allows collections of procedures and data declarations to be grouped, separately compiled, and selectively utilized by other programs as they are needed. A procedure may be invoked either by the main program or by another procedure. The invoking program determines when the procedure is to be activated, what values are to be supplied to it, and what variables are to hold the results.

Certain functions are of such widespread importance in numerical applications that they are provided as "standard function procedures" in Modula-2. As such, they need not be defined before they are invoked. These are listed in Figure 14-8. It is noteworthy to observe that Modula-2 does not directly embed the usual collection of trigonometric and logarithmic functions. These are assumed to be implemented in an additional standard module called MathLib0, and include procedures named "sqrt," "exp," "ln," "sin," "cos," "arctan," "real," and "entier."

Any of these standard procedures may be invoked by using a "procedure call" in place of an ordinary variable or constant in an expression. This has the following form:

name (e)

FIGURE 14-8
STANDARD PROCEDURES IN MODULA-2

Procedure	Name	Arguments
Absolute value of e	ABS	Any arithmetic expression e
Capital letter equivalent of c	CAP	Any character c
Character equivalent of e	CHR	Any enumeration or subrange e
Decrement x	DEC	Any numeric variable x
Conversion to REAL of e	FLOAT	Any CARDINAL expression e
High subscript bound of a	HIGH	Any array a
Increment x	INC	Any numeric variable x
Is e odd?	ODD	Any INTEGER expression e
Integer equivalent of c	ORD	Any character c
Truncation of e	TRUNC	Any arithmetic expression e
The value of e in type t	VAL(t,e)	Any INTEGER expression e and type t = CHAR, INTEGER, CARDINAL, or enumeration.

Here, "name" denotes the procedure's name and e denotes the expression whose value is the actual argument to which the procedure is applied.

Defining Function Procedures When the Modula-2 standard procedures or implementaion-defined modules do not provide the kind of computation desired, the programmer may define a new function by way of a "function procedure declaration." It can then be invoked using a function call, in the same way that the standard procedures are invoked.

Because a (programmer-written) function procedure call appears in the same context as a standard function procedure call, it must always deliver a single value as a result. The type (REAL, INTEGER, BOOLEAN, CHAR, or enumeration) of that result is identified at the beginning of its declaration, whose general form is as follows:

```
PROCEDURE name (formal parameters) : type;
  locals
BEGIN
  statements
END name
```

Here, "name" denotes the procedure's name, "formal parameters" denotes a list of the names and types of the parameters, separated by semicolons, and "type" denotes the type of the result. "Locals" denotes the declaration of any local variables used by the procedure, and "statements" comprises the procedure's body.

To illustrate, let's write a function which computes the factorial of an integer *n*, defined as follows:

$$\text{factorial}(n) = n \times (n - 1) \times \cdots \times 3 \times 2 \quad \text{for } n > 1$$
$$= 1 \quad \text{for } n \leqslant 1$$

The one parameter, *n*, is an INTEGER, and the result will also be an INTEGER. When writing the function body, we treat *n* as if it were an ordinary INTEGER variable whose factorial we are computing. The declaration can thus be written as follows:

```
PROCEDURE factorial (n: INTEGER): INTEGER;
  VAR i, f: INTEGER;
BEGIN
  f := 1;
  FOR i := 2 TO n DO
    f := f * i
  END;
  RETURN f
END factorial
```

The function's body must contain at least one "**RETURN** statement," which designates the value of the result to be returned to the point of the call. In our example, the result is the final value of f, as designated by the last statement.

Invoking Functions As mentioned, a function may be invoked only by execution of a function call within an expression. The function call takes the following general form:

name (actual parameters)

Here, "name" denotes the name of the function to be invoked and "actual parameters" denotes a list of expressions, separated by commas. These actual parameters define the particular values with which the formal parameters will be associated during execution of the body. Therefore, there must be exactly as many actual parameters in the function designator as there are formal parameters in the function declaration. Furthermore, a left-right, one-to-one correspondence is assumed between the actual and formal parameters as they are listed.

An invocation of the function involves the following steps. First, each formal parameter is assigned the current value of its corresponding actual parameter. Second, the body is executed. Third, control is returned to the expression which contained the function call when the **RETURN** statement is executed. The result returned is the value of the expression following the word **RETURN.** To illustrate, suppose we want to compute the binomial coefficients

$$a_i = \frac{N!}{i!\,(N - i)!} \qquad \text{for } i = 0, 1, \ldots, N$$

for the familiar polynomial:

$$(x + y)^N = a_N x^N + a_{N-1} x^{N-1} y + \cdots + a_i x^i y^{N-i} + \cdots + a_0 y^N$$

We can write the following program which reads N and prints the desired sequence of coefficients a:

```
MODULE coefficients;
  FROM InOut IMPORT WriteInt, WriteLn, ReadInt, Done;
  FROM MathLib IMPORT factorial;
  VAR N, a, i: INTEGER;
BEGIN
  ReadInt(N);
  FOR i := 0 TO N DO
      a := factorial (N) / (factorial (i) * factorial (N - i));
      WriteInt (i); WriteInt (a); WriteLn
  END
END coefficients.
```

In this program, note that we have specified linkage to the independently compiled procedure "factorial" by **IMPORT**ing it from a module called MathLib, which is assumed to exist and to contain that procedure (among others). Execution of the three procedure calls to factorial occurs as usual, with the actual parameter called by value in each case.

Writing and Invoking Nonfunction Procedures Procedures which return results through their parameters are called "proper procedures" in Modula-2. These differ from function procedures in the following ways:

1 They typically deliver several results, rather than just one.

2 Each one of its results is identified with an additional formal parameter, called a "varying parameter."

3 Its body therefore contains statements which assign to each of those varying parameters its designated result, in lieu of an explicit expression in the **RETURN** statement.

The proper procedure declaration is otherwise the same as the function procedure declaration, with the omission of the type suffix in its heading, as given in the following form:

```
PROCEDURE name (formal parameters; varying parameters);
  locals
BEGIN
  statements
END name
```

Here, "name," "formal parameters," "locals," and "statements" have the same meaning as they did for functions. The varying parameters are each preceded by the word **VAR** to designate that they are called by reference rather than by value.

The "procedure call statement" invokes a procedure, and has the following form.

name (actual parameters)

Here, "name" identifies the procedure being invoked, while "actual parameters" denotes a list of expressions and variables which, respectively, designate value passed to the procedure body and results received from the procedure body at the time of invocation.

The formal-actual parameter correspondence is the same as described above for function procedures, except that the values of all actual parameters corresponding to **VAR** parameters are linked by address. Thus, each such actual parameter must be an ordinary variable, and not an expression. When we define proper procedures, every formal parameter which designates a value to be returned by the procedure should be preceded by **VAR**; if it is not, the corresponding actual parameter will never receive its intended result.

Suppose we redeclare the factorial function as a procedure with the parameter f added to designate the resulting factorial.

```
PROCEDURE factorial (n: INTEGER; VAR f: INTEGER);
  VAR i: INTEGER;
BEGIN
  f := 1;
  FOR i := 2 TO n DO
    f := f * i
  END;
  RETURN
END factorial
```

Now the main program which computes the binomial coefficients can be rewritten to make use of this proper procedure "factorial" as follows:

```
MODULE coefficients;
  FROM InOut IMPORT WriteInt, WriteLn, ReadInt, Done;
  FROM MathLib IMPORT factorial;
  VAR N, Nfact, n1, n2, i, a: INTEGER;
BEGIN
  ReadInt (N);
  factorial (N, Nfact);
  FOR i := 0 TO N DO
    factorial (i, n1);
    factorial (N - i, n2);
    a := Nfact / (n1 * n2);
    WriteInt (i); WriteInt (a); WriteLn
  END
END coefficients.
```

Note here that new variables Nfact, n1, and n2, are used to hold intermediate results delivered by the varying parameters. Below is another example in which a procedure computes and returns more than one value. It also illustrates one way by which an array containing an arbitrary number of elements can be accommodated as a formal parameter. We will name the procedure MMM. Its task is to compute the mean, maximum value, and minimum value in an n-element array A of REAL values.

```
PROCEDURE MMM (A: ARRAY OF REAL; VAR mean, max, min: REAL);
  VAR i, n: INTEGER;
BEGIN
  n := HIGH (A);
  mean := A[1]; max := A[1]; min := A[1];
  FOR i := 2 TO n DO
    mean := mean + A[i];
    IF max < A[i] THEN
      max := A[i]
    ELSIF min > A[i] THEN
      min := A[i]
    END
  END;
  mean := mean/n
END MMM
```

Note here that varying parameters mean, max, and min will hold the results. Moreover, the standard procedure HIGH is used to determine the value of the local variable n, corresponding to the size of A.

The following main program program uses MMM as it reads ten values into REAL array X, computes their mean, maximum, and minimum, and displays the results:

```
MODULE statistics;
  FROM InOut IMPORT WriteString, Write Ln;
  FROM RealInOut IMPORT ReadReal, WriteReal;
  FROM MathLib IMPORT MMM;
  VAR X: ARRAY [1 . . 10] OF REAL; xbar, xmax, xmin: REAL;
BEGIN
  ReadReal (X);
  MMM (X, xbar, xmax, xmin);
  WriteString (''mean = ''); WriteReal (xbar); WriteLn;
  WriteString (''minimum =''); WriteReal (xmin); Writeln;
  WriteString (''maximum =''); WriteReal (xmax)
END statistics.
```

Note here that in the procedure call, each actual parameter, X, xbar, xmax, and xmin agrees in its type with that of its corresponding formal parameter A, mean, max, and min, respectively.

Modules Still more useful in Modula-2 is the ability to collect several related procedures, functions, and declarations into a single unit called a "module." Some modules, such as InOut, are predefined and can be immediately used by a program by simply including an **IMPORT** statement at the beginning of the program. Other modules can be defined by the programmer and separately compiled for later use. One can easily conceive, for instance, of a database module, a string processing module, a list processing module, or a statistical module like SPSS for development and wide distribution as a shared tool for diverse groups of programmers.

The mechanism for defining a module divides it into two parts, its "definition part" and its "implementation part." The definition part identifies the module's constituent procedures, parameters, types, and other declarations. The implementation part includes the detailed procedure bodies as well. The purpose of this separation is to allow the program which uses the module access to the relevant information about procedure names, parameter types, and shared variables without inheriting the tedium of each procedure's particular code. This separation also encourages top-down design, allowing separate compilation and use of definition parts of modules before their implementations are fully developed.

The definition part of a module has the following general form:

```
DEFINITION MODULE name;
   FROM other-module IMPORT names;
   EXPORT QUALIFIED list;
   declarations
   procedure-headings
END name.
```

Here, the module "name" is defined, and the next line identifies a list of "names" of procedures and external variables taken from an "other-module." "List," in turn, identifies the names of procedures and declarations which are defined herein and may be accessed by programs which use this module itself. "Declarations" actually declare the types and variables which are intrinsic to this module, and "procedure-headings" is a list of this module's procedures with their respective parameters and types.

The implementation part of a module is similar to the definition part, except that the detailed bodies of its constituent procedures are fully declared. It has the following form:

```
IMPLEMENTATION MODULE name;
   FROM other-module IMPORT names;
   EXPORT QUALIFIED list;
   declarations
   procedure-declarations
END name.
```

Here, the word **IMPLEMENTATION** is optional. In fact, it is often omitted, in which case the reader should note that even the simplest program (such as the one at the beginning of the chapter) is a special case of an implementation module. For another example, suppose we want to develop a package of arithmetic operations for COMPLEX numbers. The definition part could be as follows:

```
DEFINITION MODULE ComplexArithmetic;
  EXPORT COMPLEX, csum, cdif, cprod, cquot, cabs;
  TYPE COMPLEX = RECORD
       REALPART: FLOAT;
       IMAGPART: FLOAT
    END;
  PROCEDURE csum (X, Y: COMPLEX): COMPLEX;
  PROCEDURE cdif (X, Y: COMPLEX): COMPLEX;
  PROCEDURE cprod (X, Y: COMPLEX): COMPLEX;
  PROCEDURE cquot (X, Y: COMPLEX): COMPLEX;
  PROCEDURE cabs (X: COMPLEX): COMPLEX;
END ComplexArithmetic.
```

The implementation part can occur separately by simply filling in the bodies of the respective procedures at a later time. For instance, our ComplexArithmetic module's implementation part begins as follows:

```
IMPLEMENTATION MODULE ComplexArithmetic;
  EXPORT COMPLEX, csum, cdif, cprod, cquot, cabs;
  TYPE COMPLEX = RECORD
       REALPART: FLOAT;
       IMAGPART: FLOAT
    END;
  PROCEDURE csum (X, Y: COMPLEX): COMPLEX;
       SUM: COMPLEX;
  BEGIN
       SUM.REALPART := X.REALPART + Y.REALPART;
       SUM.IMAGPART := X.IMAGPART + Y.IMAGPART;
       RETURN SUM
  END csum;
  PROCEDURE cdif (X, Y: COMPLEX): COMPLEX;
       ⋮
END ComplexArithmetic.
```

Now, any program that wishes to use the procedures of ComplexArithmetic should contain the following **IMPORT** statement:

```
FROM ComplexArithmetic IMPORT Complex, csum, cdif, cprod, cquot, cabs;
```

and all of these procedures are immediately accessible to the program.

14-2.8 Additional Features

Modula-2 has two additional features that have not been introduced, namely "list processing" and "concurrency." The former allows for powerful dynamic storage management to be implemented, while the latter supports the control of asynchronous processing.

Modula-2's list processing facilities are useful in systems programming applications where stacks, queues, trees, or similar data structures must be maintained. To support this, a "pointer type" must be declared in the program as follows:

```
TYPE ptr = POINTER TO node;
```

which means that "the type 'ptr' is defined as a pointer to a record of type 'node'."

Moreover, the record type 'node' can be declared to characterize a typical entry, or "node," in a linked list or stack. For instance, if we wish to create a linked list of fifteen-character names, a typical node would be defined as follows:

```
TYPE node = RECORD
               name: ARRAY [1..15] OF CHAR;
               fptr: ptr
            END
```

Here, the node has two parts, one for the name itself, and one for the pointer ("fptr") that will link this node to the next one in the list. Thus, the following picture

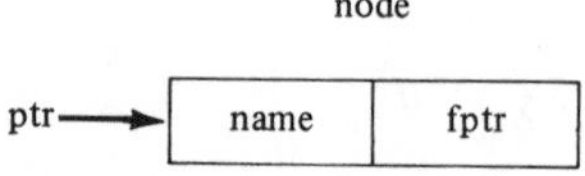

shows that a node in a linked list is identified by variables of type "ptr," and consists of two parts, a "name" and a "fptr," which in turn is of type ptr and serves as a *link* to the next node in the list.

The special value NIL is the designation that a pointer points nowhere, and is represented graphically as follows:

Assuming the above **TYPE** declarations, we may declare variables head, p, and q of type ptr in the usual way:

```
VAR head, p, q: ptr;
```

Two useful procedures, called NEW and DISPOSE, are provided by the standard module Storage in Modula-2. These allow individual nodes to be created and destroyed, and must be accessed through the following **IMPORT** statement:

FROM Storage **IMPORT** ALLOCATE, DEALLOCATE;

The procedure NEW is invoked with a pointer variable as a parameter. Continuing our example, the statement

NEW(p)

will create a node and set the variable p to point to it as shown:

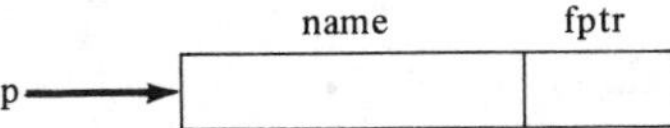

Note that no *value* is stored in the node as a result of this statement; only the node is created.

To reference the value of an entry in a node, we use the notation pointer ^. entry where "pointer" is a variable which currently points to that node. Thus, for example, p^. name denotes the "name" entry in the node to which p currently points.

Conversely, to destroy a node the procedure DISPOSE is invoked, with a pointer to the node in question supplied as a parameter. Thus,

DISPOSE(p)

will cause the node currently referenced by p, together with its value, to become inaccessible to the program.

A pointer valuable may be set to point to the same node as another by using a simple assignment statement. For instance, to make q point to the same node as p, we simply say:

q := p

To combine these ideas into a functional example, consider the following Modula-2 program which develops a linked list from a series of fifteen-character names given as input, as shown in Figures 14-9 and 14-10.

```
MODULE Lister;
   FROM Storage IMPORT ALLOCATE, DEALLOCATE;
   FROM InOut IMPORT ReadString, Done;
   TYPE ptr = POINTER TO node;
```

```
        node = RECORD
          name: ARRAY [1 . . 15] OF CHAR;
          fptr: ptr
        END;
    VAR p, q, head: ptr;
  BEGIN
    NEW(p);
    head := p; q := NIL;
    ReadString (p^.name);
    WHILE Done DO
      q := p;
      NEW(p);
      q^.fptr := p;
      ReadString(p^.name)
    END;
    DISPOSE(p); (* end of input – get rid of extra node *)
    IF q # NIL
      THEN q^.ftpr := NIL
      ELSE head := NIL
    END
  END Lister.
```

The first statement causes a single node to be created, as shown in Figure 14-11. The next three statements set ''head'' to point to this node, q to NIL, and the first ''name'' in the input data to be read and stored in this node. Thus, after the first three statements within the **WHILE** loop are executed, the list is partially constructed as shown in Figure 14-12.

Note that each time through this loop, a NEW node is prepared for receiving the next input name just before the statement ''ReadString (p^.name)'' is reached. Thus, upon end of input the situation is as shown in Figure 14-13, with an extra node that will not be utilized. The last two statements in the program clean up this loose end, disposing of the extra node and setting the last node's fptr to NIL (if there is one).

Concurrent Processes The specification and control of asynchronous processes in Modula-2 is realized by its facilities for definition and activation of concurrent procedures. Such procedures are embedded within modules, and as such have two parts: a

FIGURE 14-9

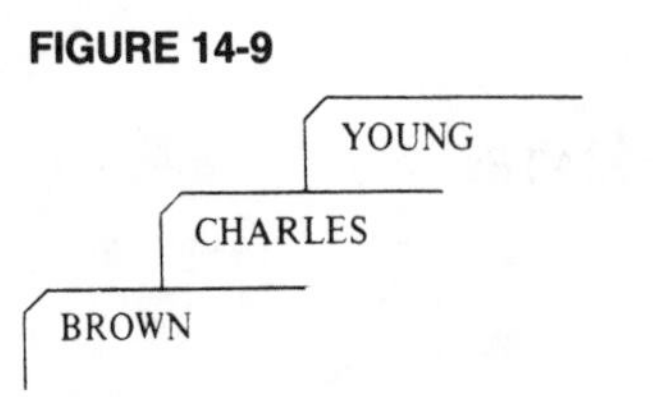

FIGURE 14-10

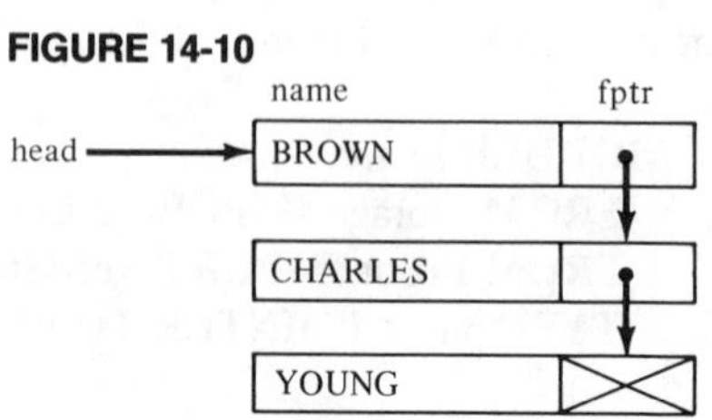

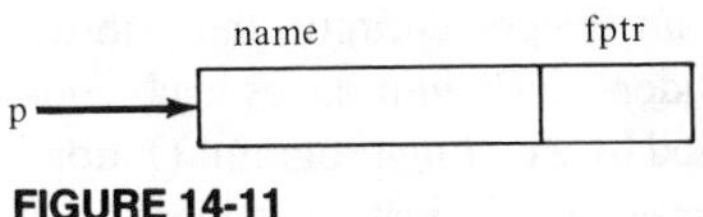

FIGURE 14-11

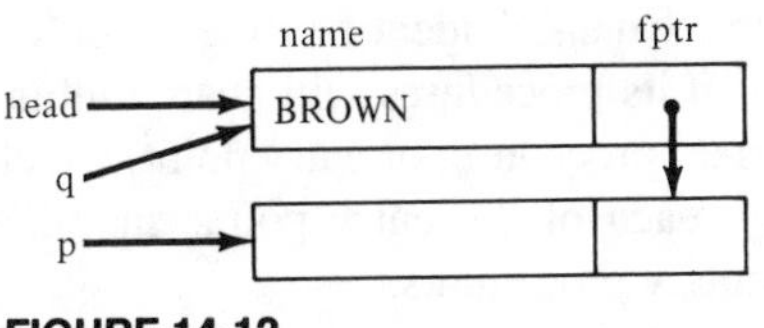

FIGURE 14-12

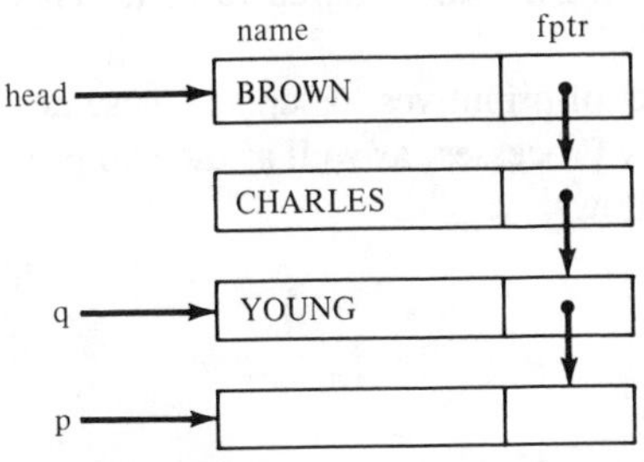

FIGURE 14-13

DEFINITION and an **IMPLEMENTATION**. The definition identifies the particular procedures, or "entry points," which can be asynchronously activated by a program, while the implementation defines the algorithms contained within these entry points and the conditions under which they may be activated. Thus, the definition and implementation modules have the following forms:

```
DEFINITION MODULE name [priority];
  EXPORT QUALIFIED list;
  IMPORT list;
  declarations
PROCEDURE identifier (formal parameters);
PROCEDURE identifier (formal parameters);
  :
END name.

IMPLEMENTATION MODULE name;
  EXPORT QUALIFIED list;
  IMPORT list;
  declarations
PROCEDURE identifier (formal parameters);
  locals
BEGIN
  statements
END identifier;
PROCEDURE identifier (formal parameters);
  :
END name.
```

Here, ''name'' identifies the module, ''priority'' is an integer defining the priority which its procedures will share within the system, ''identifier'' introduces each concurrent procedure, or entry point, which can be activated by a calling program. Optionally, each of the entry points may have ''formal parameters,'' just as if they were ordinary procedures.

The ''declarations'' indicate variables which may be *shared* by the concurrently executing procedures, and special variables called ''signals'' which help to prevent more than one such procedure from simultaneously accessing the same shared variable. This kind of control is known as ''mutual exclusion.''

The standard module ''Processes'' contains a set of primitives to support these notions. Specifically, the type SIGNAL is exported by Processes, as well as the two procedures SEND and WAIT. They are invoked as follows:

```
SEND(signal)
WAIT(signal)
```

where ''signal'' denotes any variable of type SIGNAL. Invocation of SEND sends the indicated signal, while another procedure may suspend its own action (until such signal is sent) by giving a WAIT with the same signal. If several procedures are simultaneously WAITing for the same signal to be sent, they are queued.

A module which contains procedures that guarantee mutual exclusion in this way is called a ''monitor.'' Procedures which are defined within a monitor may be activated by procedure calls from other modules, in any order and asynchronously. Mutual exclusion is controlled by use of signals, SENDs, and WAITs among the procedures within the monitor themselves. To illustrate these notions, consider the problem of a single buffer, in which two kinds of events can take place:

1 A value is placed in the buffer.
2 A value is taken from the buffer.

The buffer can hold only one value at a time, so that neither event can occur twice in a row (before the other event occurs), and event **1** must occur first. However, the timing in which values are presented to enter the buffer is undetermined. The following module BufferIO characterizes this situation:

```
DEFINITION MODULE BufferIO [1];
  EXPORT INSERT, TAKE;
  FROM Processes IMPORT SIGNAL, SEND, WAIT, Init;
  IsFull, IsEmpty: SIGNAL;
  BUFFER: INTEGER;
  PROCEDURE TAKE (VAR I: INTEGER);
  PROCEDURE INSERT (I: INTEGER);
END BufferIO.

IMPLEMENTATION MODULE BufferIO [1];
  EXPORT INSERT, TAKE;
  FROM Processes IMPORT SIGNAL, SEND, WAIT, Init;
```

```
    IsFull, IsEmpty: SIGNAL;
    BUFFER: INTEGER;

    PROCEDURE TAKE (VAR I: INTEGER);
    BEGIN
      WAIT(IsFull);          (* Wait for buffer to be full *)
      I := BUFFER;           (* Transfer value from it *)
      SIGNAL(IsEmpty)        (* Signal that buffer is empty *)
    END TAKE;

    PROCEDURE INSERT (I: INTEGER);
    BEGIN
      WAIT(IsEmpty);       (* Wait for buffer to be empty *)
      BUFFER := I;         (* Transfer value to it *)
      SIGNAL(IsFull)       (* Signal that buffer is full *)
    END INSERT;
  BEGIN
    Init(IsFull); Init(IsEmpty)
  END BufferIO.
```

The signals IsFull and IsEmpty report the status of the BUFFER. Procedure TAKE waits for the BUFFER to become full before it can perform its task, after which it signals that the BUFFER is empty. Similarly, procedure INSERT waits for the BUFFER to become empty, performs its task, and signals that the BUFFER has become full.

The calls for these procedures are themselves mutually asynchronous; one or more may be attempting to send values to the buffer and others may be wanting to retrieve values from it. There is only one buffer, however, and when more than one request occurs, duplicate requests are placed in a waiting queue until they can be satisfied. To insert a value into the buffer, the calling procedure gives a "call statement":

```
INSERT (value)
```

To retrieve a value from the buffer, a calling procedure gives the following call statement:

```
TAKE (value)
```

Such calling procedures are not in any way synchronized with each other, or knowledgeable about each other's existence. All synchronization of INSERT and TAKE requests is managed by the BufferIO module itself. We shall give a more substantial example of asynchronous processing in the next section.

14-3 APPLICATIONS OF MODULA-2

Now that the reader has a working knowledge of Modula-2, we present and discuss a Modula-2 solution to Case Study 5—Job Scheduler. This discussion will exhibit various characteristics of Modula-2 as it is used in systems programming applications.

Following that discussion we will briefly explain implementation dependent extensions of Modula-2, especially those found in the standard system modules. We conclude the chapter with an overall evaluation of Modula-2, using this case study and the evaluation criteria discussed in Chapter 1.

14-3.1 Modula-2 Case Study Implementation

Case Study 5—Job Scheduler is defined as a Modula-2 ''monitor''—a module named JobScheduler in which three principal activities are taking place asynchronously. These activities are: insertion of a new job into the queue (procedure NEWJOB), activation of the next job from the queue in storage (procedure ACTIVATE), and deactivation of a terminated job from storage (procedure DEACTIVATE). A fourth principal activity, COMPACTIFY, is called by ACTIVATE in situations where storage cannot be allocated because of fragmentation. The principal shared variables and SIGNALS used by these procedures are given in the definition module for JobScheduler shown in Figure 14-14.

Here, we see that the job queue is represented as a linked list, with HEAD pointing to the next job in the queue ready for scheduling. The lists of active storage blocks (Active) and available storage blocks (Asl) are defined as arrays of MAXBLOCKS entries, representing an upper bound on the number of jobs that can be active (blocks that can be available) at one time. Each block in this list contains a job identification (Jobno), a starting address (Startaddress), and a size (Blocksize), each given as an integer representing thousands of bytes. That is, a value 2000 means 2000k bytes, or 2 megabytes.

Four signals are maintained by these procedures, and are called Qready, Qempty, Aslready, and Aslempty. Qready is signaled by procedure NEWJOB as soon as it has added a new job to the queue. Qempty is signaled by the procedure ACTIVATE if it schedules the *last* job from the queue. Aslready is signaled by either DEACTIVATE or the auxiliary procedure COMPACTIFY, as a result of finding a block on the available space list which is at least as large as that required by the next job on the queue. Aslempty is signaled when the converse is true.

The implementation of this module is described in Figures 14-15 through 14-18, where the bodies of the principal procedures are shown. Sufficient commentary is provided so that their logic should be clear.

This case study was compiled on the Modula-2 implementation shown in Figure 14-19 but was not executed because the compiler available to the author does not yet support asynchronous processes. The efficiency of this compilation is summarized in Figure 14-19.

14-3.2 Implementation Dependent Extensions of Modula-2

Although there are few implementations of Modula-2 at this writing, the language definition [4] expects that implementations will provide several ''standard modules'' beyond the basic language description. Some of these have already been mentioned in this chapter, such as MathLib0, InOut, and Storage. Others are also suggested, such as a string handling module, a screen graphics module, and so forth. It is too early in the life

```
DEFINITION MODULE JobScheduler;

     FROM Processes IMPORT SIGNAL, SEND, WAIT, Init;
     FROM Storage IMPORT ALLOCATE, DEALLOCATE;
     EXPORT QUALIFIED NEWJOB, DEACTIVATE;


     PROCEDURE NEWJOB (Jobno, Jobsize: CARDINAL);
       (* This procedure adds a new job to the queue.  The
          signal Qready is issued when that is complete.
       *)

     PROCEDURE ACTIVATE;
       (* This procedure removes the next job from the head
          of the queue and allocates a block of storage for
          it, if space is available.
       *)

     PROCEDURE DEACTIVATE (Jobno: CARDINAL);
       (* This procedure removes an active job from the list
          of active jobs in storage.
       *)

     PROCEDURE COMPACTIFY;
       (* This procedure regroups the jobs in storage, so that
          all fragments are combined into a single contiguous
          storage block.
       *)

END JobScheduler.
```

FIGURE 14-14

```
IMPLEMENTATION MODULE JobScheduler [1];
     FROM Processes IMPORT SIGNAL, SEND, WAIT, Init;
     FROM Storage IMPORT ALLOCATE, DEALLOCATE;
     CONST HIMEM = 2000;

     TYPE JQptr = POINTER TO Jobqueue;
     TYPE Jobqueue = RECORD
               Jobno: CARDINAL;
               Jobsize: CARDINAL;
               Previousjob: JQptr;
               Nextjob: JQptr
          END;
     VAR HEAD, TAIL: JQptr;

     TYPE ASptr = POINTER TO Asl;
     TYPE Asl = RECORD
               Jobno: CARDINAL;
               Startaddress: CARDINAL;
               Blocksize: CARDINAL;
               Nextblock: ASptr
          END;
     VAR AslHEAD: ASptr;
         Qready, Aslready, Aslempty: SIGNAL;
```

FIGURE 14-15

```
PROCEDURE NEWJOB (Jobno, Jobsize: CARDINAL);
     VAR P: JQptr;
     (* This procedure adds a new job to the queue,
        accommodating the case where the queue is
        initially empty.  The signal Qready is sent in
        either case. *)
BEGIN
     NEW(P);
     P^.Jobno:=Jobno;
     P^.Jobsize:=Jobsize;
     P^.Previousjob:=NIL;
     IF TAIL=NIL THEN                    (* queue is empty *)
          HEAD:=P;
          TAIL:=P;
          P^.Nextjob:=NIL;
     ELSE TAIL^.Previousjob:=P;     (* insert at tail *)
          P^.Nextjob:=TAIL;
          TAIL:=P
     END;
     SEND (Qready)    (* indicate that queue has new entry *)
END NEWJOB;
```

FIGURE 14-15 (*Continued*)

FIGURE 14-16

```
PROCEDURE ACTIVATE;
     VAR P: JQptr;
         I, J: ASptr;
     (* This procedure removes the next job from the HEAD of
        the job queue and allocates a block of storage for
        it, provided that both the queue has at least one
        job in it (Qready) and there is space to accommodate
        it (Aslready). *)
BEGIN
     WAIT (Qready);
     WAIT (Aslready);
     I:=AslHEAD;        (* search Asl for the place to insert *)
     WHILE I # NIL DO
        IF (I^.Jobno=0) AND (I^.Blocksize>=HEAD^.Jobsize) THEN
           I^.Jobno:=HEAD^.Jobno;
           IF I^.Blocksize>HEAD^.Jobsize THEN
              NEW(J); (* add a block for the remaining
                          available space out of this block *)
              J^.Jobno:=0;
              J^.Startaddress:=I^.Startaddress+I^.Blocksize;
              J^.Blocksize:=I^.Blocksize-HEAD^.Jobsize;
              J^.Nextblock:=I^.Nextblock;
              I^.Blocksize:=HEAD^.Jobsize;
              I^.Nextblock:=J
           END;
           P:=HEAD;             (* delete HEAD node in queue *)
           HEAD:=HEAD^.Previousjob;
           DISPOSE(P);
           RETURN
        END;
        I:=I^.Nextblock
     END;
     SEND (Aslempty);
     RETURN
END ACTIVATE;
```

```
PROCEDURE DEACTIVATE (Jobno: CARDINAL);
     VAR I: ASptr;
     (* This procedure deletes an active job from the Asl *)
BEGIN
     I:=AslHEAD;
     WHILE I # NIL DO
        IF I^.Jobno = Jobno THEN
           I^.Jobno:=0;
           RETURN
        END;
        I:=I^.Nextblock
     END;
END DEACTIVATE;
```

FIGURE 14-17

FIGURE 14-18

```
PROCEDURE COMPACTIFY;
     VAR I, J, K: ASptr;
         Tempsize: CARDINAL;
     (* This procedure regroups the jobs in Asl, so that
        they are contiguous, and all blocks of available
        space are compressed into one contiguous block.
        It then signals either Aslempty or Aslready,
        depending on whether that new block is large enough
        to accommodate the job at the head of the queue. *)
BEGIN
     WAIT (Aslempty);
     I:=AslHEAD;
     WHILE I^.Nextblock # NIL DO
        J:=I^.Nextblock;
        IF I^.Jobno=0 THEN     (* available block; look for
                                  combining with the next one *)
           IF J^.Jobno=0 THEN
              I^.Blocksize:=I^.Blocksize+J^.Blocksize;
              I^.Nextblock:=J^.Nextblock;
              DISPOSE (J)
           ELSE          (* move available block downward *)
              I^.Jobno:=J^.Jobno;
              Tempsize:=I^.Blocksize;
              I^.Blocksize:=J^.Blocksize;
              J^.Jobno:=0;
              J^.Startaddress:=I^.Startaddress+I^.Blocksize;
              J^.Blocksize:=Tempsize
           END
        END;
        I:=J
     END;
         (* Now check to see if the available block is
            adequate to accommodate the next job on the
            queue. *)
     IF I^.Blocksize>=HEAD^.Jobsize THEN
        SEND (Aslready)
     ELSE
        SEND (Aslempty)
     END
END COMPACTIFY;
```

```
BEGIN
     HEAD:=NIL; TAIL:=NIL;       (* initialize job queue *)
     NEW(AslHEAD);               (* initialize Asl *)
     AslHEAD^.Jobno:=0; AslHEAD^.Startaddress:=0;
     AslHEAD^.Blocksize:=HIMEM;
     AslHEAD^.Nextblock:=NIL;
     Init (Qready); Init (Aslready); Init (Aslempty)
END JobScheduler.
```

FIGURE 14-18 *(Continued)*

FIGURE 14-19
EFFICIENCY OF MODULA-2 CASE STUDY 5 PROGRAM

Implementation	Compile speed	Execution speed
1 Digital VAX-750/UNIX Modula-2	21.4 sec	na

of Modula-2 to tell which particular standard modules will emerge and find their way into various implementations.

14-3.3 Overall Evaluation of Modula-2

From our case study experience, we evaluate Modula-2 using the nine criteria of Chapter 1 as follows:

1 Expressivity	Good
2 Well-definedness	Excellent
3 Data types and structures	Excellent
4 Modularity	Excellent
5 Input-output facilities	Fair
6 Portability	Good
7 Efficiency	Good
8 Pedagogy	Fair
9 Generality	Good

An insistence on strong typing and simplicity of syntax are major factors in Modula-2's excellent ''well-definedness.'' Well-conceived and rigorous syntactic and semantic definitions are also important here. Factors which contribute to Modula-2's excellent ''data types'' include its type definition and abstraction mechanisms, while its excellent ''modularity'' derives from the module concept, and related facilities for information hiding, independent compilation, and library functions.

We find Modula-2 to be weakest in ''input-output facilities'' and ''pedagogy.'' Its standard input-output procedures are drearily like those of its predecessors, which have not dramatically improved since the early 1960s. Modula-2's weak pedagogy is due mainly to its newness, and that should improve as familiarity is gained and more useful textbooks are written for it.

In all other criteria, Modula-2 is judged to be good. Its "efficiency" is quite good for such a powerful language, and its "portability" and "generality" hold much promise for more widespread applications in the future. Indeed, if for some reason Ada fails to live up to its advanced billing, Modula-2 will become a very viable alternative for embedded systems programming and real time control. Outside of the systems programming area, the future of Modula-2 is difficult to anticipate at this early stage in its life.

EXERCISES

1 Let x, y, and z be REAL variables, and let i, j, and k be INTEGER variables. Assume that they have the following values:

```
x = 2.5      i = 1
y = -10      j = -5
z = 8        k = 12
```

Compute the result delivered by evaluating each of the following arithmetic expressions:

(a) x + y * z	**(e)** i − 1
(b) (x + y) * z	**(f)** i **DIV** j* k
(c) (x + y)/(z − 3)	**(g)** i/j * k
(d) x + y/(z − 3)	**(h)** 4 * i + k **DIV** j

2 Suppose we have a 5 × 5 **ARRAY** A of REAL values. The "Trace" of A is defined as the sum of its diagonal elements. For instance, if A's elements are the following:

$$\begin{bmatrix} 3 & 2 & -1 & 9 & 0 \\ 0 & 1 & 5 & 6 & 7 \\ 2 & 4 & 6 & 8 & 7 \\ -9 & 2 & 3 & 7 & 10 \\ -1 & -2 & -3 & -4 & -5 \end{bmatrix}$$

then its Trace is 3 + 1 + 6 + 7+ (−5) = 12.

(a) Write a declaration for A.

(b) Write an input statement which will store these values in A, assuming they are typed row by row as input lines.

(c) Write a **FOR** loop which will compute the Trace of A.

(d) Write another **FOR** loop which will leave the maximum value from A in the REAL variable named Amaxim, and leave that value's row and column numbers in the INTEGER variables named Arow and Acol.

3 Write a function procedure named Trace which will compute the Trace of any n × n REAL **ARRAY** A.

4 Rewrite the function procedure of Exercise 3 as a proper procedure.

5 If your installation has a different Modula-2 compiler than the ones used here, adapt our Modula-2 Case Study 5 implementation to run under that compiler. How difficult was that adaptation? What features does your Modula-2 system have that make the program easier to write? More difficult?

6 Implement Case Study 4—Missionaries and Cannibals in Modula-2. Evaluate Modula-2 as an AI programming language from this experience.

7 Implement Case Study 0 (which you defined at the end of Chapter 1) in Modula-2. Evaluate Modula-2's performance and suitability for this application.

8 Consider implementing Case Study 2—Employee File Maintenance in Modula-2. What are Modula-2's strengths for data processing applications such as this? What are its weaknesses?

9 Modula-2 has no "go to" statement, a familiar fixture in most other languages, and apparently has no need for it. Review the history of the "go to" statement controversy, and discuss the relevant issues pro and con.

10 Consider the BufferIO module written in section 14-2.8. What changes would be necessary to accommodate a buffer in which N messages ($N \leq 10$) could be simultaneously stored, rather than just one. Are additional signals needed?

11 Write a Modula-2 procedure that will sort its three parameters into ascending sequence, assuming they are all INTEGERs.

12 Write a procedure which, given an array A of integers, counts the number of positive entries (Npos), the number of negative entries (Nneg), and the number of zero entries (Nzero) that it contains.

13 Trace execution of the BufferIO module in section 14-2.8, given the following sequence of invocations for INSERT and TAKE from various sources.

```
INSERT(1)
TAKE(X)
TAKE(X)
INSERT(2)
INSERT(3)
INSERT(4)
INSERT(5)
TAKE(X)
INSERT(6)
INSERT(7)
TAKE(X)
TAKE(X)
INSERT(8)
TAKE(X)
```

REFERENCES

1 Niklaus Wirth, "The Personal Computer Lilith," Report 40, Institute for Informatik, ETH Zurich, Switzerland, April 1981.

2 Niklaus Wirth, "Modula: a Language for Modular Multiprogramming," *Software—Practice and Experience* 7:3–35 (1977).

3 Niklaus Wirth, *Programming in Modula-2*, 2d corrected ed., Springer-Verlag, New York, 1983.

4 Wirth, *Programming in Modula-2*.

CHAPTER **15**

LANGUAGE DESIGN: PRAGMATICS

The pragmatic aspects of language design are perhaps the broadest and the most influential on future trends in programming languages. They are also more subtly shifting and difficult to characterize then the subjects of "syntax" and "semantics." In this chapter, we try to identify the principal forces that currently influence the incorporation of new programming language features and the dissolution of old ones. We conclude the text with a comparative evaluation of the eleven languages presented, together with some observations on the process of language evaluation itself.

15-1 THE ART AND SCIENCE OF LANGUAGE DESIGN

In this book, we have seen programming languages evolve from two principal sources: the genius of an individual person (LISP and Modula-2 for example) and the consorted efforts of a committee or a community (COBOL and Ada for example). Individually designed languages tend to be "cleaner" in content and style, and more distinctive as well. Committee-designed languages tend, on the other hand, to represent the *union* of several interests and are therefore more laden with baggage and features than they might otherwise be. Of course, there are exceptions to these generalizations, as seen in the proliferation of dialects of LISP on the one hand, and in the unusual clarity and focus of Ada on the other.

Various language designers have, from time to time, discussed their art itself. For instance, C. A. R. Hoare published his thoughts on the subject in 1973,[1] and Niklaus Wirth did the same in 1974.[2] In these and other similar papers, the overriding advice for language designers is to combine simplicity and functionality. The ultimate goal of a language should be to allow the programmer to think clearly about the complexity of the presented problem rather than the complexity of the programming language itself. Judging from the evolution of programming languages studied in this book, that goal seems much easier to state than it is to reach.

15-2 THE ART AND SCIENCE OF PROGRAMMING

Our discussion leads also to an examination of more fundamental issues on the nature of programming itself. Programming is, on the one hand, an artistic or creative endeavor, and on the other, a scientific endeavor. Knuth's three famous volumes, for instance, are entitled *The Art of Computer Programming*.[3] Gries' recent book, conversely, is entitled *The Science of Programming*.[4]

As an artist, the programmer begins with an understanding of the medium, or application area. The art of programming seems therefore to be the development of creative solutions to problems, so that the overall quality of activity within that application area will be enhanced.

As a scientist, the programmer begins with a clearly defined set of principles, or axioms of programming. He or she then applies them systematically to a problem, in such a way that at any stage in the process the (mathematical) correctness of the program can be routinely demonstrated.

The implications for language design of these two philosophies of programming are significant. The art of programming demands a variety of "tools," or a "programming environment" within which the total process of program development can take place. The science of programming demands a language which supports the axiomatic proof of program behavior. Although the latter has been under study for several years, it has not yet been significantly embedded within contemporary languages. An early version of Ada had a facility called the "**assert** statement," which provided a mechanism for formalizing "assertions" about programs, but that facility did not ultimately survive in the Ada standard.

Nevertheless, good programming must necessarily combine both an artistic spirit and a methodology based on scientific principles. In the next several paragraphs, we shall examine some of the more concrete developments in programming methodology and their implications for language design.

The Von Neumann Bottleneck For several years, a general discontent has been expressed, in various ways, with the programming process and its productivity (or lack thereof). We noted at the beginning of the Ada chapter, for instance, that Ada was designed as a vehicle to address the "software crisis" that had developed in embedded systems programming.

Two different lines of response to this problem have developed in the last few years. On the one hand, the need to develop a more refined "programming environment" has been addressed by such languages as C (within the context of the UNIX operating system) and Ada (within the context of the newly conceived Ada Programming Support Environment [APSE]).[5]

On the other hand, John Backus has observed that the problem is rooted in the so-called "von Neumann bottleneck."[6] In his 1977 Turing Award lecture, Backus strongly criticized contemporary programming languages as growing increasingly complex but retaining inherent defects at their heart. These defects are based in large part on the underlying von Neumann machine architecture (exemplified by contemporary machines) which have motivated the basic control structures in most languages since the 1960s.

Software Engineering "Software engineering" is a general approach to alleviating the software crisis and facilitating the development of large and/or complex software products, borrowing its methodologies from other traditional engineering disciplines. Software engineering emerged in the 1960s as a separate discipline, and it encompasses the entire software development life cycle from the initial feasibility study to the ongoing maintenance of the final product.

Software engineering is a broad and comprehensive topic for study. Within the context of programming language design, the needs of software engineering have been more effectively addressed by current languages than by older ones. Most notable among these are Ada, C, and Modula-2, since they explicitly support abstraction and modular design at an efficient level of implementation. Two recent texts, one by Grady Booch[7] and the other by Richard Wiener and Richard Sincovec,[8] provide excellent introductions to software engineering using Ada and Modula-2 as vehicles.

Logic Programming "Logic programming" is an attempt to define an alternative programming style from the conventional von Neumann style. In it, the programmer describes a process indirectly, by defining a set of assertions, or conditions, which must be satisfied or "true" in order for the process to complete its task. The resulting algorithm itself is not completely under the control of the programmer, yet the programmer must master the underlying control mechanisms in order to specify a correct set of assertions. Moreover, the backtracking and control mechanism provided by PROLOG appears to be sometimes inefficient, and the programmer has few tools available for governing that mechanism.

We saw an example of logic programming in our study of PROLOG in Chapter 11. Other languages have also been developed for logic programming, most notably an extension of LISP known as LOGLISP.[9] These languages appear to be useful not only as vehicles for logic programming, but also as a constructive medium for expressing the unification of a program with its database. The PROLOG family-tree illustration in Chapter 11 is a good example of this unification. Here, traditional considerations for "input-output" and "file processing" become less important than the logical relationships within the database itself.

Yet logic programming is, by its unusual nature, difficult to assimilate for persons who have been trained in the von Neumann style. It appears, in its present infancy, to be difficult to teach as well; the current scarcity of good textbooks on the subject tends to reinforce this belief. It may, therefore, be too soon to tell what the overall impact of logic programming will be on the future of programming and programming languages.

Functional Programming In 1977, John Backus advocated a "functional style" of programming, based on pure LISP constructs and a higher level of data abstraction such as that found in APL. The aim here is to base a programming language on elementary forms of function definition, and thus provide a simple, clear, and elegant medium for expressing algorithms. It is possible that functional programming had been in practice for several years before, although it may not have been identified as such or seen as a means of escape from the von Neumann bottleneck.

Clearly, LISP was the first functional programming language to be widely used. The recent text by Peter Henderson[10] is an excellent exposition of functional programming, its style and its uses. More recently, C can be said to embody a functional programming style as well, since every executable construct in the language is an instance of an expression, which consists of a series of applications of functions to arguments and delivers a result. Functional programming languages are also known as "applicative languages" for this reason.

Data Abstraction In recent languages, we have seen a trend toward unification and generalization of data types. Generally, the idea of providing a language mechanism which unifies the *representation* and the *operations* of a programmer-defined data type is known as "data abstraction." Explicit facilities for data abstraction appear in Ada in the form of packages, and in Modula-2 in the form of modules.

The usefulness of these notions in the context of software engineering and large system development is clear. In fact, the activity of data abstraction has been conducted for several years earlier, as the development of statistical packages (SPSS [statistical package for the social sciences], SAS [statistical analysis system], BMDP [biomedical data processing]) and other application-oriented packages can attest. The recent embedding of data abstraction facilities in programming languages gives formal endorsement of this practice for programmers at large.

15-3 THE PROGRAMMING ENVIRONMENT

The design of particular programming language features has recently been given less attention than the design of "programming environments." Broadly, a programming environment includes all the facilities and tools which a software designer or programmer requires in the design, development, testing, implementation, and maintenance of a system of programs. Thus, text editors, compilers, interpreters, diagnostic tools, optimizers, measurement tools, and other aids comprise a complete programming environment.

The first effective formal link between a programming language and the programming environment was perhaps achieved by C and its host operating system UNIX. Comprising a highly portable library and set of tools, UNIX has become a "standard" operating environment for software design inside and outside the academic community. Similarly, INTERLISP has provided the same comprehensive set of tools as an environment for LISP programming within the artificial intelligence community. Even more recently, the development of "LISP machines" has attempted to build into the hardware such a complete set of tools.

However, a strong link exists between the programming environment and a particular programming language. In addition to C and LISP, other languages make strong commitments to the need for a modern programming environment. Recent developments in the design process for Ada have produced the working document called STONEMAN,[11] which contains a set of requirements for a programming support environment for Ada called APSE. It is a complex set of specifications whose contribution to the development of "universals" for programming environments remains to be seen. At a more concrete level, a recent Sigsoft/Sigplan symposium reflects the current level of vitality and progress in the development of programming environments in several different programming language settings.[12]

15-4 LANGUAGE COMPARISON AND EVALUATION

Sooner or later, every language designer and programmer comes to the point of deciding which of the myriad of programming languages and features are good, which are bad, and why. Such decisions often raise heated debates among the best of professionals and students alike. The languages which emerge, or fail to emerge, do so for various reasons. Historically, we think that languages tend to improve along with the art and science of programming itself, but this is difficult to quantify.

Some attempts have been made to formulate objective criteria for language evaluation and comparison. The oldest criteria, and the most quantifiable, are the efficiency of a language's implementation; measured in compile speed, execution speed, storage requirements, and so forth. In the past, the choice of a language was strongly dictated by the performance of several benchmark problems (not unlike our case study problems), using these measures for comparing of language A with language B with the same benchmark problem.

More recently, attention has been redirected at the quality of a language's expressive power, the portability of programs and programmers, and its well-definedness and internal consistency. Important papers on language comparison methodology have been written by Alan Feuer and Narian Gehani[13] and Niklaus Wirth,[14] as well as the Ada STEELMAN requirements[15] document itself.

Particular language comparisons and evaluations have also been extensively conducted in the past few years. Most significant among these was the comprehensive evaluation of twenty-two candidate languages for the DOD, using the STEELMAN requirements, which resulted in the conclusion that the new language Ada was needed. Other language evaluations and comparisons have been conducted by Brian Kernighan,[16] B. A. Wichmann,[17] M. Shaw et al.,[18] and H. J. Boom and E. DeJong.[19] Such papers are varied in their completeness, objectivity, and points of view.

Our own comparisons are based on the nine evaluation criteria presented in Chapter 1, and applied at the end of each of the eleven language chapters. Our conclusions are mixed, of course, and not all language pairs in this book lend themselves to a direct comparison for reasons cited elsewhere. Our comparisons are divided into five groups, one for each of the application areas characterized by a case study problem. We compare Pascal, FORTRAN, and APL for scientific programming, COBOL and PL/I for data processing, SNOBOL and C for text processing, LISP and PROLOG for artificial intelligence, and Ada and Modula-2 for systems programming.

Pascal, FORTRAN, and APL for Scientific Programming Our evaluations of Pascal, FORTRAN, and APL are summarized below, and are based primarily on our experience with Case Study 1—Matrix Inversion.

	Pascal	FORTRAN	APL
1 Expressivity	Good	Fair	Fair
2 Well-definedness	Excellent	Good	Good
3 Data types and structures	Fair	Fair	Good
4 Modularity	Good	Good	Fair
5 Input-output facilities	Good	Good	Fair
6 Portability	Excellent	Good	Poor
7 Efficiency	Good	Excellent	Good
8 Pedagogy	Good	Good	Fair
9 Generality	Fair	Fair	Poor

From this experience, we conclude that Pascal is the best defined and most portable among the three, APL has the best data structure support, and FORTRAN is the most efficient. None of these results is particularly surprising, except perhaps for the arguable alternative position that FORTRAN is at least as portable as Pascal.

COBOL and PL/I for Data Processing In the data processing application area, our experience with PL/I and COBOL in Case Study 2—Employee File Maintenance yields the following summary results:

	COBOL	PL/I
1 Expressivity	Fair	Fair
2 Well-definedness	Good	Good
3 Data types and structures	Fair	Good
4 Modularity	Fair	Good
5 Input-output facilities	Excellent	Excellent
6 Portability	Good	Poor
7 Efficiency	Excellent	Poor
8 Pedagogy	Poor	Good
9 Generality	Fair	Excellent

This summary leads to the conclusion that PL/I is superior to COBOL in data structures, modularity, pedagogy, and generality. On the other hand, COBOL excels in portability and efficiency. These results tend to corroborate similar widely accepted opinions about these two languages in comparison with each other.

SNOBOL and C for Text Processing In the text processing area, we can compare SNOBOL and C, based on our experience with Case Study 3—Text Formatter. Our conclusions are summarized below.

	SNOBOL	C
1 Expressivity	Fair	Good
2 Well-definedness	Excellent	Excellent
3 Data types and structures	Good	Good
4 Modularity	Fair	Excellent
5 Input-output facilities	Fair	Good
6 Portability	Good	Excellent
7 Efficiency	Good	Excellent
8 Pedagogy	Fair	Fair
9 Generality	Poor	Good

Here, C is clearly superior, overshadowing SNOBOL in six of the nine categories. This difference is primarily attributable to C's relative youthfulness combined with the lack of recent progress in upgrading SNOBOL with modern control and data structures. Moreover, C's strength extends into the systems programming area, for which it was principally designed. Finally, C contains the most unified approach, in our opinion, to procedures and functions among all the languages covered in this text, virtually eliminating the artificial dichotomy that has existed between them for decades.

We also note that the evolution of ICON, a recently designed successor to SNOBOL, responds favorably to all of SNOBOL's weaknesses. The fact that ICON incorporates C's best features promises the future success of this young language.

LISP and PROLOG for Artificial Intelligence For artificial intelligence applications, we can compare LISP and PROLOG on the basis of our Case Study 4—Missionaries and Cannibals problem. The results are summarized below.

	LISP	PROLOG
1 Expressivity	Good	Good
2 Well-definedness	Excellent	Excellent
3 Data types and structures	Good	Good
4 Modularity	Excellent	Good
5 Input-output facilities	Poor	Good
6 Portability	Fair	Poor
7 Efficiency	Good	Fair
8 Pedagogy	Fair	Poor
9 Generality	Poor	Poor

These results reflect a bit of a standoff, with LISP slightly better in modularity and efficiency, and PROLOG slightly better in input-output facilities. Notably, neither rates particularly well in portability, pedagogy, or generality. Weak portability exists for LISP because of the proliferation of dialects, while PROLOG is weak in portability because it is not widely implemented. Neither is particularly efficient because both are principally interpreted languages. Neither is particularly general because they were never designed for general use.

Ada and Modula-2 for Systems Programming Finally, in the area of systems programming, we can compare Ada and Modula-2, based on our experience with Case Study 5—Job Scheduler. Our comparisons are summarized below.

	Ada	Modula-2
1 Expressivity	Good	Good
2 Well-definedness	Good	Excellent
3 Data types and structures	Good	Excellent
4 Modularity	Excellent	Excellent
5 Input-output facilities	Good	Fair
6 Portability	Good	Good
7 Efficiency	Fair	Good
8 Pedagogy	Good	Fair
9 Generality	Excellent	Good

To our knowledge, these two languages have not yet been compared head-to-head in the systems programming area. This is principally due to their relative youthfulness. In any event, we conclude that Ada's input-output facilities, pedagogy, and generality are superior to those of Modula-2. On the other hand, Modula-2 is superior in well-definedness, data types and structures, and efficiency. However, Modula-2 may soon catch up with Ada in pedagogy as new textbooks are developed for it. Similarly, Ada may catch up with Modula-2 in efficiency as improved compilers become available in the future.

15-5 CONCLUSIONS

Our conclusions in the 1977 edition of this text were guardedly hopeful in their outlook for the "future of programming languages." There, we expressed the hope that languages would expand their built-in functional capabilities, improve upon their efficiency, begin to include lowercase characters in their character sets, increase their declarative content so that large application packages could be more easily developed, and improve their generic functional capabilities.

For the most part, these hopes have been realized in the last eight years. Tremendous advances have been achieved in programming language design. Especially notable has been Ada's design process, which momentarily fused the best efforts from academia, industry, and government in a monumental effort. In this, the resulting language design may be less important in the long run than the dialog that was created in the process. The design of future languages and programming environments will surely benefit from such a fusion.

EXERCISES

1 Comparatively evaluate the languages in which you have implemented your Case Study 0 problem, using the nine criteria presented in Chapter 1. How do your conclusions differ from ours?

2 Read Backus's 1978 paper (cited in Ref. 6), and comment on the "von Neumann bottleneck," as it relates to programming, language design, and language implementation.
3 Read references (cited in Refs. 5 and 7) on the Ada programming support environment, or so-called APSE, and comment on their relation to environments with which you are already familiar (for instance, in C, LISP, Pascal, and so forth).
4 Read references on "LISP machines" (cited in Ref. 10) and comment on their potential effect on programming, language design, and language implementation.
5 Read the STEELMAN (cited in Ref. 15) requirements, and compare them with our nine criteria for language evaluation. To what extent would these requirements be appropriate to other than systems programming applications?
6 Obtain current statistics on programming language usage, using recent issues of *Datamation, DataPro* reports, and so forth. Evaluate the trends, and predict which of the current languages will be prevalent over the next decade.
7 Compare and contrast the terms "structured programming," "modular programming," and "software engineering," and evaluate our eleven languages' strengths and weaknesses for each of them.
8 Portability of a language is often achieved by compiling into an abstract assembly language and then assembling into the native code for each of several cpu's via an appropriate set of macros. For instance, the UCSD P-system is such an abstract assembly language, hosting the compilation of Pascal, FORTRAN, and Modula-2 for several different machines. Comment on the advantages and disadvantages of this approach, in the context of the other eight language evaluation criteria (besides portability).
9 A programming language design tends either to evolve out of the work of a committee or to be the product of essentially one person's individual effort. Comment on which of these two approaches tends to produce a better language, and give reasons and examples to support your conclusions.
10 A recent survey of data processing programmers revealed that about 71 percent of all programming was done in COBOL, RPG, or FORTRAN, 8 percent was done in assembly language, 5 percent was done in PL/I, and the remaining 16 percent was done in other languages. Comment on these findings, in light of the languages and applications which you know.
11 Under what conditions can we meaningfully compare COBOL and PL/I? Pascal and Ada? FORTRAN and Modula-2? C and PROLOG?
12 For scientific applications, would you consider APL, FORTRAN, Pascal, or PL/I to be the better language? Are there alternatives better than any of these? Explain.
13 What is "default" when used in the context of language design? Compare the use of default in the definitions of PL/I, Pascal, LISP, and Ada.
14 Contrast the approach used in the design of Ada with that used in the design of other languages. How do they differ, and what advantages and disadvantages do you see in such an approach?

REFERENCES

1 C. A. R., Hoare, "Hints on Programming Language Design," *Sigact/Sigplan Symposium on Principles of Programming Languages,* October 1973.
2 Niklaus Wirth, "On the Design of Programming Languages," *Proc IFIP Congress 74,* North Holland, 1974, pp. 386–393.
3 Donald Knuth, *The Art of Computer Programming,* vols. 1, 2, 3, Addison-Wesley, Boston, 1983.
4 David Gries, *The Science of Programming,* Springer-Verlag, New York, 1981.

5 *Requirements for the Programming Environment for the Common High Order Language, STONEMAN,* Department of Defense, Washington, D.C., 1980.
6 John Backus, ''Can Programming Be Liberated from the von Neumann Style? A Functional Style and its Algebra of Programs,'' *Communications of the ACM* 21(8): 613–641 (August 1978).
7 Grady Booch, *Software Engineering with Ada,* Benjamin Cummings, Boston, 1983.
8 Richard Wiener and Richard Sincovec, *Software Engineering with Modula-2 and Ada,* Wiley, New York, 1984.
9 Peter Henderson, ed., *Proc Sigsoft/Sigplan Symposium on Practical Software Development Environments,* ACM, New York, April 1984.
10 Peter Henderson, *Functional Programming: Application and Implementation,* Prentice-Hall, Englewood Cliffs, N.J., 1980.
11 *Requirements for the Programming Environment . . ., STONEMAN.*
12 Peter Henderson, ed., *Proc Sigsoft/Sigplan Symposium.*
13 Alan Feuer and Narian Gehani, eds., *Comparing and Assessing Programming Languages: Ada C Pascal,* Prentice-Hall, Englewood Cliffs, N.J., 1984.
14 Niklaus Wirth, ''Programming Languages: What to Demand and How to Assess Them,'' *Software Engineering,* Academic Press, New York, 1977.
15 *STEELMAN Requirements for DoD High Order Computer Programming Languages,* Department of Defense, Washington, D.C., 1978.
16 Brian Kernighan, ''Why Pascal Is Not My Favorite Programming Language,'' CS Tech Report 100, Bell Laboratories, Murray Hill, N.J., 1981.
17 B. A. Wichmann, ''A Comparison of Pascal and Ada,'' *The Computer Journal* 25 (2) (1982).
18 Shaw, M. et al., ''A Comparison of Programming Languages for Software Engineering,'' *Software—Practice and Experience* 11: 1–52 (1981).
19 H. J. Boom and E. DeJong, ''A Critical Comparison of Several Programming Languages,'' *Software—Practice and Experience* 10(6): 435–483 (June 1980).

APPENDIX **A**

CASE STUDY 1—MATRIX INVERSION

This problem occurs in a variety of scientific applications, including regression analysis, linear programming, and the solution of differential equations. Matrix inversion has such heavy usage that scientific installations typically have a packaged routine for it. Nevertheless, the programming involved in the solution of this problem is representative of that found in many scientific applications.

We assume throughout this case study that the reader is familiar with matrix algebra. The following definitions and notations will be used in our discussion of this problem.

Definition: A square matrix is an $n \times n$ array of numbers, for any integer $n > 0$.

For example, the matrix A below has $4 \times 4 = 16$ numbers.

$$A = \begin{bmatrix} 4 & 7 & 6 & 8 \\ 3 & 8 & 2 & -1 \\ -9 & 0 & 1 & -2 \\ 16 & 3 & 9 & -3 \end{bmatrix}$$

A row is any horizontal line of values in the matrix, while a column is any vertical line of values. Thus, our matrix A has four distinct rows and four distinct columns. The rows and columns are numbered in ascending order from the topmost row and the leftmost column. Thus, we speak of row 3 of A when we are talking about the values of $-9, 0, 1, -2$, and column 4 when we are talking about $8, -1, -2, -3$.

A value within a matrix is identified by a "subscript," which is a pair of integers to identify its row number and column number, respectively, within the matrix. For example, if we write A_{42}, we are talking about the value in the fourth row and second column of the matrix A.

Definition (matrix multiplication): If A and B are $n \times n$ matrices, then their product AB is the $n \times n$ matrix C whose values are defined as follows:

$$C_{ij} = \sum_{k=1}^{n} A_{ik}B_{kj} \qquad \text{for each } i, j = 1, \ldots, n$$

One particular kind of square matrix has the property that whenever it is multiplied by some other matrix, say A, the result is A itself. This is called an "identity matrix," and is denoted by I. It always has 1's on the diagonal and 0's everywhere else. The following is the 4×4 identity matrix:

$$I = \begin{bmatrix} 1 & 0 & 0 & 0 \\ 0 & 1 & 0 & 0 \\ 0 & 0 & 1 & 0 \\ 0 & 0 & 0 & 1 \end{bmatrix}$$

The reader should verify, for example, that $IA = AI = A$ for the 4×4 matrix A given above.

Definition: The "inverse" of an $n \times n$ matrix A is an $n \times n$ square matrix (denoted by A^{-1}) which has the property that, when it is multiplied by A, the result is the $n \times n$ identity matrix I. That is,

$$AA^{-1} = A^{-1}A = I$$

It is easy to verify that an identity matrix has itself as its own inverse. For another example, the reader should verify that the matrix

$$\begin{bmatrix} 3 & 2 \\ 2 & 1 \end{bmatrix}$$

has

$$\begin{bmatrix} -1 & 2 \\ 2 & -3 \end{bmatrix}$$

as its inverse.

Not every square matrix has an inverse. For instance, there is no 2×2 matrix which, when multiplied by the matrix

$$\begin{bmatrix} 1 & 2 \\ 2 & 4 \end{bmatrix}$$

will yield the 2×2 identity matrix. Thus, no matter what algorithm we use to find an inverse for an arbitrary square matrix, it must allow for the possibility that the inverse does not exist. On the other hand, if we determine that there is an inverse, that inverse is unique. That is, no square matrix has more than one inverse.

An Algorithm for Matrix Inversion Here, we briefly discuss and present an algorithm for computing the inverse of an $n \times n$ square matrix. The method used is known as "Gaussian elimination.'' This algorithm will be followed in those language chapters which use matrix inversion as a case study. The problem is as follows:

> Given an integer n and an $n \times n$ matrix, find either A's inverse or the fact that A has no inverse.

This method exploits the following properties, beginning with the identity $A = IA$:

1 If we multiply all values of a given row of the left-hand A by an arbitrary constant k, yielding A', and then multiply all values of the same row of I by k, yielding I', then the identity is not lost. That is, $A' = I'A$.

2 If we replace any row of the left-hand A by the row which results from subtracting the corresponding values of some other row of A, yielding A'', and then replace the same row of I by the row which results from subtracting the corresponding values of that same other row of I, yielding I'', then the identity is not lost. That is, $A'' = I''A$.

3 If we interchange any two rows of the left-hand A, yielding A''', and then interchange the same two rows of I, yielding I''', then the identity is not lost. That is, $A''' = I'''A$.

The Gaussian elimination method itself requires performing a series of such ''row operations,'' with the goal of systematically reducing A, the original left-hand side of the identity, to the ''triangular'' form shown below.

$$\begin{matrix} A_{11} & A_{12} & \cdots & A_{1n} \\ 0 & A_{22} & \cdots & A_{2n} \\ \cdots & \cdots & \cdots & \cdots \\ 0 & 0 & \cdots & A_{nn} \end{matrix}$$

This form has all zeros in its lower left ''triangle'' and no zeros on its diagonal. Simultaneously, an identical series of row operations are performed on I. At the time this form is reached, then the inverse can be computed directly from the resulting A and I by ''back substitution,'' which is defined in the algorithm which follows.

Step **1** (Triangularization) Consider each row j from 1 to $n - 1$ as the ''pivot row.''

A (Row interchange) Among rows j through n, find the one (call it the kth) with the absolutely largest value in its jth column. That is,

$$A_{kj} = \max |A_{pj}| \qquad \text{for all } p = j, \ldots, n$$

Interchange the kth and jth rows of both I and A.

B Reduce all elements in the jth column of A which lie below A_{jj} to zeros as follows:

If $A_{jj} \neq 0$ then for each $p = j + 1, \ldots, n$

(1) Compute $S = A_{pj};/A_{jj}$

(2) For each $k = 1, \ldots, n$ recompute both

$$A_{pk} = A_{pk} - A_{jk} \times S$$
$$I_{pk} = I_{pk} - I_{jk} \times S$$

Step **2** (Back substitution, leaving A^{-1} in I) For each $j = n, n - 1, \ldots, 1$ in turn, if $A_{jj} \neq 0$ perform the following steps for each $k = 1, \ldots, n$:

A Compute $S = \sum_{p=j+1}^{n} A_{jp} I_{pk}$

B Compute $I_{jk} = (I_{jk} - S)/A_{jj}$

We finally note that the original matrix A has no inverse if at any point in this process $A_{jj} = 0$.

To illustrate the Gaussian elimination algorithm, we compute the inverse of the 4 × 4 matrix given above. We start with the two matrices A and I, as shown below.

$$A = \begin{bmatrix} 4 & 7 & 6 & 8 \\ 3 & 8 & 2 & -1 \\ -9 & 0 & 1 & -2 \\ 16 & 3 & 9 & -3 \end{bmatrix} \qquad I = \begin{bmatrix} 1 & 0 & 0 & 0 \\ 0 & 1 & 0 & 0 \\ 0 & 0 & 1 & 0 \\ 0 & 0 & 0 & 1 \end{bmatrix}$$

At step 1, we begin by considering the first row as the pivot row, and look for the absolutely largest element in that column. This occurs in the fourth row, so the first and fourth rows of A and I are interchanged (step 1a) as shown below.

$$A = \begin{bmatrix} 16 & 3 & 9 & -3 \\ 3 & 8 & 2 & -1 \\ -9 & 0 & 1 & -2 \\ 4 & 7 & 6 & 8 \end{bmatrix} \qquad I = \begin{bmatrix} 0 & 0 & 0 & 1 \\ 0 & 1 & 0 & 0 \\ 0 & 0 & 1 & 0 \\ 1 & 0 & 0 & 0 \end{bmatrix}$$

Step 1b then causes the first column of A, below the first pivot element, to be reduced to zeros leaving A and I as shown here.

$$A = \begin{bmatrix} 16 & 3 & 9 & -3 \\ 0 & 7.4375 & 0.3125 & -0.4375 \\ 0 & 1.6875 & 6.0625 & -0.6875 \\ 0 & 6.25 & 3.75 & 8.75 \end{bmatrix} \qquad I = \begin{bmatrix} 0 & 0 & 0 & 1 \\ 0 & 1 & 0 & -0.1875 \\ 0 & 0 & 1 & 0.5625 \\ 1 & 0 & 0 & -0.25 \end{bmatrix}$$

At the completion of step 1, A will have become triangularized as shown below.

$$A = \begin{bmatrix} 16 & 3 & 9 & -3 \\ 0 & 7.4375 & 0.3125 & -0.4375 \\ 0 & 0 & 5.9915 & -3.5882 \\ 0 & 0 & 0 & 11.2061 \end{bmatrix}$$

Back substitution leaves A unchanged and I with values shown below.

$$I = \begin{bmatrix} -0.01389 & 0.00563 & -0.08448 & 0.01739 \\ 0.00300 & 0.13391 & -0.00876 & -0.03078 \\ 0.05344 & -0.07571 & 0.13579 & 0.07722 \\ 0.08923 & -0.06320 & -0.05193 & -0.03967 \end{bmatrix}$$

The final result is only a close approximation to A^{-1}, since the values computed along the way retained only five-digit accuracy. The reader should check this result by multiplying the resulting A^{-1} by the original A. That (matrix) product should be nearly identical to the 4 × 4 identity matrix.

APPENDIX **B**

CASE STUDY 2—EMPLOYEE FILE MAINTENANCE

A classical data processing application is the payroll application. An effective payroll system has many important parts, one being that subsystem which maintains the employee master file. This case study will concentrate on the problem of employee master file maintenance.

Our hypothetical firm employs about 6000 people. The master file contains one record for each employee and is stored on random access storage. The information for an employee falls into the following two categories:

1 Descriptive: the employee's name, address, social security number, and so forth
2 Payroll-related: salary rate, deductions, year-to-date gross pay, and so forth

A full record description for an employee is shown in Table B-1. As the table shows, the length of a record is 200 characters.

Due both to the high incidence of changes to the file and the need for keeping it current on each working day, the file is maintained on a daily basis. It is organized so that an arbitrary record may be updated randomly. Since the social security numbers of all employees are mutually unique, the social security number (SS#) serves as the key to uniquely identify an individual employee's record.

Furthermore, since this file contains important information, it should be protected from careless errors during a maintenance run. The maintenance program will therefore be required to perform certain validifying checks to ensure the correctness of all changes which are made.

The maintenance functions to be performed by the program fall into three classes: additions, deletions, and changes. An addition occurs when a new employee is hired by the company. In that event, a new record must be added to the file, indicating SS#, NAME, ADDRESS, SEX, MARITAL, BIRTH, DATE-EMPLOYED, JOB-STATUS, and DEDUCTIONS. The YEAR-TO-DATE information must be set to zero. A deletion occurs when an employee ceases to be employed by the firm. In that event, a record must be deleted from the file. A change occurs when any of the recorded information about an employee must be changed. For example, when an employee moves to a new address the ADDRESS must be changed, when an employee is promoted

TABLE B-1
EMPLOYEE MASTER FILE RECORD LAYOUT

Item	Record position	Description
SPARE	1	
SS#	2–11	The employee's social security number, with check digit
NAME		The employee's name
LAST	12–26	Last name
FIRST	27–41	First name
MIDDLE	42–51	Middle name or initial
ADDRESS		The employee's home address
STREET	52–66	Street, PO box, or RFD number
CITY	67–81	City
STATE	82–83	State
ZIP	84–88	Zip code
SEX	89	M or F
MARITAL	90	S for unmarried, M for married
BIRTH	91–96	Date of birth, mmddyy
DATE-EMPLOYED	97–102	Date employed by the firm
JOB-STATUS		Present job status information
POSITION	103–104	Job position code
DATE	105–110	Date hired at this position
DEPT	111–113	Department employing code
SALARY		Salary information
BASIS	114	H = hourly, W = weekly, M = monthly
RATE	115–121	$xxxxx.xx gross pay per BASIS
DEDUCTIONS		Information for withholding
#DEPENDENTS	122–123	Number of dependents
HEALTH-INS	124–128	$xxx.xx withheld per month
LIFE-INS	129–133	Same for life insurance
CREDIT-UNION	134–138	Same for credit union account
STOCK-PURCHASE	139–143	Same for stock purchase plan
YEAR-TO-DATE		Year-to-date payroll information
GROSS	144–151	Gross pay $xxxxxx.xx
FED-TAX	152–158	Federal income tax $xxxxx.xx
FICA	159–164	Social security tax $xxxx.xx
STATE-TAX	165–170	State income tax $xxxx.xx
HEALTH-INS	171–175	Health insurance premiums $xxx.xx
LIFE-INS	176–180	Life insurance premiums $xxx.xx
CREDIT-UNION	181–186	Credit union $xxxx.xx
STOCK-PURCHASE	187–192	Stock purchase $xxxx.xx
NET	193–200	Net pay $xxxxxx.xx

the JOB-STATUS must be changed, and when an employee is married the NAME, MARITAL, and certain DEDUCTIONS may change.

Thus for each maintenance run a second file is required, containing the additions, deletions, and changes to be made to the master file. We will call this second file the "update file." Unlike the master file, the update file may contain errors. Each record must, therefore, be edited for validity by the maintenance program before that record is allowed to affect the master file. In the event that an update record is found to be invalid in some respect, both the record and a diagnostic message should be printed and the invalid update record should be dropped from the run. An update record will have one of the three formats shown in Figure B-1, depending on whether it is an addition, a deletion, or a change.

The maintenance program cannot change an employee's year-to-date payroll information or social security number. Position 1 of the update record identifies the function (addition, deletion, or change) to be performed. For an addition, all indicated items must be present and valid. For a change, only those items to be changed must be filled in and the remaining items (i.e., those which are not to be changed) are to be left blank. For a deletion, positions 12–150 of the update record should be blank.

The maintenance program should check the validity of all update records in the following way:

1 The record contains A, C, or D in position 1.

2 The record contains a valid SS#. Specifically, the SS# must be composed of ten decimal digits and must have a valid check digit. The check digit is the rightmost digit of the SS# and is used strictly to provide a measure of confidence that the first nine digits are correctly recorded. There are different schemes for defining check digits. The one we will use is as follows:

a Divide by 11 that number which is the first nine digits of the SS#.

b Identify as the check digit the rightmost digit of the quotient. For example, if the employee's

FIGURE B-1
Update record formats.

Addition

Position 1	2-11	12-51	52-88	89	90	91-96	97-102	103-121	122-143	144-150
A	Social Security Number	Name	Address	Sex	Marital	Birth	Date Employed	Job Status	Deductions	Blank

Deletion

Position 1	2-11	12-150
D	Social Security Number	Blank

Change

Position 1	2-11	12-143	144-150
C	Social Security Number	Item to be changed is filled in; all other items are left blank.	Blank

social security number is 425-32-8219, we divide 425328219 by 11, obtaining a quotient of 38666201 and a remainder of 8. The check digit is thus 1, and the SS# would be properly encoded as 4253282191.

3 The remainder of the record is valid.

a If the record is deletion, then it must be blank in positions 12–150 and there must be a corresponding record with the same SS# on the master file.

b If the record is an addition, then its fields must conform to both the ''basic validity rules'' listed in Table B-2 and the ''extended validity rules'' listed in Table B-3. Also the master file must not contain a record with the same SS# as that of the addition.

TABLE B-2
BASIC VALIDITY RULES FOR ADDITIONS AND CHANGES

Item	Validity
NAME	LAST, FIRST, and MIDDLE should be each composed entirely of alphabetic and blank characters. MIDDLE may be entirely blank, but LAST and FIRST may not.
ADDRESS	STREET should be composed entirely of alphabetic, numeric, and blank characters, but not all blank. CITY should be composed entirely of alphabetic and blank characters, but not all blank. STATE should be one of the valid two-letter state abbreviations, and ZIP should contain five decimal digits.
SEX	M or F.
MARITAL	M or S.
BIRTH	Should be in the form mmddyy, where mm is a two-digit integer between 1 and 12, dd is a two-digit integer between 01 and 31, and yy is a two-digit integer denoting the year of birth (e.g., 52 denotes the year 1952).
DATE-EMPLOYED	Same as for BIRTH.
POSITION	A two-digit number which is among the following valid position codes for the firm: 01, 05, 10, 15–19, 20, 25, 30, 35, 40–45, 60, 70, 80, 90, 99.
DATE	Same as for BIRTH.
DEPT	A three-digit number which is among the following valid department numbers for the firm: 001–060, 100–143, 300–320, 400–420, 500–530.
BASIS	H, W, or M.
RATE	A seven-digit, zero-filled, decimal number, indicating the number of cents paid the employee per hour, week, or month.
#DEPENDENTS	A two-digit, zero-filled decimal number between 00 and 20 inclusive.
HEALTH-INS	A five-digit, zero-filled decimal number, indicating an amount withheld in cents per month.
LIFE-INS	Same as HEALTH-INS.
CREDIT-UNION	Same as HEALTH-INS.
STOCK-PURCHASE	Same as HEALTH-INS.

TABLE B-3
EXTENDED VALIDITY RULES FOR ADDITIONS AND CHANGES

Item	Validity
BIRTH DATE-EMPLOYED DATE	All dates should pass a "reasonability" test; specifically, BIRTH should precede DATE-EMPLOYED and DATE-EMPLOYED should not follow DATE.
POSITION BASIS RATE	POSITION codes 01–20 are hourly paid positions (BASIS = H), codes 25–60 are weekly paid positions (BASIS = W), and all others are monthly paid positions. Furthermore, the firm's salary policy dictates that the following RATE ranges not be exceeded:

BASIS	RATE range
H	\$1.25 to \$10.00 per hour
W	\$60 to \$400 per 35-hour week
M	\$400 to \$10,000 per month

Item	Validity
HEALTH-INS LIFE-INS	The premiums are fixed at \$6 per month for HEALTH-INS and \$3, \$5, \$7, or \$8 per month for LIFE-INS. Each of these is optional, however; an employee's nonsubscription is indicated by zeros (00000).
CREDIT-UNION STOCK-PURCHASE	Neither of these amounts may exceed 5% of an employee's estimated monthly gross pay. The latter is computed for hourly employees by multiplying RATE by 160, and for weekly employees by multiplying RATE by 4.4.

4 If the record is a change, then its nonblank fields must conform to the basic validity rules listed in Table B-2 and there must exist a corresponding record (i.e., with the same SS#) on the master file. Too, the net effect of the change on the master file record must leave that record valid according to the extended validity rules in Table B-3. Furthermore, all change records must heed the following convention for NAME, ADDRESS, JOB-STATUS, and DEDUCTIONS changes: Whenever a NAME, ADDRESS, JOB-STATUS, or DEDUCTIONS change occurs, all of its subitems must appear on the update record.

These rules, like any, are not foolproof in ensuring the integrity of the employee master file. However, they do protect the file from contamination by most types of errors.

To illustrate the functions performed by the master file maintenance program, we have constructed the small employee master file illustrated in Figure B-2. A hypothetical set of update records is shown in Figure B-3. When the maintenance program is applied to this master file and these updates, it should detect and list errors as shown in Figure B-4, and leave the master file updated as shown in Figure B-5. The reader is encouraged to hand-trace the maintenance process using these records, in order to gain working familiarity with this case study.

```
 015338529KNAPP       EDWARD    J       81 GALVESTON STPIKESVILLE    PA12301MM0215290621508001017241 5M031250004006000080
00000015625
 016494037 7COMOLLI   ELSIE     N       1219 POTOMAC AVBOSTON        IL60482FM11073508015219041575120H000072504006000070
00000000000
 0164952114BOLEN      JOHN      W       3 MAIN ST-APT 4COUNCIL BLUFFS IC70013MS081236090157411101740 38W002050001006000030
00020000200
 0164982309SISSMAN    SOPHIE            4700 CONN RD   CENTERBURY    VA22210FS013037040167300901733 01W001350001006000030
00000103000
 0251773086TUNNEY     OSCAR     PAUL    4 FIELDING ST  PITTSBURGH    NC73201MM120442010163450415733 20W002450002006000050
00000000000
 0311971454MOREHEAD   MATTIE    B       318 E MAIN ST  ST LOUIS      DC02007FM122452082572150325763 01H000062500000000000
00200000000
 0312021236GEORBER    THORNTON          HAVERFORD LN   NEW YORK      CA90003MM091852021070100115755 12H000045003006000070
00000000000
 1427569888CARROTT    C         COLIN   1107 BLADEBURY WASHINGTON    RI01523MS030654090176190901761 20H000073501000000070
00250000000
 1448830112HENRY      HANK      H       4702 CONN RD   CENTERBURY    VA22210MS020754082375150515765 11H000063001006000030
00300000000
 1450932233ABBOTT     DORIS             1200 PENN BLVD MIAMI         MA01543FS061354082575200101761 24H000090001006000030
00000000000
```

FIGURE B-2
Sample employee master file records.

```
A1192343920LEATHERBURY   LEONARD     P      773 MAIN ST      MIDDLEVILLE   MO64207MM04164609017619090176530H0000900060060000050
00000000000
A1183762951KENNARD       KEN                44 FROSTY WAY    MAYBERRY      ND78888MS08294509017630090176410W0016000000060000080
00000001000
A0123432100CONCEPT       CALVIN      K      RFD #3           CLEARVIEW     IL65432MM01112509017630090176019H0000975250060000030
00000000000
A0223022305STELLE        THADDEUS           8 COLONEL ST     SANDERS       KY33294MM02273209017640090176055W0022500020060000070
00000000000
C0164982309HENRY         SOPHIE      S      4702 CONN RD     CENTERBURY    VA22210 M                                 00006000030
00000002500
C1448830112                                                                        M                                 02006000030
00300000000
C0164940377                                                                                      2CC90176120H0000785

D0164952111

A1297462301TEAXEL        AXEL               CEDAR GROVE      GAINESVILLE   OH40204MM12164909017615091176032H0000555080050000000
00000000000
C1450932233                                                                                                         01010001000
01000010000
A0156938160PAYNE         WAYNE       S      18 KNOX PIKE     GATORADE      FL28947MS10313009017670090176043M0105000010060000000
00000000000
D1427569888

C0312021247                                                                                                         04

D0251773086

C0153038529                                                                                      80G10172415M3150000

C0311971454                                 VACATION LANE    SILVERTON     MD21134

A0569819890RICE          RIMSEY      W      240 NORTH ST     ALBERTA       WY82305FS09134509017630090176425W0015000010060000000
00000000000
A1238124608BRISTON       BILLY       JOE    100 KINGFIELD    KINGSTOWN     AL99800MS04045309017616090176318H0000375010060000000
00000001500
C0164952114                                                                                           122W0021500

A1170117037MOSS          MICKEY      J      APT#304 RTE 1    IVY           CO71234FS05255009017620090176101H0000950010060000080
00000000000
```

FIGURE B-3
Some update records.

```
EMPLOYEE FILE MAINTENANCE ERROR LOG                                              PAGE   1

RECORD CONTENTS                                                                                       ERROR DESCRIPTION

A0123432100CONCEPT          CALVIN            K          RFD #3        CLEARVIEW       IL65432MM0111250901 INVALID BASIS, RATE
7630090176019H00009752500600003000000000000                                                            , OR #DEPENDENTS.

D0164952111                                                                                           INVALID SS#.

A1297462301TRAXEL           AXEL                         CEDAR GROVE   GAINESVILLE     OH40204MM1218490901 INVALID HEALTH OR L
761509117603 2H0000555080050000000000000000                                                             IFE INS.

C1450932233                                                                                           INVALID HEALTH OR L
                         010100010000100001 0000                                                      IFE INS. INVALID CR
                                                                                                      EDIT-UNION OR STOCK
                                                                                                      -PURCHASE.

C0312021247                                                                                           INVALID SS#.
                         04

C0153038529                                                                                           INVALID POSITION, B
  80010172415M3150000                                                                                 ASIS, OR RATE.

A0569819890RICE             RIMSEY            W          240 NORTH ST  ALBERTA         WY82305FS0913450901 INVALID POSITION OR
76300901764 25W0015000010060000000000000000                                                             DEPT.

C0164952114                                                                                           INVALID BIRTH DATE,
          122W0021500                                                                                  DATE EMPLOYED, OR
                                                                                                      DATE. INVALID POSIT
                                                                                                      ION OR DEPT.

END MAINTENANCE RUN

    2 DELETIONS,
    4 CHANGES, AND
    6 ADDITIONS WERE MADE.
    8 ERRONEOUS UPDATES WERE DISCARDED.
```

FIGURE B-4
Maintenance error log.

```
 0153038529KNAPP              EDWARD          J       81 GALVESTON STRIKESVILLE      PA12301MM0219290621
5080010172415M03125000400600008000000015625

 0156938160PAYNE              WAYNE           S       18 KNOX PIKE    GATORADE       FL28947MS1031300901
7670090176043M01050000100600000000000000000

 0164940377COMOLLI            ELSIE           N       1219 POTOMAC AVBOSTON          IL60482FM1107350801
5220090176120H00007850400600007000000000000

 0164952114BOLEN              JOHN            W       3 MAIN ST-APT 4COUNCIL BLUFFS  IO70013MS0812360901
5741110174038W00225000100600003000020000200

 0164982309HENRY              SOPHIE          S       4702 CONN RD    CENTERBURY     VA22210FM0130370401
6730090173301W00135000000600003000000002500

 0223022305STELLE             THADDEUS                8 COLONEL ST    SANDERS        KY33294MM0227320901
7640090176055W00225000200600007000000000000

 0311971454MOORHEAD           MATTIE          B       VACATION LANE   SILVERTON      MD21134FM1224520825
7215032576301H00006250000000000000020000000

 0312021236GERBER             THORNTON                HAVERFORD LN    NEW YORK       CA90003MM0918520210
7010011575512H00004500300600007000000000000

 1170117037MOSS               MICKEY          J       APT#304 RTE 1   IVY            CO07123FS0525500901
7620090176101H00009500100600008000000000000

 1183762951KENNARD            KEN                     44 FROSTY WAY   MAYBERRY       ND78888MS0829450901
7630090176410W00160000100600008000000001000

 1192343920LEATHERBURY        LEONARD         P       773 MAIN ST     MIDDLEVILLE    MO64207MM0416460901
7619090176530H00009000600600005000000000000

 1238124608BEISTON            BILLY           JOE     100 KINGFIELD   KINGSTOWN      AL99800MS0404530901
7616090176318H00003750100600000000000001500

 14488301124HENRY             HANK            H       4702 CONN RD    CENTERBURY     VA22210MM0207540823
7515051576511H00006300200600003000030000000

 1450932233ABBOTT             DORIS                   1200 PENN BLVD MIAMI           MA01543FS0613540825
7520010176124H00009000100600003000000000000
```

FIGURE B-5
Updated master file records.

APPENDIX **C**

CASE STUDY 3— TEXT FORMATTER

Many typists use word processing software as an aid to their work, either on a dedicated word processor or on a terminal connected to a time-sharing computer. Such software permits interactive editing and subsequent printing of a body of text with great ease, compared with manual typing methods. For instance, this text was prepared using word processing software on a microcomputer.

This case study reflects the programming required for printing such a text in accordance with specifications given by the typist. Because of the magnitude of the general problem, we will constrain it somewhat here. Our constrained problem will nevertheless demonstrate the basic nature of text formatting as an algorithmic problem.

We will assume that a text may be any sequence of characters from the following set:

A B . . Z a b . . . z	(letters)
0 1 . . . 9	(digits)
b̸ ¢ . < (+ & !	
$ *) : − / , %	(special characters)
_ < ? # @ ‘ = ″	

Consider, for example, the text shown in Figure C-1. The purpose of this case study problem will be to read any such text and display it in accordance with certain user-specified formatting requirements.

THE CENTER SECTION, KNOTS IN THE NATURAL SILK TWIST, BESIDES BEING WORKED IN A VARIETY OF PICOTS AND BOBBLES, ALSO CONTAINS SQUARE KNOTS, OVERHAND KNOTS, AND REVERSED DOUBLE HALF HITCHES. IN ADDITION, THERE ARE ANGLED AREAS OF DOUBLE HALF HITCHES. THE SIDE AREAS IN YELLOW LINEN ARE DOMINATED BY ANGLING DOUBLE HALF HITCHES, SQUARE KNOTS, HALF KNOTS, OVERHAND KNOTS AND SINNETS OF HALF KNOTS THAT TWIST IN OPPOSITE DIRECTIONS.

IN THE BOTTOM HALF OF THE HANGING, THE YELLOW AND WHITE AREAS APPEAR SEPARATE. BUT WHILE THE COLORS ARE INDEPENDENT OF EACH OTHER, THE DESIGN IS NOT. THE BEGINNING OF THIS AREA IS A GOOD EXAMPLE OF THE VARIATIONS THAT CAN BE OBTAINED BY ANGLING THE DOUBLE HALF HITCH. AS STATED PREVIOUSLY, THE HALF HITCH IS THE MOST PRACTICAL KNOT FOR OBTAINING VARIATIONS.

FIGURE C-1
Sample text.

Specifically, the user may give one or more of the "format controls" in the following table for printing:

Format control	Meaning	Default
WIDTH = W	The number of characters on each printed line. W cannot exceed 120 or be less than 40.	WIDTH = 80
LINES = L	The number of lines on each printed page. L cannot exceed 60 or be less than 20.	LINES = 60
TABS = t	The location on a line (t) of first tab setting. The value of t cannot exceed 20 or be less than 3.	TABS = 5
HEADING = h	Position the heading at the left (h = L), center (h = C), or right (h = R), at the top of the page.	HEADING = C
SPACING = s	Single-space (s = 1), double-space (s = 2), or single-space with double-space between paragraphs (s = 3).	SPACING = 1
BREAK = b	Sentence may break between pages (b = 0), sentence may not break between pages (b = 1), or paragraph may not break between pages (b = 2).	BREAK = 0

The input will be provided in a file of eighty-character records. Each record will contain a record sequence number in positions 71–80, and the text itself in positions 1–70, as shown in Figure C-2. In addition, the following encoding conventions will be followed:

1 Each heading within the text will be immediately preceded and immediately followed by the sequence)H, will not exceed forty characters in length, and will not be split between two records.

2 The beginning of a paragraph will be immediately preceded by the two-character sequence)P.

```
)P THE CENTER SECTION, KNOTS IN THE NATURAL SILK TWIST, BESIDES BEING 0000010000
WORKED IN A VARIETY OF PICOTS AND BOBBLES, ALSO CONTAINS SQUARE KNOTS,0000020000
 OVERHAND KNOTS, AND REVERSED DOUBLE HALF-HITCHES.   IN ADDITION, THER0000030000
E ARE ANGLED AREAS OF DOUBLE HALF-HITCHES.    THE SIDE AREAS IN  YELL0000040000
OW LINEN ARE DOMINATED BY ANGLING DOUBLE HALF-HITCHES, SQUARE KNOTS,  0000050000
HALF KNOTS, OVERHAND KNOTS, AND SINNETS OF HALF KNOTS THAT TWIST      0000060000
IN OPPOSITE DIRECTIONS.  )P IN THE BOTTOM HALF OF THE HANGING, THE YEL0000070000
LOW AND WHITE AREAS APPEAR SEPARATE.  BUT WHILE THE COLORS ARE INDEPEN0000080000
DENT OF EACH OTHER, THE DESIGN IS NOT.     THE BEGINNING  OF THIS AREA0000090000
 IS A GOOD EXAMPLE OF THE VARIATIONS THAT CAN BE OBTAINED BY ANGLING  0000100000
THE DOUBLE HALF-HITCH KNOT.  AS STATED PREVIOUSLY, THE HALF HITCH IS  0000110000
THE MOST PRACTICAL KNOT FOR OBTAINING VARIATIONS.                     0000120000
```

FIGURE C-2
Input encoding of the sample text.

3 Each sentence will be terminated by one of the following two-character sequences (b̸ denotes blank):

.b̸   !b̸   ?b̸

4 Adjacent words in the text will be separated either by a blank or by one of the following two-character sequences:

,b̸   b̸(   )b̸   :b̸   ;b̸

5 An individual word can be a sequence of any nonblank characters, which additionally does not contain either of the sequences)H or)P.

6 Whenever the blank (b̸) occurs in the text, any number of blanks may immediately follow it. These will be known as "superfluous blanks."

The output text will be printed according to the format controls specified. Furthermore, the following requirements will be met:

1 The text will be aligned vertically at both left and right margins, except that paragraphs will be indented to the first tab position.

2 Pages will be numbered sequentially with the page number appearing at the right margin of the first line on each page.

3 No word will be split between two lines.

4 Superfluous blanks within the text will be deleted, except when they are needed to align the text at the right margin.

5 The heading (if present) will begin on the second line of each page and one blank will separate it from the text.

6 A page break will be forced whenever a new heading line is encountered.

To clarify the meaning of these various conventions, let's look at what the sample text in Figure C-1 would look like if it were presented as the file shown in Figure C-2. Assuming that the default format controls are used, the printed results for this text will be as shown in Figure C-3.

To illustrate the effect of adjusting format controls, Figure C-4 shows the printed results when the following format controls are used:

WIDTH = 60   SPACING = 3

In order to preserve the integrity of the program, certain possible inconsistencies between the text and its printing conventions will be checked and resolved as follows:

```
                                                                     PAGE  1.

     THE CENTER SECTION, KNOTS IN THE NATURAL SILK TWIST, BESIDES BEING WORKED IN
A VARIETY OF PICOTS AND BOBBLES, ALSO CONTAINS SQUARE KNOTS, OVERHAND KNOTS, AND
REVERSED DOUBLE HALF-HITCHES. IN ADDITION, THERE  ARE  ANGLED  AREAS  OF  DOUBLE
HALF-HITCHES. THE SIDE AREAS IN YELLOW LINEN ARE  DOMINATED  BY  ANGLING  DOUBLE
HALF-HITCHES, SQUARE-KNOTS, HALF KNOTS, OVERHAND  KNOTS,  AND  SINNETS  OF  HALF
KNOTS THAT TWIST IN OPPOSITE DIRECTIONS.
     IN THE BOTTOM HALF OF  THE  HANGING, THE  YELLOW  AND  WHITE  AREAS  APPEAR
SEPARATE. BUT WHILE THE COLORS ARE INDEPENDENT OF EACH OTHER, THE DESIGN IS NOT.
THE BEGINNING OF THIS AREA IS A GOOD EXAMPLE  OF  THE  VARIATIONS  THAT  CAN  BE
OBTAINED BY ANGLING THE DOUBLE HALF-HITCH KNOT. AS STATED PREVIOUSLY,  THE  HALF
HITCH IS THE MOST PRACTICAL KNOT FOR OBTAINING VARIATIONS.
```

FIGURE C-3
Printed results with default format controls.

```
                                                     PAGE  1.

     THE CENTER SECTION, KNOTS IN  THE  NATURAL  SILK  TWIST,
BESIDES BEING WORKED IN A VARIETY  OF  PICOTS  AND  BOBBLES,
ALSO CONTAINS SQUARE KNOTS,  OVERHAND  KNOTS,  AND  REVERSED
DOUBLE HALF-HITCHES. IN ADDITION, THERE ARE ANGLED AREAS  OF
DOUBLE HALF-HITCHES. THE SIDE  AREAS  IN  YELLOW  LINEN  ARE
DOMINATED BY ANGLING DOUBLE HALF-HITCHES, SQUARE KNOTS, HALF
KNOTS, OVERHAND KNOTS, AND SINNETS OF HALF KNOTS THAT  TWIST
IN OPPOSITE DIRECTIONS.

     IN THE BOTTOM HALF OF THE HANGING, THE YELLOW AND  WHITE
AREAS APPEAR SEPARATE. BUT WHILE THE COLORS ARE  INDEPENDENT
OF EACH OTHER, THE DESIGN IS NOT. THE BEGINNING OF THIS AREA
IS A GOOD EXAMPLE OF THE VARIATIONS THAT CAN BE OBTAINED  BY
ANGLING THE DOUBLE HALF-HITCH KNOT.  AS  STATED  PREVIOUSLY,
THE HALF HITCH IS THE  MOST  PRACTICAL  KNOT  FOR  OBTAINING
VARIATIONS.
```

FIGURE C-4
Printed results with adjusted format controls.

1 If the length of any word in the text exceeds the length of a line, then the word will be broken between two or more lines.

2 If the length of a sentence exceeds a single page, then the BREAK format control will be temporarily set to BREAK = 0 (if it is defined as 1 or 2) to permit completion of the sentence on the next page(s).

3 If the length of a paragraph exceeds a single page, then the BREAK format control will be temporarily set to BREAK = 0 (if defined as 2) to permit completion of that paragraph on the next page(s).

The first two of these possibilities will seldom occur in practice, while the third may occasionally occur. Nevertheless, the program must be prepared to handle such "worst case" eventualities.

This case study will be implemented according to the guidelines described above and using the following techniques. Two working buffers will be used by the program. The first, called TEXTIN, will contain a portion of the input text to be formatted. The second, called TEXTOUT, will contain an image of a complete printed page as it is being developed. TEXTIN will be large enough to hold several lines of printed text. Whenever the particular text in TEXTIN becomes exhausted, a routine called READTXT will be summoned to replenish it from the input file. That replenishment will be done in such a way that superfluous blanks are "squeezed out" as the text is read. Similarly, whenever TEXTOUT becomes full, it will be displayed and reinitialized with appropriate heading, page number, and blank lines.

The file (called TEXT) containing the input text is typically stored on disk. A second file (called CONTROLS) containing the user's format control specifications, will be separate from the first. That file may be empty, which will indicate that the user wants the default values to be taken. Otherwise, it may contain one or more of the format controls. In the latter event, the format controls may be entered in any order and separated from each other by any number of blanks. No format control, however, may contain any embedded blanks. For example, the format controls used for the output shown in Figure C-4 may be given as follows:

WIDTH = 60   SPACING = 3

The program should read and check these controls for validity before proceeding with the text. However, the program will do no validity checking of the text itself. Specifically, the sequence number in positions 71–80 of each text itself can be ignored by the program.

APPENDIX **D**

CASE STUDY 4— MISSIONARIES AND CANNIBALS

A classical example of artificial intelligence programming is found in the ''missionaries and cannibals'' problem. This is a popular problem because it demonstrates some of the issues in AI in a simple and interesting way. Its solution involves the development of a list structure, or graph, representing all the possible moves that can be made from each state, and then interrogating that list structure in order to develop an orderly path to the solution. As an AI problem, ''missionaries and cannibals'' exhibits intelligent behavior in the sense that the program solves a puzzle by simulating the sequence of decisions which lead to a solution.

Briefly, this problem can be described as follows: three missionaries and three cannibals stand on the left bank of a river, and all of them want to cross over to the right side. There is one boat available, but it can hold no more than two people (missionaries and/or cannibals) at one crossing. Moreover, if the missionaries are, at any time, outnumbered by the cannibals on either bank, they will be devoured by the cannibals. A solution must be found which shows the number of missionaries and cannibals on each bank after each crossing of the boat, ends with all six beings on the right bank (with no devouring in the meantime), and involves a minimum number of crossings.

In solving this kind of problem, an effective representation scheme must be found. One such scheme would be to define as a ''state'' a series of M's and C's (denoting individual missionaries and cannibals), one B (denoting the boat), and a slash (denoting the position of the river between them. For example, the following state

MMCCB/MC

shows two missionaries and two cannibals on the left bank with the boat, and one of each on the right side.

Given the limitations of the boat, the following diagram shows three possible crossings which can be made from the initial state to a next state:

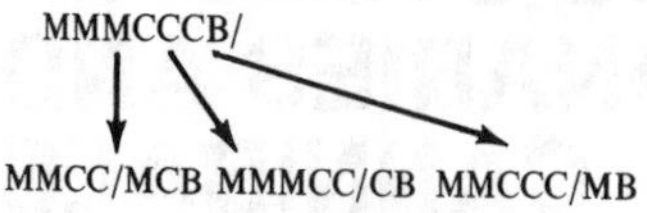

```
MMMCCCB/
   |    \         \
   v     v          v
MMCC/MCB MMMCC/CB MMCCC/MB
```

Here, we note that the two leftmost alternatives are feasible, since no devouring takes place, but the rightmost one is not and therefore does not lead to a solution.

In general, there are a finite number of possible states, and therefore a finite transition graph for the solution may be developed. Whenever a "dead end" (no pun intended) state appears, no further transitions from that state need to be tried. We can also eliminate all transitions which lead to a state already visited, or "loops." For instance, if the middle crossing above is followed immediately by the cannibal taking the boat back to the left bank, the original starting state will be revisited.

A partial transition graph for the solution to the missionaries and cannibals problem is shown on the next page. Here, underlined states indicate either dead ends or loops, from which no further transitions would lead to a minimal solution.

The output of this program should be a display of the sequence of states which leads to a solution, traversing the graph thus generated. That is:

MMMCCCB/
MMCC/MCB
MMMCCB/C
MMM/CCCB
MMMCB/CC
MC/MMCCB
MMCCB/MC
CC/MMMCB
CCCB/MMM
C/MMMCCB
MCB/MMCC
/MMMCCCB

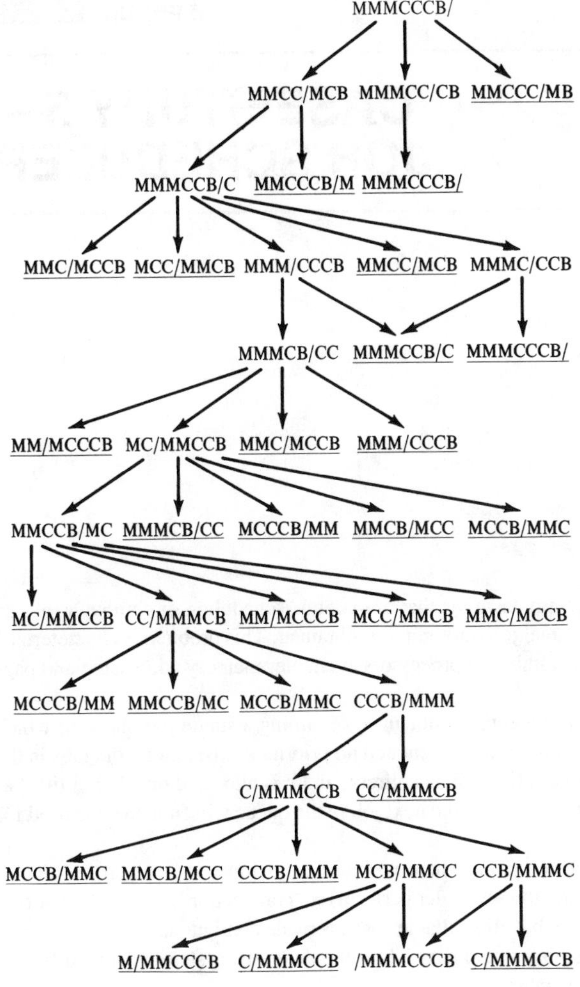
MMMCCCB/
MMCC/MCB
MMMCC/CB
MMCCC/MB
MMMCCB/C
MMCCCB/M
MMMCCCB/
MMC/MCCB
MCC/MMCB
MMM/CCCB
MMCC/MCB
MMMC/CCB
MMMCB/CC
MMMCCB/C
MMMCCCB/
MM/MCCCB
MC/MMCCB
MMC/MCCB
MMM/CCCB
MMCCB/MC
MMMCB/CC
MCCCB/MM
MMCB/MCC
MCCB/MMC
MC/MMCCB
CC/MMMCB
MM/MCCCB
MCC/MMCB
MMC/MCCB
MCCCB/MM
MMCCB/MC
MCCB/MMC
CCCB/MMM
C/MMMCCB
CC/MMMCB
MCCB/MMC
MMCB/MCC
CCCB/MMM
MCB/MMCC
CCB/MMMC
M/MMCCCB
C/MMMCCB
/MMMCCCB
C/MMMCCB

APPENDIX **E**

CASE STUDY 5—JOB SCHEDULER

A pivotal problem of operating system design is that of dynamic scheduling of computer jobs so that optimal use of memory and optimal job throughput is obtained. This problem is characterized in different ways depending on the number of processors available, memory addressing and paging schemes, and so forth.

Here, we take a limited view of the entire problem by assuming a single job queue in which each job j1, j2, . . . has a fixed memory requirement and no priorities exist among the jobs in the queue. Moreover, available memory is fixed in its entirety, and it is allocated on a ''first fit'' basis; that is, the first block of memory in which the next job in the queue will fit is the one used for allocation to the job.

Finally, when the system reaches a point where *no* block of memory is large enough to accommodate the next job in the queue, the scheduler performs a ''compaction'' routine by shifting all active jobs upward in memory so that all available space is made contiguous. Now another attempt may be made to allocate memory to the next job; if this fails, the system must wait for the first termination of an active job to occur.

To illustrate, suppose we have the following queue of jobs j1, j2, . . . , j7 with storage requirements (in k bytes) shown below, and a 2mb memory space shown on the right:

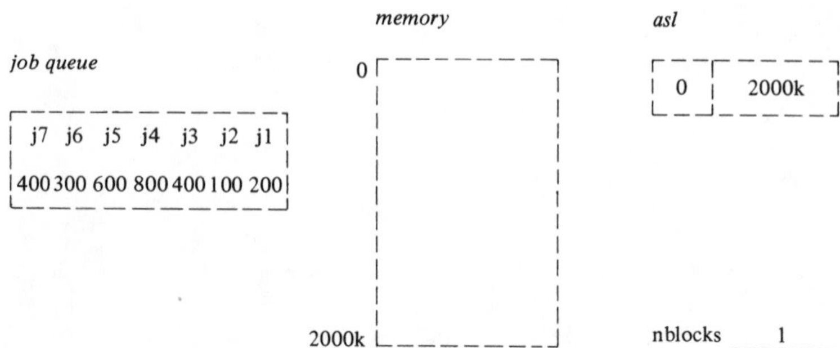

Here, note the "available space list" *asl* and the "number of blocks" of available memory *nblocks* initialized appropriately. An entry in asl gives the starting address and length (in this case 0 and 2000k) of a contiguous block of memory which is available for scheduling.

Now the jobs should be taken from the queue, allocated blocks of memory, and initiated, until the memory requirements of the next job in the queue cannot be accommodated. This is shown below for our example, assuming that none of the first few jobs thus initiated has yet terminated.

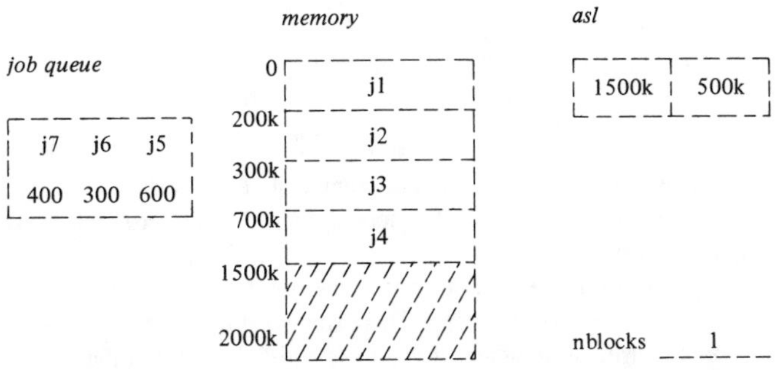

Now the available block in asl has systematically been reduced to 500k bytes, not large enough to accommodate the memory needs of job j5.

The first response to this situation is to try and compactify memory by shifting the active jobs and recovering fragmented memory blocks. At this time, that strategy doesn't help, so the system waits for one of the active jobs to terminate.

Suppose now that job j3 terminates. This frees a 400k block, and the result is shown below.

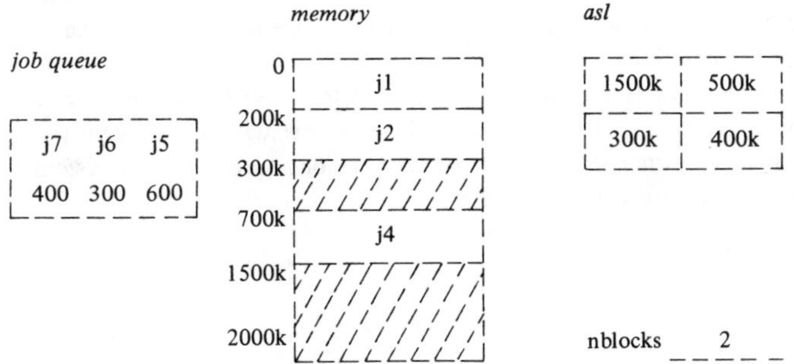

Now two blocks are available, but neither is adequate for accommodating job j5. Thus, compactification takes place again, making space for job j5, and the situation changes as shown on the next page.

Thus, the program's task is to manage memory and the available space list, assuming a dynamically growing job queue and an asynchronous sequence of active job terminations. The program should try to compactify memory whenever it has become too fragmented to accommodate

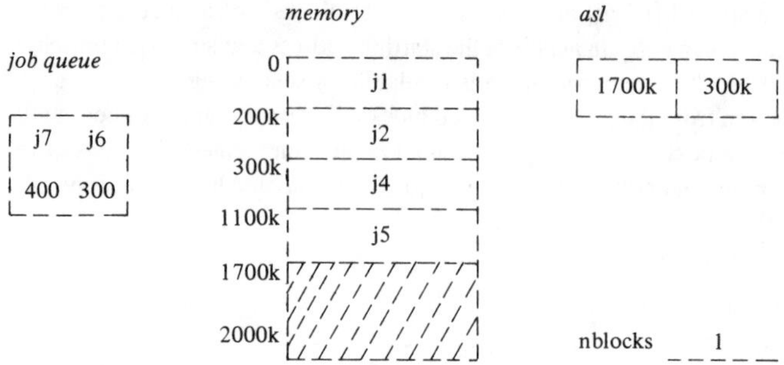

the next job in the queue, and enter a wait state if the result of compactification does not satisfy the next job's memory needs. The wait state is terminated as soon as an active job terminates, in which case compactification can be retried.

A sample of the input (sequence of job queue arrivals and active job terminations) and expected output for this program are shown on the next page. There, the notation A denotes an arrival in the job queue and T denotes a termination of an active job. ''Active'' is a list of the ''na'' active memory blocks, and ''asl'' is a list of the ''nblocks'' of available memory, as described above.

Each of these steps involves one of the following principal activities for the program:

1 Initiating a new job in memory
2 Termination of a job in memory
3 Compactification of memory
4 Waiting

These activities in turn affect the asl and active lists in a different way. Moreover, the events which force these activities to occur are not synchronized among themselves. That is, the arrival of a new job in the queue may occur either before, after, or simultaneously with the termination of an active job in memory. It is the program's task to effectively manage the job queue, the active list, and the asl under these conditions.

The general problem of scheduling is far more complex than this case study can address. Here, we give only the barest elements, so that a reasonable basis for evaluation of systems programming languages is available. Further study of this problem belongs properly in a systems programming, operating systems, or software engineering course.

Event	na	active	nblocks	asl
	0		1	0,2000k
A j1 200k	1	j1 0,199k	1	200k,2000k
A j2 100k	2	j1 0,199k j2 200k,299k	1	300k,2000k
A j3 400k	3	j1 0,199k j2 200k,299k j3 300k,699k	1	700k,2000k
A j4 800k	4	j1 0,199k j2 200k,299k j3 300k,699k j4 700k,1499k	1	1500k,2000k
A j5 600k A j6 300k A j7 400k				
T j3	3	j1 0,199k j2 200k,299k j4 700k,1499k	2	1500k,2000k 300k, 699k
Compactify	3	j1 0,199k j2 200k,299k j4 300k,1099k	1	1100k,2000k
Schedule j5	4	j1 0,199k j2 200k,299k j4 300k,1099k j5 1100k,1699k	1	1700k,2000k
T j1	3	j2 200k,299k j4 300k,1099k j5 1100k,1699k	2	1700k,2000k 0,199k
T j4	2	j2 200k,299k j5 1100k,1699k	3	1700k,2000k 0,199k 300k,1099k

INDEX

60.''[2] This report became the accepted definition of ALGOL for its various implementations, throughout the 1960s. During this period, ALGOL became extremely popular among computer scientists, particularly in Europe. Although most U.S. computer manufacturers gave ALGOL only limited support, interest in it nevertheless flourished. Its rigorous definition marked new standards for language design and implementation. ALGOL became a universal language for defining published algorithms in journals.

On the other hand, experience with this new tool uncovered many weaknesses and difficulties with ALGOL.[3] Various proposals were offered during the 1960s to extend, revise, and update ALGOL. Niklaus Wirth, an original member of the ALGOL working committees, developed a refinement known as ALGOL W.[4] Later, the ALGOL working group itself developed an elaborate and far-reaching extension known as ''ALGOL 68.''[5] While earlier versions of ALGOL had been scientific programming languages, ALGOL 68 was intentionally a general-purpose language with applications across a broad range of interests. The ''Report on the Algorithmic Language ALGOL 68'' was a large and complex document, describing an enormous language. Implementers had difficulty developing compilers for ALGOL 68, and there was disagreement among the members of the working group over the possibility that this new language had been too ambitious to be practical.

At this time, Wirth was designing a more narrowly defined successor to ALGOL 60, and called it ''Pascal.'' Its first compiler was implemented in 1970, and a revised version was defined and implemented in 1973.[6] This *Pascal User Manual and Report* became the universally accepted standard definition of Pascal, which was formally standardized in 1983,[7] and is now implemented on most computers, from micros to mainframes.

In spite of its strong improvements over ALGOL—especially in the area of input-output, files, records, dynamic storage management, and control structures—Pascal too has been scrutinized for its weaknesses.[8] Successors have already been proposed in the new languages Ada and Modula-2. The latter is designed by Wirth himself, and shows considerable promise in the area of systems programming. However, before we examine the future of the ALGOL tradition we begin this text with a careful study of Pascal itself.

2-1.2 Implementations and Variations of Pascal

The version of Pascal that we will discuss in this chapter is defined in the *Pascal User Manual and Report*[9] and the ANSI standard,[10] and is known as ''Standard Pascal.'' This is implemented on a variety of computers, including at least the following:

Apple
Burroughs
CDC
Commodore
Digital
IBM
Radio Shack
Univac

Most Pascal implementations include extensions to the language described in the report which enhance its usefulness. The most notable extended version is UCSD Pascal,[11] developed at the University of California at San Diego for use on a wide variety of microcomputers.

2-1.3 Major Applications of Pascal

Although some of its extensions render Pascal a general-purpose language, it was clearly intended to serve as a language for teaching algorithm design and programming methodology. Like ALGOL, Pascal has played a unique role as the principal language used for publishing algorithms in journals and texts. Its well-definedness gives authors an expressive precision and elegance not found in many other languages. Thus, it is not surprising to find Pascal as the main teaching language for computer science at the university level.

2-2 WRITING PASCAL PROGRAMS

A Pascal program, in its simplest form, consists of a series of declarations (for variables, files, arrays, etc.) followed by a series of statements enclosed within **begin** and **end. Begin** and **end** themselves are ''reserved words'' in Pascal, and thus cannot be used as variable names or for any other purpose in individual programs. A complete list of Pascal reserved words is given in section 2-2.2. **Boldface** will be used *throughout* the text to denote reserved words for *every* language that we study.

Below is a simple Pascal program which computes and displays the average of an indeterminate number of input numbers. For instance, if the input were 85.5, 87.5, 89.5, and 91.5, the result displayed would be 88.5. The program uses the variable X to hold a single input number and the variable N to determine the number of input numbers in the process. The variables SUM and AV connote the numbers' sum and average, respectively.

```
program Averager (input, output);

     { This program computes the average AV of N input
       numbers X }

     var X, SUM, AV: real;
        N: integer;

     begin
        N:=0; SUM:=0;
        read (X);
        while not eof do
           begin
                N:=N+1;
                SUM:=SUM+X;
                read (X)
           end;
        AV:=SUM/N;
        writeln (N:5, ' numbers were given');
        writeln (AV:5:1, ' is their average')
     end.
```

The different types of statements in this program will be explained later. Generally, we see that the semicolon is used to separate statements and **begin** . . . **end** are used to group statements. Thus, the statements following "**while not** eof **do**" are treated as a group to be repeated until the end of the input (eof) occurs. Note also that the format of a Pascal program is freely determined by the programmer. The style of indenting shown here is a fairly conventional one that facilitates program readability. Note also that comments in a Pascal program may be inserted anywhere, provided that they are enclosed within the delimiters { and }. Alternately, the delimiters (* and *) can be used for the same purpose. Finally, we see that the full upper- and lowercase alphabet (A–Z and a–z) can be used in writing Pascal programs. This feature is not always supported, however, since some hardware only carries the uppercase letters (A–Z) in its character set.

2-2.1 Elementary Data Types and Values

The basic Pascal data types are numbers, which may be **real** or **integer**; logical values, which are called **Boolean**; and single American Standard Code for Information Interchange (ASCII) characters, which are called **char**.

An **integer** number is a sequence of decimal digits (0, . . . , 9), which may be preceded by a sign, + or −. A **real** number is either an **integer**, a decimal fraction, an exponent part, or some combination of these. The "exponent part" consists of the symbol E followed by an integer, denoting multiplication by that integer power of 10. Thus, for example, the **real** number −5.33E−4 consists of the integer −5, the decimal fraction .33, and the exponent part E−4, and is equivalent to the number −0.000533. Of course, the number −0.000533 is also a legitimate **real** number and represents the same value as −5.33E−4. Additional examples of Pascal number representations are given below.

Number	Integer representation	Real representation
0	0	0.0
0.5		0.5
−1	−1	−1.0
22.55		22.55
		0.2255E2

Each number has, of course, several equivalent **real** representations. The range of valid **integer** and **real** numbers depends upon the host computer where the language is implemented. For example, the computer can have a 32-bit word size and thus accommodates **integers** from -2^{31} to $+2^{31}-1$ and **reals** with a magnitude from 10^{75} down to 10^{-75} and a precision of 6–7 decimal digits.

The **Boolean** data values are **true** and **false**. They are used primarily in the evaluation of conditional expressions which appear in **if** statements and **while** statements.

The **char** data type provides the basis for string processing in Pascal. A **char** data value is a single character (a letter, digit, or special character) enclosed in quotes, as in the following examples.

'A'   '7'   ' '   '+'   '$'   'a'

The set of characters available as **char** values depends on the implementation. Thus, lowercase letters and certain special characters (such as | or \) may not be available on all computers where Pascal is supported.

A "string" in Pascal is a series of characters enclosed in quotes, as shown in the following examples.

'SALES SUMMARY REPORT'
'5/15/83'
'May 15, 1983'

Although standard Pascal does not support string variables or string processing functions, certain Pascal extensions (such as UCSD Pascal) do. We shall examine these later in the chapter.

Two additional data type classifications in Pascal are the "scalar type" and the "subrange type." These provide a building block for the programmer to define additional basic classes of data beyond the four that are provided by the language.

A "scalar type" is just a list of identifiers, or names, enclosed in parentheses. The following are three examples of scalar types:

(club, diamond, heart, spade)
(N, S, E, W)
(Mon, Tue, Wed, Thu, Fri, Sat, Sun)

The first would be appropriate for a variable that keeps track of the suits in a bridge game. The second would be useful for recording wind direction, and the third would perhaps be helpful in a calendar print program. The basic idea behind scalar types is to provide the programmer with a means for declaring variables using values that fit the application directly, rather than some awkward codification of **integer** values instead. The effect is to make programs more intelligible statements of their purpose, and we shall exhibit this later in the chapter.

The "subrange type" also allows the programmer to define new data types from old ones. It permits the definition of a contiguous range of integers, such as 1 to 10, as the only values that a variable can assume. It is written as a pair of integers with two dots (..) between them. Thus, the subrange 1..10 denotes the integers from 1 to 10. This data type is particularly useful for automatically ensuring that an array's *sub*script is within the proper *range;* hence the name "subrange."

Scalar and subrange types are defined at the beginning of a Pascal program by way of the "type declaration," which has the following form:

```
type identifier = type;
     identifier = type;
       .
       .
       .
```

Here, "identifier" may be any name that is appropriate to the newly defined type, and "type" may be either a scalar or a subrange type as described above. Thus, the following type declarations can be made:

```
type digits = 0..9;
     days = (Mon, Tue, Wed, Thu, Fri, Sat, Sun);
     suit = (club, diamond, heart, spade);
     direction = (N, S, E, W);
```

The "constant declaration" is another device that can be used at the beginning of a Pascal program to identify a numerical value by name. It has the following form:

```
const identifier = value;
```

For instance, if we wanted to define a very small number, say 10^{-5}, as "epsilon" in a mathematical computation, we could write:

```
const epsilon = E-5;
```

This allows us to use the word "epsilon" as a synonym for 10^{-5} wherever it is needed throughout the program. The advantage of this device becomes clear when we want to change the value of epsilon (to, for example, 10^{-8}) throughout the program. To accomplish this, we would need to change only the declaration to:

```
const epsilon = E-8;
```

and the change would be automatically effected.

2-2.2 Names, Variables, and Declarations

A Pascal variable is a name which is associated with a value during execution of the program. The value of a variable may be changed by the program as execution proceeds. A variable name is called an "identifier," which formally is defined as follows:

> An *identifier* is a sequence of one or more letters (a–z, A–Z) and/or digits (0–9), the first of which must be a letter.

All variables used in a Pascal program *must* be declared within the type declaration, which appears near the beginning of the program and has the following general form:

```
var identifier list: type;
    identifier list: type;
    .
    .
    .
```

Here, "type" may be one of **integer**, **real**, **Boolean**, **char**, or any scalar or subrange type, and "identifier list" denotes a list of those variable names, separated by commas, whose values are to be of the designated type. For instance, the foregoing sample program had in it the following type declaration:

```
var X, SUM, AV: real;
    N: integer;
```

which declares the three variables X, SUM, and AV will each contain a **real** value, while the variable N will contain an **integer**.

Unlike other languages, variables' values so declared cannot be initialized here, nor can they be assumed to automatically be assigned an initial value by the system. The values of all variables in a Pascal program are initially *undefined*. Finally, Pascal identifiers must not be identical with any of the language's "reserved words." A full list of the Pascal reserved words is given in Figure 2-1.

2-2.3 Arrays and Other Data Structures

The three internal data structures provided by Pascal are "arrays," "records," and "sets." Arrays are usually associated with mathematical and list processing, records are associated with files and dynamic data structures, and sets are a relatively novel data type that have diverse uses as we shall see.

An array is declared via an "array declaration," which has the following form:

```
var identifier: array [size] of type;
    identifier: array [size] of type;
    .
    .
    .
```

Here "type" denotes the type of all values stored in the array, "identifier" names the array, and "size" is a (list of) subrange(s) defining the subscript range in each of the

FIGURE 2-1
PASCAL RESERVED WORDS

and	**array**	**begin**	**case**	**const**
div	**do**	**downto**	**else**	**end**
file	**for**	**function**	**goto**	**if**
in	**label**	**mod**	**nil**	**not**
of	**or**	**packed**	**procedure**	**program**
record	**repeat**	**set**	**then**	**to**
type	**until**	**var**	**while**	**with**

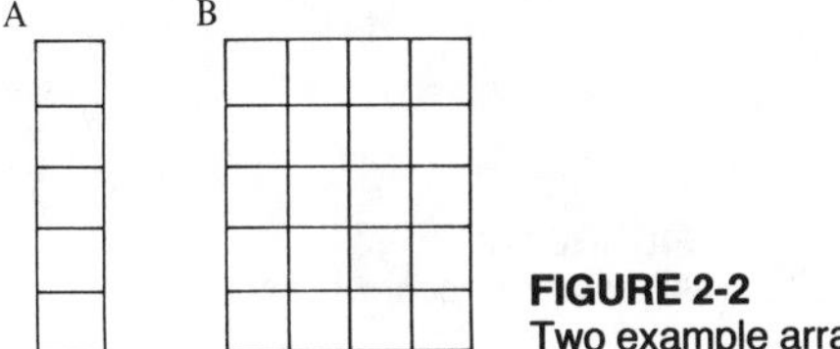

FIGURE 2-2
Two example arrays.

array's dimensions. For example, suppose we want to define an array A of one dimension and five **integer** entries, and an array B of two dimensions with five rows and four columns of **real** entries, as shown in Figure 2-2. Then we would declare A and B as follows:

```
var A: array [1..5] of integer;
    B: array [1..5,1..4] of real;
```

Now, to reference a single entry in an array, we write an "indexed variable." For A above, we can reference any of the first, second, . . . , or fifth entries by writing the indexed variables A[1], A[2], . . . , or A[5], respectively. In a similar fashion, we can reference a single entry in B by identifying its row number and its column number in an indexed variable. For instance, the entry in the second row and third column of B is referenced by writing B[2,3]. The integers within the brackets, [ ], of an indexed variable are known as "subscripts" or "indexes."

A special kind of array, called a **packed array of char**, is used for declaring fixed-length character string variables in standard Pascal. For instance, the declaration

```
var name: packed array [1..25] of char;
```

declares "name" as a fixed-length 25-character string variable. Individual characters within "name" may be accessed by using an appropriate indexed variable, such as name[1], name[2], and so forth. However, this is an awkward device in practice, since standard Pascal provides neither varying-length string variables nor string manipulation functions. Thus, any reasonable text processing applications in Pascal must depend upon the UCSD Pascal extensions which are more robust. There, one has the built-in string data type and a useful set of string functions to accompany it.

The "record" is Pascal's vehicle for defining an entry in a file or a linked list. Such an entry is typically composed of varying types of elements. An example record is shown in Figure 2-3. Here, we see a record comprising a name, a social security number, a gross pay amount, and an address. Each of these "fields" in the record has a different type; the name is a 25-character string, the social security number is an integer (which may alternately be defined as a nine-character string), the gross pay is a decimal number, and the address is a 40-character string.

Alternately, a record can be described as a tree to display its structure and name its

|ALLENƀB.ƀTUCKERƀƀƀƀƀƀƀƀƀ|

|275407437|

|25400.00|

|1800ƀBULLƀRUN,ƀALEXANDRIA,ƀVA.ƀ22200ƀƀƀƀ|

FIGURE 2-3
An example record.

nodes, as shown in Figure 2-4. A record in Pascal is viewed as a new data type, and thus is defined by a type declaration, as follows:

```
type identifier = record
                      identifier: type;
                      identifier: type;
                      .
                      .
                      .
                      identifier: type
                  end;
```

Here, the first "identifier" names the record as a whole, while the others name and assign types to each of its constituent fields. Thus, the above example record structure is characterized in the following type declaration:

```
type person = record
                  name: packed array [1..25] of char;
                  ssnumber: packed array [1..9] of char;
                  grosspay: real;
                  address: packed array [1..40] of char
              end;
```

Having defined the new type "person," we can proceed to declare variables with this type, as in the variable PER below.

```
var PER: person;
```

FIGURE 2-4

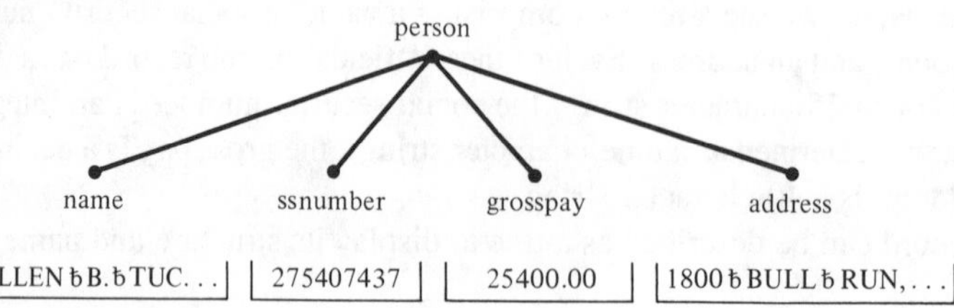

Alternately, we can give the **record** description for the variable PER directly when we declare it as follows:

```
var PER: record
           name: packed array [1..25] of char;
             .
             .
             .
         end;
```

Records, like trees, can have multiple levels of structure, as shown in the following refinement of our example:

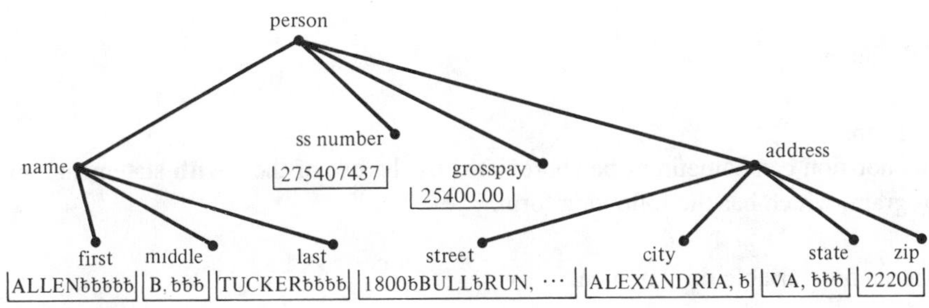

FIGURE 2-5

In this case, we embed an additional **record** description in place of each elementary type in our structure where a nonleaf node appears. Thus, the type "person" is refined as follows:

```
type person = record
                name: record
                   first: packed array [1..10] of char;
                   middle: packed array [1..5] of char;
                   last: packed array [1..10] of char
                end;
                ssnumber: packed array [1..9] of char;
                grosspay: real;
                address: record
                   street: packed array [1..17] of char;
                   city: packed array [1..12] of char;
                   state: packed array [1..6] of char;
                   zip: packed array [1..5] of char
                end
              end;
```

In all these declarations, we emphasize that only the record structure is declared; no initial values can be stored in such a record variable at the time of declaration. That cannot be done until the body of the program begins execution.

To reference an *entire record* within a Pascal program, only the name of a variable declared with that record type needs to be given. For example, the name "PER" references collectively all four fields of a "person" record. On the other hand, to reference a *single field* of a record, we "qualify" the variable by following it with a dot (.) and the corresponding field name. For example, to reference a "person" record's name field we say

PER.name

To reference the address, we say

PER.address

and so forth.

This notation can sometimes be abbreviated by the use of the "**with** statement" in the program, which has the following form:

with record variable **do** statement

Here, the "record variable" is named once, and then all references to fields within that record variable can be made *without* the prefixed qualifier and dot (.). For instance,

with PER **do** . . . name
. . . address

denotes a statement containing references to PER.name and PER.address. But since the **with** PER **do** has been prefixed to the statements, all such references can be written simply as name and address instead.

A final data structure in Pascal is the *set*. A set is a finite collection of elements which share the same (scalar) type. A set variable is declared in the following way:

var identifier: **set of** type

Here, "name" identifies the set variable, while "type" may be any of the standard types (**real**, **integer**, **Boolean**, or **char**) or programmer-defined types (subrange or scalar). Thus, for example, if we have

type digits = 0. .9;
days = (Mon,Tue,Wed,Thu,Fri,Sat,Sun);

then we can declare the following variables:

```
var weekend: set of days;
    odds: set of digits;
    vowels: set of char;
```

Correspondingly, a set *value* is just a list of values of its constituent type, separated by commas and enclosed in brackets [ ]. Thus, the following set values are appropriate to the set variables weekend, odds, and vowels declared above, respectively:

weekend [Sat, Sun]
odds [1,3,5,7,9]
vowels ['a', 'e', 'i', 'o', 'u']

In the following section, we shall see how set variables' values may be assigned and manipulated, using operations that are common to set algebra.

2-2.4 Basic Statements

Pascal declarations, whose purpose is to define the variables, arrays, and other data structures play a passive role in a program. Statements, on the other hand, are executable and thus describe the active aspect of the program. The following is a list of the Pascal statements and a general description of their purpose:

Statement	Purpose
Assignment statement	To perform a series of arithmetic operations (addition, subtraction, etc.) or logical operations (comparison, negation, etc.) and "assign" the final result as the new value of a variable or array element.
Compound statement	To identify a series of statements to be treated as a single statement.
Procedure statement	To invoke a procedure (subprogram).
Goto statement	To alter the sequence of program statement execution by transferring control to a statement which does not immediately follow in the program text.
Conditional statement **Case** statement	To select a statement for execution depending on whether or not a particular condition is **true.**
For statement **Repeat** statement **While** statement	To repeat execution of a sequence of statements.

The assignment and compound statements will be discussed in this section. The procedure statement, together with the procedure declaration, will be discussed in sections 2-2.6 and 2-2.7. The rest are control statements, and will be discussed in section 2-2.5.

The statements themselves in a Pascal program are *separated* by semicolons (;). The reader should note that the semicolon is a statement separator and not a statement terminator, as it is in other languages.

The compound statement is Pascal's device for grouping several statements so that they can be treated as one. This is especially valuable in the specification of loops, as we shall see. The form of the compound statement is

begin S; S;. . .S **end**

where S denotes any other Pascal statement. An example of the compound statement appears in the averaging program at the beginning of section 2-2.

The assignment statement has the following basic form:

variable := expression

Here, "variable" denotes the name of a variable or array reference, and "expression" denotes a calculation, reference, or constant which will give a value. Examples of assignment statements are given in the averaging program such as the following:

N := N + 1

The type of value designated by the expression on the right of the assignment operator ":=" must agree with that of the variable on the left. That may be any **integer**, **real**, **set**, or programmer-defined type, but it must agree. In this sense, Pascal is said to be a "strongly typed" language.

Expressions can be "arithmetic expressions," delivering **real** or **integer** results; "Boolean expressions," delivering **Boolean** results; or "set expressions," delivering **set** results. Trivially, an expression can also be a string constant, in which the variable on the left must be a **packed array of char** of the same length.

The simplest form of arithmetic expression is called a factor, which may be either an unsigned number, a (simple or subscripted) variable, a function designator, or an arithmetic expression enclosed in parentheses. For instance, the number 0 which appears in the assignment statement N := 0 in our example program is a factor.

The value and type resulting from evaluation of a factor are determined as follows:

- If the factor is a number, then that number (and its type) is the result of the evaluation.
- If the factor is a variable, then the result is the current value of the variable.
- If the factor is a function designator, then the result is that value which is returned by application of the designated function to the designated argument(s); see section 2-2.7 for a full description of function designators.
- If the factor is an expression in parentheses, then the result is that value which occurs from evaluation of that expression. For example, the value and type resulting from evaluation for the primary "0" is the value 0 of type **integer**.

An arithmetic expression may be either a factor or a series of factors, each separated from the next by one of the following arithmetic operators.

Arithmetic operator	Meaning
+	Addition
−	Subtraction
*	Multiplication
/	Division
div	Integer division
mod	Integer remainder

(Note here that Pascal provides *no* exponentiation operator, as most languages do.)

For instance, the first two arithmetic expressions below appear on the right-hand sides of assignment statements in the example program.

N + 1
SUM/N
3 + B * (C − D)

The first denotes addition of two values. The second denotes division of two values. The third is a series of three factors; the first two are separated by +, while the second and third are separated by *. The third primary is itself an arithmetic expression "C − D," enclosed in parentheses.

The value and type resulting from evaluation of an arithmetic expression depends upon the value and type of each primary it contains, combined with Pascal's precedence rules for defining the order in which a series of two or more arithmetic operations are carried out.

Operator	Precedence
+ −	1
* / **div mod**	2

The sequence in which operations are carried out is generally in descending order of precedence (starting with all operations of precedence 2) and then from left to right (when there are two or more operators of the same precedence). The type of the result of evaluation of an arithmetic expression will be **integer** when all its primaries are integer; otherwise the result will have **real** type (but see point 1 below). All operators carry their usual meanings, with the following exceptions and clarifications:

1 The result of "a/b" is **real**, regardless of the types of a and b.

2 The result of "a **div** b" is **integer**, and a and b must themselves be **integer**. The result is the **integer** quotient a/b, obtained from truncation.

3 The result of "a **mod** b" is **integer**; a and b must themselves be **integer**. The result is the **integer** remainder of a/b.

What does all this mean? It simply means that if we write

3 + B * C

then the product of B and C is computed first, and that result is added to 3. If we wanted, on the other hand, to multiply the sum of 3 and 2 by C, then we would override the precedence of "*" over "+" by using parentheses as follows:

(3 + B) * C

Reconsidering the third expression listed above, we can now number the operators according to the order in which they will be executed:

```
3 + B * (C - D)
  ↑   ↑    ↑
 (3) (2)  (1)
```

Note that if we had not parenthesized "C − D" then the implied order would have been as follows:

```
3 + B * C - D
  ↑   ↑   ↑
 (2) (1) (3)
```

The result of evaluating this expression will be a **real** value if any of B, C, or D is **real**. Otherwise, it will be **integer**. Assuming that B, C, and D have **integer** values 3, 1, and 5 respectively, the expression's result will be −9, computed as follows:

```
  3 + B * (C - D)
= 3 + 3 * (1 - 5)
= 3 + 3 * (-4)
= 3 + (-12)
= -9
```

Boolean expressions are formed using arithmetic expressions, Boolean values, relational operators, logical operators, and parentheses. The simplest form of Boolean expression is the "Boolean factor." It can be (1) a Boolean value (**true** or **false**), (2) a variable of type **Boolean**, (3) a function designator (see section 2-2.7), (4) a "relation," or (5) a Boolean expression enclosed in parentheses. A relation is a pair of arithmetic expressions, for example a and b, separated by one of the following relational operators:

Relational operator	Meaning of "a operator b"
<	a is less than b
<=	a is not greater than b
=	a is equal to b
>=	a is not less than b
>	a is greater than b
<>	a is not equal to b

The result of evaluating a Boolean factor is **true** or **false**, accordingly, as (1) the Boolean value is **true** or **false**, (2) the value of the **Boolean** variable is **true** or **false**, (3) the value returned by the function designator is **true** or **false**, (4) the indicated relation between the values of the two arithmetic expressions is satisfied or not, or (5) the value of the Boolean expression within the parentheses is **true** or **false**, respectively.

For instance, the factor

h <= 5

gives the result **true** or **false**, respectively, as the current value of the variable h is less than or equal to 5 or not.

Another kind of Boolean factor can be formed using the operator **in,** denoting set membership. If a is an element, and S is a **set** containing the same type of values as a, then "a **in** S" denotes a test to see whether a is a member of S.

A Boolean expression can be either a Boolean primary or a series of Boolean primaries, each possibly preceded by the logical operator **not**, and each separated from the next by one of the logical operators **and** and **or**.

For instance, the following are Boolean expressions:

(h <= 5) **and** (h > 0)
a **or** b **or** c

In the first, the test is to see whether the value of h is less than or equal to 5 and greater than 0. The second is a test to see whether at least one of a, b, and c is **true** or not.

The evaluation of a Boolean expression yields a **Boolean** result, and depends on the current value of each Boolean factor in the expression, the definition of the logical operators, and Pascal's precedence rules for defining the order in which two or more (relational or logical) operators are applied in an expression. The logical operator **not** has equal precedence with prefix −; **and** has equal precedence with symbols *, /, **div**, and **mod**; **or** has equal precedence with signs + and −. The relational operators <, >, <=, >=, =, <>, and **in** have lower precedence than the rest, and are equal in precedence among themselves.

These precedence rules give rather unusual evaluations for some expressions, like the following:

a < b **and** c > d

Here, the expression "b **and** c" is evaluated *first,* so the implied ordering is as if we had written "a < (b **and** c) < d." Thus, we must add parentheses in this case to get the usual ordering:

(a < b) **and** (c < d)

The meaning of each logical operator, when applied to two Boolean primaries, a and b, is defined in the following table for each of the possible pairs of values for a and b.

Value of a	Value of b	a and b	a or b	not a
true	true	true	true	false
	false	false	true	
false	true	false	true	true
	false	false	false	

As another example, the following Boolean expression

a **or** b **and** c

has the value **true** or **false**, respectively, as the following statement is or is not **true**:

Either a is **true**
or both b and c are **true**

However, if we write "(a **or** b) **and** c", we have said:

Both (a or b) is **true**
and c is **true**

"Set expressions" are formed using some of the operators described above, but with sets or set variables as operands. These operators and their meaning for set operands S and T are summarized below.

Set operator op	Precedence	Result	Meaning
=	0	**Boolean**	S equals T
<>	0	**Boolean**	S is not equal T
<=	0	**Boolean**	S is subset of T
+	1	**set**	S union T
−	1	**set**	S difference T
*	2	**set**	S intersect T

Note here that the given precedence of these operators further applied to sets is the same as for the other uses.

For example, suppose the set variable S, T, and U have the following values:

S [Mon, Wed, Fri]
T [Mon, Tue, Wed]
U [Mon]

Then the following expressions have values shown on the right:

Sat **in** S	**false**
S + T	[Mon, Tue, Wed, Fri]
S * T	[Mon, Wed]
S − T	[Fri]
S = T	**false**
U <= S	**true**
U <> S	**true**

2-2.5 Control Structures

In this section, the Pascal statements that control the structure of program execution are presented and illustrated.

Goto Statements The basic form of the go to statement is the following:

goto label

Here, "label" denotes any unsigned integer, which can be the label of some other statement in the program by preceding that statement with that same integer and a colon (:). When executed, the **goto** statement serves to interrupt the normal (textual) sequence of statement execution by transferring control to the statement having the indicated label. For instance, the **goto** statement:

goto 11

causes the statement labeled 11 to be the next one executed, rather than the statement following this one.

Conditional Statements The form of the conditional statement may be one of the following:

(i) if B **then** S1
(ii) if B **then** S1 **else** S2

Here, B denotes any Boolean expression, while S1 and S2 denote any statements. A conditional statement of form (i) is executed in two steps. First, the Boolean expression B is evaluated. Second, if the result is **true**, then the statement S1 is executed. Otherwise, S1 is not executed.

Form (ii) is executed also in two steps. As before, the Boolean expression is first evaluated. Second, either S1 or S2 is executed (and the other one is not executed) depending on whether the result of evaluating B is **true** or **false**, respectively.

Form (i) of the conditional statement is illustrated in the following example:

```
if a < b then
    begin
      a := a + 1;
      b := b - 1
    end
```

Here, the Boolean expression is "a < b," while the statement S1 is the compound statement "**begin** a := a + 1; b := b − 1 **end**."

For a more practical example, consider writing a Pascal program segment to solve for the real roots x of the quadratic equation.

$$ax^2 + bx + c = 0 \qquad \text{(for } a \text{ not 0)}$$

where a, b, and c, are **real** and given.

The number of roots and their values can be determined by first computing the discriminant d from a, b, and c as follows.

$$d = b^2 - 4ac$$

If $d < 0$ then there are no real roots. If $d = 0$, then there is one real root x_1, given by the calculation $x_1 = -b/(2a)$. If $d > 0$, then there are two roots, x_1 and x_2, given by the following calculations:

$$x_1 = \frac{-b + \sqrt{d}}{2a}$$

$$x_2 = \frac{-b - \sqrt{d}}{2a}$$

The Pascal program segment to compute the number of roots, say NROOTS, and their values x1 and x2, given the coefficients a, b, and c, can be written as follows:

```
d := b*b - 4*a*c;
if d < 0
then NROOTS := 0
else if d = 0
  then begin
         NROOTS := 1;
         x1 := -b / (2 * a)
    end
  else begin
         NROOTS := 2;
         x1 := (-b + SQRT (d) ) / (2 * a);
         x2 := (-b - SQRT (d) ) / (2 * a)
    end
```

Both conditional statements in this example are of form 2. The notation SQRT (d) is a function reference, denoting the calculation of the square root of d. This will be discussed in section 2-2.7.

For Statements and Iterative Loops Much of programming concerns the proper specification of iterative loops where the number of steps is counted. Pascal provides several forms of the **for** statement as an aid to specifying such loops.

A controlled loop may be described as the repeated execution of a sequence of statements until a certain specified condition becomes **true.** Many such loops are "counter-controlled" loops, in which a control variable is initialized and tested and incremented each time the sequence of statements is executed. When the variable is incremented beyond a specific limit, the loop's execution terminates. This is pictured in two different

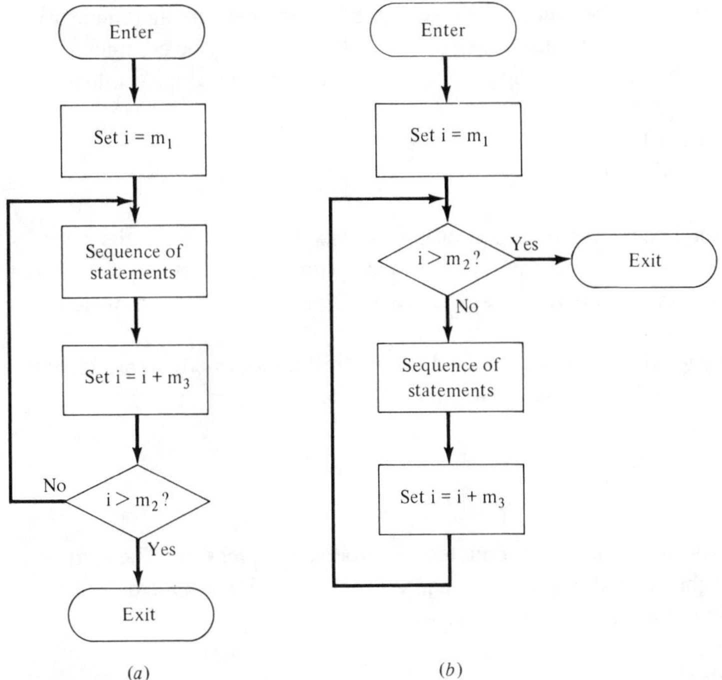

FIGURE 2-6
Two forms of iterative loops.

forms in the flowcharts in Figure 2-6. In the figure, i denotes the control variable and m_1, m_2, and m_3 denote arithmetic expressions which are the initial value, the limit, and the increment value for the control variable, respectively.

Flowchart (*b*) can be written equivalently as a Pascal "**for** statement" as follows:

```
for i := m1 to m2 do
        begin
             sequence of statements
        end
```

For instance, the following loop denotes summation in SUM of the integers from 1 to 10:

```
for i := 1 to 10 do
      SUM := SUM + i
```

assuming that SUM is initially 0.

As indicated, the single **for** statement incorporates the initialization, test, and increment steps of the loop depicted in flowchart (*b*).

Two other points should be noted when using **for** loops. First, the increment value in a **for** statement need not be positive. For instance, the SUM may be computed in reverse order in the example above simply by rewriting the **for** statement as follows:

for i := 10 **downto** 1 **do**
  SUM := SUM + i

When the step value is negative, the test for exit in flowchart (*b*) changes its sense as shown in Figure 2.7. Finally, the value of the loop-control variable upon normal exit from the loop is undefined. Note that this differs from the flowchart version, which suggests otherwise.

The **while** and **repeat** statements are used for controlling loops which are repeated for an indeterminate number of times. They have the following forms:

while B **do** S
repeat S **until** B

Here, S denotes any statement and B denotes any Boolean expression. The semantics of these forms are shown in Figures 2-8(*a*) and 2-8(*b*), respectively. One common use of this form occurs in the example program, where we see:

while not eof **do**
 begin
 .
 .
 .
 end

Here, S is the compound statement and B is the expression "**not** eof," denoting that "end of the input file" has not yet occurred. Further discussion of this special **Boolean** variable "eof" is given in section 2-2.6.

Another use for these forms occurs in numerical analysis, where a sequence of approximations is computed until a specific convergence condition is satisfied. For example, suppose we are developing an approximation to $\sqrt{A}$ by Newton's method. There the next approximation, Y, is computed from the previous one, X, by the formula:

$$Y = 0.5\left(X + \frac{A}{X}\right)$$

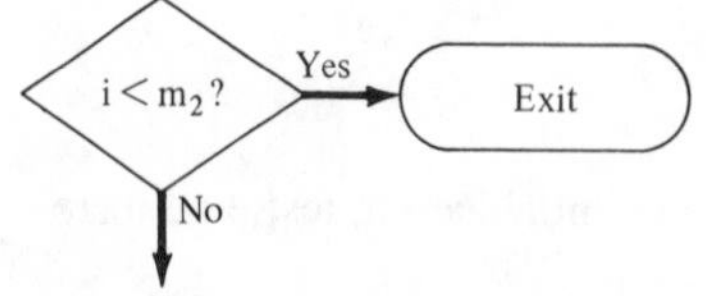

FIGURE 2-7

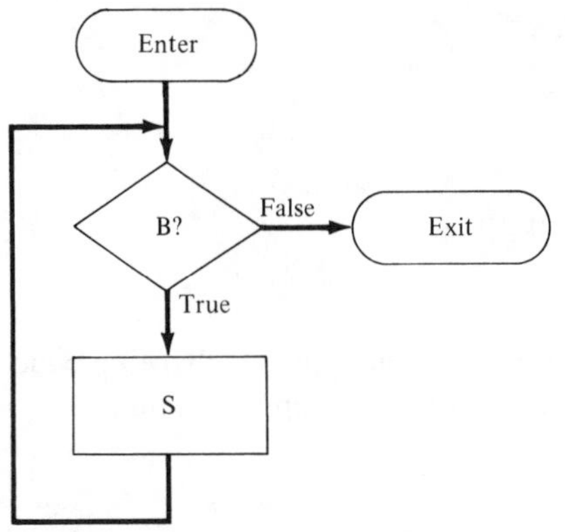

FIGURE 2-8*a*
The **while** statement.

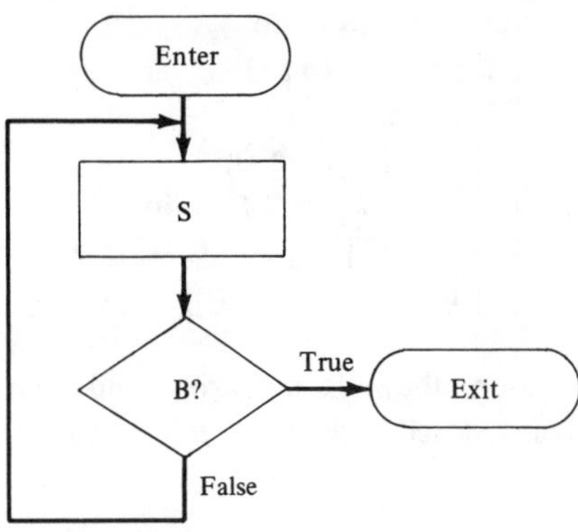

FIGURE 2-8*b*
The **repeat** statement.

This is repeated until the absolute value of the difference between two successive approximations is sufficiently small, say less than 0.0001. The following loop will exit when that condition occurs.

```
Y := 0.5 * (X - A / X);
while abs (Y - X) >= 0.0001 do
  begin
    X := Y;
    Y : = 0.5 * (X + A / X)
  end
```

Here, abs (Y – X) denotes the function reference "absolute value of (Y – X)." Alternately, this loop can be specified by the **repeat** statement:

```
repeat
  X := Y;
  Y := 0.5 * (X + A / X)
until abs (Y – X) < 0.0001
```

Before we leave this section, it is necessary to make two additional points about loops. First, although it is permissible to transfer out of a loop prematurely, it is not permissible to transfer directly into a loop from outside it. Any transfer to a loop must be made by way of its first statement, so that the control variable and test may be properly initialized. Second, a loop may be nested completely within another loop, as illustrated by the following *matrix multiplication* example.

```
for i := 1 to m do
  for j := 1 to p do
    begin
      C [i, j] := 0;
      for k := 1 to n do
        { C [i, j] := C [i, j] + A[i,k] * B [k, j]
    end
```

Here, the $m \times n$ matrix A and the $n \times p$ matrix B are multiplied, with their product being stored in the $m \times p$ matrix C. The ijth element of C is computed as follows:

$$C_{ij} = \sum_{k=1}^{n} A_{ik}B_{kj} \qquad \text{for } i = 1, \ldots, m \text{ and } j = 1, \ldots, p$$

The braces on the program segment's left indicate the nesting of **for** statements. The reader should note that the "innermost" assignment statement is executed n times for each one of the $m \times p$ entries in C, or $m \times n \times p$ times altogether.

The Case Statement The **case** statement provides selection of one from a series of alternative statements, depending on the value of an expression. It has the following form:

```
case e of
  v1: S1;
  v2: S2;
    .
    .
    .
  vn: Sn
end
```

Here, e denotes an expression, v1, . . . , vn denote lists of alternate values that e can have, and each of S1, . . . , Sn denotes the corresponding statement to be executed for each value. For example, suppose we want to take one of four different actions depending on whether the current wind direction DIR is N, S, E, or W respectively. This can be specified in a **case** statement as follows:

```
case DIR of
  N: {action 1};
  S: {action 2};
  E: {action 3};
  W: {action 4}
end
```

Thus, the **case** is equivalent to a nest of **if** . . . **then** . . . **else** statements. The above example can be given equivalently as:

```
if DIR = N then {action 1}
   else if DIR = S then {action 2}
      else if DIR = E then {action 3}
         else if DIR = W then {action 4}
```

which is substantially more tedious to write.

2-2.6. Input-Output Conventions

A "file" is a sequence of data elements stored on an auxiliary storage device, such as a disk, a tape, or an interactive terminal. All data elements in a file are of the same type, such as **char**, **integer**, or a particular program-defined **record** type.

A Pascal file type is declared in the following general way:

type identifier = **file of** type;

Here "identifier" names the file and "type" gives the type of its constituent elements. For example,

type employees = **file of** person;

defines a file type "employees" whose elements are of type "person." If person in turn is assumed to have the definition given in section 2-2.3, then each element of this kind of file will be a **record** containing a name, social security number, gross pay, and address.

One or more specific files of this type may then be declared in the usual way. For example, the following defines two files, "active" and "retired," each containing records of type "person."

var active, retired: employees;

Alternatively, these can be declared without the intermediate declaration of the type "employees" as follows:

var active, retired: **file of** person;

"Text files" are a special class of file in which input and output is done at the terminal. A text file is one whose element type is **char**, and whose data is divided into lines of text, with each line terminated by control characters (typically a carriage return and a line feed). Two "standard" text files are predefined in Pascal, and are named "input" and "output." In fact, the heading of a typical Pascal program may have the form:

program name (input, output);

to designate that this program will use these standard text files during execution. These standard files are predeclared, as if we had written:

var input, output: **file of char**;

Moreover, the "standard" Boolean functions eof and eoln are also provided. These are set to **true** whenever the file "input" is at the end of its data (eof) or the end of an individual line (eoln).

Input and output from the standard files "input" and "output" are performed via the read, write, readln, and writeln procedures, which are given in the following way:

Input	Output
read (variable list)	write (expression list)
readln (variable list)	writeln (expression list)

Here, "variable list" denotes any list of variables into which input data will be stored, and "expression list" denotes any list of expressions whose values will be transferred to the output file. The suffix "-ln" (on read*ln* and write*ln*) denotes passage to the end of a *line* (of input or output) after the operation has been completed. Thus, a series of readln's is distinguished from a series of read's by the fact that each readln will pass over *an entire line* of data while each read may not. Similarly, a series of writeln's will produce output vertically (as a series of lines), while a series of write's will not.

The data input and output is otherwise taken as a continuous *stream* of values, and each successive read (or write) operation will proceed to the next successive value (or position) in the stream. For example, consider the following series of three input lines.

```
-14
  8     3
 12
```

If we have an integer variable named I then the following read statements:

```
read (I);
read (I);
read (I)
```

will leave the values of I successively as −14, 8, and 3. However, if these read's had instead been readln's, then the values of I would have been −14, 8, and 12 instead, since each readln automatically passes to the end of a line after it is executed.

The Boolean system function "eof" will become **true** whenever a read or a readln is attempted which passes the end of the input file. Otherwise, it remains **false**. Thus, the familiar loop structure:

```
read (x);
while not eof do
  begin
    .
    .
    .
    read (x)
  end
```

provides for handling the data one value at a time, as long as "**not** eof" remains **true** (i.e., eof remains **false**).

The function "eoln" will become **true** whenever a read or readln is attempted which passes the end of a line (a carriage return) in the input file. It should be noted that readln *always* passes the end of a line, by its nature, and thus always leaves eoln **true**.

The write and writeln statements provide output to the standard text file (usually the terminal screen or a printed listing). For example, if NAME is a **packed array** of twenty characters with value 'BUCK   ', and SCORE is an **integer** variable with value −11, then

```
writeln (NAME, SCORE)
```

will display the values

```
BUCK          -14
```

and then proceed to the beginning of the next line. If write had been given instead of writeln, the output would be the same but the next line would *not* automatically be available for the display of subsequent output.

The spacing between adjacent output values is determined by the presence of preset tab positions on the output line. Typically, these are at positions 1, 21, 41, and 61 as shown:

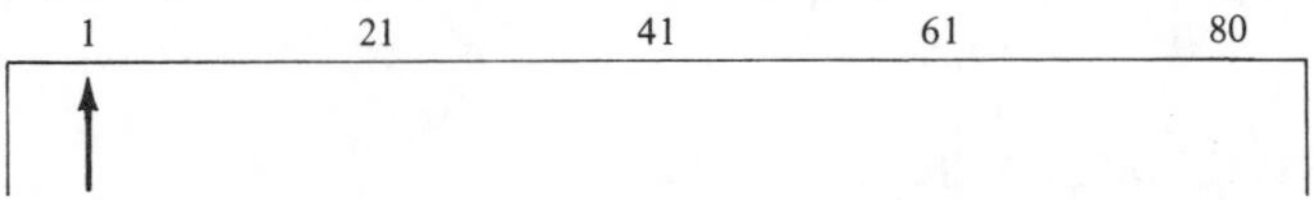

Each separate item displayed is thus adjusted at the next available tab position on the line.

To override this "default" spacing, items in a write or writeln statement can be affixed with a format specification, of the form:

(i) :p
or **(ii)** :p :q

Here, "p" denotes the total number of horizontal positions required by the item, while "q" denotes the number of decimal digits for a **real** value. Thus, if the **integer** variable SCORE has the value − 14 and the **real** variable AV has the value 10.25, the statement

writeln (SCORE:5, AV:8:2)

will have the following output (the letter b denotes a blank space in the output):

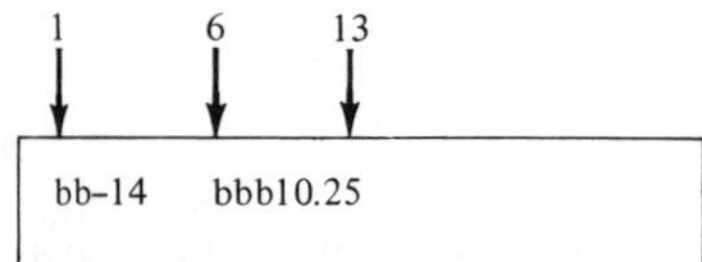

To transfer input and output from disk or tape (sequential) files, the get and put statements are used, respectively. When such a file is used, a "buffer" is automatically provided for holding a single record from the file. The buffer's name is composed out of the file's name and the up arrow (↑). Thus, if the file named "active" is a file of "person" (from the foregoing discussion), we have the buffer named "active↑" automatically provided:

name	ssnumber	grosspay	address

active↑

To open a file for input, we use the following statement:

reset (filename, systemname)

Similarly, the statement

rewrite (filename, systemname)

opens a file for output. In these forms, the "systemname" is the name by which the file is known to the operating system of the computer where the program is run. For example, the statement

reset (active, 'ACTIVE.EMPLOYEES')

opens the system file named ACTIVE.EMPLOYEES and identifies it with the name "active," which is the name by which that file will be known by the program.

To transfer the next sequential record from an input file to its buffer, the get statement is used:

```
get (filename)
```

The put statement has the reverse effect, transferring a single record from the buffer to an output file.

```
put (filename)
```

Thus, if we are processing the file "active" for input, we would use a single reset statement, and a series of get statements of the form:

```
get (active)
```

to retrieve individual records. Moreover, an extension of the eof function can be written in the following way:

```
eof (filename)
```

to detect the end of an input file named "filename." Thus, the following loop displays a list of the individual names of all employees in the active file.

```
reset (active, 'ACTIVE.EMPLOYEES');
get (active);
while not eof (active) do
  begin
    writeln (active↑.name);
    get (active)
  end
```

On the other hand, to process a file for output, we use a single rewrite statement, followed by a series of put statements which transfer individual records from the output file buffer to the file itself. Thus, the following code will save in a separate file called 'ACTIVE.NAMES' the names (only) of all records in the file *active*.

```
reset (active, 'ACTIVE.EMPLOYEES');
rewrite (anames, 'ACTIVE.NAMES'):
get (active);
while not eof (active) do
  begin
    anames↑ := active↑.name;
    put (anames);
    get (active)
  end
```

In this loop, the assignment ''anames↑ := active↑.name'' transfers the *name* field (active↑.name) out of an active record to the buffer (anames↑) in preparation for the put statement which subsequently transfers the name to the output file anames.

2-2.7 Subprograms, Functions, and Libraries

Most practical programming tasks are large enough to justify segmenting the program into a number of functional units, all linked together by a ''main'' program which controls the sequence in which these units will be executed. The other advantage of program segmentation is that it permits the reuse of code without rewriting and debugging it each time it is needed.

Pascal provides facilities which enable such segmentation. A Pascal subprogram is called a ''procedure'' or a ''function,'' and is defined by way of a ''procedure declaration'' or ''function declaration,'' respectively. It may be invoked either by the main program or by another subprogram. The invoking program determines when the subprogram is to be activated, what values are to be supplied to it, and what variables are to hold the results.

Certain functions are of such widespread importance in numerical applications that they are provided as ''standard functions'' in Pascal. As such, they need not be defined before they are invoked. The standard functions are listed in Figure 2-9. As the reader can see, these functions perform arithmetic calculations like the trigonometric sine and cosine, the square root, and the natural logarithm. There are also some special functions which have more marginal usage with scalar, subrange, and character types.

Any of these functions may be invoked by using a ''function designator'' in place of

FIGURE 2-9
THE PASCAL STANDARD FUNCTIONS

Function	Name	Arguments (*e*)
Absolute value of *e*	abs	Any arithmetic expression *e*
Arctangent of *e*	arctan	Any arithmetic expression *e*
Character equivalent of *e*	chr	Any scalar or subrange *e*
Cosine of *e*	cos	Any expression *e* representing an angle in radians
Exponential of *e*	exp	Any arithmetic expression *e*
Natural logarithm of *e*	ln	Any expression *e* > 0
Integer equivalent of *c*	ord	Any character value of *c*
Is *e* odd?	odd	Any **integer** expression *e*
Predecessor of *e*	pred	Any scalar or subrange *e*
Rounding of *e*	round	Any arithmetic expression *e*
Sine of *e*	sin	Any expression *e* representing an angle in radians
Square of *e*	sqr	Any arithmetic expression *e*
Square root of *e*	sqrt	Any arithmetic expression *e*
Successor of *e*	succ	Any scalar or subrange *e*
Truncation of *e*	trunc	Any arithmetic expression *e*

an ordinary variable or constant in an arithmetic expression. A function designator is written in the following way:

name (e)

Here, "name" denotes the standard function's name and e denotes the expression whose value is the actual argument to which the function is applied. For example, suppose we have **real** variables a, b, and c; the values of a and b are 2 and 3, respectively; and we want to compute c as follows:

$$c = \frac{a + b}{\sqrt{a^2 + b^2}}$$

Then we can use the standard functions "sqr" and "sqrt" as follows:

```
c := (a + b) / sqrt (sqr (a) + sqr (b))
```

Note that the expression sqr (a) + sqr (b) is first evaluated, then the result, 13, is passed as the argument to the function sqrt, and that result is (a close approximation to) the square root of 13, say 3.60555. This value then becomes the divisor for the remaining evaluation.

It is important also to mention that most of the standard functions are *generic*. That is, they accept as an argument any arithmetic expression *e*, whether it is **integer** or **real**, and the result delivered is usually **real**. Exceptions are odd which delivers a **Boolean** result; trunc, round, and ord which deliver **integer** results; and succ, pred, and chr which deliver subrange or scalar results.

Writing Functions When the Pascal standard functions do not provide the kind of computation desired, the programmer may define a new function by way of a "function declaration." It can then be invoked using a function designator, in the same way that the standard functions are invoked.

Because a (programmer-written) function is invoked in the same context as a standard function, it must always deliver a single value as a result. The type (**real**, **integer**, **Boolean**, **char**, or scalar) of that result is identified at the beginning of the declaration, whose general form is as follows:

function heading body

Here, "heading" denotes a description of the parameters required by the function and the result delivered by it, while "body" denotes the function's local variables and the sequence of statements that will be executed when it is invoked.

To illustrate, let's write a function which computes the factorial of an integer n, defined as follows.

$$\text{factorial}(n) = n \times (n-1) \times \cdots \times 3 \times 2 \qquad \text{for } n > 1$$
$$= 1 \qquad \text{for } n = 1$$

The one parameter, *n,* is an **integer**, and the result will also be an **integer**. When writing the function body, we treat *n* as if it were an ordinary **integer** variable whose factorial we are computing. The function declaration can thus be written as follows:

```
                 heading
       ┌───────────────────────────────┐
function factorial (n: integer): integer;
           ⎧ var i, f: integer;
           ⎪   begin
           ⎪     f := 1;
  body     ⎨     for i := 2 to n do
           ⎪       f := f * i;
           ⎪     factorial := f
           ⎩   end
```

Note the delineation of the procedure's heading and body by braces. The heading itself has the following general form:

name (formal parameters) : type;

Here, ''name'' denotes the procedure's name, ''formal parameters'' denotes a list of the names and types of the parameters, separated by semicolons, and ''type'' denotes the type of the result delivered by the function. The body of a function is always a compound statement, following the declaration of local variables.

The function's body must contain at least one statement whose execution will cause a value to be assigned to the function's name. This designates the particular value of the result to be returned to the invoking program. In our example, the result is so designated by the last assignment statement.

Invoking Functions As mentioned, a function may be invoked only by execution of a function designator within an expression. The function designator takes the following general form:

name (actual parameters)

Here, ''name'' denotes the name of the function to be invoked and ''actual parameters'' denotes a list of expressions, separated by commas. These actual parameters define the particular values with which the formal parameters will be associated during execution of the body. Therefore, there must be exactly as many actual parameters in the function designator as there are formal parameters in the function declaration. Furthermore, a left-right one-to-one correspondence is assumed between the actual and formal parameters as they are listed.

An invocation of the function involves the following steps. First, each formal parameter is assigned the current value of its corresponding actual parameter. (This treatment of final-actual correspondence is known as "call by value.") Second, the body is executed. Third, control is returned to the expression which contained the function designator after the body's last statement is executed. The result returned is the last value assigned the function name during execution of the body.

To illustrate, suppose we want to compute the binomial coefficients

$$a_i = \frac{N!}{i!\,(N - i)!} \qquad \text{for } i = 0, 1, \ldots, N$$

for the familiar polynomial:

$$(x + y)^N = a_N x^N + a_{N-1} x^{N-1} y + \cdots + a_i x^i y^{N-i} + \cdots + a_0 y^N$$

We can write the following program which reads N and prints the desired sequence of coefficients a.

```
program coefficients (input, output);
  var N, a, i: integer;
    begin
      read (N);
      for i := 0 to N do
        begin
          a := factorial (N)/ (factorial (i) * factorial (N-i));
          writeln ('a[' :2, i:2, ']=' :2, a:3)
        end
    end.
```

We will focus attention on the underlined assignment statement which contains three different function designators invoking the function "factorial."

The first invocation occurs as "factorial (N)." Suppose that the actual value of N is 4. First, the formal parameter n is assigned the value 4 of N (its corresponding actual parameter). Second, the body

```
begin
  f := 1;
  for i := 2 to n do
    f := f * i;
  factorial := f
end
```

is executed, leaving "factorial" with the correctly computed factorial of N, or 24. This is then returned to the expression, whose subsequent evaluation will be as follows:

```
24/ (factorial (i) * factorial (N-i))
```

The next invocation is "factorial (i)," which similarly causes the value 1 to be returned, and the expression to be reduced as follows:

24/ (1 * factorial (N − i))

The third invocation will leave the following:

24/ (1 * 6)

The expression's final result can now be computed.

Writing and Invoking Procedures Often a subprogram is required which will compute a number of results rather than just one, or else compute a result which is an **array** rather than a simple variable. For these situations, the *function* is not appropriate, and a *procedure* is needed instead. It differs from the function in the following ways.

1 Its name is not associated with any of the results it delivers.
2 Each one of the results it delivers (in addition to each one of the "inputs" it requires) is identified with an additional formal parameter, called a "varying parameter."
3 Its body therefore contains statements which assign to each of those varying parameters its designated result, in lieu of assigning any result to the procedure name itself.

The procedure declaration is otherwise the same as the function declaration, with the omission of the type suffix in its heading, as shown:

procedure name (formal parameters; varying parameters); body

Here, "name," "formal parameters," and "body" have the same meaning as they did for functions. The "varying parameters" are each preceded by the word **var** to designate that they will carry results *from* the procedure rather than actual values *to* it.

The procedure is invoked with a "procedure statement" which has the following form:

name (actual parameters)

Here, "name" identifies the procedure being invoked, while "actual parameters" denotes a list of expressions and variables which, respectively, designate value passed to the procedure body and results received from the procedure body at the time of invocation.

The formal-actual parameter correspondence is the same as described above for functions and function designators, except that the values of those actual parameters that correspond to varying parameters are *not* copied to them. Instead, each varying parameter is taken as a "synonym" for its corresponding actual parameter *throughout* execution of the body. (This treatment of formal-actual correspondence is known as "call by reference," in contrast to "call by value" discussed above.) Thus, each such *actual* parameter must be an ordinary variable, and not an expression. That is, it must be prepared to hold *output from* the procedure. Because of these semantics, one must be careful which formal parameters are to be designated **var** in the procedure declaration. Specifically, every formal parameter which designates a value to be returned by the procedure should be preceded by **var**; if it is not, then the corresponding actual parameter will never receive the intended result!

Suppose we redeclare the factorial function as a procedure with the parameter f added to designate the resulting factorial.

```
procedure factorial (n: integer; var f: integer);
  var i: integer;
  begin
    f :=1 ;
    for i := 2 to n do
      f := f * i
  end
```

Now the main program which computes the binomial coefficients can be rewritten to make use of this procedure "factorial" as follows:

```
program coefficients (input, output);
  var N, Nfact, n1, n2, i, a: integer;
  begin
    read (N);
    factorial (N, Nfact);
    for i := 0 to n do
      begin
        factorial (i, n1);
        factorial (N - i, n2);
        a := Nfact/ (n1 * n2);
        writeln ('a[' :2, i:2, ']=':2, a:3)
      end
  end.
```

Note here that new variables Nfact, n1, and n2 are used to hold intermediate results delivered by the varying parameters. Below is another example in which a procedure computes and returns more than one value. It also illustrates one way by which an array containing an arbitrary number of elements can be accommodated as a formal parameter. We will name the procedure MMM. Its task is to compute the mean, maximum value, and the minimum value in an n-element array A of **real** values, assuming n is no greater than 50.

```
type ary = array [1. .50] of real;
procedure MMM (A:ary; n:integer; var mean, max, min: real);
   var i: integer;
   begin
      mean := A [1]; max := A [1]; min := A [1];
      for i := 2 to n do
         begin
            mean := mean + A [i];
            if max <A [i] then max := A [i]
            else if min >A [i] then min := A [i]
         end;
      mean := mean/n
   end
```

Note here that varying parameters mean, max, and min will hold the results. The following main program uses MMM as it reads 10 values into **real** array X, computes their mean, maximum, and minimum, and prints the results.

```
program statistics (input, output);
   var X: array [1..50] of real;
      xbar, xmax, xmin: real;
      i: integer;
   begin
      for i: = 1 to 10 do read (X[i]);
      MMM (X,10,xbar,xmax,xmin);
      writeln ('mean =', xbar);
      writeln ('minimum =', xmin);
      writeln ('maximum =', xmax)
   end.
```

Note here that in the procedure statement, each actual parameter X, 10, xbar, xmax, and xmin agrees in its type with that of its corresponding formal parameter A, n, mean, max, and min, respectively. Note also that executing that procedure statement will leave in xbar, xmax, and xmin, respectively, the mean, maximum, and the minimum value in array X, as computed by the procedure MMM. Finally, note that X is declared with the same dimensionality as the parameter A, and this is strictly required (even if we are using just 10 of its entries).

Recursion Some scientific applications deal with functions that are defined recursively. Uses of recursive function definitions are found extensively in calculus, number theory, formal language theory, and artificial intelligence.

Pascal permits direct definition of recursively defined functions in its programs. To illustrate, let us consider again the factorial function, which may be redefined recursively as follows:

$$\text{factorial}(n) = \begin{cases} 1 & \text{if } n < 2 \\ n \times \text{factorial}(n - 1) & \text{if } n >= 2 \end{cases}$$

This definition can be directly encoded in Pascal as a recursive function in the following way:

```
function factorial (n: integer) : integer;
  begin
    if n < 2 then factorial := 1
    else factorial := n * factorial (n - 1)
  end
```

Note here that factorial invokes itself each time the expression n * factorial (n − 1) is evaluated. Thus, this leads to the following sequence of invocations for the evaluation of factorial (4).

Invocation	Value of n	Result returned
1	4	4 * factorial (3)
2	3	3 * factorial (2)
3	2	2 * factorial (1)
4	1	1

Many problems are more clearly expressed via recursion rather than a conventional **for** loop, although the factorial is not one of them. More motivation may be gained for the value of recursion when one studies AI applications, as shown in Case Study 5 and implemented in later chapters.

2-2.8 Additional Features

Pascal has two additional features that have not yet been introduced, namely "variant records" and "list processing." The former allows storage for different types of records to be shared, while the latter allows storage to be dynamically allocated in blocks, and then linked together to simulate queues, stacks, trees, and other dynamic data structures.

The use of "variant records" is dictated by the need to redefine a storage area in two or more different ways. For example, suppose we have a file of employee records which have two different forms, depending on whether the employee is active or retired.

Active employee	Retired employee
Name	Name
Address	Address
Social security number	Social security number
Status (A)	Status (R)
Job classification	Years of service
Gross pay	Pension
Deductions	

Here, we note that *both* record types have the same first four fields, and then they diverge. The active record (status = A) has job classification, gross pay, and deductions information, while the retired record (status = R) has years of service and pension information. Yet the processing of an employee file involves reading a record into the file's buffer *without* regard to (or prior knowledge of) its type. Thus, the buffer must be defined in such a way that will alternately accommodate *either* type in the *same* memory space. This kind of definition is sometimes known as "overlay defining," "equivalencing," or "redefining" in other languages. In Pascal it is known as a "variant record."

To define a variant record, a **case** statement is embedded within the record at the spot where the variations diverge, as shown below for our example:

```
type string20 = packed array [1. .20] of char;
     string9 = packed array [1. .9] of char;
     employee = record
          name: string20;
          address: string20;
          socialsecurityno: string9;
          case status: char of
             'A': (jobclass: integer;
                   grosspay: real;
                   deductions: real);
             'R': (yearsofservice: integer;
                   pension: real)
          end
     end;
```

Here, we see that each variation within the record is distinguished by a different value of the "status" field ('A' or 'R') and its constituent fields are enclosed in parentheses following that value.

Pascal "list processing" facilities are its only provision for dynamic storage allocation. These facilities are useful in systems programming applications where stacks, queues, trees, or similar data structures must be maintained. To support this, a *pointer type* must be declared in the program as follows:

```
type ptr = ↑entry;
```

Here, the prefix up arrow is to be read as "points to"; thus we read "the type 'ptr' is defined as a pointer to a record of type 'entry.' " Moreover, the type "entry" characterizes a typical entry, or *node,* in the linked list or stack. For instance, if we wish to create a linked list of fifteen-character names, a typical entry would be defined as follows:

```
type entry = record
                 name: packed array [1. .15] of char;
                 fptr: ptr
             end;
```

Here, the node has two parts, one for the name itself, and one for the pointer (fptr) that will link this node to the next one in the list. Thus, the following picture

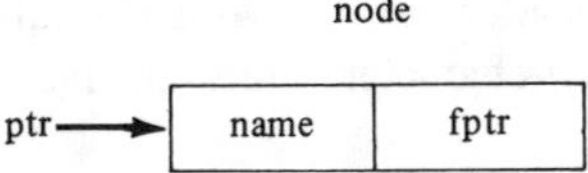

shows that a node in a linked list is identified by a variable of type ptr, and consists of two parts, a "name" and an "fptr," which in turn is of type ptr and serves as a *link* to the next entry in the list.

The special value **nil** is the designation that a pointer is indicated graphically as follows:

Assuming the above **type** declarations, we may declare variables "head'," "p", and "q" of type ptr in the usual way:

```
var head,p,q: ptr;
```

Two standard procedures are provided in Pascal which allow individual nodes to be created and destroyed. These are called "new" and "dispose." The procedure "new" is invoked with a pointer variable as a parameter. Continuing our example, the statement

```
new (p)
```

will create a node and set the variable p to point to it: Note that no *value* is stored in the node as a result of this statement; only the node is created.

Conversely, to destroy a node the procedure "dispose" is invoked, with a pointer to the node in question supplied as a parameter. Thus,

```
dispose (p)
```

will cause the node currently referenced by p, together with its value, to become inaccessible to the program.

A pointer variable may be set to point to the same node as another by using a simple assignment statement. For instance, to make q point to the same node as p, we simply say

```
q := p
```

with the result shown below:

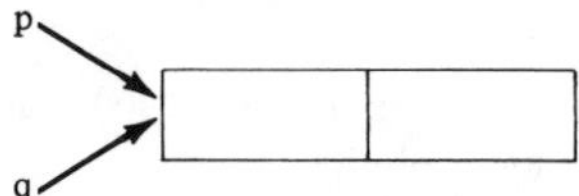

To combine these ideas into a functional example, consider the following Pascal program which develops a linked list from a series of fifteen-character names given as input, as shown in Figures 2-10 and 2-11.

```
program lister (input, output);
  type ptr = ↑entry;
    entry = record
          name: packed array [1..15] of char;
          fptr: ptr
      end;
  var p,q,head: ptr;
  begin
    new(p);
    head := p; q := nil;
    read (p↑.name);
    while not eof do
      begin
        q := p;
        new (p);
        q↑.fptr := p;
        read (p↑.name)
      end;
    dispose (p); {end of input—get rid of extra node}
    if q <> nil then q↑.fptr := nil
    else head := nil
  end.
```

The first statement causes a single node to be created, as shown in Figure 2-12. The next three statements set ''head'' to point to this node, q to **nil**, and the first ''name'' in the input data to be read and stored in this node. Thus, after the first three statements within the **while** loop are executed, the list is partially constructed as shown in Figure 2-13.

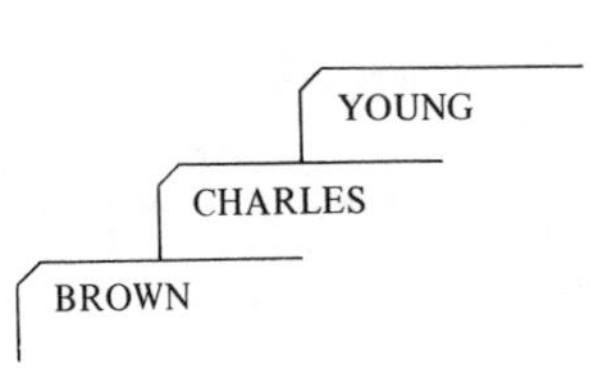

FIGURE 2-10

FIGURE 2-11

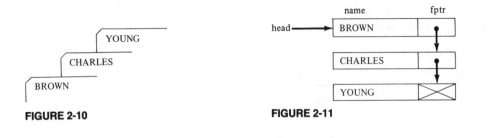

Note that each time through this loop, a *new* node is prepared for receiving the next input name just before the statement "read (p↑.name)" is reached. Thus, upon end of input the situation is as shown in Figure 2-14, with an extra node that will not be utilized.

The last two statements in the program clean up this loose end, disposing of the extra node and setting the last node's fptr to **nil** (if there is one).

2-3 APPLICATIONS OF PASCAL

Now that the reader has a working knowledge of Pascal, we will present and discuss a Pascal solution to Case Study 1—Matrix Inversion. This discussion will exhibit various concepts of Pascal as it is used in scientific applications. After this, we will introduce major implementation-dependent extensions of Pascal, especially those found in the University of California at San Diego (UCSD) implementation. We conclude this chapter with an overall evaluation of Pascal, using this case study and the evaluation criteria discussed in Chapter 1.

2-3.1 Pascal Case Study Implementation

The Pascal implementation of Case Study 1 was run on the following two computers and compilers.

1 Digital VAX 750/UNIX Pascal
2 IBM PC Turbo Pascal

The algorithm described in Appendix A for this case study was coded as a Pascal procedure named INVERT shown in Figure 2-15. To exercise INVERT, a main program named CASE1 is used, as shown in Figure 2-16.

FIGURE 2-12

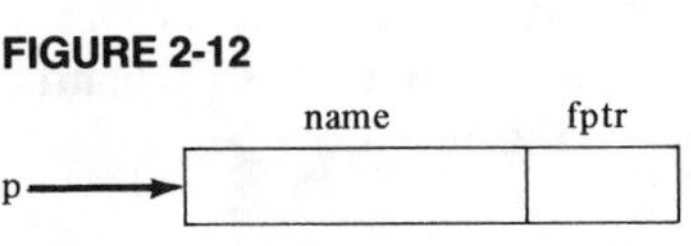

FIGURE 2-13

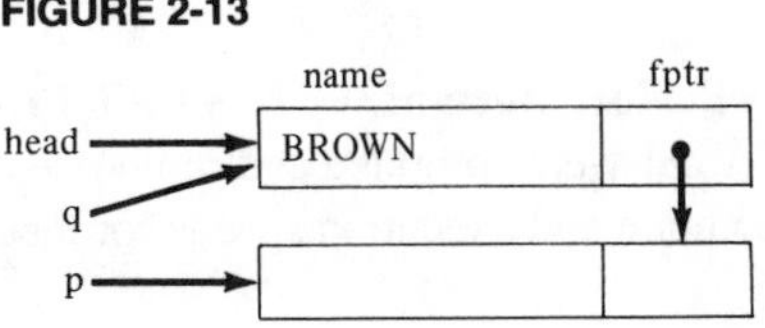

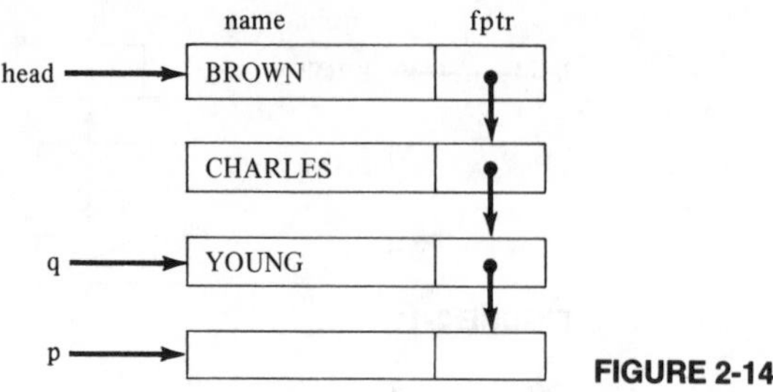

FIGURE 2-14

The main program reads from the input an integer n, which gives the size of the arrays (A, Ainv, and so forth) which will be used in the calculations. Note that since Pascal does not permit dynamic array declaration, a *maximum* size (here, 20) must be postulated. This number is arbitrary and can be larger to the extent that the available memory of the host computer allows it. The auxiliary procedure "outarray" is defined to *display* an n × n array, and is invoked for displays at different places within the main program. The values are then read into A, and INVERT is invoked to compute A's inverse, Ainv. The remainder of the program CASE1 is concerned with displaying the result.

The procedure INVERT is a straightforward encoding of the algorithm described in Appendix A. We should note that the actual procedure declaration for INVERT must be embedded within CASE1. However, some implementations allow the option to compile procedures separately.

Accuracy and Reliability of the INVERT Procedure Accuracy of the result delivered by a numerical algorithm depends upon three factors: the nature of the algorithm, the nature of the data, and the maximum number of significant digits for a **real** value that is carried by the implementation.

By its nature, the matrix inversion algorithm sometimes delivers inaccurate results. One way to guard against this event is to give a reasonable test for zero. That is, *exact* zeros are generally not attained in the machine representation of **real** data, so that the test for $A_{JJ} = 0$ is normally written as follows:

if abs (A[j,j]) < E−8 **then** . . .

That is, the test for zero becomes one of whether or not the computed value of A_{JJ} had become sufficiently *close* to zero that it could be considered to be effectively zero. The maximum number of significant (decimal) digits allowed for a **real** value by the IBM and Digital computers is 16.

Performance of the INVERT Procedure The INVERT procedure and program CASE1 were compiled and run on two systems, using as data a single 20 × 20 matrix. Compile and execution speeds for these runs are shown in Figure 2-17.

FIGURE 2-15
Pascal procedure INVERT for Case Study 1.

```
procedure INVERT(A:array20; var B:array20;
                 n:integer; var error:Boolean);
     {Compute the inverse B of the n x n matrix A.  Set error
     to true or false, depending on whether or not the inverse
     can be computed.}

     var j,k,l,jmax: integer;
         Amax, Ahold, Bhold, S: real;
     label 99, 100;

  begin
        for j:=1 to n-1 do     {Initialize B and error}
          begin
             B[j,j]:=1;
             for k:=j+1 to n do
               begin B[k,j]:=0; B[j,k]:=0 end
          end;
        B[n,n]:=1;
        error:=false;
        for j:=1 to n-1 do     {Perform step 1 -- row interchange}
          begin
             Amax:=abs(A[j,j]);
             jmax:=j;
             for k:=j+1 to n do
               if abs(A[k,j])>Amax
               then begin Amax:=abs(A[k,j]); jmax:=k end;
             if j<>jmax then for l:=1 to n do
               begin
                  Ahold:=A[j,l]; A[j,l]:=A[jmax,l]; A[jmax,l]:=Ahold;
                  Bhold:=B[j,l]; B[j,l]:=B[jmax,l]; B[jmax,l]:=Bhold
               end;
             if abs(A[j,j])<1E-8 then goto 99;
             for l:=j+1 to n do
               begin
                  S:=A[l,j]/A[j,j];
                  for k:=1 to n do
                     begin
                       A[l,k]:=A[l,k]-A[j,k]*S;
                       B[l,k]:=B[l,k]-B[j,k]*S
                     end
               end
          end;
        for j:=n downto 1 do  {Perform step 2 -- back substitute.}
          begin
             if abs(A[j,j])<1E-8 then goto 99;
             for k:=1 to n do
               begin
                  S:=0;
                  for l:=j+1 to n do
                    S:=S+A[j,l]*B[l,k];
                  B[j,k]:=(B[j,k]-S)/A[j,j]
               end
          end;
        goto 100;
   99: error:=true;
  100:
  end;
```

FIGURE 2-16
Pascal Main Program CASE1 for Case Study 1.

```
program CASE1 (input,output);

type array20 = array[1..20,1..20] of real;

var i, j, k, n: integer;
     error: Boolean;
     A, B, Ainv, Prod: array20;

procedure outarray (var A: array20; n: integer);
     {This utility procedure displays an nxn array as output}
     var i,j: integer;
  begin
     for i:=1 to n do
       begin
         for j:=1 to n do
           write (A[i,j]:8:4);
         writeln
       end
  end;

  begin
     writeln ('enter the matrix size');
     readln(n);
     while not eof(input) do
       begin                    {read an nxn matrix into A}
        writeln ('enter the matrix, row by row');
        for i:=1 to n do
          begin
           for j:=1 to n do
              read(A[i,j]);
           readln
          end;

        writeln('The matrix A = ');
        outarray (A, n);
        INVERT (A, Ainv, n, error);

        if not error
        then begin
              writeln('Its inverse = ');
              outarray (Ainv, n);  {display the inverse}
              for i:=1 to n do     {compute the product of A and Ainv}
                for j:=1 to n do
                  begin
                     Prod[i,j]:=0;
                     for k:=1 to n do
                        Prod[i,j]:=Prod[i,j]+A[i,k]*Ainv[k,j]
                  end;
              writeln('Their product = ');
              outarray (Prod, n);  {display the product}
             end
        else writeln('Its inverse cannot be computed');

        writeln ('enter the matrix size');
        readln(n)
       end  {of while loop}
  end.
```

FIGURE 2-17
EFFICIENCY OF PASCAL CASE STUDY 1 PROGRAM

Implementation	Compile speed	Execution speed
1 Digital VAX-750/UNIX Pascal	5.1 sec	8.5 sec
2 IBM PC/DOS Turbo Pascal	3.4 sec	28.3 sec

2-3.2 Implementation-Dependent Extensions of Pascal

The most widely known extensions of Pascal are found in the version developed at the University of California at San Diego, known as UCSD Pascal. Its principal extensions are in the areas of string processing, random access files, and graphics.

While string processing is not really supported by standard Pascal, UCSD Pascal provides the additional data type **string**. A string is any sequence of characters enclosed between apostrophes ('). Moreover, a variable can be declared to have type string, and thus contain a string value. String assignment, input, output, and concatenation are also supported. Moreover, a strong collection of functions and procedures for string manipulation is also provided, so that reasonable text processing can be done if one has access to these UCSD Pascal extensions.

UCSD Pascal's random access file processing procedures are an extension of its sequential file procedures. The special procedure "seek" is provided to position the file reading-writing mechanism to an arbitrary record in the file. Any subsequent get or put statement, therefore, accesses that record rather than the next sequential one.

Finally, UCSD Pascal provides so-called "turtle graphics" procedures which allow the programmer to realize graphical, as well as numerical display of results. These are useful in a variety of applications, including statistics, games, and various interactive programs. They are based on the idea that the program controls the motion of a "turtle," or cursor, around on a screen which is divided into a rectangular array of finely divided points. As the turtle moves, its trail across the screen is visible, and thus a graphical image can be displayed.

2-3.3 Overall Evaluation of Pascal

From our case study experience, we evaluate Pascal using the nine criteria of Chapter 1 as follows:

1 Expressivity	Good
2 Well-definedness	Excellent
3 Data types and structures	Fair
4 Modularity	Good
5 Input-output facilities	Good
6 Portability	Excellent
7 Efficiency	Good
8 Pedagogy	Good
9 Generality	Fair

An insistence on strong typing and static data structures are major factors in Pascal's excellent "well-definedness." Well-conceived and simple syntax and semantic definitions are also important here. These factors also contribute to Pascal's excellent "portability," since the standard version is implemented on almost all hardware, from micros to mainframes. The only warning that should be issued here is to UCSD Pascal users who later try to "port" programs to a non-UCSD system; UCSD extensions are not generally supported by the other Pascal compilers.

We judge Pascal as only fair in "data types and structures" and "generality." In the former case, its severe restrictions on arrays—when used as parameters, when used in input, output, and arithmetic, when initialized, and when declared—are a major factor. Arrays are important in all programming domains, and failure to be able to generalize an array's size or to perform array I/O or arithmetic in a single statement, are serious handicaps. In the latter case, standard Pascal does not permit reasonable support for string manipulation and random access files. Moreover, separate compilation of procedures and functions are not defined in standard Pascal, and thus the development of general libraries is discouraged.

In all other criteria, Pascal is judged to be good. Its textbooks are improving rapidly, its efficiency is comparable with FORTRAN and superior to PL/I, it has good sequential file processing facilities, its procedure and function declaration facilities are about the same as in most other languages, and its expressivity is good.

EXERCISES

1 Let x, y, and z be **real** variables, and let i, j, and k be **integer** variables. Assume that they have the following values.

$x = 2.5$ $\quad i = 1$
$y = -10$ $\quad j = -5$
$z = 8$ $\quad k = 12$

Compute the result delivered by evaluating each of the following arithmetic expressions.

(a) $x + y * z$ **(e)** $i - 1$
(b) $(x + y) * z$ **(f)** i **div** $j * k$
(c) $(x + y)/z - 3$ **(g)** $i/j * k$
(d) $x + y/(z - 3)$ **(h)** $4 * i + k$ **div** j

2 Suppose we have a 5 × 5 **array** A of **real** values. The "Trace" of A is defined as the sum of its diagonal elements. For instance, if A's elements are the following,

$$\begin{bmatrix} 3 & 2 & -1 & 9 & 0 \\ 0 & 1 & 5 & 6 & 7 \\ 2 & 4 & 6 & 8 & 7 \\ -9 & 2 & 3 & 7 & 10 \\ -1 & -2 & -3 & -4 & -5 \end{bmatrix}$$

then its Trace is $3 + 1 + 6 + 7 + (-5) = 12$.

(a) Write a declaration for A.

(b) Write an input statement which will store these values in A, assuming they are typed row by row as input lines.

(c) Write a **for** loop which will compute the Trace of A.
(d) Write another **for** loop which will leave the maximum value from A in the **real** variable named Amaxim, and leave that value's row and column numbers in the **integer** variables named Arow and Acol.

3 Write a function named "Trace" which will compute the Trace of any $n \times n$ **real array** A, where $n <= 20$.
4 Rewrite the function of Exercise 3 as a procedure.
5 Given a "telephone directory" file whose records are structured as follows:

```
type phones = record
                name: packed array[1. .15] of char;
                phone: packed array[1. .7] of char
              end;
```

Write Pascal statements that will display all persons whose names begin with the letter 'A,' together with their phone numbers.
6 Write a Pascal procedure that will sort its three parameters into ascending sequence, assuming they are all **integer.**
7 Write a procedure which, given an array A of n integers, counts the number of positive entries (Npos), the number of negative entries (Nneg), and the number of zero entries (Nzero) that it contains.
8 Revise the averaging program given at the beginning of the chapter so that it averages only the positive numbers in the input, rather than all of them.
9 Write a procedure named "Zeros" which counts the number of zero entries in an $m \times n$ array A of integers.
10 If your installation has a different Pascal compiler than the ones used here, adapt our Pascal Case Study 1 implementation to run under that compiler. How difficult was that adaptation? What features does your Pascal system have that make the program easier to write? More difficult?
11 Implement Case Study 4—Missionaries and Cannibals in Pascal. Evaluate Pascal as an AI programming language from this experience.
12 Implement Case Study 0 (which you defined at the end of Chapter 1) in Pascal. Evaluate Pascal's performance and suitability for this application.
13 Consider implementing Case Study 2—Employee File Maintenance in Pascal. What are Pascal's strengths for data processing applications such as this? What are its weaknesses?

REFERENCES

1 "Preliminary Report—International Algebraic Language," *Communications of the ACM* 1: 8 (1958).
2 Peter Naur, ed., "Revised Report on the Algorithmic Language ALGOL 60," *Numerische Mathematik* 4: 420 (1963).
3 D. E. Knuth, "The Remaining Troublespots in Algol 60," *Communications of the ACM* 10: 611 (1967).
4 Niklaus Wirth and C. A. R. Hoare, "A Contribution to the Development of Algol," *Communications of the ACM* 9:413 (1966).
5 Aad van Wijngaarden, ed., "Report on the Algorithmic Language Algol 68," *Numerische Mathematik* 14:79 (1969).
6 Niklaus Wirth and Kathleen Jensen, *Pascal User Manual and Report,* 2d ed., New York, Springer-Verlag, 1978.

7 *IEEE Standard Pascal Computer Programming Language,* American National Standards Institute, ANSI/IEEE 770 X3.97, New York, 1983.
8 J. Welsh, W. J. Sneeringer, and C. A. R. Hoare, ''Ambiguities and Insecurities in Pascal,'' *Software Practice and Experience* p. 685 (1977).
9 Wirth and Jensen, *Pascal User Manual.*
10 *IEEE Standard Pascal.*
11 Kenneth Bowles, *Problem Solving Using Pascal,* New York, Springer-Verlag, 1977.

CHAPTER 3

FORTRAN

3-1 INTRODUCTION TO FORTRAN

FORTRAN, originating in 1954, is the oldest and perhaps the strongest surviving high-level language. Since then, the FORTRAN (*For*mula *Tran*slating System) family has been the most widely used language for scientific and engineering programming applications. In addition, the FORTRAN language style has engendered a number of dialects, each responding to a different need to "bend" the language to fit some special situation. Over the years, FORTRAN has shown remarkable durability and flexibility in keeping up with changing styles and demands of programming as they have developed.

3-1.1 Brief History of FORTRAN

The original member of the family, FORTRAN I, came into existence in 1954 and was implemented on the IBM 704 computer in 1956. Two years later, FORTRAN II appeared. It contained a number of significant enhancements to FORTRAN I, including the subroutine definition and invocation facility. Between 1958 and 1963, FORTRAN was implemented on a number of computers. FORTRAN III was developed during this period but, because it contained too many machine-dependent features, was never implemented for public use.

In 1962, FORTRAN IV was developed for the IBM 7090/7094 computers. During that same year, the American Standards Association formed a committee to define a standard version of FORTRAN. This effort was a response to the differences that had begun to proliferate among the various FORTRAN implementations, which made it impossible to transfer a program from one computer to another with confidence that the program would both run and run correctly. This committee produced two standard versions of FORTRAN in 1966. One was called ''Basic FORTRAN'' and was similar to FORTRAN II. the other was called simply ''FORTRAN'' and was similar in its features to FORTRAN IV.[1]

In 1977, major extensions to FORTRAN were added, and the standard was accordingly revised.[2] This version, known as FORTRAN 77, added features to the language that improved its structured programming, string processing, and file processing capabilities. Like the 1966 standard, FORTRAN 77 has a distinguished subset defined for it. Moreover, FORTRAN 77 properly includes the 1966 standard as a subset, so that ''upward compatibility'' is maintained for programs which were written before the new standard was installed. Unless otherwise noted, we shall limit our discussion to FORTRAN 77 throughout the remainder of this chapter.

3-1.2 Implementations and Variations of FORTRAN

FORTRAN is implemented on nearly all computers, including the following:

Apple
Burroughs
Control Data
Data General
Digital
Honeywell
IBM
Univac

Implementations of FORTRAN are designed to conform to the standard version. The most significant divergence from the standard arises out of different machines' word sizes and number representations, which affect the accuracy of sensitive mathematical calculations. Another divergence occurs when different implementations add language extensions to the standard, thus limiting portability of programs which use these extensions.

Our discussion includes only those elements of FORTRAN which appear in the standard, except where otherwise noted. Furthermore, we include only those features which are essential to provide a clear and useful introduction to FORTRAN.

3-1.3 Major Applications of FORTRAN

Almost all FORTRAN usage falls within the scientific and engineering application area. Recent extensions allow FORTRAN to be marginally useful in data processing and text processing applications as well, but it is not considered a serious alternative to other languages specifically designed for work in these areas.

3.2 WRITING FORTRAN PROGRAMS

A FORTRAN program, in its simplest form, consists of a PROGRAM statement, a series of declarations for variables and arrays, a series of executable statements, and finally the statement END which marks the physical end of the program. Generally, the declarations and statements of a program are written one per line, and there is no explicit punctuation mark that can be used to delimit statements from each other. Certain words, such as END and IF, have special use in a FORTRAN program, and the programmer should avoid using these as variable names.

The simple FORTRAN program below computes and displays the average of an indeterminate number of input numbers. For example, if the input were 85.5, 87.5, 89.5, and 91.5 the result displayed would be 88.5. The program uses the variable X to hold a single input number and the variable N to determine the number of input numbers in the process. The variables SUM and AV contain the numbers' sum and average, respectively.

```
      PROGRAM AVRAGE

C     THIS PROGRAM COMPUTES THE AVERAGE (AV) OF N INPUT NUMBERS (X)

      REAL SUM, AV, X
      INTEGER N

      N=0
      SUM=0
 10   READ (5, *, END=20) X
         N=N+1
         SUM=SUM+X
         GO TO 10

 20   AV=SUM/N
      PRINT *, N, ' NUMBERS WERE GIVEN'
      PRINT *, AV, ' IS THEIR AVERAGE'
      END
```

Here, we see that the first line serves only to name the program, and in general this line is optional. The next line is an example of a FORTRAN "comment," which is always distinguished by the letter C in the first position of the line. The next two lines serve to identify (declare) the four variables in the program and, in many cases, such declarations are optional too! The remaining lines represent the executable statements of the program itself. Here, we see a loop between lines numbered 10 and 20, and the final two PRINT statements which display the results.

When typing a FORTRAN program, rather strict formatting conventions must be followed. Any statement which is numbered must have its number placed within positions 1–5 of the line. Position 6 is reserved for continuing a very long statement onto a second line. More than one statement on a line is not possible in standard FORTRAN. The body of a statement (or its continuation) must be entirely contained within positions 7–72 of the line. The program above suggests that most statements begin exactly in position 7, while the statements within a loop are indented to another tab position to set the loop apart. We shall examine the statements individually, and in detail, later in the chapter.

3-2.1 Elementary Data Types and Values

The FORTRAN data types are INTEGER, REAL, DOUBLE PRECISION, COMPLEX, LOGICAL, and CHARACTER. An INTEGER constant is written as a sequence of digits, possibly preceded by a sign. A REAL constant is written either in ordinary decimal notation or in exponential notation. The former consists of an integer, a decimal point, and (optionally) a decimal fraction. The latter is formed by appending the letter E and an integer exponent on the right of an ordinary decimal number. This indicates a scaling of the number by the (given) integer power of 10. The following examples show some numbers and their corresponding INTEGER and REAL representations.

Number	INTEGER representation	REAL representation
0	0	0.
0.5		0.5
−1	−1	−1.
22.55		22.55 *or* 0.2255E2
−0.0055		−0.0055 *or* −0.55E−2

Note that there are several equivalent representations for each REAL constant. Also, the range of valid INTEGER and REAL constants is implementation dependent, as is the number of significant digits for REAL constants. Most implementations allow at least six or seven significant digits for REALs in the normal representation so that, for instance, the number 222.55555 is typically rounded to 222.5556 when it is stored.

To permit more accuracy when the situation warrants it, FORTRAN has a DOUBLE PRECISION alternative for REAL values. Its use doubles the amount of storage reserved for the representation of a number so that, typically, 16 significant digits can be retained. Whenever a DOUBLE PRECISION value is written, the letter D is used in place of the letter E in its exponential representation. If it is written in ordinary decimal representation, its number of significant digits portrays implicitly whether or not DOUBLE PRECISION will be used.

The COMPLEX and LOGICAL data types have such limited usage that we will not discuss them at any length in this chapter. Briefly, COMPLEX denotes a complex number in the algebraic sense, and its real and imaginary parts are written as a pair of REALs enclosed in parentheses and separated by a comma. For example, the COMPLEX value (3.2, 1.5) represents the complex number $3.2 + 1.5i$. LOGICAL denotes the Boolean values "true" and "false," which are written in FORTRAN as .TRUE. and .FALSE., respectively. COMPLEX and LOGICAL values may be manipulated by a FORTRAN program in ways similar to ordinary numerical values.

The CHARACTER data type allows the programmer to store and manipulate nonnumeric information, such as headings and other documentation for program output. This is illustrated in the two PRINT statements of the example program. A CHARACTER string in FORTRAN is written as a sequence of characters enclosed in apostrophes ('), as in the following examples:

'SALES SUMMARY REPORT'
'5/15/84'
'MAY 15, 1984'

Each CHARACTER string has associated with it a ''length,'' which is a count of the total number of characters (including blanks) that are enclosed within the apostrophes. The above examples, therefore, have lengths 20, 7, and 12, respectively.

An alternative form for strings is preserved from older versions of FORTRAN, and is known as the ''Hollerith constant.'' It is written by placing the string length and the letter H in front of the string itself (in lieu of the enclosing apostrophes), as shown by the following rewriting of the above examples:

```
20HSALES SUMMARY REPORT
7H5/15/84
12HMAY 15, 1984
```

This has more limited convenience within a program than the other form, and is thus rarely used.

3-2.2 Names, Variables, and Declarations

A FORTRAN variables has a name and a value. The name is written as a string of six or fewer alphabetic (A–Z) and numeric (0–9) characters, the first of which must be alphabetic. That name identifies a unique storage location which is permanently assigned to the variable *throughout* program execution, and which holds the variable's value.

The ''type'' of a variable can be defined either explicitly or implicitly, depending on whether or not the variable is listed in a ''type declaration.'' The latter has the form:

type variable list

Here, ''type'' denotes any of the types REAL, INTEGER, DOUBLE PRECISION, COMPLEX, LOGICAL, or CHARACTER. ''Variable list'' denotes a list of variable names, separated by commas, whose values are to be the designated type. For example, the following are type declarations:

```
REAL N, P1, X, Y
INTEGER H, I, J
```

The first indicates that each of the variables names N, P1, X, and Y will have a REAL value during execution, and the second indicates that H, I, and J will designate storage locations which will hold INTEGER values.

Variables which are not declared explicitly in this way are implicitly assigned a type by way of the following rule for ''implicit typing'':

> If the variable's name begins with any of the letters I, J, K, L, M, or N then its type is INTEGER; otherwise, its type is REAL.

Considering again the seven variables declared in the type declarations above, we see that only the variable N needs to be explicitly declared as REAL, and only the variable H needs to be explicitly declared as INTEGER; the others would have been typed correctly by the implicit typing rule. However, we should quickly add that explicit declaration of variables in a program is a good documentation practice, even in cases where the type would have been correctly assigned without it.

Variables whose values are type CHARACTER must be declared with their associated *lengths* as well as their type. The form of this declaration is thus slightly different:

CHARACTER variable*length list

Here, ''variable*length list'' denotes a list of variables, each with an integer length appended on the right with an asterisk (*). Thus, for example,

CHARACTER TITLE*25, DATE*8

declares the variable TITLE to hold a character string of length 25 or less, and the variable DATE to hold a string of length 8 or less.

3-2.3 Arrays and Other Data Structures

The only data structuring facility provided by FORTRAN is the ''array.'' Arrays in FORTRAN may have from one to seven dimensions. Three examples are illustrated by the arrays named A, B, and C in Figure 3-1.

As shown, the one-dimensional array A can hold five values, the two-dimensional array B has five rows and four columns (twenty values), and the three-dimensional array C has five rows, four columns, and two layers (forty values).

All values in an array must be of the same type, which is established at the time the array is declared. An array's dimensionality and number of entries in each dimension are also established at the time of declaration, and remains invariant throughout program execution. To declare an array, one of the following forms must be used:

type name (size)
DIMENSION name (size)

The first form is used when the array's type is to be explicitly chosen, while the second is used when the implicit typing rule is desired. The first form is, thus, generally preferred. Here, ''name'' denotes the name of the array, and ''size'' defines its dimensionality and number of entries in each dimension. The latter is specified by writing a series of integers, one for each dimension and separated by commas, giving the number of entries in the respective dimensions. For example, the following three declarations are possible for the arrays A, B, and C shown in Figure 3-1:

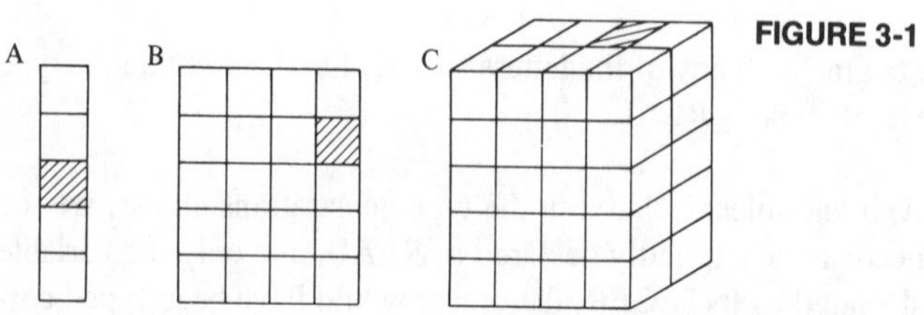

FIGURE 3-1

```
DIMENSION A(5)
INTEGER B(5,4)
DOUBLE PRECISION C(5,4,2)
```

Here, A becomes implicitly typed REAL, while the types of B and C are explicitly designated.

Several additional conveniences are available for array declaration. For example, several arrays can be listed in the same declaration, and ordinary variables can be intermixed within an explicit type declaration for arrays. To illustrate,

```
DIMENSION A(5), B(5,4), C(5,4,2)
INTEGER D(2,7), H
```

declares the REAL arrays A, B, and C, the INTEGER array D, and the INTEGER variable H.

To reference the value of an entry within an array, the programmer follows the array name by a list of ''subscripts'' enclosed in parentheses and separated by commas. These subscripts identify the location of the desired entry by giving its row number, its column number, and so forth, depending on the number of dimensions in the array. For instance, a one-dimensional array would have a single subscript, a two-dimensional array would have two, and so forth. For example, if we write A(3), we are referencing the third entry in the array as shown in Figure 3-1. If we write B(2,4), we are referencing the entry in the second row and fourth column of B. If we write C(1,3,2), the entry in the first row, third column, and second layer is referenced. These three particular examples are shaded in Figure 3-1.

Initialization of Variables and Arrays It is often convenient to have the initial values of variables and arrays assigned initially, that is, at the outset of program execution. This is accomplished in FORTRAN via the DATA statement, which has the following form:

```
DATA names / values /
```

Here, ''names'' denotes any list of variable or array names, separated by commas, and ''values'' denotes a corresponding list of constant values to be assigned to them, and in the same order listed. Any value in the list may be repeated by placing the repetition factor and an asterisk before the value itself. For instance, the values

```
0,0,0,0
```

may alternatively be written as

```
4*0
```

using the repetition factor 4.

To illustrate initialization, suppose we have the REAL variable X, the 25-character variable TITLE, and the 5 × 4 INTEGER array B that were discussed above. These may be initialized using the following DATA statement:

```
      DATA X, TITLE, B / 3.59847E-5, '1984 ANNUAL BUDGET',
     -  17,18,19,20,0,42,3,47,48,0,0,0,19,49,-2,-10,
     -  -11,-12,22,-3 /
```

[The use of a dash (−) in position 6 of the second and third lines here denotes the continuation of the DATA statement, which would not fit altogether on one line.]

The effect here will be to initialize X as 3.59847E−5, TITLE as '1984 ANNUAL BUDGET,' and B as shown below.

B

17	42	00	-10
18	03	00	-11
19	47	19	-12
20	48	49	22
00	00	-2	-3

Note here that the values for B are stored column-by-column, which is known as "column-major" order, which is assumed by FORTRAN for all two-dimensional and higher-dimensional arrays.

3-2.4 Basic Statements

The FORTRAN statements fall into two classes; nonexecutable and executable. The nonexecutable statements are the declarations, the END statement, and certain other statements that are declarative in nature. The executable statements and a brief description of their purpose are summarized below.

Executable statement	Purpose
Assignment statement	To perform arithmetic calculations and assign the result as the new value of a variable or array entry.
GO TO statement	To transfer control to a statement which does not immediately follow.
IF statement	To conditionally execute a series of statements or conditionally transfer control to a statement out of sequence.
DO statement	To repeat the execution of a sequence of statements which immediately follows.
STOP statement	To stop execution of the program.
READ statement	To transfer data from an input file (e.g., a terminal or punched cards) to a series of variables in storage.
WRITE statement PRINT statement	To transfer data from storage to an output file (e.g., a terminal screen or printer).
CALL statement	To invoke a subprogram.
RETURN statement	To return control from a subprogram to the invoking program.

This section describes the assignment statement and the next section describes the GO TO, IF, DO, and STOP statements. Section 3-2.6 describes the READ, WRITE, and PRINT statements and their uses for performing input-output operations in FORTRAN. Section 3-2.7 describes the CALL and RETURN statements and their uses with subprogram definition and invocation.

Assignment Statement The assignment statement is written in the following way:

reference = expression

Here, ''reference'' denotes a variable name or an array reference, and ''expression'' denotes any computation whose result will become the new value of the reference at the time the assignment statement is executed.

Note that several assignment statements appeared in the example program. The first one,

```
N = 0
```

assigns the value 0 to N. The last one,

```
20 AV = SUM/N
```

specifies the division of the value of SUM by the value of N, and the subsequent assignment of the result as the new value of AV.

The ''expression'' on the right of an assignment statement describes how the assigned value is to be computed. A FORTRAN expression may be one of three types, ''arithmetic expression,'' ''logical expression,'' or ''string expression.'' the type depends on whether the result is to be an arithmetic (INTEGER, REAL, DOUBLE PRECISION, or COMPLEX), LOGICAL, or CHARACTER value.

The simplest form of arithmetic expression, called a ''factor,'' may be any of the following:

1 An arithmetic constant
2 A reference (variable or array entry)
3 A ''function reference'' (to be discussed in section 3-2.7)

For example, the constant 0 is a factor.

The value and type resulting from execution of a factor are determined as follows:

1 For an arithmetic constant, the value and type of the constant is that of the result.

2 For a reference, the value and type of the given variable or array entry is that of the result.

3 For a function reference, the value and type of the result are discussed in section 3-2.7.

For example, the constant 0, when used on the right of an assignment statement, denotes the INTEGER value 0.

An arithmetic expression may also be formed by combining factors with one or more of the arithmetic operations +, −, *, /, or ** (exponentiation), according to the following rule:

If E1 and E2 are arbitrary arithmetic expressions, and P is any of the above operators, the following are also valid arithmetic expressions:

1 E1 P E2
2 (E1)
3 − E1 (provided that the sign − is not preceded immediately by another operator)

Thus, the following arithmetic expressions are valid under these rules:

N + 1
SUM/N

The first denotes addition of two values, and the second denotes division. They are formed directly under rule 1 above.

The value and type resulting from evaluation of an arithmetic expression depends upon the values and types of its constituent factors, as well as the priority rules which govern the order in which two or more operations in the expression will be carried out. The priorities of the arithmetic operators are as follows:

Operator		**Priority**
+ −	(add and subtract)	0
* /	(multiply and divide)	1
**	(exponentiate)	2

These priorities determine the order of evaluation in the following way:

1 If the expression contains no parenthesized subexpressions, then:
  a All priority 2 operations are evaluated first, and from left to right.
  b All priority 1 operations are evaluated next, and from left to right.
  c All priority 0 operations are evaluated next, and from left to right.
2 If the expression has parenthesized subexpressions, each of them is separately evaluated (by these rules), from left to right and from the innermost to the outermost, before any nonparenthesized operations are evaluated.

Thus, if we write the expression

A + B * C

then the product B * C is evaluated first, and that result is subsequently added to A. Moreover, if we want to designate that the sum A + B should be evaluated *before* multiplying by C, these rules require that the subexpression A + B be enclosed in parentheses, as shown:

```
(A + B) * C
```

Considering a more complex expression:

```
5 + 3 * (H - 4)
  ↑   ↑     ↑
  3   2     1
```

the numbers below it indicate the order in which the operations will be carried out. Note here that if we had not parenthesized the subexpression H − 4, the implied order of evaluation would have been as follows:

```
5 + 3 * H - 4
  ↑   ↑   ↑
  2   1   3
```

The result of evaluating an arithmetic expression is thus the result of performing the indicated operations on the values of the factors in the indicated order. The type of that result is determined by the types of the operands, as follows:

1 If the expression contains one or more REAL or DOUBLE PRECISION factors, then the result will be REAL or DOUBLE PRECISION accordingly.

2 Otherwise, the expression contains all INTEGER factors, and the result will be INTEGER.

For instance, reconsider the expression 5 + 3 * (H − 4). If the factor H is REAL, then the result of evaluation will be REAL. Otherwise, the result will be INTEGER.

A final question regarding the assignment statement arises when the result of evaluating the expression on the right has a different type than that of the reference on the left. When the result is INTEGER and the reference is REAL (or DOUBLE PRECISION), the result is converted automatically to the equivalent REAL value. In the opposite case, where the result is REAL and the reference is INTEGER, the result is *truncated* to the nearest integer. (These kinds of conversion are commonly referred to as ''coercion.'') For example, suppose that X is a REAL variable and I is an INTEGER variable. Then the assignment X = 5 will leave the equivalent REAL value 5.0 in X, while the assignment I = 3.5 will leave the truncated value 3 in I.

String Assignment The assignment statement may also be used to assign a character string value to a CHARACTER variable. In this case, the ''concatenation operator'' (//) and the ''substring reference'' can be used to form a ''string expression'' on the right of the assignment statement. To illustrate, suppose we have the fifteen-character variables S and T, declared and initialized as follows:

```
CHARACTER S*15, T*15
DATA S, T / 'HELLO', '' /
```

Here, the values are stored in S and T as shown:

```
|HELLO|   |_|
 S         T
```

The associated lengths of S and T are 5 and 0, respectively.

"Concatenation" (//) of two strings results in the formation of a single string by placing them together. For instance, the expression S//' THERE' forms the single string 'HELLO THERE.' An assignment statement with this expression on the right, such as

```
T=S // ' THERE'
```

will assign the resulting string to the CHARACTER variable on the left. In this case, T is changed as follows:

```
|HELLO THERE|
 T
```

and has a new length of 11 (including the blank!).

A "substring reference" allows an embedded portion of a string to be extracted and treated as a separate entity. It has the form

```
reference ( start : end )
```

where "reference" denotes the CHARACTER variable where the embedded portion is stored, and "start" and "end" are INTEGER-valued expressions which denote the position of the first and last character of that portion within the string. For example, given the variable T shown above, the following substring references can be designated:

Substring reference	**Result**
T(1:5)	'HELLO'
T(7:11)	'THERE'
T(I:J), with I=7 and J=9	'THE'

This, too, can be used in an assignment statement, perhaps combined with concatenation, to achieve powerful effects.

3-2.5 Control Structures

STOP Statement The general form of the STOP statement is the following:

STOP

Execution of the STOP statement causes program execution to stop. The STOP statement is not required in a program. If it is omitted, program execution will stop when it reaches the END statement:

GO TO Statement The GO TO statement has the following form:

GO TO n

Here, n denotes the statement number of an executable statement elsewhere in the program. Execution of the GO TO statement causes a transfer of control to the statement numbered n. In the example program, the statement GO TO 10 causes transfer of control unconditionally to the statement numbered 10 at the top of the loop.

IF Statement The IF statement may be written in any of the three following forms:

(i) IF (a) n_1, n_2, n_3
(ii) IF (b) s
(iii) IF (b) THEN
    ss_1
ELSE
    ss_2
ENDIF

Here (a) denotes any arithmetic expression; n_1, n_2, and n_3 denote the statement numbers of other executable statements; (b) denotes any "logical expression"; s denotes any executable statement except an IF or a DO; and ss_1 and ss_2 denote any sequence of executable statements.

Execution of form (i) occurs in two steps. First, the arithmetic expression a is evaluated. Second, if the result of that evaluation is negative, zero, or positive, control is transferred to statement n_1, n_2, or n_3 respectively. For instance, consider the following statements:

```
  IF (H-6) 4,4,5
4 H = H + 1
5 ——
```

Execution of this IF statement will first evaluate the expression H − 6. If the result is less than or equal to 0, statement numbered 4 will be the next to be executed. Otherwise, statement numbered 5 will be next, and statement 4 will be effectively skipped.

Execution of form (ii) also occurs in two steps. First, the logical expression b is evaluated (see below). Second the statement s is executed, but only if the result of that evaluation is .TRUE. For instance, consider the following statements:

```
     IF (H.GT.6) GO TO 5
  4  H = H + 1
  5  ——
```

The logical expression H.GT.6 asks whether or not H is greater than 6. If so, the statement GO TO 5 is executed, and statement 4 is thus effectively skipped. If not, GO TO 5 is not executed, and control passes through to statement 4. Thus, this example is an equivalent rewriting of the previous example.

Form (iii) of the IF statement, called the "block IF," allows one or another sequence of statements to be executed depending on whether the logical expression b is .TRUE. or not. Suppose, for example, that we want to compute a tax, FEDTAX, as 22 percent of GROSS pay, provided that the latter is under $18000, and 25 percent of GROSS pay otherwise. Then we can perform this calculation as follows:

```
IF (GROSS.LT.18000) THEN
   FEDTAX = .22 * GROSS
ELSE
   FEDTAX = .25 * GROSS
ENDIF
```

To define this calculation without form (iii), we would have to either duplicate the test b or add GO TO statements and labels. For instance, here is a version using form (ii):

```
IF (GROSS.LT.18000) FEDTAX = .22 * GROSS
IF (GROSS.GE.18000) FEDTAX = .25 * GROSS
```

This is not only a bit awkward, but it could *not* have been used if *more* than one statement were needed to perform the calculations resulting from GROSS.LT.18000 being .TRUE..

Logical expressions are formed using "relational operators" and "logical operators," together with arithmetic expressions. The FORTRAN relational operators and their meanings are summarized below.

Relational operator	Operands	Meaning
.LT.	arithmetic	less than
.LE.		less than or equal
.GT.		greater than
.GE.		greater than or equal
.EQ.		equal
.NE.		not equal
.LLE.	string	lexically less than or equal
.LLT.		lexically less than
.LGE.		lexically greater than or equal
.LGT.		lexically greater than

If E_1 and E_2 denote arbitrary expressions and R denotes any of these relational operators, then a logical expression can be formed as:

E_1 R E_2

Evaluation of a logical expression gives the result .TRUE. or .FALSE. by first evaluating the expressions E_1 and E_2 separately. These two results are then compared to see whether the relation R holds between them, and the result .TRUE. or .FALSE. is obtained accordingly. For arithmetic operands, these relations are based on the natural ordering among numbers. For string operands, the relations are based on the ordinary dictionary (lexical) ordering.

Often we need to write a logical expression which tests whether two or more such relations are simultaneously .TRUE., or else whether at least one of a series of relations is .TRUE.. This can be done by using the .AND. and .OR. operators, respectively, as follows:

(i) B_1 .AND. B_2
(ii) B_1 .OR. B_2

Here, B_1 and B_2 denote arbitrary logical expressions.

For instance, if we want to test the condition that either the value of the variable H is greater than 5 or the value of the array entry A(1) is not zero, we would write the following logical expression:

H.GT.5 .OR. A(1).NE.0

Since forms (i) and (ii) allow B_1 and B_2 to be arbitrary expressions, ambiguity in the order of evaluation is avoided by the rule that relational operators have higher precedence than logical operators. Moreover, the logical operator .AND. has higher precedence than the logical operator .OR.. Finally, the arithmetic and string operators have higher precedence than the relational and logical operators. Thus, the expression

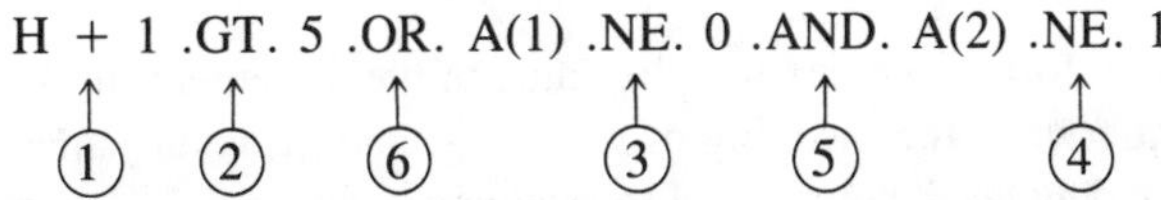

is evaluated in the order shown by the numbers below it. To override this order, parentheses can be used, as for ordinary arithmetic expressions.

DO Statements and Iteration Only rarely does a program not contain at least one instance of a "loop." Loops which are repeated a counted number of times are characterized in Figure 3-2, and are frequently used in FORTRAN. In this figure, i denotes a variable which controls the number of times the "sequence of statements" is repeated; m_1, m_2, and m_3 denote arbitrary arithmetic expressions.

While most loops can be written equivalently in either of the two forms in Figure 3-2, it is important to notice the case where the equivalence does not hold. That is, form (*a*) does not permit the sequence of statements to be executed zero times, in the event that the initial value m_1 is greater than m_3. Form (*b*) does permit this possibility, and thus is superior to form (*a*) in general.

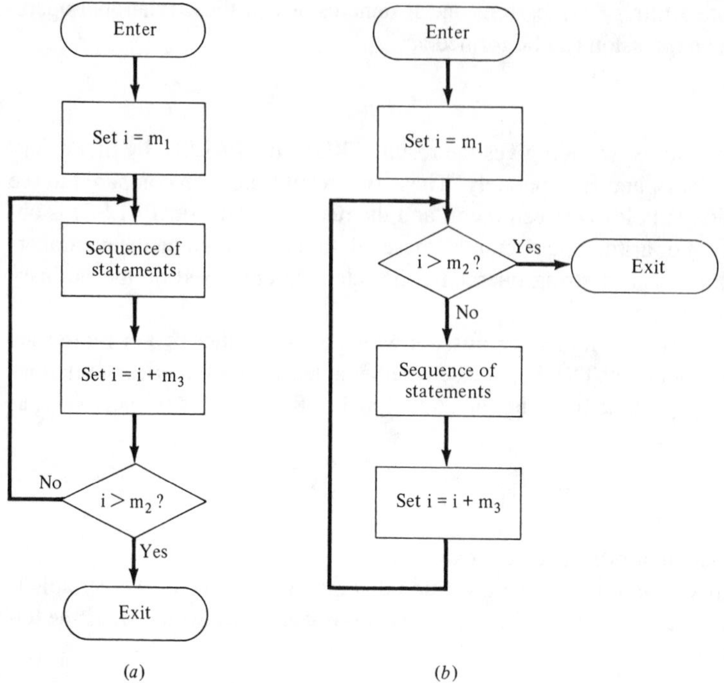

(*a*) (*b*)

FIGURE 3-2

Loops of this kind occur frequently enough that a special facility, the DO statement, is provided to facilitate their definition. This statement embodies the logic of flowchart (*b*) in Figure 3-2, and is written in either of the following two forms:

(i) DO n i = m_1,m_2
(ii) DO n i = m_1,m_2,m_3

Form (i) is used in preference to form (ii) whenever the value of the increment, m_3 is 1, and that is the usual case. Otherwise, the meaning of i, m_1, m_2, and m_3 is the same as in the flowchart. The integer n denotes the number of the statement which is the last one in the "sequence of statements," in order to mark the extent of the sequence to be repeated.

To illustrate, suppose we want to write a sequence of statements that will initialize the values of a five-entry array A with the values 5, 4, 3, 2, and 1, respectively. That is, for each value of I, the value of A(I) will be 6 − I. This can be written in either of the following two equivalent ways, without or with a DO statement, as shown below.

```
       I = 1
10     IF (I.GT.5) GO TO 20
         A(I) = 6 - I
         I = I + 1
         GO TO 10
20     ——
```

```
       DO 10 I = 1,5
10       A(I) = 6 - I
```

As the reader can see, the DO statement affords a great deal of coding economy, since it essentially combines three statements (initialization, test, and increment of the control variable) into one.

A number of constraints must be followed when using the DO statement. First, the last statement in the "sequence of statements" must not be a GO TO, an IF, or another DO statement. If this would logically be the case, the following statement must be added to mark the end of the sequence:

```
n CONTINUE
```

Many programmers *always* use CONTINUE to mark the end of a DO loop, as a matter of good programming style.

Second, although execution of the sequence of statements can be prematurely ended (via a GO TO out of the loop), no GO TO can be directed to any statement within the sequence from outside the loop. Third, upon normal termination of a DO loop the value of the control variable becomes undefined, and cannot be relied upon in subsequent statements of the program. Fourth, any number of DO loops may be "nested" within each other, as in the following example:

```
     DO 10 I = 1,5
       DO 20 J = 1,4
         B(I,J) = 17
20     CONTINUE
10   CONTINUE
```

Here, we intend to initialize all 20 entries in the 5 × 4 array B to the value 17. The outer loop traverses each of the five rows of B, while the inner loop passes through each of the four columns (entries in the individual rows). It should be clear that the above nested DO loops are equivalent to the following non-DO loops:

```
     I = 1
10   IF (I.GT.5) GO TO 40
       J = 1
20       IF (J.GT.4) GO TO 30
         B(I,J) = 17
         J = J + 1
         GO TO 20
30     I = I + 1
       GO TO 10
40   ——
```

Note here and in the previous example, that the nested loops are indented to portray the different control structures. Note also the proliferation of labels and GO TO statements that occcurs when the DO statement is not used.

3-2.6 Input-Output Conventions

FORTRAN has facilities for sequentially reading or writing data in input or output files, which usually include the terminal screen, punched cards, magnetic tape, magnetic disk, and printed paper. An "input file" is any collection of data which resides on a single medium, and is used to supply input data to the program. An "output file" serves the same purpose for data produced by the program. A program may have any number of input and/or output files associated with it during execution.

The data stored in a file is organized into a sequence of records. Each record has an associated length (total number of characters required to hold all of its data values), which is usually the same for all records in the file. For instance, the records in a punched card file are the individual cards' data, and thus the record length is 80. The records in a print file are the individual lines of print, and are typically either 80 or 132 characters in length. For magnetic tape or disk files, the record length varies among applications, and has no such natural "default" value.

The FORMAT Statement The FORMAT statement is a nonexecutable statement which defines the layout of the individual data values within a record of a file. This statement is always numbered, and is thereby associated with a particular READ or WRITE statement which is directing input or output to that particular file. The FORMAT statement has the following form:

n FORMAT (format codes)

Here, n denotes the number of the FORMAT statement, and therefore must be unique within the program. The "format codes" are listed consecutively and separated by commas. Each format code describes either the layout of a particular data value or the position within the record of the next data value to be described.

To illustrate, consider the following record layout for a punched card input file whose record has the following fields:

Field positions	Field contents
1–5	A five-digit INTEGER value
6–17	A REAL value in E notation, with five-digit mantissa
18–21	Four 1-digit INTEGER values
22–30	Blank (ƀ)
31–36	A REAL value with two decimal digits
37–40	Blank (ƀ)
41–50	A REAL value with five decimal digits
51–79	Blank
80	A one-digit INTEGER value

For example, the card image in Figure 3-3 shows a typical input record for this file. To write a FORMAT statement for this record, we must define a "format code" for each

Column	1–5	6–17	18	19	20	21	22–30	31–36	37–40	41–50	51–79	80
	00237	–0.32971E+06	5	0	3	2	ƀƀ. . .ƀ	ƀ43.21	ƀƀƀƀ	ƀƀ37.00031	ƀƀ...	4

FIGURE 3-3

field. Moreover, the format codes must be written in the same order that the fields occur, and blank (skipped) fields must also be accommodated by appropriate FORMAT codes. The possible FORMAT codes and their uses are summarized below.

Format code	Use
Fw.d *or* Gw.s	REAL decimal value
Ew.d *or* Gw.s	REAL E-notation value
Dw.d *or* Gw.s	DOUBLE PRECISION value
Iw	INTEGER value
Aw *or* A	CHARACTER value
wX	One or more blanks in the record
Tn	Tab to position in the record
/	Skip to the beginning of the next record

Here, w denotes the width of the field in the record, d denotes the number of digits to the right of the decimal point, and s denotes the total number of significant digits in the value. Moreover, vertical spacing in a print file can be controlled by placing one of the following character strings as the first code in a FORMAT statement:

Code	Meaning
' '	Single-space before printing the line
'0'	Double-space
'1'	Skip to the top of the next page
'+'	Suppress spacing

With this information, we return to the above example and write an appropriate FORMAT statement for a record:

```
100 FORMAT (I5,E12.5,I1,I1,I1,I1,9X,F6.2,4X,F10.5,T80,I1)
```

The FORMAT codes that appear here correspond one for one and left to right with the data values and blank gaps that appear in the record. Also, some variations are possible, as summarized below:

1 If two or more identical FORMAT codes appear in succession, they can be replaced by one, preceded by a repetition factor. For example, I1,I1,I1,I1 can be replaced by 4I1.

2 Leading and trailing zeros need not be given in a numeric data value, although each such value must be right-justified within its field. For example, if ƀƀ237 is entered in positions 1–5 of the above record, it will be interpreted properly as 237. However, if it is entered as 237ƀƀ, this will be interpreted as 23700!

3 Any REAL value need not be entered with a decimal point. If the point is typed, its position will take precedence over that implied by the FORMAT code. For example, the value 23.75 would be interpreted as 23.75 even if it were read using, say, a FORMAT code of F5.1. If the point is not given for a REAL value, the FORMAT code will govern its interpretation. For instance, 02375 will be interpreted as 237.5 if it is read under the FORMAT code F5.1.

4 More than one record may be described in a single FORMAT code; a skip to the beginning of the next record is designated by placing a slash (/) at the appropriate place among the codes.

5 The "generalized" FORMAT code, Gw.s, is used to allow a field to contain either an INTEGER or a REAL value. The nature of the value thus governs its interpretation; an INTEGER value will thus have the same effect as Iw, while a REAL value will have the same effect as Fw.s, Ew.s, or Dw.s, depending on how it is written.

READ and WRITE Statements To read data from an input file into a series of variables, the READ statement is used. It can have the following form:

```
READ (u,f) references
```

Here, u denotes the integer "unit number" associated with the file, and f denotes the number of the FORMAT statement that describes the format of the data to be read. "References" is a list of variables and/or array entries in which the data to be read will be stored when the READ statement is executed. They are associated in a left to right manner with the corresponding codes in FORMAT statement numbered f.

Unit number assignments to files vary among implementations. For our purposes, we will assume the following unit assignments to input-output devices:

Unit number	I/O device
1 *or* 2	A magnetic tape file
3 *or* 4	A magnetic disk file
5	A card or terminal input file
6	A print or terminal output file
7	A card output file

To illustrate, reconsider the example card layout given above, and its corresponding FORMAT statement numbered 100. Suppose we want to read data from such a card into the variables declared below:

```
INTEGER L,M(4),K
REAL X,Y,Z
```

To accomplish this, we can give the following READ statement:

```
READ (5,100) L,X,M(1),M(2),M(3),M(4),Y,Z,K
```

Here, the input-output unit number 5 designates that the data is on cards, and the number 100 designates that its layout is as defined in FORMAT statement 100. Execution of this statement with the example data shown in Figure 3-3 will leave the variables with values shown in Figure 3-4.

The following additional conventions should be remembered when defining an input operation.

First, an array may be read simply by inserting the array name in the READ statement. For instance, in the above statement we could have written M in place of the list M(1),M(2),M(3),M(4).

Second, an "implied DO" may be used to define the order of storing elements in an array within a READ statement. For example, the implied DO (M(I),I = 1,4) could have been used to replace M(1),M(2),M(3),M(4) in the above READ statement. Also, implied DO's may be nested. For instance, if B is a 5 × 4 array then the statement

```
READ (5,200) ((B(I,J),I = 1,5),J = 1,4)
```

will store values in B in column-major order, while the statement

```
READ (5,200) ((B(I,J),J = 1,4),I = 1,5)
```

will store them in row-major order.

Third, each new execution of a READ statement begins automatically at the *beginning* of the *next* record in the file, regardless of where the last one ended. Thus, if a READ statement fails to read *all* the data on a record, no subsequently executed READ statement can retrieve the remaining values on that record.

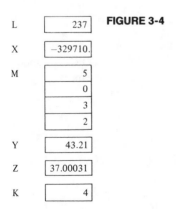

L	237
X	−329710.
M	5
	0
	3
	2
Y	43.21
Z	37.00031
K	4

FIGURE 3-4

Finally, if this same file had been on magnetic tape or disk instead of cards, the only change required for the READ statement would be a renumbering of the input-output unit accordingly. On some systems this change is not even necessary, since system control commands can be given to redefine unit number 5 as a tape or a disk file for the duration of the program run.

The WRITE statement is used to transfer values from memory to a record in an output file. Its general form is as follows:

```
WRITE (u,f) expressions
```

Here, u and f have the same meaning as for READ statements, while "expressions" denotes a list of expressions (usually variables) whose values are to be transferred. To illustrate, suppose we have variables and values shown in Figure 3-5. Suppose further that we want to display and document these values as shown in Figure 3-6. This can be accomplished in the following way:

```
      WRITE (6,300) K,L,X,Y
300   FORMAT ('1','K= ',I5,T21,'L= ',I5,T41,'X= ',F6.0,T61,'Y= ',F7.2)
```

As for the READ statement, the WRITE statement always begins its output at the first position of a new record (line of print). Moreover, for printed output, the first character in the FORMAT statement must specify the appropriate carriage control ('1' in the above example).

The value displayed for a variable depends upon the corresponding FORMAT code. For instance, suppose the variable Y has the value 43.21. The following table shows what is displayed for each of four different FORMAT codes applied to Y:

Format code	Value displayed
F4.0	ƀƀ43
F7.4	43.2100
F6.2	ƀ43.21
F4.2	****

In the last case, the value displayed indicates an error; that the value of Y has more significant digits to the left of the decimal point than are allowed by the FORMAT code. Rather than truncate a leading significant digit in the value displayed, the message **** appears instead.

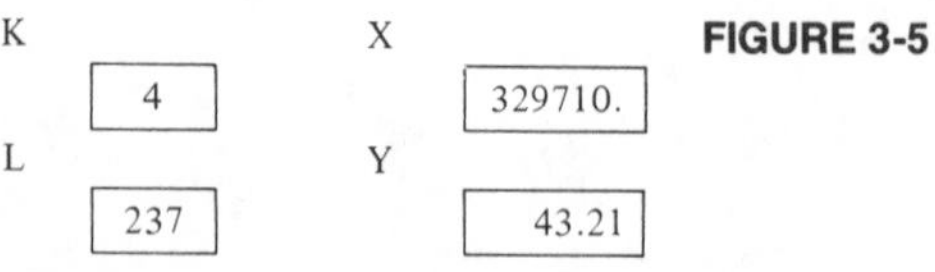

FIGURE 3-5

```
        Position
        1             21             41              61
Line 1  K = bbbb4     L = bb237      X = 329710      Y = bb43.21
```

FIGURE 3-6

List-Directed I/O When input comes from the terminal or output goes to the printer, it is often more convenient to avoid the tedious formatting conventions described above. This is possible when the input data is separated from each other by commas or spaces, or the output data values will be sent to preset tab positions on each line. To accomplish this "list-directed I/O," the following alternate forms of the READ and WRITE statements are used:

READ *, references *instead of* READ (5,f) references
PRINT *, expressions *instead of* WRITE (6,f) expressions

Concurrently, the corresponding FORMAT statements (f) need not be written.

To illustrate, suppose the input data in Figure 3-3 had been presented with *spaces* between the individual values, as shown:

237 −0.32971E6 5 0 3 2 43.21 37.00031 4

Then the original READ and FORMAT statements can be replaced by the following:

READ *,L,X,M,Y,Z,K

Here, we are also using the fact that FORTRAN identifies two "standard" files: one for input and one for output. When these are used, their corresponding unit numbers (usually 5 and 6, respectively) can be omitted from all corresponding READ, WRITE, and PRINT statements. Thus, the following are equivalent:

READ *, references
READ (5,*) references

and so are these:

PRINT *, expressions
WRITE (6,*) expressions

Other Input-Output Options Two additional options are important for the READ statement, and deserve mention. They are placed after the FORMAT number (or *), and serve the following purposes:

Option	Purpose
END = n	Transfer to the statement numbered n if the end of the input file is raised by this READ statement.
ERR = n	Transfer to the statement numbered n if an error occurs during this READ statement.

An example of the END option appears in the sample program at the beginning of this chapter:

```
10 READ (5,*,END=20) X
```

This says, literally, to transfer to statement 20 if an attempt to read a value into X is unsuccessful because the end of the input file has been reached.

The ERR option is used to help the program enforce input data validity. For instance, if an INTEGER is expected and a CHARACTER value actually appears in the input, this data error should transfer control away from the normal processing loop. We could extend, for example, the above READ statement as follows:

```
10 READ (5,*,END=20,ERR=90) X
```

This will pass control to statement 90 if the value being read is not a properly formed number.

Direct Access I/O So far, we have dealt only with *sequential* input-output; data is accessed in the same sequence in which it is stored. FORTRAN also provides for ''direct access I/O,'' in which each record in a file is referenced via a unique ''record number'' from 1 to n (the number of records in the file). Thus, an individual record may be read 0, 1, or several times in the same run of the program, and records may be accessed in any order.

To access record number r in a random access file, the specification REC = r is added to the READ or WRITE statement, following the FORMAT number. For example, suppose we want to access record 34, and then record 19, in the random access file on I/O unit 2. Then we would write:

```
READ (2,100,REC=34) references
READ (2,100,REC=19) references
```

Here, 100 designates an appropriate FORMAT statement for the file, and ''references'' designates the corresponding list of references where each record's data values will be stored.

Other File Manipulation Statements The special nature of direct access files, and the special functions that are associated with disk and tape files, require a number of additional FORTRAN statements in order to properly manage them. These statements are briefly described below, but the interested reader will need to consult an advanced FORTRAN text or reference manual in order to gain a full appreciation of their uses.

Statement	Purpose
BACKSPACE u	Reposition the sequential input file on unit u to the *previous* record.
ENDFILE u	Mark end-of-file on the sequential file on unit u.
REWIND u	Reposition the file on unit u to the *first* record.
OPEN(u,specs)	Establish a connection between the program and the file on unit u, at the beginning of program execution. The "specs" designate characteristics of the file that would not normally be assumed by the system (e.g., the spec ACCESS = 'DIRECT' is needed to override sequential access, which is otherwise assumed).
CLOSE(u,specs)	To disconnect the program from the file on unit u, at the time the program is finished with it.
INQUIRE(UNIT=u,specs)	To learn about the current status of the file on unit u, by way of variables given in the "specs."

Sophisticated file processing functions like these are quite new to FORTRAN. For most FORTRAN applications, these functions are not needed; the ''default specs'' are generally assumed. Moreover, omission of the explicit OPEN and CLOSE statements will cause the file to be automatically opened at the beginning of execution, and closed at the end of execution of the program. The advantage of using these is that the programmer gains some run-time control over the handling of files. The disadvantage is that programs containing such statements tend to be less portable, since different implementations often have different input-output conventions and default actions built within their operating systems.

3-2.7 Subprograms, Functions, and Libraries

Most programming tasks are large enough to warrant dividing them into a number of functional units, all linked together by a main program which controls the sequence in which they are executed. Another advantage of such segmentation is that it permits the reuse of code without rewriting it. FORTRAN supports two main kinds of subprogram: the ''function'' and the ''subroutine.''

Certain functions are of such widespread utility that they are defined as an integral part of the FORTRAN language. These are called the FORTRAN ''intrinsic functions,'' and a partial list is given below. As the reader can see, they perform trigonometric, logarithmic, and string processing functions.

Function	Name	Argument(s)	Argument values
Exponential	EXP	x	
Natural logarithm	LOG	x	Any $x > 0$
Common logarithm	LOG10	x	Any $x > 0$
Sine	SIN	x	Any x, an angle in radians
Cosine	COS	x	Any x, an angle in radians
Tangent	TAN	x	Any x, an angle in radians not close to n/2,3n/2, . . .
Square root	SQRT	x	Any $x > 0$
Absolute value	ABS	x	
Maximum value	MAX	$x_1,x_2, \ldots$	
Minimum value	MIN	$x_1,x_2, \ldots$	
Integer remainder	MOD	x_1,x_2	Any x_1,x_2 with $x_2 > 0$
Length	LEN	s	Any string s
Position of substring s_2 in s_1	INDEX	s_1,s_2	Any strings s_1,s_2

In this list, the symbol x denotes any arithmetic expression, and the symbol s denotes any string expression. The functions MAX and MIN have an indefinite number of arguments, while the others have exactly the number shown.

Writing Functions In the event that the intrinsic functions are not adequate for a particular application, the programmer may define additional ones by writing appropriate functions and/or subroutines.

A function is always written with a ''FUNCTION statement' at its beginning and an ''END statement'' at its end. The FUNCTION statement serves to name the function, identify the type of result that the function will deliver, and identify the arguments that will be needed for proper invocation. Between it and the END statement is the function's ''body,'' which describes the function's calculation itself. The FUNCTION statement has the following form:

type FUNCTION name (arguments)

Here, ''type'' denotes the type of result to be returned by the function, ''name'' denotes the function's name, and ''arguments'' denotes a list of arguments that the function will require when it is invoked, separated by commas. ''Type'' may be omitted in cases where the function's name would implicitly suggest the desired type, according to the implicit typing rules for ordinary variables. The arguments here are individual names, and are called ''dummy arguments.''

To illustrate the writing of a function, consider the problem of defining the calculation of the factorial of an integer n, under the following definition:

$$\begin{aligned} \text{factorial}(n) &= n \times (n-1) \times \cdots \times 2 \qquad \text{for } n > 1 \\ &= 1 \qquad \text{for } n \leq 1 \end{aligned}$$

Here, we identify the argument as n, and the result as the computed *factorial*, also an integer. Thus, the function (which we shall name FACT) can be defined as follows:

```
      INTEGER FUNCTION FACT (N)
      INTEGER N,I,F              }
      F = 1                      }
      DO 10 I = 2,N              }
        F = F * I                }  body
   10 CONTINUE                   }
      FACT = F                   }
      RETURN                     }
      END                        }
```

Here, the FUNCTION statement names the function FACT, identifies the argument N, and prescribes that the result returned will be INTEGER in type. The indicated "body" of the function defines the actual calculation of the factorial, according to the definition. It uses the dummy argument N just as if it were an ordinary variable in a main program. It also uses the "local variables" I and F in the process, and declares them appropriately.

However, there are two main differences between this definition and its counterpart in a main program. First, N is merely a placeholder for an actual argument that will be passed at the time when FACT is actually invoked (see below). That actual argument's value at each different invocation will cause a different resulting factorial to be computed accordingly. Second, the function name FACT itself serves as a basis for defining the result to be returned to the invoking program. In this case, it is assigned the resulting value of F just before the end of the program. Note also here that the new statement RETURN is given to cause control to be passed back to the point in the invoking program where FACT was originally activated.

Invoking Functions No function, whether it is an intrinsic function or a programmer-defined function, will be executed until it is invoked. To do this, a so-called "function reference" is given as a factor within an expression, in the following form:

name(arguments)

Here, "name" denotes the name of the function to be invoked, and "arguments" denotes the actual values to which the function will be applied in order to deliver a result. These arguments may be, in general, any expressions, provided that their respective types and values are consistent with those required by the corresponding dummy arguments in the function definition. The correspondence between these arguments and the dummy arguments must be one for one, and from left to right. For instance, any function reference which invokes FACT must provide exactly one argument, which may be any expression of INTEGER type.

Since the function reference appears as a factor within an expression, the result returned by that invocation may influence a more complex calculation. For example, consider the following assignment statement:

```
C = (A + B)/SQRT(A**2 + B**2)
```

Here, the SQRT function is invoked to provide the denominator in a subsequent division operation. Moreover, the argument itself is an expression whose result must be evaluated *before* the function SQRT is invoked.

For another example, consider the use of our function FACT to compute the coefficients $a_n, a_{n-1}, \ldots, a_0$ in the following polynomial:

$$(x + y)^n = a_n x^n + a_{n-1} x^{n-1} y + \cdots + a_0 y^n$$

Here, the integer-valued a_i's can be computed by the following formula:

$$a_i = \mathit{factorial}\,(n)/(\mathit{factorial}\,(i) * \mathit{factorial}\,(n-i))$$
$$\text{for each } i = 0,1, \ldots, n.$$

In the following program segment, we compute and display each of these $n + 1$ values in succession. Here, we assume that the INTEGER variable N has already been assigned a proper value, and that the variables A and I are of type INTEGER.

```
      DO 10 I = 0,N
         A = FACT(N)/(FACT(I) * FACT(N - I))
         PRINT *, A
10    CONTINUE
```

Note here the similarity between the definition of the coefficients a_i and the assignment statement which actually computes them.

Writing Subroutines A subroutine must be used whenever the result consists of more than one value. When written, it begins with a "SUBROUTINE statement" and ends with an "END statement." Between the two appears the body of the subroutine which, like that of a function, describes the computation. The SUBROUTINE statement has the following general form:

```
SUBROUTINE name (arguments)
```

Here, the "name" serves to name the subroutine, and "arguments" is a list of dummy arguments which designate both values to be supplied by the invocation to the subroutine and results to be delivered by the subroutine to the invoking program. The results delivered by a subroutine are, therefore, not associated with the subroutine's name as they are with the function.

To illustrate, we rewrite the factorial function as a subroutine, in which the additional argument F designates the result to be returned.

```
      SUBROUTINE FACT(N,F)
      INTEGER N,F,I
      F = 1
      DO 10 I = 2,N
        F = F * I
   10 CONTINUE
      RETURN
      END
```

The logic here is exactly the same as that in the function. The only difference is the method by which the result is returned.

Below is another example which demonstrates how a subroutine may return several results, and also how an array of arbitrary size may be accommodated. We name this subroutine MMM, and its task is to compute the MEAN, MINimum, and MAXimum value of an N-element array A of REAL values.

```
      SUBROUTINE MMM(A, N, MEAN, MIN, MAX)
      INTEGER N,I
      REAL MEAN, MIN, MAX, A(N)
      MEAN = A(1)
      MIN = A(1)
      MAX = A(1)
      DO 10 I = 2,N
        MEAN = MEAN + A(I)
        IF (A(I).LT.MIN) MIN = A(I)
        IF (A(I).GT.MAX) MAX = A(I)
   10 CONTINUE
      MEAN = MEAN/N
      RETURN
      END
```

Note that the first two dummy arguments, A and N, denote inputs to the subroutine and the last three denote output results returned by it.

Invoking Subroutines A subroutine is not executed until it is invoked, which is accomplished by a "CALL statement." This has the following form:

```
CALL name (arguments)
```

Here, "name" identifies the subroutine to be invoked, and "arguments" denotes a list of expressions and variables which gives the actual values to be passed to the subroutine and the actual memory locations where the results will be stored. As in the case of functions, the arguments in a CALL statement are associated one to one with their corresponding dummy arguments in the subroutine definition. They must agree, therefore, in type and number. Moreover, each argument which corresponds to an output to be delivered by the subroutine *must* be a variable of the same type.

For example, suppose we want to invoke the FACT subroutine to compute the coefficients in the polynomial expansion described above. Then we must supply two arguments, one designating the number whose factorial will be computed and the other designating a variable to hold the result. Thus, we can rewrite the calling program segment as follows:

```
      CALL FACT(N, NFACT)
      DO 10 I = 0,N
        CALL FACT(I,N1)
        CALL FACT(N - I,N2)
        A = NFACT/(N1 * N2)
        PRINT *,A
 10   CONTINUE
```

Here, we have assumed additionally that N1 and N2 are also INTEGER variables designating the factorials of I and N − I, respectively.

As another example, let us write a main program which, using MMM, will read 100 values into the REAL array X, compute their mean, minimum, and maximum values, and will display the results.

```
DIMENSION X(100)
REAL XMEAN, XMIN, XMAX
READ *,X
CALL MMM(X,100,XMEAN,XMIN,XMAX)
PRINT *,'MEAN=',XMEAN,'MIN=',XMIN,'MAX=',XMAX
END
```

Note here that the type of each argument agrees with that of its corresponding dummy argument. The actual arguments XMEAN, XMIN, and XMAX are necessarily variables, since they contain the results of the invocation.

3-2.8 Additional Features

The Use of COMMON A calling program may communicate with a subprogram by using a so-called "COMMON area," as an alternative to using arguments. This is illustrated in Figure 3-7. This figure shows a main program and several subprograms which each have their own local variables, but which share several variables "in common" among each other, or globally. Unlike a local variable, a common variable is known to all subprograms which declare it to be in this common area.

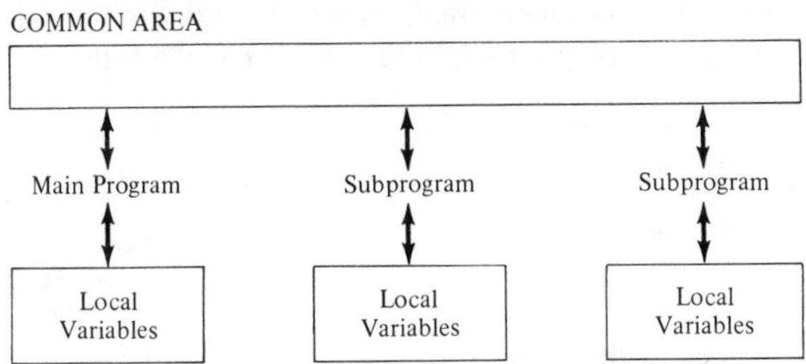

FIGURE 3-7

For example, the array A in the subroutine MMM could have been designated as a COMMON array rather than a dummy argument, by changing its declaration as follows:

```
DIMENSION A(100)
COMMON A
```

The second line here is the "COMMON statement" which actually causes this effect. Now, any invocation of MMM must predeclare and initialize *this* array A (rather than the array X, in the example above), and then *omit* it in the CALL statement. Moreover, the above pair of statements must appear in the *calling* program as well as the subroutine, in order that the linkage of the name A to both can be properly established.

Equivalence The "EQUIVALENCE statement" allows two variable names to be made synonymous, and thus share the same storage location. Its form is as follows:

EQUIVALENCE $(v_1,v_2),(v_3,v_4), \ldots$

For example, if we want to be able to alternately refer to the separate elements in an array A by three different names (for example, GROSS, TAX, and NET), we can do so by writing the following:

```
REAL A(3)
EQUIVALENCE (A(1),GROSS),(A(2),TAX),(A(3),NET)
```

Having done this, we establish the following array and equivalent names:

GROSS	↔	A(1)	
TAX	↔	A(2)	
NET	↔	A(3)	

Thereafter, all subsequent references to, say A(2) in the program could be rewritten as TAX (perhaps to improve the program's readability) without any effect on the results.

BLOCK DATA The "BLOCK DATA subprogram" is used to initialize the values of COMMON variables at the outset of program execution. It has the following form:

```
BLOCK DATA
  COMMON and DATA statements
END
```

Here, the form of the DATA statement is the same as it is for initializing ordinary variables and arrays.

3-3 APPLICATIONS OF FORTRAN

Now that we have established a good working knowledge of FORTRAN, we shall develop and discuss its application to Case Study 1—Matrix Inversion. This discussion will reveal several practical aspects of using FORTRAN in scientific applications. Also in this section, we shall summarize several implementation-dependent extensions of FORTRAN, mainly focusing on the WATFIV and WATFIV-S compilers. Finally, we give an overall evaluation of FORTRAN, using the nine evaluation criteria introduced in Chapter 1.

3-3.1 FORTRAN Case Study Implementation

The FORTRAN case study program was run on each of the following computers and operating systems:

1. Digital VAX 11/750 UNIX
2. IBM PC (UCSD P-System)

The algorithm described in Appendix A for this case study was coded as a FORTRAN subroutine named INVERT. It is shown in Figure 3-8. To exercise it, we wrote a main program named CASE1 which is shown in Figure 3-9. The main program reads an integer N, and then reads N × N values into the array A. It then invokes INVERT to compute the inverse and finally displays the results accordingly. A particular matrix and its corresponding output are shown in Appendix A.

Accuracy and Reliability of the Program Accuracy of the results delivered by a numerical algorithm depends upon the accuracy of data representation in the implementation, as well as the sensitivity of the algorithm to the data itself. For example, the matrix inversion algorithm can, for certain kinds of matrices, deliver totally inaccurate results. Thus, in writing such programs, the scientific programmer can take certain precautions against such loss of control. One such precaution occurs in the routine declaration of DOUBLE PRECISION accuracy for all variables and arrays. Another occurs in the way that a test for zero is specified. Note, for example, that we have given the test for $A_{JJ} = 0$ in the following way:

```
IF (ABS(A(J,J)).LT.1D-8) . . .
```

FIGURE 3-8
INVERT subroutine for FORTRAN Case Study 1.

```
      SUBROUTINE INVERT(A,B,N,ERROR)

C COMPUTE THE INVERSE B OF AN N X N MATRIX A, AND SET ERROR
C TO 0 IF SUCCESSFUL.  IF NOT, SET ERROR TO 1.  IN EITHER
C CASE, THE ORIGINAL MATRIX A IS DESTROYED IN THE PROCESS.

      INTEGER N,ERROR
      DOUBLE PRECISION A(N,N),B(N,N),AMAX,AHOLD,BHOLD,S,ABS

C INITIALIZE B AND ERROR

      DO 10 J=1,N-1
         B(J,J)=1
         DO 20 K=J+1,N
           B(J,K)=0
           B(K,J)=0
 20      CONTINUE
 10   CONTINUE
      B(N,N)=1
      ERROR=0

C PERFORM STEP 1 -- TRIANGULARIZE A

      DO 30 J=1,N-1

C                     ----- ROW INTERCHANGE -----

         AMAX=ABS(A(J,J))
         JMAX=J
         DO 40 K=J+1,N
           IF (ABS(A(K,J)).LE.AMAX) GO TO 40
           AMAX=ABS(A(K,J))
           JMAX=K
 40      CONTINUE
         IF (J.EQ.JMAX) GO TO 50
         DO 60 L=1,N
           AHOLD=A(J,L)
           A(J,L)=A(JMAX,L)
           A(JMAX,L)=AHOLD
           BHOLD=B(J,L)
           B(J,L)=B(JMAX,L)
           B(JMAX,L)=BHOLD
 60      CONTINUE
C                     ----- REDUCE A -----

 50      IF (ABS(A(J,J)).LT.1D-8) GO TO 110
         DO 70 L=J+1,N
           S=A(L,J)/A(J,J)
           DO 80 K=1,N
              A(L,K)=A(L,K)-S*A(J,K)
              B(L,K)=B(L,K)-S*B(J,K)
 80        CONTINUE
 70      CONTINUE
 30   CONTINUE

C PERFORM STEP 2 -- BACK SUBSTITUTION

      DO 90 JJ=1,N
         J=N+1-JJ
         IF (ABS(A(J,J)).LT.1D-8) GO TO 110
         DO 100 K=1,N
           S=0
           DO 105 L=J+1,N
              S=S+A(J,L)*B(L,K)
 105       CONTINUE
           B(J,K)=(B(J,K)-S)/A(J,J)
 100     CONTINUE
 90   CONTINUE
      RETURN
 110  ERROR=1
      RETURN
      END
```

```
      PROGRAM CASE1

      DOUBLE PRECISION A(20,20),AINV(20,20),PROD(20,20),
     -                 B(20,20),P
      INTEGER N,ERROR
500   FORMAT (' ',6G20.13)

10    READ (5,*,END=99) N
         PRINT *, 'THE MATRIX A ='
         DO 20 I=1,N
           READ (5,*) (A(I,J),J=1,N)
           WRITE (6,500) (A(I,J),J=1,N)
           DO 30 J=1,N
              B(I,J)=A(I,J)
30         CONTINUE
20       CONTINUE

         CALL INVERT (A,AINV,N,ERROR)
         IF (ERROR.EQ.0) GO TO 60

         PRINT *, 'ITS INVERSE CANNOT BE COMPUTED'
50       PRINT *, 'REDUCED A ='
         DO 40 I=1,N
           WRITE (6,500) (A(I,J),J=1,N)
40       CONTINUE
         GO TO 10

60       PRINT *, 'ITS INVERSE ='
         DO 70 I=1,N
           WRITE (6,500) (AINV(I,J),J=1,N)
           DO 80 J=1,N
              P=0
              DO 90 K=1,N
                P=P+B(I,K)*AINV(K,J)
90            CONTINUE
              PROD(I,J)=P
80         CONTINUE
70       CONTINUE
         PRINT *, 'THEIR PRODUCT ='
         DO 100 I=1,N
           WRITE (6,500) (PROD(I,J),J=1,N)
100      CONTINUE
         GO TO 50
99    STOP
      END
```

FIGURE 3-9
FORTRAN main program for Case Study 1.

Here, we are admitting that any value of A(J,J) which is within 10^{-8} of zero in either direction is close enough to be considered as zero. In other words, exact zero is seldom attained, even in cases where the algebraic calculations, had they been carried out precisely by hand, would have attained it.

Performance of the Program The program CASE1 was run on each of the implementations listed above. Their respective compile and execution speeds for a sample 20 × 20 matrix are shown in Figure 3-10. Execution speed includes input-output time as well as matrix inversion time.

FIGURE 3-10
EFFICIENCY OF FORTRAN CASE STUDY 1 PROGRAM

Implementation	Compile speed	Execution speed
1 Digital VAX-750/UNIX	6.6 sec	5.9 sec
2 IBM PC/UCSD	63.2 sec	22.4 sec

3-3.2 Implementation-Dependent Extensions of FORTRAN

Most FORTRAN compilers implement more features of the language, in addition to the standard features. Sometimes these extensions prove so valuable that they show up in future standards of the language. Such is the case for the WATFIV and WATFIV-S compilers developed at the University of Waterloo.[3]

Debugging Features of WATFIV WATFIV was designed for use in the student environment, where typically the ratio of compile runs to execution runs of a program is quite high, and the need for high-quality compile-time and execution-time diagnostics dominates the need for run-time efficiency.

Many compilers do not check for variables which have not been initialized before they are used in a calculation. For example, the following "program"

```
PRINT *, I
END
```

might deliver an output of, for example, 1199608416, which might be the value in the storage area assigned to I at the time the program executes. WATFIV, however, will treat this as a run-time error, delivering the following message,

```
UUUUUUUUUU
```

which says that the value of I is "undefined."

Another common run-time error is that in which the subscript for an array is out of its allowable range. Consider the following:

```
REAL A(10),B(2)
B(1) = 0
I = 11
A(I) = 1
PRINT *, B(1)
END
```

Some implementations will not flag this as an error when the assignment A(I) = 1 is reached. Moreover, the result displayed from the PRINT statement may well be identical with the value of the mythical A(11)! WATFIV, on the other hand, will methodically and clearly flag this kind of an error as follows:

```
*** ERROR *** SUBSCRIPT NUMBER 1 OF A HAS THE VALUE 11
```

Another common error involves passing an inappropriate argument upon calling a subroutine, as in the following:

```
CALL SUB(3,I)
END
SUBROUTINE SUB(A,B)
B = A + 1
END
```

Some compilers will not check this error, while WATFIV will deliver the following message:

```
*** ERROR *** INVALID TYPE OF ARGUMENT IN REFERENCE TO SUB-
              PROGRAM SUB
```

These and similar common errors illustrate that there is wide variance among implementations of FORTRAN in their compile-time and run-time support for program development.

Structured Programming Support and WATFIV-S Before the 1977 FORTRAN standard was adopted, the language suffered from a virtual absence of structured programming support. Now, the standard has incorporated at least the IF . . .THEN . . .ELSE control structure, but its designers curiously omitted the WHILE and CASE control structures which had by then become central elements in the structured programming vernacular.

These control structures are, however, present in some implementations, including WATFIV-S where they originated. In general, the WHILE statement has the following WATFIV-S form:

```
WHILE (condition) DO
  statements
END WHILE
```

and the CASE statement has the following WATFIV-S form:

```
DO CASE case1
  statements
CASE case2
  statements
.
.
.
```

```
CASE caseN
   statements
IF NONE DO
   statements
END CASE
```

The WHILE structure provides a looping mechanism which can specify an arbitrary "condition" as a basis for continuing the loop. The CASE structure gives a convenient method to select one from among several sequences of "statements" according to which of a number of alternative conditions is .TRUE., and is a clearer form of expression than the nested IF, which would have to be written otherwise.

3-3.3 Overall Evaluation of FORTRAN

From our case study experience, we evaluate FORTRAN using the nine criteria of Chapter 1 as follows:

1 Expressivity	Fair
2 Well-definedness	Good
3 Data types and structures	Fair
4 Modularity	Good
5 Input-output facilities	Good
6 Portability	Good
7 Efficiency	Excellent
8 Pedagogy	Good
9 Generality	Fair

FORTRAN ranks excellent in its "efficiency," and good in most other categories. Its fair "expressivity" stems mainly from its lack of a complete set of control structures (especially the very valuable WHILE), and its line-oriented syntax.

Its fair "data types and structures" arises from the absence of facilities for defining records hierarchically and its inability to support dynamic storage allocation in any form. Of course, this contributes positively to its run-time efficiency, so there is a trade-off here.

FORTRAN's fair "generality" occurs because it really doesn't comprehensively support file processing or text processing applications, even though some facilities of this sort were added in the 1977 standard. One still cannot consider FORTRAN to be a serious alternative for such applications if one has access to languages which were specifically designed for them.

In general, FORTRAN appears to be continuing solidly as the main scientific and engineering language in the 1980s, just as it was in prior decades. The vast amount of software already developed and in productive use will continue to discourage any wholesale abandonment of FORTRAN in the near future.

EXERCISES

1 Let X, Y, and Z be REAL variables, and I, J, and K be INTEGER variables, with the following values:

X	2.5	I	1
Y	−10.0	J	−5
Z	8.0	K	12

Determine the value and type returned by each of the following arithmetic expressions:

(a) X + Y * Z **(e)** I − 1
(b) (X + Y) * Z **(f)** I − 1.5
(c) (X + Y)/Z − 3 **(g)** I/J * K
(d) (X + Y)/(Z − 3) **(h)** 4 * I + K/J

2 Suppose we have a 5 × 5 array A of REAL values. The "trace" of A is defined as the sum of its diagonal elements (A_{ii}, for i = 1, . . . ,5). For instance, if A is as follows:

$$\begin{bmatrix} 3 & 2 & -1 & 9 & 0 \\ 0 & 1 & 5 & 6 & 7 \\ 2 & 4 & 6 & 8 & 10 \\ -9 & 2 & 3 & 7 & 4 \\ -1 & -2 & -3 & -4 & -5 \end{bmatrix}$$

then its trace will be the sum 3 + 1 + 6 + 7 + (−5) = 12.

(a) Write a DIMENSION statement for A.
(b) Write a DATA statement that will initialize A as shown.
(c) Give a DO loop which will compute the trace of A.
(d) Give another DO loop which will leave the maximum value from A in the REAL variable AMAX, and store the row and column numbers where that maximum was found in the INTEGER variables ROW and COL, respectively.

3 Write a function named TRACE which will compute the trace of any N × N matrix A of REAL values.

4 Rewrite TRACE as an equivalent subroutine, adding an appropriate argument to hold the result.

5 An integer N, between 1 and 20, is in columns 1-2 of the first line of an input file, followed by exactly N lines which each contain N values shown in Figure 3-11. Write a program which will accomplish the following:

(a) Read and store N and the next N × N values in the first N rows and first N columns in a 20 × 20 array A.
(b) Print the values of N and A, in the layout shown in Figure 3-12.
(c) Determine whether or not A is symmetric (that is, $A_{ij} = A_{ji}$ for all i and j from 1 to N), and print one of the following accordingly:

A IS SYMMETRIC
A IS NOT SYMMETRIC

FIGURE 3-11

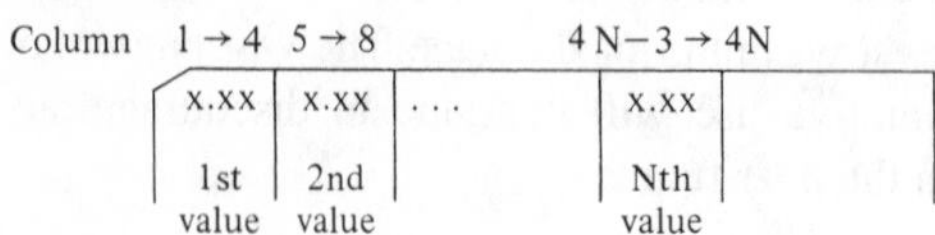

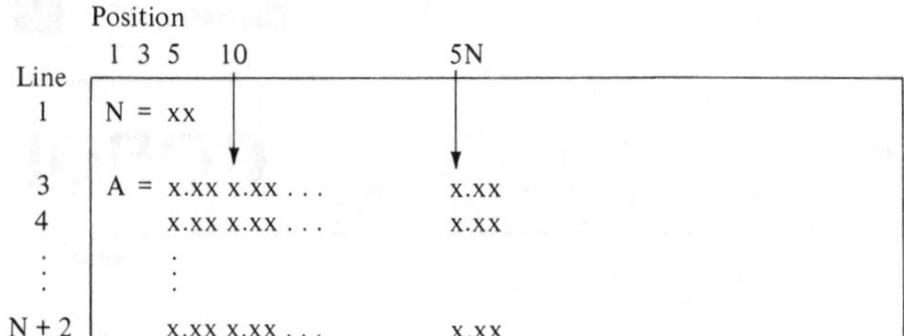

FIGURE 3-12

6 Write a FORTRAN subroutine that will sort its three parameters into ascending sequence, assuming they are all INTEGERs.

7 Write a subroutine which, given an array A of N integers, counts the number of positive entries (NPOS), the number of negative entries (NNEG), and the number of zero entries (NZERO) that it contains.

8 If your FORTRAN system differs from the ones used here, run the Case Study 1 program on it. Does it compile successfully? Does it execute properly? Are the results the same? Reevaluate FORTRAN's portability on the basis of this experiment.

9 Implement your Case Study 0 program in FORTRAN. Evaluate FORTRAN using the nine criteria, and compare your results with ours.

10 Consider implementing Case Study 3—Text Formatter in FORTRAN. What limitations appear to hinder the implementation? Can it be done well? Discuss the utility of FORTRAN for text processing in general, using this problem as a basis.

REFERENCES

1 *USA Standard FORTRAN,* USA Standards Institute, USAS X3.9–1966, New York, 1966.

2 *American National Standard FORTRAN,* American National Standards Institute, ANS X3.9–1977, New York, 1977.

3 *WATFIV Users Guide,* University of Waterloo, Waterloo, Ontario, Canada, 1981.

CHAPTER 4

COBOL

4-1 INTRODUCTION TO COBOL

COBOL (*Co*mmon *B*usiness *O*riented *L*anguage) is the most widely used language for data processing applications. It was designed and refined as a common language that would enable programs and programming techniques to be easily shared and transferred from one machine to another. Furthermore, COBOL is an English-like language; its syntax was designed so the casual observer as well as the programmer could intelligently read a program and understand it. In this chapter, we will study COBOL and assess how well it has achieved these goals.

4-1.1 Brief History of COBOL

In the late 1950s, data processing groups began to realize the need for a common data processing language. In May 1959, representative computer manufacturers and users from industry and government met in Washington D.C. to discuss the feasibility and desirability of such a development.

The CODASYL (Conference on Data Systems Languages) Committee was thus formed, and soon thereafter it had developed a draft description for such a language. A revised version of that draft was published in April 1960 and became known as ''COBOL-60.'' The second version, ''COBOL-61,'' was published the following year, and became widely implemented. In 1963 an extended version of COBOL, called

"COBOL-61 Extended," was published. Further extensions and refinements to the language were made in a 1965 version, called "COBOL, Edition 1965." This version was finally approved as an American National Standard in 1968.[1]

Meanwhile, COBOL development continued and new versions were published in 1968, 1969, 1970, and 1973 in the *COBOL Journal of Development*. A revised American National Standard for COBOL was approved in 1974.[2] This standard reflects all COBOL modifications which had been published since the 1968 COBOL standard. Since the 1974 Standard was adopted, the CODASYL Committee continues to review refinements to the standard. A draft revision was prepared in 1981,[3] and its adoption is under consideration at this writing.

4-1.2 Implementations and Variations of COBOL

The version of COBOL which we will discuss in this chapter is the 1974 American National Standard COBOL. COBOL is implemented on most medium and large computers, as well as some micros, including the following:

Burroughs
Control Data
Digital
Honeywell
IBM
Radio Shack
Univac

All of these implementations support at least the features of the 1974 Standard. Many support various extensions to the language. Moreover, limited versions of COBOL are available on microcomputers, such as the Radio Shack TRS 80 and the IBM PC.

In addition to the manufacturer-supplied implementations of COBOL, other implementations have been developed by software houses and university groups. Perhaps the best known among these is WATBOL, a fast-compiling implementation of COBOL developed at the University of Waterloo.[4]

4-1.3 Major Applications of COBOL

The application area for which COBOL was designed is the data processing area. Although COBOL can be used in scientific or text processing applications, it is seldom done in practice. COBOL is, however, well suited to data processing applications, since it contains such powerful built-in functional elements as a report-writer feature, a table-search function, and a sort facility. Essentially, these features of COBOL are designed to aid the programmer in organizing, accessing, updating, reordering, and reporting data in files.

4-2 WRITING COBOL PROGRAMS

A COBOL program is composed of four "divisions," whose purposes are briefly summarized below:

Division name	Purpose
IDENTIFICATION DIVISION	Identifies the program, its author(s), its purpose, and any other general operational characteristics.
ENVIRONMENT DIVISION	Specifies certain characteristics of the physical computer on which the program is run, especially the input-output devices used by the program.
DATA DIVISION	Describes the variables, files, and organization of storage used by the program, including record layouts, arrays, and working constants.
PROCEDURE DIVISION	Describes the algorithm itself.

The four divisions must occur in the above order within a COBOL program. Each one is delineated by the occurrence of its respective name at its beginning. That name must be written exactly as shown above, followed by a period.

The next level of organization within the division is the "section." Each section comprises "paragraphs," which are in turn composed of "sentences." Sentences are formed out of "statements," which are made up of "clauses," which come from "words" and, finally, "characters." These COBOL notions roughly parallel their usage in ordinary English, as we shall see.

Certain words in COBOL are "reserved words," and as such cannot be used by the programmer for naming variables or any other purpose beyond that for which they are reserved. A complete list of the COBOL reserved words is given in section 4-2.2, and these appear in **boldface** throughout the remainder of the chapter.

Below is a simple COBOL program which computes and displays the average of an indeterminate number of values. For instance, if the values are 85.5, 87.5, 89.5, and 91.5, then the output will be 88.5. The program uses the variable X to hold a single input value and the variable N to keep track of the number of values that occur. The variables SUMX and AV denote the computed sum and average of the numbers, respectively.

```
IDENTIFICATION DIVISION.
  PROGRAM-ID.  AVERAGER.

ENVIRONMENT DIVISION.
CONFIGURATION SECTION.
  SOURCE-COMPUTER.  IBM-PC.
  OBJECT-COMPUTER.  IBM-PC.
```

```
INPUT-OUTPUT SECTION.
  FILE-CONTROL.
    SELECT INFILE ASSIGN TO DISK.
    SELECT OUTFILE ASSIGN TO PRINTER.

DATA DIVISION.
FILE SECTION.
  FD INFILE LABEL RECORDS STANDARD,
          VALUE OF FILE-ID IS "B:SCORES".
  01  A-RECORD.
    02  A-NUMBER       PICTURE X(5).
    02  FILLER         PICTURE X(75).
  FD OUTFILE LABEL RECORDS OMITTED.
  01  A-LINE.
    02  MSG            PICTURE X(20).
    02  AV-OUT         PICTURE -9(5).9.
    02  FILLER         PICTURE X(52).

WORKING-STORAGE SECTION.
  77  X                PICTURE S99V9.
  77  SUMX             PICTURE S9(5)V9 VALUE 0.
  77  AV               PICTURE S9(5)V9.
  77  N                PICTURE S9(5)   VALUE 0.
  77  EOF              PICTURE X(3)      VALUE "NO".

PROCEDURE DIVISION.
INITIALIZE.
    OPEN INPUT INFILE, OUTPUT OUTFILE.
    READ INFILE AT END MOVE "YES" TO EOF.
    PERFORM READ-LOOP UNTIL EOF = "YES".

* END OF FILE PROCESSING: DISPLAY AVERAGE AND STOP.
        COMPUTE AV = SUMX / N.
        MOVE "THE AVERAGE =" TO MSG.
        MOVE AV TO AV-OUT.
        WRITE A-LINE AFTER ADVANCING 1 LINES.
        CLOSE INFILE, OUTFILE.
        STOP RUN.

* LOOP FOR EACH INPUT DATA VALUE READ.
READ-LOOP.
    MOVE A-NUMBER TO X.
    ADD X TO SUMX.
    ADD 1 TO N.
    READ INFILE AT END MOVE "YES" TO EOF.
```

As we can see, the program is highly stylized; division and section names must appear in ''margin A'' of each line, defined as positions 8–11. So must all paragraph names (such as INITIALIZE and READ-LOOP), 77-level variable declarations (such as X and N), 01-level record declarations (such as A-LINE and A-RECORD), and file descriptions (FD's). The remaining program text must appear in ''margin B,'' defined as positions 12–72 of each line.

However, statements within the **PROCEDURE DIVISION** can continue from one line to the next without special notation, and several statements may appear on a single line. The period (.) marks the end of each sentence in the **PROCEDURE DIVISION**. Many of these in the example program are self-explanatory; the verbs **READ**, **WRITE**, and **ADD** have their usual connotations. The words **PERFORM** . . . **UNTIL** denote a looping control structure (like **repeat** . . . **until** or **while** . . . **do** in other languages).

The paragraph being repeated, however, need not immediately follow the **PERFORM** statement itself.

Much attention must be paid in COBOL to the file and record structures and the conversion of data from one representation to another. Each file must be declared in the **FILE-CONTROL SECTION** of the **ENVIRONMENT DIVISION**, and its associated record structure is defined in the **FILE SECTION** of the **DATA DIVISION**. Most input-output operations in COBOL are record-oriented rather than stream-oriented, so these conventions are standard overhead when writing a program.

Comments in COBOL are designated by placing an asterisk (*) in position 7 of each line that contains one. Two such comments appear in the **PROCEDURE DIVISION** of the example program. Individual words within the COBOL statements themselves are always separated by a blank space (denoted by b̸) and the punctuation (commas, periods, parentheses) is placed as it is in ordinary English.

4-2.1 Elementary Data Types and Values

A COBOL data value may be represented as a "literal," which may be "numeric" or "nonnumeric." Numeric literals are written as ordinary decimal numbers. They may have up to eighteen decimal digits, possibly preceded by a sign + or −, and possibly containing an embedded decimal point (.). The following are examples of COBOL numeric literals.

1.73   0   −17   250

Figurative constant	Class of values represented
ZERO **ZEROS** **ZEROES**	A numeric or nonnumeric literal composed entirely of zeros, such as "0" and "00" and "000."
SPACE **SPACES**	A nonnumeric literal composed entirely of blanks (b̸), such as "b" and "b̸b̸" and "b̸b̸b̸".
HIGH-VALUE **HIGH-VALUES**	A nonnumeric literal composed entirely of the highest value in the collating sequence for the implementation's character set, such as "9" and "99" and "999".
LOW-VALUE **LOW-VALUES**	A nonnumeric literal composed entirely of the lowest value in the collating sequence for the implementation's character set, such as "b̸" and "b̸b̸" and "b̸b̸b̸".
ALL literal	A nonnumeric literal composed of a sequence of occurrences of 'literal'; e.g., ALL "14" means "14" or "1414" or "141414", etc.

A nonnumeric literal is any string, enclosed in quotes (”), of characters from the implementation-defined character set. That set must contain at least the following fifty-one characters that comprise the COBOL character set.

b̸(blank) . < (+ $ ∗) ; − / , > = “ A B . . . Z 0 1 . . . 9

Furthermore, if the literal itself is to contain a quote (“”), then that quote must be written twice in succession so that it may be distinquished from an enclosing quote. The following are examples of COBOL nonnumeric literals.

“ABC”
“Ab̸Bb̸C”
“WHAT”“Sb̸THIS?”

Note that blanks (b̸) are significant within a literal, so that the first two literals are *not* equivalent in any sense.

Certain values may be represented alternatively as “figurative constants.” A figurative constant is a COBOL word which denotes a class of literal values. (See bottom page 107.)

As shown, each figurative constant except the last may be written in more than one way. The particular value represented by an occurrence of a figurative constant in the program depends upon the context in which it is used.

4-2.2 Names, Variables, and Declarations

A COBOL variable is called an “elementary data item,” composed of a “data name” and an associated value that may change while the program is executing. A data name must be either a “user-defined word” or **FILLER** and must be both unique in the program and not among the COBOL “reserved words” (see Figure 4-1).

A *user-defined word* is a sequence of at most 30 alphabetic (A–Z), numeric (0–9), and dash (-) characters, except that dash (-) may not be the first or last character.

Additionally, a COBOL data name must contain at least one alphabetic (A–Z) character. The following are valid COBOL data names.

GROSS-PAY X N19 19N

“Procedure names” are used to label sections and paragraphs in the program. Unlike data names, they are not required to contain an alphabetic character.

In Figure 4-1 an underlined part of a reserved word indicates an allowable abbreviation for the word. For example, the word **CORRESPONDING** may be written more briefly as **CORR** without any change in its meaning.

All variables in a COBOL program must be declared within the program's Data Di-

ACCEPT
ACCESS
ADD
ADVANCING
AFTER
ALL
ALPHABETIC
ALSO
ALTER
ALTERNATE
AND
ARE
AREAS
ASCENDING
ASSIGN
AT
AUTHOR
BEFORE
BLANK
BLOCK
BOTTOM
BY
CALL
CANCEL
CD
CF
CH
CHARACTER
CHARACTERS
CLOCK-UNITS
CLOSE
COBOL
CODE
CODE-SET
COLLATING
COLUMN
COMMA
COMMUNICATION
COMPUTATIONAL
COMPUTE
CONFIGURATION
CONTAINS
CONTROL
CONTROLS
COPY
CORRESPONDING
COUNT
CURRENCY
DATA
DATE
DATE-COMPILED
DATE-WRITTEN
DAY
DEBUG-CONTENTS
DEBUG-ITEM
DEBUG-LINE
DEBUG-NAME
DEBUG-SUB-1
DEBUG-SUB-2
DEBUG-SUB-3
DEBUGGING
DECIMAL-POINT
DECLARATIVES
DELETE
DELIMITED
DELIMITER
DEPENDING
DESCENDING
DESTINATION
DETAIL
DISABLE
DISPLAY
DIVIDE
DIVISION
DOWN
DUPLICATES
DYNAMIC
EGI
ELSE
EMI
ENABLE
END
END-OF-PAGE
ENTER
ENVIRONMENT
EOP
EQUAL
ERROR
ESI
EVERY
EXCEPTION
EXIT
EXTEND
FD
FILE
FILE-CONTROL
FILLER
FINAL
FIRST
FOOTING
FOR
FROM
GENERATE
GIVING
GO
GREATER
GROUP
HEADING
HIGH-VALUES
I-O
I-O-CONTROL
IDENTIFICATION
IF
IN
INDEX
INDEXED
INDICATE
INITIAL
INITIATE
INPUT
INPUT-OUTPUT
INSPECT
INSTALLATION
INTO
INVALID
IS
JUSTIFIED
KEY
LABEL
LAST
LEADING
LEFT
LENGTH
LESS
LIMIT
LIMITS
LINAGE
LINAGE-COUNTER
LINE
LINE-COUNTER
LINES
LINKAGE
LOCK
LOW-VALUES
MEMORY
MERGE
MESSAGE
MODE
MODULES
MOVE
MULTIPLE
MULTIPLY
NATIVE
NEGATIVE
NEXT
NO
NOT
NOTE
NUMBER
NUMERIC
OBJECT-COMPUTER
OCCURS
OF
OFF
OMITTED
ON
OPEN
OPTIONAL
OR
ORGANIZATION
OUTPUT
OVERFLOW
PAGE
PAGE-COUNTER
PERFORM
PF
PH
PICTURE
PLUS
POINTER
POSITION
POSITIVE
PRINTING
PROCEDURE
PROCEDURES
PROCEED
PROGRAM
PROGRAM-ID
QUEUE
QUOTES
RANDOM
RD
READ
RECEIVE
RECORD
RECORDS
REDEFINES
REEL
REFERENCES
RELATIVE
RELEASE
REMAINDER
REMOVAL
RENAMES
REPLACING
REPORT
REPORTING
REPORTS
RERUN
RESERVE
RESET
RETURN
REVERSED
REWIND
REWRITE
RF
RH
RIGHT
ROUNDED
RUN
SAME
SD
SEARCH
SECTION
SECURITY
SEGMENT
SEGMENT-LIMIT
SELECT
SEND
SENTENCE
SEPARATE
SEQUENCE
SEQUENTIAL
SET
SIGN
SIZE
SORT
SORT-MERGE
SOURCE
SOURCE-COMPUTER
SPACES
SPECIAL-NAMES
STANDARD
STANDARD-1
START
STATUS
STOP
STRING
SUB-QUEUE-1
SUB-QUEUE-2
SUB-QUEUE-3
SUBTRACT
SUM
SUPPRESS
SYMBOLIC
SYNCHRONIZED
TABLE
TALLYING
TAPE
TERMINAL
TERMINATE
TEXT
THAN
THROUGH
TIME
TIMES
TO
TOP
TRAILING
TYPE
UNIT
UNSTRING
UNTIL
UP
UPON
USAGE
USE
USING
VALUE
VALUES
VARYING
WHEN
WITH
WORDS
WORKING-STORAGE
WRITE
ZERO
ZEROES
+
−
*
/
**
>
<
=

FIGURE 4-1

vision. A variable may occur by itself, as an entry within a table (i.e., an array), or as an element within a data structure in one of the following ways:

(i) 77 data-name description
(ii) Level data-name description

Form (i) is used when a variable occurs as an independent item, while form (ii) is used when it occurs either as an entry within a table or as an element within a data structure. Here, ''data-name'' identifies the variable. ''Description'' denotes a series of clauses which describe the range and kind of values the variable can contain. ''Level'' denotes a two-digit number which identifies the hierarchical level of the variable within the table or data structure.

The different clauses which can occur in a variable's description are summarized below:

Clause	Purpose
REDEFINES clause	Causes a variable to share the same storage as another variable (see section 4-2.8).
JUSTIFIED clause	Causes a nonnumeric variable's value to be right-justified (with blank-fill on the left) rather than left-justified (see section 4-2.8).
PICTURE clause	Identifies whether the variable will have numeric or nonnumeric values, as well as the range of values it can accommodate. It also may describe any editing characteristics (e.g., "$") that might be inserted when its value is displayed.
USAGE clause	Identifies how a variable will be represented internally, and thus what kinds of operations can be performed on its value.
VALUE clause	Causes an initial value to be assigned to the variable at the beginning of program execution.

Among these, the **PICTURE** clause is the most important, since it describes the nature of the variable. The **PICTURE** clause has the following general form.

PICTURE [IS] string

(Hereafter in this chapter, the enclosure of a word—**IS**, in this case—within brackets will denote that the word is optional in the statement.) ''String'' describes the variable's class (alphabetic, numeric, or alphanumeric), range of values, and other editing characteristics. It is written as a sequence of characters from the following list:

PICTURE character	Meaning
A	A single alphabetic (A–Z) or blank (ƀ) character position.
B	A single blank character position.
S	A numeric sign (+ or −) position which will not appear when the value is printed.
V	The position of a decimal point within a numeric value, which will not appear when the value is printed.
X	A single alphanumeric character position.
Z	A leading zero position in a numeric value, which will suppress its appearance when the value is printed.
9	A single decimal digit (0–9) position in a numeric value.
$	The position of a leading dollar sign to be displayed with a numeric value.
−	A numeric sign position, which will appear as "−" when the value printed is negative, and as "ƀ" otherwise.

A variable is said to be alphabetic, alphanumeric, numeric, alphanumeric edited, or numeric edited according to the appearance of its **PICTURE** clause. These five classes are defined and illustrated in the following paragraphs.

Alphabetic Variable **PICTURE** clause contains a sequence of A's, denoting that the variable can contain any nonnumeric value which has only alphabetic (A–Z) and/or blank (ƀ) characters. The number defines the length of any value that the variable may have. For example, that the variable named TITLE shall contain a fifteen-character alphabetic value is declared in either of the following two equivalent ways (assuming TITLE is not part of a table or other structure).

77 TITLE **PIC** AAAAAAAAAAAAAAA.
77 TITLE **PIC** A(15).

The value of TITLE may thus be any fifteen-character value, as long as it is composed of only blanks (ƀ) and letters (A–Z). For example, TITLE's value may be "ANNUALƀREPORTƀƀ". THE "A(15)" in the second version is a convenient way to abbreviate a sequence of fifteen consecutive A's.

Alphanumeric Variable **PICTURE** clause contains a sequence of X's, denoting that the variable can contain any nonnumeric value which has alphabetic (A–Z), numeric (0–9), or special (ƀ, +, *, etc.) characters. The number of X's defines the length of the value of the variable. For example, that the variable named TITLE shall contain *any* fifteen-character value is declared in either of the following two ways.

77 TITLE **PIC** XXXXXXXXXXXXXXX.
77 TITLE **PIC** X(15).

For example, TITLE's value may be either "ANNUALƀREPORTƀƀ" or "1984ƀ REPORTƀƀƀƀ" or any other fifteen-character value.

Numeric Variable **PICTURE** clause contains a sequence of 9s, optionally headed by S and optionally containing V. The number of 9s denotes the number of decimal digits in the variable's value. The presence of S denotes that negative, as well as positive, values may be assigned to the variable. The position of V among the 9s denotes the (fixed) position of a decimal point in the variable's value. For example, assuming that the variable named GROSS-PAY shall contain a numeric value in the range 0 to 99999.99, the variable I shall contain a numeric value in the range 0 to 999, and the variable NET-INCOME shall contain a value in the range −99999.99 to 99999.99 we have the following:

77 GROSS-PAY	**PIC** 99999V99.
77 I	**PIC** 999.
77 NET-INCOME	**PIC** S99999V99.

Alphanumeric Edited Variable **PICTURE** clause contains a sequence of the characters A, X, 9, and B. The variable's value is dictated by the particular sequence of A's, X's and 9s in its **PICTURE** clause, and additionally each occurrence of B indicates the presence of an embedded blank in the variable's value. For example, suppose the variable TITLE were declared as follows:

77 TITLE **PIC** 9999BA(10).

This says that TITLE may contain any fifteen-character string whose first four characters are numeric (0–9), whose fifth character is blank (ƀ), and whose remaining characters are alphabetic (A–Z) or blank (ƀ). Thus, TITLE may again have the value "1984ƀREPORT".

Numeric Edited Variable PICTURE clause contains a sequence of the following characters.

B V Z 9 . − $

The meanings of B, V, and 9 are the same as above. Additionally, one or more *leading* 9s in the **PICTURE** string may be written as Z's, to indicate suppression of leading zeros when the value is printed. Similarly, the occurrence of V in the **PICTURE** string may be replaced by period (.) to indicate the position of the decimal point which additionally will appear when the value is printed. The $ may be written before the leftmost 9 or Z to indicate printing of a dollar sign. Additional dollar signs may be written in place of leading 9s or Z's to indicate a dollar sign which will "float" rightward to appear beside the leftmost (significant) digit when the value is printed. Finally, the minus sign (−) may be written at the extreme left of the **PICTURE** string to denote sign insertion on the left of the printed value when it is negative.

Too, the minus sign (−) is similar to S in the numeric variable's **PICTURE,** in the sense that it permits the variable to have negative, as well as nonnegative, values. For example, suppose that GROSS-PAY and NET-INCOME were to contain the same range of values as described above, but were to be displayed *with* decimal points. Additionally, suppose that leading zeros were to be suppressed (replaced by ƀ) in the display of NET-INCOME, and that a "floating dollar sign" were to be displayed immediately before the leftmost significant digit of GROSS-PAY. Then they would be declared as follows.

77 GROSS-PAY **PIC** $$$$$$.99
77 NET-INCOME **PIC** −ZZZZZ.99.

If the value of GROSS-PAY were, for example, 03571.52 then it would be displayed as ƀ$3571.52. If the value of NET-INCOME were −00025.53 then it would be printed as −ƀƀƀ25.53. We should note that the minus sign (−) may also be designated to float by using the same convention as for $.

The **USAGE** clause may be written for a variable to specify the manner which its value is represented in storage. It has the following form.

$$[\textbf{USAGE [IS]}] \left\{ \begin{array}{l} \textbf{DISPLAY} \\ \textbf{COMPUTATIONAL} \\ \textbf{INDEX} \end{array} \right\}$$

[Enclosure of a list within braces ({ and }) signifies that one of the alternatives enclosed must be selected.] If the **DISPLAY** alternative is chosen, then the variable's value is stored in exactly the form that it will be printed. If the **COMPUTATIONAL** alternative is chosen, then the variable must be numeric. In that case, its value will be stored in binary form. If the **INDEX** alternative is chosen, then the variable must be numeric and can be used only in restricted ways (see the **SEARCH** and **SET** statements in section 4-2.4). If, on the other hand, the **USAGE** clause is omitted, then it is assumed to be **DISPLAY** by default.

The **VALUE** clause is used when a variable is to be initialized to a constant value at the beginning of the program's execution. It has the following general form.

VALUE [IS] literal

Here, "literal" denotes either a numeric literal, a nonnumeric literal, or a figurative constant.

For example, suppose the above variables, named "TITLE," "I," and "GROSS-PAY," were to be initialized with the values "ANNUALƀREPORTƀƀ", "0", and "3571.52", respectively, at the beginning of execution. Suppose additionally that the variable I were to be used heavily in arithmetic calculations. Then they would be declared as follows:

```
77 TITLE        PIC X(15) VALUE "ANNUALbREPORTbb".
77 I            PIC 999 VALUE 0 COMP.
77 GROSS-PAY    PIC $$$$$$.99 VALUE "b3571.52".
```

Note here that the **PICTURE** and **VALUE** clauses have been written in the abbreviated form in all three declarations.

4-2.3 Arrays and Other Data Structures

COBOL provides two ways in which a single data name may be associated with more than one value. One is the so-called "table" (known as an "array" in other languages) and the other is the so-called "record description entry."

A table is a one-, two-, or three-dimensional collection of values, all of which have the same characteristics. Consider, for example, Figure 4-2 in which A is a one-dimensional table of five entries, each a three-digit nonnegative integer, and B is a two-dimensional table with five rows and four entries in each row, each entry a two-digit integer.

A one-dimensional table is declared in the following way:

```
01 table-name.
   02 entry-name description OCCURS clause
```

A two-dimensional table is declared in the following way:

```
01 table-name.
   02 row-name OCCURS clause.
      03 entry-name description OCCURS clause.
```

A three-dimensional table is declared in the following way:

```
01 table-name.
   02 row-name OCCURS clause.
      03 column-name OCCURS clause.
         04 entry-name description OCCURS clause.
```

In each of these cases, "table-name" denotes any unique user-defined word which names the table, while "description" denotes the particular clauses (e.g., **PICTURE** clause) which describe the nature of a typical entry in the table. These are written exactly as in an ordinary 77-level (single-valued) variable. "Row-name," "column-name," and "entry-name" denote user-defined words which name a table's typical row, column, and individual entry.

A
006
035
217
001
023

B			
17	42	00	–10
18	03	00	–11
19	47	19	–12
20	48	49	22
00	00	–2	–3

FIGURE 4-2

''**OCCURS** clause'' is used to define the number of elements in each dimension of the table. It has the following two principal forms:

(i) **OCCURS** integer [**TIMES**] [**INDEXED** [**BY**] indices]
(ii) **OCCURS** integer-1 **TO** integer-2 [**TIMES**]
[**DEPENDING** [**ON**] data-name]
[**INDEXED** [**BY**] indices]

Here, ''integer'' denotes the number of entries in the dimension where the **OCCURS** clause appears. ''Integer-1'' and ''integer-2'' denote lower and upper bounds for the number of entries in a given dimension. When the **DEPENDING ON** option of form (ii) is used, then the value of ''data-name'' defines the dimension's current number of entries throughout program execution. ''Date-name'' itself must be separately defined as a numeric variable. The **INDEXED BY** option is used when an entry in the table is referenced by one or more variables whose usage is **INDEX.** These variables' names are then listed as ''indexes'' within that option.

Returning to our example tables, we can declare A and B (but not their given values) as follows.

```
01 TABLE-A.
   02 A PIC 999 OCCURS 5.
01 TABLE-B.
   02 ROW-B OCCURS 5.
      03 B PIC S99 OCCURS 4.
```

The values shown in the diagrams for A and B cannot be initialized from within A's or B's declaration. The **VALUE** clause can be used to initialize a table, but only if all entries are to have the same value and, in addition, all entries have **USAGE DISPLAY** (as opposed to **COMP** or **INDEX**). Thus, initialization of arrays is usually deferred to the Procedure Division.

An ordinary variable's value is referenced from within the Procedure Division by giving its name. However, an entry in a table is referenced in one of two ways, depending on whether or not the table is indexed (i.e., contains an **INDEXED BY** option in its declaration).

If the table is not indexed, then an individual entry is referenced using "subscripts" as follows.

entry-name (subscript [, subscript] [, subscript])

Here, "entry-name" denotes the name of an individual entry in the table's declaration (e.g., A and B are the entry-names in our declarations). The number of "subscripts" given must agree with the number (1, 2, or 3) of dimensions in the table's declaration. Also, a blank space must separate the entry-name from the left parentheses, and separate the subscripts as well. Each subscript must be either a numeric literal or the name of a numeric variable. The subscript's value must be within the range permitted by the **OCCURS** clause for the dimension.

For example, when referring to the third element in the table A, we would write the following.

A (3)

When referring to the Ith entry in A, we would write:

A (I)

Here, I must be a numeric variable with value from 1 to 5, since A has 5 entries.

Similarly, when referring to the item in the third row and second columnn of B, we would write the following.

B (3, 2)

The item in the Ith row and Jth column of B is referenced by

B (I, J)

where I and J must be numeric variables whose values are in the ranges 1 to 5 and 1 to 4, respectively.

If, on the other hand, the table is indexed, then an individual element in the table may be referenced by a similar expression, having the following form.

```
entry-name (index-name [{±} integer]
                 [, index-name [ {±} integer]]
                 [, index-name [ {±} integer]])
```

Here, the "entry-name" again denotes the name of an individual entry in the table's declaration, and the number of occurrences of "index-name" is the same as the number of dimensions (1, 2, or 3) in the table.

Suppose, for example, that table B were redeclared as follows.

```
01 TABLE-B.
   02 TABLE-B OCCURS 5 INDEXED BY I.
      03 B OCCURS 4 PIC S99 INDEXED BY J.
```

Here, B represents the same configuration (5 × 4) of the same kinds of values as in its previous declaration. However, the variables I and J are identified as "indexes" for referencing a row and column, respectively, in B. Now, I and J must have values in the range 1 to 5 and 1 to 4, respectively, when they are used as indexes to reference a single element in B. Again the expression

B (I, J)

references the item in the Ith row and Jth column of B.

A bit more flexibility is available when indexes are used instead of subscripts to reference an item in a table. For instance, the expression

B (I + 1, J − 2)

references the entry in the (I + 1)st row and (J − 2)d column of B. Uses for subscripts and indices will be illustrated when we discuss COBOL's table-handling facilities in section 4-2.4.

A "record description entry" is the description of a structured collection of individual variables which generally are not all of the same type. For example, we may describe a record named PERSON as a collection of four variables; a 25-character alphanumeric NAME, a 9-digit numeric social security (SS-NO), a numeric GROSS-PAY in the range 0 to 99999.99, and a 40-character alphanumeric PADDRESS. (Note that the preferred name, ADDRESS, is a reserved word, and thus cannot be used for this purpose.) A set of sample data for one PERSON appears in Figure 4-3. This particular example shows two levels of structure, at the elementary level are four variables, and at a higher level is the variable PERSON, which includes all four as subordinates. Another way to picture a record description entry is in the form of a tree. There, the name (e.g., PERSON) of the record description entry is the "root" of the tree, and the individual elements are its "leaves." This is illustrated in Figure 4-4 for the example.

To define a record description entry in COBOL, one writes "level numbers" prefixed to the various names in the structure. The name of the entire structure (e.g., PER-

|ALLENƀB.ƀTUCKERƀƀƀƀƀƀƀƀƀƀ|

|275407437|

|25400.00|

|1800ƀBULLƀRUN,ƀALEXANDRIA,ƀVA.ƀ22200ƀƀƀƀ|

FIGURE 4-3

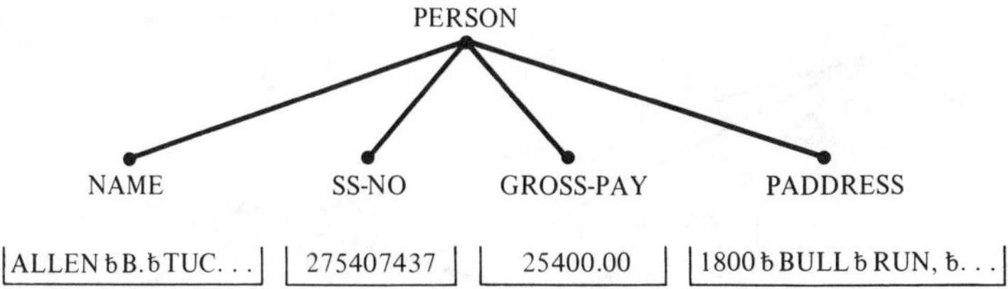

FIGURE 4-4

SON) is prefixed by level number 01; the names of all items at the next level are prefixed by level number 02, and so on. Within an individual level, names are listed from left to right. Thus, the above structure could be defined in the following way.

```
01 PERSON.
   02 NAME          PIC X(25).
   02 SS-NO         PIC 9(9).
   02 GROSS-PAY     PIC 9(5)V99.
   02 PADDRESS      PIC X(40).
```

Note also that each individual item of a record description entry must be terminated by a period (.), and that the elementary items are the only ones which have a **PICTURE** clause.

Some of the variables at level 02 in this example can themselves be structured. The tree in Figure 4-5 shows how NAME can be subdivided into three items and PADDRESS into four. If this were done, then we would have the following corresponding record description entry.

```
01 PERSON.
   02 NAME.
      03 NFIRST        PIC X(10).
      03 MIDDLE        PIC X(5).
      03 NLAST         PIC X(10).
   02 SS-NO            PIC 9(9).
   02 GROSS-PAY        PIC 9(5)V99.
   02 PADDRESS.
      03 STREET        PIC X(17).
      03 CITY          PIC X(12).
      03 STATE         PIC X(6).
      03 ZIP           PIC 9(5).
```

Notice again that only those variables which are not themselves subdivided have **PICTURE** clauses. These are known as the ''elementary items,'' and correspond to the leaves in the tree description. The other items in a record description entry are known

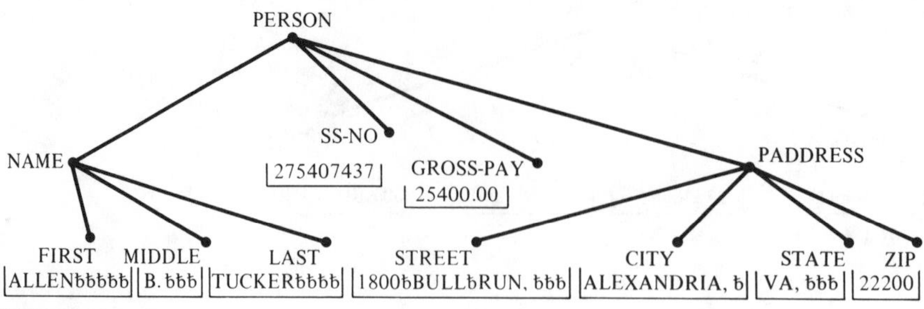

FIGURE 4-5

as "group items." In this example, PERSON, NAME, and PADDRESS are group items.

To reference an entire record description entry from within the Procedure Division of a COBOL program, one simply gives that entry's name, which appears at the 01 level. For instance, to reference the entire collection of values defined in the above example, one uses the name PERSON. Thus, all record description entries within a single COBOL program must have mutually unique names (i.e., unique at the 01 level).

However, names at subordinate levels (e.g., 02, 03, etc.) within a record description entry may be identical with subordinate names of another record description entry. Suppose, for example, that we wanted to simultaneously store the NAME, SS-NO, GROSS-PAY, and PADDRESS of two different persons, say PERSON-A and PERSON-B. Then we would write the following record description entries.

```
01 PERSON-A.
   02 NAME            PIC X(25).
   02 SS-NO           PIC 9(9).
   02 GROSS-PAY       PIC 9(5)V99.
   02 PADDRESS        PIC X(40).
01 PERSON-B.
   02 NAME            PIC X(25).
   02 SS-NO           PIC 9(9).
   02 GROSS-PAY       PIC 9(5)V99.
   02 PADDRESS        PIC X(40).
```

To reference, for example, the SS-NO of PERSON-A, we write a "qualified reference" as follows:

```
SS-NO OF PERSON-A
```

If, on the other hand, we wanted to reference PERSON-B's SS-NO, we would write the following:

```
SS-NO OF PERSON-B
```

Such qualification is necessary only when the indicated name (SS-NO, in this case) is not unique. If it were unique, then the name itself would be adequate to unambiguously reference the item.

We note also that a table can occur within a record description entry, as well as by itself. For example, suppose that we wanted to store the last *five* addresses for each PERSON, rather than just the current one. Then we could rewrite the record description entry for a person as follows.

```
01 PERSON.
   02 NAME          PIC X(25).
   02 SS-NO         PIC 9(9).
   02 GROSS-PAY     PIC 9(5)V99.
   02 PADDRESS      PIC X(40) OCCURS 5.
```

The use of subscripts, indexes, and qualification for tables occurring in this way is exactly the same as described in the foregoing paragraphs.

4-2.4 Basic Statements

We will not discuss *all* of the COBOL statements in this chapter, because of the importance of focusing attention on the most widely used ones. Specifically, we will exclude the ACCEPT, ALTER, CANCEL, DISABLE, ENABLE, ENTER, RECEIVE, SEND, START, SUPPRESS, and USE statements. The ones we will cover are listed in the following table, together with a brief description of their purpose in a COBOL program.

Statement	Purpose
ADD statement **SUBTRACT** statement **MULTIPLY** statement **DIVIDE** statement **COMPUTE** statement	To perform one or more arithmetic (add, subtract, . . .) operations and then assign the result as the new value of a variable or table entry.
CALL statement **EXIT PROGRAM** statement	To initiate execution of a subprogram, and to return control from the subprogram to the calling program, respectively. These are discussed in section 4-2.7.
CLOSE statement **DELETE** statement **OPEN** statement **READ** statement **REWRITE** statement **WRITE** statement	To perform the various input-output operations. These are discussed in section 4-2.6.
COPY statement	To cause insertion of source text from a library into a COBOL program at compile time. This is discussed in section 4-2.8.

(cont'd)

Statement	Purpose
GENERATE statement **INITIATE** statement **TERMINATE** statement	To aid in the generation of reports. These are discussed in section 4-2.8.
GO TO statement **IF** statement **PERFORM** statement	To control the sequence of program statement execution. See section 4-2.5.
INSPECT statement **SEARCH** statement **SET** statement	To search a character string or table.
MERGE statement **RELEASE** statement **RETURN** statement **SORT** statement	To sort a file or merge two files. These are discussed in section 4-2.8.
MOVE statement **STRING** statement **UNSTRING** statement	To move, concatenante, or separate data values, respectively.

In the remainder of this section, we will discuss all the statements listed above which are not designated for discussion in another section. To begin our discussion, consider the simple COBOL program at the beginning of the chapter.

The reader should recognize the declarations of variables (X, AV, etc.) and record description entries (A-LINE) within the Data Division. The statements which actually control program execution occur within the Procedure Division. Let us focus attention for a moment on this program's Procedure Division. In general, it may consist of one or more "sections." Each section consists of one or more "paragraphs," and each paragraph consists of one or more "statements."

A section always begins with a "section header," which has the following form.

section-name **SECTION.**

Here, "section-name" names the section and must be a unique, nonreserved user-defined word. In the special case that the Procedure Division has only one section, its section header may be omitted. This is the case for our sample program.

A "paragraph" always has the following form:

paragraph-name. sentence-sequence

Here, "paragraph-name" names the paragraph and may be any unique, nonreserved, user-defined word. "Sentence-sequence" denotes a sequence of sentences which comprise the paragraph. The end of a paragraph is delimited by the beginning of the next paragraph (or by the end of the program if there are no more paragraphs). The example program's Procedure Division contains two paragraphs, named INITIALIZE and READ-LOOP.

Arithmetic Expressions Arithmetic expressions are used in a COBOL program to designate a series of arithmetic calculations. They appear in the **COMPUTE** and **IF** statements. An arithmetic expression may be any one of the following:

(i) A numeric elementary variable name
(ii) A numeric literal
(iii) Two arithmetic expressions separated by an "arithmetic operator"
(iv) An arithmetic expression enclosed in parentheses

The "arithmetic operators" and their meanings appear in the following list.

Arithmetic operator	Meaning
+	Addition
−	Subtraction
*	Multiplication
/	Division
**	Exponentiation

Each of these operators is always infixed and always has two operands. For instance, the arithmetic expression

```
H + 2
```

denotes addition of the value of the variable named H and the numeric literal 2.

When two or more arithmetic operations are specified, they are exectued sequentially. For instance, if we want to add the value of I to the sum H + 2, then we write the following:

```
H + 2 + I
  ↑   ↑
 (1) (2)
```

Here, the addition H + 2 takes place first, and the addition of that sum and the value of I takes place second, as shown by the numbers below the expression.

A series of two or more operations within an arithmetic expression is generally carried out from left to right, with the following two exceptions. First there is a hierarchy among the operators, so that all exponentiations (**) are performed first, all multiplications (*) and divisions (/) are performed next, and all additions (+) and subtractions (−) are performed last. This means that

```
H + 2 * I
  ↑   ↑
 (2) (1)
```

denotes the sum of H and 2 * I, rather than the product of H + 2 and I.

Second, whenever the ordering thus defined is not desired, the programmer may override it by enclosing in parentheses the operations that should instead be performed first. For instance, to specify the product of H + 2 and I, the programmer writes the following:

```
(H + 2) * I
    ↑   ↑
   (1) (2)
```

Notice the very careful spacing that has been used in writing these arithmetic expressions, and recall that COBOL requires at least one blank space (ƀ) before and after every arithmetic operator within an arithmetic expression. Thus, for instance,

6−I

and 6 − I

are *not* equivalent, and only the latter is acceptable.

Arithmetic Statements The five COBOL arithmetic statements are the **ADD, SUBTRACT, MULTIPLY, DIVIDE,** and **COMPUTE** statements. These statements have the following options in common.

ROUNDED option
SIZE ERROR option

These options will be discussed and illustrated at the end of this section. The **ADD** statement may be written in either of the following forms.

(i) **ADD** value-list **TO** identifier-list [**ROUNDED**]
[**SIZE ERROR** option]
(ii) **ADD** value, value-list **GIVING** identifier-list [**ROUNDED**]
[**SIZE ERROR** option]

Here, "value-list" denotes a list of one or more numeric identifiers and/or literals, mutually separated by comma-blank (,ƀ). "Identifier-list" denotes a list of one or more numeric identifiers, mutually separated by comma-blank (,ƀ). "Value" denotes a single numeric identifier or literal.

Execution of form (i) leaves in each identifier of "identifier-list" the result of adding to its current value the sum of all the values in "value-list." The example program contains an illustration of form (i) as follows:

ADD 1 **TO** N

Here, "value-list" has only one value, which is added to the current value of the variable named N.

Execution of form (ii) leaves in each identifier of "identifier-list" the result of adding the identifier or literal ''value'' and the sum of the identifiers and literals in ''value-list.'' The following statement is equivalent to the example above.

ADD 1, N **GIVING** N

The **SUBTRACT** statement may be written in either of the following forms.

(i) **SUBTRACT** value-list **FROM** identifier-list [**ROUNDED**]
    [**SIZE ERROR** option]
(ii) **SUBTRACT** value-list **FROM** identifier [**ROUNDED**]
    GIVING identifier-list
    [**SIZE ERROR** option]

Here, ''value-list'' and ''identifier-list'' have the same denotations as they did in the **ADD** statement.

Execution of form (i) leaves in each identifier of ''identifier-list'' the result of subtracting from its current value the sum of all the values in ''value-list.'' For example,

SUBTRACT 1 **FROM** I

leaves as the new value of I the result of subtracting 1 from its current value.

Execution of form (ii) leaves in each identifier of ''identifier-list'' the result of subtracting from the current value of ''identifier'' the sum of all the values in ''value-list.'' The current value of ''identifier,'' however, is not affected by this execution unless it appears also in ''identifier-list.'' For example, to leave in the variable H the result of subtracting 1 from the variable I, we could write the following.

SUBTRACT 1 **FROM** I **GIVING** H

The current value of I here is not affected.

The **MULTIPLY** and **DIVIDE** statements have the following forms, respectively.

MULTIPLY value-1 **BY** value-2 [**GIVING** identifier-3] [**ROUNDED**]
  [**SIZE ERROR** option]
DIVIDE value-1 **BY** value-2 **GIVING** identifier-3 [**ROUNDED**]
  [**REMAINDER** identifier-4]
  [**SIZE ERROR** option]

Here, ''value-1'' and ''value-2'' each denotes a numeric identifier or literal, while ''identifier-3'' and ''identifier-4'' denote numeric identifiers.

Execution of the **MULTIPLY** statement leaves in identifier-3 the product of value-1 and value-2. If the **GIVING** option is omitted, then value-2 *must* be an identifier, and the product becomes that identifier's new value. For example,

MULTIPLY 3 **BY** H **GIVING** I

leaves in I the product of 3 and the current value of H. However,

MULTIPLY 3 **BY** H

leaves that product as the new value of H.

Execution of the **DIVIDE** statement leaves in identifier-3 the quotient of value-1 and value-2. Additionally, if the **REMAINDER** option is included, the result of subtracting from value-1 the product of value-2 and the quotient is defined as the "remainder," and it is stored in identifier-4. For example,

DIVIDE 5 **BY** 2 **GIVING** I **REMAINDER** J

leaves in I the value 2 and in J the value 1.

The **COMPUTE** statement permits several arithmetic operations to be designated, with the result assigned to an identifier. It is similar to the assignment statement of most other languages, and has the following general form.

COMPUTE identifier [**ROUNDED**] = arithmetic expression
[**SIZE ERROR** option]

Here, "identifier" denotes any numeric variable. Execution of the **COMPUTE** statement causes the numeric result of evaluating the arithmetic expression to become the new value of the identifier. For instance, the following **COMPUTE** statement can be written in place of the first **ADD** statement in the sample program.

COMPUTE SUMX = SUMX + X

The **ROUNDED** option allows rounding of the final result of an arithmetic operation before it is assigned to the identifier which is the "target" of the result. It may be used for any of the five arithmetic statements described above. It is specified by placing the reserved word **ROUNDED** immediately after those target identifiers for which the result should be rounded. We illustrate this using the **MULTIPLY** statement, assuming that the following declarations have been made:

77 HOURS **PIC** 9(2)V9.
77 RATE **PIC** 9V99.
77 GROSS-PAY **PIC** 9(5)V99.

Suppose that we want to compute a person's GROSS-PAY as the product of the HOURS worked (say 37.5) and the RATE per hour (say $5.25), rounding to the nearest penny. Then we would write the following.

MULTIPLY HOURS **BY** RATE **GIVING** GROSS-PAY **ROUNDED**

This would leave GROSS-PAY at $196.88, the result of rounding the product $196.875 to two decimal places. Omission of the **ROUNDED** option would have left GROSS-

PAY at $196.87. The decimal place to which rounding takes place is always the rightmost decimal digit of the target identifier.

A "size error condition" arises whenever the result of performing an arithmetic operation has more significant digits than the number allowed by the target variable's **PICTURE** clause. Also, the size error condition arises whenever division by zero is attempted. For example, if GROSS-PAY had been declared with **PICTURE** 9(2)V99 rather than 9(5)V99 and the above **MULTIPLY** statement had been executed, a size error condition would have been raised.

If an arithmetic statement in which a size error condition occurs does not contain a **SIZE ERROR** option, then the resulting value of the target identifier becomes undefined. On the other hand, the arithmetic statement may contain a **SIZE ERROR** option, which has the following general form.

[ON] **SIZE ERROR** statement

Here, "statement" denotes any imperative statement, such as a **GO TO** statement that would transfer control to an error-handling paragraph whenever the size error condition arises. If the arithmetic statement contains the **SIZE ERROR** option, then the current value of the target identifier is not changed and the "statement" is executed, whenever execution of the arithmetic statement causes the size error condition to arise. If that condition does not arise, execution of the statement proceeds normally. Continuing the example, where GROSS-PAY is declared with **PICTURE** 9(2)V99, consider the following statement.

```
MULTIPLY RATE BY HOURS GIVING GROSS-PAY
   ON SIZE ERROR GO TO BAD-GROSS
```

Execution of this statement will leave in GROSS-PAY the correct product of RATE and HOURS, provided it does not exceed 99.99. If it does, however, then the size error condition will be raised and control will pass to the paragraph named BAD-GROSS.

The MOVE statement The **MOVE** statement causes one or more values to be assigned to one or more variables. It has the following basic form.

MOVE value **TO** identifier-list

Here, "value" denotes either an identifier or a literal, while "identifier-list" denotes a list of one or more identifiers, which are mutually separated by comma-space (,ƀ).

Execution of the **MOVE** statement causes "value" to become the new value of each identifier in "identifier-list." For instance, the first **MOVE** statement in the example program causes the variable MSG to have the value THE AVERAGE =.

On the other hand, "value" and "identifier-list" may designate group items, rather than elementary items. In this case, each one should be identically structured, so that the result of the **MOVE** is identical with that which would occur if it were replaced by a sequence of **MOVE** statements, one for each pair of corresponding elementary items in the two groups.

When "value" and "identifier-list" designate elementary items, they should belong to the same category. That is, they should either be both numeric or both nonnumeric (i.e., alphabetic, alphanumeric, or alphanumeric edited). For instance, in **MOVE** 1 **TO** N, both 1 and N are numeric.

Furthermore, whenever an identifier in "identifier-list" has a **PICTURE** which is not the same as that of "value," then *conversion* of "value" takes place before it is moved to the identifier. Conversion from one *numeric* value to another is accomplished by decimal point alignment, adding leading zeros, truncating leading digits, adding decimal zeros or truncating decimal digits from "value," as required by the identifier's **PICTURE.** Conversion from one *nonnumeric value* to another requires only that the length of the value being moved be made equal to the length of the identifier where it will be stored. This is accomplished by either truncating right-hand characters or adding right-hand blanks (ƀ) to "value." The following examples illustrate the results of some common **MOVE** operations:

Value to be moved	PICTURE of result	Value after the move
3.19	9V9	3.1
	V99	.19
	99V999	03.190
"TEXT"	X(3)	"TEX"
	X(4)	"TEXT"
	X(5)	"TEXTƀ"

We emphasize here that conversion occurs *only* when both "value" and "identifier" are *elementary* items. When they are not, the **MOVE** operation takes place without regard for either the value's type or the result's **PICTURE.** It is executed as if an elementary nonnumeric value were moved to another elementary nonnumeric item, with padding or truncation on the right as required. For example, execution of

MOVE "TEXT" **TO** C, D

where C and D are defined as follows:

01 C.
  02 C1 **PIC** X.
  02 C2 **PIC** X.
01 D.
  02 D1 **PIC** X(3).
  02 D2 **PIC** X(3).

will leave the following results in C and D:

C1 T   D1 TEX
C2 E   D2 Tƀƀ

This rule suggests some strong advice. That is, when moving data from one group to another, be sure that the two groups are identically structured and that corresponding elements have identical **PICTURE**s.

STRING and UNSTRING Statements The **STRING** and **UNSTRING** statements provide COBOL with a primitive character-manipulation facility. The **STRING** statement allows concatenation of several nonnumeric values (strings) into one, while the **UNSTRING** statement allows decomposing a single string into several. Their forms are as follows:

```
STRING value-list-1 [DELIMITED [BY] {value-1}]
                                    {SIZE   }
   [ ,  value-list-2 [DELIMITED [BY] {value-2}]
                                     {SIZE   }
   .
   .
   .

   INTO identifier [[WITH] POINTER ptr]
   [; [ON] OVERFLOW statement]

UNSTRING identifier [DELIMITED [BY] delimiter-list]
   INTO identifier-list
   [;[ON] OVERFLOW statement]
```

Here, ''value-list-1'' and ''value-list-2'' denote lists of elementary nonnumeric items or literals that are mutually separated by comma-space (,b̸). ''Value-1'' and ''value-2'' each denotes an individual nonnumeric elementary item or literal. ''Identifier'' denotes a nonnumeric identifer, ''identifier-list'' denotes a list of the same that are mutually separated by comma-space (,b̸), and ''ptr'' denotes a numeric identifier. ''Statement'' denotes any unconditional statement. ''Delimiter-list'' denotes a list of one or more nonnumeric identifiers and /or literals, mutually separated by the word **OR**.

Execution of the **STRING** statement causes ''identifier'' to be filled from left to right with the result of concatenating the values in value-list-1, value-list-2, . . . , in the order in which they are written. If that result has more characters than allowed by identifier's **PICTURE,** then the **OVERFLOW** condition is raised, and ''statement'' is executed (if the **ON OVERFLOW** clause is present). Otherwise (either the **OVERFLOW** condition is not raised or the **ON OVERFLOW** clause is not present), control passes to the next statement following. If, on the other hand, the result is not as long as that allowed by identifier's **PICTURE,** the remaining (rightmost) characters in ''identifier'' are kept unchanged.

When the **DELIMITED BY SIZE** alternative is used, each of the values in the corresponding value-list is taken in its entirety. When, on the other hand, the **DELIMITED BY** value-1 alternative is used, the first (leftmost) occurrence of ''value-1'' within each of the values in the corresponding value-list delimits the end of the value. If ''value-1'' does not occur within one or more of the values in value-list, then the entire value is used, as in the **SIZE** alternative. When the **WITH POINTER** (ptr) option is specified, the current integer value of ptr dictates the position in ''identifier'' where the leftmost character of ''value-list-1'' will be stored.

The INSPECT Statement COBOL character manipulation is enhanced by the **INSPECT** statement. It permits the program to search a character string for occurrences of some other character string, possibly replacing such occurrences by yet another string. The form of the **INSPECT** statement is as follows:

```
INSPECT identifier-1

  [                      { ALL value-1     }
  [ TALLYING id-2 FOR    { LEADING value-1 }
  [                      { CHARACTERS      }

        [[ { BEFORE }                      ]]
        [[ {        }  INITIAL value-2     ]]
        [[ { AFTER  }                      ]]

  [             { CHARACTERS      }
  [             { ALL value-3     }
  [ REPLACING   { LEADING value-3 }  By value-4
  [             { FIRST value-3   }

        [[ { BEFORE }                      ]]
        [[ {        }  INITIAL value-5     ]]
        [[ { AFTER  }                      ]]
```

Here, ''identifier-1'' denotes any data item whose usage is **DISPLAY**. ''Id-2'' denotes any elementary numeric data item, which serves to count the number of occurrences of the designated string ''value-1'' in ''identifier-1.'' ''Value-1,'' ''value-2,'' ''value-3,'' ''value-4,'' and ''value-5'' each denotes a nonnumeric elementary identifier or a literal.

When the **BEFORE** (or **AFTER**) option is included, the ending point (or starting point, respectively) of the search is identified as the position in ''identifier-1'' immediately before (after) the leftmost occurrence of ''value-2'' or ''value-5.'' When it is omitted, the ending point and starting point are identified as the right and left ends of ''identifier-1,'' respectively.

Execution of the **INSPECT** statement thus occurs as follows. If the **TALLYING** option is included, then ''id-2'' will be left with the total number of characters counted. Counting is governed by the choice given after the word **FOR.** ''**ALL** value-1'' dictates that the total number of occurrences of ''value-1'' from the starting point to the ending point of the search be counted. ''**LEADING** value-1'' dictates that only those occurrences of ''value-1'' that occur before any non-''value-1'' be counted. **CHARACTERS** dictates that the total number of characters from the starting to the ending point be counted. In all of these cases, ''id-1'' is *not* initialized by the **INSPECT** statement, and this must be done elsewhere in the program.

If the **REPLACING** option is included, then the starting and ending points for replacement of characters within "identifier-1" are similarly defined, depending on the presence or absence of "value-5." Here, "value-3" identifies the characters to be replaced (or else **CHARACTERS** designates that all characters be replaced), while "value-4" designates the value which will replace the characters. Either the **TALLYING** option or the REPLACING option must be present in an **INSPECT** statement.

The SEARCH and SET Statements While **INSPECT** allows searching a character string for a particular value, the **SEARCH** statement allows searching a table for a particular value. The **SET** statement is used to assign a value to an **INDEX** variable that is associated with the table being searched. These statements have the following forms:

(i) **SEARCH** identifier-1 [**VARYING** index]
[**AT END** statement-1]
WHEN condition statement-2

$$\textbf{(ii) SET}\ \text{index-list} \left\{ \begin{array}{l} \textbf{TO} \\ \textbf{UP BY} \\ \textbf{DOWN BY} \end{array} \right\} \text{value}$$

Here, "identifier-1" identifies the table to be searched. It must be a group-level name which contains both an **OCCURS** clause and an **INDEXED BY** clause. "Index" denotes an index variable, which is defined in an "**INDEXED BY** var" part of the table's **OCCURS** clause. "Index-list" denotes a list of such items, mutually separated by comma-space (,ƀ). "Statement-1" and "statement-2" both denote imperative statements. "Value" denotes either an index variable or an integer constant.

When executed, the **SEARCH** statement performs a search of the indicated table, varying the table's own index (and, concurrently, the "index" if the **VARYING** clause is present) until either the designated "condition" is true or the end of the table is reached. Accordingly, either "statement-2" or "statement-1" is executed and the other is skipped. When "statement-1" is not specified and the search reaches the end of the table before "condition" becomes true, control passes to the next sentence.

Execution of the **SET** statement causes each variable in "index-list" to be initialized at (**TO**), incremented by (**UP BY**), or decremented by (**DOWN BY**) the integer "value." Consider the following example, where the table named "TABLE-A" is searched for the first occurrence of zero. Here, TABLE-A and index I are declared as follows:

01 TABLE-A.
02 A **PIC** S99 **OCCURS** 5 **INDEXED BY** I.

A
43
19
−5
0
−19

FIGURE 4-6

Note that our mention of I as an index in the declaration of TABLE-A implicitly declares I. Now assume that A has the values given in Figure 4-6. Then the search is designated as follows:

```
SET I TO 1.
SEARCH TABLE-A
   AT END GO TO ZERO-NOT-FOUND
   WHEN A (I) = 0 GO TO ZERO-FOUND.
```

Execution of the search will pass control to ZERO-FOUND, leaving I with value 4.

4-2.5 Control Structures

The GO TO Statement The statements in a COBOL program are generally executed in the order in which they are written, unless a statement which can alter that order is encountered. One such statement is the **GO TO** statement, which has either of the following forms:

(i) GO TO procedure-name
(ii) GO TO procedure-name-list **DEPENDING** [**ON**] identifier

Here, "procedure-name" denotes any paragraph-name or section-name appearing in the Procedure Division. "Procedure-name-list" denotes a list of one or more (for example, n) procedure-names, which are mutually separated by comma-space (,b̸). "Identifier" denotes the name of an elementary numeric variable which can have integer values only.

When executed, form (i) of the **GO TO** statement causes control to pass directly to the first statement within the first sentence of the paragraph or section having the indicated procedure-name. For example, execution of the statement

```
GO TO LOOP
```

causes control to pass to the first statement in the paragraph named LOOP.

Form (ii) of the **GO TO** statement causes control to pass directly to the beginning of the first, second, . . . , or nth named paragraph (or section) in the procedure-name-list depending on whether the current value of identifer is 1, 2, . . . , or n, respectively. If, on the other hand, the current value of identifier is not within this range, the next statement following the **GO TO** statement is executed.

The STOP statement The **STOP** statement causes program execution to cease. It has the following form:

STOP RUN

The **STOP** statement is not necessarily the last statement in the program. Its position(s) in the Procedure Division is (are) dictated by the logical point(s) where program execution could cease. The only **STOP** statement in the example program occurs at the end of the first paragraph.

Conditions and IF statements An **IF** statement is used to test whether a so-called "condition" is true or false, and then select the subsequent sequence of statement execution accordingly.

Conditions serve to specify relations that exist among variables and values. COBOL allows specification of conditions in a variety of ways. Conditions fall into the following categories:

Relations
Class conditions
Condition-name conditions
Sign conditions

A relation consists of any two arithmetic expressions (a and b) separated by a relational operator that must be preceded and followed by blank (ƀ). The relational operators (op) and the meanings of "a op b" are as follows:

Relational operator (op)	Meaning of "a op b"
=	a and b are equal
<	a is less than b
>	a is greater than b
NOT =	a and b are not equal
NOT <	a is not less than b
NOT >	a is not greater than b

For example, the following relation

H < 6

is true exactly when the value of H is less than 6.

A relation can also be written using nonnumeric literals and nonnumeric variables instead of arithmetic expressions. For example, to specify a test of whether or not the current value of a nonnumeric variable NAME is "ALLEN B. TUCKER" the following relation can be written:

NAME = "ALLENƀB.ƀTUCKER"

Evaluation of this delivers the value "true" or "false" as the current value as Name is or is not identical (character by character) with the literal "ALLENƀB.ƀTUCKER".

The relations < and > are defined for nonnumeric values on the basis of an implementation-dependent collating sequence among characters in the COBOL character set. For our purposes, we will assume that sequence to be the order in which the characters are listed in section 4-2.1. For example, "A" < "B" is true, "B" < "C" is true, and so forth. Now, for two nonnumeric literals, for example, "a" and "b", the relation "a < b" is true if one of the following is true:

1 a and b have the same number of characters, the first k (for some k > 0) characters in a are respectively identical with the first k characters in b, and the k + 1st character in a is less than the k + 1st character in b.

2 a and b do *not* have the same number of characters, but the result of extending the shorter of the two with enough blanks at its right to make their lengths identical leaves 1 true. The relation "a = b" is similarly defined when the lengths of a and b are not identical.

The relation "a > b" for nonnumeric values is true whenever neither "a < b" nor "a = b" is true. The relations "a **NOT** < b", "a **NOT** = b", and "a **NOT** > b" are defined for nonnumeric values as they were for arithmetic expressions.

A class condition is used to test whether a value is numeric or alphabetic. It may be written as follows:

$$\text{identifier } \textbf{IS [NOT]} \left\{ \begin{array}{l} \textbf{NUMERIC} \\ \textbf{ALPHABETIC} \end{array} \right\}$$

Here, "identifier" denotes any identifier whose **USAGE** is **DISPLAY**. Evaluation of a class condition yields the value "true" or "false" as the identifier's current value does or does not satisfy the indicated test, respectively. For example, reconsider the variable NAME used above, and assume that it has the value "ALLENƀB.ƀTUCKER". Then the conditions

NAME **IS NUMERIC**
NAME **IS ALPHABETIC**

both yield the value "false," since (1) the value of NAME is not a number, and (2) the value of NAME contains a character (specifically, ".") which is not alphabetic or blank.

A condition-name condition is used to test whether an elementary variable's current value satisfies a particular condition, as defined by a "condition-name" in the variable's declaration. This is done by following the variable's declaration immediately by an "88-level" condition-name declaration as follows:

88 condition-name **VALUE**-clause-list.

Here, "condition-name" denotes any user-defined word, while "**VALUE**-clause-list" denotes a sequence of one or more **VALUE** clauses which are mutually separated by comma-blank (,b̸). A **VALUE** clause has either of the following forms:

(i) VALUE [IS] literal-1
(ii) VALUES [ARE] literal-1 **THROUGH** literal-2

Here, "literal-1" and "literal-2" denote any numeric or nonnumeric literal which is consistent with the variable's **PICTURE**. For instance, suppose we declare the variable GROSS-PAY as follows:

```
02 GROSS-PAY            PIC 9(5)V99.
   88 LOW-PAY               VALUES 0 THROUGH 5000.
   88 AVERAGE-PAY           VALUE 6000.
   88 HIGH-PAY              VALUES 20000 THROUGH 99999.
```

Here, we have defined three condition-names to be associated with the variable GROSS-PAY: LOW-PAY, AVERAGE-PAY, and HIGH-PAY. Each identifies a value, or range of values, for GROSS-PAY by an explicit name.

Now, the condition-name condition is written simply by stating any condition-name which has been defined for some variable. Its evaluation yields the value "true" or "false," respectively, as the current value of that condition-name's associated variable falls within the range of values identified by that condition name. For example, if the condition-name

LOW-PAY

is written, and the value of GROSS-PAY is currently 25400.00, then the value "false" will be returned. The condition-names AVERAGE-PAY and HIGH-PAY will yield the values "false" and "true," respectively, since only the range defined for HIGH-PAY is satisfied by the value 25400.

A sign condition is used to test whether the current value of an arithmetic expression is positive, negative, or zero. It has the following form.

$$\text{arithmetic expression } \textbf{IS [NOT]} \left\{ \begin{array}{l} \textbf{POSITIVE} \\ \textbf{NEGATIVE} \\ \textbf{ZERO} \end{array} \right\}$$

Evaluation of this condition yields the value "true" or "false," accordingly as the expression's value does or does not satisfy the indicated condition.

Finally, several of these conditions may be combined, using the logical operators **AND** and **OR**. Evaluation of

C_1 **AND** C_2

where C_1 and C_2 denote any of the four kinds of conditions described above, yields the value "true" or "false" accordingly as both C_1 and C_2 are true or not. Similarly,

C_1 **OR** C_2

is "true" or "false" accordingly as either one of C_1 or C_2 is "true" or not. **AND** has higher priority than **OR**, so that

C_1 **OR** C_2 **AND** C_3

means C_1 **OR** (C_2 **AND** C_3) rather than (C_1 **OR** C_2) **AND** C_3. As suggested here, priority may be overridden by appropriate use of parentheses.

An **IF** statement may be written in one of the following ways:

(i) **IF** condition statement-1
(ii) **IF** condition statement-1 **ELSE** statement-2

Here, "condition" denotes any of the conditions discussed above, while "statement-1" and "statement-2" each denotes any (sequence of) statement(s), containing at most one conditional statement.

Execution of form (i) proceeds in two major steps. First, the designated "condition" is evaluated. Second, if that result is "true" then control passes to the (first statement in the sequence of) statement(s) designated by "statement-1." Otherwise, control passes to the first statement of the next sentence textually following the **IF** statement.

Execution of form (ii) proceeds also in two steps. First, the designated "condition" is evaluated. Second, control passes either to (the beginning of) "statement-1" or to (the beginning of) "statement-2," depending respectively on whether that result is "true" or "false."

The PERFORM Statement Much of programming is concerned with proper specification of controlled loops. COBOL provides the **PERFORM** statement as an aid to writing such loops.

A "controlled loop" is the repeated execution of a sequence of statements until a certain condition becomes true. Many such loops are "counter-controlled," which means that a counting variable is initialized and then incremented and tested each time a sequence of statements is executed. This is pictured in two different forms in Figure 4-7. Here, i denotes the control variable, while m_1, m_2, and m_3 denote numeric variables or numeric literals which are, respectively, the initial value, the limit value, and the increment value for the control variable. Flowchart (*b*) can be written using the **PERFORM** statement as follows:

PERFORM procedure-name
  VARYING i **FROM** m_1 **BY** m_3 **UNTIL** i $> m_2$
procedure-name. | Sequence of statements |

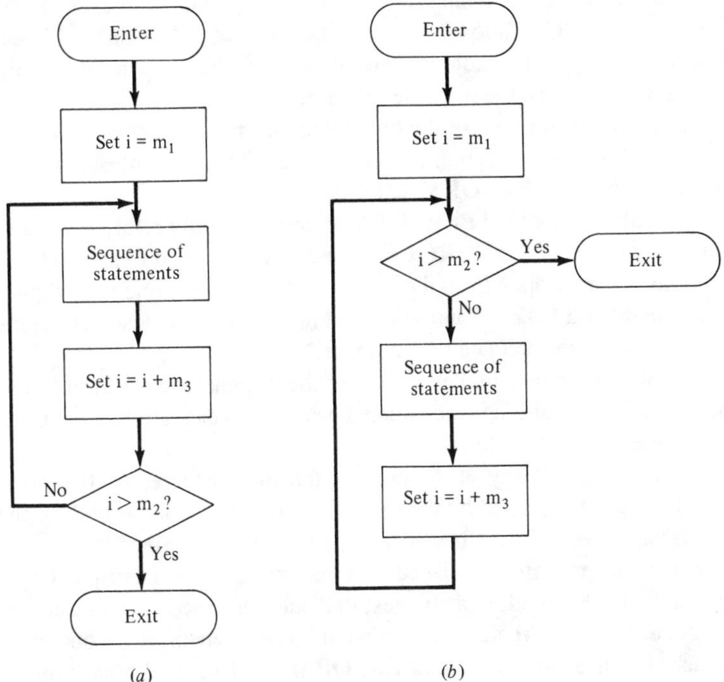

(*a*) (*b*)

FIGURE 4-7

For instance, the following **PERFORM** statement will execute each of the **MOVE** and **COMPUTE** statements five times.

```
        PERFORM LOOP VARYING H FROM 1 BY 1 UNTIL H > 5.
        .
        .
        .
LOOP.   MOVE 1 TO B (H, 1)
        COMPUTE B (H, 2) = 5 + 3 * (H - A (H)).
```

More generally, the **PERFORM** statement has several different forms. Some of them are as follows:

(i) PERFORM pn-1 [**THROUGH** pn-2] [number **TIMES**]
(ii) PERFORM pn-1 [**THROUGH** pn-2] **UNTIL** condition-1
(iii) PERFORM pn-1 [**THROUGH** pn-2]
  VARYING i **FROM** m_1 **BY** m_3 **UNTIL** condition-1
  [**AFTER** j **FROM** n_1 **BY** n_3 **UNTIL** condition-2
  [**AFTER** k **FROM** p_1 **BY** p_3 **UNTIL** condition-3]]

Here, pn-1 and pn-2 denote procedure names, and "number" denotes an integer-valued variable or integer constant. "Condition-1," "condition-2," and "condition-3" denote arbitrary conditions; i, j, and k denote numeric variables; while m_1, m_3, n_1, n_3, p_1, and p_3 each denotes a numeric variable or numeric literal.

Execution of form (i), without either of the two indicated options, causes execution of all statements in the paragraph or section named pn-1, after which control passes to the next statement following the **PERFORM** statement.

In fact, execution of all forms of the **PERFORM** statement finally return control to the next statement following it. If the **THROUGH** pn-2 option is used in any of these forms, then all sections or paragraphs from the one named pn-1 to the one named pn-2 are executed. If the "number **TIMES**" option is used in form (i), the designated pn's are executed the number of times dictated by "number."

Execution of form (ii) causes repeated execution of the designated pn's until "condition-1" becomes true. The condition is reevaluated *before* each execution of the pn's, so that the pn's may be executed zero times.

Execution of form (iii) without any of the options shown is depicted by flowchart (*b*), with the test in Figure 4-8 replaced by the one in Figure 4-9. If one or both of the options are included, then two or three "nested" loops would be described.

Note that the loop being repeated is placed in a remote location from the **PERFORM** statement itself. If, like in other languages, that paragraph had been placed immediately *following* the **PERFORM** statement, it would have been executed one *extra* time. This is an unusual control structure; the **PERFORM** acts like an internal subroutine call as well as a loop control statement.

4-2.6 Input-Output Conventions COBOL provide extensive facilities for reading and writing data values during program executions. A COBOL "file" is a collection of records, each one formatted into fields in the same way as the next. A file may be accessed sequentially by a program for either input or output, or randomly for either input, output, or input-output (i.e., records may be both read and written).

Sequential access takes a file's records in the order in which they are stored. Random access takes a file's records in no particular order, as dictated by the program. Thus any record in a randomly accessed file may be read (written) zero, one, or more times in a single program run.

For each file accessed by a COBOL program, the following must be included in the program:

1 In the Environment Division, identify the physical device class (e.g., card reader, magnetic tape) where the file is stored.

2 In the File Section of the Data Division, define the file's attributes and a buffer area (by way of a record description entry) into (from) which records will be read (written) from (to) the file.

3 In the Procedure Division, provide statements which will read (write) records from (to) the file, as well as statements which will "open" and "close" the file.

Device Assignment in the Environment Division Whenever a program uses a file, its Environment Division must contain an "Input-Output Section" and a "File-Control Paragraph." The file-control paragraph contains for each file a "file-control-

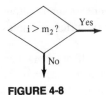

FIGURE 4-8

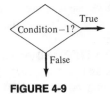

FIGURE 4-9

entry,'' which principally assigns the file to a particular (implementation-dependent) physical input-output device. The Input-Output Section is thus headed as follows.

INPUT-OUTPUT SECTION.
  FILE-CONTROL. file-control-entry . . .

Here, the ellipses indicate one or more instances of a file-control-entry. Each file-control-entry has the following form:

```
SELECT file-name ASSIGN TO device-name
    [RESERVE integer AREAS]
    [ORGANIZATION IS { SEQUENTIAL | INDEXED }]
    [ACCESS MODE IS { SEQUENTIAL | RANDOM }]
    [RECORD KEY IS data-name].
```

Here, ''file-name'' serves to name the file and ''device-name'' is implementation dependent. The following are valid device-names for IBM OS COBOL implementations:

Device-name	Meaning
DA-S-ddname	Some direct-access (DA) device and a sequentially organized (S) file.
DA-I-ddname	Same, except that the file has indexed (I) organization.
UT-S-ddname	Some magnetic tape (UT) device and a sequentially organized file.
UR-S-ddname	Some unit record (UR) device—card reader, card punch, or line printer—and a sequentially organized file.

Here, a file whose organization is indexed may be accessed either sequentially or randomly, but must reside on a direct-access device. Also, ''ddname'' denotes a one- to eight-character name which appears on the data-definition job control statement for that file at execution time.

The **RESERVE** clause is optional, and is used to specify the number of input-output buffers (**AREAS**) to be assigned to the file. If omitted, the number of buffers is implementation dependent.

The **ORGANIZATION** and **ACCESS** clauses are also optional. If omitted, then **SEQUENTIAL** is assumed for each. If a file has **INDEXED** organization, then its **ACCESS MODE** may be either **SEQUENTIAL** or **RANDOM.**

When organization is **INDEXED** and **ACCESS MODE** is **RANDOM** for a file, then an individual record is retrieved by its ''key.'' The key of a record is a value which uniquely distinguishes that record from all others in the file. For example, the key for an employee master file can be an employee's social security number, so that no two employees will have the same key. Thus, for random access to an **INDEXED** file, the **RECORD KEY** clause identifies the ''data-name'' (or field) within the file's record description entry which serves as the key for the file. This clause is, of course, not used for **SEQUENTIAL** access.

For example, suppose we have an input punched-card file named CARDS, an output print file named PAPER, and an output magnetic tape file named MAG-TAPE. Then a program with these three files would have the following Input-Output Section in its Environment Division:

```
INPUT-OUTPUT SECTION.
  FILE-CONTROL.
    SELECT CARDS        ASSIGN TO UR-S-SYSIN.
    SELECT PAPER        ASSIGN TO UR-S-SYSPRINT.
    SELECT MAG-TAPE     ASSIGN TO UT-S-TAPEDD.
```

File and Record Definition in the Data Division For each file used by a program, there must be one file description which is immediately followed by one or more record descriptions, in the File Section of the Data Division. Basic organization of the Data Division is as follows:

```
DATA DIVISION.
FILE SECTION.
{file-description
record-description. . .}. . .
WORKING-STORAGE SECTION.
{declarations of variables, tables, and records}
```

A ''file-description'' has the following form.

```
FD file-name
    [BLOCK [CONTAINS] integer-1 [CHARACTERS]]
    [RECORD [CONTAINS] integer-2 [CHARACTERS]]
    LABEL RECORDS ARE { STANDARD }
                      { OMITTED  }
    [LINAGE IS value LINES].
```

Position	1-10	11-15	16-30	31-32	33	34-35	36-38	39-47	48-80
	Name			Age	Height		Weight	Social Security Number	. . .
	First	Middle	Last		Feet	Inches			

FIGURE 4-10

Here, "file-name" must be the same as the file's file-name given in its **SELECT** clause in the Environment Division. The **BLOCK CONTAINS** clause is used when each physical record in the file contains more than one logical record (i.e., the records are "blocked"). In this case, "integer-1" denotes the total number of characters in a physical record. When the file's records are unblocked, the **BLOCK CONTAINS** clause is not required.

The **RECORD CONTAINS** clause identifies the number of characters in a logical record, denoted by "integer-2." This clause may be omitted when the logical record length is fixed by the file's device class, which is implementation dependent.

The **LABEL RECORDS** clause is always present, and identifies whether or not the file has **STANDARD** labels. The format of file labels is implementation dependent.

The **LINAGE** clause may be used only for print files. It defines the number of lines on a logical page as "value." "Value" itself denotes any integer-valued variable or constant. If the **LINAGE** clause is present, a system-generated **LINAGE-COUNTER** is available to the program. It contains an integer value which defines the next line to be written on the current page. Its value is maintained by the system and it may be referenced by the program.

Following the file's "file-description" is one or more of the "record descriptions," which define the structure and layout of a logical record in the file. Sometimes a file's records will have two, three, or more different structures, and thus will require two, three, or more different record-descriptions. The form of an individual record description is the same as that defined in section 4-2.2 for a record-description entry. Additionally, the number of character positions defined in the combined **PICTURE** clauses of the elementary items of a record description must be the same as the file's logical record size.

For example, reconsider the three files named CARDS, PAPER, and MAG-TAPE presented in the previous section, and assume additionally that the CARDS file is an input deck of standard 80-character punched cards, the PAPER file is an output file of 132-character-per-line paper, and the MAG-TAPE file is a sequence of 80-character records, combined into 800-character blocks. Furthermore, the tape file has standard labels (but the others do not) and a tape record has the layout shown in Figure 4-10. Then we could write file and record descriptions in the Data Division for these files as follows:

```
FD CARDS
    RECORD CONTAINS 80 CHARACTERS
    LABEL RECORDS ARE OMITTED.
```

```
01 CARDS-RECORD.
   02 CARD PIC X(80).
FD PAPER
   RECORD CONTAINS 133 CHARACTERS
   LABEL RECORDS ARE OMITTED
   LINAGE IS 60 LINES.
01 PAPER-RECORD.
   02 FILLER PIC X.
   02 DATA-LINE PIC X(132).
FD MAG-TAPE
   BLOCK CONTAINS 800 CHARACTERS
   RECORD CONTAINS 80 CHARACTERS
   LABEL RECORDS ARE STANDARD.
01 MAG-TAPE-RECORD.
   02 NAME.
      03 NFIRST      PIC X(10)
      03 MIDDLE      PIC X(5).
      03 LAST        PIC X(15).
   02 AGE            PIC 99.
   02 HEIGHT.
      03 FEET        PIC 9.
      03 INCHES      PIC 99.
   02 WEIGHT         PIC 999.
   02 SS-NO          PIC 9(9).
   02 FILLER         PIC X(33).
```

We should point out that the reserved word **FILLER** can be used to name any portion of a record which will not be referenced in the Procedure Division. This is the case for positions 48–80 of our MAG-TAPE-RECORD.

Note also that the PAPER file's record is 133 (not 132) characters long, with provision for one leading position at the beginning of its record description. This is an implementation-dependent characteristic. The extra position is used by the system for controlling vertical printer spacing, as dictated by **WRITE** statements (see below) for that file.

File Accessing in the Procedure Division A file is accessed during execution of a COBOL program whenever an **OPEN**, **CLOSE**, **READ**, **WRITE**, **REWRITE**, or **DELETE** statement is executed.

The **OPEN** statement initiates access to a file. No records may be read (written) from (to) a file before the file is opened. The **OPEN** statement has the following form:

```
     { INPUT  }
OPEN { OUTPUT } file-name-list
     { I-O    }
```

Here, ''file-name-list'' denotes a list of names of the files to be opened, mutually separated by comma-space (,b̸). The choice of **INPUT**, **OUTPUT**, or **I-O** depends on how the file is to be accessed. When the file is opened for **INPUT**, records may only be read from the file (sequentially or randomly) using the **READ** statement. When the file is opened for **OUTPUT**, records may be written to the file (sequentially or randomly) using the **WRITE** statement. When the file is opened for **I-O**, records may be read from the file (sequentially or randomly) using the **READ** statement, (re)written to the file randomly using the **WRITE** or **REWRITE** statement, rewritten to the file sequentially using the **REWRITE** statement, or deleted from the file (sequentially or randomly) using the **DELETE** statement.

The **CLOSE** statement terminates access to the file. It should occur only after all other accesses to the file have been completed. Its form is as follows:

CLOSE file-name-list

Execution of a **CLOSE** statement effectively disconnects the listed files from use by the program. However, any of these files may be subsequently accessed after another **OPEN** statement for that file has been executed.

The **READ** statement is used to transfer a single logical record from a file to the program. It has the following form:

READ file-name [**RECORD**]
  [**AT END** statement-1]
  [**INVALID KEY** statement-2]

Here, ''file-name'' denotes the file from which a record is to be read. The record itself is transferred to the area described by the record-description entry (or entries) for that file's description, and no conversion is performed. ''Statement-1'' denotes an imperative statement to be executed when end-of-file occurs. ''Statement-2'' denotes an imperative statement to be executed when an attempt to read a record from a randomly accessed file has been unsuccessfully made. That is, there is no record in the file whose key matches the current value of the variable whose data-name appears in the **RECORD KEY** clause of the file's **SELECT** statement in the Input-Output Section of the Environment Division. We will illustrate this in our COBOL program for Case Study 2 —Employee File Maintenance at the end of the chapter.

The **WRITE** statement is used to transfer a single record from the program to a file. It has the following form:

WRITE record-name

$$\text{[\textbf{AFTER} [\textbf{ADVANCING}]} \left\{ \begin{array}{l} \text{value \textbf{LINES}} \\ \text{\textbf{PAGE}} \end{array} \right\} \text{]}$$

[**AT END-OF-PAGE** statement-1]
[**INVALID KEY** statement-2]

''Record-name'' denotes the group-level name of some record-description entry for the file. The **AFTER** clause is used only for print files, and ''value'' denotes an integer variable or constant which denotes the number of lines to advance before the line is printed. The **PAGE** alternative denotes a skip to the top of the next page. The **AT END-OF-PAGE** clause is also used only for print files, and ''statement-1'' denotes an imperative statement to be executed whenever the last line of the current page has been reached.

The **INVALID KEY** clause is only used when the file had **INDEXED** organization. If it is accessed *sequentially,* the **INVALID KEY** condition occurs when an attempt is made to write a record whose key is less then or equal to that of the most recently written record. If the file is accessed *randomly,* the **INVALID KEY** condition occurs whenever an attempt is made to write a record whose key is *identical* with that of some other record in the file. In either case, ''statement-2'' denotes an imperative statement to be executed whenever the **INVALID KEY** condition occurs.

The **REWRITE** statement causes a record to be *replaced* in a file that resides on a direct access (DA) device. The file may be either a sequential or an indexed file. It has the following form:

REWRITE record-name
  [**INVALID KEY** statement-2]

If the file is sequential, then the most recently read record is replaced by that stored in ''record-name.'' If the file is indexed, the **INVALID KEY** clause is specified and has the same purpose as in the **WRITE** statement. Furthermore, if the file is an indexed file and is accessed sequentially, the most recently read record will be replaced by the one stored in ''record-name,'' and the **INVALID KEY** condition will be raised if its key is not identical with that of the most recently read record. If the indexed file is accessed randomly, the effect is the same as that of a **WRITE** statement. In either case, the file must have been opened in the input-output mode before any **REWRITE** statement can be executed.

Finally, the **DELETE** statement causes a record to be deleted from an **INDEXED** file. It has the following form:

DELETE file-name [**RECORD**]
  [**INVALID KEY** statement-2]

The file must be opened in the input-output mode for a **DELETE** statement to be valid for it, but it may be accessed either sequentially or randomly. If it is accessed sequentially, then the most recently read record is deleted. If it is accessed randomly, then the record whose key matches the current value of the variable containing the file's key is deleted from the file. Raising of the **INVALID KEY** condition on a **DELETE** statement is the same as that for the **REWRITE** statement.

To illustrate some of these statements, let us reconsider the files CARDS, PAPER, and MAG-TAPE defined above. The following Procedure Division statements will read the CARDS file, print it (doubled-spaced), and copy it to magnetic tape.

```
           OPEN INPUT CARDS, OUTPUT PAPER,
             OUTPUT MAG-TAPE.
       L1. MOVE SPACES TO DATA-LINE.
           WRITE PAPER-RECORD AFTER ADVANCING PAGE.
     LOOP. READ CARDS AT END GO TO ALL-DONE.
           MOVE CARD TO DATA-LINE, MAG-TAPE-RECORD.
           WRITE PAPER-RECORD AFTER ADVANCING 2 LINES
             AT END-OF-PAGE GO TO L1.
           GO TO LOOP.
 ALL-DONE. CLOSE CARDS, PAPER, MAG-TAPE.
           STOP RUN.
```

Further illustrations of these statements appear in the example program at the beginning of the chapter, as well as in the COBOL program for Case Study 2 at the end of the chapter.

4-2.7 Subprograms, Functions, and Libraries

In most programming situations, the task is large enough to warrant subdividing it into a number of functional blocks, or ''subprograms.'' These subprograms are linked together by a main program which controls the sequence in which they will be executed. COBOL provides facilities for writing subprograms. A COBOL subprogram is a complete program that has certain additional features which allow it to be invoked during the execution of another COBOL program or subprogram. In this section, we describe and illustrate these facilities. Our COBOL Case Study 2 program, shown in section 4-3.2, also illustrates COBOL subprograms.

Writing Subprograms The subprogram itself is actually a definition of a task, such as computing a factorial, to be performed. In COBOL, the following special provisions must be made when writing a subprogram.

1 The Data Division must contain a Linkage Section which defines the nature and structure of all variables that will be ''passed'' to the subprogram from the invoking program.

2 The Procedure Division header must be expanded to identify those variables and the order in which they should be given at the time the invoking program calls the subprogram.

3 The Procedure Division should contain an **EXIT** statement at location(s) where control should logically return to the invoking programs.

The Linkage Section immediately follows the Working-Storage Section in the Data Division. It contains a declaration of each parameter that will be passed to the subprogram, according to the same conventions used for defining ordinary variables and record-description entries in the Working-Storage Section. It begins with the following section header:

LINKAGE SECTION.

The Procedure Division header for subprograms has the following general form:

PROCEDURE DIVISION USING parameter-list.

Here, ''parameter-list'' denotes a list of the parameters defined in the Linkage Section, mutually separated by comma-space (,b̸).

The Procedure Division itself is written just as though it were an ordinary program performing its designated task. However, when it has completed the task, it must return control to the invoking program using the following statement:

p-name. **EXIT PROGRAM**.

As indicated, the **EXIT PROGRAM** statement must appear in a paragraph (named ''p-name'') by itself.

Two very good examples of COBOL subprograms appear in the solution for CASE Study 2, in Figures 4-12 and 4-13. They are called BVALID and EVALID, respectively. Each one of them has as its parameters EMPLOYEE, MSG, and MSG-PTR.

Invoking Subprograms Once written, a subprogram is invoked from another program via the **CALL** statement. The **CALL** statement also lists the particular variable(s) that will be identified with the subprogram's parameter throughout execution of the subprogram for the invocation. The **CALL** statement has the following form:

CALL 'name' **USING** variable-list

Here, ''name'' denotes the subprogram's name as defined in the **PROGRAM-ID** paragraph of its Identification Division. ''Variable-list'' denotes a list of those variables in the calling program's Data Division which are to be accessed by the subprogram during this particular invocation. There is a one-to-one, left-right correspondence between the variables in ''variable-list'' and the parameters in the subprogram's ''parameter-list.''

To illustrate, look at the COBOL main program for Case Study 2, shown in Figure 4-11. There, the subprograms BVALID and EVALID, each with the same variable-list, are called: EMPLOYEE, MSG, and MSG-PTR.

4-2.8 Additional Features

Although we cannot cover all of the various COBOL features in this chapter, several important additional features are presented in this section. The following are discussed in the paragraphs below:

- Additional COBOL stylistic options
- The **VALUE**, **REDEFINES**, and **JUSTIFIED** clauses
- The Debug and Library facilities
- The Sort-Merge facility
- The Report-Writer facility

Additional COBOL Stylistic Options The Identification Division in a COBOL program serves mainly as documentation. Although only its division header and the **PROGRAM-ID** paragraph are required there, additional paragraphs can optionally be written to further document the program. The general Identification Division syntax is as follows:

IDENTIFICATION DIVISION.
PROGRAM-ID. program-name.
[**AUTHOR**. comment.]
[**INSTALLATION**. comment.]
[**DATE-WRITTEN**. comment.]
[**DATE-COMPILED**. comment.]
[**SECURITY**. comment.]

Here, ''program-name'' denotes the name of the program and may be any unique non-reserved word (perhaps subject to other implementation-dependent restrictions). ''Comment'' denotes any private documentary information that identifies the author, the installation, and so forth.

The order of the four divisions, as well as the order of the various sections within the Environment and Data Divisions, must not vary. Additionally all 77-level items in the Working-Storage and Linkage sections of a program must physically precede all record descriptions in that section. The ordering of individual 77-level items or record-description entries among themselves, however, is immaterial.

Positions 1–6 of a line are normally left blank. Position 7 serves one of two purposes, as follows. If it contains an asterisk (*), the remainder of the line is taken as commentary documentation for the program. If it contains a dash (−), the remainder of the line has the continuation of a literal constant which would not entirely fit on the previous line. This is illustrated in the COBOL case study program in section 4-3.1.

Area A (positions 8–11) of the line is reserved for division headers, section headers, paragraph names, 01-level items in record-description entries, 77-level items and file-description (**FD**) entries. Each of these must begin *somewhere* within Area A, although not necessarily in position 8. All other elements of a program—principally words, statements, sentences, and non-01-level items of record-description entries—must be entirely within Area B, but need not begin exactly in position 12. Moreover, any such element may continue from one line of the program to the next, provided that its continuation is in Area B.

The VALUE, REDEFINES, and JUSTIFIED clauses One way to initialize the value of either a variable or elementary item in a record-description entry at the beginning of program execution is to give that initial value in a "**VALUE** clause," which has the following form:

VALUE [IS] literal

Here, "literal" denotes any numeric or nonnumeric constant which is consistent with the variable's **PICTURE**. For example, if we want to initialize the numeric variable named I with value 0 we could write either of the following declarations:

77 I **PIC** S9(5) **VALUE** 0.
77 I **PIC** S9(5) **VALUE ZERO**.

We note that this has rather restricted use, since a variable having the **OCCURS** clause or the **REDEFINES** clause cannot be initialized in this way. Furthermore, this convention can only be used in the Working-Storage Section of the Data Division.

The **REDEFINES** clause allows the program to rename a storage area in two or more different ways. This is useful, for instance, when a single eighty-character value is to be treated occasionally as eighty contiguous single-character values. It has the following form:

REDEFINES data-name

Here, "data-name" denotes the name of the area being redefined. The item which redefines that area must be declared immediately after it. For our example, consider the following declarations:

01 CARD-AREA.
  02 CARD **PIC** X(80).
  02 CARD-POS **REDEFINES** CARD **PIC** X **OCCURS** 80.

Now, if we want to reference the entire CARD-AREA as a single entity, we write CARD. If, on the other hand, we want to reference the Ith position (where I is an integer-valued variable) of the *same* CARD-AREA, we write CARD-POS (I).

The **JUSTIFIED** clause allows nonnumeric data being moved to a receiving area to be right-justified, rather than left-justified (which normally occurs if the **JUSTIFIED** clause is omitted). It has the following form:

JUSTIFIED [RIGHT]

This clause can be only used at the elementary level. For example, suppose we redeclare the CARD area as follows:

```
01 CARD-AREA.
   02 CARD PIC X(80) JUSTIFIED RIGHT.
```

Then the execution of the following **MOVE** statement

```
MOVE "ALLEN" TO CARD
```

leaves CARD with the value "ALLEN" in its rightmost five (rather than leftmost five) positions and blank-filled on the left (rather than on the right).

The Debug and Library Facilities To serve the programmer's needs for (1) tracing execution and dumping intermediate results during program testing, and (2) continually changing and extending existing programs, COBOL has facilities that ease the tedium of program modification and testing.

The Debug facility allows the programmer to add a "debugging algorithm" to a program while it is being tested. That algorithm may specify conditions under which to dump certain variables' values, initiate program trace, and so forth.

The Library facility permits the programmer to save certain often-used segments of COBOL source programs in a library, and then have one or more of them dynamically inserted into a program at compile time. A natural use for this facility occurs when a large record description (e.g., an employee master file's record description) is shared among several programs that use it. This permits writing and editing that record description only once, and then obtaining an automatic copy of it as it is needed, eliminating duplication of effort and the errors that would occur therein.

The Sort-Merge and Report-Writer Facilities File sorting and merging occurs so frequently in data processing applications that COBOL provides a very powerful facility to directly specify these actions within a program. To specify a file sort or merge, the program must make the following provisions.

1 Identify the file to be sorted (merged) in the File-Control paragraph of the Environment Division.

2 Describe the file to be sorted (merged) and its record layout in Sort Description (**SD**) entries of the File Section in the Data Division.

3 Specify that the sort or merge function be executed by writing a **SORT** or **MERGE** statement within the Procedure Division. Additional processing of records, as they either enter into or exit from the **SORT** or **MERGE** operation, is provided by the **RELEASE** and **RETURN** statements, respectively.

COBOL applications usually require one or more carefully formatted reports to be produced by the program. Coding for these reports can be extremely tedious using the ordinary COBOL output facilities described in section 4-2.6. The Report-Writer facility eases this burden by allowing the programmer to specify the physical layout of a report, rather than the program logic that would be required to produce that report.

To use the Report-Writer facility, a COBOL program must have the following elements.

In the Data Division:

1 A file-description (**FD**) entry in the File Section that identifies the output file where each report is to be written.

2 A Report Section, containing a description of each report to be generated.

In the Procedure Division:

1 Initialize the generation of a report, using the **INITIATE** statement.

2 Perform the generation of a report, using the **GENERATE** statement.

3 Complete the generation of a report, using the **TERMINATE** statement.

The program must also establish access to a sequential input file, whose individual records supply the basic data for the report. That file must be sorted according to some known set of fields, known as "controls." Whenever a record is read whose controls differ from those of the previous record, a "control break" is said to occur.

Space limitations prevent us from further describing the Sort-Merge and Report-Writer facilities in this book. The interested reader is referred to a COBOL text or reference manual for more detailed information.

4-3 APPLICATIONS OF COBOL

Now that the reader has a working knowledge of COBOL, we present and discuss a COBOL solution for Case Study 2—Employee File Maintenance. This presentation will expose some of the practical aspects of using COBOL in data processing applications. Following that, we will discuss certain implementation-dependent aspects of COBOL. Finally, we will give an overall evaluation of COBOL, using the nine evaluation criteria.

4-3.1 COBOL Case Study Implementation

The case study program was run using the following compiler and computer.

IBM 4341 OS/VS1 COBOL

It was implemented as a COBOL main program (called CASE2) and two subprograms (called BVALID and EVALID). These are shown in Figures 4-11, 4-12, and 4-13, respectively.

The main program, CASE2, controls the overall process. It reads an update record from the file UPDATES, verifies its SS-NO and its sequence, reads a corresponding record from the employee file (EMPFILE) if necessary, and performs the addition, change, or deletion appropriately.

The subprogram BVALID checks the satisfaction of the basic validity rules for an individual addition or change record. Similarly, EVALID checks the satisfaction of the extended validity rules. Note that when an error is found by either of these subprograms, an appropriate error message is placed within an available (blank) part of MSG. If MSG remains blank throughout the processing of a single update record, then the record is error-free. Otherwise, the error message MSG is printed (by EPRINT) together with the erroneous record.

This program was run using the master file, UPDATES file, and resulting master file given in Appendix B. The results of this run are shown in Figure 4-14, and indicate the efficiency of COBOL in the data processing application area.

4-3.2 Implementation-Dependent Extensions of COBOL

The implementation of COBOL presented here generally supports all the features of the 1974 COBOL standard. Moreover, many COBOL systems go far beyond the standard in supporting features that further enhance the quality of COBOL programming. In this section, we summarize the additional features found in two such compilers, the WATBOL compiler developed at the University of Waterloo,[4] and the IBM OS COBOL compiler.[5]

WATBOL Extensions of COBOL The WATBOL compiler contains facilities that enhance COBOL usage in a student programming environment. Its compile speed is unusually fast, and its compile-time and run-time diagnostics are unusually clear.

IBM OS Extensions of COBOL IBM's COBOL compiler supports interactive syntax checking at an on-line terminal as the program is being developed. Moreover, a number of compiler options are avilable which permit the selective generation of documentary information, such as cross-reference listings, storage maps and run-time statistics. Additional debugging statements are available, which supplement those found in the standard version's Debug Facility. Finally, this compiler supports floating-point data types and arithmetic, so that limited scientific applications can be done in COBOL.

4-3.3 Overall Evaluation of COBOL

This evaluation is based on our experience with COBOL in implementing Case Study 2, as shown in section 4.3.1.

1 Expressivity	Fair
2 Well-definedness	Good
3 Data types and structures	Fair
4 Modularity	Fair
5 Input-output facilities	Excellent
6 Portability	Good
7 Efficiency	Excellent
8 Pedagogy	Poor
9 Generality	Fair

```
 IDENTIFICATION DIVISION.
 PROGRAM-ID.  CASE2.

* COBOL IMPLEMENTATION OF CASE STUDY 2 - EMPLOYEE FILE MAINTENANCE.
* SUBPROGRAM 'BVALID' CHECKS ADDITIONS AND CHANGES AGAINST THE
* BASIC VALIDITY RULES.  'EVALID' CHECKS THE EXTENDED VALIDITY
* RULES.

 ENVIRONMENT DIVISION.
 CONFIGURATION SECTION.
   SOURCE-COMPUTER.  IBM-4341.
   OBJECT-COMPUTER.  IBM-4341.

 INPUT-OUTPUT SECTION.
   FILE-CONTROL.
     SELECT EMPFILE ASSIGN TO DA-I-EMPFILE,
                    NOMINAL KEY IS NSS-NO,
                    RECORD KEY IS SS-NO,
                    ACCESS MODE IS RANDOM.
     SELECT UPDATES ASSIGN TO UT-S-UPDATES.
     SELECT PAPER   ASSIGN TO UR-S-SYSPRINT.

 DATA DIVISION.
 FILE SECTION.
   FD EMPFILE RECORD CONTAINS 200 CHARACTERS
              LABEL RECORDS ARE STANDARD.
   01  EMPLOYEE.
     02  DELETE-CODE             PIC X.
     02  SS-NO                   PIC 9(10).
     02  EDATA                   PIC X(132).
     02  EDATA-FIELDS REDEFINES EDATA.
       03  ENAME               PIC X(40).
       03  EADDRESS            PIC X(37).
       03  ESEX                PIC X.
       03  EMARITAL            PIC X.
       03  EBIRTH              PIC X(6).
       03  EDATE               PIC X(6).
       03  EJOB-STATUS         PIC X(19).
       03  EDEDUCTIONS         PIC X(22).
     02  YEAR-TO-DATE.
       03  GROSS               PIC 9(6)V99.
       03  FED-TAX             PIC 9(5)V99.
       03  FICA                PIC 9(4)V99.
       03  STATE-TAX           PIC 9(4)V99.
       03  HEALTH-INS          PIC 999V99.
       03  LIFE-INS            PIC 9(4)V99.
       03  CREDIT-UNION        PIC 999V99.
       03  STOCK-PURCHASE      PIC 9(4)V99.
       03  NET                 PIC 9(6)V99.


   FD UPDATES RECORD CONTAINS 150 CHARACTERS
              LABEL RECORDS ARE STANDARD.
   01  URECORD.
     02  UCODE                 PIC X.
       88  ADDITION VALUE 'A'.
       88  DELETION VALUE 'D'.
       88  CHANGE   VALUE 'C'.
     02  USS-NO                PIC 9(10).
     02  USS-NO-A REDEFINES USS-NO.
       03  USS-VAL             PIC 9(9).
       03  USS-CK              PIC 9.
```

FIGURE 4-11

```
    02  UDATA                 PIC X(132).
    02  UDATA-FLDS REDEFINES UDATA.
      03  UNAME               PIC X(40).
      03  UADDRESS            PIC X(37).
      03  USEX                PIC X.
      03  UMARITAL            PIC X.
      03  UBIRTH              PIC X(6).
      03  UDATE               PIC X(6).
      03  UJOB-STATUS         PIC X(19).
      03  UDEDUCTIONS         PIC X(22).
    02  FILLER                PIC X(7).

  FD PAPER RECORD CONTAINS 133 CHARACTERS
           LABEL RECORDS ARE OMITTED.
  01 PRINT-LINE.
    02  FILLER                PIC X.
    02  A-LINE.
      03  DATA-AREA           PIC X(100).
      03  FILLER              PIC X.
      03  MSG-AREA            PIC X(19).
    03  FILLER                PIC X(12).

WORKING-STORAGE SECTION.
  77  NSS-NO                  PIC 9(10).
  77  MSG                     PIC X(150).
  77  MSG-PTR                 PIC 9(5) COMPUTATIONAL.
  77  MSG-PTRA                PIC 9(5) COMPUTATIONAL VALUE 0.
  77  REST-AREA               PIC X(50).
  77  NR                      PIC 9(5) VALUE 0.
  01  HEADING-LINE-1.
    02  FILLER                PIC X.
    02  HDG-A PIC X(79)   VALUE 'FILE MAINTENANCE ERROR LOG'.
    02  HDG-B PIC X(5)    VALUE 'PAGE '.
    02  PNO   PIC 9(3)    VALUE 0.
  01  HEADING-LINE-2.
    02  FILLER                PIC X.
    02  HDG-C PIC X(101)  VALUE 'RECORD CONTENTS'.
    02  HDG-D PIC X(19)   VALUE 'ERROR DESCRIPTION'.
  01  QUO.
    02  Q                     PIC 9(9).
    02  QR REDEFINES Q.
      03  FILLER              PIC 9(8).
      03  Q-UNITS             PIC 9.


  01  FOOTING-LINE-1.
    02  FILLER                PIC X.
    02  FTG-A  PIC X(25)  VALUE 'END MAINTENANCE RUN.'.
    02  FILLER PIC X(107) VALUE SPACES.
  01  FOOTING-LINE-2.
    02  FILLER                PIC X.
    02  ND                    PIC 9(5) VALUE 0.
    02  FTG-B                 PIC X(15) VALUE ' DELETIONS,   '.
    02  NA                    PIC 9(5) VALUE 0.
    02  FTG-C                 PIC X(15) VALUE ' ADDITIONS,   '.
    02  NC                    PIC 9(5) VALUE 0.
    02  FTG-D                 PIC X(15) VALUE ' CHANGES,     '.
    02  NE                    PIC 9(5) VALUE 0.
    02  FTG-E                 PIC X(15) VALUE ' ERRORS.      '.
    02  FILLER                PIC X(52) VALUE SPACES.

PROCEDURE DIVISION.
INITIALIZATION.
    OPEN INPUT UPDATES, OUTPUT PAPER, I-O EMPFILE.
    PERFORM HEADING-PRINT.
    PERFORM MAIN-LOOP VARYING NR FROM 0 BY 1 UNTIL NR < 0.
```

FIGURE 4-11 *(Continued)*

```
MAIN-LOOP.
    MOVE SPACES TO MSG.
    MOVE 1 TO MSG-PTR.
    READ UPDATES            AT END GO TO END-OF-RUN.
    PERFORM SS-CHECK.
    IF MSG NOT = SPACES     GO TO MAIN-LOOP-END.
    MOVE USS-NO TO SS-NO, NSS-NO.
    IF DELETION PERFORM PROCESS-DELETION
      ELSE IF ADDITION PERFORM PROCESS-ADDITION
        ELSE IF CHANGE PERFORM PROCESS-CHANGE
          ELSE STRING MSG, 'INVALID UPDATE CODE. '
               DELIMITED BY SIZE INTO MSG WITH POINTER MSG-PTR.
MAIN-LOOP-END.
    IF MSG NOT = SPACES PERFORM EPRINT.

SS-CHECK.
* CHECK VALIDITY OF UPDATE'S SOCIAL SECURITY NUMBER.
    IF USS-NO NOT NUMERIC
      STRING 'INVALID SS-NO.' DELIMITED BY SIZE INTO MSG
              WITH POINTER MSG-PTR
      ELSE DIVIDE USS-VAL BY 11 GIVING Q
           IF Q-UNITS NOT = USS-CK
             STRING 'INVALID SS-NO. ' DELIMITED BY SIZE INTO MSG
                    WITH POINTER MSG-PTR.

PROCESS-DELETION.
    IF UDATA NOT = SPACES
      STRING 'INVALID UPDATE RECORD. ' DELIMITED BY SIZE
             INTO MSG WITH POINTER MSG-PTR
      ELSE READ EMPFILE
           INVALID KEY STRING 'DELETION NOT ON FILE. '
                DELIMITED BY SIZE INTO MSG WITH POINTER MSG-PTR.
    IF MSG = SPACES
      ADD 1 TO ND
      MOVE HIGH-VALUES TO DELETE-CODE
      REWRITE EMPLOYEE.

PROCESS-ADDITION.
    READ EMPFILE
      INVALID KEY GO TO ADD-OK.
    STRING 'ADDITION SS-NO ALREADY ON FILE. '
      DELIMITED BY SIZE INTO MSG WITH POINTER MSG-PTR.
    GO TO ADD-EXIT.
ADD-OK.
    MOVE UDATA TO EDATA.
    MOVE LOW-VALUES TO DELETE-CODE.
    MOVE ZEROS TO YEAR-TO-DATE.
    CALL 'BVALID' USING EMPLOYEE, MSG, MSG-PTR.
    IF MSG = SPACES
      CALL 'EVALID' USING EMPLOYEE, MSG, MSG-PTR
      IF MSG = SPACES
        WRITE EMPLOYEE
        ADD 1 TO NA.
ADD-EXIT. EXIT.
```

FIGURE 4-11 *(Continued)*

```
PROCESS-CHANGE.
    READ EMPFILE
      INVALID KEY STRING 'CHANGE SS-NO NOT ON FILE. '
        DELIMITED BY SIZE INTO MSG WITH POINTER MSG-PTR.
    IF MSG NOT = SPACES GO TO CHG-EXIT.
    IF UNAME        NOT = SPACES MOVE UNAME        TO ENAME        .
    IF UADDRESS     NOT = SPACES MOVE UADDRESS     TO EADDRESS     .
    IF USEX         NOT = SPACES MOVE USEX         TO ESEX         .
    IF UMARITAL     NOT = SPACES MOVE UMARITAL     TO EMARITAL     .
    IF UBIRTH       NOT = SPACES MOVE UBIRTH       TO EBIRTH       .
    IF UDATE        NOT = SPACES MOVE UDATE        TO EDATE        .
    IF UJOB-STATUS NOT = SPACES MOVE UJOB-STATUS TO EJOB-STATUS.
    IF UDEDUCTIONS NOT = SPACES MOVE UDEDUCTIONS TO EDEDUCTIONS.
    CALL 'BVALID' USING EMPLOYEE, MSG, MSG-PTR.
    IF MSG = SPACES
      CALL 'EVALID' USING EMPLOYEE, MSG, MSG-PTR
      IF MSG = SPACES
        REWRITE EMPLOYEE
        ADD 1 TO NC.
CHG-EXIT. EXIT.

EPRINT.
* PRINT AN ERROR UPDATE RECORD AND MESSAGES.
    ADD 1 TO NE.
    MOVE 1 TO MSG-PTRA.
    UNSTRING URECORD INTO DATA-AREA, REST-AREA.
    UNSTRING MSG INTO MSG-AREA WITH POINTER MSG-PTRA.
    WRITE PRINT-LINE AFTER ADVANCING 2 LINES
      AT END-OF-PAGE PERFORM HEADING-PRINT.
    MOVE REST-AREA TO DATA-AREA.
    UNSTRING MSG INTO MSG-AREA WITH POINTER MSG-PTRA.
    WRITE PRINT-LINE AFTER ADVANCING 1 LINES
      AT END-OF-PAGE PERFORM HEADING-PRINT.
    MOVE SPACES TO DATA-AREA.
EP-LOOP.
    IF MSG-PTRA > MSG-PTR GO TO EP-EXIT.
    UNSTRING MSG INTO MSG-AREA WITH POINTER MSG-PTRA.
    WRITE PRINT-LINE AFTER ADVANCING 1 LINES
      AT END-OF-PAGE PERFORM HEADING-PRINT.
    GO TO EP-LOOP.
EP-EXIT. EXIT.

HEADING-PRINT.
    ADD 1 TO PNO.
    WRITE PRINT-LINE FROM HEADING-LINE-1 AFTER ADVANCING PAGE.
    WRITE PRINT-LINE FROM HEADING-LINE-2 AFTER ADVANCING 2 LINES.

END-OF-RUN.
    WRITE PRINT-LINE FROM FOOTING-LINE-1 AFTER ADVANCING PAGE.
    WRITE PRINT-LINE FROM FOOTING-LINE-2 AFTER ADVANCING 2 LINES.
    CLOSE EMPFILE, UPDATES, PAPER.
    STOP RUN.
```

FIGURE 4-11 (*Continued*)

```
 IDENTIFICATION DIVISION.
 PROGRAM-ID.  BVALID.
* SUBPROGRAM TO CHECK AN EMPLOYEE RECORD'S COMPLIANCE WITH THE
* BASIC VALIDITY RULES, AND LEAVE AN APPROPRIATE MESSAGE IN 'MSG'
* FOR EACH ERROR DETECTED.
 ENVIRONMENT DIVISION.
 CONFIGURATION SECTION.
   SOURCE-COMPUTER.  IBM-4341.
   OBJECT-COMPUTER.  IBM-4341.

 DATA DIVISION.
 WORKING-STORAGE SECTION.
   77  Q                         PIC 9(5) COMPUTATIONAL.
   77  R                         PIC 9(5) COMPUTATIONAL.
   01  DATE-FORMS.
     02  D                       PIC X(6).
     02  MMDDYY REDEFINES D.
       03  MM                    PIC 99.
       03  DD                    PIC 99.
       03  YY                    PIC 99.
   01  DTBL.
     02  DATEX  PIC X(24) VALUE '312831303130313130313031'.
     02  DATES  REDEFINES DATEX PIC 99 OCCURS 12.
   01  DATE-VALIDITY.
     02  DATE-VALIDITY-CODE      PIC X.
       88  VALID-DATE            VALUE 'Y'.
       88  INVALID-DATE          VALUE 'N'.

 LINKAGE SECTION.
   77  MSG                       PIC X(150).
   77  MSG-PTR                   PIC 9(5) COMPUTATIONAL.
   01  EMPLOYEE.
     02  FILLER                  PIC X.
     02  SS-NO                   PIC 9(10).
     02  NAME.
       03  NLAST                 PIC X(15).
       03  NFIRST                PIC X(15).
       03  NMIDDLE               PIC X(10).
     02  EADDRESS.
       03  STREET                PIC X(15).
       03  CITY                  PIC X(15).
       03  STATE                 PIC X(2).
         88  VALID-STATE VALUES     'AL' 'AK' 'AR' 'AZ' 'CA' 'CO'
     'CT' 'DL' 'FL' 'GA' 'HA' 'ID' 'IL' 'IN' 'IO' 'KA' 'KY' 'LA'
     'MA' 'MD' 'ME' 'MI' 'MN' 'MO' 'MS' 'MT' 'NB' 'NE' 'NH' 'NJ'
     'NM' 'NY' 'NC' 'ND' 'OH' 'OK' 'OR' 'PA' 'RI' 'SC' 'SD' 'TN'
     'TX' 'UT' 'VA' 'VT' 'WA' 'WI' 'WV' 'WY'.
       03  ZIP                   PIC X(5).
     02  SEX                     PIC X.
         88  VALID-SEX               VALUES 'M' 'F'.
     02  MARITAL                 PIC X.
         88  VALID-MARITAL           VALUES 'S' 'M'.
     02  BIRTH                   PIC X(6).
     02  DATE-EMPLOYED           PIC X(6).
     02  JOB-STATUS.
       03  POSN                  PIC 99.
         88  VALID-POSITION VALUES 1, 5, 10, 15 THRU 19, 20, 25,
             30, 35, 40 THRU 45, 60, 70, 80, 90, 99.
       03  DAT                   PIC X(6).
       03  DEPT                  PIC 999.
         88  VALID-DEPT VALUES 1 THRU 60, 100 THRU 143, 300 THRU
             320, 400 THRU 420, 500 THRU 530.
```

FIGURE 4-12

```
      03  SALARY.
        04  SBASIS             PIC X.
          88  VALID-BASIS VALUES 'H' 'W' 'M'.
        04  RATE               PIC 9(5)V99.
    02  DEDUCTIONS.
      03  NO-DEPENDENTS        PIC 99.
      03  HEALTH-INS           PIC 999V99.
      03  LIFE-INS             PIC 999V99.
      03  CREDIT-UNION         PIC 999V99.
      03  STOCK-PURCHASE       PIC 999V99.
    02  YEAR-TO-DATE           PIC X(57).

PROCEDURE DIVISION USING EMPLOYEE, MSG, MSG-PTR.
BEGIN-BVALID.
    IF NLAST IS ALPHABETIC AND NLAST NOT = SPACES AND
       NFIRST IS ALPHABETIC AND NFIRST NOT = SPACES
       NEXT SENTENCE
    ELSE STRING 'INVALID NAME. '
            DELIMITED BY SIZE INTO MSG WITH POINTER MSG-PTR.

    IF STREET NOT = SPACES AND
       CITY IS ALPHABETIC AND CITY NOT = SPACES AND
       VALID-STATE AND
       ZIP IS NUMERIC
       NEXT SENTENCE
    ELSE STRING 'INVALID ADDRESS. '
            DELIMITED BY SIZE INTO MSG WITH POINTER MSG-PTR.

    IF VALID-SEX AND VALID-MARITAL
       NEXT SENTENCE
    ELSE STRING 'INVALID SEX OR MARITAL. '
            DELIMITED BY SIZE INTO MSG WITH POINTER MSG-PTR.
    MOVE 'Y' TO DATE-VALIDITY-CODE.
    MOVE BIRTH TO D.             PERFORM ISDATE.
    MOVE DATE-EMPLOYED TO D.  PERFORM ISDATE.
    MOVE DAT TO D.               PERFORM ISDATE.
    IF INVALID-DATE
       STRING 'INVALID BIRTH-DATE, DATE-EMPLOYED, OR DATE. '
            DELIMITED BY SIZE INTO MSG WITH POINTER MSG-PTR.
    IF POSN IS NUMERIC AND DEPT IS NUMERIC
       IF VALID-POSITION AND VALID-DEPT
         NEXT SENTENCE
         ELSE STRING 'INVALID POSITION OR DEPT. '
            DELIMITED BY SIZE INTO MSG WITH POINTER MSG-PTR
    ELSE STRING 'INVALID POSITION OR DEPT. '
         DELIMITED BY SIZE INTO MSG WITH POINTER MSG-PTR.

    IF VALID-BASIS AND RATE IS NUMERIC
                AND NO-DEPENDENTS IS NUMERIC
       IF NO-DEPENDENTS NOT > 20
         NEXT SENTENCE
         ELSE STRING 'INVALID NO OF DEPENDENTS. '
            DELIMITED BY SIZE INTO MSG WITH POINTER MSG-PTR
    ELSE STRING 'INVALID BASIS, RATE, OR NO OF DEPENDENTS. '
         DELIMITED BY SIZE INTO MSG WITH POINTER MSG-PTR.

    IF HEALTH-INS IS NUMERIC AND LIFE-INS IS NUMERIC AND
       CREDIT-UNION IS NUMERIC AND STOCK-PURCHASE IS NUMERIC
       NEXT SENTENCE
    ELSE STRING 'INVALID INSURANCE, CREDIT-UNION, OR STOCK. '
         DELIMITED BY SIZE INTO MSG WITH POINTER MSG-PTR.
```

FIGURE 4-12 *(Continued)*

```
END-BVALID. EXIT PROGRAM.

* SET DATE-VALIDITY-CODE TO 'N' IF D IS NOT A VALID DATE.
ISDATE.
    IF MM NOT NUMERIC OR DD NOT NUMERIC OR YY NOT NUMERIC
       MOVE 'N' TO DATE-VALIDITY-CODE
    ELSE IF MM < 1 OR MM > 12 MOVE 'N' TO DATE-VALIDITY-CODE
         ELSE DIVIDE YY BY 4 GIVING Q REMAINDER R
              IF R = 0 DIVIDE YY BY 100 GIVING Q REMAINDER R
                       IF R = 0 MOVE 28 TO DATES (2)
                       ELSE MOVE 29 TO DATES (2)
              ELSE MOVE 28 TO DATES (2).
    IF VALID-DATE
       IF DD < 1 OR DD > DATES (MM)
          MOVE 'N' TO DATE-VALIDITY-CODE.
END-ISDATE. EXIT.
```

FIGURE 4-12 *(Continued)*

COBOL's fair "expressivity" stems from the basic problem that in order to express a little, one has to write a lot. Even a "null program," one which does nothing, requires a minimum of about 150 symbols (division headers, section headers, etc.)! Moreover, the inability to abbreviate most keywords or express arithmetic using simple expressions compounds this problem. The argument that an English-like syntax makes programs self-documenting and easy to pass among programmers is questionable at best.

COBOL's fair "data types and structures" stems mainly from its lack of support for any dynamic storage allocation; all storage is allocated at compile time, statically, and thus many dynamic processes can be at best simulated using static storage in large amounts. Also, there are some nit-picking restrictions on the use of some clauses in the Data Division which also make programming unnecessarily difficult. Among these are the inability to initialize an array (table) with multiple different values and the unnecessary dichotomy between the "index" and the "integer variable" when dealing with tables and subscripts.

COBOL's "modularity" is also deemed fair, mainly because of its cumbersome support for subroutines and its lack of provision for external, or common, variables. Morever, its structured programming support is somewhat restricted as well. For example, consider the following valid COBOL sentence:

IF condition
  statement-1
  statement-2
  READ filename **AT END** statement-3
  statement-4.

Here, assume also that each of "statement-1" through "statement-4" is an unconditional statement. Our intention is that all of the last four lines be executed when "condition" is true. However, a closer look at COBOL syntax will reveal that "statement-4"

```
 IDENTIFICATION DIVISION.
 PROGRAM-ID.  EVALID.
* SUBPROGRAM TO CHECK AN EMPLOYEE RECORD'S VALIDITY IN ACCORDANCE
* WITH THE EXTENDED VALIDITY RULES.  AS ERRORS ARE FOUND,
* APPROPRIATE MESSAGES ARE LEFT IN MSG.
 ENVIRONMENT DIVISION.
 CONFIGURATION SECTION.
   SOURCE-COMPUTER.  IBM-4341.
   OBJECT-COMPUTER.  IBM-4341.

 DATA DIVISION.
 WORKING-STORAGE SECTION.
   77  EGROSS                 PIC 9(8)V99.

 LINKAGE SECTION.
   77  MSG                    PIC X(150).
   77  MSG-PTR                PIC 9(5) COMPUTATIONAL.
   01  EMPLOYEE.
     02  FILLER               PIC X.
     02  SS-NO                PIC 9(10).
     02  NAME.
       03  NLAST              PIC X(15).
       03  NFIRST             PIC X(15).
       03  NMIDDLE            PIC X(10).
     02  EADDRESS.
       03  STREET             PIC X(15).
       03  CITY               PIC X(15).
       03  STATE              PIC X(2).
       03  ZIP                PIC X(5).
     02  SEX                  PIC X.
     02  MARITAL              PIC X.
     02  BIRTH.
       03  FILLER             PIC XXXX.
       03  BIRTH-YEAR         PIC 99.
     02  DATE-EMPLOYED.
       03  FILLER             PIC XXXX.
       03  EMPLOYED-YEAR      PIC 99.
     02  JOB-STATUS.
       03  POSN               PIC 99.
       03  DAT.
         04  FILLER           PIC XXXX.
         04  DATE-YEAR        PIC 99.
       03  DEPT               PIC 999.
       03  SALARY.
         04  SBASIS           PIC X.
         04  RATE             PIC 9(5)V99.
     02  DEDUCTIONS.
       03  NO-DEPENDENTS      PIC 99.
       03  HEALTH-INS         PIC 999V99.
         88  VALID-HEALTH-INS     VALUES 0, 6.
       03  LIFE-INS           PIC 999V99.
         88  VALID-LIFE-INS       VALUES 0, 3, 5, 7, 8.
       03  CREDIT-UNION       PIC 999V99.
       03  STOCK-PURCHASE     PIC 999V99.
     02  YEAR-TO-DATE         PIC X(57).

 PROCEDURE DIVISION USING EMPLOYEE, MSG, MSG-PTR.
 BEGIN-EVALID.
     IF BIRTH-YEAR NOT < EMPLOYED-YEAR OR
        EMPLOYED-YEAR > DATE-YEAR
     STRING 'INCONSISTENT DATES. '
        DELIMITED BY SIZE INTO MSG WITH POINTER MSG-PTR.
```

FIGURE 4-13

```
    IF POSN NOT > 20 AND SBASIS = 'H' AND
       RATE NOT < 1.25 AND RATE NOT > 10.00
       NEXT SENTENCE
    ELSE IF POSN NOT < 25 AND POSN NOT > 60 AND SBASIS = 'W' AND
       RATE NOT < 60 AND RATE NOT > 400
       NEXT SENTENCE
    ELSE IF POSN > 60 AND SBASIS = 'M' AND
       RATE NOT < 400 AND RATE NOT > 10000
       NEXT SENTENCE
    ELSE STRING 'INVALID POSITION, BASIS, OR RATE. '
            DELIMITED BY SIZE INTO MSG WITH POINTER MSG-PTR.

    IF VALID-HEALTH-INS AND VALID-LIFE-INS
       NEXT SENTENCE
    ELSE STRING 'INVALID HEALTH OR LIFE INSURANCE. '
            DELIMITED BY SIZE INTO MSG WITH POINTER MSG-PTR.

    IF SBASIS = 'M'
       MOVE RATE TO EGROSS
    ELSE IF SBASIS = 'W'
       MULTIPLY 4.4 BY RATE GIVING EGROSS
    ELSE MULTIPLY 160 BY RATE GIVING EGROSS.
    MULTIPLY EGROSS BY 0.05 GIVING EGROSS.
    IF CREDIT-UNION > EGROSS OR STOCK-PURCHASE > EGROSS
       STRING 'INVALID CREDIT UNION OR STOCK PURCHASE. '
          DELIMITED BY SIZE INTO MSG WITH POINTER MSG-PTR.

END-EVALID. EXIT PROGRAM.
```

FIGURE 4-13 *(Continued)*

is executed (together with "statement-3") *only* if end-of-file occurs upon execution of the **READ** statement.

COBOL's excellent input-output facilities arise out of its strong support for the various file manipulation functions found in data processing applications. Moreover, its Sort-Merge, Report-Writer, and other special features greatly simplify the task of the data processing programmer.

Efficiency is excellent in COBOL mainly because nothing occurs "by default" in a program. If a conversion of data from one form to another is needed, the program must explicitly specify this. Moreover, all storage is statically allocated, which eliminates the overhead required for dynamic storage management.

Our poor view of COBOL "pedagogy" stems from the fact that it is very difficult to introduce it to the novice without teaching a lot of overhead that is functionally useless.

FIGURE 4-14
EFFICIENCY OF COBOL CASE STUDY 2 PROGRAM

Implementation	Compile speed	Execution speed
1 IBM 4341 OS/VS1 COBOL	3.5 sec	0.1 sec

A great deal must be known about input-output requirements, conversion, and the limitations of the arithmetic statements before even the simplest program is written. The vast assortment of COBOL textbooks now on the market doesn't do much to alleviate this problem. The ''simple'' example program at the beginning of this chatper illustrates this point very well.

Finally, COBOL's fair ''generality'' arises simply from the observation that it was intended all along to be just a data processing language. It's not likely that a scientist or a systems programmer would ever be tempted to choose COBOL over, say, FORTRAN or Assembly language for a serious task.

EXERCISES

1 Write a COBOL (sub)program which will be called to convert a date in any one of the following three forms to any other.
(a) yyddd (e.g., 85165)
(b) MMMbDD,bYYYY (e.g., JUNb14,b1985)
(c) MM/dd/yy (e.g., 6/14/85)
Also, the program should check the validity of the date before it converts it, returning an appropriate error indication if the date is invalid.

2 If the COBOL standard did not have the **STRING** and **UNSTRING** statements, how could they be simulated?

3 The **STRING**, **UNSTRING**, and **INSPECT** statements are a key to COBOL's utility in the text processing application area. Try using COBOL to implement Case Study 3—Text Formatter, and evaluate it from your results.

4 Given a ''telephone directory'' file NAMES whose records are structured as follows:

```
01 PHONES.
   02 NAME    PIC X(15).
   02 PHONE   PIC X(17).
```

Write COBOL statements that will display all persons whose names begin with the letter ''A'', together with their phone numbers.

5 Revise the averaging program given at the beginning of the chapter so that it averages only the *positive* numbers in the input, rather than all of them.

6 Write a subprogram named ZEROS which counts the number of zero entries in an M × N table A of **PIC** 9(5) values.

7 What are the main differences between a COBOL **PERFORM** statement and a Pascal **for** statement?

8 What is the main difference between a numeric variable and a numeric edited variable, in terms of how it can be used within the PROCEDURE DIVISION?

9 For each of the COBOL characteristics given below, discuss how it influences the nine evaluation criteria given in Chapter 1.
(a) Use of the period at the end of a group of statements.
(b) Reserved words.
(c) The Sort and Report-Writer features.
(d) The **VALUE** clause.
(e) The use of blanks within a statement.

10 Given the following declarations:

```
01 DAY-TABLE.
   02 FIRST-DAY OCCURS 12 PIC 999.
01 YYDDD.
   02 YY          PIC 9.
   02 DDD         PIC 999.
01 MMDDYY.
   02 MM          PIC 99.
   02 DD          PIC 99.
   02 YY          PIC 99.
```

Assume also that the array FIRST-DAY contains the day of the year on which the first day of each month falls [i.e., FIRST-DAY (1) is 001, FIRST-DAY (2) is 032, and so forth]. Write COBOL statements which will convert a date stored in YYDDD to an equivalent month, day, and year and store the result in MMDDYY. For instance, if YYDDD is 85033, your statements should leave 020285 in MMDDYY. (Accommodate leap years.)

11 If your computer, operation system, or COBOL compiler differs from the ones used here, rerun our case study program. Does it compile successfully? Does it execute properly? If your answer to either of these questions is no, what changes must be made so that they will compile and execute properly?

12 If Case Study 0 (which you defined at the end of Chapter 1) is a data processing application, implement it in COBOL. Gather and record its efficiency as we did for Case Study 2.

13 If your COBOL system supports floating-point arithmetic, try implementing Case Study 1—Matrix Inversion in COBOL. Evaluate COBOL as a scientific language from your results.

REFERENCES

1 *American National Standard Programming Language COBOL,* American National Standards Institute (ANSI), ANS X3.23–1968, New York, 1968.

2 *American National Standard Programming Language COBOL,* ANSI, ANS X3.23–1974, New York, 1974.

3 *Draft Proposed Revised X3.23 ANS Programming Language COBOL,* Technical Committee X3J4, ANSI, New York, September 1981.

4 WATBOL Users Guide, University of Waterloo, Waterloo, Ontario, 1978.

5 *IBM VS COBOL for OS/VS,* IBM Corporation, White Plains, N.Y., 1981.

CHAPTER **5**

PL/I

5-1 INTRODUCTION TO PL/I

PL/I is a general-purpose language, designed intentionally to support scientific, data processing, text processing, and systems programming applications at a very high level. In this chapter we will study PL/I and evaluate its effectiveness in the data processing area, and also evaluate the advantages and disadvantages of general-purpose languages, as exemplified by PL/I.

5-1.1 Brief History of PL/I

The first version of PL/I was presented by the Advanced Language Development Committee of the SHARE FORTRAN project.[1] This version was called NPL (New Programming Language). It was first implemented in 1965 by IBM, under the name PL/I.

PL/I was slow to gain acceptance in the 1960s. Its first compilers were inefficient and unreliable. Although its programming features were many and varied, PL/I was not considered an acceptable alternative to the established languages of the time, notably COBOL and FORTRAN. However, PL/I did later gain significant usage, and has steadily improved in the efficiency of its compilers.

In February 1975 a Draft Proposed Standard for PL/I was published jointly by Technical Committee X3J1-PL/I of the American National Standards Institute and Technical Committee TC10-PL/I of the European Computer Manufacturers Association. These two groups adopted the draft standard in 1976.[2] We will use this standard version of PL/I as our basis for discussion and evaluation in this chapter.

More recently, recognition has been given to the fact that some features of PL/I are so extensive that they become difficult to teach, implement, or effectively utilize. In response, a refinement of Standard PL/I, called "Subset/G PL/I," was developed and standardized in 1981.[3] Subset/G was designed to preserve the most useful features of PL/I, including its general-purpose flavor, while deleting generalizations that were of little use, difficult to implement, or inappropriate to good programming practice. Moreover, Subset/G is implemented on microcomputers (unlike the full Standard PL/I), thus widening the range of PL/I's applications.

5-1.2 Implementations and Variation of PL/I

Since its first implementation in 1965, PL/I compilers have been developed for a number of computer systems, including the following:

Burroughs
CDC
Digital
Honeywell
IBM

Subset compilers have also been developed for PL/I by Microsoft for various microcomputers that run under the CP/M operating system,[4] and by Cornell University.[5] Implementations of PL/I are not, nevertheless, as widespread as those of other languages. This is mainly due to PL/I's overall complexity and the industry's general reluctance to migrate away from older languages which have more efficient implementations.

5-1.3 Major Applications of PL/I

Unlike most other languages, PL/I is intentionally designed as a general-purpose language. It was intended to be equally effective in scientific, data processing, text processing, and systems programming applications, and to replace the dominant language in each of these areas. However, that has not occurred; FORTRAN is still dominant in scientific and engineering applications, COBOL still prevails in data processing, and assembly language is still the preferred systems programming language. PL/I has been used effectively, however, in the design and implementation of *large* systems that require robust and advanced programming features for file processing and text processing combined within a *single* language.

Our PL/I program for Case Study 2 will allow us to directly evaluate PL/I for data processing applications, and will thus permit direct comparison with COBOL in Chapter 4.

5-2 WRITING PL/I PROGRAMS

A PL/I program, in its simplest form, consists of a PROCEDURE statement, a series of declarations (for variables, files, arrays, etc.), one or more "on units" for handling exceptions, a series of statements, and finally an END statement. There are no "reserved words" in PL/I, and thus any series of letters can be used for variable names or any other purpose within an individual program.

Below is a simple PL/I program which computes and displays the average of an indeterminate number of input numbers. For instance, if the input were 85.5, 87.5, 89.5, and 91.5 the result displayed would be 88.5. The program uses the variable X to hold a single input number and the variable N to determine the number of input numbers in the process. The variables SUM and AV connote the numbers' sum and average, respectively.

```
AVERAGE: PROCEDURE OPTIONS (MAIN);

     /* THIS PROGRAM COMPUTES THE AVERAGE 'AV' OF 'N' INPUT
      NUMBERS 'X' */

     DCL (X, SUM, AV) FLOAT,
          N FIXED BINARY;

     ON ENDFILE(SYSIN) BEGIN;
          AV=SUM/N;
          PUT SKIP LIST (N, ' NUMBERS WERE GIVEN');
          PUT SKIP LIST (AV, ' IS THEIR AVERAGE');
          STOP;
        END;

        N=0; SUM=0;
        GET LIST (X);
        DO WHILE('1'B);
           N=N+1;
           SUM=SUM+X;
           GET LIST (X);
        END;

     END AVERAGE;
```

The different types of statements in this program will be explained later. Generally, the semicolon is used to terminate statements and DO . . . END, BEGIN . . . END, and PROCEDURE . . . END are used to group statements. Thus, the statements following "DO WHILE('1'B);" are treated as a group to be repeated until the end of the input "ENDFILE(SYSIN)" occurs. Note that the format of a PL/I program is freely determined by the programmer. The style of indenting shown here is a fairly conventional one that facilitates program readability. Note also that comments in a PL/I program may be inserted anywhere, provided that they are enclosed within the delimiters /* and */. We see that only the uppercase alphabet (A–Z) can be used in writing PL/I programs. This restriction is extended to the lowercase letters by some PL/I compilers.

The on unit "ON ENDFILE(SYSIN) BEGIN; . . . END;" is PL/I's device for handling the end-of-file exception. It is executed only after "end of file" actually occurs, despite its initial position in the program text. The remaining statements in the program are executed as expected. More discussion of each individual statement type will be presented throughout the remainder of the chapter.

5-2.1 Elementary Data Types and Values

PL/I data types fall into two classes, "problem data" and "program control data." PL/I's problem data includes character strings, numbers and other values that occur as input, output, and working values in the program. Program control data includes such items as statements labels and linked list pointers.

PL/I's problem data occurs in two classes: "arithmetic" and "string." An arithmetic data value is a number, and as such has the following attributes:

Attribute	**Options**
Base	DECIMAL or BINARY
Mode	REAL or COMPLEX
Scale	FIXED or FLOAT
Precision	(p,q) or (p)

The "options" listed here are written in uppercase letters to identify that they are part of the PL/I language. In addition, many of these PL/I "keywords" can be abbreviated. A keyword's proper abbreviation is indicated throughout this chapter by underlining those letters which compose it. For example, COMPLEX can be equivalently written as CPLX, DECIMAL as DEC, and so forth.

A REAL FIXED DECIMAL arithmetic data value is an ordinary decimal number, with or without a fractional part, such as the following:

1.73 0 −17 250

A REAL FIXED BINARY data value is a binary number, with or without a fractional part, and written with a "B" at its right end, such as the following:

1.01B 0B −11B 11111010B

The precision of a REAL FIXED (DECIMAL or BINARY) arithmetic data value is always of the form (p,q); p and q are positive integers defining that value's total number of digits and total number of fractional digits, respectively. For instance, the REAL FIXED DECIMAL constant 1.73 has precision (3,2), as does the REAL FIXED BINARY constant 1.01B. The *maximum* precision for a FIXED arithmetic data value is implementation dependent, but typically the maximum value for p or q is 31 (for BINARY) and 15 (for DECIMAL).

A REAL FLOAT DECIMAL arithmetic data value is an ordinary decimal number followed by an exponent part which indicates multiplication by a power of 10. For example, the number 105000 may be written as a REAL FLOAT DECIMAL value as 1.05E5. This coding convention describes the number 1.05×10^5 or 105000. A REAL FLOAT BINARY value, similarly, is written as a binary number followed by an exponent part, which indicates multiplication by a power of 2. For example, the binary number 101000 may be written as a REAL FLOAT BINARY number as 1.01E5B, which denotes 1.01×2^5. The symbol "B" distinguishes the value as BINARY rather than DECIMAL.

The precision for a REAL FLOAT (DECIMAL or BINARY) arithmetic data value is always of the form (p), where p is an integer which defines that value's total number of *significant* (decimal or binary) digits. For instance, the REAL FLOAT DECIMAL constant 1.05E5 has precision (3), since it has 3 significant digits. Similarly, 1.01E5B has precision (3). The precision with which a FLOAT value is actually stored is implementation dependent, but typically is at least (6) for "single precision" and at least (16) for double precision.

A COMPLEX value is written in two parts: a real part followed by an imaginary part. The imaginary part is identified by writing the letter I at its right end. Although PL/I fully supports COMPLEX arithmetic, we will not discuss it further in this chapter.

Generally, FLOAT data are used in scientific calculations, since they can represent a wide range of values. FIXED DECIMAL data are generally preferred in data processing since they represent decimal fractions exactly. For instance, the number 10.53 will be converted to binary if it is stored in FLOAT, and thus accuracy will be lost. If it is stored in FIXED DECIMAL, however, the number is not converted to binary and no accuracy is lost. Finally, FIXED BINARY data are usually preferred for performing integer arithmetic, as in integer counters, loop-control variables, and so forth.

The other class of PL/I problem data is "string data." A PL/I string may be either a character string (denoted by the attribute CHARACTER) or a bit string (denoted by the attribute BIT). A character string is a sequence of zero or more characters taken from an (implementation-defined) alphabet. For most PL/I implementations, the alphabet contains at least the following characters:

ƀ(blank) . (+ & $ *) ; – / , % ? : # @ ' = "
A B C D E F G H I J K L M N O P Q R S T U V W X Y Z
0 1 2 3 4 5 6 7 8 9

Furthermore, we will assume that they are ordered exactly as they are written here. That is, "ƀ" is less than ".", which is less than "(", and so forth.

When written within a PL/I program a character string is enclosed by an apostrophe ('). Here are five examples of character strings.

```
'ABC'
'AƀBƀC'
''
'WHAT''SƀTHIS?'
(5)'ABC'
```

The first two strings are not equivalent, remembering that the blank (ƀ) is significant within a character string. The third string contains no characters. The fourth string illustrates how to represent an embedded apostrophe within the string proper; write it twice. The fifth string illustrates how a repetition of a shorter string can be abbreviated.

In addition to its value, a character string always has an associated length: the number of characters contained within it. The lengths of the five character strings above are, respectively, 3, 5, 0, 12, and 15. Note that the occurrence of a quote (') within a string contributes only one character to the length, even though it is written twice.

A "bit string" is a sequence of zero or more binary digits. When written in a PL/I program, a bit string is enclosed in apostrophes and followed immediately by B. Here are five examples of bit strings.

'0'B
'1'B
''B
'01001'B
(3)'01'B

Like the character strings, bit strings have the length attribute. The lengths of the above bit strings are 1, 1, 0, 5, and 6 respectively.

An important use for bit strings in PL/I programming is for representing logical (truth) values. Specifically, the bit strings '0'B and '1'B are interpreted as "false" and "true," respectively, when they are used in this way.

5-2.2 Names, Variables, and Declarations

A PL/I variable name may be any sequence of alphabetic (A–Z,@,#,$), numeric (0–9), and/or break (_) characters, the first of which must be alphabetic. The following are valid variable names:

X
GROSS_PAY
#19

Some implementations impose a maximum length on variable names. When the variable is associated with exactly one value, then it is said to be an "element." When it is associated with more than one value, the variable is either an "array variable" or a "structure variable."

Every element variable in a PL/I program has a set of attributes associated with it. Those attributes describe the type of value which may be assigned to that variable during program execution. Suppose X, GROSS_PAY, and TITLE are variables in a program. Let X have the attributes REAL FLOAT DECIMAL and precision (6). Let GROSS_PAY have the attributes REAL FIXED DECIMAL and precision (7,2). Finally, let TITLE have the attributes CHARACTER and length (25). This means that

1 X may contain any arithmetic data value which is REAL FLOAT DECIMAL and has six or fewer significant decimal digits. For example, the value of X may be 3.5984E−5.

2 GROSS_PAY may contain any arithmetic data value which is REAL FIXED DECIMAL and whose value lies within the range −99999.99 to 99999.99. For example, the value of GROSS_PAY may be 23400.00.

3 TITLE may contain any character string data value which has a length of 25 characters. For example, the value of TITLE may be '1984ƀANNUALƀBUDGETƀREPORT', or perhaps '1984ƀANNUALƀBUDGETƀƀƀƀƀƀ'.

The attributes associated with a variable are established either by explicit declaration or by default. That is, when a variable's attributes are not explicitly declared, the system assigns attributes to it according to a well-defined set of rules.

To declare a variable's attributes explicitly, the programmer writes a "declaration statement" which may take the following form:

```
DECLARE name attributes;
```

Here, "name" identifies the variable's name and "attributes" denotes a sequence of attributes which are to be associated with that name. Continuing the examples presented above, we could declare attributes for the variables X, GROSS_PAY, and TITLE as follows:

```
DECLARE X FLOAT DECIMAL (6);
DECLARE GROSS_PAY FIXED DECIMAL (7,2);
DECLARE TITLE CHARACTER (25);
```

This series of declarations could have been written more briefly by both using abbreviations for keywords and combining several variables into one declaration, as shown here.

```
DCL X FLOAT DEC (6),
   GROSS_PAY FIXED DEC (7,2),
   TITLE CHAR (25);
```

Another kind of abbreviation is useful when several variables all have the same attributes. For example, if Y and Z both have the same attributes as X above, then the three can be declared as follows:

```
DCL (X,Y,Z) FLOAT DEC (6);
```

Finally, any FIXED precision (p,q) in which q = 0 can be abbreviated simply as (p).

There is another attribute, called VARYING, which allows the length, as well as the value, of a character or bit string variable to change during program execution. For example, if we redeclare TITLE as follows:

```
DCL TITLE CHAR (25) VARYING;
```

then we permit any character string, of length 0 to 25 inclusive, to become the value of TITLE.

It is not always necessary to explicitly declare a variable in a program. A variable exists in a program as soon as its name is used in an executable statement, whether or not it has been declared. Furthermore, not all attributes for a declared variable need to be explicitly written. When one or more attributes for a declared variable are omitted, or when the variable is totally undeclared, its attributes are assigned, by "default," as follows:

1 When the variable is either undeclared or none of its attributes appear in its declaration: if its name begins with I, J, K, L, M, or N then it is assigned the attributes REAL FIXED BINARY. If its name begins with any other letter, the variable is assigned the attributes REAL FLOAT DECIMAL. (This convention is a carryover from FORTRAN.)

2 When an arithmetic variable is declared and at least one, but not all, of its mode, scale, and base attributes is missing in the declaration, then the missing one(s) are assigned from the following list:

Attribute missing	Assign
Mode	REAL
Scale	FLOAT
Base	DECIMAL

3 When an arithmetic variable is declared without a precision attribute, then the latter is assigned according to the "default" precision available for the implementation. For IBM mainframe implementations, the defaults are as follows:

Scale and base	Precision assigned
FIXED DECIMAL	(5,0)
FIXED BINARY	(15,0)
FLOAT DECIMAL	(6)
FLOAT BINARY	(21)

4 When a bit or character string variable is declared without a length attribute, its length is assigned as 1.

Thus, for example, we did not need to declare the variable X in the foregoing example, although we did have to declare GROSS_PAY and TITLE. If we did not, then they would both have defaulted to REAL FLOAT DEC (6). A modest abbreviation for our declaration of GROSS_PAY, however, is still possible:

```
DCL GROSS_PAY FIXED (7,2);
```

Omission of REAL or COMPLEX (mode) here defaults to REAL, and omission of DECIMAL or BIN (base) here defaults to DECIMAL.

PL/I provides an alternative method of declaring certain arithmetic and string variables: the PICTURE specification. This kind of declaration was borrowed from COBOL and has the following form:

```
DCL name PICTURE 'specification';
```

For instance, to declare a character variable like TITLE in the foregoing example, we could have equivalently said one of the following:

```
DCL TITLE PIC 'XXXXXXXXXXXXXXXXXXXXXXXXX';
DCL TITLE PIC '(25)X';
```

Here, "X" is the character specification, and the number of X's gives the length of the string.

To declare a REAL FIXED DECIMAL variable, such as GROSS_PAY in the foregoing example, we could have alternatively given the following PICTURE specification:

```
DCL GROSS_PAY PIC '99999V99';
```

Specifically, 9 is the decimal digit specification, and the number of 9s defines the number of digits accommodated by the variable. Also, the position of "V" locates the decimal point. If V is omitted, the decimal point is assumed to be at the right of the rightmost 9. Thus, we have here the equivalent of declaring GROSS_PAY to be REAL FIXED DECIMAL (7,2).

This PICTURE specification offers, however, a bit more flexibility than its alternative REAL FIXED DECIMAL (7,2), since one can include editing characters, such as ($) and (.), to control printing of the value of the variable. For example, if GROSS_PAY were redeclared as follows,

```
DCL GROSS_PAY '$99999V.99';
```

had the value 23400.00, and then were printed, the result would be $23400.00.

5-2.3 Arrays and Other Data Structures

PL/I provides two ways in which a variable may represent a number of values, rather than just one; the "array" and the "structure." An array can be an n-dimensional collection of elements, all of which have the same attributes. For instance, an array named "A" may be a one-dimensional list of five elements, each having the attributes REAL FLOAT DEC (6). Similarly, B may be a two-dimensional array, with five rows and four columns of elements, each having the attributes REAL FIXED DEC (2,0). A and B are illustrated in Figure 5-1.

A

1.50000 E0
2.70000 E-3
1.49999 E1
0.00000 E0
1.11001 E17

B

17	42	00	-10
18	03	00	-11
19	47	19	-12
20	48	49	22
00	00	-2	-3

FIGURE 5-1

To define an array, its dimensionality *n*, and the number of elements in each dimension, the program must declare the array in the following way.

DCL name (size) attributes;

Here ''name'' identifies the array's name, ''size'' defines its dimensionality and number of elements in each dimension, and ''attributes'' identifies the attributes possessed by all elements in the array. If one or more attributes are omitted, they will be assigned (by default) according to the same rules as for ordinary variables.

''Size'' may appear as a sequence of one or more integers, separated by commas. The number of integers identifies the number of dimensions in the array, while the value of each one identifies the number of elements in the dimension. For example,

DCL A(5) FLOAT DEC (6);

defines an array A with one dimension and five elements. Similarly,

DCL B(5,4) FIXED DEC (2,0);

defines an array B with two dimensions, five elements in the first dimension (rows), and four elements in the second dimension (columns). Thus, these declarations define the arrays A and B as pictured in Figure 5-1 (but not the values shown there).

The size of a PL/I array need not be constant, even though that is the case for these two arrays. In general, an array may be declared with a variable number of elements in each dimension, as suggested by the following:

DLC A(N) FLOAT DEC (6);

Further discussion of this and other dynamic storage allocation features of PL/I appears in section 5-2.8.

The PL/I ''structure'' is the second way by which multiple valued variables may be defined. The individual elements of a structure typically have different attributes from each other. For example, a structure named PERSON may have four different elements; a NAME which is a twenty-five-character string, a social security number (SS#) which is a nine-digit numeric character value, a GROSS_PAY which is a REAL FIXED DECIMAL (7,2) value, and an ADDRESS which is a 40-character string. Figure 5-2 is a set of example data for one PERSON.

```
ALLENƀB.ƀTUCKERƀƀƀƀƀƀƀƀƀƀ

275407437

25400.00

1800ƀBULLƀRUN, ƀALEXANDRIA, ƀVA. ƀ22200ƀƀƀƀ
```

FIGURE 5-2

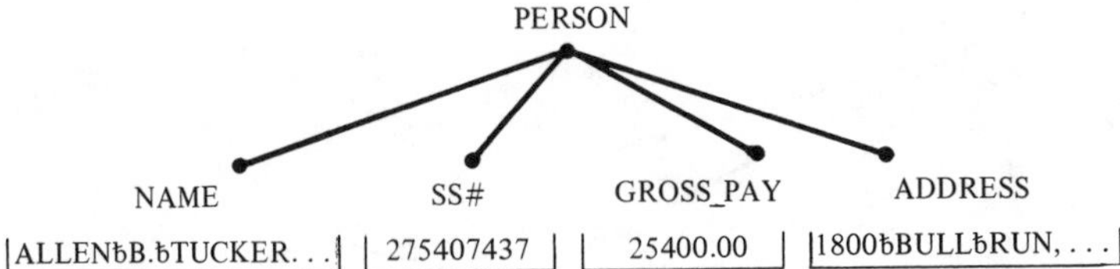

FIGURE 5-3

This kind of structure is often represented as a tree structure, as shown in Figure 5-3. In this representation, two distinct levels of identification are apparent. At the elementary level are four variables, and at a higher level is the variable PERSON, which includes all four as subordinates.

To define a structure in PL/I, we write a declaration in which the individual level of each variable within the structure is defined by an integer prefixed to it. This, too, is notation borrowed from COBOL. Thus, in our example, we prefix the integer 1 to PERSON, and 2 to all variables at the next level. Within an individual level, variables are ordered from left to right as they appear on the tree. Thus, the above structure would be declared as follows:

```
DCL 1 PERSON,
        2 NAME          CHAR (25),
        2 SS#           PIC '(9)9',
        2 GROSS_PAY     FIXED DEC (7,2),
        2 ADDRESS       CHAR (40);
```

Note also that the individual elements in the structure are separated by commas, while the entire declaration is terminated by a semicolon.

Some of the variables at level 2 in this example can themselves be structures. For example, NAME can subdivide into FIRST, MIDDLE, and LAST, and ADDRESS can subdivide into STREET, CITY, STATE, and ZIP, as illustrated in the tree in Figure 5-4. To declare this, we would write the following:

```
DCL 1 PERSON,
        2 NAME,
           3 FIRST CHAR (10),
           3 MIDDLE CHAR (5),
           3 LAST CHAR (10),
        2 SS# PIC '(9)9',
        2 GROSS_PAY FIXED DEC (7,2),
        2 ADDRESS,
           3 STREET CHAR (17),
           3 CITY CHAR (12),
           3 STATE CHAR (6),
           3 ZIP PIC '99999';
```

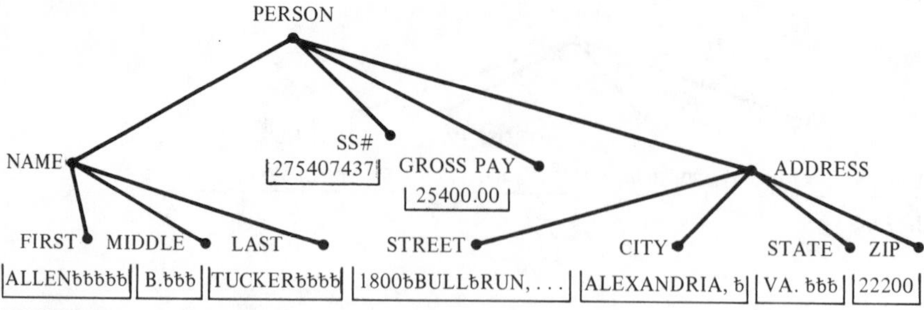

FIGURE 5-4

Notice here that only those variables within a structure which are not themselves subdivided have attributes associated with them.

To reference a single array element within the PL/I program, we give the array name, followed by a list of subscripts enclosed in parentheses. The number of subscripts given must be identical with the number of dimensions in the array as declared. Recalling the arrays A and B above, we may reference the fourth element within A by writing A(4). Similarly, to reference the element in the third row and second column of B, we would write B(3,2). Moreover, the subscripts in an array reference need not be integer constants. For instance, if I is an integer-valued variable whose value is, for example, 4 then the expression A(I) is equivalent to A(4). However, if the value of I changes to 2, then the same expression A(I) is now equivalent to A(2). Similarly, if I and J are both integer-valued variables, then the expression B(I,J) references the element in the Ith row and the Jth column of B.

Another way to reference selected elements of an array is by using the so-called "cross section." Consider once again the 5 × 4 array B defined above. If we want to reference all elements in a single row of B, say the second row, then we can write B(2,*). Similarly, we can reference the entire fourth column of B by writing B(*,4). These two cross sections of B are pictured in Figure 5-5.

Thus, a cross section serves to reduce the dimensionality of an array; the result is an array of fewer dimensions. In this example, we took one-dimensional cross sections B(2,*) and B(*,4) from the two-dimensional array B. As with single elements, cross sections may be defined by the use of variables instead of constants. For instance, B(I,*) denotes the Ith row of B and B(*,J) denotes the Jth column. The use of cross sections is especially convenient in applications using matrix algebra.

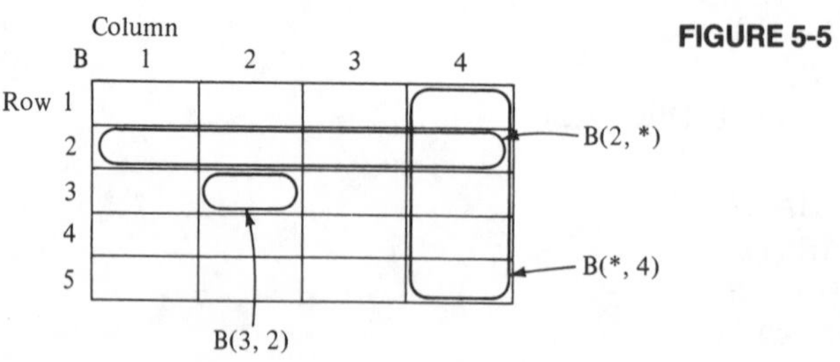

FIGURE 5-5

To reference an entire structure, we give the structures's name, such as PERSON for the example shown above. To reference a substructure within a structure, that substructure's name is given. To reference a single element within a structure, only that element's name needs to be given. In addition, it is possible to have two different elements (or substructures) with the same name, as shown in the following example:

```
DCL 1 PERSON_A,
        2 NAME CHAR (25),
        2 SS# PIC '(9)9',
        2 GROSS_PAY FIXED DEC (7,2),
        2 ADDRESS CHAR (40),
    1 PERSON_B,
        2 NAME CHAR (25),
        2 SS# PIC '(9)9',
        2 GROSS_PAY FIXED DEC (7,2),
        2 ADDRESS CHAR (40);
```

These two structures, PERSON_A and PERSON_B, have identically named elements, even though the structures themselves must have mutually unique names. In order to distinguish the SS#, for example, of PERSON_A from that of PERSON_B, a "qualified name" must be given. If PERSON_B's SS# is to be referenced, then the qualified name PERSON_B.SS# must be written, while PERSON_A's SS# is referenced by PERSON_A.SS#.

Finally, we note that PL/I permits arrays to occur within structures and structures to occur within arrays.

Initialization of Variables, Arrays, and Structures The initial value of a variable, array, or structure can be established at the beginning of PL/I program execution by giving the "INITIAL attribute" within its declaration. This has the following form:

<u>INIT</u>IAL (value-list)

Here, "value-list" denotes a list of values to be assigned to the declared variable, array, or structure. Each value may be a constant or a repetitive specification, which abbreviates a list of identical constants.

For example, reconsider the variables X and TITLE and the array B that were discussed in the previous section. The values that were shown there may be initialized in the following way:

```
DCL X FLOAT DEC (6) INIT(3.59847E-5),
    TITLE CHAR (25) INIT ('1984 ANNUAL BUDGET'),
    B(5,4) FIXED DEC (2,0) INIT(17,42,0,-10,18,3,0,
       -11,19,47,19,-12,20,48,49,22,0,0,-2,-3);
```

The elementary items in a structure are initialized similarly.

Two points should be made about the use of the INITIAL attribute. First, when an array is initialized, the list of values are assigned in *row-major* order. Second, if several adjacent (or all) entries in an array are to be initialized to the same value, the number of repetitions for that value may be indicated by placing that number before it, enclosed in parentheses. For example, if we want to initialize all the entries of B to the value zero, we can write the following:

```
DCL B(5,4) FIXED DEC (2,0) INIT ((20)0);
```

Note carefully that the specification INIT (0) would have initialized only B(1,1) to zero, leaving undefined the values of the remaining entries in B.

5-2.4 Basic Statements

Due to space limitations, this chapter will not cover all the PL/I statements. Specifically, we will exclude the DELAY, DISPLAY, ENTRY, EXIT, HALT, LOCATE, REVERT, UNLOCK, and WAIT statements. The ones that we will cover are summarized on page 175.

In the remainder of this section, we will introduce the use of expressions and the assignment statement in PL/I. The remaining statements in this list are introduced in the sections indicated. Our discussion will use as an illustration the sample program presented at the beginning of this chapter.

Expressions The PL/I "expression" is a very general device for specifying any of a wide variety of computations, on numbers or strings, and with simple variables, arrays, or structures. For strictly pedagogical purposes, we partition expression into the following classes:

- Elementary expressions
    - Arithmetic expressions
    - String expressions
    - Logical expressions
- Array expressions
- Structure expressions

The "elementary expressions" have the common characteristic that their execution yields a single value as a result. For an "arithmetic expression," that result is a numeric value. For a "string expression," the result is a character or bit string, and for a "logical expression" the result is always a one-bit string value. In this context, the values '1'B and '0'B are interpreted "true" and "false" respectively.

An arithmetic expression may be either a single term or a series of terms separated by arithmetic operators, and perhaps by parentheses (as described below). A single term may be either a numeric constant, a numeric variable, a numeric function, or a numeric array reference, as illustrated by the following examples:

```
10    SUM    GROSS_PAY    SQRT (X)    A(I)
```

Statement	Purpose
ALLOCATE statement FREE statement	To accomplish dynamic storage allocation, which will be discussed in section 5-2.8.
Assignment statement	To perform a series of arithmetic or string operations, and assign the result to a variable, array, or structure.
BEGIN statement	To delimit the scope of a dynamic array or the statements of an on unit. Its uses are discussed in section 5-2.8.
CALL statement RETURN statement	To invoke a subprogram, and to return control to the invocation. These are discussed in section 5-2.7.
CLOSE statement OPEN statement GET statement PUT statement FORMAT statement READ statement WRITE statement	To perform the various input-output operations. These will be discussed in section 5-2.6
DECLARE statement	To define variables and their attributes, as introduced in section 5-2.2, and further discussed in later sections.
DO statement	To delimit the beginning of a group of statements to be either repeated or conditionally executed. See section 5-2.5.
END statement	To delimit the end of a group of statements headed by DO, BEGIN, or PROCEDURE. END will be illustrated in this and later sections.
GO TO statement IF statement SELECT statement STOP statement	To alter the textual sequence of statement execution, as illustrated in section 5-2.5.
ON statement	To describe an action to be taken in the event that an exceptional condition occurs during program execution. See sections 5-2.6 and 5-2.8.
PROCEDURE statement	To identify the beginning of a PL/I program or subprogram. It will be discussed in section 5-2.7.

Each of these terms denotes a single value; the first is a constant, the next two are variable names, the fourth is a function reference (see section 5-2.7), and the last is an array reference.

The arithmetic operators and their meanings are as follows:

Operator	Meaning
+	Addition
−	Subtraction
*	Multiplication
/	Division
**	Exponentiation

Each of these operators always has two operands, as shown in the following example.

```
N + 1
```

This comes from the example program, and denotes addition of the value of the variable N and the constant 1.

A series of two or more operations are generally carried out from left to right, with the following exceptions. First, according to the hierarchy among the operators, all the exponentiations (**) are performed first (from right to left), all multiplications (*) and divisions (/) are performed next (from left to right), and finally all additions (+) and subtractions (−) are performed (from left to right). This means that

```
H + 2 * I
  ↑   ↑
 (2) (1)
```

denotes the sum of H and 2 * I rather than the product of H + 2 and I. The numbered arrows below the expression indicate the order in which the operations are performed.

Second, when this ordering is not what is desired, the programmer may enclose in parentheses the operations to be performed first. For instance, to specify the product of H + 2 and I, we can write the following:

```
(H + 2) * I
   ↑    ↑
  (1)  (2)
```

Here the addition will take place first, as the numbered arrows indicate.

A "string expression" may be a single term or a series of terms separated by the operator ||, which denotes concatenation. A single term in a string expression may be either a string constant or a string-valued variable, array reference, or function reference, as illustrated below.

```
'ABABAB'    NAME    S(1)    SUBSTR (NAME, 1, 5)
```

The concatenation operator || forms one string as a result of juxtaposing two strings. For instance, if we want to concatenate 'ABA' and 'BAB' to form the one string 'ABABAB', we could write the following.

```
'ABA'|| 'BAB'
```

Although concatenation is the only PL/I string operator, PL/I's capability for supporting text processing applications is made extensive by its powerful string functions, as we shall later see in sections 5-2.7. and 5-3.1.

A "logical expression" is either a 1-bit string constant ('0'B or '1'B), a 1-bit variable, a function reference which returns a 1-bit string constant as a result, a relation between two arithmetic expressions or two string expressions, or a series of such logical expressions connected by the logical operators & (and), | (or), and ¬ (not). A relation is formed by separating two expressions by one of the relational operators <, <=, =, ¬=, >=, or >.

The relational operators and the logical operators & and | are all binary operators, while the logical operator ¬ is a unary prefix operator. The relational operators share the same precedence with each other in an expression. They have higher precedence than the logical operators, and lower precedence than the arithmetic operators. Furthermore, "&" has precedence over "|", and "¬" has precedence over both "&" and "|." Parentheses are used in logical expressions to override this precedence, just as for arithmetic expressions. Thus, for example,

```
0 < H & H < 5
```

has the interpretation given above. On the other hand, the expression

```
P | Q & (H <= 5 | NAME = 'ALLEN')
↑   ↑      ↑    ↑        ↑
(5) (4)    (1)  (3)      (2)
```

is evaluated in the order indicated by the numbered arrows, since the parentheses override the precedence that "&" would otherwise have over the second "|."

The relations <, <=, ¬=, >=, and >, when applied to arithmetic expressions, reflect the usual ordering that exists among the numbers. That is, the expression

```
H <= 5
```

is a test of whether the value of H is less than or equal to 5 in the numerical sense. When applied to string expressions, the relations reflect the so-called "collating sequence," or predefined ordering that exists among the characters in the character set.

PL/I expressions can contain arrays or structures, in addition to elementary values, as operands. An expression which contains one or more array names is called an "array expression," and its execution yields an array, rather that a single value, as the result. An expression which contains structure names is called a "structure expression," and its execution yields a structure as the result. Although there is a natural analogy between the PL/I array and the algebraic notion of matrix, note that the analogy breaks down in the case of multiplication. That is, array multiplication (A * B) does *not* represent the matrix product.

There are some general considerations to be kept in mind when writing array expressions. First, the number of dimensions and number of elements in each dimension must be the same for all arrays referenced in a single expression. For instance, the only array that we can add to a 4 × 3 array is another 4 × 3 array. Second, array cross sections can be used in arithmetic expressions. For instance, if we want to compute the one-dimensional, three-element array which is formed by taking the product of corresponding elements from the third row of a two-dimensional array A and the second row of another array B, we would write the following expression:

```
A(3,*) * B(2,*)
```

In this case, A and B must have the same number of columns.

Coercion in Expression Evaluation The mode, base, and scale attributes of the result of executing an arithmetic operation are defined in the following table, for cases where one operand does not agree in all of its attributes with the other:

One operand's attributes	Other operand's attributes	Result's attributes
REAL	COMPLEX	COMPLEX
FIXED	FLOAT	FLOAT
DECIMAL	BINARY	BINARY

If the two operands agree in all these attributes, then the result carries their common attributes. The precision of the result depends both upon the nature of the arithmetic operation and the implementation. Generally, that precision is adequate to accommodate the largest or smallest value that would reasonably be achieved by executing that operation. For instance, I + 1 will yield a result with attributes FIXED BIN (15,0) if those of I are FIXED BIN (15,0). The precision of the result of an arithmetic operation is also bound by implementation-dependent maxima and minima, as was discussed for numeric constants in section 5-2.1.

When the result of a FIXED (DEC or BIN) arithmetic operation is so large that it exceeds the maximum precision allowed by the implementation, the so-called FIXEDOVERFLOW condition is raised. For example, if we perform the following FIXED DECIMAL addition,

```
999999999999999 + 1
```

the result will have 16 significant digits. Raising the FIXEDOVERFLOW condition causes the program's execution to be interrupted. Whether execution resumes, and from what place, may then be determined by the programmer. More will be said about the handling of conditions in later sections of the chapter.

The Assignment Statement In order to assign the result of evaluating an expression to a variable, array, or structure, the assignment statement is used. It has the following form:

```
variable = expression;
```

Here, ''variable'' denotes either an elementary variable, an array variable, or a structure variable, and ''expression'' denotes an elementary expression, array expression, or structure expression accordingly.

When an assignment statement is executed, the expression on its right is first evaluated. The result of that evaluation then becomes the new value of the variable. For example, the following assignment appears in the example program at the beginning of the chapter:

```
N = N + 1;
```

Assuming for the moment that the current value of N is 2, then this assignment will first compute the sum N + 1, and that result (3) then becomes the new value of the variable N.

The variable on the left of the assignment's equal sign (=) may also be an array reference. For instance, if A is an array of 10 integer values, the assignment statement A(3) = N + 1 will leave the sum N + 1 in the third entry in A.

More than one variable may be listed on the left of the assignment's equal sign, in which case a multiple assignment is indicated. This is a convenient device for initializing several variables to the same value. For instance, we could write

```
I,J,K = 0;
```

to initialize the variables I, J, and K to zero. This is slightly more convenient to write than the following equivalent sequence of statements:

```
I = 0; J = 0; K = 0;
```

If the result designated by the expression on the right of the assignment's ''='' sign has different attributes from those of the variable on the left, then ''conversion'' will occur. ''Conversion'' is PL/I's terminology for the coercion of a value with a given type to an equivalent value with a different type. For example, the value 15 has attributes REAL FIXED DEC (2,0). If we convert it to an equivalent value in REAL FIXED BIN (15,0), the resulting equivalent value will be 000000000001111B.

PL/I conversion rules are difficult to master in general. Sometimes the result of conversion is not what one would even logically expect to occur. In most cases, however, the result of conversion is reasonable and well defined. For instance, a character string containing a valid number, like '1.23', will be converted to its equivalent arithmetic value, 1.23. Some conversions are impossible, however. For instance, if we were asked to convert the character string 'ALLEN' to an ''equivalent'' arithmetic value, we would throw up our hands. Situations like this one will cause the so-called ''CONVERSION condition'' to be raised. This is an exceptional condition which causes program execution to be interrupted. Whether execution is resumed, and from what point in the program, can be determined by the programmer.

PL/I also provides the array assignment and structure assignment statements. For instance, if we want to set all elements of an array named A to some elementary value such as 0, then we may write

```
A = 0;
```

Similarly, we may assign such a value to a cross section of an array by designating that cross section on the left of the assignment. Finally, we may initialize all elements of a structure to a single value in a similar fashion, by giving that structure's name on the left.

Moreover, we can directly assign to an array B the values of corresponding elements in an array D by simply writing the following:

```
B = D;
```

In cases like this, the array on the left of the assignment must agree, in dimensionality and number of elements in each dimension, with the array (expression) on the right.

5-2.5 Control Structures

In this section, we illustrate the PL/I statements which are used to control the flow of program execution; the GO TO, STOP, IF, SELECT, and DO statements.

The GO TO statement The statements in a PL/I program are generally executed in the order in which they are written, unless a statement is encountered which can alter that order. One such statement is the GO TO statement, which has the following general form:

```
GO TO label;
```

Here, "label" denotes the label of some other statement between the program's first (PROCEDURE) statement and its END statement (including the END statement itself). Any PL/I executable statement can thus be the "target" of a GO TO statement. This excludes the PROCEDURE statement, the DECLARE statement, the FORMAT statement, and the ON statement.

A statement is labeled by prefixing it with a "label" and a colon(:) as shown:

```
label : statement
```

Here, "label" may be any sequence of characters, the first of which is alphabetic (A–Z,$,@,#), and the rest of which are alphabetic, numeric (0–9), or the break character (_).

The STOP Statement The STOP statement simply causes program execution to cease. It may be included or not if program execution would normally cease upon reaching the program's END (last) statement. Otherwise, it must be placed at whatever place in the program where execution should cease. It is always written as follows:

```
STOP;
```

The IF Statement When a statement or sequence of statements, S, is to be executed only when a certain condition designated by the logical expression, e, is true (i.e., has the value '1'B), the IF statement is used. It has either of the following two forms:

(i) IF e THEN S
(ii) IF e THEN S_1 ELSE S_2

Here, e designates the logical expression, while S, S_1, and S_2 designate any executable statement, "DO group," or "BEGIN block." DO groups and BEGIN blocks are very important in this context for writing well-structured programs, and we shall discuss them later. Note also that no semicolon explicitly appears to terminate the IF statement. However, S, S_1, and S_2 each terminates with a semicolon, so that the semicolon will appear in any event.

Execution of form (i) of the IF statement occurs in two steps. First, the expression e is evaluated, giving a true or false result. If the result is true, then S is executed. Otherwise, S is bypassed. Execution of form (ii) is similar, except that either S_1 or S_2 is executed, and the other is bypassed, depending on whether the result of evaluating e is true or false, respectively.

A DO group has several forms, most of which will be discussed in a later paragraph. We introduce its simplest form here, however, because of its natural association with the IF statement. The simplest form of the DO group is composed of a sequence of executable statements headed by "DO;" and ended by "END;". When a DO group appears as the statement S in form (i) or form (ii) of the IF statement, its effect is to delimit an entire *series* of statements that will be conditionally executed.

As an example, consider the problem of solving, for real roots x, the quadratic equation,

$$ax^2 + bx + c = 0 \qquad (a \neq 0)$$

where a, b, and c are given. The number of roots and their values can be determined by first computing the discriminant d from a, b, and c as follows:

$$d = b^2 - 4ac$$

If $d < 0$, then there are no real roots. If $d = 0$, then there is one real root $x1$, given by

$$x1 = \frac{-b}{2a}$$

If $d > 0$, then there are two real roots, $x1$ and $x2$, given by

$$x1 = \frac{-b + \sqrt{d}}{2a}$$

$$x2 = \frac{-b - \sqrt{d}}{2a}$$

The program segment to compute the number of roots, NROOTS, and their values, say X1 and X2, given coefficients A, B, and C, can be written as follows:

```
D = B ** 2 - 4 * A * C;
IF D < 0 THEN NROOTS = 0;
ELSE IF D = 0
  THEN DO;
      NROOTS = 1;
      X1 = -B/(2 * A);
    END;
  ELSE DO;
      NROOTS = 2;
      X1 = (-B + D ** .5)/(2 * A);
      X2 = (-B - D ** .5)/(2 * A);
    END;
```

As shown, the ELSE of the first IF statement is followed by another IF statement of form (ii). Each part of that statement contains a separate DO group.

The SELECT Statement The SELECT statement provides selection of one from a series of alternative statements, depending on the value of an expression. It has the following form:

```
SELECT;
  WHEN (e1) S1
  WHEN (e2) S2
      .
      .
      .
  OTHERWISE Sn
END;
```

Here, the e's denote logical expressions, and the S's denote the corresponding statements to be executed as any of the e's is true, taken in order from the first to the last. If none of the e's is true, the OTHERWISE statement allows Sn to be executed instead. Thus, this is a convenient way of abbreviating a series of nested IF . . . THEN . . . ELSE statements.

For example, reconsider the roots calculation above, and its rewriting with the use of SELECT. It has the following form:

```
D = B ** 2 - 4 * A * C;
SELECT;
  WHEN (D<0) NROOTS = 0;
  WHEN (D=0) DO;
        NROOTS = 1;
        X1 = -B/(2 * A);
      END;
  OTHERWISE DO;
        NROOTS = 2;
        X1 = (-B + D ** .5)/(2 * A);
        X2 = (-B-D ** .5)/(2 * A);
      END;
END;
```

The DO Statement and Loops Much of programming is concerned with the writing of controlled loops. PL/I provides several forms of the DO statement for this purpose.

A controlled loop is the repeated execution of a sequence of statements until a specific condition becomes true. Many such loops are "counter-controlled" loops, in which a counting variable is initialized and then incremented and tested each time the sequence of statements is executed. When the variable is incremented beyond a specific limit, the loop's execution terminates. This is pictured in two different forms in Figure 5-6. Here, i denotes the loop-control variable, while m_1, m_2, and m_3 denote expressions which are, respectively, the initial value, the limit value, and the increment value for the control variable. The logic of flowchart (*b*) in Figure 5-6 can be encoded as a "DO loop" as follows:

DO i = m_1 TO m_2 BY m_3

Sequence of statements

END;

For instance, the following loop can be written to compute the SUM of the five elements in an array A:

```
SUM = 0;
DO I = 1 TO 5 BY 1;
  SUM = SUM + A (I);
END;
```

As indicated, the single DO statement incorporates the initialization, test, and increment steps of the loop depicted in flowchart (*b*).

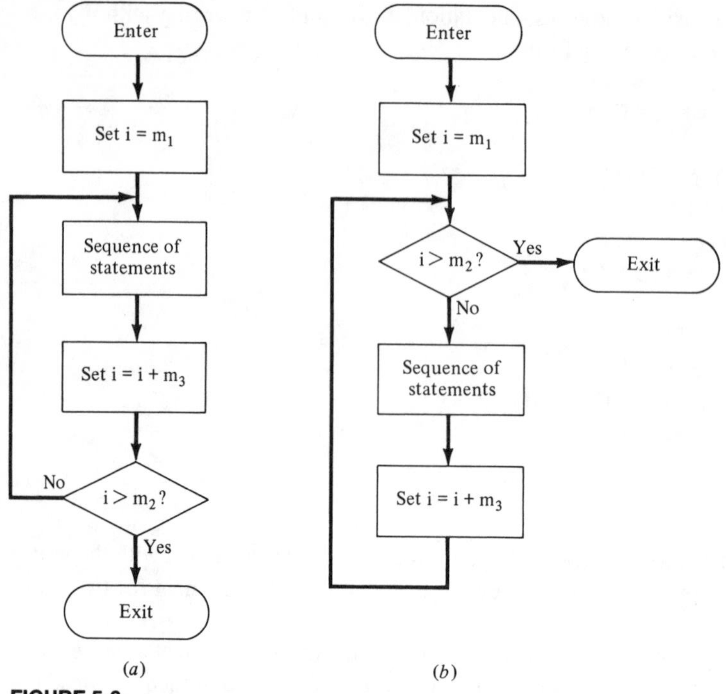

FIGURE 5-6

There are many other forms in which the DO statement may be written, in order to permit a variety of commonly used loops to be conveniently described. We will discuss what we consider to be the most useful among these forms, as follows:

1 DO i = m_1 TO m_2 BY m_3;
2 DO i = m_1 TO m_2;
3 DO i = m_1 BY m_3;
4 DO i = v_1, v_2, . . . , v_n;
5 DO WHILE (e);

Here, i denotes a variable; m_1, m_2, m_3, v_1, v_2, . . . , v_n denote arithmetic expressions; and e denotes a logical expression. In each of these forms, the DO statement is used to control the repeated execution of some sequence of statements. That sequence is always terminated by an END statement, no matter which form of the DO statement is used. In the next few paragraphs we describe the meaning of each of these forms, and illustrate a case where it is useful.

Form 1 has already been illustrated in the above example. In general, the increment m_3 can be negative as well as positive, as shown in the following rendition of the DO statement in the above example:

DO I = 5 TO 1 BY −1;

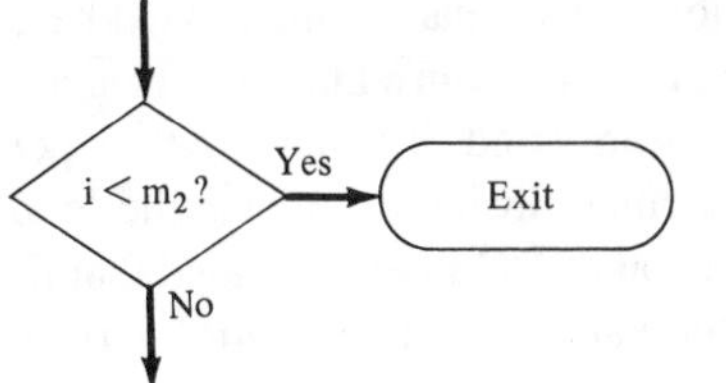

FIGURE 5-7

If m_3 is negative, then the sense of the test performed before execution of the sequence of statements in flowchart (*b*) is reversed, as shown in Figure 5-7.

Form 2 is an abbreviation of form 1 when the increment value m_3 is 1. Form 3 is used when exit from the loop is not naturally specifiable by either an upper limit or a WHILE clause. Its meaning is the same as that of form 1, except that no test for exit is performed. The programmer must ensure that such a loop remains controlled by providing some other means by which the loop will eventually terminate.

Form 4 is used when the succession of values taken on by the loop-control variable is not a sequence having a constant increment or decrement. For example, suppose we want to execute a sequence of statements once for each of the following values of H: 1, 3, and 4. Then we would use form 4 as follows.

```
DO H = 1, 3, 4;
   [Sequence of statements]
END;
```

This is equivalent to the repeated writing of "Sequence of statements" shown in Figure 5-8.

Form 5 is used when exit from the loop is taken only when a certain condition, specified by e, becomes false. This test is performed before each execution of the loop, so that it may be executed zero times.

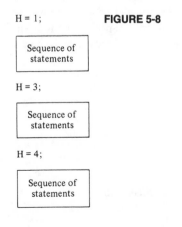

```
H = 1;
[Sequence of statements]
H = 3;
[Sequence of statements]
H = 4;
[Sequence of statements]
```

FIGURE 5-8

There are several restrictions on the use of DO loops that must be mentioned here. First, it is impermissable to transfer control to any statement within a DO loop from outside it, unless the transfer is to the DO statement itself. Second, it is nevertheless permissable to transfer from within the loop to any statement inside or outside the loop. Third, a DO loop may be completely nested within another DO loop, provided that the rules for transfer of control are followed. Fourth, the value of a loop-control variable should not explicitly be altered from inside the loop.

5-2.6 Input-Output Conventions

PL/I facilities for input-output file processing are extensive. They fall into two different classes called "stream I/O" and "record I/O." When data are read or written by a program using stream I/O, that data is considered to form a continuous sequence, or stream, of individual values. Indeed, the individual records are taken as if they were attached end to end, to form one very long record accommodating all data values in the file.

For example, consider the input data in Figure 5-9. When read as input under stream I/O, this data appears to the program in a left-to-right order, as if the cards were attached, as in Figure 5-10. Under stream I/O, it is the individual data value, rather than the individual record, which is the fundamental unit of input or output.

Stream input operations are always specified by a GET statement, while stream output operations are specified by a PUT statement. When the GET statement is executed, a number of individual data values are read from the current position of the data stream. When the PUT statement is executed, a number of data values are placed into the current position of the data stream. After completion of either of these statements, the current position of the data stream is advanced.

We can visualize this by picturing an imaginary pointer initially placed at the first value in the data stream, as shown in Figure 5-11. When the first GET statement is executed, assume that two values are read as input 'BUCK' and −14. Now the current position of the pointer is moved past these two, as shown in Figure 5-12. The next execution of a GET statement will cause data to be read beginning with 'JONES'.

When data is read or written using *record I/O,* the file is taken as a collection of records. Any individual input or output operation causes the transfer of an entire record. Record I/O may take place sequentially or randomly. Random file processing is an important alternative for many applications, as we will see in Case Study 2 at the end of the chapter.

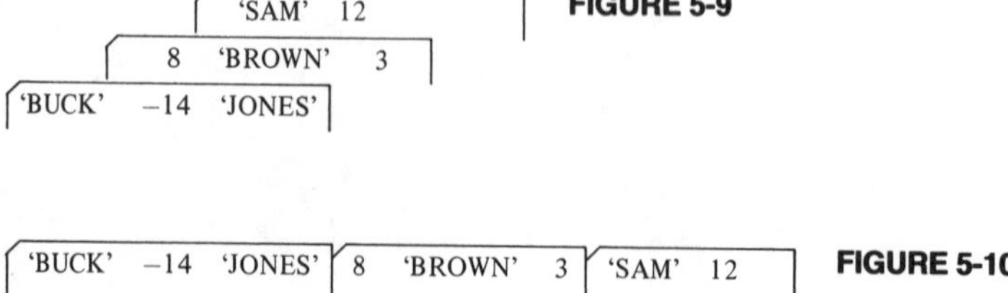

FIGURE 5-9

FIGURE 5-10

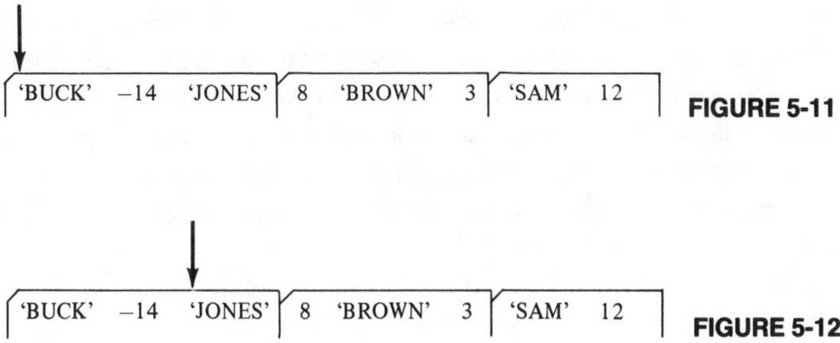

FIGURE 5-11

FIGURE 5-12

Record input operations are specified by a READ statement, while record output operations are specified by a WRITE or a REWRITE statement. When a READ statement is executed (for a sequential file) the next *record* in the file is read. Similarly, when a WRITE statement is executed the next record is written to the file.

Stream I/O When stream I/O is used, the data in a file may appear either as a sequence of data values separated from each other by blanks or as a sequence of records which are identically laid out (formatted), as illustrated in Figure 5-13. In the former case the program uses so-called ''list-directed'' I/O, while in the latter case the program uses ''edit-directed'' I/O to access the data.

List-directed input is specified by a GET statement in one of the following forms.

(i) GET LIST (variable-list);
(ii) GET FILE (filename) LIST (variable-list);

Here, ''variable-list'' is a list of the names of the variables, separated by commas, which will be assigned the values of the data read. Suppose, for example, that we have the following variables declared in a program.

```
DCL NAME CHAR (10),
    SCORE FIXED DEC (3,0);
```

Then the following GET statement, when executed with the data shown in the previous section, will cause the variables NAME and SCORE to take on the values 'BUCKƀƀ ƀƀƀƀ' and − 14, respectively.

```
GET LIST (NAME, SCORE);
```

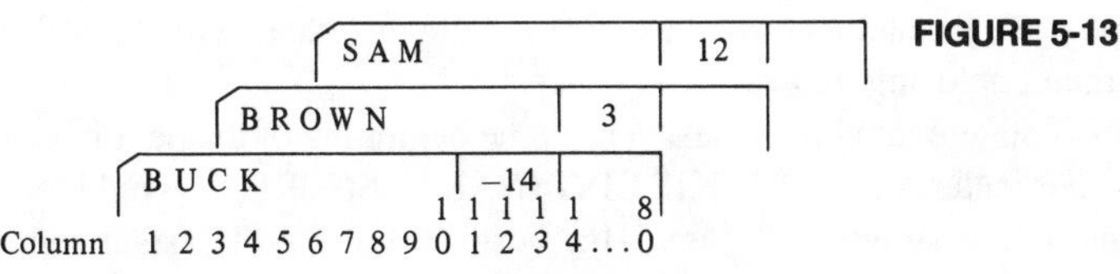

FIGURE 5-13

The order in which the variables are listed in the GET statement defines the order in which input values are assigned. Note also that character string data is represented with its enclosing apostrophes. Note finally that individual data values are separated from each other by at least one blank space when read under list-directed input.

The difference between forms (i) and (ii) of the GET statement is that form (i) takes input data from the "standard input file," while form (ii) allows data to be taken from any particular file, as designated by "filename."

Every file used by a PL/I program, whether for input or for output, has a unique file name. The file name may be any sequence which begins with an alphabetic (A–Z,@,#,$) character and contains only alphabetic, numeric (0–9), and/or break(_) characters. Because they are used so commonly, two particular files are singled out and designated as the "standard input file" and the "standard output file." These are given preassigned file names by the system, usually SYSIN (for punched card or keyboard input) and SYSPRINT (for printed or terminal screen output).

Similarly, *list-directed output* is specified by a PUT statement in one of the following forms:

(i) PUT LIST (expression-list);
(ii) PUT SKIP LIST (expression-list);
(iii) PUT FILE (filename) LIST (expression-list);

Here, "expression-list" designates any number of expressions, separated by commas. Form (i) or (ii) is used when the standard output file SYSPRINT is desired. Otherwise, form (iii) is used in order to direct output to a different file, given by "filename." When executed, the PUT statement causes the values of the listed expressions to be transferred to the file, and in the order they are listed.

For example, reconsider the variables NAME and SCORE declared above, and with values 'BUCKƀƀƀƀƀƀ' and −14, respectively. If we want to print these values, we could say the following:

```
PUT LIST (NAME, SCORE);
```

The particular location where these values are printed depends upon both the current position of the output file and the (system-defined) tab settings for that file.

For printer or terminal output each line is segmented into a fixed number of horizontal tab positions. For this chapter, we will assume that they are positions 1, 21, 41, 61, 81, and 101 on a 120-character line size.

Suppose the current position of the print file is as shown in Figure 5-14 when the above PUT statement is executed. Then execution will leave the values of NAME and SCORE as shown in Figure 5-15. Note that the current position has also changed in preparation for the next PUT statement to be executed. Note also that character strings are printed *without* their enclosing quotes.

Form (ii) of the PUT statement will cause a skip to the beginning of the next line before printing begins. For instance, "PUT SKIP LIST (NAME, SCORE);" would leave the results printed instead, as shown in Figure 5-16. Form (iii) of the PUT statement is used when the output is destined for a file different from the standard output file. In this

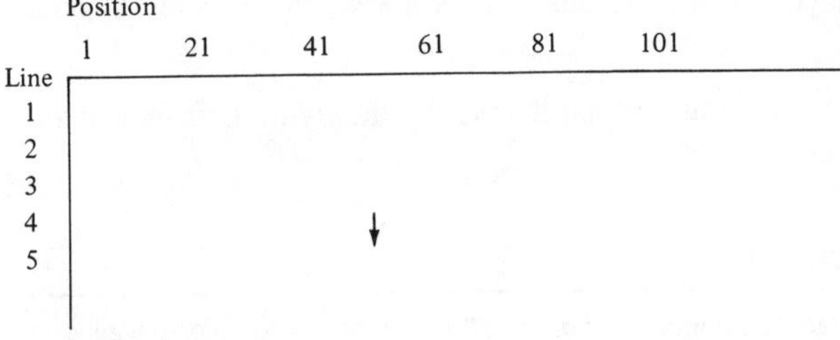

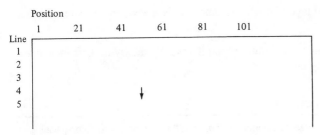

FIGURE 5-14

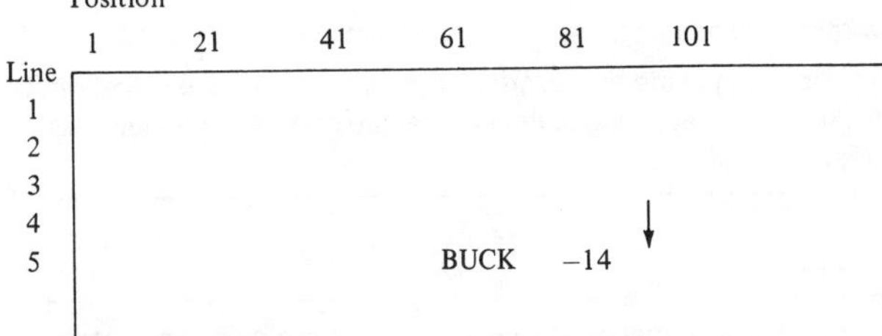

FIGURE 5-15

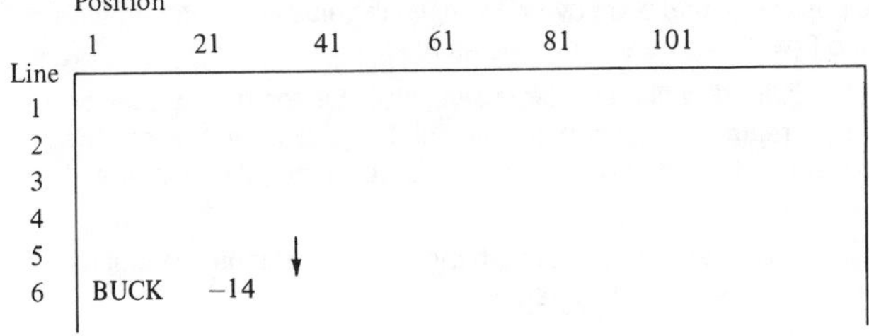

FIGURE 5-16

case the file may not be printed, and individual data values will be separated by a single blank space adjusted to preset tab positions.

Edit-directed input is specified by a GET statement in one of the following forms:

(i) GET EDIT (variable-list) (format-list);
(ii) GET FILE (filename) EDIT (variable-list) (format-list);

The choice between form (i) and form (ii) is again governed by whether input is to be read from the standard input file or not. The ''variable-list'' serves the same purpose as it did for the list-directed GET statement. The ''format-list'' describes the layout and form of the individual data values in the record (e.g., card) where they reside. (This formatting notation is inherited directly from FORTRAN.) It is composed of a sequence of format items, each of which serves one of the following purposes:

1 It controls the location from which the next data value is to be read, and is thus called a ''control format item.''

2 It describes the physical layout in which a data item is stored, and is called a "data format item."

Some commonly used control and data format items, together with their meanings, are described in the following tables:

Control format item	Meaning (input)
COLUMN(n)	Skip forward to column (position) n in the current record before reading the next value. Here, n may be any integer expression. If column n has already been passed in the current record, column n of the next record is accessed instead.
X(n)	Skip forward n positions past the present position in the input stream.
SKIP(n)	Skip to the beginning of the *n*th record beyond the current one in the input stream. A skip to the beginning of the next record can be abbreviated as SKIP rather than SKIP(1).

Data format item	Meaning (input)
F(w,d)	A FIXED DECIMAL arithmetic data value, stored in the next w positions in the input stream. Here, w and d can be any integer-valued expression. Here, d denotes the number of digits, from right to left, to be taken as the value's fractional part. However, if the value already has a decimal point, then the position of that point overrides d. If the value is an integer, then d = 0 and F(w,0) can be abbreviated as F(w).
E(w,d)	A FLOAT DECIMAL arithmetic data value, stored in the next w positions in the input stream. Here, d denotes the number of digits in the mantissa which follow the decimal point, and is overridden if the point appears explicitly in the number.
A(w)	A character string data value, stored in the next w positions (without its enclosing quotes) in the input stream.
B(w)	A BIT string data value, stored in the next w positions (without its enclosing quotes or "B"), in the input stream.

To illustrate how these work, the statement below uses edit-directed input to read the first two data values from the formatted data shown in Figure 5-13 into NAME and SCORE.

```
GET EDIT (NAME, SCORE) (COL(1), A(10), F(3,0));
```

Here, there is a left-to-right matching of the variables listed with the data format items listed. For each variable the corresponding format item is used to control the interpretation of the value which will be assigned to it. Second, the individual format items are obeyed from left to right (as they appear), when the statement is executed. That is, this statement says literally the following: "Proceed to column 1 of the next record. The next ten columns (1–10) will contain a character string which should be stored in NAME, and the next three columns will contain a three-digit integer, which should be stored in SCORE."

Edit-directed output is specified by a PUT statement in one of the following forms:

(i) PUT EDIT (variable-list) (format-list);
(ii) PUT FILE (filename) EDIT (variable-list) (format-list);

Again, the choice between form (i) and form (ii) is governed by whether or not output is to be directed to the standard output file, SYSPRINT. The ''variable-list'' serves the same purpose as it did for the list-directed PUT statement. The format list is identical in purpose to the format list accompanying edit-directed input; it describes the layout and form of the individual data values in the output file.

The various kinds of control and data format items for output are similar to those used for edit-directed input. Their meanings for edit-directed output are described below.

Control format item	Meaning (output)
PAGE	Skip forward to the first position (column) on the first line of the next page before printing the next value.
LINE(n)	Skip forward to the first position on the *n*th line on the current page before printing the next value.
COLUMN(n)	Skip forward on the current line to the *n*th column for printing the next data value.
X(n)	Skip forward n positions in the stream from the current position.
SKIP(n)	Skip forward to the beginning of the *n*th line following the present one. SKIP(1) may be abbreviated as simply SKIP.

Data format item	Meaning (output)
F(w,d)	An arithmetic value will be stored in the next w positions of the output stream, rounded to d digits on the right of the decimal point. For an integer, F(w,0) can be abbreviated as F(w).
E(w,d)	An arithmetic value is stored in the next w positions of the output stream, rounded to d digits on the right of the decimal point, as shown below. $\underbrace{\text{x.xxx}\ldots\text{x}}_{d}\ \text{E} \pm \text{yy}$ The interpretation of this value is the same as that for FLOAT data values.
A(w)	A character string value is written in the next w positions of the output stream, without its enclosing quotes; "(w)" may be omitted here, in which case the remaining "A" specification implies a value of w identical with the length of the character string being written.
B(w)	A BIT string value is written in the next w positions of the output stream, without its enclosing quotes or "B." Again, "(w)" may be omitted, in which case it is assumed to be identical with the length of the bit string being written.
p'picture-spec'	A numeric character data value is stored in the output stream, as specified by the "picture-spec."

The PAGE and LINE control format items described above apply only to files which are destined for the printer—so-called "print files."

To illustrate, let's apply edit-directed output to print the values of NAME and SCORE, which are declared and initialized as follows:

```
DCL NAME CHAR (10) INIT ('BUCK'),
    SCORE FIXED DEC(3) INIT (-14);
```

Suppose the current position of the output data stream is the first position of the first line on a page. Then the following statement

```
PUT EDIT (NAME, SCORE) (A(10), X(10), F(3,0));
```

will leave the values printed as shown in Figure 5-17. The same result would have been obtained if the "A(10)" format had been replaced by "A" (since the length of NAME is 10), the "F(3,0)" format item had been replaced by "F(3)", or the "X(10)" format item had been replaced by "COL(21)".

Finally, some points about stream I/O for arrays and structures should be made. An array or structure may be read (written) under stream I/O in a variety of ways. To illustrate, consider the following declarations:

```
DCL B(5,4) FIXED DEC (2,0),
    1 S,
      2 T FIXED DEC (3,2),
      2 U CHAR (5),
      2 V FLOAT DEC (6);
```

To read the next twenty values into B, and then the next three values into S, we could say any of the following, equivalently:

```
  (i) GET LIST (B(1,1), B(1,2), B(1,3), B(1,4),
                B(2,1), . . . , B(5,4), T, U, V);
 (ii) GET LIST (((B(I,J)DO J = 1 TO 4) DO I = 1 TO 5), T, U, V);
(iii) GET LIST ((B(I,*) DO I = 1 TO 5), S);
 (iv) GET LIST (B,S);
```

Record I/O In this section, we will discuss two different modes of accessing files using record I/O; "sequential" input and output, and "direct" input, output, and up-

FIGURE 5-17

```
        Position
                    111        2222
        123456789012.....0123...
Line   ________________________________
  1   |BUCKƀƀƀƀƀƀ          -14
  2   |
  3   |
```

date. Sequential accessing takes a file's records in the order in which they are physically stored. Direct accessing takes a file's records in a random order, as dictated by the program. Thus any record in a directly accessed file may be read or written zero, one, or more items in a single program run.

To define a file's attributes, the file declaration is used. Its form is as follows:

$$\text{DCL filename FILE RECORD} \begin{Bmatrix} \text{SEQUENTIAL} \\ \text{DIRECT} \end{Bmatrix} \begin{Bmatrix} \text{INPUT} \\ \text{OUTPUT} \\ \text{UPDATE} \end{Bmatrix} ;$$

Here, "filename" is the name of the file, and the keywords FILE and RECORD (as opposed to STREAM) identify that record I/O, as opposed to stream I/O, will be used. One of the alternatives in braces is given to indicate SEQUENTIAL or DIRECT access, and one is given to indicate whether the file is to be used for INPUT, OUTPUT or UPDATE. "UPDATE" means that records may be both read and written in the file in a single run of the program.

To process an INPUT RECORD file sequentially, the following statement may be used:

```
READ FILE (filename) INTO (variable);
```

Here, "filename" identifies the file itself, and "variable" identifies the location where a record's contents will be stored. For example, suppose we have a file named CARDS and a variable named CARD declared as follows:

```
DCL  CARDS FILE RECORD INPUT SEQUENTIAL,
     CARD CHAR (80);
```

Then the following statement,

```
READ FILE (CARDS) INTO (CARD);
```

causes the next record in the file CARDS to be read and stored in CARD.

We have assumed here that the length of a record is eighty characters; the variable into which an input record is read should generally be the same length as that of a record in the file. Yet the variable need not be declared with the CHARACTER attribute. Alternatively, it may be useful to define a structure to accommodate an input record.

For example, assume that a card contains information for a person, as shown in Figure 5-18. The following structure would accommodate a single such record:

```
DCL 1 PERSON,
      2 NAME,
        3 FIRST CHAR (10),
        3 MIDDLE CHAR (5),
        3 LAST CHAR (15),
```

```
2 AGE PIC '99',
2 HEIGHT,
  3 FEET PIC '9',
  3 INCHES PIC '99',
2 WEIGHT PIC '99',
2 SS# PIC '(9)9',
2 REST CHAR (33);
```

The following READ statement would store a record from the file CARDS into this structure, filling all its elementary fields with values:

```
READ FILE (CARDS) INTO (PERSON);
```

It is important to emphasize that record I/O, unlike stream I/O, performs no conversions of data. Thus, the program must be sure that the data items as stored in the record will match exactly the attributes of the variables where the data items will be stored upon execution of a READ statement. Moreover, in most implementations, the *internal* representations of FIXED (FLOAT) DECIMAL (BINARY) values are *not* identical with their *external* representations; conversion is required to get from one to the other. Thus, record I/O is appropriate only for values whose internal representations are identical with their representations in the file (mainly CHARACTER and PICTURE values).

To process an OUTPUT RECORD file SEQUENTIALLY the following statement is used:

```
WRITE FILE (filename) FROM (variable);
```

Here, "filename" and "variable" identify the file and the location from which the record will be written, respectively. For example, if we want to produce a file of card images, we might declare the output file as follows:

```
DCL IMAGES FILE RECORD OUTPUT SEQUENTIAL;
```

We then would use the following WRITE statement to produce a single card image from CARD in the file IMAGES:

```
WRITE FILE (IMAGES) FROM (CARD);
```

FIGURE 5-18

Column	1-10	11-15	16-30	31-32	33	34-35	36-38	39-47	48-80
	Name			Age	Height		Weight	Social Security Number	ƀƀ. . .ƀ
	First	Middle	Last		Feet	Inches			

To process a RECORD file DIRECTly, whether for INPUT, OUTPUT, or UPDATE, each record must have associated with it a "key," which serves to uniquely identify the record and thus distinguish it from all other records in the file. For input, the READ statement must be modified to specify the KEY, in the following way:

READ FILE (filename) INTO (variable) KEY (expression);

The "expression" here defines the desired record's KEY.

To illustrate, suppose our file of PERSONs described above is to be processed DIRECTly, and that the SS# (positions 39–47) serves as each record's key. If we want to read directly from this file the record with SS# = '012301234', then we would give the following READ statement:

READ FILE (CARDS) INTO (PERSON) KEY ('012301234')

If a record exists in that file with that key, then it will be retrieved and stored in the structure PERSON. If not, the KEY condition will be raised.

To process a DIRECT RECORD file for OUTPUT, the WRITE statement must also identify the particular key of the record to be stored. Thus, the WRITE statement takes the following form:

WRITE FILE (filename) FROM (variable) KEYFROM (expression);

The value of the "expression" is interpreted as a character string and inserted into the position of the record where the key is stored. For example, if we want to add to our file (now declared as OUTPUT rather than INPUT) a record which is stored in PERSON, with KEY = '012301234', we would write the following:

WRITE FILE (CARDS) FROM (PERSON) KEYFROM ('012301234');

If a record already exists in that file with an identical key, the KEY condition will be raised.

To process a DIRECT RECORD file for UPDATE, three alternative operations can be specified:

1 Change an existing record on the file.
2 Add a new record to the file.
3 Delete an existing record from the file.

The first operation is achieved by the following pair of statements:

READ FILE (filename) INTO (variable) KEY (expression);
REWRITE FILE (filename) FROM (variable) KEY (expression);

The two statements are often separated by other statements which make changes to the record read and stored in "variable." In any event, the record which is finally rewritten from the "variable" replaces in the file the record that was just read.

The second operation, adding a record, is achieved by a WRITE statement as follows:

WRITE FILE (filename) FROM (variable) KEYFROM (expression);

The program must assure that the "expression" designating the new record's key is distinct from all other records' keys in the file. Otherwise, the KEY condition will be raised and the addition will not be made.

The third operation, deleting a record, is achieved by the following statement:

DELETE FILE (filename) KEY (expression);

The result of executing this statement is that that record on the file whose key matches the "expression" is deleted from the file. If there is no such record, the KEY condition is raised.

Input-Output Conditions The foregoing discussion noted that certain extraordinary conditions may be raised upon the occurrence of unexpected events during execution of different input-output operations. The most common among these are the ENDFILE condition, the ENDPAGE condition, the KEY condition, and the TRANSMIT condition.

The ENDFILE condition is raised when a sequential input operation (READ or GET statement) is to be executed but there is no more data remaining in the file.

The ENDPAGE condition is raised when a PUT statement is being executed for a print file and causes the last line of the current page to be passed.

The KEY condition may be raised when a direct record input or output operation is to be executed. The various situations which can cause the KEY condition to be raised are defined in the preceding section.

The TRANSMIT condition may be raised during *any* input or output operation. It means that an uncorrectable transmission error has occurred during a read or write operation, and thus the current record was not properly transferred from (or to) the file.

When any one of these conditions is raised for a file, the action that takes place depends upon whether or not the program contains a so-called "on-unit" for that condition and that file. If such an on-unit is absent from the program, the action that takes place is defined as follows:

Condition	Action in the absence of an on-unit
ENDFILE KEY TRANSMIT	Print a message indicating that the condition has occurred, and then raise the ERROR condition.
ENDPAGE	Skip to the top of the next page and then resume executing the PUT statement at the point where the ENDPAGE condition was raised.

Raising the ERROR condition usually means that program execution stops.

If the programmer prefers that some other action take place when one of these conditions takes place, then a so-called ''ON statement'' for that condition may be written. It has the following form:

ON condition (filename) on-unit;

Here, ''condition'' is one of the conditions ENDFILE, ENDPAGE, KEY or TRANSMIT, while ''filename'' identifies the particular file for which the indicated condition's occurrence is being trapped. For example, if two different sequential input files are being processed by a program, then two different ON statements may be provided for the condition ENDFILE. The ''on-unit'' designates what action should take place when the designated condition occurs with the designated file. The on-unit may be either a single statement or a sequence of statements headed by ''BEGIN;'' and terminated by ''END;''. Such a sequence is called a ''BEGIN block,'' and an example of this kind of ON statement appears in the sample program at the beginning of the chapter.

If the on-unit contains neither a STOP statement nor a GO TO statement that would cause control to transfer into another part of the program, then execution of the on-unit is immediately followed by a ''normal return'' of control to the point in the program near where the condition originally was raised. The exact return point depends upon the particular condition that occurs, as defined in the following list:

Condition	Point of normal return
ENDFILE	The statement immediately following the particular GET or READ statement where ENDFILE was raised.
ENDPAGE	The PUT statement that was being executed when ENDPAGE was raised is resumed at the point in its data list where it was interrupted.
KEY	The statement immediately following the input-output (READ, WRITE, REWRITE, or DELETE) statement where KEY was raised. The input-output statement itself, however, will not have taken place.
TRANSMIT	The statement immediately following the input-output statement where TRANSMIT was raised. The input-output statement itself, however, will not have taken place.

5-2.7 Subprograms, Functions, and Libraries

A PL/I subprogram is a procedure which may be invoked during execution of the main program [designated by ''PROCEDURE OPTIONS (MAIN)''] or another subprogram. A PL/I subprogram is classified as either a ''function procedure'' or a ''subroutine procedure.'' In either case, there are two aspects to the use of subprograms, writing them and invoking them.

Certain functions have such widespread utility that they are provided as part of the PL/I language. They are known as the ''built-in functions,'' and have been predefined as function procedures. Thus, when one of these functions—such as finding a square root—is required, the program needs only to invoke it. PL/I provides a large collection of built-in functions. From among these, we describe in Tables 5-1, 5-2, and 5-3 those which are the most useful in the various application areas.

TABLE 5-1
SOME OF PL/I's ARITHMETIC BUILT-IN FUNCTIONS

Function	Name	Arguments	Result
Absolute value	ABS	x	The absolute value of x.
Ceiling	CEIL	x	The smallest integer i for which $i \geq x$.
Cosine	COS	x	The cosine of x, where angle x is given in radians.
Exponential	EXP	x	The result of raising e to the power x.
Natural logarithm	LOG	x	The natural logarithm of x, where $x > 0$.
Common logarithm	LOG10	x	The logarithm (to the base 10) of x, where $x > 0$.
Maximum value	MAX	$x_1, x_2, \ldots, x_n$	The largest value among the given x's ($n \geq 2$).
Minimum value	MIN	$x_1, x_2, \ldots, x_n$	The smallest value among the given x's ($n \geq 2$).
Remainder	MOD	x_1, x_2	The remainder of x_1/x_2.
Sine	SIN	x	The sine of x, where x is an angle in radians.
Square root	SQRT	x	The square root of x, where $x \geq 0$.

For each of the arithmetic functions shown in Table 5-1, its argument(s) may be any numeric-valued expression x. These functions are therefore generic, in the sense that they can be applied to a numeric argument with attributes FIXED or FLOAT, DEC or BIN, and so forth. The result returned by any of these functions generally has attributes which are consistent with those of its argument(s) and the nature of the function itself.

Similarly, the array built-in functions (Table 5-2) are generic, in the sense that each may be applied to an array of any size, dimensionality, and appropriate attributes. The

TABLE 5-2
SOME OF PL/I's ARRAY BUILT-IN FUNCTIONS

Function	Name	Arguments	Result
High bound	HBOUND	a,i	For the ith dimension of the array a, the highest subscript value.
Product	PROD	a	The product of all elements in the array a.
Sum	SUM	a	The sum of all elements in the array a.

TABLE 5-3
SOME OF PL/I's STRING BUILT-IN FUNCTIONS

Function	Name	Arguments	Result
Index	INDEX	*s,t*	If the string *t* occurs in the string *s*, then the result is an integer $i > 0$ defining the position of the leftmost character of the first occurrence of *t* in *s*. Otherwise, the result is 0.
Length	LENGTH	*s*	The length of string *s*.
Substring	SUBSTR	*s,i,j*	The substring within the string *s* which begins in the position *i* and has length *j*. If *j* is omitted, then the substring extends to the end of *s*.
Verify	VERIFY	*s,t*	If all characters of the string *s* are also in the string *t*, then the result is 0. Otherwise the result is an integer $i > 0$ defining the position of the leftmost character in s which is not in *t*.

result returned by HBOUND is an integer, while the other two return results whose attributes are identical with those of the array itself.

A function is invoked by using a "function reference" in place of a variable or constant in an expression. A function reference has the following form:

name (arguments)

Here, "name" denotes the name of the function and "arguments" denotes a list of expressions (separated by commas) which describe the values to which the function is to be applied. When invoked, the function returns a single value as a result, and that result subsequently becomes an operand in the remaining evaluation of the expression in which the function reference appears. For example, suppose we have variables *A, B,* and *C,* that the values of *A* and *B* are 2 and 3, respectively, and we want to compute *C* as follows:

$$C = \frac{A + B}{\sqrt{A^2 + B^2}}$$

For this, we can use the built-in function SQRT as follows:

```
C = (A + B) / SQRT (A ** 2 + B ** 2);
       ↑   ↑          ↑    ↑    ↑
       1   5          2    4    3
```

As shown, the function reference calls for evaluation of A ** 2 + B ** 2, yielding 13, which is passed to the SQRT function. The result returned is a close approximation to the square root of 13, say 3.60555. This value then becomes the divisor in the remaining evaluation of the expression.

To illustrate how various other built-in functions may be used, assume that we have the variables and values shown in Figure 5-19. The following function references, when executed, would deliver the results shown on the right:

Function reference	Result delivered
COS(Y)	−0.970958E0
SUM(A)	15
SUM(A * B(*,3))	The "inner product" of A and the third column of B; A(1) * B(1,3) + A(2) * B(2,3) + · · · + A(5) * B(5,3) = 5.
SUBSTRING (S,I,6)	'IMES.b̸'
SUBSTR (S,I)	'IMES.b̸b̸b̸b̸'
INDEX (S,'THE')	2
INDEX (S,'THEb̸$')	12
INDEX (S,'?')	0
VERIFY (S,'b̸')	2 (the position in S of the leftmost *non*blank character)
INDEX (SUBSTR (S, VERIFY (S,'b̸')),'b̸')	6 (the position of the leftmost blank within that substring of S which begins 'THESEb̸ARE . . .')

Note that these last two examples illustrate how the INDEX and VERIFY built-in functions can be used to easily isolate a word (i.e., a sequence of characters followed by a blank) within a text. Specifically, VERIFY locates the word's leftmost character and INDEX locates its rightmost.

Writing Function Definitions When the program requires the performance of a function which is not among the built-in functions, the programmer can define a "function procedure" and then invoke it in the same way that a built-in function is invoked. Because a programmer-written function is invoked in generally the same way as a built-in function, it must always deliver a single value as a result. Procedures which expressly deliver several different results must be written as "subroutine procedures." These will be discussed in a later section.

To define a function procedure, the programmer must (1) identify the particular parameters which will be required for the function to deliver a result, (2) determine the attributes of these parameters, together with the attributes of the delivered result, (3) determine the algorithm to be used for the function's definition, and (4) set this all down as a PL/I function procedure. To illustrate these tasks, consider the problem of writing a function subprogram which will deliver as a result the factorial of a given integer *n*.

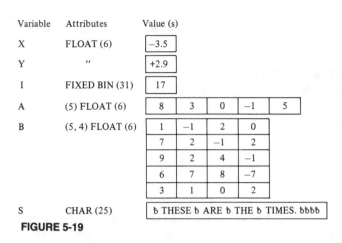

Variable	Attributes	Value (s)				
X	FLOAT (6)	−3.5				
Y	"	+2.9				
I	FIXED BIN (31)	17				
A	(5) FLOAT (6)	8	3	0	−1	5
B	(5, 4) FLOAT (6)	1	−1	2	0	
		7	2	−1	2	
		9	2	4	−1	
		6	7	8	−7	
		3	1	0	2	
S	CHAR (25)	ƀ THESE ƀ ARE ƀ THE ƀ TIMES. ƀƀƀƀ				

FIGURE 5-19

Here, one parameter, an integer *n*, is required and the factorial is defined as follows:

$$\text{fact}(n) = n \times (n - 1) \times \cdots \times 3 \times 2 \qquad \text{if } n > 1$$
$$= 1 \qquad \text{if } n \leqslant 1$$

The result to be returned is thus an integer, which is either 1 (if $n \leqslant 1$) or the product of the first *n* positive integers (if $n > 1$).

To define a PL/I function, we must begin with a PROCEDURE statement of the following form:

```
entry-name: PROCEDURE (parameter-list) RETURNS (attributes);
```

Here, "entry-name" denotes the procedure's name and the optional "parameter-list" denotes a list of parameters separated by commas. The attributes of the result returned are determined either by default or from the "attributes" part of the optional RETURNS clause shown here, if that clause is present. The rules for assigning attributes by *default* to the returned value are the same as those for ordinary variables.

Following the procedure statement is the body of the procedure, which defines the computations that will take place when the function is invoked. The function is written like an ordinary program segment, except that parameters are used where variable names would otherwise occur in the program segment. The procedure's body is always terminated by an END statement as follows:

```
END entry-name;
```

Here, "entry-name" must be identical with the function name given in its PROCEDURE statement.

To illustrate, we write a function procedure named "FACT" to compute the factorial of an integer n. Here, the parameter N denotes the number whose factorial will be computed.

```
FACT: PROC (N) RETURNS (FIXED BIN);
   DCL (F, I, N) FIXED BIN;
      F = 1;
      DO I = 2 TO N;
         F = F * I;
      END;
      RETURN (F);
END FACT;
```

Note that the procedure's body designates the factorial calculation as if N were an ordinary variable. As a parameter, N takes the place of a value which will be supplied at the time the function is invoked. At those places where it is logically appropriate to return the computed result to the calling program, the function must have a RETURN statement, whose form is as follows:

```
RETURN (expression);
```

The value of this "expression" is returned to the calling program. Since that result must be a single value, the expression must be one which delivers one value, be it arithmetic or string. In this example, notice that the computed value of the variable F is returned to the calling program. Both F and I are "local" variables within the function, and serve only temporary purposes.

Invoking Functions Functions which are defined in the program are invoked the same way as the built-in functions: by using a function reference. However, some additional considerations apply to programmer-defined functions, which are discussed below. To illustrate, suppose we want to compute the binomial coefficients

$$a_i = \frac{n!}{i!\,(n - i)!} \qquad i = 0, 1, \ldots, n$$

Then we could write the following program, which prints the desired sequence of coefficients, given by A in the program:

```
P: PROC OPTIONS (MAIN);
   DCL (A, I, N) FIXED BIN,
      FACT ENTRY RETURNS (FIXED BIN);
   GET LIST (N);
   DO I = 0 TO N;
      A = FACT(N) / (FACT(I) * FACT(N-I));
      PUT SKIP LIST (I, A);
   END;
END P;
```

We focus attention on the two underlined parts of this program. The *first* serves to identify the attributes of the result returned by the FACT function. The *second* highlights three invocations of the function FACT.

Each argument of a function reference may be any expression, as shown by N, I, and N − I in these three invocations, respectively. Such arguments are evaluated before the function is invoked. Of course, a function reference must always contain exactly as many arguments as there are parmeters in the function's definition. A left-right, one-to-one correspondence is established between the arguments and the parameters.

When the function is invoked, the following steps take place:

1 Each argument's name, or its value, replaces each occurrence of the corresponding parameter in the body.

2 The resulting body is executed as if it were part of the calling program.

3 The result returned by the invocation is given by the expression in the RETURN statement when it is executed.

It is important to remember, when writing and invoking functions, the PL/I convention for associating parameters with arguments at the time of an invocation.

1 When an argument agrees in all its attributes with its corresponding parameter, it is associated "by reference" with the parameter. That is, all references to the parameter within the procedure actually take place in the location where the value of the corresponding argument is stored.

2 If one or more arguments disagrees in any of its attributes with its corresponding parameter, a so-called "dummy argument" is created, which is a *copy* of the value of the argument, and used in the procedure throughout the invocation. Since that copy resides in a different (system-defined) storage location than the original argument, the value of the original argument is *not changed* by the invocation. This is usually referred to as "call by value," and is generally acceptable for arguments which are used as input to the procedure. The opposite situation, "call by reference," is a *necessary* condition for arguments whose values may be changed by the procedure. In the case of functions, however, normal usage dictates that all of the arguments are used strictly as input to the function, and thus the notion of "call by reference" is not relevant. For subroutines, this is quite a different matter, as we shall see in the next section.

3 If the argument is not a simple variable name (i.e., is a constant or an expression with operators), then a dummy argument is automatically created by the invocation.

The form of an entry declaration is slightly more general than the one underlined in the example above.

DCL entry-name ENTRY (attributes-list) RETURNS (attributes);

Here, "attributes-list" denotes a list of attributes, each separated from the next by a comma. The number of attributes in the list is identical with the number of parameters in the function itself. Each one must agree with the attributes of its corresponding parameter in the function's definition.

Writing Subroutine Definitions A subroutine does not return a value to the calling program in the same way that a function does. The result returned by a subroutine can be one or more elementary values, arrays, or structures. Additional parameters are provided in the subroutines's definition to designate each of these results. In a subroutine definition, the RETURN statement must not contain an expression (since one result may not be returned). Instead, those parameters which designate results returned by the subroutine are written in an appropriate context within the subroutine's body, in order to allow values to be assigned to their corresponding arguments at the time of invocation.

We illustrate these conventions by rewriting the function FACT as a subroutine. In this rewriting, the additional parameter F is used to designate the resulting factorial. Recall that F was an ordinary variable in the original function definition.

```
FACT: PROC (N, F);
   DCL (N, F, I) FIXED BIN;
      F = 1;
      DO I = 2 TO N;
         F = F * I;
      END;
      RETURN;
END FACT;
```

Comparing this with the original function definition, note that the RETURN statement does not include an expression. This gives only the point at which control will return to the calling program. Note also that the RETURNS clause is omitted in the first line, since no result is returned as for functions.

Below is another example to illustrate two additional features: a subroutine which computes several results (rather than just one), and the handling of arrays in subroutine definitions. Here, we write a subroutine which, for any one-dimensional array, computes the mean, maximum value, and minimum value. For this problem, we identify four parameters. A designates the array supplied by the calling program, while MEAN, MAX, and MIN designate the results to be computed by the subroutine. We name the subroutine MMM.

```
MMM: PROC (A, MEAN, MAX, MIN);
        DCL A(*) FLOAT DEC,
           (MEAN, MAX, MIN) FLOAT DEC,
           (I, N) FIXED BIN;
        N = HBOUND (A,1);
        MEAN, MAX, MIN = A(1);       /* INITIALIZE RESULTS*/
        DO I = 2 TO N;
           MEAN = MEAN + A(I);
           IF A (I) > MAX THEN MAX = A(I);
           ELSE IF A (I) < MIN THEN MIN = A(I);
        END;
        MEAN = MEAN/N;
END MMM;
```

This subprogram can adapt itself to any one-dimensional array, regardless of its size. Recall that the function HBOUND is used to determine the highest subscript value (number of elements) in an array.

Invoking a Subroutine A subroutine is invoked by a CALL statement, whose general form is as follows.

CALL entry-name (argument-list);

Here, ''entry-name'' identifies the name of the subroutine being invoked, and the optional ''argument-list'' gives the actual arguments to be used for this particular invocation. For example, we rewrite below the program which computed the binomial coefficients, using the subroutine FACT rather than the function FACT.

```
P: PROC OPTIONS (MAIN);
   DCL (A, I, N, F1, F2, F3) FIXED BIN,
      FACT ENTRY (FIXED BIN, FIXED BIN);
   GET LIST (N);
   CALL FACT (N, F1);
   DO I = 0 TO N;
      CALL FACT (I, F2);
      CALL FACT (N-I, F3);
      A = F1/(F2 * F3);
      PUT SKIP LIST (I, A);
   END;
END P;
```

The most noticeable difference between this and the original version is the addition of three new variables, F1, F2, and F3. These hold the results computed by the three different calls to the FACT subroutine. Note also that the ENTRY declaration for FACT does not have a RETURNS clause. That clause is meaningful only for functions.

The argument-parameter correspondence for subroutines is exactly like that for functions. Note specifically that the arguments F1, F2, and F3 *must* necessarily agree in their attributes with the corresponding parameter F in the subroutine definition. Failure to do this would have forced dummy arguments to be created, and thus prevented the subroutine from properly returning the computed factorial to the argument F1, F2, or F3. In other words, parameters which designate results returned by the subroutine must necessarily be called ''by reference'' and not ''by value.''

Internal Subprograms, EXTERNAL Variables, and Side Effects So far, we have discussed PL/I subprogramming facilities as if the calling program and the called subprogram were mutually external to each other, and the only way that information can be passed between the two is through the use of parameters and corresponding arguments. Other options, however, are available. A subprogram's definition may be embedded totally within the (sub)program that invokes it. Information may be passed between the invoking program and the subprogram in other ways than by the use of parameters. In this section we present these alternatives.

The range of statements which can reference a variable is known as the variable's "scope." This is defined in such a way that no two variables with the same name can be referenced by the same statement. The scope of a PL/I variable includes just the statements in that procedure (or BEGIN block) where it is declared, excluding any procedures which are internal to that procedure and which themselves contain a declaration of a variable with the same name. If the variable is *undeclared*, its scope includes the procedure in which it is referenced together with all procedures in which it is embedded that do not themselves declare a variable with the same name. These two situations are depicted below.

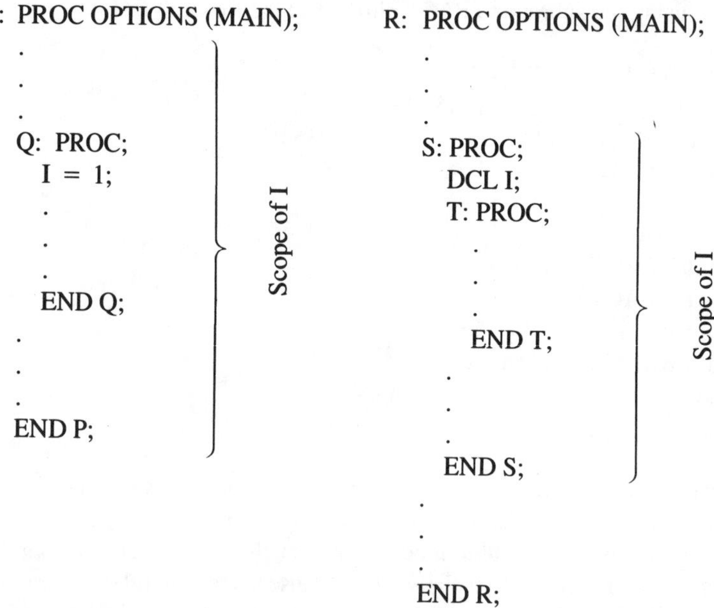

In the left-hand example, the variable I is assumed undeclared in P and Q, and thus its scope includes all statements in both procedures. In the right-hand example, I is declared in procedure S, and thus its scope is delimited to all statements throughout S and T (assuming I is undeclared in T), but *no* statements in procedure R may reference I.

When two procedures are mutually external, they may still share the same variable by declaring it EXTERAL in *both* procedures. In the example below, both procedures U and V share the variable I in common.

```
U: PROC;
   DCL I EXTERNAL;
   .
   .
```

```
      .
      END U;
V:    PROC;
      DCL I EXTERNAL;
      .
      .
      .
      END V;
```

Here, if I had not been given the EXTERNAL attribute, each procedure would have had access to its own *local* variable I.

Another question to be considered when defining subprograms is that of so-called "side effects." A side effect is the alteration by a subprogram of the value of a variable which is not an argument in the invocation, and is not local to the subprogram. Most side effects in actual practice are undesirable and unnecessary. For example, if the internally embedded function FACT had failed to declare, and thus delimit the scope of, its local variable I, this undesirable kind of side effect would have arisen. Some side effects are intentional and should be explicitly documented when they occur.

Recursion Some applicatons require the use of functions that are defined recursively. That is, the function may invoke istelf during its execution. Instances of recursion are found throughout mathematics, the theory of computing, and artificial intelligence.

PL/I supports recursive functions by requiring that the word RECURSIVE appear in the procedure heading. For example, consider the recursive definition of the factorial function.

$$\begin{aligned} \text{factorial }(n) &= 1 && \text{if } n < 2 \\ &= n \times \text{factorial }(n-1) && \text{if } n \geqslant 2 \end{aligned}$$

This definition can be directly encoded in PL/I as a recursive procedure as follows:

```
FACT: PROC (N) RETURNS (FIXED BIN) RECURSIVE;
   DCL N FIXED BIN;
   IF N < 2 THEN RETURN (1);
   ELSE RETURN (N * FACT (N - 1));
END FACT;
```

5-2.8 Additional Features

Although it would be impossible to do justice to *all* the additional features of PL/I in this section, we will dwell on the following three topics in the paragraphs below:

- Program preparation and layout
- Conditions, interrupts, and on-units
- Storage classes and dynamic storage allocation

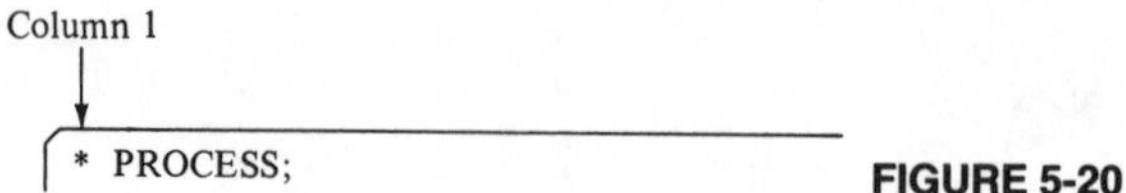

FIGURE 5-20

Program Preparation and Layout When typed at a terminal, a PL/I program may be laid out in a fairly free-form manner. Some implementations require that the program not use column 1 or columns 73–80 of each line. Beyond that, however, there is no required starting position for statements or statement labels.

When a PL/I program has one or more EXTERNAL subprograms, some implementations require that the subprograms be separated from each other and from the main program by a special delimiter line. This line usually has the form shown in Figure 5-20. Additional compiler options can also be specified on this line. The interested reader is referred to specific compiler documentation for further information.

Any number of blank spaces may be inserted anywhere within a PL/I statement except within a variable name, statement label, procedure name, or PL/I keyword. For example, DECLARE must not contain any embedded blanks. On the other hand, no two adjacent PL/I keywords or names may be written *without* at least one blank space between them. For instance, the following are not equivalent:

```
DCL X FLOAT DEC;
DCL X FLOATDEC;
DCL XFLOAT DEC;
DCLX FLOAT DEC;
```

The second and fourth of these are invalid statements, the first declares a variable named X, and the third declares a variable named XFLOAT.

Conditions, Interrupts, and On-Units In earlier sections we have mentioned a number of so-called "conditions" that can be raised in the event that an exceptional event occurred during execution of a program. In addition to those we mentioned, PL/I has a number of other conditions. The most important of these conditions are summarized in the following table:

Condition	**Meaning**
CONVERSION	A character string value, such as 'ABC', cannot be converted to an equivalent arithmetic value.
FIXEDOVERFLOW	An arithmetic operation has a FIXED result which exceeds the maximum precision allowed by the implementation.
OVERFLOW	A FLOAT value exceeds the maximum allowed by the implementation.
SIZE	A high-order significant digit is dropped when a value is assigned to a FIXED variable.
(cont'd)	

Condition	Meaning
UNDERFLOW	A FLOAT value is smaller than the minimum allowed by the implementation.
ZERODIVIDE	The denominator in a division (/) is zero.
ENDFILE	An attempt was made to read from a sequential input file after the last record had already been read.
ENDPAGE	An attempt was made to execute a PUT statement for a print file whose output would exceed the last line of the page.
KEY	(1) An attempt was made to read a record from a DIRECT file, and no record exists on the file with the specified key, or (2) an attempt was made to write a record to a DIRECT file and there was already a record on the file with the same key.
TRANSMIT	A physical input-output device error occurred during the transmission of a record to or from the device.
SUBSCRIPTRANGE	A subscript is outside its range for the array in question.
STRINGRANGE	A SUBSTR function reference improperly describes a substring which is partly or fully outside the string in question.
CHECK	One of the variables in the so-called "check-list" has been assigned a new value, or a statement whose label appears in the check list has been executed.

The uses of these conditions are individually illustrated below. Here, we first describe what happens when *any* of these conditions occurs during program execution.

First, each condition is said to be in one of two states at any time during program execution: ''enabled'' and ''disabled.'' Program execution is, in fact, interrupted upon the occurrence of one of these conditions only if that condition is enabled at the time the condition occurs. If the condition is disabled, program execution continues as if the condition had never occurred.

Certain of these conditions are *permanently* enabled by the system throughout program execution. Those are ENDFILE, ENDPAGE, KEY, and TRANSMIT. Certain other of these conditions are initially enabled by the system, but may be explicitly disabled with the program. Those are CONVERSION, FIXEDOVERFLOW, OVERFLOW, and ZERODIVIDE. The rest of these are initially disabled by the system, but may be explicitly enabled within the program.

To enable a condition within the program, a so-called ''condition prefix'' is added at the top of the program. This has the following form:

(condition-list);

Here, ''condition-list'' denotes a list of those conditions, separated by commas. For example, if we wanted to enable the SIZE and SUBSCRIPTRANGE conditions throughout execution of program P, we would write the following:

```
(SIZE, SUBRG):
P:PROC OPTIONS (MAIN);
.
.
.
END P;
```

Similarly, to *disable* one or more otherwise-enabled conditions throughout execution of a program, we write a condition prefix in which each of the disabled conditions is written with NO attached to its left end. For example, if we want also to disable the CONVERSION condition in the above program, we may rewrite the condition prefix as follows:

```
(SIZE, SUBRG, NOCONV):
```

Now suppose that an enabled condition actually arises and program execution is interrupted. What happens next depends upon whether the program wants to take its own action when the condition arises, or is willing to accept the ''Standard System Action'' for that condition. This choice is indicated by the presence or absence in the program of an ON statement for that condition, respectively.

Suppose for the moment that no ON statement is present in our program for any condition, and that all conditions are enabled. The following table tells what will occur as the Standard system action when one of these conditions arises:

Condition(s)	**Standard system action**
CONVERSION FIXEDOVERFLOW OVERFLOW SIZE UNDERFLOW ZERODIVIDE ENDFILE KEY TRANSMIT SUBSCRIPTRANGE	An error message is displayed and execution terminates.
ENDPAGE	The print file is advanced to the top of the next page, and execution of the output statement resumes as if ENDPAGE had not occurred.
STRINGRANGE	Execution continues with some string different from the ill-specified substring.
CHECK	This is a special condition used for program tracing, and will be discussed separately.

We have already seen the use of ON statements to control program execution when an input-output condition arises, in the example program at the beginning of the chapter. The general form of an ON statement is the following:

```
ON condition on-unit
```

Here, "condition" denotes any of the conditions listed above, and "on-unit" denotes either a single statement or a BEGIN block.

A BEGIN block, like a DO group, is used to delimit an entire sequence of statements. It has the following form:

```
BEGIN;
   Sequence of
   statements
END;
```

When used as an on-unit, the BEGIN block may contain any statement except RETURN.

To further illustrate the use of ON statements, consider the following program:

```
P: PROC OPTIONS (MAIN);
       DCL (I, NZ) FIXED BIN INIT (0);
       ON ENDFILE (SYSIN) BEGIN;
          PUT SKIP LIST (NZ, 'DIVISIONS BY ZERO.');
          STOP;
       END;
       ON ZDIV NZ = NZ + 1;
LOOP:  DO I = 1 BY 1;
          GET LIST (A, B);
          C = A/B;
       END;
END P;
```

The purpose of this program is simply to read pairs of numbers, A and B, divide the first by the second, and keep track of the number of times division by zero occurs.

Execution begins with the statement labeled LOOP. This DO loop continues normally until one of the two conditions, ENDFILE (SYSIN) or ZDIV, occurs. ZDIV can occur only during execution of the statement "C = A/B;". When that condition arises, the program is interrupted and the ON statement for ZDIV is executed. Thus the counter NZ is incremented.

Now, when execution of an ON statement terminates without either a transfer back to the program (via a GO TO statement in the on-unit) or a termination of the program (via a STOP statement in the on-unit), this causes so-called "normal return" to occur. The particular point in the program where control returns in this fashion depends on the particular condition that arose. The table below describes the point of normal return for each of the conditions discussed here:

Condition	Normal return from an on-unit
CONVERSION	Conversion is retried with the string which caused the condition to arise, within the statement where it arose.
FIXEDOVERFLOW OVERFLOW SIZE UNDERFLOW ZERODIVIDE	Control returns to a point immediately following the statement where the condition arose. The numerical result where the condition was raised becomes undefined.
ENDFILE KEY TRANSMIT	Control returns to the statement immediately following the input-output statement which caused the condition to arise.
ENDPAGE	Control returns to that point in the PUT statement which caused the condition to arise.
SUBSCRIPTRANGE STRINGRANGE CHECK	Control returns to a point immediately following that place in the statement where the condition arose.

Returning to our example program, we now see that control will return from the ON statement to assign the undefined result of A/0 to C, in the statement "C = A/B;". The loop then continues, exercising the statement "NZ = NZ + 1;" whenever the condition ZDIV arises, until finally the condition ENDFILE (SYSIN) arises. At that point, the other ON statement takes control and execution stops upon reaching the STOP statement. If "Normal return" had been allowed to occur here, control would have passed back improperly to the loop.

Finally, we should mention that the CHECK condition is PL/I's main vehicle for program tracing and checking of intermediate results during program development. Although it is a debugging tool the CHECK condition is an intrinsic part of the PL/I language.

To display the value of a variable, for example I, whenever it is assigned a new value (by execution of an assignment or input statement), we append a CHECK prefix to the program as follows:

```
(CHECK (I)):
```

When we want a statement label, for example L, displayed each time that statement is executed, we append a CHECK prefix to the program as follows.

```
(CHECK (L)):
```

Of course, use of the CHECK prefix generally degrades execution speed of the program, and it should be used only during program development.

Storage Classes and Dynamic Storage Allocation Often a program cannot predict its storage requirements for certain variables and arrays until after it has begun executing. PL/I has extensive facilities for dynamic storage allocation, and these allow PL/I to be substantially useful in systems programming applications, where it is needed most.

Every PL/I variable (including arrays and structures) has a ''storage class'' attribute, which defines when, how, and by whom its storage is allocated. A variable's storage class can be any of the following:

Storage class	Meaning
STATIC	Storage is allocated once for the variable, and its initial value (if any) is assigned by the system when the program is loaded for execution.
AUTOMATIC	Storage is allocated for the variable and its initial value (if any) is reassigned by the system each time the procedure, or BEGIN block, that declares it begins execution.
CONTROLLED	Storage is allocated for the variable by the program upon execution of an ALLOCATE statement. Until that time, the variable may not be referenced, since its storage does not yet exist. However, several "copies" of the variable may exist simultaneously, in which case only the most recently allocated copy can be referenced by the program.
BASED	Like CONTROLLED variables, storage is allocated by the program. Unlike CONTROLLED, a BASED variable may exist in several "copies" and all may be referenced at the same time by the program.

If the program does not explicitly declare a variable's storage class, AUTOMATIC is assigned by default.

The STATIC storage class is the most efficient in time, since stroage is allocated and initial values are assigned when the program is first loaded for execution. Because AUTOMATIC is generally the most widely used storage class, it occurs by default. The system allocates storage for an AUTOMATIC variable, but not until the PROCEDURE or BEGIN block in which it is declared actually begins execution. This accommodates, for example, the important situation where the program cannot predict the size N of an array A before execution begins.

The CONTROLLED storage class passes responsibility for allocating and freeing a variable's storage to the program. Storage allocation occurs upon execution of an ALLOCATE statement, and deallocation occurs upon execution of a FREE statement. They have the following basic forms:

```
ALLOCATE variable-list;
FREE variable-list;
```

Here, "variable-list" denotes a list of one or more variable (including array or structure) names, each of which must have the CONTROLLED attribute.

A CONTROLLED variable, for example X, cannot be referenced until after an "ALLOCATE X;" statement is executed. A reference to X, as in "Y = X + 1;", refers to that instance of X which was most recently allocated. The next most recently allocated instance of X is accessible only after a "FREE X;" statement is executed, which deallocates the most recently allocated instance of X. Thus, a series of allocations for the same variable creates a pushdown stack, whose top is identified as the most recently allocated instance of the variable. ALLOCATE and FREE, in this setting, tend to simulate the stack's elementary "push" and "pop" operations.

However, when the CONTROLLED variable is an array whose size is unpredictable, its allocation can be done explicitly in the program as follows. First, the array's unknown size is indicated by "*" in its declaration. For example,

```
DCL A(*) FLOAT CONTROLLED;
```

declares A to be a one-dimensional array of an unknown number of FLOAT values, for which storage will be allocated and freed by the program.

The BASED storage class is similar to the CONTROLLED storage class, with the additional capability that all existing (rather than just the most recently allocated) copies of a BASED variable may be referenced at any time during program execution.

The mechanism for referencing a BASED variable is the so-called "POINTER variable." This is a different kind of variable from the ones we have discussed so far. A POINTER variable's sole purpose is to *point to,* or reference, a BASED variable. This is illustrated in Figure 5-21. Here, if we want to refer to that instance of B whose value is 15, we would write the following "qualified reference" to B:

```
P → B
```

The other instance is referenced by "Q → B".

Although any number of different pointer variables may be used to reference a BASED variable, *one* must be identified uniquely as the BASED variable's "home pointer." This is done at the time of declaration as follows:

```
DCL variable BASED (pointer-variable);
```

For example, we may write

```
DCL B FIXED BASED (P);
```

to declare that B is BASED and its home pointer is P.

When storage is allocated for a BASED variable, one of the following forms of the ALLOCATE statement must be used:

(i) ALLOCATE variable;
(ii) ALLOCATE variable SET (pointer-variable);

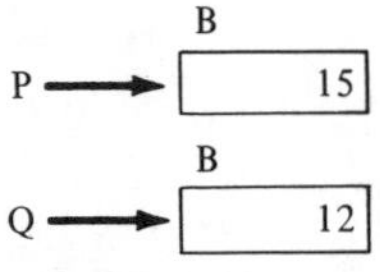

FIGURE 5-21

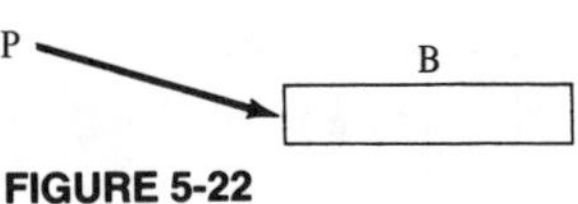

FIGURE 5-22

Form (i) causes a new version of the "variable" to be created, and sets that variable's home pointer to point to it. Form (ii) is equivalent to form (i), except that the particular pointer variable is given explicitly. Thus either of the following

```
ALLOCATE B;
ALLOCATE B SET (P);
```

causes storage to be allocated for B and P to point to that version, as shown in Figure 5-22. The following statements cause (1) another version of B to be allocated and referenced by Q, and (2) the values 15 and 12 to be assigned the two versions, respectively, as shown in Figure 5-21:

```
ALLOCATE B SET (Q);
P → B = 15;
Q → B = 12;
```

As shown here, the particular version of a BASED variable in question may be explicitly specified by a "qualified reference," such as P → B or Q → B above. Moreover, when the desired version is the one referenced by the based variable's home pointer, the qualification "P→" may be dropped. Thus, for instance, the second statement above may be equivalently rewritten as "B = 15;".

Pointer variables may be declared either by their identification as a BASED variable's home pointer or explicitly, with the POINTER attribute. For instance, the pointer Q used above must be declared as follows:

```
DCL Q PTR;
```

A pointer variable may be assigned a value by execution of an ALLOCATE statement or by execution of an assignment statement. For instance,

```
Q = P;
```

assigns to Q the value of P. Effectively, this makes Q reference the same version of a based variable as P currently does (Figure 5-23).

There is a special value "NULL" which, when assigned to a pointer variable, means

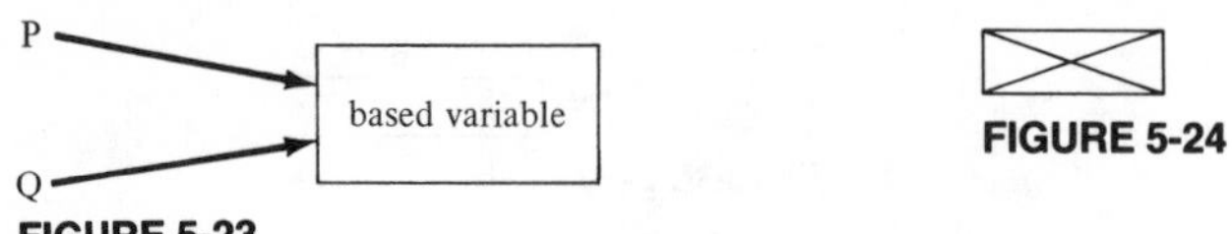

FIGURE 5-23

FIGURE 5-24

that it "points nowhere." The NULL value is depicted in Figure 5-24 for the pointer Q. NULL can be assigned to Q in the following way:

```
Q = NULL;
```

5-3 APPLICATIONS OF PL/I

Now that the reader has a working knowledge of PL/I, we present and discuss a PL/I solution for Case Study 2—Employee File Maintenance. This presentation will illustrate the use of PL/I in data processing applications. Following that discussion, we present certain implementation-dependent features of PL/I. Finally, we give an overall evaluation of PL/I.

5-3.1 PL/I Case Study Implementation

The PL/I case study program was run on the following computer and compiler:

1 IBM 4341 OS/VS PL/I Optimizing Compiler

Case Study 2—Employee File Maintenance in PL/I

This case study was implemented as a PL/I main program (CASE2) and four external subprograms (NUMERIC, EPRINT, BVALID, and EVALID). These are shown in Figures 5-25 to 5-29.

The main program, CASE2, controls the overall process. It reads an update record from the file UPDATES, verifies its SS# and its sequence, reads a corresponding record from the file EMPFILE (if necessary), and performs the addition, change, or deletion appropriately.

The subprogram NUMERIC serves to answer the question of whether or not an arbitrary string is composed entirely of digits. The subprogram EPRINT prints an erroneous update record, as well as a message (MSG) indicating the nature of the error. The subprogram BVALID checks for satisfaction of the basic validity rules by an individual addition or change update record. Similarly, EVALID checks for satisfaction of the extended validity rules. Note that, when an error is found by either of these subprograms, the string MSG is appended with an appropriate message describing the nature of the error.

We also note that certain commonly accessed items are declared as EXTERNAL to these various subprograms, so that the cumbersome linkage by way of parameters and arguments can be avoided. These items include the current employee record, MRECORD, as well as error message string, MSG.

```
CASE2: PROCEDURE OPTIONS(MAIN);

/* PL/I IMPLEMENTATION OF CASE STUDY 2 -- EMPLOYEE FILE MAINTENANCE

   THE MAIN PROGRAM USES THE FOLLOWING AUXILIARY SUBPROGRAMS:
       BVALID - CHECKS AN ADDITION OR CHANGE AGAINST THE BASIC
                VALIDITY RULES
       EVALID - CHECKS THE SAME AGAINST THE EXTENDED VALIDITY RULES
       EPRINT - DISPLAYS AN ERRORONEOUS UPDATE RECORD
       NUMERIC - CHECKS WHETHER OR NOT A STRING CONTAINS ONLY DECIMAL
                 DIGITS

   THESE PROGRAMS SHARE A MASTER FILE RECORD AND AN UPDATE RECORD,
   WHICH ARE DECLARED 'EXTERNAL' AMONG THEM.
*/

DECLARE NUMERIC ENTRY(CHAR(*)) RETURNS(BIT),
      (BVALID, EVALID) ENTRY RETURNS(BIT),
      EPRINT ENTRY,

        EMPFILE FILE RECORD UPDATE DIRECT ENV(INDEXED),
        UPDATES FILE RECORD INPUT SEQUENTIAL,

      1 URECORD EXTERNAL,            /* UPDATE RECORD LAYOUT */
        2 UCODE           CHAR(1),        /* A=ADDITION, D=DELETION,
                                             C=CHANGE */
        2 USS#            CHAR(10),       /* SOCIAL SECURITY NUMBER */
        2 UDATA           CHAR(139),      /* UPDATE RECORD DETAILS */

      MRECORD CHAR(200) EXTERNAL,    /* EMPLOYEE MASTER FILE RECORD */
      1 EMPLOYEE DEFINED MRECORD,
        2 SPARE           CHAR(1),
        2 SS#             CHAR(10),       /* SOCIAL SECURITY NUMBER */
        2 FILLER          CHAR(132),
        2 YEAR_TO_DATE,
          3 GROSS         PIC'(6)9V99',
          3 FED_TAX       PIC'(5)9V99',
          3 FICA          PIC'(4)9V99',
          3 STATE_TAX     PIC'(4)9V99',
          3 HEALTH_INS    PIC'(3)9V99',
          3 LIFE_INS      PIC'(3)9V99',
          3 CREDIT_UNION  PIC'(4)9V99',
          3 STOCK_PURCHASE PIC'(4)9V99',
          3 NET           PIC'(6)9V99',

      (MSG CHAR(150) VARYING, NE FIXED BIN INIT(0)) EXTERNAL,

      (PNO, NA, ND, NC, NR) FIXED BIN INIT(0), /* LOCAL VARIABLES */
      KEYRAISED BIT;

ON ENDFILE(UPDATES) BEGIN;
        PUT SKIP(2) EDIT('END MAINTENANCE RUN',
                         ND, ' DELETIONS,',
                         NC, ' CHANGES, AND',
                         NA, ' ADDITIONS WERE MADE.',
                         NE, ' ERRONEOUS UPDATES WERE DISCARDED.')
                        (A, SKIP(2), (4)(F(5), A, SKIP));
        CLOSE FILE(UPDATES), FILE(EMPFILE);
        GO TO END_CASE2;
        END;
```

FIGURE 5-25

```
ON KEY(EMPFILE) BEGIN;
         KEYRAISED='1'B;
         IF UCODE='D' THEN DO;
            MSG=MSG||'RECORD TO BE DELETED NOT ON EMPLOYEE FILE.' ;
            CALL EPRINT;
            END;
         IF UCODE='C' THEN DO;
            MSG=MSG||'RECORD TO BE CHANGED NOT ON EMPLOYEE FILE.' ;
            CALL EPRINT;
            END;
         END;

ON ENDPAGE(SYSPRINT) BEGIN;
         PNO=PNO+1;
         PUT EDIT('EMPLOYEE FILE MAINTENANCE ERROR LOG',
                  'PAGE', PNO, 'RECORD CONTENTS', 'ERROR DESCRIPTION')
                 (PAGE, A, COL(80), A, F(4), SKIP(2), A, COL(102), A);
         PUT SKIP(2);
         END;

/* MAIN CONTROL LOOP FOR THE PROGRAM */
      SIGNAL ENDPAGE(SYSPRINT);
      DO  NR=0 BY 1;            /* REPEAT AS LONG AS RECORDS REMAIN */
        MSG='';
        KEYRAISED='0'B;
        READ FILE(UPDATES) INTO(URECORD);
        IF NUMERIC(USS#)
          THEN IF MOD(SUBSTR(USS#,1,9)/11,10) ^= SUBSTR(USS#,10,1)
               THEN MSG=MSG||'INVALID SS#. ';
          ELSE MSG=MSG||'INVALID SS#. ';
        IF MSG^='' THEN CALL EPRINT;
        ELSE IF UCODE='D'                    /* PROCESS A DELETION */
             THEN IF UDATA^=' ' THEN DO;
                    MSG=MSG||'INVALID DELETION RECORD. ';
                    CALL EPRINT;
                    END;
                  ELSE DO;
                    DELETE FILE(EMPFILE) KEY(USS#);
                    IF ^KEYRAISED THEN ND=ND+1;
                    END;

        ELSE IF UCODE='A' THEN DO;          /* PROCESS AN ADDITION */
                  READ FILE(EMPFILE) INTO(MRECORD) KEY(USS#);
                  IF ^KEYRAISED THEN DO;
                    MSG=MSG||'SS# OF ADDITION ALREADY ON FILE. ';
                    CALL EPRINT;
                    END;
                  ELSE DO;
                    SS#=USS#;
                    SUBSTR(MRECORD,12,139)=UDATA;
                    YEAR_TO_DATE=0;
                    IF ^BVALID THEN CALL EPRINT;
                    ELSE IF ^EVALID THEN CALL EPRINT;
                         ELSE DO;
                           WRITE FILE(EMPFILE) FROM(MRECORD)
                                 KEYFROM(SS#);
                           NA=NA+1;
                           END;
                    END;
                  END;
```

FIGURE 5-25 *(Continued)*

```
ELSE IF UCODE='C' THEN DO;          /* PROCESS A CHANGE */
        READ FILE(EMPFILE) INTO(MRECORD) KEY(USS#);
        IF ^KEYRAISED THEN DO;
          IF SUBSTR(UDATA,  1,40) ^= ' '  /* NAME CHANGE */
          THEN SUBSTR(MRECORD, 12,40) = SUBSTR(UDATA,  1,40);
          IF SUBSTR(UDATA, 41,37) ^= ' '  /* ADDRESS     */
          THEN SUBSTR(MRECORD, 52,37) = SUBSTR(UDATA, 41,37);
          IF SUBSTR(UDATA, 78, 1) ^= ' '  /* SEX         */
          THEN SUBSTR(MRECORD, 89, 1) = SUBSTR(UDATA, 78, 1);
          IF SUBSTR(UDATA, 79, 1) ^= ' '  /* MARITAL     */
          THEN SUBSTR(MRECORD, 90, 1) = SUBSTR(UDATA, 79, 1);
          IF SUBSTR(UDATA, 80, 6) ^= ' '  /* BIRTH       */
          THEN SUBSTR(MRECORD, 91, 6) = SUBSTR(UDATA, 80, 6);
          IF SUBSTR(UDATA, 86, 6) ^= ' '  /* DATE EMPLOYED */
          THEN SUBSTR(MRECORD, 97, 6) = SUBSTR(UDATA, 86, 6);
          IF SUBSTR(UDATA, 92,19) ^= ' '  /* JOB STATUS  */
          THEN SUBSTR(MRECORD,103,19) = SUBSTR(UDATA, 92,19);
          IF SUBSTR(UDATA,111,22) ^= ' '  /* DEDUCTIONS  */
          THEN SUBSTR(MRECORD,122,22) = SUBSTR(UDATA,111,22);

          IF ^BVALID THEN CALL EPRINT;
          ELSE IF ^EVALID THEN CALL EPRINT;
               ELSE DO;
                 REWRITE FILE(EMPFILE) FROM(MRECORD) KEY(SS#);
                 NC=NC+1;
                 END;
          END;
        END;
ELSE DO;
  MSG=MSG||'INVALID UPDATE CODE. ';
  CALL EPRINT;
  END;
END;

END_CASE2: END CASE2;
```

FIGURE 5-25 (*Continued*)

```
NUMERIC: PROCEDURE(S) RETURNS(BIT);
       /* DETERMINE WHETHER OR NOT THE STRING S IS COMPRISED
          ENTIRELY OF DIGITS */
       DCL S CHAR(*);
       IF VERIFY(S,'0123456789')=0
         THEN RETURN('0'B);
         ELSE RETURN('1'B);
       END NUMERIC;
```

FIGURE 5-26

```
EPRINT: PROCEDURE;
       /* THIS PROCEDURE PRINTS AN ERROR UPDATE RECORD AND
          THE CORRESPONDING ERROR MESSAGE */
       DCL (MSG CHAR(150) VAR, URECORD CHAR(150),
            NE FIXED BIN INIT(0)) EXTERNAL;
       PUT SKIP(2) EDIT(SUBSTR(URECORD,1,100),MSG)
                       (A,COL(102),A(19));
       IF LENGTH(MSG)>19 THEN MSG=SUBSTR(MSG,20); ELSE MSG='';
       PUT SKIP EDIT(SUBSTR(URECORD,101),MSG)
                    (A,COL(102),A(19));
       IF LENGTH(MSG)>19 THEN MSG=SUBSTR(MSG,20); ELSE MSG='';
       NE=NE+1;
       DO WHILE(MSG^='');
          PUT SKIP EDIT(MSG)(COL(102),A(19));
          IF LENGTH(MSG)>19 THEN MSG=SUBSTR(MSG,20); ELSE MSG='';
          END;
       END EPRINT;
```

FIGURE 5-27

```
BVALID: PROCEDURE RETURNS(BIT);
      /* CHECK THE RECORD FOR COMPLIANCE WITH THE BASIC
         VALIDITY RULES. */
      DCL NUMERIC ENTRY(CHAR(*)) RETURNS(BIT),
          MSG CHAR(150) VAR EXTERNAL,
          MRECORD CHAR(200) EXTERNAL,
          1 EMPLOYEE DEFINED MRECORD,
            2 SPARE         CHAR(1),
            2 SS#           PIC'(10)9',
            2 NAME,
              3 LAST        CHAR(15),
              3 FIRST       CHAR(15),
              3 MIDDLE      CHAR(10),
            2 ADDRESS,
              3 STREET      CHAR(15),
              3 CITY        CHAR(15),
              3 STATE       CHAR(2),
              3 ZIP         CHAR(5),
            2 SEX              CHAR(1),
            2 MARITAL          CHAR(1),
            2 BIRTH            CHAR(6),
            2 DATE_EMPLOYED CHAR(6),
            2 JOB_STATUS,
              3 POSITION CHAR(2),
              3 DATE     CHAR(6),
              3 DEPT     CHAR(3),
              3 SALARY,
                4 BASIS        CHAR(1),
                4 RATE         PIC'(5)9V99',
            2 DEDUCTIONS,
              3 #DEPENDENTS       PIC'99',
              3 HEALTH_INS        PIC'999V99',
              3 LIFE_INS          PIC'999V99',
              3 CREDIT_UNION      PIC'999V99',
              3 STOCK_PURCHASE PIC'999V99',
            2 YEAR_TO_DATE        CHAR(57);

      DCL ALPHA CHAR(26) STATIC INIT('ABCDEFGHIJKLMNOPQRSTUVWXYZ'),
          STATES(50) CHAR(2) STATIC INIT('AL','AK','AZ','CA','CO',
              'CT','DL','FL','GA','HA','ID','IL','IN','IO','KA',
              'KY','LA','MA','MD','ME','MI','MN','MO','MS','MT',
              'NB','NE','NH','NJ','NM','NY','NC','ND','OH','OK',
              'OR','PA','RI','SC','SD','TN','TX','UT','VA','VT',
              'WA','WI','WV','WY'),
          ESW BIT,
          POSITIONS(23) PIC'99' STATIC INIT(1,5,10,15,16,17,18,19,
              20,25,30,35,40,41,42,43,44,45,60,70,80,90,99);

      HASALPHA: PROCEDURE(S) RETURNS(BIT);
          /* DETERMINE WHETHER A STRING S HAS AT LEAST ONE ALPHA-
             BETIC CHARACTER */
          DCL S CHAR(*), I FIXED BIN;
          DO I=1 TO LENGTH(S);
             IF VERIFY(SUBSTR(S,I,1),ALPHA)=0
               THEN RETURN('1'B);
             END;
          RETURN('0'B);
          END HASALPHA;

      ISDATE: PROCEDURE(D) RETURNS(BIT);
          /* DETERMINE WHETHER OR NOT THE SIX-CHARACTER STRING D
             IS A VALID DATE OF THE FORM MMDDYY */
          DCL D CHAR(6),
              (MM,DD,YY) PIC'99',
              DTBL(12) PIC'99' STATIC INIT(31,28,31,30,31,30,31,
                                      31,30,31,30,31);
```

FIGURE 5-28

```
        IF ^NUMERIC(D) THEN RETURN('0'B);
        MM=SUBSTR(D,1,2); DD=SUBSTR(D,3,2); YY=SUBSTR(D,5,2);
        IF MM<1|MM>12 THEN RETURN('0'B);
        IF MOD(YY,4)=0 & MOD(YY,100)^=0 THEN DTBL(2)=29;
          ELSE DTBL(2)=28;
        IF DD<1 | DD>DTBL(MM) THEN RETURN('0'B);
        RETURN('1'B);
        END ISDATE;

    ESW='1'B;                   /* ASSUME VALID INITIALLY */

    /* VALIDIFY NAME */
    IF ^(HASALPHA(LAST) & HASALPHA(FIRST) &
         (HASALPHA(MIDDLE) | MIDDLE=' '))
    THEN DO; MSG=MSG||'INVALID NAME. '; ESW='0'B; END;

    /* VALIDIFY ADDRESS */
    IF ^(HASALPHA(STREET) & HASALPHA(CITY) & NUMERIC(ZIP))
    THEN DO; MSG=MSG||'INVALID ADDRESS. '; ESW='0'B; END;
    ELSE DO;
           DO I=1 TO 50 WHILE(STATE^=STATES(I));
           END;
           IF I>50
           THEN DO; MSG=MSG||'INVALID ADDRESS. '; ESW='0'B; END;
         END;

    /* VALIDIFY SEX AND MARITAL STATUS */
    IF ^(SEX='M' | SEX='F')
    THEN DO; MSG=MSG||'INVALID SEX. '; ESW='0'B; END;
    IF ^(MARITAL='M' | MARITAL='S')
    THEN DO; MSG=MSG||'INVALID MARITAL STATUS. '; ESW='0'B; END;
.pa
     /* VALIDIFY BIRTH, EMPLOYED, AND CURRENT DATE */
    IF ^(ISDATE(BIRTH) & ISDATE(DATE_EMPLOYED) & ISDATE(DATE))
    THEN DO;
           MSG=MSG||'INVALID BIRTH DATE, DATE EMPLOYED, OR DATE. ';
           ESW='0'B;
         END;

    /* VALIDIFY POSITION AND DEPARTMENT */
    IF ^(NUMERIC(POSITION) & NUMERIC(DEPARTMENT))
    THEN DO; MSG=MSG||'INVALID POSITION OR DEPT. '; ESW='0'B; END;
    ELSE DO;
           DO I=1 TO 23 WHILE(POSITION^=POSITIONS(I));
           END;
           IF I>23 | ^(DEPT>=1&DEPT<=60 | DEPT>=100&DEPT<=143 |
                       DEPT>=300&DEPT<=320 | DEPT>=400&DEPT<=420 |
                       DEPT>=500&DEPT<=530)
           THEN DO; MSG=MSG||'INVALID POSITION OR DEPT. '; ESW='0'B;
                END;
         END;

    /* VALIDIFY BASIS, RATE, AND NUMBER OF DEPENDENTS */
    IF ^(BASIS='H' | BASIS='W' | BASIS='M') |
       ^(NUMERIC(RATE) & NUMERIC(#DEPENDENTS) & #DEPENDENTS<=20)
    THEN DO;
           MSG=MSG||'INVALID BASIS, RATE, OR DEPENDENTS. ';
           ESW='0'B;
         END;

    /* VALIDIFY HEALTH & LIFE INS, CREDIT UNION, STOCK PURCHASE */
    IF ^(NUMERIC(HEALTH_INS) & NUMERIC(LIFE_INS) &
         NUMERIC(CREDIT_UNION) & NUMERIC(STOCK_PURCHASE))
THEN DO;
       MSG=MSG||'INVALID INS, CREDIT UNION OR STOCK PURCHASE. ';
       ESW='0'B;
     END;

RETURN(ESW);
END BVALID;
```

FIGURE 5-28 (*Continued*)

```
EVALID: PROCEDURE RETURNS(BIT);
       /* CHECK THE EXTENDED VALIDITY RULES AGAINST THE RECORD.
          IF INVALID, ADD AN ERROR MESSAGE AND RETURN '0'B.
          OTHERWISE, RETURN '1'B */

       DCL MSG CHAR(150) VAR EXTERNAL,
           MRECORD CHAR(200) EXTERNAL,
           1 EMPLOYEE DEFINED MRECORD,
             2 SPARE          CHAR(1),
             2 SS#            PIC'(10)9',
             2 NAME           CHAR(40),
             2 ADDRESS        CHAR(37),
             2 SEX            CHAR(1),
             2 MARITAL        CHAR(1),
             2 BIRTH          CHAR(6),
             2 DATE_EMPLOYED  CHAR(6),
             2 JOB_STATUS,
               3 POSITION        CHAR(2),
               3 DATE            CHAR(6),
               3 DEPT            CHAR(3),
               3 SALARY,
                 4 BASIS            CHAR(1),
                 4 RATE             PIC'(5)9V99',
             2 DEDUCTIONS,
               3 #DEPENDENTS     PIC'99',
               3 HEALTH_INS      PIC'999V99',
               3 LIFE_INS        PIC'999V99',
               3 CREDIT_UNION    PIC'999V99',
               3 STOCK_PURCHASE  PIC'999V99',
             2 YEAR_TO_DATE      CHAR(57);

       DCL ESW BIT,                         /* ERROR SWITCH */
           EGROSS PIC'(5)9V99';             /* ESTIMATED MONTHLY GROSS */

       ESW='1'B;                    /* ASSUME INITIALLY VALID */

       /* CHECK CONSISTENCY OF BIRTH, EMPLOYED, AND CURRENT DATES */
       IF SUBSTR(BIRTH,5)>=SUBSTR(DATE_EMPLOYED,5) |
          SUBSTR(DATE_EMPLOYED,5)>SUBSTR(DATE,5)
       THEN DO; MSG=MSG||'INCONSISTENT DATES. '; ESW='0'B; END;

       /* CHECK CONSISTENCY OF POSITION, BASIS, AND RATE */
       IF POSITION<=20 &
          (BASIS^='H' | RATE<1.25 | RATE>10.00)
       THEN DO;
               MSG=MSG||'INVALID POSITION, BASIS, OR RATE. ';
               ESW='0'B;
            END;
       ELSE IF POSITION>=25 & POSITION<=60 &
               (BASIS^='W' | RATE<60 | RATE>400)
            THEN DO;
                    MSG=MSG||'INVALID POSITION, BASIS, OR RATE. ';
                    ESW='0'B;
                 END;
```

FIGURE 5-29

```
/* CHECK CONSISTENCY OF HEALTH AND LIFE INSURANCE */
IF ^(HEALTH_INS=0 | HEALTH_INS=6.00) |
    ^(LIFE_INS=0 | LIFE_INS=3 | LIFE_INS=5 |
      LIFE_INS=7 | LIFE_INS=8)
THEN DO; MSG=MSG||'INVALID HEALTH OR LIFE INS. '; ESW='1'B; END;

/* CHECK CREDIT UNION AND STOCK PURCHASE */
IF BASIS='M' THEN EGROSS=RATE;
ELSE IF BASIS='W' THEN EGROSS=4.4*RATE;
     ELSE EGROSS=160*RATE;
IF CREDIT_UNION>.05*EGROSS | STOCK_PURCHASE>.05*EGROSS
THEN DO;
        MSG=MSG||'INVALID CREDIT UNION OR STOCK PURCHASE. ';
        ESW='1'B;
     END;

RETURN(ESW);
END EVALID;
```

FIGURE 5-29 (*Continued*)

FIGURE 5-30
EFFICIENCY OF PL/I CASE STUDY 2 PROGRAM

Implementation	Compile speed	Execution speed
1 IBM 4341 OS/VS1 PL/I Optimizer	5.3 sec	0.3 sec

Reliability and Maintainability of the Program The class of programs which this case study exemplifies must be particularly reliable and maintainable. That is, the program must be written defensively, so that invalid data will not cause abnormal termination before all update records have been processed. It must, in addition, generate valid employee records in every case.

The program satisfies these requirements in the following ways. First, the various validity-checking parts of the program assume no more than the fact that an individual update record is a string of characters. Only after checking that a given item is NUMERIC will the program treat that item as a number. Second, the program performs all the tests on an individual update record that are required by the basic and extended validity rules.

Performance of the Program This program was run in the compiling mode listed above. The results of this run are shown in Figure 5-30.

5-3.2 Implementation-Dependent Features of PL/I

The implementations of PL/I presented here differ not only in their performance but also in the PL/I language features which they support. The PL/I Optimizing Compiler generally supports all the standard PL/I features, as presented in this chapter. However, PL/C does not support all the standard PL/I language features. In this section, we present the important differences (1) between the PL/I optimizer and the standard, and (2) between the standard and PL/C.

The PL/I Optimizer and the Standard The PL/I Optimizing compiler has five "levels" of diagnostic message, depending on the severity of the error. A "warning" occurs when a valid, but unlikely, statement is encountered. An ''error'' occurs when a minor (syntactic) error is detected and an attempt to fix the error was made by the compiler. A ''severe error'' occurs when the nature of the error prevents the compiler from making any reasonable attempt to correct it. Finally, a ''termination error'' occurs when the error is so severe that compilation cannot continue. The compiler has an aggressive strategy toward error correction. When an error occurs, an informatory message is printed, indicating the nature of the error and the statement in the program where it occurs.

In addition to the availability of the CHECK condition for program trace and intermediate results, the PL/I Optimizer provides a number of additional debugging facilities. It can produce an alphabetized cross-reference listing of variables, labels, and entry names. It has an option which gives in the program listing a graphic indication of the program's structure: the nesting of internal procedures, BEGIN blocks, and DO groups.

The PL/I Optimizer additionally provides the options FLOW and COUNT. When used, FLOW produces a listing of the flow of control during program execution. COUNT produces a table showing the number of times each statement was executed in a given run.

However, none of these diagnostic features, debugging facilities, or compiler options is included in the standard. Comparing the PL/I Optimizer with the PL/I standard, we also note major differences in the following areas:

Conditions
Compile-time facilities
Built-in functions
Multitasking
Environment attributes in record I/O

All the PL/I conditions given in this chapter, with the exception of CHECK, are included in the standard. There are a few additional conditions available in the Optimizer which are also not included in the standard. The standard contains a condition, ''string size,'' which is not implemented by the Optimizer.

The Optimizer supports a so-called ''compile-time'' facility, which provides a limited macro capability for the language. Perhaps the most useful statement in this facility is the ''%INCLUDE statement,'' which allows the programmer to catalog a commonly used segment of code (such as a structure definition of a large record layout) in a source program library, and then have it automatically inserted into the program text at compile time.

All the PL/I built-in functions presented in this chapter are included in the standard. However, the optimizing compiler has a number of built-in functions which are not included in the standard. Notable among these are the inverse trigonometric functions (arcsine, arccosine, etc.), certain array built-in functions, and certain other built-in functions related to multitasking.

On the other hand, the standard includes certain built-in functions which are not currently supported by the optimizing compiler. Notable among these are some additional string built-in functions and a ''dot product'' built-in function.

The optimizing compiler supports a so-called "multitasking" facility. This essentially allows the programmer to subdivide a program into a number of tasks, which may execute asynchronously. This facility is not included in the standard.

Because they are too hardware-specific, the I/O ENVIRONMENT attributes supported by the optimizing compiler are not included in the standard. The standard explicitly states that the particular choice of ENVIRONMENT attributes will vary among implementations.

PL/C and the PL/I standard A general comparison of PL/C with the standard leaves the clear conclusion that PL/C is a subset of PL/I. Because of its special diagnostic features and compiling efficiency, PL/C is especially attractive for use in the classroom setting. This setting also justifies the active use of a PL/I subset instead of the entire language, to simplify the environment for teaching programming principles. The special features which PL/C does support tend to favor the scientific and text processing application over the data processing and systems programming applications.

PL/C differs from the draft standard in the following general areas:

- Compiler options, diagnostics, error correction, and debugging facilities
- Direct-access record I/O
- The DEFINED and PICTURE attributes
- The CONTROLLED and BASED storage classes, and POINTER variables
- Certain built-in functions and conditions

PL/C has compiler options, diagnostics, error correction, and debugging facilities which are generally similar with those of the Optimizer. These are too implementation dependent to be included in the standard. PL/C's debugging statements are somewhat more extensive, including the following additional statements:

Statement	Meaning
PUT FLOW;	Print the recent flow history during execution.
PUT SNAP;	Print the recent subprogram calling history.
PUT ALL;	Print the current values of all elementary variables.
PUT ARRAY;	Print the current values of all arrays.

PL/C also tends to correct compile-time errors more aggressively than the Optimizer, with the overall goal of initiating a program's execution wherever possible.

Its exclusion of direct-access record I/O facilities, as well as the DEFINED and PICTURE attributes, renders PL/C far less adequate for data processing applications than the other implementations. That, specifically, prevented our implementing Case Study 2—Employee File Maintenance in PL/C. Its exclusion of CONTROLLED and BASED storage classes, as well as POINTER variables, renders PL/C far less adequate for systems programming than the Optimizer.

PL/C includes one built-in function (RAND) which generates pseudorandom numbers. It is not included in either the standard or the Optimizer. PL/C also includes certain other built-in functions which are not in the standard. Notable among these are the inverse trigonometric functions (arcsine, arccosine, etc.) and certain array built-in functions. The standard includes certain built-in functions which are not currently supported by PL/C. Included here are those related to BASED, CONTROLLED, and POINTER variables, certain additional string built-in functions, and a dot product built-in function.

Similarly, certain conditions included in the standard are not in PL/C. They are the KEY condition, the AREA condition, and the STRINGSIZE condition. Those conditions which are included in PL/C do not, however, all have the same initial status as their counterparts under the Optimizer. Most notable among these are the SIZE, STRINGRANGE, and SUBSCRIPTRANGE conditions, which are all initially enabled in PL/C. This is consistent with PL/C's emphasis on providing maximum diagnostic support for program development.

5-3.3 Overall Evaluation of PL/I

We evaluate PL/I on the basis of the experience shown in sections 5-3.1 and 5-3.2. Our conclusions are summarized as follows, for data processing and text processing applications:

1 Expressivity	Fair
2 Well-definedness	Good
3 Data types and structures	Good
4 Modularity	Good
5 Input-output facilities	Excellent
6 Portability	Poor
7 Efficiency	Poor
8 Pedagogy	Good
9 Generality	Excellent

PL/I's "expressivity" is generally comparable with that of its contemporaries; its control structures adequately support structured programming, its subprogramming features are complete, and its broad coverage of diverse data types all contribute to this conclusion. A minor hindrance is its failure to distinguish between the assignment operator (=) and the equality operator (=), and its noninsistence on variable declaration. The latter can often lead to subtle debugging problems, which causes inordinate dependency on the compiler's "cross-reference" listing during program development.

Another negative influence on PL/I's expressivity is its "default" conversion conventions, and the prevailing attitude that "some conversion will be made, no matter what the situation." This often leads to the generation of unwanted side effects *by the system*, especially during the evaluation of an assignment statement in which a variable was not declared, its type defaulted to FLOAT, and what was thought to be a fixed-point arithmetic calculation turned out to be quite different.

PL/I's "input-output facilities" are excellent, since they include the full range of data processing file operations, in addition to the general stream I/O conventions found in other applications. In fact, PL/I has proven to be quite robust in supporting the development of complex database applications.

PL/I also scores excellent ratings in its "generality." We have already seen its direct utility in the data processing application area. The reader will be asked to demonstrate its utility in the scientific and systems programming areas, where it has also been productively used. As a scientific language, PL/I's array built-in functions are especially useful, and as a systems programming language its dynamic storage management features are most appropriate.

On the other hand, PL/I's poor rating in the "portability" and "efficiency" categories stems largely from its strong IBM mainframe orientation and its sheer size and complexity, respectively. Since its standardization, PL/I has, in fact, been implemented on diverse machines. However, the enthusiasm with which those implementations have been supported by other-than-IBM manufacturers is warm at best. The PL/I manuals in, say, a Digital VAX installation will (if they are there at all) most likely be covered with dust.

A brief comparison of the efficiency of PL/I with that of COBOL in Case Study 2 (see Chapter 4) shows the price one pays for having a language which does everything for everyone. Its lack of comparable compile speed and execution speed with COBOL and FORTRAN continues to be PL/I's main handicap in head-to-head competition as a production programming language.

PL/I's good "pedagogy" comes from the development of effective subset compilers, such as PL/C, and related textbooks for teaching the language in a modular fashion. Its CHECK feature and related program development tools also contribute to PL/I's strength in this area.

REFERENCES

1 G. Radin and H. P. Rogoway, "Highlights of a New Programming Language," *Communications of the ACM* 8:9 (1965).

2 *American National Standard Programming Language PL/I,* American National Standards Institute, ANS X3.53, New York, 1976; *Standard for PL/I,* European Computer Manufacturers Association, Standard ECMA-50, Geneva, 1976.

3 *American National Standard Programming Language PL/I General Purpose Subset,* American National Standards Institute, ANS X3.74, New York, 1981.

4 *PL/I-80 Users Guide,* Microsoft Corporation, 1980.

5 R. W. Conway and D. Gries, *A Primer on PL/I, PL/C, and PL/CT,* Winthrop, 1976.

6 *PL/I Optimizing Compiler: Language Reference Manual,* IBM Corporation, White Plains, N.Y., 1983.

EXERCISES

1 Let X, Y, and Z be REAL FLOAT DEC variables, and let I, J, and K be REAL FIXED BIN variables, with the following values:

```
X =    2.5      I =   1
Y = -10.0       J =  -5
Z =    8.0      K =  12
```

Compute the result delivered by each of the following arithmetic expressions, and determine each result's attributes:

(a) X + Y * Z
(b) (X + Y) * Z
(c) (X + Y)/Z − 3
(d) X + Y/(Z − 3)
(e) I − 1
(f) I − 1.5
(g) I/J * K
(h) 4*I − K/J

2 Suppose we have a 5 × 5 array A of REAL FLOAT DEC values. The "Trace" of A is defined as the sum of its diagonal elements. For instance if A's elements are the following:

$$\begin{bmatrix} 3 & 2 & -1 & 9 & 0 \\ 0 & 1 & 5 & 6 & 7 \\ 2 & 4 & 6 & 8 & 10 \\ -9 & 2 & 3 & 7 & 4 \\ -1 & -2 & -3 & -4 & -5 \end{bmatrix}$$

then its Trace is 3 + 1 + 6 + 7 + (−5) = 12.

(a) Write a declaration for A which will cause it to be initialized with the values shown.
(b) Write statements which will compute the Trace, T, of A.
(c) Write a loop which will find the largest (maximum) value in A, store it in AMAXIMUM, and store that value's row and column numbers in ROW and COL, respectively.

3 Write a function named TRACE which will compute the Trace of any N × N array A of REAL FLOAT DEC values. Let A be the *only* parameter!

4 Rewrite this function as a subroutine with two parameters, A and T (the result).

5 An integer N is entered in positions 1–2 of an input line. N lines follow that line, each with N values stored in its as shown in Figure 5-31. Write a program which accomplishes the following:

(a) Read N, and read the N × N values into an N × N array, in row-major order. Storage allocation for A should be deferred until after N has been determined.
(b) Print N and the array, A, one row per line, as shown in Figure 5-32.

FIGURE 5-31

Column	1 → 4	5 → 8		2N−3 → 2N
	X.XX	X.XX	. . .	X.XX
	1st value	2d value		Nth value

FIGURE 5-32

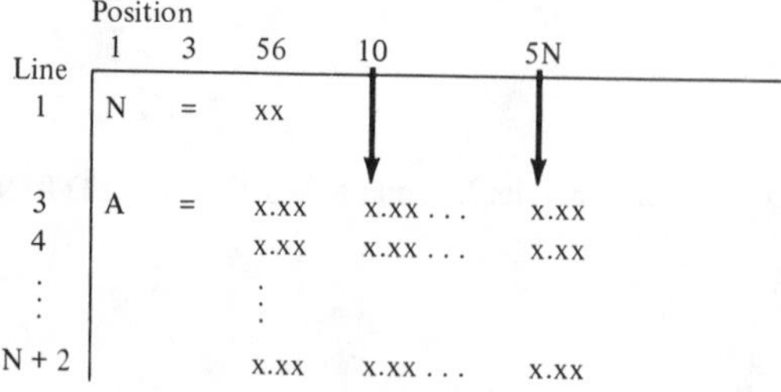

(c) Determine whether or not A is symmetric (i.e., $A_{ij} = A_{ji}$ for all i, j = 1, . . . , N) and prints one of the following messages, on output line 32, accordingly:

A IS SYMMETRIC
A IS NOT SYMMETRIC

6 If your computer, operating system, or PL/I compiler differs from the one used here, rerun our programs at your installation. Do they compile successfully? Do they execute properly? If not, make appropriate changes that will allow them to run.

7 Gather and record performance statistics for this program, as we did for Case Study 2.

8 Implement Case Study 1—Matrix Inversion in PL/I. Contrast its efficiency with that of Pascal or FORTRAN, using comparable information from the corresponding program in Chapter 2 or 3.

9 Consider implementing Case Study 4—Missionaries and Cannibals in PL/I. How would you evaluate PL/I as an artificial intelligence programming language?

10 Consider implementing Case Study 5—Job Scheduler in PL/I. How would you evaluate PL/I as a systems programming language.

11 Modify our PL/I implementation of Case Study 2 to reflect the following changes in the definition of the case study:

(a) The HEALTH INSURANCE deduction can be either $6 or $10.

(b) A new BASIS has been added, "bi-weekly," with code B. Its rate is valid if it is within the range defined by doubling the weekly range.

Make all changes to the program that these redefinitions require, and then test the resulting program.

CHAPTER **6**

LANGUAGE DESIGN: SYNTAX

After having taken a firsthand look at four prominent and diverse programming languages in the previous four chapters, we now shift to a different style of study. In this chapter, we examine the main developments that led to current methods in defining the "syntax" of programming languages.

The "syntax" of a programming language, broadly speaking, is that set of rules and writing conventions that allow the formation of correct programs in a language, from the point of view of "representation" only. That is, syntax has nothing to do with "meaning," or run-time behavior of a program. For example, Figure 6-1 has syntactically correct, yet meaningless Pascal and FORTRAN programs.

Yet syntax is a prerequisite to meaningful expression, just as it is in English. Thus, a programming language must have a good syntactic definition *before* it can properly support the development of meaningful programs.

There are several reasonable approaches to the syntactic description of a programming language, and along with each comes various strengths and weaknesses. These approaches are viewed from two perspectives; the language designer's and the programmer's. The language designer aims to achieve a clean implementation of the language, while the programmer wants maximum expressivity and convenience in a particular programming domain. Thus, good languages tend to incorporate these two aims when they are complementary, and to compromise them when they are not.

6-1 CHARACTER SET

The "character set" of a language is simply that set of symbols from which all programs are composed. Several different approaches to character set selection have been taken by different languages.

```
program P;
  begin
  end.
```

```
END
```

FIGURE 6-1
Syntactically correct Pascal (left) and FORTRAN (right) programs.

In the 1950s and 1960s, ALGOL and FORTRAN were among the most visible languages. Their respective character sets are shown in Figure 6-2. The FORTRAN designers felt that a minimum functional character set—only uppercase letters, digits, and thirteen special symbols—was appropriate for programming. The main reason for this decision at the time was the need for FORTRAN to conform in its typing to the limits of the "standard" programming tool of the day, the IBM 026 keypunch. Moreover, FORTRAN was most strongly supported by IBM, so that the close association between its character set and the 026 punched card codes is not surprising.

The ALGOL designers felt, on the other hand, that the character set should support the *publication* of programs in journals and books. Thus, the ALGOL character set includes upper- and lowercase letters and an extensive complement of special symbols for punctuation and mathematical expression. Some felt in the early 1960s that extensive character sets would soon be supported by computer hardware as well. Thus, the ALGOL character set would serve to inspire better hardware design rather than conform to the limits of current hardware.

Because the character set is such a fundamental element of programming language design and, more generally, of data representation in computers, strong efforts were made to develop an (international) standard character set and internal machine representation. As a result, two alphabets have emerged and become the de facto standards

FIGURE 6-2*a*
THE ALGOL CHARACTER SET

A B C D E F G H I J K L M N O P Q R S T U V W X Y Z
a b c d e f g h i j k l m n o p q r s t u v w x y z
0 1 2 3 4 5 6 7 8 9
$<$ $\leq$ $=$ $>$ $\geq$ $\neq$ $\neg$ $\wedge$ $\vee$ $\supset$ $\equiv$
$+$ $-$ $\times$ $\div$ $\neq$, . ; : $_{10}$ ' " ( ) [ ] b̸ (blank)

FIGURE 6-2*b*
THE FORTRAN CHARACTER SET

A B C D E F G H I J K L M N O P Q R S T U V W X Y Z
0 1 2 3 4 5 6 7 8 9
= + − * / ( ) , . $ ' : b̸ (blank)

for the industry. One is called ASCII (American Standard Code for Information Interchange), and the other is called EBCDIC (Extended Binary Coded Decimal Interchange Code), put forth by the American National Standards Institute and by IBM, respectively. These character sets are shown in Figure 6-3.

Most current programming language designs conform in their character sets to one or both of these standards. For instance, the Ada standard identifies the ASCII code as its basis for representing all character string values and Ada programs themselves.

Yet some do not conform to either of these two standards. As we can see, the ALGOL character set contains several symbols that are not among either the ASCII or the EBCDIC set. As a more striking exception, the APL character set has a *large* number of symbols which are unique unto itself. Most of these symbols denote special APL functions as we shall see in our study of APL in Chapter 9. Yet any implementation of APL must accommodate this diverse set of characters by either providing a specially designed keyboard (see Figure 6-4) or an alternative transliteration scheme for the special characters in APL.

Their need for special character sets tends to make these programming languages less accessible for general use. The cost of designing or purchasing a special keyboard

FIGURE 6-3*a*
ASCII CHARACTER SET

bits 1,2,3								bits 4,5,6,7
000	001	010	011	100	101	110	111	
NUL	DLE	SP	0	@	P	`	p	0000
SOH	DC1	!	1	A	Q	a	q	0001
STX	DC2	''	2	B	R	b	r	0010
ETX	DC3	#	3	C	S	c	s	0011
EOT	DC4	$	4	D	T	d	t	0100
ENQ	NAK	%	5	E	U	e	u	0101
ACK	SYN	&	6	F	V	f	v	0110
BEL	ETB	'	7	G	W	g	w	0111
BS	CAN	(	8	H	X	h	x	1000
HT	EM	)	9	I	Y	i	y	1001
LF	SUB	*	:	J	Z	j	z	1010
VT	ESC	+	;	K	[	k	{	1011
FF	FS	,	<	L	\	l	|	1100
CR	GS	-	=	M	]	m	}	1101
SO	RS	.	>	N	^	n	~	1110
SI	US	/	?	O	_	o	DEL	1111

FIGURE 6-3*b*
EBCDIC CHARACTER SET

<table>
<tr><td colspan="16">bits 0,1,2,3</td><td>bits 4,5,6,7</td></tr>
<tr><td>0000</td><td>0001</td><td>0010</td><td>0011</td><td>0100</td><td>0101</td><td>0110</td><td>0111</td><td>1000</td><td>1001</td><td>1010</td><td>1011</td><td>1100</td><td>1101</td><td>1110</td><td>1111</td><td></td></tr>
<tr><td>NUL</td><td>DLE</td><td>DS</td><td></td><td>SP</td><td>&</td><td>-</td><td></td><td></td><td></td><td></td><td></td><td>{</td><td>}</td><td>\</td><td>0</td><td>0000</td></tr>
<tr><td>SOH</td><td>DC1</td><td>SOS</td><td></td><td></td><td></td><td>/</td><td></td><td>a</td><td>j</td><td>~</td><td></td><td>A</td><td>J</td><td></td><td>1</td><td>0001</td></tr>
<tr><td>STX</td><td>DC2</td><td>FS</td><td>SYN</td><td></td><td></td><td></td><td></td><td>b</td><td>k</td><td>s</td><td></td><td>B</td><td>K</td><td>S</td><td>2</td><td>0010</td></tr>
<tr><td>ETX</td><td>TM</td><td></td><td></td><td></td><td></td><td></td><td></td><td>c</td><td>l</td><td>t</td><td></td><td>C</td><td>L</td><td>T</td><td>3</td><td>0011</td></tr>
<tr><td>PF</td><td>RES</td><td>BYP</td><td>PN</td><td></td><td></td><td></td><td></td><td>d</td><td>m</td><td>u</td><td></td><td>D</td><td>M</td><td>U</td><td>4</td><td>0100</td></tr>
<tr><td>HT</td><td>NL</td><td>LF</td><td>RS</td><td></td><td></td><td></td><td></td><td>e</td><td>n</td><td>v</td><td></td><td>E</td><td>N</td><td>V</td><td>5</td><td>0101</td></tr>
<tr><td>LC</td><td>BS</td><td>ETB</td><td>UC</td><td></td><td></td><td></td><td></td><td>f</td><td>o</td><td>w</td><td></td><td>F</td><td>O</td><td>W</td><td>6</td><td>0110</td></tr>
<tr><td>DEL</td><td>IL</td><td>ESC</td><td>EOT</td><td></td><td></td><td></td><td></td><td>g</td><td>p</td><td>x</td><td></td><td>G</td><td>P</td><td>X</td><td>7</td><td>0111</td></tr>
<tr><td>GE</td><td>CAN</td><td></td><td></td><td></td><td></td><td></td><td></td><td>h</td><td>q</td><td>y</td><td></td><td>H</td><td>Q</td><td>Y</td><td>8</td><td>1000</td></tr>
<tr><td>RLF</td><td>EM</td><td></td><td></td><td></td><td></td><td></td><td>`</td><td>i</td><td>r</td><td>z</td><td></td><td>I</td><td>R</td><td>Z</td><td>9</td><td>1001</td></tr>
<tr><td>SMM</td><td>CC</td><td>SM</td><td></td><td>c</td><td>!</td><td>:</td><td>:</td><td></td><td></td><td></td><td></td><td></td><td></td><td></td><td>|</td><td>1010</td></tr>
<tr><td>VT</td><td>CU1</td><td>CU2</td><td>CU3</td><td>.</td><td>$</td><td>,</td><td>#</td><td></td><td></td><td></td><td></td><td></td><td></td><td></td><td></td><td>1011</td></tr>
<tr><td>FF</td><td>IFS</td><td></td><td>DC4</td><td><</td><td>*</td><td>%</td><td>@</td><td></td><td></td><td></td><td></td><td></td><td></td><td></td><td></td><td>1100</td></tr>
<tr><td>CR</td><td>IGS</td><td>ENQ</td><td>NAK</td><td>(</td><td>)</td><td>—</td><td>'</td><td></td><td></td><td></td><td></td><td></td><td></td><td></td><td></td><td>1101</td></tr>
<tr><td>SO</td><td>IRS</td><td>ACK</td><td></td><td>+</td><td>;</td><td>></td><td>=</td><td></td><td></td><td></td><td></td><td></td><td></td><td></td><td></td><td>1110</td></tr>
<tr><td>SI</td><td>IUS</td><td>BEL</td><td>SUB</td><td>|</td><td>¬</td><td>?</td><td>"</td><td></td><td></td><td></td><td></td><td></td><td></td><td></td><td>EO</td><td>1111</td></tr>
</table>

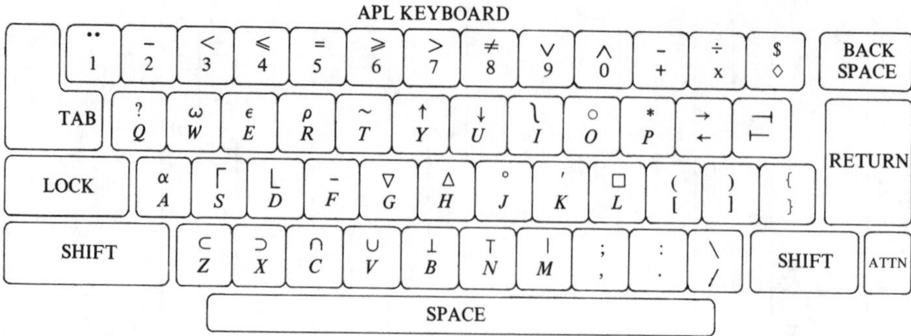

FIGURE 6-4
The APL keyboard.

and terminal is an important deterrent. The question of whether the extra benefit of having special symbols for special functions outweighs this cost remains open.

6-2 VOCABULARY

The "vocabulary" of a programming language is that set of characters and words from which programs are constructed. For example, in Figure 6-5, the Pascal program is on the left and the constituent vocabulary items are listed on the right.

The elements of a language's vocabulary are called its "tokens." These tokens are usually divided into classes according to their role in the language. For instance, we have tokens which are "identifiers" (P, x, y, read, and write), "constants" (2.5), "operators" (:=, +), and "delimiters" (**program**, **var**, :, ;, (,), ., **begin**, and **end**).

The set of tokens for a programming language is defined in such a way that permits efficient recognition by a compiler (a process called "lexical analysis") and clear expression by a programmer. An efficient recognizer should, in a single pass over the program text, be able to separate the program into its constituent tokens and classify them as it goes.

FIGURE 6-5
PASCAL PROGRAM (LEFT) AND ITS VOCABULARY (RIGHT)

program P;	**program**	P	;
var x,y: **integer**;	**var**	x	:
begin	**integer**	y	(
read(x);	**begin**	read	)
y := x + 2.5;	**end**	write	:=
write(y)	2.5	+	.
end.			

Recognition of single-symbol tokens (such as +) is straightforward. Identifiers and constants require a bit more attention in order that they be unambiguously defined and classified. One way of doing this is by using a metalinguistic device such as a "context-free grammar" to define these classes. This is a common formalism for defining the syntax of programming languages, originally developed by Noam Chomsky in the 1950s for defining the syntactic structure of English.[1] The context-free grammar was later adapted by Backus and Naur, and used for the syntactic description of ALGOL in 1962.[2] As such, this adaptation was named "Backus-Naur form," or commonly BNF. Since then, BNF or one of its many variants has become a standard tool for defining the syntax of various programming languages.

To illustrate, suppose we want to define that class of tokens which are "identifiers," according to the following understanding.

> An identifier is defined as any letter, followed optionally by any sequence of letters and/or digits.

In English, this kind of definition is awkward, but what we are defining is a class of tokens like the following:

x
y
Alpha
x1
x2
SUM

In BNF, we use the following metalinguistic symbols as shorthand notation:

::= means "is defined as."
{ } means "any sequence of 0 or more of the items enclosed."
[ ] means "either 0 or one concurrence of the items enclosed."
| means "or" in the exclusive sense.

Items which compose BNF "rules" are either names of token *classes* (such as "identifier"), or single symbols of the language's alphabet.

A BNF rule always has a single token class name on its left, followed by ::=, followed by a sequence of token class names and/or symbols, separated possibly by | and grouped possibly by { }. Thus, for example, the following BNF rule defines exactly what we mean by the token class "letter":

letter ::= a | b | c | . . . | z | A | B | C | . . . | Z

In English, we would interpret this definition as "a letter is defined as either 'a' or 'b' or 'c' or . . . or 'z' or 'A' or 'B' or 'C' or . . . 'Z'." [Here, we have also taken the liberty of abbreviating the definition with ellipses (. . .) because the implied sequence is obvious without writing it all out in detail. Technically, however, this is not properly part of the BNF definition mechanism.] Similarly, the class "digit" is defined as follows:

digit ::= 0 | 1 | 2 | 3 | 4 | 5 | 6 | 7 | 8 | 9

Having these elementary definitions, we can build new rules which are based on them, such as the following:

identifier ::= letter {letter | digit}

That is, "an identifier is defined as a letter, followed by 0 or more occurrences of a letter or a digit." The same approach can be used to define the class "number," based on the elementary classes "natural," "integer," and "digit."

natural ::= digit {digit}
integer ::= [+ | −] natural
number ::= integer | [+ | −] . natural | integer . natural.

Here, the class "natural" includes the unsigned integers, like 0, 7, 32, and 4435. The class "integer" allows *signed* natural numbers, like −7 and +32. Finally, the class "number" includes integers, and adds decimal fractions (like .7 and −.32) and decimal numbers (like −7.32 and 32.7). Thus, the definition is both complete and concise, and allows for efficient recognition of such tokens by a lexical analyzer.

Another issue that confronts language designers is the treatment of delimiters in the vocabulary that are complete words (like **begin**, **end**, and **program**). This is important because the language usually allows variable names, procedure names, and statement labels as well to be defined as identifiers, and it is thus conceivable for programmers to choose identifiers like "begin" and "end" as variable names. So, how can confusion be avoided when the compiler encounters the word "begin" in a program?

One solution is to prescribe in the language definition that all such tokens are "reserved words." That is, they are excluded by fiat from the class of identifiers that a program can define for its own use. This approach is taken for instance in Pascal, Ada, and COBOL. Pascal's list of reserved words is quite short (see Chapter 2), compared with Ada's (see Chapter 13) and COBOL's (see Chapter 4). The advantage of the "reserved word" approach is that it simplifies lexical analysis by the compiler. The disadvantage is that a *long* reserved word list encumbers the programmer, since it usually takes out of circulation words which would naturally be chosen as identifiers in a program (for instance, SUM is a reserved word in COBOL).

The second solution is to designate these as "keywords" by requiring that they be explicitly flagged in the program text by special delimiters or typing conventions. This approach is taken by some ALGOL and BASIC implementations, for instance. On one implementation, each keyword is set apart in the program text by keying a leading apostrophe ('). The above Pascal program would appear as follows if we had to use this convention:

```
'PROGRAM P;
  'VAR X, Y: 'INTEGER;
    'BEGIN
      READ(X);
      Y := X + 2.5;
      WRITE(Y)
    'END.
```

Now the tokens PROGRAM, BEGIN, END, and so forth are free for use within the program as variable names. However, this convention makes program preparation much more tedious, while it keeps the compiler's lexical analysis process simple.

The third solution is to *allow* these tokens to be used *also* as identifiers in the program, and place the burden of distinguishing between the two uses of an identifier on the context in which it appears in the program. The definition of PL/I, for instance, takes this approach, and the following (bizarre) kinds of statements are therefore possible:

```
IF IF = 1 THEN IF = 0;
DO DO = IF TO THEN;
```

In the first example, the variable "IF" is tested and conditionally reassigned the value "0," using an IF statement. In the second, the loop variable "DO" is initialized to the value of the variable "IF" and the loop is repeated until its value reaches that of the variable "THEN," using a DO statement.

Of course, programmers who write these kinds of statements deserve whatever consequences they get! Moreover, a significant burden is placed on the compiler to support such "freedom of expression," and it is not altogether clear that the results are worth the effort.

6-3 SYNTACTIC STRUCTURE

The complete syntactic definition of a programming language seeks to fully define the set of all strings of symbols that form correct programs, from a grammatical point of view. Some languages (FORTRAN, COBOL, BASIC, SNOBOL) are defined syntactically on the basis of a program *line,* and the end of each line is thus a hidden delimiter in the text of a program.

For instance, in FORTRAN a statement always begins on a new line, and there is no need for an explicit statement separator in the character set. Moreover, when a statement runs over onto a second line, explicit note must be made (nonblank in position 6) to signify that continuation. COBOL is a bit more free-form in this respect, since the period (.) plays the role of sentence delimiter and sentences can continue freely from one line to the next without any explicit denotation to designate such continuation. Yet there are certain annoying exceptions to this rule, such as for the continuation of a literal string and the special reservation of margin positions 8–11 on each line for paragraph names.

Most modern languages (Pascal, Ada, C) are syntactically free-form; the structure of a program is independent of line and tab boundaries. Statements are delimited by explicit tokens (usually ;) and labels are also distinguished by punctuation (usually :).

Some variant of BNF is typically used to define *most* of the syntax of these languages. We introduced one variant in the foregoing section, and it is used again below to show the syntactic description of some common Pascal constructs: the "statement," the "expression," and related classes of tokens.

```
statement ::= unlabeled-stmt |
      label : unlabeled-stmt
unlabeled-stmt ::= simple statement |
      structured-stmt
simple-stmt ::= assignment-stmt |
      procedure-stmt |
      goto-stmt
structured-stmt ::= compound-stmt |
      conditional-stmt |
      repetitive-stmt |
      with-stmt
compound-stmt ::= begin statement {; statement} end
conditional-stmt ::= if-stmt | case-stmt
if-stmt ::= if expression then statement |
      if expression then statement else statement
assignment-stmt ::= identifier := expression
expression ::= simple exp | simple exp relop simple exp
   relop ::= = | < > | < | <= | >= | > | in
simple exp ::= [+ | −] term | simple exp addop term
   addop ::= + | − | or
term ::= factor | term mulop factor
   mulop ::= * | / | div | mod | and
factor ::= identifier | number | ( expression ) |
      function designator | set | not factor
```

This is a fairly healthy subset of the 108 BNF rules which together comprise the Pascal syntax.[3] We see among these some common notions from our study of Pascal in Chapter 2; the "if-stmt," the "compound-stmt," and so forth.

Such a set of BNF rules defines the syntax of a programming language in the following sense. A string of tokens (from the language's character set) is a syntactically correct program (or statement or expression, etc.) in the language if it can be "derived" using the BNF rules that are appropriate to the class (program, statement, expression) in question.

The "derivation" of a particular program, statement, or expression using the BNF rules is similar to "parsing" an English sentence. In the latter, one seeks to answer the question of whether or not a given string of words is a sentence, looking first for the presence of a subject and a predicate. The syntax of English tells us that a "subject" can be any noun phrase and a "predicate" can be any verb followed possibly by an object. Thus, we can parse, or diagram in tree form, English sentences like the following:

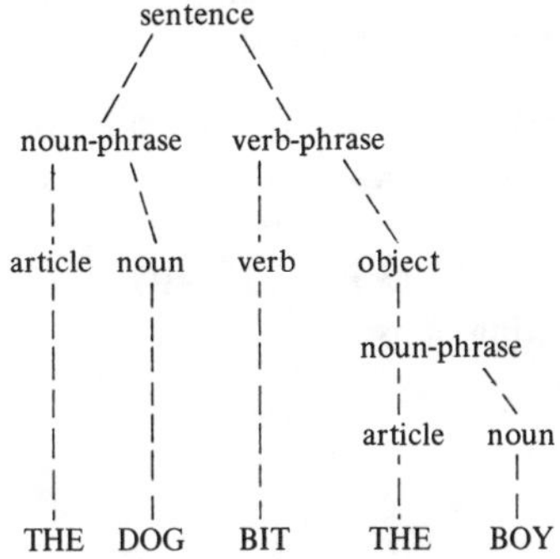

Here, the underlying grammatical rules can be expressed in BNF as follows:

sentence ::= noun-phrase verb-phrase
noun-phrase ::= noun | article noun
verb-phrase ::= verb | verb object
object ::= noun-phrase
noun ::= BOY | DOG | GIRL
article ::= A | AN | THE
verb ::= BIT | SAW | WROTE

Given the sentence "The dog bit the boy," we try to build a parse tree using these rules as follows:

1 For each word in the sentence that occurs as the right side of some rule, build a part of the parse tree as follows:

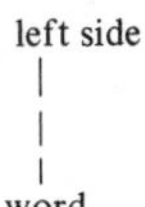

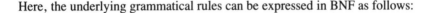

Here, "left side" denotes the left-hand side of the corresponding rule.

2 Repeat step 1 for each (group of) token class(es) that occurs among the roots of the partially constructed trees, maintaining left-to-right order among them.

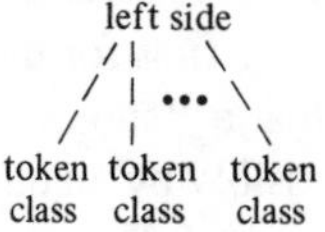

Here, the result is a subtree whose root is the left side of the appropriate rule, and whose branches lead to the token classes of the respective subtrees, taken in order.

This process will result in a *complete* parse (tree) for the string if it is a syntactically correct sentence, or will be blocked from achieving such a goal because the string is not correct in this sense.

To illustrate, suppose we want to parse the string "THE DOG BIT THE BOY" using the given grammar. From step 1, we have the following parts:

From step 2, we can group the roots "article noun," since they occur as a right side of the rule:

noun-phrase ::= noun | article noun

and arrive at the following refinements.

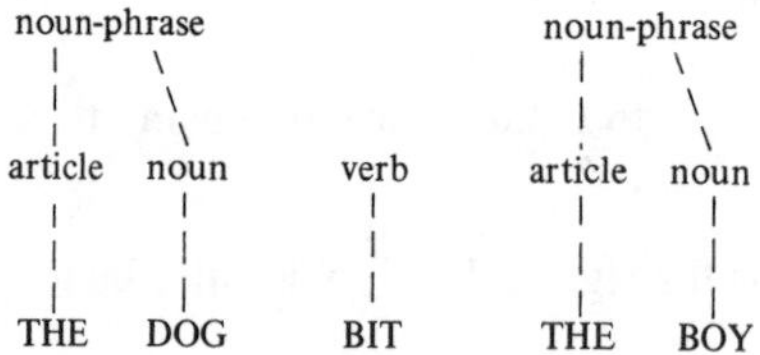

From step 2 again, we can apply the rule:

object ::= noun-phrase

and then the rule

verb-phrase ::= verb object

to arrive at the following further refinement:

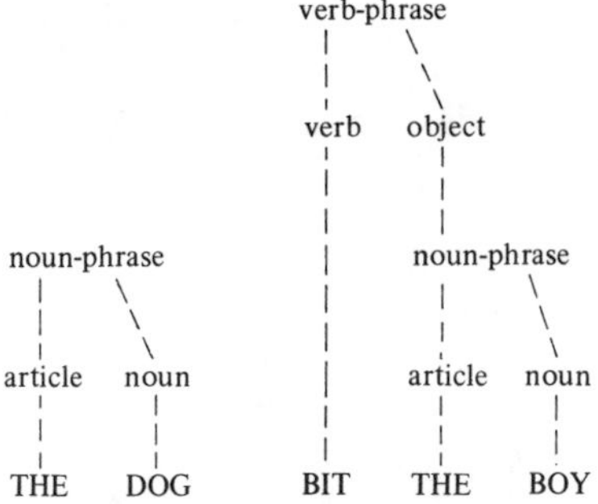

To complete the parse, application of the rule

sentence ::= noun-phrase verb-phrase

will yield the tree structure shown at the beginning of this discussion.

Returning to the BNF rules for Pascal, we can use them to parse various constituents of a Pascal program, and discover any "syntax errors" along the way. For example, suppose we want to parse the string SUM := SUM + X as an assignment-stmt. Then we must find a series of rule applications which allow the construction of a parse tree with the tokens SUM, :=, SUM, +, and X as its leaves and "assignment-stmt" as its root. Step 1 gives the following (assuming also the BNF rules for "identifier" given in the previous section):

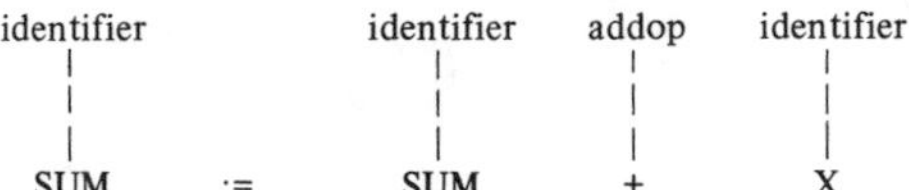

After three applications of step 2, we will have the following:

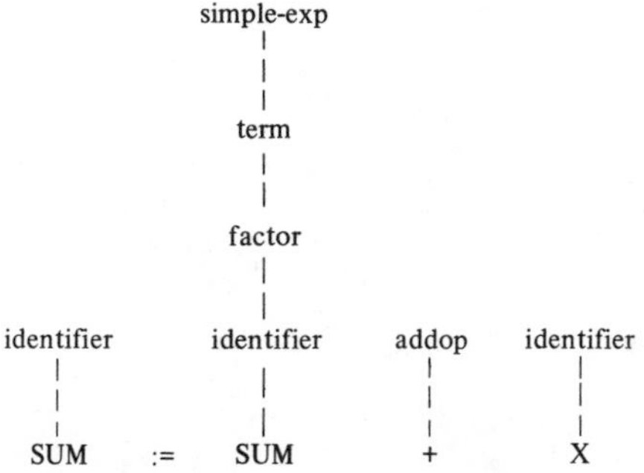

Here, the rules used were the following:

factor ::= identifier
term ::= factor
simple-exp ::= term

If we repeat this process, using only the first *two* of these rules, we can achieve the following change:

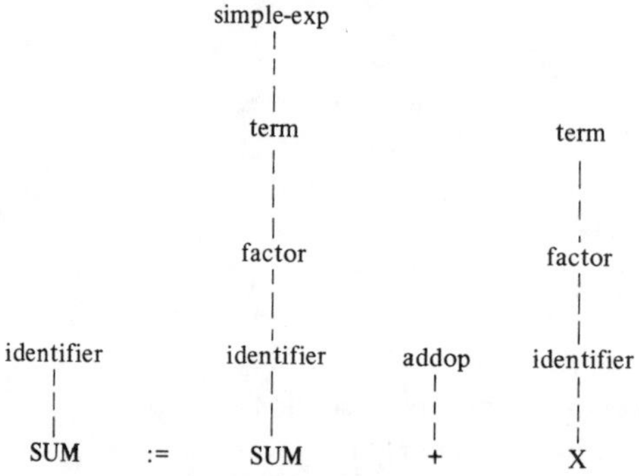

At this point, we can apply the rules for simple-exp, expression, and assignment-stmt, *in that order,* to complete the parse as follows:

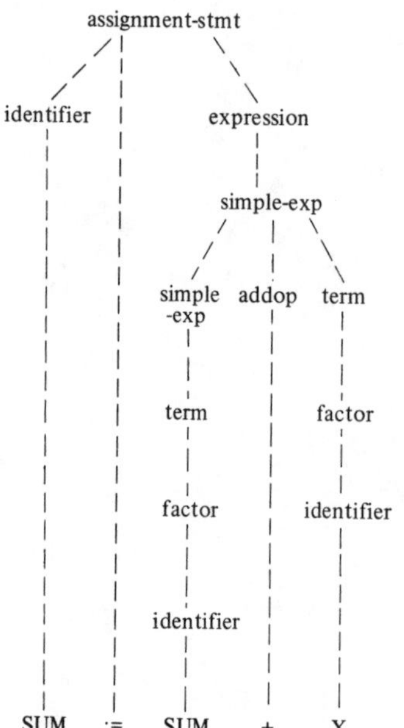

The reader may note that, in arriving at this parse, we made only "correct" choices at each step—that is, choices that would ultimately lead to a complete tree with "assignment-stmt" at its root. For instance, we could have pursued the incorrect path

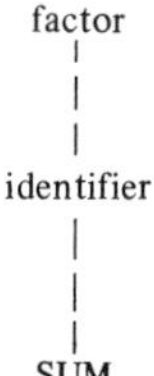

for that occurrence of SUM on the left of the assignment symbol (:=), but that would have eventually blocked the achievement of a complete parse for the whole statement.

The parsing method that we have loosely described here is known generally as "bottom-up" parsing, and it is only one of several different strategies that are commonly used by compilers. A more thorough treatment of parsing is usually reserved for a compiler course and appears in most texts on compilers.

6-4 COBOL SYNTAX DESCRIPTION

The metalanguage used to describe the COBOL syntax is more limited in scope than BNF. It is applied only to the syntax of an individual statement, rather than to the structure of an entire program. Moreover, it is designed and used in such a way to provide a vehicle for *reference manuals* to describe statement syntax to programmers, as well as to compiler writers. BNF, on the other hand, was primarily intended for use by the language designer and implementer; its pedagogical usefulness for programmers appears to be more limited.

Examples of the COBOL syntax description language appear throughout Chapter 4. Basically, its conventions are summarized as follows:

{ } encloses a vertical list of items, from which exactly one item must be selected.
[ ] encloses a sequence of items which is optional.
. . . denotes any number of repetitions of the preceding item.

For example, the following syntax appears in section 4-2.6 for the SELECT statement:

```
SELECT file-name ASSIGN TO device-name
   [RESERVE integer AREAS]
  [ORGANIZATION IS {SEQUENTIAL} ]
  [                {INDEXED   } ]
  [ACCESS MODE IS {SEQUENTIAL} ]
  [               {RANDOM    } ]
   [RECORD KEY IS data-name]
```

Thus, we see at a glance what the options and requirements of the SELECT statement are by noting the items in the lists and the enclosing delimiters (brackets or braces). Three of the many alternatives are as follows.

SELECT MYFILE **ASSIGN TO** SYSIN
SELECT MYFILE **ASSIGN TO** SYSIN
  RESERVE 4 **AREAS**
SELECT MYFILE **ASSIGN TO** SYSIN
  ORGANIZATION IS INDEXED
  ACCESS MODE IS RANDOM
  RECORD KEY IS SOCIAL-SECURITY-NO

6-5 SYNTAX DIAGRAMS

A number of alternatives and variants of BNF have thus been used to describe the syntax of different languages, although the one discussed in section 6-3 is probably the most popular. Another alternative to BNF and the COBOL conventions is the "syntax diagram," which was popularized in the formal description of Pascal. Below, for example, are syntax diagrams for the "compound-stmt" and the "if-stmt" which are equivalent to their BNF descriptions in section 6.3.

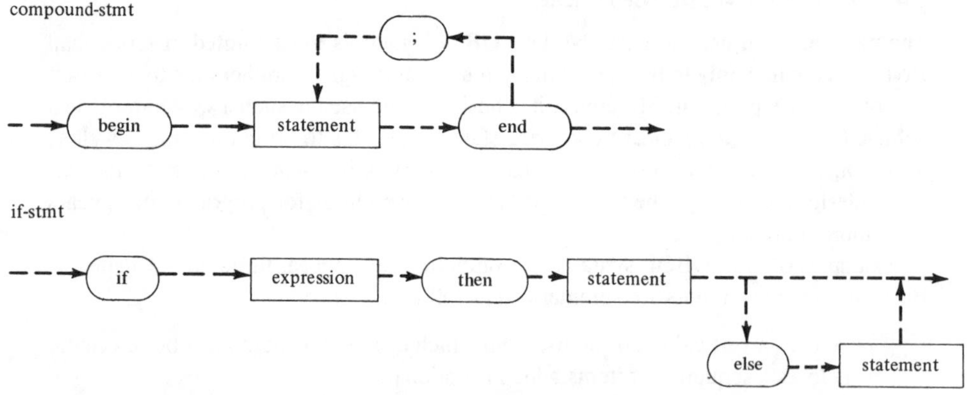

Here, the structure is that of a directed graph, with a single entrance on the left and a single exit on the right. Elements enclosed in circles (such as **begin** and **end** above) are tokens in the language, while elements enclosed in rectangles (such as "statement" and "expression") are token classes.

The syntax diagram thus gives a pictorial description of the language's formation rules; loops denote repetition of constructs, and branches denote alternatives. Thus, for instance, the form

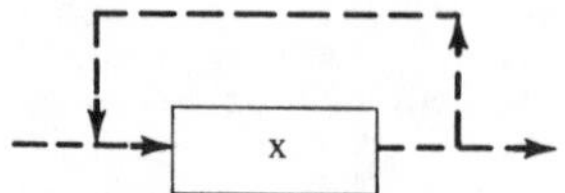

denotes x { x } in BNF, and the form

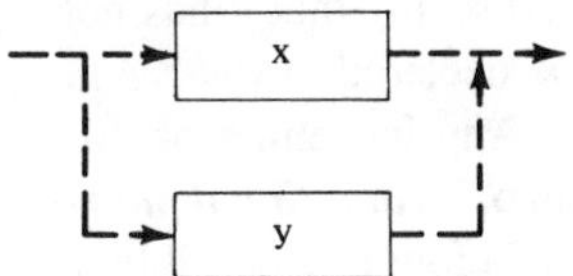

denotes x | y in BNF. Thus, the syntax diagram is no more powerful as a description device than BNF; it is an alternative which many prefer because of its descriptive quality and its simplicity.

6-6 OTHER ISSUES IN SYNTAX

A critical issue in syntax description is the question of adequacy. That is, how complete is, say, BNF in describing all the syntactic requirements of a programming language? The answer, unfortunately, is "not entirely." The overriding limitation of BNF is that it is a so-called "context-free grammar"; that is, if a language has some syntactic requirement that is sensitive to the *context* in which a construct is written in the program, then that requirement cannot be expressed in BNF.

We don't have to look too far to find such "context-sensitive" requirements within contemporary languages. For example, consider the requirement that all variables used in a program be declared. This requirement is present in Pascal, COBOL, and Ada, and is absent in FORTRAN, PL/I, and LISP.

There are two ways of handling this syntactic constraint in the language definition; either state it in English, or choose a more powerful syntax formalism than BNF. Such formalisms are available—one is called "context-sensitive grammar"[4]—but generally they are too complex and inefficient to embed within a compiler to be practical.

Ad hoc methods are generally straightforward and therefore preferred, as an approach to enforcing context-sensitive syntax requirements. To this end, the "symbol table" is one of the most important data structures managed by a compiler. The symbol table is a list of all symbols used in a program—variable names, statement labels, procedure names, and so forth—together with their attributes. The following example shows the symbol table (on the right) that would result from the Pascal program on the left:

```
program P;
  var x: integer;
    begin
      read(x);
      y := x + 2.5;
      write(y)
    end.
```

Symbol	Attributes	Declared?
P	proc-name	Y
x	integer-var	Y
y		N

Here, the compiler has identified an instance of a symbol (y) which does not appear among the declarations at the top of the program.

The requirement that all variables be declared, therefore, helps explain why declarations must appear at the *top* of the program, rather than at the bottom or somewhere else. Upon encountering the symbol y in the text above, and seeing that y has not yet been declared, the compiler can conclude that y will not be declared *anywhere* in the program, and thus can immediately flag this syntax error. Any loosening of this requirement would shift a burden onto the compiler in the form of an *additional pass* over the program text, so that all declarations could be processed before any possible references to undeclared variables are encountered.

The symbol table is also an adequate ad hoc device for enforcing the context-sensitive requirement that all variables in a declaration have mutually unique names. That is, the following declaration should raise a syntax error:

```
var x: integer;
  x: real;
```

A simple search of the symbol table as each variable in the declaration is encountered will detect any error of this type.

Uniqueness of declarations is a more complex issue when the questions of block structure and scope are introduced. That is, a variable name *may* have multiple declarations, provided that the scope of each instance of the name does not overlap with that of any other instance. Consider the following Pascal example:

```
program P;
  var x, y: integer;
  procedure Q;
    var x: real;
    begin
      .
      .
      .
    end {of Q};
  begin
    .
    .
    .
  end {of P}.
```

Here, the scope of **integer** x includes the statements of P but not Q while the scope of **real** x includes Q but not P. The scope of y, on the other hand, includes P *and* Q. All of these issues are essentially syntactic, and are handled by ad hoc methods involving the symbol table, rather than within the syntax formalism itself.

Another important issue in syntax is the problem of eliminating syntactic *ambiguity*. Generally, a language is syntactically ambiguous if it contains a construct which can be parsed in two or more different ways. For example, consider the following FORTRAN statements:

```
      DO 10 I = 1.5
         .
         .
         .
   10 CONTINUE
```

If, in FORTRAN programs, the blank space is insignificant, this apparent DO statement could be alternatively interpreted as an assignment:

```
   DO10I = 1.5
```

of the value 1.5 to the variable named DO10I.

The BNF syntax for "if-stmt," given in an earlier section, allows for ambiguity as well. Consider the following example (where s1 and s2 denote arbitrary statements) and the two correct parses which appear below it:

if x = 0 **then if** y = 0 **then** s1 **else** s2

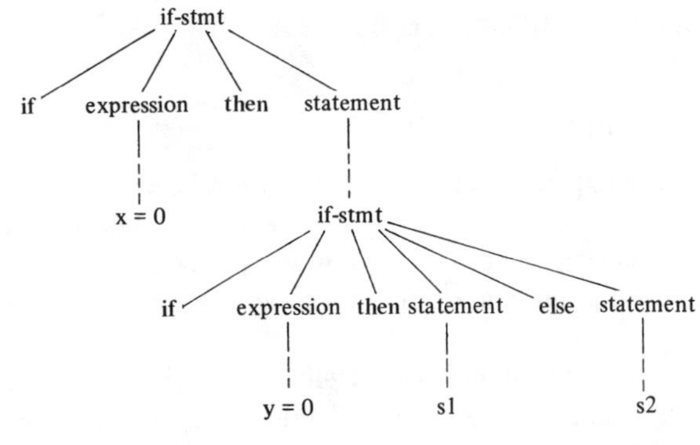

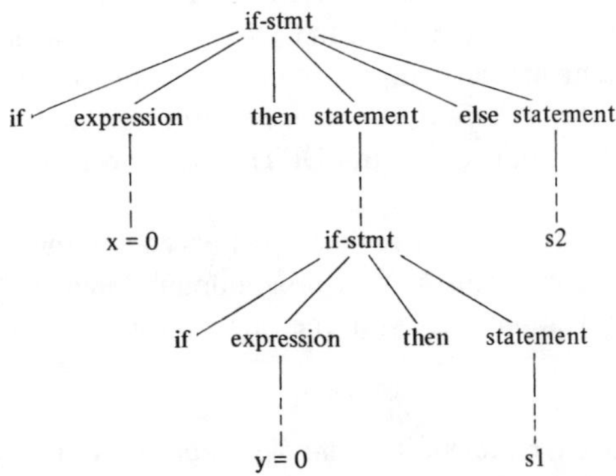

This particular instance of ambiguity is known as the "dangling else problem," and is handled in different languages by different means. Here, in the Pascal case, it is handled by the ad hoc rule that automatically associates each **else** with the nearest (innermost) **if** which precedes it. Thus, the first of the two parses above is the correct one. This particular interpretation is taken by PL/I as well.

In ALGOL, the BNF syntax simply did not allow an **if** statement to immediately follow another **if** statement. If that were desired, then the second **if** would have to be enclosed in a compound statement and, by the back door, forcing the delimiters **begin** and **end** to arbitrate the attachment of the dangling **else** clause. Thus, in ALGOL, the two parsing structures above would have been evoked by the following alternative **if** statements, respectively:

if x = 0 **then begin if** y = 0 **then** s1 **else** s2 **end**
if x = 0 **then begin if** y = 0 **then** s1 **end else** s2

In Ada, we have a slightly different strategy; all **if** statements are "closed" by a mandatory **endif** symbol, whether they have an **else** part or not. Thus, the dangling else problem does not arise in Ada. This is achieved at a slight expense in extra writing for the programmer. The two parses above would be realized by the following Ada statements, respectively:

if x = 0 **then if** y = 0 **then** s1 **else** s2 **endif endif**
if x = 0 **then if** y = 0 **then** s1 **endif else** s2 **endif**

6-7 SYNTAX AND PROGRAMMING

Some of our nine criteria for language evaluation are directly related to syntax. The quality of a language's syntactic description directly influences the tendency for programmers to make simple and conceptual errors when writing programs. Some of the most common syntactic causes of programming errors are the following:

A. Missing or Incorrect Punctuation or Other Delimiter When writing a Pascal program, the semicolon is a statement "separator." When writing in PL/I or Ada, the semicolon is a statement "terminator." When writing in BASIC, the colon separates statements, but only if two or more are on the same line. In COBOL, the period is a sentence terminator, but one or more statements can comprise a sentence with no necessary punctuation between them. Moreover, COBOL sometimes permits comma-space to separate items in a list, instead of a single space. In FORTRAN, the end of a line is implicitly a statement terminator.

With such a disparate collection of punctuation rules, even the experienced programmer leaves out an occasional punctuation mark. This area of programming language design begs for a greater degree of standardization; it is by far the single most frequent source of syntax errors in programming.[5]

B. Statement and List Bracketing Conventions for setting apart, or bracketing, groups of statements are also dissimilar among different languages. In Pascal, brackets

[ ] are reserved for array subscripts, parentheses ( ) are used for arguments in subprograms, **begin** and **end** are used for compound statements, and braces { } are used to enclose comments.

In FORTRAN, we have parentheses for arrays and subprogram arguments, IF . . . ENDIF for conditionals, and DO n . . . n CONTINUE for loops. PL/I and Ada also use parentheses for array subscripts and subprogram arguments, and a variety of different notations for statement grouping, as summarized below and compared with Pascal.

Statement grouping	Pascal	PL/I	Ada

Complete program	**program** P;
	  begin
	  :
	  end
		P: PROC;
		  :
		  END P;
			procedure P **is**
			  begin
			  :
			  end P

Looping	**while** e **do**
	  begin
	  :
	  end
		DO WHILE(e);
		:
		END;
			while e **loop**
			:
			end loop;

Selection	**case** i **of** : **end**	SELECT; : END;	**select** : **end select**;
Compounds	**begin** : **end**	DO; : END;	**begin** : **end**

Conditionals	**if** e **then**
	  begin
	  :
	  end
		IF e THEN
		  DO;
		  :
		  END;
			if e **then**
			:
			end if;

As we can see here, Pascal and Ada have more consistent conventions for grouping than does PL/I. In PL/I an END can close the bracketing for several *different* kinds of groupings, and thus causes confusion when reading a complex program. In Ada, the nature of the closure is explicitly given, thus clarifying the syntax for both the reader and the compiler! The compiler can use this extra information, of course, to perform more reliable syntax checking. Consider the following erroneous PL/I and Ada program fragments:

```
DO WHILE (e);        while e loop
   .                    .
   .                    .
   .                    .
  IF e THEN DO;          if e then
   .                      .
   .                      .
   .                      .
    END;
                          end loop
```

Both contain a missing END (or **end**), but only the Ada fragment reveals *at the point of the error* that one **end** is missing and *which* one it is. In the PL/I example, it is not obvious which END is missing; only at the conclusion of the entire program will the compiler detect that somewhere there is a missing END. This is not very good diagnostic information for large, complex programs.

C. Diversity of Metalanguage When we study different languages, we notice that each one is notoriously unique in the ways that it names token classes and other programming constructs. This is especially annoying when such differences appear to mark trivial differences, or simply give different names to essentially the same notion.

For example, the ''identifier'' in Pascal is the same as the ''data-name'' in COBOL. Arrays are called ''tables'' in COBOL, while assignment statements are called ''COMPUTE statements.'' PL/I structures are reincarnated as ''records'' in Pascal, and are called ''record description entries'' in COBOL. The reasonably well-understood notion of ''type'' in Algol-like languages refers to the set of values which a variable may have. This is similar to a PL/I variable's set of ''attributes.'' The specific types themselves are also differently named by different languages. To wit:

Pascal type	PL/I equivalent	COBOL equivalent	FORTRAN equivalent
real	FLOAT	COMP-1	REAL
integer	FIXED BIN	COMP-2	INTEGER
Boolean	BIT(1)	PIC '9'B	LOGICAL
character	CHARACTER(1)	PIC'X'	CHARACTER*1

This is only a small sample of the differences. Still greater differences will appear as we study diverse languages like APL, LISP, and PROLOG in later chapters. The languages covered so far are among the most conservative choices we could review.

6-8 SYNTAX AND SEMANTICS

Although syntax is concerned only with the form of a program, it is inextricably tied to ''semantics,'' which is the meaning of the program. Usually, semantics is defined in terms of the program's run-time behavior: what happens when the program is executed with a certain set of inputs, what statements are executed, what values are assigned to the variables, and what output is produced.

Since the basic goal of programming language design is to define the means for describing computational processes, the syntax occurs principally to serve these semantic ends. Thus, semantic goals are the original motivation for syntax design.

The connection between syntax and semantics is clearly evident in the BNF definition of arithmetic expressions and the resulting parses yielded by that definition. Consider the following abbreviated productions for Pascal-like expressions:

```
expression ::= [+ | −] term |
      expression addop term
   addop ::= + | − | or
```

term ::= factor | term mulop factor
mulop ::= * | / | **div** | **mod** | **and**
factor ::= identifier | number | (expression)

These productions govern the parse of expressions like the following:

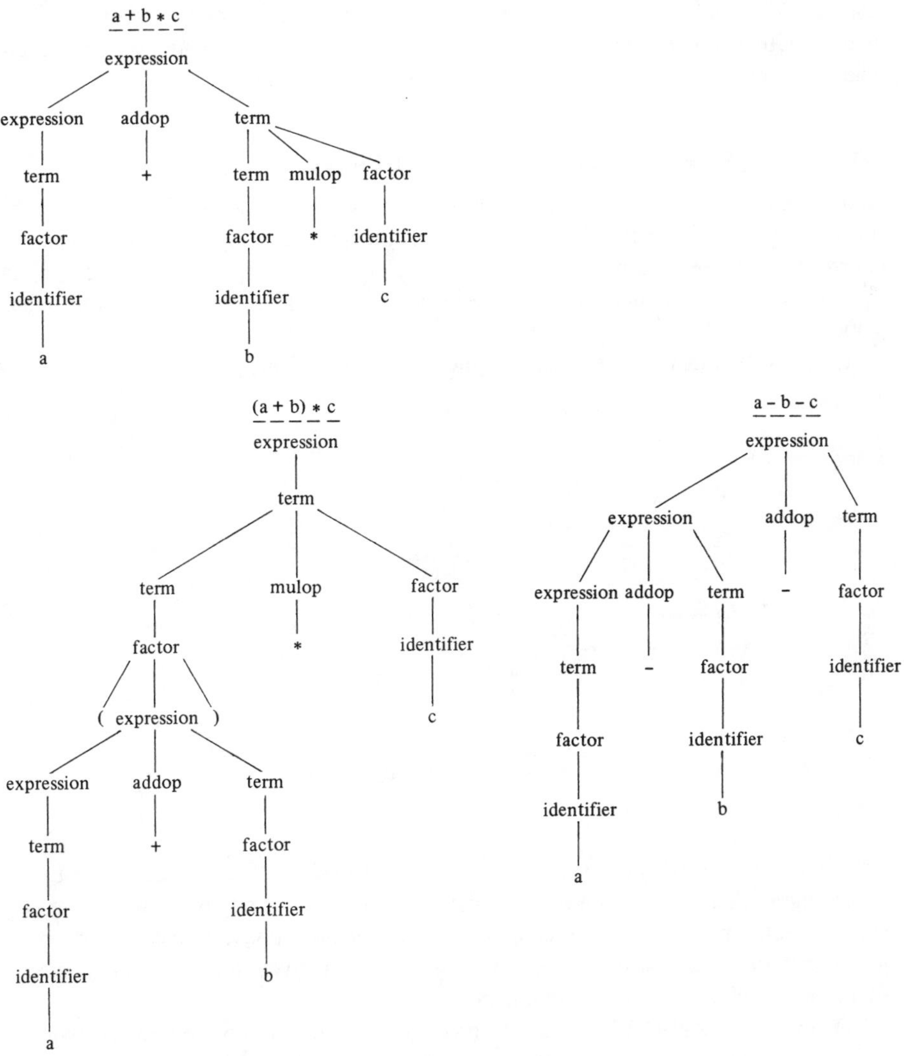

We can view a parse tree as a definition of the *order* of operations in an arithmetic expression, in a *bottom-up, left-right* sense. In the first parse above, this means that the expression a + b * c denotes multiplication of b * c followed by addition of the result to a. That is, the priority of multiplication over addition is enforced *in the syntax.*

In the second parse above, we see that parentheses can be used to override that priority. Here, the sum a + b is taken first, and that result is multiplied by c. In the third parse, the syntax is shown to enforce the *left-to-right* evaluation of operators which have the same priority. Here a − b is computed first, and c is subtracted from the result.

Moreover, the reader should become convinced that the BNF rules for expressions permit *no other* parse for any of these expressions. That is, the syntax is unambiguous.

There is a great deal more to be studied in the area of semantics of programming languages. This brief example illustrates only the essential link between syntax and semantics. Other semantic issues, such as "coercion," "storage allocation," "procedure linkage," and "array referencing," are discussed in detail in Chapter 10.

6-9 SYNTAX, SEMANTICS, AND COMPILER DESIGN

At the heart of language implementation is, of course, the design of effective compilers for the language. Compiler design is, of course, a complex subject and deserves a full course in itself. Here, however, we sketch the elementary design of a compiler, so that the links among a language's syntax, semantics, and implementation are well understood.

The basic elements of a typical compiler are shown below:

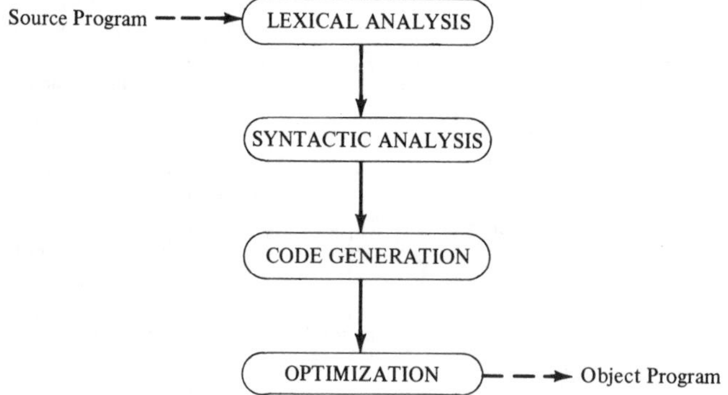

Here, the Source Program is provided to LEXICAL ANALYSIS, whose task is to recognize the basic tokens which occur in the program, and classify those which are constants, identifiers, reserved words, and so forth. Thus this phase converts the program text essentially from a string form into a serial list of language tokens. Initial construction of the symbol table occurs in this phase as well.

SYNTACTIC ANALYSIS converts this list, in turn, into a parse tree, using an internal representation of the language's grammar as its guide. Various strategies exist for syntactic analysis, since it is a relatively complex process and must be made as efficient as possible.

CODE GENERATION is basically the link between the syntax of a language and its semantics, or machine representation. That is, it converts the parse tree into an equivalent list of assembly (machine) instructions for the program. The discussion in Chapter

10 gives more detailed insight into code generation, showing the assembly code generated for several common high-level language constructs.

Finally, OPTIMIZATION attempts to refine the generated code so that its run-time performance will be improved. This is a complex process as well, as it attempts to locate semantically redundant constructs, inefficient use of registers, and so forth. Often, this phase occurs both before and after code generation, in the first case operating directly upon the parse tree itself.

The Object Program which emerges out of the compilation may be either in machine language or in some intermediate language, the latter being preferred in cases where portability is desired.

Throughout these phases, it should be clear that the symbol table plays a central role. Moreover, a thorough strategy for reporting syntactic errors, or ''diagnostics'' must be incorporated within this design as well.

Space does not permit a more thorough treatment of compiler design in this text. Several excellent texts have been written on the subject, and it deserves thorough study on its own merits outside the context of the study of programming languages.

EXERCISES

1 Design a BNF syntax for Ada if statements, as described in this chapter. Parse the following using your syntax:

if x = 0 **then** **if** y = 0 **then** s1 **else** s2 **endif** **endif**

2 Parse each of the following expressions, using the syntax given in this chapter:
(a) 1 + b * c + d
(b) 1
(c) (1 + b) * (c + d)

3 Show that the following BNF syntax is ambiguous, by finding an expression which has two or more *different* parses:

expression ::= term | expression + expression
term ::= factor | term * term
factor ::= identifier | number | (expression)

4 Give syntax charts which are equivalent to the BNF productions for ''expression'' which were given in this chapter.

5 Write a Pascal procedure that recognizes whether or not a given character string has an initial part which is a valid ''identifier,'' and if so, which returns that part. If not, the procedure should return the empty string (''). Write another procedure that does the same for ''number.''

6 Using the BNF syntax given in this chapter, parse each of the following:

(a) **if** a < b + c **then** a := 0	as an if-stmt
(b) a := b − c + d	as an assignment-stmt
(c) **begin** x := 0; y := 0 **end**	as a compound-stmt

7 Good syntax definition doesn't guarantee good semantic definition. Parse the following ''sentences'' using the BNF rules given in this chapter:
(a) THE GIRL BIT THE DOG
(b) THE DOG WROTE

8 Contrast the conventions used for separating statements in a Pascal, FORTRAN, COBOL, and PL/I program, and cite an advantage and a disadvantage of each.

9 The following syntax partially defines the structure of loops in Ada:

⟨loop⟩ ::= [⟨iterator⟩] ⟨basic loop⟩
⟨iterator⟩ ::= **while** ⟨exp⟩ |
  for ⟨var⟩ **in** ⟨subrange⟩
⟨basic loop⟩ ::= **loop** ⟨stmts⟩ **end loop**
⟨stmts⟩ ::= ⟨stmt⟩ { ⟨stmt⟩ }

Here, ⟨exp⟩, ⟨var⟩, ⟨stmt⟩, and ⟨subrange⟩ denote expressions, variables, statements, and subscript ranges in the Pascal sense. For this syntax, show an equivalent Ada loop for the familiar Pascal loop shown below, and then give its parse tree.

for i := 1 **to** 10 **do**
  begin
    ⟨stmt⟩;
    ⟨stmt⟩
  end

10 Give syntax diagrams that are equivalent to the BNF productions in the previous question.

11 FORTRAN ignores most blanks which appear in a program, but often treats them as zeros (0) when they appear as input. For instance, the sequence "1 000" represents the number 1000 in both of its appearances in the statement "IF(X .EQ. 1 000) GO TO 1 000." However, it represents the number 10000 if read under I5 format from the input. Examine the treatment of blanks in other languages which you have studied so far. Does this inconsistency appear elsewhere as well?

REFERENCES

1 N. Chomsky, *Syntactic Structures,* Mouton, The Hague, 1956.
2 P. Naur, ed., "Revised Report on the Algorithmic Language Algol 60," *Communications of the ACM* 6 (1): 1–17 (1963).
3 K. Jensen and N. Wirth, *Pascal User Manual and Report*, 2d ed., Springer-Verlag, New York, 1974.
4 N. Chomsky, *Syntactic Structures*
5 G. Ripley and Druseikis, "A Statistical Analysis of Syntax Errors," *Journal of Computer Languages* 2: 227–240 (1978).

CHAPTER 7

SNOBOL

7-1 INTRODUCTION TO SNOBOL

SNOBOL is an unusual programming language in comparison to most conventional styles, but is based on a very sound principle of pattern matching to solve string manipulation problems. Thus, SNOBOL is particularly well suited for text processing applications. It contains an unusually powerful collection of string processing functions in comparison to those of other languages. Our application of SNOBOL to Case Study 3—Text Formatter should exhibit the expressive power and utility of these facilities.

7-1.1 Brief History of SNOBOL

SNOBOL was designed in 1962 by a research group at Bell laboratories as an aid to their own applications in symbolic formula manipulation.[1] An improved and extended version, called "SNOBOL3," appeared in 1966 and was implemented on a number of machines. Further enhancements to the language produced SNOBOL4, a language with a more general-purpose flavor. The version of SNOBOL4 that we will discuss here is version 3, which was introduced in December 1969.

A new language called ICON has recently been designed as a potential successor to SNOBOL.[2] Although it contains many of SNOBOL's string processing features, ICON's syntax is much more like that of conventional languages Pascal and C. Moreover, ICON has several new features whose utility will begin to be tested over the next few years.

Substantial development of SNOBOL itself has not occurred since SNOBOL4, except for the continual implementation of the language on contemporary machines. The language has never been standardized, even though it is widely implemented on a variety of machines. Our presentation will be based on the text *The SNOBOL4 Programming Language,*[3] which is generally accepted as the "standard" definition of the language.

7-1.2 Implementations and Variations of SNOBOL

SNOBOL is implemented on a large number of computers, including the following:

Burroughs
Control Data
Digital
Honeywell
IBM
Univac

A SNOBOL4 interpreter has also been implemented on the IBM PC microcomputers at this writing, as has been the case for most other popular languages. SNOBOL is a particularly portable language, as most of its implementations are interpreters.

7-1.3 Major Applications of SNOBOL

Programming experience with SNOBOL has been almost exclusively in the text processing application area, where it excels. In this area, the basic data type is the character string. The basic operations performed on strings are those which support the analysis and synthesis of text: natural language text, algebraic formulas, and so forth. The basic unit of analysis in text processing applications is the character. A "word" is a contiguous variable-length string of nonblank characters, and thus much of text processing analysis deals with the problem of isolating and manipulating individual words.

Input-output functions in text processing applications are distinct, since the conventional fixed-length record imposes a somewhat artificial boundary on the information. A text is typically variable in length, whether we consider an input-output unit as a word, a sentence, or a paragraph. Often the input-output unit is a printed page, in which case the program must perform its own buffering. Thus, the program often has to take apart a page into paragraphs, sentences, and words, or else build a page out of words, sentences, and paragraphs. An example of these activities is given in our SNOBOL program for Case Study 6—Text Formatter, at the end of the chapter.

Recent versions of SNOBOL have facilities which render it a more general-purpose language. These facilities include floating-point arithmetic, arrays, and list structures. Although we shall introduce most of these facilities, we shall not directly evaluate SNOBOL's effectiveness in the scientific or data processing application areas. We leave that to the interested reader, with appropriate exercises at the end of this chapter.

7-2 WRITING SNOBOL PROGRAMS

A SNOBOL program, in its simplest form, consists of a series of executable statements, followed by the "END statement" which marks the physical end of the program. Generally, the statements of a program are written one statement per line, although multiple statements may appear if they are mutually separated by semicolon-space (;b̸) that can be used to delimit statements from each other. Certain words, such as END and RETURN, have special use in a SNOBOL program, should therefore not be used as variable names.

The simple SNOBOL program below computes and displays the average of an indeterminate number of input numbers. For example, if the input were 85.5, 87.5, 89.5, and 91.5 the result displayed would be 88.5. The program uses the variable X to hold a single input number and the variable N to determine the number of input numbers in the process. The variables SUM and AV contain the numbers' sum and average, respectively.

```
* THIS PROGRAM COMPUTES THE AVERAGE (AV)
* OF N INPUT NUMBERS (X)

     N = 0
     SUM = 0

LOOP X = TRIM(INPUT)            :F(DONE)
     N = N + 1
     SUM = SUM + X              :(LOOP)

DONE AV = SUM / N
     OUTPUT = N ' NUMBERS WERE GIVEN'
     OUTPUT = AV ' IS THEIR AVERAGE'
END
```

Here, we see that the first two lines are examples of a SNOBOL "comment," which is always distinguished by the character * in the first position of the line. The remaining lines represent the executable statements of the program itself. Here, we see a loop between lines labeled LOOP and DONE, and the final two OUTPUT statements which display the results.

When typing a SNOBOL program, rather strict formatting conventions must be followed. Any statement which is labeled must have its label begin in position 1 of the line. Any unlabeled statement must *not* begin in position 1. Also, any statement which exceeds the length of a single line must be continued by placing sign + in position 1.

The body of a statement comprises four distinct parts, and each part must be separated from the next by at least one space. In the program above, statements only exhibit three of these four parts, the "subject," the "object," and the "go to" parts. The "subject" is that which is normally on the left of an assignment symbol (in SNOBOL, this symbol is =), a variable name, or an array reference. The "object" is normally referred to as the expression on the right of a conventional assignment. The "go to" part is that which provides the conditional and unconditional branching from the statement. For example, the statement

```
LOOP X = TRIM(INPUT)     :F(DONE)
```

has X as its subject, TRIM(INPUT) as its object, and :F(DONE) as its go to part.

This statement operates as an ordinary assignment, with the additional consideration that the built-in function INPUT is invoked whenever a new line of input is desired.

Moreover, the abbreviations :F (DONE) denotes the conditional transfer to statement labeled DONE if the attempt to obtain input fails (F). The other go to part shown in this program is :(LOOP), which is an unconditional transfer to the statement labeled LOOP.

The remainder of this program should be relatively self-explanatory. Note that there are no declarations of variables. In SNOBOL, every variable has *generic* type, in the sense that its type changes as program execution proceeds, according to the value that was most recently assigned to it. Moreover, SNOBOL automatically initializes the values of all variables so that numeric variables are initially set to 0 and string variables are initially set to '' (empty). We shall examine all the SNOBOL statements individually, and in detail, later in the chapter.

7-2.1 Elementary Data Types and Values

The basic SNOBOL data type is the "string," which is a sequence of zero or more characters taken from the following set (this set contains only those characters which are common to *all* SNOBOL implementations):

ƀ (blank) . (+ & ! $ *) ; - / , % ? : # @ ' = "
A B C D E F G H I J K L M N O P Q R S T U V W X Y Z
0 1 2 3 4 5 6 7 8 9

When written within a SNOBOL program, a string may be enclosed either within single quotes (') or within double quotes ("). If a single (double) quote occurs as part of the string itself, then the string is enclosed within double (single) quotes. Here are four examples of strings.

'ABC'
"AbBbC"
"
"WHAT'SƀTHIS?"

A string of zero characters is called a "null" string. The third example above is null.

SNOBOL also provides the numeric data types "integer" and "real." Integer and real values are represented in their usual way, as shown by the following examples:

Integers	Reals
0	0.5
−17	3.14159
250	−0.00003

The data type "pattern" is SNOBOL's main vehicle for characterizing string manipulation activities within a program. In general, a pattern is a definition of a class of strings which share a common property. Strings may share a variety of properties, such as common substrings, common initial parts, common lengths, and so forth. There is a correspondingly rich variety of ways that a pattern may be defined. We will discuss this fully in section 7-2.3.

7-2.2 Names, Variables, and Declarations

Although different data types (string, integer, real) are identified in SNOBOL, a variable's value is not confined to one particular type throughout program execution. Rather, a variable's type is simply that of its current value. At one point during execution a variable's value may be a string such as ABC, while at another point it may be an integer such as 43.

A "variable name" is any sequence of one or more letters (A–Z) and digits (0–9), the first being a letter. The following are valid variable names:

X
S1
NAME

The existence of any particular variable, such as X, in a program is implicitly declared by its usage in the program.

7-2.3 Arrays and Other Data Structures

SNOBOL provides the "array" as a means of associating more than one value with a single name. An array is an *n*-dimensional collection of values. For instance, an array named A may be a one-dimensional list of five elements, each having the value zero, as shown in Figure 7-1. Similarly, B may be a two-dimensional array, with five rows and four columns of elements, as shown also in Figure 7-1.

To define an array's dimensionality, and possibly its initial values, the program contains a statement of the following form:

name = ARRAY (dimensionality [, initial-value])

(The use of brackets throughout this chapter will denote an optional form, in the same way that it did in the COBOL chapter.) Here, "name" denotes the name to be assigned to the array, while "dimensionality" denotes its number of dimensions and number of

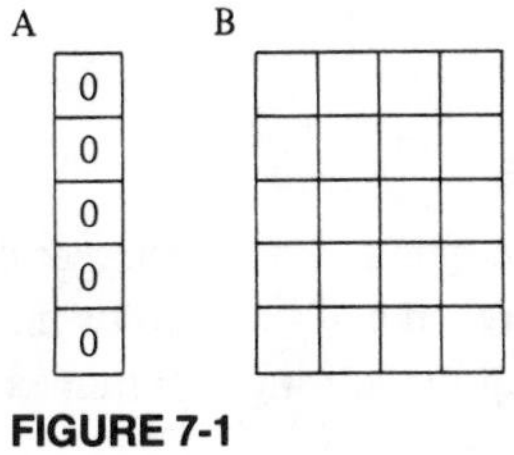

FIGURE 7-1

elements in each dimension. The optional "initial-value" denotes a value to which all elements in the array will be initialized when this statement is executed. When that option is omitted, the initial values of the array's elements are the null string. For example, to define the arrays A and B in Figure 7-1, the following statements are required:

```
A = ARRAY (5,0)
B = ARRAY ('5,4')
```

In the case of A, the dimensionality is 5 and the initial value is 0. In the case of B, the initial value is omitted and B's twenty entries are thereby initialized with the null string. Note that B's dimensionality is enclosed in quotes ('); failure to do so would declare B as a one-dimensional array of five elements with initial value 4!

An array's number of elements may be dynamically, as well as statically, declared. For instance, if M and N are variables with integer values, then the statement

```
C = ARRAY ('M,N')
```

defines the array C to have M rows and N columns, depending upon the values of M and N at the time this statement is executed.

An array element is subsequently referenced in the program by writing the array's name followed by a subscript which identifies the position of the element within the array. For example, if we want to reference the fourth element within the array A defined above, we would write A⟨4⟩. The subscripts may additionally be variables, so that A⟨I⟩ is a reference to the Ith element in A.

SNOBOL also provides the "table" and the "programmer-defined data type" as additional means of structuring data within a program. Programmer-defined data types are discussed in section 7-2.8.

A "table" is similar to a one-dimensional array, except that a table element may be referenced by a subscript of any value, whether it be integer or not. To define a table, the following statement is used:

```
name = TABLE (size, increment)
```

Here, "name" denotes the table's name, while "size" is an integer (or integer-valued variable) which denotes the number of elements in the table. "Increment" denotes an integer (-valued variable) which is the amount by which the table's size will be increased whenever the table becomes full and a new block of entries must be added. For example,

```
T = TABLE (15,5)
```

initially defines a table named T with fifteen elements. When T is full and a sixteenth entry is to be added to T, five new elements are created, increasing T's size to twenty elements. Such increments are performed as many times as required during program execution.

To reference an element within a table, we use as a subscript any arbitrary numeric or string value. For example, the reference T⟨'A'⟩, references the 'A'th element within T; i.e., the element whose subscript is *literally* A, rather than the integer value of some variable A.

SNOBOL also provides functions for manipulating arrays and tables. These will be discussed in section 7-2.8.

7-2.4 Basic Statements

There are (only) four basic statements in the SNOBOL language; the "assignment statement," the "pattern-matching statement," the "replacement statement," and the "end statement." The end statement appears last in a program and simply denotes its end. It is written simply as END, and must begin in position 1 of the line.

The assignment, pattern-matching, and replacement statements have the following general forms, respectively:

```
[label] subject = object              [go to part]
[label] [ subject [pattern] ]         [go to part]
[label] subject pattern = object      [go to part]
```

Here, "label" denotes an (optional) statement label, which is any unique name. "Subject" generally denotes a variable, array, or table entry whose current value will be changed by execution of the statement. "Pattern" denotes a pattern to be used during the statement's execution, while "object" generally denotes an expression whose value will be assigned to the subject. The optional "go to part" denotes conditional or unconditional transfer of control to another statement in the program. If this part is omitted, control will transfer directly to the next statement. The individual parts of these statement types must be separated by one or more spaces (ƀ).

As a basis for discussing these statement types we refer to the example SNOBOL program presented at the beginning of the chapter.

Expressions The "object" part of an assignment or replacement statement is an "expression" which, when evaluated, either "fails" or "delivers" a result. When the expression evaluation fails, the entire statement is said to fail.

Expressions are also used to describe the "pattern" part of a pattern-matching or replacement statement. In this context, evaluation of the pattern expression either fails or results in a collection of values which are used in the "pattern-matching" phase of the statement's execution. Again, if evaluation of the pattern expression fails, then the entire statement fails.

An expression itself may be a variable name, an array reference, a literal (number or string constant), or function call. An expression may also be formed by affixing one of the unary operators (@ , $, ?, &, -, ., \, +, or *). An expression may also be formed by writing a series of expressions which are separated by a binary operator ($, ., **, *, /, +, -, ƀ, or |). When operators are used in expressions, they must be preceded and followed by a blank space (ƀ). (SNOBOL also has a number of symbols designated as "unused operators." These may be defined by the programmer as "extensions" to the operator set.) Finally, any expression thus formed may be enclosed in parentheses. Some examples of expressions are given below.

1
N + 1
LT(I,5) I + 1
5 + 3 * (H − A⟨H⟩)

The first of these is a literal. The second is formed by separating two expressions by the binary operator "+". The third is formed by separating two expression by the binary operator "ƀ". In this, the first expression, LT(I,5), is a function call and the second is an expression formed with the binary operator "+". The fourth is formed by separating a series of expressions by binary operators. The third expression in that series is enclosed in parentheses.

Evaluation of an expression generally proceeds from left to right until either the expression fails or evaluation is completed. Left-to-right evaluation may be overridden either by the priorities among the operators or by the use of parentheses. The operators, their priorities, and their meanings are given in the following table:

Operator	Priority	Unary or binary	Meaning of "op e" or "a op b"
/	12	Unary	Negation: fails if e doesn't fail
?		Unary	Interrogation; fails if e fails
$	11	Unary	Indirect reference
$		Binary	Immediate value assignment
**	10	Binary	Exponentiation: a^b
*	8	Unary	Unevaluated expression
*		Binary	Multiplication: a × b
/	7	Binary	Division: a/b
+	6	Unary	Plus: +e
+		Binary	Addition: a + b
−	5	Unary	Negation: −e
−		Binary	Subtraction: a − b
@	4	Unary	Cursor position
ƀ	3	Binary	Concatenation: ab
|	2	Binary	Alternation: either a or b
&	1	Unary	Keyword

The meanings of many of these operators (+, −, *, /, **) should be familiar, since they are the same as in other languages. One unusual point here, however, is that integer division always yields an integer result.

The meanings of others are, however, less well known; they are used to facilitate the processing of strings. These (ƀ, |, @, &) will be illustrated in later paragraphs.

Operations within an expression are carried out in descending order of priority, and from left to right within the same priority level. Thus the two operations (ƀ and +) in the expression "LT(I,5)ƀI + 1" are carried out in the order indicated below by the numbered arrows.

```
LT(I,5) ƀ I + 1
        ↑   ↑
       (2) (1)
```

That is, the sum I + 1 is computed, and the result is then concatenated with the result of evaluating the function call "LT(I,5)." (More will be said in a later paragraph about these function calls.)

On the other hand, the use of parentheses in the expression "5 + 3 * (H − A⟨H⟩)" forces the order of evaluation to be as follows:

```
5 + 3 * (H - A⟨H⟩)
  ↑   ↑    ↑
 (3) (2)  (1)
```

Their omission would have resulted in the following order:

```
5 + 3 * H - A⟨H⟩
  ↑   ↑   ↑
 (2) (1) (3)
```

Special Function Calls and Operators Although the use of function calls will be fully discussed in section 7-2.8, we discuss some of them here because of their immediate usefulness. These are the so-called "primitive predicates." The numerical predicates are used to test whether a specified numerical relation holds between two expressions, say a and b. It is written as r(a,b), where the relation r may be any of the following:

Relation r	Requirement for r(a,b) to succeed
LT	a is less than b
LE	a is less than or equal to b
EQ	a is equal to b
NE	a is not equal to b
GE	a is greater than or equal to b
GT	a is greater than b

Evaluation of the predicate r(a,b) fails if the indicated requirement for success is not by a and b. Moreover, the null string ('') is returned when evaluation succeeds.

For instance, the predicate LT(I,5) appears in the expression "LT(I,5)ƀI + 1". This evaluation succeeds exactly when the value of I is less than 5, in which case the result is the null string. In this event, subsequent evaluation will concatenate that null string with the sum I + 1, thus leaving the same result as if the expression I + 1 were written alone. If, on the other hand, evaluation of LT(I,5) fails, then the expression itself fails and no result is delivered.

There are three object comparison predicates: IDENT, DIFFER, and LGT. Any of these may be applied to two expressions, a and b, which are not necessarily numeric. Each one is written with two arguments (which are expressions) as follows:

Object comparison predicate	**Requirement for its evaluation to succeed**
IDENT(a,b)	The values of a and b are identical, character for character.
DIFFER(a,b)	The values of a and b are not identical.
LGT(a,b)	The value of a is lexically greater than the value of b; that is, a follows b alphabetically. The collating sequence (alphabetic ordering) among the characters is implementation dependent, but generally speaking, b̸ < {all special characters} < A < B <· · · < Z < 0 < 1 < · · · < 9 for all implementations. We will not rely on any further refinements of this ordering here.

Evaluation of any of these fails when its indicated requirement for success is not met by a and b. Otherwise, the result of evaluation is the null string.,

A number of special string operators found in SNOBOL expressions deserve further explanation and illustration. For this, suppose we have the following variables and values:

Variable	**Value**
S	'b̸THESEb̸AREb̸THEb̸TIMES.b̸b̸b̸b̸'
T	'S'
U	''

If we prefix an expression e with the unary operator $, this indicates an "indirect reference." That is, the variable *actually referenced* by the expression $e is one whose *name* is the current value of e. For instance if we write $T, and the value of T is the string 'S', we are actually writing an expression whose evaluation delivers the current value of S. If, on the other hand, there is no variable whose name is identical with the current value of e then the effect of evaluation $e is to create a *new* variable with that name and null string as its value.

When used as a binary operator, "$" has a different meaning; it forces an intermediate assignment during the expression's evaluation. For instance, consider the following expression:

```
T $ Ub̸'R'
  ↑  ↑
  ①  ②
```

Here, the variable named U is assigned the value of T, which is 'S'. Then that value is concatenated with 'R', giving 'SR' as the value of the whole expression.

The operator "." can also be used either as a unary operator or as a binary operator. The expression ".v", for any variable v, returns as its result the variable's *name,* rather than its current value. This is useful when passing arguments "by name" to programmer-defined functions, as we shall illustrate in section 7-2.8. When used as a binary operator, "." designates conditional value assignment. The expression

```
e . v
```

for an expression e and a variable v, designates assignment of the value of e to the variable v, but *only* if the evaluation of e succeeds.

The unary operators "*" and "@", as well as the binary operator "|" are used principally by expression which are patterns. These will be discussed in a later section.

Finally, the unary operator "&" is prefixed to a variable whenever that variable is a SNOBOL "keyword." The SNOBOL keywords designate certain parameters and switchers that are internal to the SNOBOL system. The SNOBOL program thus has access to these "system variables" by way of the unary operator "&".

SNOBOL keywords fall into two classes, "unprotected keywords" and "protected keywords." The unprotected keywords are those to which the program can assign a value, while the protected ones are those to which only the system can assign a value. Many of the SNOBOL keywords will be introduced and illustrated later in this chapter.

Assignment Statements The assignment statement serves principally to assign a new value to a variable, array element, or table element. Recall that the assignment statement has the following form:

[label] subject = object [go to part]

Execution of the assignment statement takes place in the following sequence:

1 The subject, which may be a variable name, array reference, or table reference, is evaluated. If evaluation fails, then the statement is said to fail and the go to part is immediately processed.

2 The object, which may be any expression, is evaluated. If evaluation fails, then the statement is said to fail and the go to part is immediately processed.

3 The value of the object is assigned to the subject, and the subject is said to succeed.

4 The go to part (if present) is processed and the next statement to be executed is determined accordingly.

Failure in the evaluation of either the subject or the object may occur for any of a variety of reasons. We have already seen some of these reasons during the discussion of expressions. For example, consider the following assignment statement:

```
I = LT(I,5) I + 1
```

Suppose that, upon reaching this statement, the current value of I is 1. Then the following sequence occurs:

1 I is evaluated, and no failure occurs.

2 LR(I,5) I + 1 is evaluated, and no failure occurs since LT(I,5) succeeds. The value of this expression is thus 2.

3 That value becomes the new value of I and the statement succeeds.

If, on the other hand, the current value of I were 5, then the assignment would not take place [since failure of the object LT(I,5) I + 1 causes failure of the statement at step 2].

Failure in evaluating the subject can occur when an array reference specifies an invalid element. For instance, if A were declared as an array of five elements by the statement

A = ARRAY(5)

and A⟨6⟩ occurred on the left of an assignment statement, then the statement would fail.

Patterns and Pattern Matching The pattern is the key part of both the pattern-matching statement and the replacement statement. In this section we present and illustrate the pattern-matching process during execution of these two types of statements.

A "pattern" is an expression which represents either a single string or a set of strings. The subject of a pattern-matching or replacement statement is usually a variable name, array reference, or table reference. Pattern matching is an attempt to answer the following question:

> Does the current value of the subject contain a string which is identical to (one of) the string(s) represented by the pattern?

Pattern matching is said to succeed or fail, respectively, depending on whether the answer to this question is yes or no.

The two binary operations of concatenation (ƀ) and alternation (|) play a central role in patterns which describe sets of strings. If we write a pattern in the form

e_1ƀe_2

where e_1 and e_2 denote expressions, we are describing the (set of) string(s) formed by concatenating (any one of) the value(s) of e_1 with (any one of) the value(s) of e_2. If we write a pattern in the form

$e_1 \mid e_2$

we are describing the (set of) string(s) whose value is *either* (one of) the value(s) of e_1 *or* (one of) the value(s) of e_2.

For example, let S, T, and U again be variables with the following values:

S = 'ƀTHESEƀAREƀTHEƀTIMES.ƀƀƀƀ'
T = 'S'
U = ''

Then the pattern Tƀ'AT' describes a string of the form 'SAT' (the result of concatenating 'S' and 'AT'). On the other hand, the pattern T | 'AT' describes a string either of the form 'S' or of the form 'AT'. In the first case, a pattern match will succeed only if the subject contains a string of the form 'SAT'. In the second case, a pattern match will succeed if the subject contains either the string 'S' or the string 'AT'. For instance, if the subject were the above variable S, the pattern match of S with Tȣ'AT' would fail, while the pattern match of S with T | 'AT' would succeed.

The actual scan of the subject string, to determine whether the pattern match succeeds, takes place from left ro right, beginning with the subject's leftmost character. There is an imaginary cursor ↑ which indicates the current position in the subject string where the scan is taking place. At the beginning of the pattern match operation the cursor is pointing to the leftmost character, as shown below for our example string S. This is known as "position 0". (In general, when the cursor is at "position i" in a string it is actually pointing to the i + 1st character.)

```
S|ȣTHESEȣAREȣTHEȣTIMES.ȣȣȣȣ|
  ↑
```

If the pattern contains alternatives (indicated by "|") then the alternatives are considered in turn from left to right, beginning with the leftmost. For instance, suppose the pattern were as follows:

'S' | 'AT'

The first alternative to be tried in the match is 'S', and it is compared with a string of the same length starting at the current cursor position. That string is 'ȣ', so the match does not succeed for this particular alternative. The next alternative in the pattern is then compared with the string (of length 2) at the same cursor position.

Only after all alternatives in the pattern have been tried unsuccessfully for a given cursor position in the subject string will the cursor move, as shown below. The cursor now moves to position 1.

```
S|ȣTHESEȣAREȣTHEȣTIMES.ȣȣȣȣ|
   ↑
```

Now the alternatives are retried in the same sequence. This process continues until either an alternative succeeds for some cursor position or all cursor positions have been tried and no successful match was found. Note that pattern matching succeeds for this particular example when the cursor reaches the following position:

```
S|ȣTHESEȣAREȣTHEȣTIMES.ȣȣȣȣ|
        ↑
```

In addition to concatenation and alternation, certain other SNOBOL operators, keywords, and functions have particular usefulness in pattern matching. We illustrate the following in the remainder of this section:

Operators ".", "$", "*", and "@"
Keyword &ANCHOR
Functions LEN, SPAN, BREAK, ANY, POS, RPOS, and ARB

The binary operators "." and "$" cause intermediate value assignment during the pattern matching scan. The difference between the two is that "." causes assignment only if the entire pattern match succeeds, while "$" causes immediate assignment whether or not the pattern match succeeds. They are written as follows.

```
e . v
e $ v
```

Here, "e" denotes an expression used as part of a pattern, while "v" denotes a variable name, array reference, or table reference. As soon as a string is found in the subject which causes the pattern match with e to succeed, then "e$v" causes that string to be assigned to v. On the other hand, " e . v" causes the assignment to take place only if the *entire* pattern (of which "e . v" is a part) match succeeds.

For example, reconsider the variable S with value 'ƀTHESEƀAREƀTHEƀTIMES.ƀƀƀƀ' and the following two patterns, in which T is another variable name:

(i) ('S' | 'AT') $ T 'AT'
(ii) ('S' | 'AT') . T 'AT'

Note that both of these patterns will fail with S as the subject, since S does not contain an occurrence of either 'AST' or 'ATAT'. However, S does satisfy the pattern 'S' | 'AT', since it contains 'S' in position 4. Thus, that value will be immediately assigned to the variable T if pattern (i) is used. However, pattern (ii) will *not* result in an assignment to T, since the whole pattern match fails.

The unary operator "*" denotes an unevaluated expression. Suppose, for example, we have the following assignment statements in a SNOBOL program:

```
U = 'E'
S = 'ƀTHESEƀAREƀTHEƀTIMES.ƀƀƀƀ'
P = ('S' | 'AT') U
```

We see here that the variable P has as its value a pattern when the last assignment statement is executed. Specifically, the value of P becomes equivalent to the following:

```
'SE' | 'ATE'
```

since the value of U is 'E'. Now, consider the pattern match

```
S P
```

where S is the subject and P is the pattern. This match succeeds when 'SE' is reached in S by the cursor. If, on the other hand, we redefine P as follows,

```
P = ('S' | 'AT') * U
```

the evaluation of U in this expression will be *postponed* until P actually occurs in a pattern-matching situation. At that time, of course, the value of U may no longer be 'E', so that the pattern represented by P can *itself* vary during program execution.

The unary operator "@" is used to save the current position of the cursor during a pattern-matching operation. Specifically, the expression "@v" stores the current position of the cursor in the variable named v. For example, suppose again that S has the value 'ƀTHESEƀAREƀTHEƀTIMES.ƀƀƀƀ' and we apply the following pattern,

('S' | 'AT') @I

then the pattern match will succeed with the cursor at position 4 in S, and I will be assigned the value 4.

In many situations, the program requires that a pattern match be applied only at the beginning of the subject string. That is, if the pattern match fails for the cursor positioned at the left end of the subject string, then the pattern-matching operation should be aborted. This specification can be given by using the &ANCHOR keyword. If &ANCHOR is assigned a nonzero value, as in the statement

&ANCHOR = 1

then the pattern-matching operation is thus "anchored" at the beginning of the subject string. If &ANCHOR is zero (0), which is its default setting, pattern matching will proceed normally.

The functions in the following list have special usefulness in SNOBOL pattern-matching operations. They will be illustrated below. In this table, s denotes any string expression and i denotes any integer expression.

Function f	**Argument a**	**String which will cause a pattern match with f(a) to succeed**
ANY	s	Any single character in the subject which occurs in s.
ARB	None	Any string in the subject of arbitrary length.
BREAK	s	The *longest* nonnull string in the subject beginning with the current cursor position and not containing any of the characters in s.
LEN	i	Any string in the subject whose length is i.
NOTANY	s	Any single character in the subject which does not occur in s.
POS	i	When the subject string's length is at least i + 1, the cursor is positioned at the i + 1st character before pattern matching continues.
RPOS	i	Similarly, the cursor is positioned at the i + 1st character from the *right* end of the subject string.
SPAN	s	The *longest* nonnull string in the subject beginning at the current cursor position which contains *only* characters from s.

To illustrate these functions, consider again our familiar example, S = 'ƀTHESEƀAREƀTHEƀTIMES.ƀƀƀƀ' using several different patterns.

Pattern	String in S where the match will succeed (circled)
ANY(',.!?')	'ƀTHESEƀAREƀTHEƀTIMES.ƀƀƀƀ'
SPAN('ƀ')	'ƀTHESEƀAREƀTHEƀTIMES.ƀƀƀƀ'
SPAN('ƀ')BREAK('ƀ')	'ƀTHESEƀAREƀTHEƀTIMES.ƀƀƀƀ'
SPAN('ƀ')RPOS(0)	'ƀTHESEƀAREƀTHEƀTIMES.ƀƀƀƀ'

The position of the arrow in each of these examples indicates where the cursor will be after the pattern match succeeds. These functions can thus be used in powerful and interesting ways to isolate parts of sentences and other strings that have no explicit structure.

The Pattern-Matching and Replacement Statements Now that we have a feel for the pattern-matching process, we can proceed to examine the pattern-matching and replacement statements.

The pattern-matching statement asks the question "Will the subject match the pattern?" No direct assignment needs to be performed, unless an immediate or conditional assignment occurs within the pattern itself. The statement succeeds or fails, respectively, if the pattern match succeeds or fails,and the go to part (if present) is processed accordingly. Continuing our example, the following three pattern-matching statements will each succeed:

```
S 'S' | 'AT'
S SPAN ('ƀ') BREAK('ƀ')
S (SPAN('ƀ') BREAK ('ƀ')) $ WORD
```

The real power of these statements is that they are used to cause a conditional transfer on the basis of the success or failure of the given pattern match. The transfer itself is specified by attaching a go to part, which will be discussed in the next section. Note in the third example here that the matched substring 'ƀTHESE' in S will be immediately assigned to the variable named WORD. If the parentheses had been omitted within this pattern, the substring 'THESE' from S would be assigned instead, since the pattern match for BREAK('ƀ') would begin with the cursor at the second character in S rather than the first, and the operator ƀ yields precedence to $.

Execution of the replacement statement is a bit more complex, since the statement combines the functions of the assignment and pattern-matching statements. Recall that it has the following form:

[label] subject pattern = object [go to part]

Its execution proceeds in the following steps:

1 The subject is evaluated. If the evaluation fails, then the statement fails and the go to part is immediately processed.

2 The pattern is evaluated. If evaluation fails, then the statement fails and the go to part is immediately processed.

3 The pattern match is performed. If the pattern match fails, then the statement fails and the go to part is immediately processed. However, immediate value assignment and other "side effects" that may occur during the pattern-matching process will be carried out before the failure occurs. If the pattern match succeeds, then conditional value assignment is performed for those components of the pattern match that succeeded.

4 The object is evaluated. If evaluation fails, then the statement fails and the go to part is immediately processed.

5 The replacement is performed; i.e., the value of the object replaces that part (substring) of the subject string for which the pattern match succeeds. Thus, the subject string's length as well as its value is typically affected by the replacement.

6 The go to part is processed.

Consider the following example statements and their evaluation:

(i) S = 'ƀTHESEƀAREƀTHEƀTIMES.ƀƀƀƀ'
(ii) S SPAN('ƀ') = ''
(iii) S SPAN('ƀ') BREAK('ƀ') $ WORD1 = ''
(iv) S SPAN('ƀ') RPOS (0) = ''

Suppose at the outset of evaluation for each of statements (ii), (iii), and (iv) the value of S were as assigned in statement (i). Each of statements (ii), (iii), and (iv) will assign the null string ('') to a particular substring of S, thus deleting that substring. The substring itself is identified by the pattern in each case.

Execution of statement (ii) therefore causes deletion of leading blanks in S, as shown.

S | THESEƀAREƀTHEƀTIMES.ƀƀƀƀ |

Execution of statement (iii), on the other hand, causes deletion of all leading blanks *and* the leftmost string of nonblanks in S, with an immediate assignment of that nonblank string to WORD1, as shown.

S | ƀAREƀTHEƀTIMES.ƀƀƀƀ |
WORD1 | THESE |

Execution of statement (iv), on the other hand, causes deletion of the *rightmost* string of blanks in S, as shown.

S | ƀTHESEƀAREƀTHEƀTIMES. |

This small example should illustrate how individual words can be broken out of a sentence.

"Boundary" Conditions in Pattern Matching It is important to gain a firm understanding of precisely those conditions under which a particular pattern match will succeed or fail. Certain success and failure conditions will occur when the null string ('') occurs in a statement. We call these "boundary conditions" and describe them here.

First, recall that all variables in a SNOBOL program have the null string as initial value. Thus, if a variable appears, as, say, the object of an assignment statement before it has been assigned a value itself, then its value is (implicitly) null.

Second, all predicates (LE, EQ, etc.) return the null string ('') when their evaluation succeeds. Thus, execution of

```
I = LT(I,5) I + 1
```

when the value of I is less than 5 causes concatenation of '' with the sum I + 1, which is equivalent to the sum I + 1 by itself, when the object "LT(1,5) I + 1" is evaluated.

Third, whenever a pattern contains the null string ('') as an alternative, its appearance in a pattern match with any subject will *always* succeed! This also includes the case where the subject is null.

7-2.5 Control Structures

SNOBOL does not possess any of the usual control structures that comprise the tools of structured programming; if . . . then. . . else, do . . . while, and so forth. Its only control structures lie in the "go to" part of its basic statements.

The Go To Part of a SNOBOL Statement When the go to part of a statement is included, it has one of the following forms:

(i) :S(label1)F(label2)
(ii) :S(label1)
(iii) :F(label2)
(iv) :(label1)

Here, "label1" and "label2" denote labels of statements in the program.

When an individual SNOBOL statement is executed, its execution is said to either "succeed" or "fail." The success or failure of a statement may occur during pattern matching, as we have seen in the foregoing section. It may also be caused by other conditions, as we shall see later. The go to part is a specification of the response that should be taken, in the form of a transfer, when the statement succeeds or fails. Corresponding to the four forms above, therefore, are the following interpretations:

(i) Proceed to statement labeled "label1" if execution of the statement succeeds. Otherwise, proceed to statement labeled "label2."

(ii) Proceed to "label1" if the statement succeeds. Otherwise proceed to the next statement.

(iii) Proceed to "label2" if this statement fails. Otherwise, proceed to the next statement.

(iv) Proceed to "label1" whether or not the statement succeeds (i.e., unconditionally).

An illustration of forms (iii) and (iv) appears in the example program at the beginning of the chapter. The go to part :F(DONE) indicates a conditional transfer to statement labeled done, if the statement X = INPUT fails. The go to part :(LOOP) indicates unconditional transfer to the statement labeled LOOP. Omission of the go to part, of course, denotes an unconditional transfer to the next statement in the program text.

7-2.6 Input-Output Conventions

SNOBOL's input-output facilities are very simple and somewhat limited. The particular SNOBOL implementation used for running our case study program provides additional input-output capability. However, that capability is so implementation dependent that we will not include it here. In this section we present and discuss only those input-output facilities that are shared among all SNOBOL implementations. There are three basic files available to a SNOBOL program, and they are all sequentially accessed.

The INPUT file is a sequence of eighty-character lines. The OUTPUT file is a sequence of print lines used for output. The PUNCH file is a sequence of eighty-character records (typically punched cards) used for output.

To read a record from the INPUT file, and store its contents in a variable named v, an assignment statement of the following form is used:

```
v = INPUT      :F(eof)
```

This statement will succeed unless the last input record has already been read (i.e., "end of file" has occurred). Thus, "eof" denotes the label of some statement to be executed when end of file occurs. Of course, the go to part could have been omitted, in which case statement failure (by end of file) would transfer control to the next statement.

To write the value of an expression e to the next record of the OUTPUT file, the following assignment statement is needed:

```
OUTPUT = e
```

Similarly, to write that value to the PUNCH file, the following statement is needed:

```
PUNCH = e
```

The special variables INPUT, OUTPUT, and PUNCH may also be used in other contexts. For instance, a replacement statement may have the next INPUT record as its object, or the next INPUT record may be called from within a larger expression, such as the following:

```
TEXT = TEXT INPUT
```

Here, the next input record is appended to the right end of the current value of the variable named TEXT.

The following example is a simple two-statement SNOBOL program which lists a deck of cards:

```
LIST OUTPUT = INPUT:(LIST)
END
```

Here, the statement labeled LIST is repeated as long as there are more INPUT records to be read.

Horizontal and vertical formatting of output from a SNOBOL program is done explicitly, with no additional help from the language. Output of text, however, is a different kind of problem than output of other types of results. For example, we shall see in the SNOBOL solution to Case Study 6 the special programming required to justify OUTPUT text to the right margin as well as the left.

The most elementary aspect of vertical formatting—skipping a line—is simply accomplished by printing the null string

```
OUTPUT = ''
```

Page skipping may be accomplished either by explicitly keeping track of a line counter within the program or by filling a buffer with an entire page's worth of output before printing.

Horizontal formatting must also be done explicitly in the program. For example, the arrangement of printed results in columns must be done by explicit insertion of blanks within each line image.

Finally, we note that the unprotected keywords &INPUT and &OUTPUT may be altered to turn off input or output, or both. They are both initially set to 1. Execution of one or both of the following statements

```
&INPUT = 0
&OUTPUT = 0
```

will turn off input or output or both, accordingly. Subsequent input or output may be turned back on by reassigning some nonzero value to these keywords.

7-2.7 Subprograms, Functions, and Libraries

In most practical programming situations the task is large enough to warrant segmentation of the program into a number of functional blocks. These are often linked together by a "main" program that controls the sequence in which these functional blocks will be executed. Another advantage of program segmentation is that it permits the reuse of code without rewriting it each time it is needed.

SNOBOL provides facilities which enable such segmentation. A SNOBOL subprogram is called a "function," and it may be invoked during execution of a SNOBOL program by way of a "function call" within an expression. There are two programming aspects to the use of functions: defining them and invoking them.

Certain functions have such widespread usefulness in SNOBOL applications that they are already defined within the language. These are called the "primitive functions." We have already presented and illustrated several of the primitive functions (LE, EQ, GT, BREAK, SPAN, etc.) in earlier sections. Some additional SNOBOL primitive functions which are widely useful are described in the table below.

Primitive function	**Arguments**	**Results returned**
DUPL	s,i	A string composed of i repetitions (duplicates) of s.
REMDR	i,j	The integer remainder of *i/j*.
REPLACE	s,t,u	The result of replacing every occurrence in s of the *i*th character in t by the *i*th character in u, for each $i = 1, \ldots, n$; t and u must be the same size, *n*.
SIZE	s	The number of characters in s.
TRIM	s	The result of trimming all trailing blanks from s.

(Here, s, t, and u denote string expressions, while i and j denote integer expressions.)

Each of these can be invoked by writing an appropriate function call, which has the following general form:

function (arguments)

For example, the following function call

S = TRIM ('ƀTHESEƀAREƀTHEƀTIMES.ƀƀƀƀ')

returns and assigns to S the result of deleting all trailing blanks, as shown below:

S |ƀTHESEƀAREƀTHEƀTIMES.|

Now, the size of S (without the trailing blanks) is obtained by the function call SIZE(S). The following statement

I = SIZE(S)

thus leaves 21 as the value of I. Continuing, if we write

J = REMDR(I,8)

the value of J will become 5, which is the remainder of dividing I by 8. Execution of the statement T = REPLACE (S,'b','*') will then leave S as follows.

S |*THESE*ARE*THE*TIMES.|

Finally, if we write DUPL ('*',10) we obtain the string '**********'

Of course, function calls may be nested, in which case they are evaluated from the inside out. For example, the following statement

S = REPLACE(TRIM('ƀTHESEƀAREƀTHEƀTIMES.ƀƀƀƀ'),'ƀ','*')

leaves in S the same result that was finally achieved above.

When the programmer needs a function which is not among the primitive functions, it may be defined in the following way:

1 Invoke the primitive function DEFINE to indicate that a new function is to be defined.

2 Write a SNOBOL procedure which actually defines the logic of the function to be performed.

The invocation of DEFINE is written to name the new function, to identify its formal parameters, to identify its local variables, and to identify the entry point of the function's defining procedure. It has the following general form:

DEFINE('function(parameters) locals'[,'entry'])

Here, "function" denotes the name of the function. "Parameters" denotes a list of zero or more names, mutually separated by commas, which identify the parameters used in the function's defining procedure. "Locals" similarly identifies the local variables used in the function's definition. "Entry" is the label of the first executable statement in the function's definition. It may be omitted, in which case the function's name is assumed identical with the label in its first executable statement.

The SNOBOL procedure which defines the function may be placed anywhere outside the logical flow of the program which invokes it. (The function's DEFINE statement, however, must be executed logically before the function is invoked.) Moreover, the programmer should place such defining procedures out of line, so that control does not pass to them *unless* they are called.

Return of control from a called function is accomplished by a transfer to one of the following system labels during execution of the function's defining procedure:

RETURN—Control returns to the calling expression and the function call succeeds.
FRETURN—Control returns and the function call fails.

During execution of the defining procedure, the function's name also plays the role of a variable. As such, the value most recently assigned to it, when control returns to the calling expression via RETURN, becomes the value returned. If control returns via FRETURN, then the call fails and no value is returned.

The defining procedure for the function is written just as if it were an ordinary program segment, except that the designated parameters replace in its logic the variables that would be needed, and the function's name replaces the variable that would contain the result. To illustrate these ideas, consider the following problem.

Write a SNOBOL function definition which computes the factorial of any given integer *n*, defined as follows:

$$\text{fact}(n) = n \times (n-1) \times \cdots \times 3 \times 2 \qquad \text{if } n > 1$$
$$= 1 \qquad \text{if } n \leqslant 1$$

The function's DEFINE statement and defining procedure are given below.

```
     DEFINE ('FACT(N)I,F')
     •
     •
     •
FACT F = 1 ;I = 2
FLOOP F = LE(I,N) F *I      :F(FDONE)
     I = I + 1              :(FLOOP)
FDONE FACT = F              :(RETURN)
```

Here, the parameter is N and the local variables are I and F. The result is returned through the name FACT, and is assigned in the last statement. The statement labeled FLOOP contains the heart of the definition. That statement will continue to be executed until LE(I,N) fails, in which case control will transfer to the last statement FDONE.

To invoke such a function, the program includes a function call whose arguments are identical in number with the parameters in the function's DEFINE statement. A left-to-right, one-to-one correspondence is thus established between arguments and parameters. At the time the function call is executed, the arguments are first evaluated and their values are then assigned to the corresponding parameters. Then the function-defining procedure is executed. SNOBOL also has a "call by name" mechanism which is invoked by preceding an argument by the unary "name" operator (.) in the call. In this case, the name of the argument replaces its corresponding parameter in the procedure, rather than the value.

To illustrate, let us call the function FACT to perform the calculation of the binomial coefficients, defined as follows:

$$a_i = \frac{n!}{i!\,(n-i)!} \qquad \text{for } i = 0,1,2, \ldots, n$$

where $n!$ denotes the factorial of n.

Assume that the value of n is given as input. The following program will give the desired results:

```
     DEFINE('FACT(N)I,F')
     N = TRIM(INPUT); I = 0
LOOP OUTPUT = I 'ƀƀƀ' FACT(N) / (FACT(I) * FACT(N - I))
     I = LT(I,N) I + 1          :S(LOOP)F(END)
FACT F = 1; I = 2
FLOOP F = LE(I,N) F *I          :F(FDONE)
     I = I + 1                  :(FLOOP)
FDONE FACT = F                  :(RETURN)
END
```

Note here that the *variables* N and I in the calling program are distinct from the *parameter* N and the *local variable* I in the defining procedure for FACT. A trace of the program's execution will deliver the following result for N = 5:

```
0   1
1   5
2  10
3  10
4   5
5   1
```

When a function must change the value of one or more of its arguments, then the argument(s) should be called by name, rather than by value. For example, let us write a function which increments a variable V.

```
      DEFINE('INCR(V)')
INCR  V = V + 1        :(RETURN)
```

Now if we call this function with the expression, INCR(.I), where I is a variable with an integer value, then the name I and not its value will replace all occurrences of the corresponding parameter V in the definition. In effect, then, the statement I = I + 1 will be executed.

7-2.8 Additional Features

Among the additional featues in SNOBOL, the following are discussed in this section:

- Language extendability
- Debugging facilities

Language Extendability SNOBOL programmers may define their own data types, so that data structures more complex than the built-in ARRAY and TABLE may be defined and manipulated.

To define a new data type, the programmer gives a DATA function call, in the following form:

```
DATA('name(item-list)')
```

Here, "name" denotes the name of the new data type, while "item-list" denotes a list of names by which the new data type's individual components will be referenced.

For example, suppose we wanted to define the new data type COMPLEX for representing the real (RE) and imaginary (IM) parts of a complex number. We can do this as follows:

```
DATA('COMPLEX(RE,IM)')
```

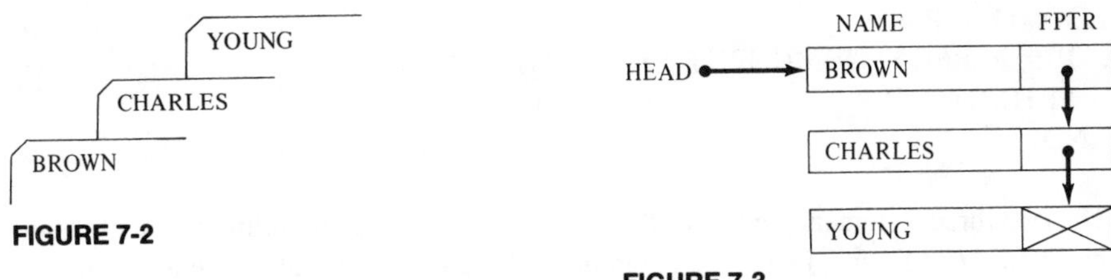

FIGURE 7-2

FIGURE 7-3

Now if we want the variables Q, R, and S to have the following COMPLEX values,

Q 1.5 + 0.3i
R −7 − 2i
S 7 + 2i

we can assign them as follows:

```
Q = COMPLEX(1.5, 0.3)
R = COMPLEX(−7, −2)
S = COMPLEX(7,2)
```

To reference an element of a variable which has a programmer-defined data type, one writes the name of that element (as defined in the DATA statement) followed by the name of that variable in parentheses. For example, the value of the real part of R is referenced by RE(R), the value of the imaginary part of Q is referenced by IM(Q).

Combining programmer-defined data types and programmer-defined functions permits the definition of a set of operations for the newly created data type. In the case of COMPLEX, for example, we are led to define the COMPLEX arithmetic functions.

The programmer-defined data type also serves as SNOBOL's vehicle for programming list processing applications. Consider the problem of creating a list of names from a deck of input cards, such as shown in Figure 7-2. Specifically, assume that the program does not know how many names are there, but wants to create an internal linked list of the form shown in Figure 7-3.

Each node of the list has the same structure, and can be defined as the data type PERSON as follows:

```
DATA ('PERSON(NAME,FPTR)')
```

Here, "FPTR" serves as a pointer which links one node (PERSON) in the list to the next. The program which creates this kind of list can be written as follows:

```
HEAD = ''
P = PERSON(TRIM(INPUT),'')      :F(END)
HEAD = P
```

```
LOOP Q = P
  P = PERSON(TRIM(INPUT,''))        :F(END)
  FPTR(Q) = P                       :(LOOP)
END
```

The first three statements initialize the list, allowing for the possibility that there may be no input (HEAD = ''). For the given data, these leave the one-element list shown in Figure 7-4. The next three statements are executed repeatedly until no more data remains. Their first execution leaves the list shown in Figure 7-5. Note that the third statement in that loop (FPTR(Q) = P) links the *P*th node with its predecessor, which is identified by Q.

SNOBOL language extendability is also provided by its facility to define new unary and binary operators. The main vehicle for this is the function OPSYN, which is invoked in the following way:

```
OPSYN (new,old,n)
```

Here, ''new'' denotes the new operator or function name being defined. ''Old'' denotes the old operator or function for which ''new'' is being defined as a synonym, and ''n'' is an integer which identifies the kind of definition as follows:

n	Meaning
0	"New" and "old" are interpreted as function names, and the new function name becomes a synonym for the old.
1	"New" and "old" are interpreted as unary operators, and the new unary operator becomes a synonym for the old.
2	"New" and "old" are interpreted as (infix) binary operators, and the new binary operator becomes a synonym for the old.

The new unary and binary operators may be selected from the following table. The symbols shown here are designated as unary and binary operators but have not been preassigned any meaning by SNOBOL.

Unassigned unary operators	Unassigned binary operators	Preassigned priorities
!	/ ?	12
%	%	9
/	#	6
#	@	4
|	&	1

Any of these unassigned unary and binary operators can be the ''new'' operator of an OPSYN definition. Note that the unassigned binary operators do have preassigned

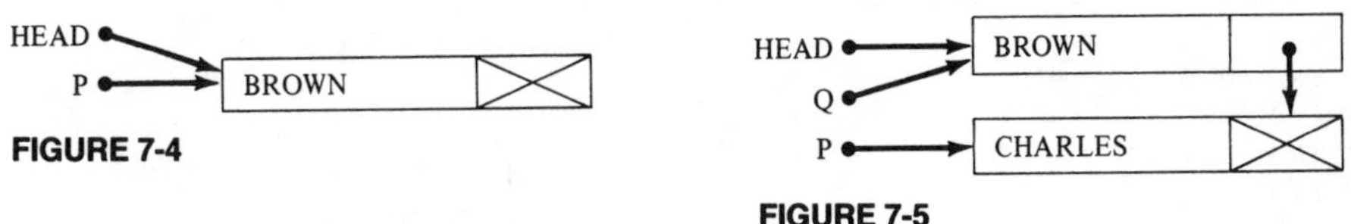

FIGURE 7-4

FIGURE 7-5

priorities. Furthermore, when the "old" part of an OPSYN definition is not a SNOBOL operator, it is assumed to be a function name. This implies, for example, that we can define functions for COMPLEX arithmetic operations (add, subtract, multiply, and divide) and then equate them to infix binary operators so that complex arithmetic expressions can be written in a natural way.

Debugging Facilities SNOBOL program execution can be traced for occurrences of certain types of actions, including the following:

Action	Meaning
VALUE	Display the value of a certain variable each time it changes during program execution.
FUNCTION	Display a message each time a certain function is called or returns control to the calling statement.
LABEL	Display the label of a statement each time that statement is executed.

To activate tracing, the system variable &TRACE must be assigned a positive integer value, indicating the maximum number of lines of tracing information desired. To invoke a particular tracing action, the following statement is written:

```
TRACE ('name', 'action')
```

Here, "name" denotes the name of the particular variable, function, or statement label to be traced, while "action" denotes the type of action (VALUE, FUNCTION, or LABEL) to be traced. For example, consider the following simple program's execution:

```
      &TRACE = 100
      TRACE ('I','VALUE')
      TRACE ('L', 'LABEL')
      X = 53
      I = 1
L     X = X ** .5
      I = LT(I,3) I + 1          :S(L)
END
```

Here, the succession of values for the variable I and the executions of statement labeled L are traced. The printed output is shown in Figure 7-6. Note that the third execution of

```
I = 1
TRANSFER TO L
I = 2
TRANSFER TO L
I = 3
TRANSFER TO L
```

FIGURE 7-6

the last statement fails, so that the value 3 is not assigned to I and control does not transfer again to the statement labeled L.

7-3 APPLICATIONS OF SNOBOL

Now that the reader has a working knowledge of SNOBOL, we present and discuss a SNOBOL solution to Case Study 3—Text Formatter. This will bring to light several practical aspects of using SNOBOL in text processing applications. Following that, we discuss certain implementation-dependent aspects of SNOBOL. Finally, the chapter ends with an overall evaluation of SNOBOL.

7-3.1 SNOBOL Case Study Implementation

The SNOBOL case study program was run using the following systems:

IBM 370/145/OS SNOBOL4
IBM 370/145/OS SPITBOL
IBM PC SNOBOL4

The program was written as a main program (CASE3) and four functions (CTLS, READTXT, MOVETXT, and JUSTIFY). These are shown in Figures 7-7 to 7-11.

Shared in common among these functions are the format controls (WIDTH, LINES, TABS, BREAK, HEADING, and SPACING), the text input buffer (TEXTIN), and the text output buffer (TEXTOUT).

The function CTLS reads and sets all format controls, either as directed explicitly by the user or by default. It also edits these user-specified controls for validity and returns with failure if one is found to be invalid. The auxiliary function INRANGE is used to check that format control values are within their proper range.

Once the format controls are thus defined, the value of WIDTH * LINES becomes the limiting size for TEXTIN. Furthermore, the main program now can define the array TEXTOUT to have LINES entries (one for each line on a page). The value of WIDTH becomes the limiting size for an individual entry in TEXTOUT.

The function READTXT fills TEXTIN from input file TEXT. Upon exit from READTXT, P1 and P2 mark the beginning and end of the currently available text in

```
* SNOBOL IMPLEMENTATION OF CASE STUDY 3 -- TEXT FORMATTER
* THE FOLLOWING FUNCTIONS ARE USED BY THE MAIN PROGRAM:

*      CTLS - READS AND SETS THE FORMAT CONTROLS
*      READTXT - READS TEXT TO FILL INPUT BUFFER 'TEXTIN'
*      MOVETXT - MOVES TEXT FROM 'TEXTIN' TO OUTPUT BUFFER 'TEXTOUT'
*      JUSTIFY - PERFORMS RIGHT MARGIN JUSTIFICATION OF 'TEXTOUT'

CASE3 DEFINE('CTLS()'); DEFINE('READTXT()'); DEFINE('MOVETXT()')
      DEFINE('JUSTIFY()')

* INITIALIZE GLOBAL VARIABLES AND FORMAT CONTROLS

      ERROR = ''
      EOFSW = ''
      P1 = 1
      P2 = 0
      CTLS()                                                   :S(START)
      OUTPUT = NE(ERROR,'') '***FORMAT CONTROL ERROR***'      :S(END)

START TEXTOUT = ARRAY(LINES)
      INPUT('TEXT',4,70)

LOOP  READTXT()                               :F(END)
      MOVETXT()                               :F(END)
      JUSTIFY()                               :F(END)

      I = 1
LOOP1   OUTPUT = TEXTOUT<I>
        I = LT(I,LINES) I + 1                      :S(LOOP1)
      :(LOOP)
```

FIGURE 7-7

TEXTIN. READTXT returns failure when both the end of the TEXT file has been reached and no more text remains in TEXTIN, as indicated by P1 becoming greater than P2.

The function MOVETXT moves text from TEXTIN to TEXTOUT, as dictated by the format controls. During this process MOVETXT must prevent a single word from being split between two lines, properly handle headings and the beginning of new paragraphs, and prevent a sentence or paragraph from being split between two pages (as dictated by the BREAK format control).

The main loop here, labeled MLOOP, is repeated once for each line moved to TEXTOUT from TEXTIN. Its logic is fairly well documented in the program listing. Once that loop completes, there is a final check to ensure that an inpermissible sentence or paragraph break has not been made at the end of a page. If one has been made, then the beginning of the inpermissibly unended sentence or paragraph is deleted from TEXTOUT and the pointer P1 is backed up within TEXTIN accordingly.

The function JUSTIFY then performs right-margin justification of the page image in TEXTOUT. Its logic is also well documented in the program listing. Finally, the resulting content of TEXTOUT is printed as a complete page by the main program CASE3.

In addition, we note the following two characteristics of the input function READTXT. First, it deletes superfluous blanks from the input as it reads. Second, it

```
*
* READ, VERIFY, AND SET FORMAT CONTROLS
*

CTLS   DEFINE('INRANGE(X,I,J)')
       DUPECHECK = TABLE(6)

* SET DEFAULT VALUES FOR FORMAT CONTROLS

       WIDTH = 80 ; LINES = 60
       TABS = 5 ; HEADING = 'C'
       SPACING = 1 ; BREAK = 0

* THE FOLLOWING PATTERN IS USED FOR IDENTIFICATION OF PROPER INPUT
* CONTROL SPECIFICATION:

       CTLSPEC = (SPAN(' ') | '')
+                (('WIDTH' | 'LINES' | 'TABS' | 'SPACING' | 'BREAK') . D
+                 '=' SPAN('0123456789') . V
+                 | 'HEADING' . D '=' ANY('LCR') . V)

* EXTRACT AND DELETE ONE SPECIFICATION AT A TIME FROM THE INPUT
CLOOP CTLREC = INPUT                               :F(RANGECHECK)
CLOOP1    CTLREC BREAK(' ')                            :F(CLOOP)
          CTLREC CTLSPEC = ''                          :F(FRETURN)
          DUPECHECK<D> = IDENT(DUPECHECK<D>,'') D :F(FRETURN)
          $D = V                                       :(CLOOP1)

* CHECK RANGE OF ALL FINAL VALUES OF FORMAT CONTROLS

RANGECHECK INRANGE(WIDTH,40,120)                   :F(FRETURN)
       INRANGE(LINES,20,60)                        :F(FRETURN)
       INRANGE(TABS,1,20)                          :F(FRETURN)
       INRANGE(SPACING,1,3)                        :F(FRETURN)
       INRANGE(BREAK,0,2)                          :F(FRETURN)S(RETURN)

*DEFINITION OF 'INRANGE' FUNCTION

INRANGE LE(X,J)                                    :F(FRETURN)
       GE(X,I)                                     :F(FRETURN)S(RETURN)
```

FIGURE 7-8

shifts the remainder of TEXTIN (that was not previously moved by MOVETXT to TEXTOUT) forward to the beginning of TEXTIN and adjusts P1 and P2 accordingly.

This program was run on the systems noted above, using as input a ninety-six-record file (containing the sample text shown in the description of Case Study 6), and the default format controls. The resulting efficiency is shown in Figure 7-12.

7-3.2 Implementation-Dependent Extension of SNOBOL

The different SNOBOL implementations are remarkably similar in their features. There is an important design difference, however, between SPITBOL and other SNOBOL systems. SPITBOL is a compiler which translates SNOBOL programs to directly executable IBM machine code. However, the SNOBOL4 system translates SNOBOL programs into an intermediate language, which is subsequently executed interpretively.

```
*
* READ FROM TEXT FILE TO 'TEXTIN' UNTIL FULL; RETURN FAILURE WHEN
* BOTH END OF FILE IS REACHED AND TEXTIN IS EMPTY.  INDICES P1 AND
* P2 POINT TO THE BEGINNING AND END OF THE ACTIVE TEXT IN 'TEXTIN'.
*
READTXT LE(P1,1)                                   :S(RLOOP)

* SHIFT TEXT BACKWARD WITHIN 'TEXTIN' AND ADJUST P1 AND P2
        TEXTIN POS(0) LEN(P1 - 1) = ''
        P2 = P2 - P1 + 1
        P1 = 1

* READ INTO REMAINDER OF 'TEXTIN', DELETING SUPERFLUOUS BLANKS
RLOOP GE(P2,WIDTH * LINES - 70)                    :S(RETURN)
        IDENT(EOFSW,'END')                         :S(ENDFILE)
        INDATA = TEXT                              :F(ENDFILE)
        IDENT(INDATA,DUPL(' ',70))                 :S(RLOOP)
        I = 1
        NSB = 0
RLOOP1  L = GT(I,SIZE(INDATA) - 1) 70 - NSB            :S(R1EXIT)
        INDATA (POS(I - 1) ARB RPOS(0)) . REST
        L = IDENT(REST,DUPL(' ',SIZE(REST))) I         :S(R1EXIT)
RLOOP2     INDATA POS(I - 1) LEN(2) . PAIR
           INDATA POS(I - 1) LEN(1) = IDENT(PAIR,'  ') '' :F(R1NEXT)
                                                          :(RLOOP2)
           NSB = NSB + 1
R1NEXT  I = I + 1                                      :(RLOOP1)

* DROP EXTRA TRAILING AND LEADING BLANKS
R1EXIT INDATA POS(L) ARB RPOS(0) = ''
        INDATA POS(0) ' '                          :F(RHOLD)
        EQ(P2,0)                                   :S(RDROP)
        TEXTIN POS(P2 - 1) ' '                     :F(RHOLD)
RDROP L = L - 1
        INDATA POS(0) LEN(1) = ''
RHOLD TEXTIN = TEXTIN INDATA
        P2 = P2 + L                                :(RLOOP)
ENDFILE EOFSW = 'END'
        LE(P1,P2)                                  :S(RETURN)F(FRETURN)
```

FIGURE 7-9

Since interpretation is inherently less efficient than direct execution of machine language, significant performance differences between SPITBOL and SNOBOL4 should be expected.

On the other hand, the SNOBOL4 system is available on a number of different computers, while SPITBOL is available only on the IBM mainframes (at this writing). The main variation in SNOBOL4, when transferring a program from one computer to another, is that different alphabets are supported by different computers.

The alphabet shown in this chapter is a subset of the full EBCDIC character set. The programmer, may, additionally, define the alphabet used by a program. This permits SNOBOL programs another level of machine independence.

These SNOBOL implementations support a number of input-output features not discussed in this chapter. Most notable among them is the ability to control input or output formats by way of FORTRAN-like format specifications. This allows some useful

```
*
* MOVE TEXT FROM 'TEXTIN' TO 'TEXTOUT'
*

MOVETXT I = 1
MOVE1 TEXTOUT<I> = ''
      I = LT(I,LINES) I + 1                     :S(MOVE1)
      PNO = PNO + 1
      NS = 0
      NP = 0
      TEXTIN POS(0) ')H'                        :F(MOVE2)

* PROCESS HEADING TEXT
      TEXTIN POS(P1) ARB . HEAD ')H'                 :F(FRETURN)
      P1 = LE(SIZE(HEAD,40)) P1 + SIZE(HEAD) + 4 :F(FRETURN)
MOVE2 I = IDENT(HEAD,'') 1                      :S(MOVE3)
         TEXTOUT<1> = IDENT(HEADING,'L') HEAD
         TEXTOUT<1> = IDENT(HEADING,'C')
+                     DUPL(' ',(WIDTH - SIZE(HEAD)) / 2) HEAD
         TEXTOUT<1> = IDENT(HEADING,'R')
+                     DUPL(' ',WIDTH - SIZE(HEAD)) HEAD
         I = 2

* NOW PERFORM THE PRINCIPAL MOVE
MOVE3 TEXTOUT<I> = DUPL(' ',WIDTH - 8) 'PAGE ' PNO '.'
      LINE1 = I + 2
      L = LINE1
      KK = EQ(SPACING,2) 2                      :S(MLOOP)
      KK = 1
MLOOP LT(P2,P1)                                 :S(CLEANUP)
         GT(L,LINES)                            :S(CLEANUP)

*     SET P1 AT FIRST NONBLANK FOR BEGINNING OF LINE
MLOOP1   TEXTIN POS(P1 - 1) ' '                      :F(MLOOP2)
         P1 = LT(P1,P2) P1 + 1                       :S(MLOOP1)F(CLEANUP)
MLOOP2   TEXTIN POS(P1 - 1) LEN(P2 - P1 + 1) . HOLD
         HOLD LEN(WIDTH) . HOLD

*     CHECK FOR BEGINNING OF HEADING
         HOLD ')H'                                   :F(NOHEAD)
         HOLD ARB . TEXTOUT<L> ')H'
         P1 = P1 + SIZE(TEXTOUT<L>)                  :(RETURN)

*     CHECK FOR BEGINNING OF PARAGRAPH
NOHEAD   HOLD ARB . TEXTOUT<L> ')P ' ARB . HOLD RPOS(0) :F(MOVELINE)
         HOLD = HOLD '   '
         EQ(SIZE(TEXTOUT<L>),0)                      :S(NEWPAR)
*     END PREVIOUS PARAGRAPH
         NP = NP + 1
         LP = L
         P1 = P1 + SIZE(TEXTOUT<L>)
         LP1 = P1 - 1
         L = EQ(SPACING,3) L + 1                     :(CHECKLINE)
NEWPAR   K = SIZE(HOLD)
         K = GT(WIDTH - TABS + 1) WIDTH - TABS + 1
         HOLD POS(K) ARB RPOS(0) = ''
         TEXTOUT<L> = DUPL(' ',TABS - 1) HOLD
         P1 = P1 + K + 3                             :(CHECKLINE)

* MOVE AN ORDINARY LINE
MOVELINE TEXTOUT<L> = HOLD
      P1 = P1 + SIZE(HOLD)
```

FIGURE 7-10

```
* CHECK FOR WORD BREAK AT END OF LINE
CHECKLINE TEXTIN POS(P1 - 1) ' '               :S(NOBREAK)
      TEXTOUT<L> POS(WIDTH - 1) ' '            :S(NOBREAK)
      I = 0
CHLOOP   TEXTOUT<L> ' ' RPOS(I)                     :S(CHOUT)
         I = I + 1                                  :(CHLOOP)
CHOUT TEXTOUT<L> LEN(I) RPOS(0) = ''
      P1 = P1 - I
NOBREAK TEXTOUT<L> RPOS(0) = DUPL(' ',WIDTH - SIZE(TEXTOUT<L>))

* CHECK FOR END OF SENTENCE ON THIS LINE
      ENDSENT = '. ' | '! ' | '? '
      I = 0
      NS = 0
NBLOOP   TEXTOUT<L> POS(I) (ARB ENDSENT) . WORDS :F(ENDMLOOP)
         NS = NS + 1
         LPS = L
         LPOS = I + 1
         I = I + SIZE(WORDS)                        :(NBLOOP)

ENDMLOOP L = L + KK                            :(MLOOP)

* NOW CHECK POSSIBLE ILLEGAL BREAK AT END OF PAGE
CLEANUP EQ(BREAK,0)                            :S(RETURN)
      EQ(NS,0)                                 :S(RETURN)
      NE(BREAK,2)                              :S(CHOPSENT)
      EQ(NP,0)                                 :S(RETURN)

* CHOP BEGINNING OF UNENDED PARAGRAPH
CHOPPAR EQ(EOFSW,1)                            :S(CHOPSENT)
      TEXTIN POS(0) ')P'                       :S(CHOPSENT)
      P1 = LP1
      I = LP + KK
CPLOOP TEXTOUT<I> = LE(I,LINES) ''             :F(RETURN)
      I = I + KK                               :(CPLOOP)

* CHOP BEGINNING OF UNENDED SENTENCE
CHOPSENT TEXTIN POS(P1 - 2) ENDSENT            :S(RETURN)
      TEXTOUT<LPS> POS(LPOS + 1) ARB RPOS(0) = ''
      I = LPS + KK
CSLOOP TEXTOUT<I> = LE(I,LINES) ''             :F(BACKUP)
      I = I + KK                               :(CSLOOP)
*REVERT P1 TO BEGINNING OF SENTENCE IN TEXTIN
BACKUP TEXTIN POS(P1 - 2) ENDSENT              :S(RETURN)
      P1 = GT(P1,2) P1 - 1                     :S(BACKUP)F(FRETURN)
```

FIGURE 7-10 *(Continued)*

```
*
* RIGHT JUSTIFY 'TEXTOUT' LINES TO MARGIN, EXCEPT FOR THOSE WHICH
* END A PARAGRAPH OR A PAGE.
*
JUSTIFY DEFINE('LASTLINE(L)'); DEFINE('ENDPAR(L)')
      L = 3
JLOOP LASTLINE(L - 1)                            :S(RETURN)
      IDENT(TEXTOUT<L>,DUPL(' ',WIDTH))          :S(ENDLOOP)
      LASTLINE(L)                                :S(ENDLOOP)
      ENDPAR(L)                                  :S(ENDLOOP)

* COUNT NW AND NS AS NUMBER OF WORDS AND SPACES AT END OF LINE
      I = 0
NSLOOP   TEXTOUT<L> ' ' RPOS(I)                       :F(NSOUT)
         I = I + 1                                    :(NSLOOP)
NSOUT NS = I
      I = 1
      NW = 0
NWLOOP   TEXTOUT<L> POS(I - 1) NOTANY(' ') ' '        :F(NCOUNT)
         NW = NW + 1
NCOUNT   I = LT(I,SIZE(TEXTOUT<L>) - 1) I + 1         :S(NWLOOP)

* NOW FILL THE LINE
NFILL LE(NW,1)                                   :S(ENDLOOP)
NFLOOP I = WIDTH - NS
NFLOOP1  GT(NS,0)                                     :F(ENDLOOP)
         TEXTOUT<L> NOTANY(' ') . X ' ' NOTANY(' ') . Y POS(I)
+                   = X '  ' Y                        :S(NFA)F(NFB)
NFA      NS = NS - 1
NFB      I = GT(I,2) I - 1                            :S(NFLOOP1)F(NFLOOP)

ENDLOOP  L = LE(L,LINES) L + 1                   :S(JLOOP)F(RETURN)

* CHECK FOR LAST NONBLANK LINE IN TEXTOUT
LASTLINE II = L + 1
LLLOOP GT(II,LINES)                              :S(RETURN)
         II = IDENT(TEXTOUT<II>,'') II + 1       :S(LLLOOP)F(FRETURN)

* CHECK FOR LAST LINE IN PARAGRAPH
ENDPAR NNB = L + 1
EPLOOP   GT(NNB,LINES)                                :S(FRETURN)
         NNB = IDENT(NNB,'') NNB + 1                  :S(EPLOOP)
      TEXTOUT<NNB> POS(0) ' '                    :S(RETURN)F(FRETURN)
END
```

FIGURE 7-11

FIGURE 7-12
EFFICIENCY OF SNOBOL CASE STUDY 3 PROGRAM

Implementation	Compile speed	Execution speed
1 IBM 370/145 SNOBOL 4	5.95 sec	1159.54 sec
2 IBM 370/145 SPITBOL	1.75 sec	112.53 sec
3 IBM PC/DOS SNOBOL	31.7 sec	10717.9 sec

functions, such as skipping to the top of a page or outputting a table of numerical values, to be conveniently specified. This also encourages the standardization of SNOBOL implementations with respect to their input-output facilities, since FORTRAN is itself standardized and widely implemented.

7-3.3 Overall Evaluation of SNOBOL

We evaluate SNOBOL in the text processing application area on the basis of the experience shown in sections 7-3.1 and 7-3.2, as follows:

1 Expressivity	Fair
2 Well-definedness	Excellent
3 Data types and structures	Good
4 Modularity	Fair
5 Input-output facilities	Fair
6 Portability	Good
7 Efficiency	Good
8 Pedagogy	Fair
9 Generality	Poor

SNOBOL's lack of structured programming constructs is probably its greatest weakness, and strongly influences the fair rating of "expressivity" given here. Its extensive and powerful pattern-matching functions compensate somewhat for this weakness. Another negative factor in expressivity is the duplicity of uses for labels (as targets for go to's and as function names) and the careful ordering that must be maintained in order that control doesn't inadvertently slip into a function definition before it is actually invoked.

SNOBOL is judged to be fair also in "modularity" and "input-output" facilities. It lacks any strong file processing support of its own, relying too much on FORTRAN's, which are relatively weak themselves! Thus, any large database applications which have text processing requirements are not likely to be done in SNOBOL.

SNOBOL's fair "pedagogy" stems from the absence of very many introductory level textbooks on the language or its applications. The book by Griswold et al.[4] is excellent, but is aimed at an advanced audience. Moreover, the absence of a SNOBOL implementation on microprocessors will be an additional pedagogical handicap if it is not corrected in the near future.

Finally, since its design is narrowly aimed at text processing, SNOBOL is not surprisingly poor in "generality." It is not conceivable that SNOBOL would be used for a scientific or data processing application in preference to the other languages that are available.

REFERENCES

1 D. J. Farber et al., "SNOBOL, A String Manipulation Language," *Journal of the ACM* 11: 21 (1964).

2 R.E. Griswold and M.T. Griswold, *The ICON Programming Language*, Prentice-Hall, Englewood Cliffs, N.J., 1983.
3 R. E. Griswold, et al., *The SNOBOL4 Programming Language*, 2d ed., Prentice Hall, Englewood Cliffs, N.J., 1971.
4 Ibid.
5 SITBOL Version 2.0, Stevens Institute of Technology, 1973.
6 Robert Dewar, SPITBOL version 2.0, Illinois Institute of Technology, 1971.

EXERCISES

1 Let S and T be variables with the following values:

S |ƀTHESEƀAREƀTHEƀTIMES'ƀƀƀƀ|
T |Xƀ + ƀA/(X + B)ƀ - ƀ1.5|

For each of the following pattern-matching specifications, determine whether or not the match succeeds. If so, identify the string (within S or T) which satisfies the pattern.

(a) S 'THE'
(b) S 'ƀTHEƀ'
(c) S 'ƀTIMESƀ'
(d) S 'THE' | ''
(e) S '' | 'THE'
(f) S NOTANY ('ƀ') ARB BREAK('.')
(g) T '(' ARB ')'
(h) T SPAN('ƀ') ARB 'ƀ'
(i) S SPAN ('ƀ') ARB 'ƀ')
(j) S SPAN('ƀ') ARB BREAK('ƀ')

2 Write a SNOBOL function named DATEF which will transform a date given in any one of the following three forms into the other two:
(a) yyddd
(b) MM/DD/YY
(c) Month DD, year
This function should also verify that the given date is valid and return failure if it is not.

3 Write a SNOBOL program that counts the number of words in a text that end with "ing" or "ed" and displays that count. Your program should also accommodate punctuation marks in a reasonable way. For example, if the text is as follows:

As the bells were ringing, we sped out of town.

your count should be 2.

4 The following SNOBOL function named STRIP will strip all leading zeros from a numeric string N of any length:

```
STRIP STRIP = N
LOOP STRIP POS(Ø)LEN(1).DIGIT (ARB RPOS(Ø)).REST
+                                    :F(RETURN)
   STRIP = EQ (DIGIT,Ø) REST :S(LOOP)F(RETURN)
```

(a) Write a DEFINE statement for STRIP, given that its only parameter is N, and all other variables are local.

(b) Write a main program which reads a series of input strings and, using STRIP, displays all integers contained therein with their leading zeros suppressed.

5 Write a SNOBOL function named SUBSTR which emulates the behavior of the PL/I function with the same name. That is, for a given string parameter S and integer parameters I and J, the function should return that substring in S beginning at position I and having length J. If I and J do not define a proper substring of S, then the result returned should be the empty string.

6 Trace execution of the following SNOBOL program, given the input data at the right:

```
LOOP      S = S TRIM(INPUT)     :F(DONE)               input
          S '-' RPOS(Ø) = ''    :S(LOOP)F(NOHYPH)      HERE IS THE
NOHYPH    S = S ' '             :(LOOP)                KEY TO STRING PRO-
DONE      OUTPUT = S                                   CESSING.
END
```

7 Augment our SNOBOL implementation of Case Study 3 so that it accommodates the following:

> There is no restriction on the length of a heading. If a heading actually exceeds the width of a line, then it should be split up and printed on two or more lines. The first line of actual text printed on the page should be adjusted accordingly.

Test and debug your revision. Was this an easy change to make? To debug?

8 Investigate SNOBOL's potential as a scientific and data processing language by

(a) Implementing Case Study 1.

(b) Implementing Case Study 2.

9 If Case Study 0 (which you defined at the end of Chapter 1) is a text processing application, implement it in SNOBOL. Gather and record performance statistics for this program. Re-evaluate SNOBOL on the basis of your experience.

CHAPTER **8**

APL

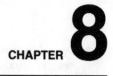

8-1 INTRODUCTION TO APL

APL (A Programming Language) is designed principally for problems which have heavy use of data in tables, vectors, and matrices, and for which quick, interactive solutions are desired. The alphabet of APL contains a large number of special symbols, outside the normal ASCII or EBCDIC character set, added for quick specification of powerful functions on arrays of numbers and character strings. APL programs are thus unusually compact and unique in style, as we shall see in this chapter.

8-1.1 Brief History of APL

APL was first formally defined and introduced by Kenneth Iverson, in his book *A Programming Language* in 1962.[1] The language is markedly the product of one person's genius and mathematical orientation.

A development effort for APL took place at IBM during the next several years. As a first stage, the APL character set (see section 8-2.2) and a linearization of the language was defined. An experimental time-sharing version of APL was implemented on the System/360 in 1966,[2] and was named "APL\360." This version has spread widely in use, and has undergone several refinements.[3]

Standardization of APL has not occurred, principally because of its unique character set's requirements for special hardware beyond that which supports the ASCII standard. As a result, APL is not widely implemented on a variety of machines.

8-1.2 Implementations and Variations of APL

Although APL development was initially supported by IBM, several recent implementations have been developed by other sources and for other machines. For example APL\5100 was designed for the IBM 5100 portable computer,[4] APL/700 was developed by Burroughs, and APL*PLUS was developed by Scientific Time Sharing Corporation.[5] The latter is now implemented on the IBM PC microcomputer as well.[6]

Throughout the two or more decades of its life, however, APL has not greatly varied as a programming language. Some notable features have been added, such as the notion of a "workspace," the time-sharing implementations, and the "shared variable" concept. However, the language is relatively free of divergent dialects, unlike many other languages. This is due mainly to APL's unique character set, and the concurrent hardware demands that it places upon implementers in the form of special keyboards, monitors, and printers.

Yet, APL has strong support among its advocates, who widely range from data processing to scientific application areas. A large APL special interest group within ACM publishes a monthly newsletter, and numerous APL conferences have been held as well. The language is very much alive, and makes a significant contribution to the field of programming languages and applications.

8-1.3 Major Application of APL

APL's main use is in the solution of scientific and mathematical problems that involve substantial use of vectors and matrices. However, it also has been used in business problems, text processing, and formal description of computer architecture. In fact, the latter purpose motivated much of IBM's early interest in the language as they sought concise means of exact functional description for the System/360 computer design.[7]

8-2 WRITING APL PROGRAMS

An APL program runs interpretively and interactively. In its simplest form, a program is a sequence of statements which begins and ends with the character **del** (∇). Usually there is one statement per line, and the lines are serially numbered on the left. The program name appears beside the **del** on the first line.

Below is a simple APL program which computes and displays the average of an indeterminate number of input numbers. For instance, if the input is 85.5, 87.5, 89.5, and 91.5, the result displayed is 88.5. The program uses the variable X to hold the input numbers and the variable N to determine the number of input numbers in the process. The variable AV connotes the resulting average.

```
    ∇ AVERAGER
[1]  ⍝ THIS PROGRAM FINDS THE AVERAGE OF ALL INPUT
[2]   'ENTER THE NUMBERS TO BE AVERAGED'
[3]   X←⎕
[4]   N←⍴X
[5]   AV←(+/X)÷N
[6]   'THE AVERAGE IS ',(⍕AV),'.'
    ∇
```

The following is the exact output of a run for this program:

```
AVERAGER
ENTER THE NUMBERS TO BE AVERAGED
⎕:
   85.5 87.5 89.5 91.5
THE AVERAGE IS 88.5.
```

Indented lines in this run indicate input by the terminal user, while the others indicate output from the program.

The first line of the program itself names it AVERAGER, while the second (numbered [1]) is an instance of an APL comment. Any line that begins with the special character ⍝ is taken as a comment. The line numbered [2] is a prompt to the screen, which asks for the input, and the next line stores it in the array variable X. The **quad** character (⎕) is a call for the input, while the left arrow (←) designates an assignment to the variable X on the left. In general, all APL variables are potentially arrays, and their size as well as their values may change as execution proceeds.

The next line assigns to N the number of values, or so-called "shape" of X, using the prefix operator **rho** (ρ). Line number [5] computes the average AV of the numbers X, using the operators +, /, and ÷. The expression +/X denotes the sum of all entries in array X, while the operator ÷ causes division of that sum by N. The line numbered [6] displays the result, together with the message 'THE AVERAGE IS'. Here, the symbol ⍕ causes conversion of the average to a formatted character string.

8-2.1 Elementary Data Types and Values

There are two elementary data types in APL, numbers and character strings. A number may be written either in ordinary decimal notation or in E-notation, as shown in the two lines below.

```
1.73       0          ¯17    250
1.73E2     1.73E¯4
```

E-notation values denote decimal numbers that are scaled by a positive or negative factor of 10. For instance, 1.73E2 denotes the number 1.73×10^2, or 173.

A character string is any series of APL characters enclosed in apostrophes, such as the following:

```
'ABC'
'A B C'
''
'WHAT''S THIS?'
'∇ρ∆⊛⎕'
```

Each such string has an associated "shape," which is its constituent number of characters, excluding the enclosing apostrophes. The shapes of the above strings are 3, 5,

0, 12, and 5, respectively. In the fourth example, an *embedded* apostrophe is represented by duplicating it. The fifth example contains some of the more unusual APL characters. A full list of the APL character set is given in Figure 8-1.

FIGURE 8-1
THE APL CHARACTER SET

A B C D E F G H I J K L M N O P Q R S T U V W X Y Z
0 1 2 3 4 5 6 7 8 9
¨ ¯ < ≤ = ≥ > ≠ ∨ ∧ + − × ÷
? ⍵ ∊ ⍴ ∼ ↑ ↓ ⍳ ○ * → ⊢ ⊣
⍺ ⌈ ⌊ _ ∇ ∆ ∘ ' ⎕ ( ) [ ] { }
⊂ ⊃ ∩ ∪ ⊥ ⊤ | ; , : . / \

The more unusual among these characters have names, which sometimes portray their meanings within the APL language.

Symbol	Name	Symbol	Name	Symbol	Name
⎕	**quad**	∇	**del**	∆	**delta**
⍴	**shape**	⌈	**ceiling**	⌊	**floor**
↑	**take**	↓	**drop**	∼	**not**
?	**roll**	/	**compress**	\	**expand**
→	**branch**	←	**specify**	,	**catenate**
⍳	**index**	|	**residue**	⊥	**decode**
⊤	**encode**				

Moreover, a few additional APL symbols are formed as composites of these basic symbols:

Symbol	Composed from
⍞	⎕ and '
⌶	⊤ and ⊥
⍕	⊤ and ∘
⍎	⊥ and ∘
⌹	⎕ and ÷
⌽	○ and |
⊖	○ and −
⍟	○ and *
⍉	○ and \
⍋	∆ and |
⍒	∇ and |
⍱	∨ and ∼
⍲	∧ and ∼
⍝	∩ and ∘

8-2.2 Names, Variables, and Declarations

An APL variable name may be any sequence of uppercase letters (A to Z), digits (0 to 9), and the character **delta** (△), provided that the first character is not a digit. Moreover, the underscored letters or **delta** (△) may also be used in variable names. Thus, the following are valid variable names in APL:

X
SIGMA
△T
Y1
$\underline{X}$

The last variable name $\underline{X}$ is distinct from the first, in the sense that they refer to different storage locations when used in the same program.

The *type* of value stored in a variable may be either numeric or character string, and may change at any time during execution of a program. Thus, the statements

```
X ← 0
X ← 'A'
```

may appear simultaneously in the same program, although this practice is usually not advised.

An APL variable is *not* explicitly declared within a program; its first use in the program implicitly activates it and assigns it a value.

8-2.3 Arrays and Other Data Structures

Variable names and operators in APL are immediately extendable to the representation and manipulation of arrays. An *array* may have any number of dimensions (referred to as its "shape") and any number of elements in each dimension. Figure 8-2 illustrates three arrays: A, B, and C. Here, A is a one-dimensional array (or "vector") with five entries, B is a two-dimensional array (or "matrix") with five rows and four columns, and C is a three-dimensional array with two layers, five rows, and four columns. To *create* each of these arrays and initialize them with the values 0 throughout, we use the *reshape* operator ρ as follows:

```
A ← 5 ρ 0
B ← 5 4 ρ 0
C ← 2 5 4 ρ 0
```

To assign different values to an array, we list the values in the order they are to be stored. Thus.

```
A ← 5 ρ 3 2 4 6 7
```

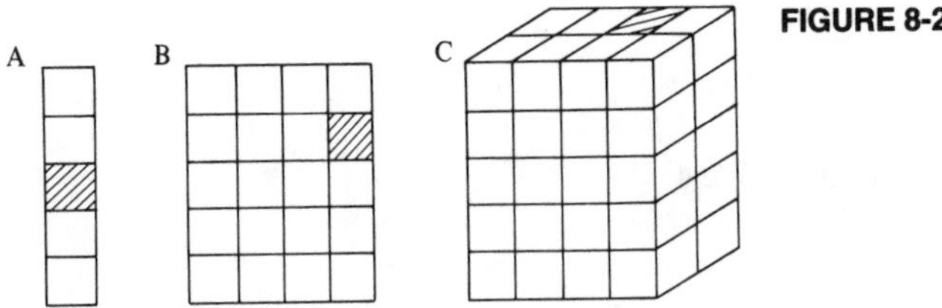

FIGURE 8-2

assigns the values 3, 2, 4, 6, and 7 to the five entries of A. Higher-dimensioned arrays are assigned values in row-major order.

To reference an element or a "subarray" of elements in an array, a subscript is placed after the array name and enclosed in brackets. Thus, for the above array A, A[3] denotes the value 4, and A[1 3 4] denotes the subarray of values, 3, 4, 6. Moreover, multiple-dimensioned arrays have their subscripts separated by semicolons. For instance, the element in row 2, column 4 of array B above is referenced by B[2;4]; the element in layer 2, row 1, and column 3 of array C above is referenced by C[2;1;3].

Moreover, a subarray of *smaller* dimension may be selected from an array by leaving out one or more subscripts. For example, the entire *second* row of B may be referenced by the expression B[2;] and the entire *fourth* column may be referenced by B[;4].

Selection of elements can also be specified by the *compression* operator (/), in conjunction with an accompanying array of 1s and 0s (denoting "select" and "don't select" respectively). Thus,

```
1 0 1 1 0 / A
```

denotes selection of the first, third, and fourth elements of the vector A to form a new three-element vector with the values 3, 4, 6. In general, we shall see that the binary values 1 and 0 are used in APL as the Boolean primitives **true** and **false** are used in other languages.

Companion to the compression operator is the *expansion* operator (\), whose purpose is to form a larger array from the elements of a smaller one. Here, the role of the 1s is to select the locations in the larger array where the elements in the smaller one will be placed, and the 0s denote locations which will be initialized to 0. For example,

```
1 0 0 1 1 0 1 0 1 \ A
```

creates the nine-element array 3 0 0 2 4 0 6 0 7, using the original values of A shown above.

A useful function in APL is the so-called "index generator" function, which generates an array of integers from 1 to a specified limit *n*. It is denoted by the symbol ⍳, and the expression ⍳ *n* generates an array of integers 1 2 3 . . . *n*. For example, the expression ⍳ 5 gives the array 1 2 3 4 5.

The "catentation" operator comma (,) is used to conjoin two or more arrays to form a larger one. For examples, suppose we want to append the integers 1, 2, and 3 to the original array A given above. This may be done in either of the following two ways:

```
A , 1 2 3
A , ⍳ 3
```

The result, in either case, is the array 3 2 4 6 7 1 2 3.

8-2.4 Basic Statements

The strength of APL lies in the power of its operators, not in the variety of its statements. In fact, there are only three basic statement forms in APL:

(i) The assignment statement
(ii) The branching statement
(iii) The expression

In this section, we shall develop the elementary form of the assignment statement and discuss basic arithmetic operators and expressions. The branching statement is discussed in section 8-2.5, while the expression is often used by itself to display output (section 8-2.6) and to invoke a function (section 8-2.7).

The assignment statement (called the "specification" in APL) has the general form shown below:

```
variable ← expression
```

Here, "variable" denotes the name of any scalar, vector, matrix, or more general structure. "Expression" denotes any series of variables, values, and operators which, when evaluated, delivers a result that will be assigned to the variable on the left.

An expression, when evaluated, may deliver a scalar value, a vector, a matrix, or a higher dimensioned array as a result. The "shape" of the variable on the left of the assignment is thus determined by that of the expression on the right. For example, the following two assignment statements

```
X ← 1
X ← ⍳ 4
```

successively assign the scalar value 1 to X, and then the four-element vector 1 2 3 4 to X.

The basic arithmetic operators in APL are used both as monadic operators and dyadic operators in expressions, and may be applied to scalars and arrays alike. These are summarized below:

	Meaning	
Operator	**Monadic**	**Dyadic**
+	identity	addition
−	negation	subtraction
×	signum	multiplication
÷	reciprocal	division
*	exponential	power

When each of these is used as a monadic operator, the operand appears after it. When used as a dyadic operator, it is placed in an infix position between the two operands.

APL expressions are always evaluated from *right to left*, with *no* implicit priority predefined for the operators. Thus, the following expression,

```
X − Y − 1
    ↑   ↑
   (2) (1)
```

is evaluated in the order shown; that is, Y − 1 is calculated first, and then the result is subtracted from X. Parentheses may be used to override this right-to-left order, as shown below:

```
(X − Y) − 1
    ↑    ↑
   (1)  (2)
```

These operators, when applied to arrays, are extended in the usual way. For instance, the expression Y + 1 when the array Y is

1 2 3 4

will leave the result as 2 3 4 5. We can also add two arrays, say X and Y, using the same operator. The expression X + Y can only be formed when X and Y have the *same shape;* that is, they are both four-element vectors, or both 5 × 4 matrices, and so forth. If that is not the case, a LENGTH ERROR will result.

Most of the operators are self-explanatory. The monadic operator × denotes the "signum" of its operand, which is defined as −1, 0, or +1 accordingly as the operand is negative, zero, or positive. The monadic operator ∗ denotes the exponential of its operand; raising the mathematical constant *e* to that power.

These operators can also be combined with reduction (/) to deliver a scalar result from vector or matrix operands. We saw one example of this in the sample program at the beginning of the chapter. For another example, if X and Y are three-element vectors, say 2 3 4 and 1 3 2 respectively, then their inner product, INPROD, which is the sum of the products of corresponding entries in X and Y, can be defined as follows:

```
INPROD ← + / X × Y
```

Recalling that evaluation takes place from right to left, we first have X × Y yielding the vector

2 9 8

and then the subsequent sum-reduction gives the result 2 + 9 + 8 = 19.

Operators can also be used to give Boolean results, which are represented by the integers 1 and 0. The APL relational and logical operators are summarized as follows:

Operator (op)	Meaning of a op b
$<$	a less than b
$\leqslant$	a not greater than b
$=$	a equal b
$\geqslant$	a not less than b
$>$	a greater than b
$\neq$	a not equal b
∧	a and b are both 1 (true)
I	a and b are not both 1
∨	either a or b is 1
⍱	neither a nor b is 1

A final monadic operator ~ is used to *negate* a relation, so that ~a is 1 (true) whenever a is 0 (false), and vice versa.

These operators, too, are evaluated from right to left, and have no built-in precedence among them. Thus, for instance, to test whether the value of H is between 0 and 5, we must use parentheses as shown:

$$(0 < H) \wedge (H < 5)$$

Here, the second pair of parentheses, strictly speaking, is optional. Here too, the result may be a scalar or a vector, depending on the nature of the argument H. For instance, if H is the vector 1 4 7 then the above expression gives as a result the *vector* 1 1 0, since 1 and 4 are between 0 and 5 but 7 is not.

8-2.5 Control Structures

The only way to alter the sequence of execution in an APL program is to use the conditional or unconditional branching statement. No explicit provision for structured programming is made in APL, and none is contemplated.

Any APL statement may be labeled by simply preceding it with a statement label and a colon (:). For instance,

```
L: X ← Y
```

is an assignment statement with the label L. Labels may be formed by the same conventions as variable names. Only those statements to which branching will take place need to be labeled.

If we want to *unconditionally* transfer control to a statement elsewhere in the program, we just give a right arrow (→) followed by that statement's label. For instance,

```
→ L
```

transfers control to statement labeled L, and is equivalent to **goto** L in other languages.

Conditional transfer is affected in APL by using one of the following (slightly more intricate) forms:

```
→ label × ⍳ expression
→ (expression) / label
```

This is to be read, "if expression is 1 (true), then transfer to label." For example,

```
   → L × ⍳ A < B
or → (A < B) / L
```

will transfer to L if A is less than B.

Branching can also be specified using the prefixed *number* of the statement rather than introducing a label. However, this is dangerous because all such branches must be adjusted whenever the statements in a program are renumbered.

To illustrate, suppose we want to write an APL program which computes a federal TAX as 22 percent of GROSS pay if the latter is less than $18,000, and 25 percent of GROSS otherwise:

```
     ∇ TAXCALC
[1]   'ENTER GROSS PAY'
[2]   GROSS ← ⎕
[3]   → LESS × ⍳ GROSS < 18000
[4]   TAX ← .25 × GROSS
[5]   → DISPLAY
[6] LESS: TAX ← .22 × GROSS
[7] DISPLAY: 'THE TAX IS $', ⍕ TAX
[8] ∇
ENTER GROSS PAY
      20000
THE TAX IS $5000
```

Here, line [3] says "if GROSS is less than 18000 then transfer to the line labeled LESS." For the example input data, that is not true, so lines 4, 5, and 7 are executed to obtain the result.

Often, the use of branching statements like this can be avoided by judicious coding. For example, the above could have been rewritten *without* branching by preassigning the value .22 or .25 to the variable MULT:

```
[3] MULT ← ((GROSS < 18000) × .22) + ((GROSS ≥ 18000) × .25)
```

Here, if GROSS is 20000, the expression GROSS < 18000 is 0 and the expression GROSS ≥ 18000 is 1. Thus, the correct multiplier will be assigned to MULT.

Loops Loops in APL, when needed, are also specified by conditional and unconditional branching statements. Because APL's functions are so powerful, however, the need for explicit looping through the individual elements of an array, one by one, is far less than in other languages.

The following loop computes the SUM of all entries in the array X, using explicit branching.

```
   SUM ← 0
   I ← 1
LOOP: → (I > ρ X) / EXIT
   SUM ← SUM + X[I]
   I ← I + 1
   → LOOP
EXIT:
```

However, we wouldn't ordinarily use this form, since the statement below does the same summation much more briefly, and without the usual housekeeping required by a loop.

```
SUM ← + / X
```

This is an example illustrating the uniqueness of APL's programming style, and the danger inherent in applying habits learned with other languages directly in APL.

The following example shows an APL rendition of the common **do . . . while** construct, applied to the approximation of the square root of a number A by Newton's method. Here, the next approximation Y is computed from the previous one X by the formula $Y = .5(X + A/X)$. This is repeated until the difference between X and Y becomes sufficiently small in absolute value, say less than .0001.

```
LOOP: → (|(Y − X) ≤ .0001) / OUT
   X ← Y
   Y ← .5 × (X + A ÷ X)
   → LOOP
OUT:
```

8-2.6 Input-Output Conventions

As we have seen, input to an APL program is nominally obtained by the **quad** operator, and output on the screen is specified by a character string, or a sequence of character strings separated by a comma (,). The example program at the beginning of the chapter, for instance, has the input statement:

```
X ← □
```

and the output statement:

```
'THE AVERAGE IS ', (⍕AV), '.'
```

Here, the formatting operator ⍕ is needed to convert the numeric value of AV to a character string, so that it can be concatenated with the rest of the message.

A slight variation of the **quad** operator is the **quote quad** operator. It is used when accepting character input, rather than numbers. For instance, the following statement

X ← ⍞

accepts the next string of characters as input, up to the carriage return, and assigns it to X. The string must be typed without its enclosing quotes. For instance, if we type the following in response to this statement,

1800 BULL RUN, ALEXANDRIA, VA.

that string will literally become the value of X.

Additional input-output facilities are available in APL, so that *data files* can be created and accessed on direct access storage by an APL program. Furthermore, the creation and maintenance of *program files* is supported in APL through the notion of "workspaces" and related functions which allow easy manipulation of programs in those workspaces. Both the data-file facilities and the program-file facilities are implementation dependent, and the functions described below are the ones provided by the APL*PLUS system. Other systems' file support is discussed in section 8-3.2.

Data Files To initialize, or create, a new file in APL the ⎕FCREATE command is used. It has the following form:

'name' ⎕FCREATE tie-number

Here, "name" serves to name the file for the system, and can be any sequence of letters and digits, beginning with a letter. "Tie-number" may be any positive integer, and serves to identify the file for the program. That is, all transfers of data to and from the file are given by commands which specify its particular tie-number.

If, on the other hand, we wish to access a file that has already been created by another program, we must first "tie" it to the program using the ⎕FTIE command:

'name' ⎕FTIE tie-number

Here, "name" again denotes the system name for the file, and "tie-number" denotes the number by which it will be referenced from within the program.

Once a file has been either created by or tied to the program, individual components may be stored into the file or retrieved from the file using one of the following functions:

data ⎕FAPPEND tie-number
variable ← ⎕FREAD tie-number component-number
data ⎕FREPLACE tie-number component-number

The first function appends "data" as the next sequential component of the file identified by "tie-number." The second reads the data from component "component-number'' of file ''tie-number'' and stores it in ''variable.'' The last function replaces the component ''component-number'' in file ''tie-number'' by the given ''data.''

In general, an APL file is viewed as a series of components, each having an associated component-number 1, 2, 3, . . . , *n* and *n* is the total number of components in the file. Each component may be a single value or a collection of values, of any type. The APL notion of component is thus similar to the common notion or ''record'' in other languages.

Files are generally created *serially* in APL, by way of a single ⎕FCREATE followed by a series of ⎕FAPPEND's. Yet they may be accessed either *serially* or *randomly,* since the ⎕FREAD allows specification of the ''component-number'' whenever a component is retrieved. Individual components may also be *randomly updated* in a file using the ⎕FREPLACE command, once the components are known to be present in the file.

At the end of processing a file (or files), the program *must* deactivate, or ''untie'' it from the program's grasp. This is done by the following command:

⎕FUNTIE tie-number(s)

Here, ''tie-numbers'' denotes the file(s) which are to be deactivated.

Several utility commands are available to the program to determine the status of its files. These are summarized below.

⎕FSIZE tie-number. This gives the size of the file ''tie-number'' as four integers: the starting component number, the ending component number, the number of bytes occupied by the file, and the growth limit for the file (0 means ''no limit'').

⎕FNAMES. This gives the names of all current tied files for the program.

⎕FNUMS. This gives the tie numbers of all currently tied files for the program.

'name' ⎕FERASE tie-number. This erases the file ''tie-number'' which has the system name of ''name.''

⎕FLIB. This gives *all* files that are accessible to the program, whether they have been tied or not.

To illustrate, suppose we want to write an APL program that will create a file of names and scores, as illustrated in Figure 8-3. Here, the names and scores are typed individually and appended to the file in pairs. That is, for this example, BUCK and ¯14 will be appended as the first component, BROWN and 3 as the second, and SAM and 12 as the third. The file will be named 'SCORES' for the system, and will be assigned tie-number 1 for the duration of the program

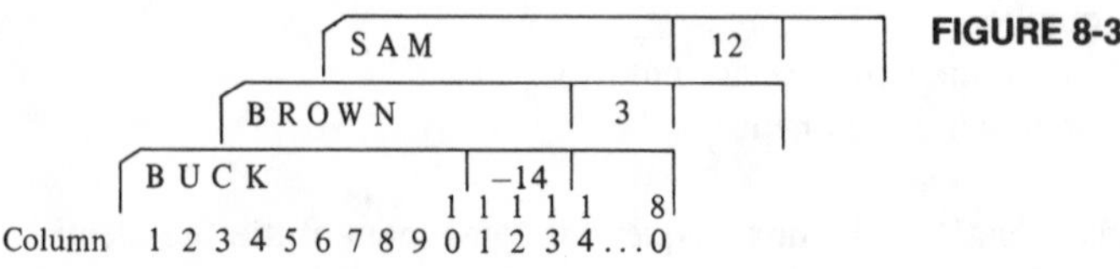

FIGURE 8-3

```
      ∇FILESCORES
[1]   'SCORES' ⎕FCREATE 1
[2] LOOP: 'ENTER NEXT NAME AND SCORE'
[3]   NAME ← ⍞
[4]   → ((ρ NAME) = 0) / DONE
[5]   SCORE ← ⎕
[6]   NAME SCORE ⎕FAPPEND 1
[7]   → LOOP
[8] DONE: ⎕FUNTIE 1
[9] ∇
```

In this program, each repetition of the loop (lines [2] through [7]) captures a name and score from the terminal and appends it to the file 'SCORES'. A test for the end of the input appears in line [4], where the shape of NAME is examined to see if it is empty. If so, the statement DONE is reached, and the file is untied from the program. Thus, the ⎕FCREATE and ⎕FUNTIE functions are similar to the *open* and *close* functions of many other programming languages.

To access components from this file at a later time, the ⎕FTIE function is used, together with several instances of the ⎕FREAD function. The following APL program, for instance, reads all components, lists them, and reports the maximum score in the file. Note how the ⎕FSIZE command is used here to control the number of times the loop is repeated (NCOMPS is the number of components in the file).

```
       ∇MAXSCORE
[1]     'SCORES' ⎕FTIE 1
[2]     NCOMPS ← ⎕FSIZE 1 [2] − 1
[3]     I ← 1
[4]     NAME SCORE ⎕FREAD 1 I ⍝ READ THE ITH COMPONENT
[5]     MAXSCORE ← SCORE
[6]  LOOP: NAME, ' ', ⍕ SCORE ⍝ OUTPUT THE RECORD
[7]     I ← I + 1
[8]     → (I>NCOMPS) / DONE
[9]     NAME SCORE ⎕FREAD 1 I
[10]    → (SCORE <MAXSCORE) / LOOP
[11]    MAXSCORE ← SCORE
[12]    → LOOP
[13] DONE: 'THE MAXIMUM SCORE IS ',⍕ SCORE
[14]    ⎕FUNTIE 1
[15] ∇
```

Program Files Unlike many other languages, APL has intrinsic facilities for the creation and maintenance of data files and program files. The latter is called a "workspace." APL has a complete set of functions available for manipulating programs in these workspaces as program development proceeds.

When we sit down to begin an APL session, we automatically have access to a single workspace, called the "active workspace." This is where we enter new programs, define functions, and so forth for the duration of the session. But when we terminate the session, all programs and functions in the active workspace are lost, unless we save them (ahead of time) in a *permanent* workspace.

To save the current workspace as a permanent workspace, we use the following command:

)SAVE wsname

Here, "wsname" is the name we choose for this workspace. For instance, suppose we want to save as a permanent workspace named FILEMAINT the two programs in the previous paragraphs—FILESCORES and MAXSCORE—which we assume are currently residing in the active workspace. To save these, we write the following:

)SAVE FILEMAINT

Now we are free to terminate the session, without fear of losing our programs.

Later, when we want to resume work on these programs, we can enter the following command at the beginning of a new session:

)LOAD FILEMAINT

This will load our active workspace with a copy of the programs from the workspace FILEMAINT, which we had previously saved.

The following commands for keeping track of the programs in workspaces are also useful:

)CLEAR. Clears the active workspace of all functions, variables, and programs.

)FNS. Lists alphabetically the names of all functions and programs in the active workspace.

)VARS. Lists alphabetically all variables in the active workspace.

)ERASE *n*1, *n*2, ... Erases *selectively* those functions, programs, and variables named *n*1, *n*2, . . . in the active workspace, and leaves the rest intact.

)DROP wsname. Deletes the workspace named "wsname" from the system.

)COPY wsname *n*1, *n*2, ... Copies the functions and variables *n*1, *n*2, . . . from the active workspace into the permanent workspace "wsname."

8-2.7 Subprograms, Functions, and Libraries

In addition to the operators presented in previous sections, APL provides a variety of additional operators which perform functions like those found on an electronic calculator. These are summarized and illustrated below. Also in this section, we illustrate APL's facilities for defining and invoking functions.

The following monadic functions augment the basic arithmetic operators in APL:

Monadic operator (op)	Name	Meaning of "op X"
?	**roll**	A random integer between 1 and X
○	**pi times**	The product 3.14159X
⍟	**log**	Natural logarithm of X
⌈	**ceiling**	Smallest integer ⩾ X
⌊	**floor**	Largest integer ⩽ X
!	**factorial**	The factorial of X (X > 1), or 1 (X ⩽ 1).

When any of these operators is applied to a vector or matrix X, rather than a scalar, the effect is propagated across all elements of the vector or matrix. For instance, if

X ← 3 2 4

then !X will give the vector result 6 2 24, which are the respective factorials. Moreover, each of these operators has dyadic counterparts which extend their meanings in the following ways:

Dyadic operator (op)	Name	Meaning of X op Y
?	**deal**	A random selection of X integers from the sequence 1, . . . ,Y without repetition.
○	**sine**	**1** ○ Y is the sine of Y radians
	cosine	**2** ○ Y is the cosine of Y radians
	tangent	**3** ○ Y is the tangent of Y radians
	sinh	**5** ○ Y is the hyperbolic sine
	cosh	**6** ○ Y is the hyperbolic cosine
	tanh	**7** ○ Y is the hyperbolic tangent
		¯X ○ Y is the *inverse* (arc) trigonometric function, where X = 1,2,3,5,6,7 as defined above, and the result is in radians
⍟	**log**	Logarithm of Y to the base X
⌈	**max**	The maximum of X and Y
⌊	**min**	The minimum of X and Y
!	**combinations**	The number of combinations of Y taken X at a time, or !Y / (!X × !(Y − X))
∣	**residue**	The integer or fractional remainder when dividing Y by X.

This collection is therefore more extensive than that found in most other languages (few others contain the equivalent of "?" and "!"). This distinction is more dramatic when we consider that each of these functions is applicable to operands which are vectors and matrices, as well as scalars.

Writing Function Definitions When the program requires the performance of a function which is not among the set of operators provided by APL, and is not defined within one of the workspaces provided with the APL system, the programmer may define it, and then may later use it in the same way that any of the APL operators is used.

APL functions fall into two classes; those that return an explicit result (scalar or array) and those that do not. Moreover, functions may have 0, 1, or 2 arguments (which may themselves be scalar or array) in addition to the result. These alternatives give rise to the six forms of function definition ''header,'' each beginning with the **del** character, which are summarized below.

Number of arguments	**No explicit result**	**Explicit result**
0	∇ name	∇ result ← name
1	∇ name arg	∇ result ← name arg
2	∇ name arg1 arg2	∇ result ← name arg1 arg2

Here, ''name'' denotes the function name, ''result'' denotes the result returned by the function, and ''arg'' denotes an argument to the function. The reader should recognize the *simplest* form among these as being identical with the form of an APL program header line. In fact, an APL program is just one instance of the more general notion of a function, and thus can be invoked by any other function or program as well! Note also that a function with *one* argument has the same appearance as any *monadic* APL operator, while a function with *two* arguments has the same form as any *dyadic* APL operator.

When a function has arguments, their corresponding values must be provided at the time it is invoked. Moreover, only when a function returns an explicit result may it be invoked from within an expression with other operators or function invocations.

The body of a function definition is written just as if it were an ordinary program, and the arguments and result (if any) are treated as if they were ordinary variables. At the time of invocation, the arguments are called by value, and the result (if present) must appear on the left of some executable assignment statement within the body of the function definition.That body is terminated by a single line containing only the **del** character.

To illustrate these points, let us assume momentarily that the factorial operator is not predefined in APL, and that we wish to define a function FACT which will provide this calculation. One argument, N, is needed and the result will be designated by F. The function is defined below.

```
    ∇ F ← FACT N
[1] F ← 1
[2] → (N < 2) / 0
[3] F ← × / ⍳ N
[4] → 0
[5] ∇
```

Here, line [1] preassigns the result F as 1, and line [2] then looks to see if the value of N is less than 2, in which case control returns to the invocation. Here, the special branching instruction "→0" denotes a transfer to the calling program, or return of control. In the other case, line [3] computes the factorial F as the "product-reduction" of the first N integers, given by "⍳ N", followed by a return in line [4].

Invoking Functions To invoke a function, we just name it and provide the appropriate number of argument values as expressions. When the function returns a result, the invocation may be embedded within a larger expression. For instance, the factorial of 4 is invoked simply as

```
FACT 4
```

with result returned as 24. Moreover, the combinatorial problem built in as the dyadic operator "!", and defined as

$$a_i = \frac{n!}{i!\,(n-i)!} \qquad \text{for } i = 0, 1, \ldots, n$$

can be defined by the following program segment, using the FACT function defined above.

```
      A ← (N + 1) ρ FACT N
      I ← 0
Loop: A [I + 1] ← A [I + 1] × (FACT I) ÷ (FACT N − I)
      I ← I + 1
      → (I ≤ N) / Loop
```

Recall that these operations are done from right to left, so that no additional parentheses are needed. Here, I contains the integers 0, 1, . . . , N while the vector A contains the N + 1 corresponding coefficients.

The reader should note not only that the FACT function is unnecessary, but also that this program segment is unnecessary, since the dyadic operator ! calculates the binomial coefficients directly. Thus, the single statement

```
A ← (0 , ⍳ N) ! N
```

is a preferred substitute for the above program segment.

Functions That Return No Explicit Results These are often known in other languages as "subroutines" or "procedures," and they are distinguished from ordinary functions by the fact that several different (or no) results are returned to the invocation. In APL, returning several different results is possible only through the use of *global* variables, since arguments are always called by value. That is, when we invoke a function, a *copy* of each operand value is assigned to a temporary storage location for its corresponding argument, and therefore the operand itself cannot be affected by the function's execution. (More discussion of "call by value" and other linkage conventions appears in Chapter 10.)

To obtain multiple results from a function, therefore, they must be identified with separate global variables when the function is defined. For example, suppose we want to write a function which computes, for a vector A, its mean, maximum, and minimum values, assuming the global variables MEAN, MAX, and MIN respectively.

```
    ∇ MMM A
[1] N ← ρ A
[2] MEAN ← (+/A) ÷N
[3] MAX ← ⌈ A
[4] MIN ← ⌊ A
[5] → 0
[6] ∇
```

Here, we find the size of A, or N, and use it to compute the mean in line [2]. The MAX and MIN are given directly by the monadic operators ⌈ and ⌊.

Local Variables and Side Effects Some variables in a function definition have only local use, and they should not have scope outside the function body in which they are used. Such is the case, for instance, with the variable N in the foregoing function MMM. However, unless otherwise specified, *all* variables used in an APL program and its associated functions are *global* in scope. Thus, potentially disastrous side effects can occur unless names are well chosen and scopes are properly localized.

To declare that a variable should have its scope localized to the body of a particular function, that variable is listed in the function header immediately after the argument(s), with a preceding semicolon. For example, the above function MMM should have its header rewritten as follows:

```
∇ MMM A; N
```

This properly localizes the scope of N. Now any other variables named N may be used elsewhere in the program without their values being inadvertently destroyed by the function MMM.

8-2.8 Additional Features

APL functions are, as we can see, powerfully associated with vector and matrix arithmetic operations. To solidify this association, the following monadic operators are defined in the language.

Monadic operator (op)	Name	Meaning of op X
⌽	reverse	Reverses the elements in X, column by column if X is a matrix.
⊖		Reverses X, row by row.
⍉	transpose	For an m x n matrix X, this produces the n x m matrix Y, in which $Y_{ji} = X_{ij}$ for all i = 1, . . . , m and j = 1, . . . , n.
⌹	inverse	For an n × n matrix X, this produces its inverse Y, so that XY = I and I is the identity matrix. If the inverse does not exist, then a DOMAIN ERROR results.
⍋	grade up	These produce a vector of subscripts which reflect an increasing (decreasing) ordering among the elements of X.
⍒	grade down	

Thus, for example, if A and B are as follows:

```
A ← 3 7 6 8
B ← 2 2 ρ 1 2 3 4
```

then the following results are directly obtained:

Operation	Meaning	Result
⌽A	reverse A	8 6 7 3
⊖B	reverse B row-wise	2 1 4 3
⍉B	reverse B column-wise	1 3 2 4
⌹B	invert B	−2 1 1.5 ¯.5
⍋A	grade up A	1 3 2 4
⍒A	grade down A	4 2 3 1

Note that the **grade up** and **grade down** operators give an immediate solution to the problem of array sorting. In particular,

```
A ← A[⍋A]     sorts A into ascending order
A ← A[⍒A]     sorts A into descending order
```

Some of these operators have dyadic counterparts which are useful. For instance, the dyadic operator ⌹ defines matrix division, while the dyadic ⌽ and ⊖ operators can be used to describe more intricate kinds of reversal and rotation.

Two very useful dyadic operators are the inner product (.) and the outer product (°). The inner product, when used with any two scalar functions f1 and f2, and any two vectors or matrices X and Y, is written as follows:

```
X f1 . f2 Y
```

It specifies the *pairwise application* of function f2 to corresponding elements of X and Y, and then *reduction* of the result with function f1. Thus, for example, the inner product·can be used in its ordinary algebraic sense as follows:

X + .× Y

for *n*-element vectors X and Y, and this is equivalent to

+/X × Y

using the reduction operator /. However, if X and Y are two matrices, say m × n and n × p, the expression

X +.× Y

defines the ordinary *matrix product,* an m × p matrix in which the *ij*th element is the inner product of the *i*th row of X and the *j*th column of Y.

The *outer product* operator can be applied to any vectors X and Y in the following way:

X°.f Y

Here, f denotes any scalar dyadic operator. The result is a table, with ρX rows and ρY columns, in which each entry results from applying f to a distinct pair of entries in X and Y. For example,

1 2 3 °.× 4 5

gives a 3 × 2 table in which each entry is a product, as shown:

```
 4  5
 8 10
12 15
```

Finally, APL contains a few additional operators, ⊤ , ⊥, and ⍎, whose usage is so marginal that they will not be discussed in this chapter.

8-3 APPLICATIONS OF APL

It is evident that APL is especially styled for quick and compact solutions of mathematical and statistical problems. It is not generally useful outside that domain, since its file handling facilities are rather limited and its dynamic storage and string processing functions are limited. Many have espoused APL as a language for solving business problems, especially those that have tabular representations in ''spreadsheet'' form. However, the recent advent of packaged programs on microcomputers for such problems seems to have eclipsed APL's utility there.

8-3.1 APL Case Study Implementation

We shall use APL to solve Case Study 1—Matrix Inversion, as discussed in Appendix A. This becomes a trivial problem, since the APL operator ⌹ computes the inverse in a single step. Our only task is to develop appropriate input and output instructions to complete the case study.

The program is named CASE1, and is shown in Figure 8-4. A 20 × 20 array is entered as A, its inverse is computed as AINV, and their product is finally computed as PROD. All three are displayed with appropriate messages.

```
    ∇ CASE1
[1]  ⍝CASE STUDY 1 - MATRIX INVERSION IN APL
[2]  ⍝FOR A 20X20 ARRAY
[3]   'ENTER THE MATRIX'
[4]   A← 20 20 ⍴⎕
[5]   A
[6]   AINV←⌹A
[7]   'ITS INVERSE IS'
[8]   AINV
[9]   PROD←A+.×AINV
[10]  'THEIR PRODUCT IS'
[11]  PROD
    ∇
```

FIGURE 8-4
Case Study 1—Matrix Inversion in APL.

When the matrix has no inverse, which occurs if the rows are not linearly independent, a run-time error will be raised. Unfortunately, APL does not provide facilities to trap a run-time error and thus avoid system-level termination of the program. If we wanted to faithfully replicate the error detection conditions that are in the case study description itself (Appendix A), we would *not* use the operator ⌹, but would use explicit row operations instead. This would make the inverse calculation somewhat longer, but the result would still favorably compare with that found in other languages.

This program was run on an APL*PLUS system for an IBM PC, and on a VAX/UNIX system. The resulting efficiency of these runs is summarized in Figure 8-5, for a single 20 × 20 matrix as input.

8-3.2 Implementation-Dependent Extensions of APL

The main variations among implementations of APL are its file processing conventions and program library facilities. We have shown these for the APL*PLUS system in section 8-2.6. Here, we discuss the main differences between this system and two other prominent APL implementations: APL.SV (which runs on IBM's OS/VS systems), and APL/700 (which runs on Burroughs B6700 and 7700 systems).

FIGURE 8-5
EFFICIENCY OF APL CASE STUDY 1 PROGRAM

Implementation	Compile speed	Execution speed
1 Digital VAX-750/UNIX APL	na	8.5 sec
2 IBM PC APL*PLUS	na	50.4 sec

The APL.SV implementation has input-output facilities which are adapted from IBM's OS/VS file processing and accessing conventions. Thus, the style of these facilities is reminiscent of OS JCL (Job Control Language), a highly stylized and rigidly formatted language for describing specific characteristics of files. This, in general, is not a solution which was designed in the style and spirit of APL. Moreover, it was a modest adaptation of facilities which already existed for other operating environments.

On the other hand, the APL/700 file processing facilities amount to an extension of the APL special (composite) symbol set, using new symbols for the primitive file input-output functions. For example, the composite formed by placing → inside the **quad** symbol denotes a file write operation, while the composite of ← and **quad** denotes a file read. Similarly, composing ∧ and **quad** gives the file create function (like our ⎕FCREATE), and composing ∨ and **quad** gives the file destroy function (like ⎕FERASE). Finally, composing either ↑ or ↓ with **quad** gives the file open or the file close function, respectively.

Neither of these implementations differ significantly from the APL*PLUS implementation covered in this chapter. However, APL is not standardized, so that its portability from one implementation to another is not guaranteed, even if we ignore differences among input-output functions. For example, thorough testing should precede the transport of software which uses the matrix inversion function, since it may perform differently from one implementation to another.

8-3.3 Overall Evaluation of APL

With the experience of the foregoing sections, we can evaluate APL in the scientific application area. Our conclusions are summarized as follows:

	Criterion	Rating
1	Expressivity	Fair
2	Well-definedness	Good
3	Data types and structures	Good
4	Modularity	Fair
5	Input-output facilities	Fair
6	Portability	Poor
7	Efficiency	Good
8	Pedagogy	Fair
9	Generality	Poor

APL's best features are its "well-definedness" and its "data types and structures." Its definition is concise and rigorous, for the particular functions which its character set defines. Its fully dynamic approach to vectors and matrices allows very powerful functions to be defined using very few symbols. The need for explicit looping statements, as in other languages, is nearly eliminated in APL due to the generality of its functions.

On the negative side, APL's weakest characteristics are its "portability" and its "generality." Portability is hampered by its complete lack of standardization for file I/O and program management environment. Generality was never intended in the design of APL, so its limitations in this respect are not surprising. Yet, not all the world is expressible in an n-dimensional rectangular structure, and most applications demand a less rigid approach to record definition, dynamic lists, trees, and so forth.

Mild handicaps also exist in APL's "expressivity," "modularity," and "pedagogy." The unique list of function symbols defined exclusively for APL does little to encourage intuition on the part of the programmer or the reader of a program, even though it renders significant savings in program size. Modularity is hampered by the absence of call-by-reference arguments, lack of provision for explicit declaration of variables and their scopes, and the limitations of function definitions to one or two arguments.

EXERCISES

1 If X, Y, and Z are scalars with values 3, 7, and 2, and A and B are vectors with values 3, 4, 7 and 1, 2, 8, what is the result of each of the following APL expressions?

(a) X × Y + Z
(b) A + X
(c) A + 2 × B
(d) (A ÷ Y) + B
(e) ⌈ A − B
(f) ⍳ A[Z] + 3

2 The "trace" of an N × N matrix A is defined as the sum of its diagonal elements, A_{ii} for i = 1, . . . , N. Write APL statements which compute the trace of A.

3 Define the trace calculation from question 2 as an APL function. Show how it would be invoked to compute the trace T of the following array:

$$\begin{bmatrix} 3 & 2 & -1 & 9 & 0 \\ 0 & 1 & 5 & 6 & 7 \\ 2 & 4 & 6 & 8 & 10 \\ -9 & 2 & 3 & 7 & 4 \\ -1 & -2 & -3 & -4 & -5 \end{bmatrix}$$

4 If your case study problem is a mathematical application, implement it in APL. How does your experience compare with ours, in terms of your overall evaluation of APL using the nine criteria?

5 Some applications in the text processing area are suitable for APL, using the general notion of a character string as an APL vector of characters. Assuming S is such a vector, define functions which perform each of the following text processing actions:

(a) SUBSTR extracts the substring T from string S, beginning at position I and with length J.
(b) INDEX searches string S for the leftmost occurrence of string T, and returns the position of that occurrence. If T does not occur within S, INDEX returns the value 0.

6 Using the functions defined in question 5, write an APL program which counts the number of words and sentences in a free-running input text, stored in an external file named "TEXT." Assume that a sentence is terminated with any one of the character sequences ".", "?", and "!". Assume also that a word is any sequence of nonblank characters terminated by a blank, an end-of-line, or an end-of-file, and that no word is split between two lines.

7 Apply APL to the solution of Case Study 3—Text Formatter, using some of the techniques suggested in questions 5 and 6. Is APL adaptable to the text processing area? If so, evaluate it using your experience.

8 Adapt our solution to Case Study 1 to the exact requirements of Appendix A, by explicitly specifying the steps of the algorithm, and testing for singularity after each stage of triangularization.

REFERENCES

1 Kenneth E. Iverson, *A Programming Language,* Wiley, New York, 1962.
2 A. D Falkoff and K. E. Iverson, *APL\360,* IBM Corp., White Plains, N.Y., 1966.
3 A. D Falkoff and K. E. Iverson, *APL\360 User's Manual,* IBM Corp., White Plains, N.Y., 1968; A. D Falkoff and K. E. Iverson, *APLSV User's Manual,* IBM Corp., White Plains, N.Y., 1973.
4 *APL PLUS File Subsystem Instruction Manual,* Scientific Time Sharing Corp., Washington, D.C., 1970.
5 *APL PLUS/PC,* Scientific Time Sharing Corp., Rockville, Md., 1982.
6 A. D. Falkoff, K. E. Iverson, and E. H. Sussenguth, "A Formal Description of System/360," *IBM Systems Journal* 4: 198–262 (October 1964).
7 Ibid.

CHAPTER 9

LISP

9-1 INTRODUCTION TO LISP

LISP (List Processor) was a language originally designed for symbolic formula manipulation. Later it emerged as the *lingua franca* of the artificial intelligence community. LISP is unparalleled in its ability for expressing recursive algorithms which manipulate dynamic data structures. It also has an unusual expressiveness and simplicity of style in this domain. LISP is very well defined, since its basic structure arises out of the lambda calculus. In this chapter, we shall explore the main features of LISP, and employ it in artificial intelligence applications.

9-1.1 Brief History of LISP

The LISP language was developed by John McCarthy during the period 1956 to 1958,[1] and was first implemented during the 1959–1962 period.[2] McCarthy's work during these early years was involved with representing world information in a formal language, and developing a reasoning program that would make inferences from it. The representations were in list structure form, and the language was a variant of the lambda calculus. The latter then evolved into LISP as we know it.

During this first implementation period (1959–1962), the original "pure LISP" had many features added to it. Among them were property lists, efficient numerical arithmetic, free variables, the "prog" feature, and the "eval" function. All these combined to become known as LISP 1.5.[3]

LISP was first implemented experimentally on an IBM 704 in 1960, and a LISP interpreter was implemented for productive use in 1962. It then appeared on the Digital PDP-1 in 1963, and later on the PDP-6 and PDP-10. The 704 implementation led to versions on the IBM 7090, 360, and other 360-like machines. Since 1962, a number of LISP dialects have evolved, including principally MACLISP[4] and INTERLISP.[5] Also notable among recent developments are the Berkeley compiler called "Franz Lisp"[6] and the direct execution concept on "LISP machines."

Although LISP has never been standardized, software aids are available which facilitate conversion of programs from MACLISP to INTERLISP.[7] Moreover, efforts have been made to develop a "standard" version of LISP,[8] which is close to MACLISP. The most recent effort is known as COMMON LISP. Whether or not these efforts will arrive at a useful and uniform standard remains to be seen.

9-1.2 Implementations and Variations of LISP

The two principal LISP dialects, MACLISP and INTERLISP, are implemented on a wide variety of machines in an interpretive and interactive programming environment. At least one implementation, Franz Lisp, runs in a compiled mode as well. LISP implementations appear on at least the following machines:

Apple II and //e
Burroughs B1700
Digital PDP-10, PDP-11, and VAX
Honeywell Multics
IBM PC, 370, 4300, and similar machines
LMI Lambda
Symbolics 3600
Univac 1100
Xerox LISP Machine

In the earliest implementation of LISP, on the IBM 704 computer, the hardware actually left a permanent mark on the language's instruction set. Later in this chapter, we will introduce the elementary LISP functions named **car** and **cdr.** These allow separation of a list structure into two parts, its head and its tail, respectively. The names of these functions, however, come from two registers in the 704, the "Address Register" and the "Decrement Register," which contained the necessary information to reference a list's head and tail, respectively. Thus, **car** and **cdr** originally stood for "contents of the Address Register" and "contents of the Decrement Register," respectively. Although the 704 has long since become obsolete, these two function names remain at the heart of the LISP language.

9-1.3 Major Applications of LISP

The general area for which LISP was designed is artificial intelligence, whose applications deal with data in the form of symbols and structures of symbolic expressions. Its earliest applications included programs which performed symbolic differentiation, integration, and mathematical theorem verification, since these were the principal AI programming activities of the 1960s.

More recent AI applications have grown into the areas of natural language understanding, computer vision, robotics, knowledge representation, and expert systems. In all of these areas, LISP has been the predominant programming vehicle for developing experimental systems.

9-2 WRITING LISP PROGRAMS

A LISP program usually runs interpretively and interactively. In its simplest form, a program or a function is represented as a fully parenthesized expression with all operators given in prefix form. All variables have values which are either scalars (called "atoms") or fully parenthesized expressions (called "lists").

Below is a simple LISP program which computes and displays the average of a list of input numbers. (Although this particular problem is the antithesis of those for which LISP is typically used, we shall use it to illustrate the elementary syntax, and develop a basis for teaching the language which is similar to that which we use in all other language chapters.) For instance, if the input is the list

(85.5 87.5 89.5 91.5)

then the result displayed will be the value 88.5. The variable x is used here to hold the input list, and the variable n is used to determine how many values there are. The variable av ultimately contains the computed average.

```
(defun sum (x)          ; compute the sum of a list x
     (cond ((null x) 0)
           ((atom x) x)
           (t (+ (car x) (sum (cdr x)]

(defun count (x)        ; count the number of values in x
     (cond ((null x) 0)
           ((atom x) 1)
           (t (add1 (count (cdr x)]

(defun average ()       ; main program begins here
     (princ "enter the list to be averaged")
     (setq x (read))
     (setq n (count x))
     (setq av (/ (sum x) n))
     (princ "the average = ")
     (print av)]
```

The program is composed of three LISP functions, each indicated by the "defun" heading (short for "define function"). The first function "sum" computes the arithmetic sum of the elements in the list x. The second, "count," computes the *number* of values in the list. The third function, "average," is the main program and controls the input (using "read"), the calculation of the average "av," and the output (using "print").

Comments in a LISP program begin with the special delimiter semicolon (;), and extend to the end of the line. Variables are generally undeclared, and have global scope. Bound variables, which are local to a function, may also be specified.

Loops in LISP are often given by recursion rather than by iteration. Thus, for example, calculation of the *sum* is done by the following recursive definition:

If the list is empty (i.e., "null"), the sum is 0.

If the list has one entry, the sum is that entry.

If the list is longer than one entry, the sum is the result of adding the first entry (i.e., the "car") and the sum of the list composed of the remaining entries (i.e., the "cdr").

Thus, if the list is (1 2 3), then its sum is 1 plus the sum of the list (2 3), and so forth.

LISP syntactic structure is very simple. The program is a fully parenthesized expression, in which all functions appear as prefix operators. In some LISP implementations, there are two classes of parentheses, () and []. The brackets are used to specify multiple closure. The right bracket,], can be used at the end of a function definition to effectively close *all* open left parentheses, (, which precede it. This avoids the need to count and explicitly balance right parentheses in many cases. We shall make use of this convention hereafter.

Note finally that there is no fundamental difference in structure between a LISP program and its data. This characteristic leads to strong inherent facilities for programs to manipulate other programs, as we shall see. Also, this provides a basic uniformity of expression not found in other languages. Thus, this brief example provides the flavor of LISP programming. Further details are left to later sections of this chapter.

9-2.1 Elementary Data Types and Values

The elementary data types in LISP are "numbers" and "symbols." A number is a value which is either an integer or a real (decimal) number. The following are examples of numbers:

```
0        -17      234      49.5
10.5E-5      -7E4
```

The last two examples are abbreviations for scientific notation, where E stands for "times 10 to the power" as it does in other languages.

A symbol comprises any string of characters which does not represent a decimal number. The following are valid LISP symbols:

```
av       orange
alpha    NOUN
A1       2+3
```

A LISP "atom" is either a number or a symbol. Atoms are the basic building blocks for all data structures in LISP, as we shall see in section 9-2.4.

Certain atoms have preassigned meanings in LISP, as follows, and should therefore not be used for other purposes.

Atom	Meaning
t	Denotes the logical value **true**
nil	Denotes either the logical value **false** or the empty list ( ), depending on the context in which it appears.

Many other atoms have preassigned meanings, in the sense that they are predefined LISP functions. These so-called "primitive functions" are given in Figure 9-1.

The functions listed here are those which are common to most LISP implementations, and form the "heart" of the language. Notations enclosed in parentheses indicate alternative representations in some implementations, such as "+" instead of "plus." Additional functions appear in one or another implementation, but are not common to others. Some of these are discussed in section 9-3.2.

A LISP function is always written in the following general form:

```
(name arg1 arg2 . . . )
```

Here, "name" identifies the function and "arg1," "arg2," . . . denote the arguments to which the function is to be applied. For instance,

```
(+ 2 3)
```

denotes the sum 2 + 3, while

```
(list 2 3)
```

FIGURE 9-1
THE MAIN PRIMITIVE FUNCTIONS IN LISP

abs	and	append	apply	assoc	atom
car	cdr	close	cond	cons	difference (−)
defun (de, df)	dm (macro)	eq	equal	eval	explode
expt	fix	fixp	float	floatp	function
gensym	get	getd	go	greaterp (gt)	intern
lambda	length	lessp (lt)	list	map	mapc
mapcan	mapcar	mapcon	maplist	max	min
nconc	not	null	numberp	open	or
princ	print	prin1	prog	progn	put
quote (')	quotient (/)	read	remainder	remob	remprop
return	reverse	rplaca	rplacd	set	setq
subst	plus (+)	terpri	times (*)		

denotes the construction of a list whose elements are 2 and 3, which is represented as:

```
(2 3)
```

Functions may be arbitrarily nested, in which case they are evaluated from the "inside out." Thus,

```
(+ (* 2 3) 4)
```

denotes the sum of 2 * 3 and 4. Moreover, a list of functions is evaluated from left to right. For instance,

```
(-(+ 2 3) (* 3 4))
```

denotes the difference of the sum 2 + 3 *followed by* the product 3 * 4.

9-2.2 Names, Variables, and Declarations

A LISP variable has a name, which may be any symbol, and a value which may be either an atom or a list. The following are examples of LISP variable names:

```
x
av
ALPHA
eaten
```

(Some implementations do not permit lowercase letters, but we shall assume them throughout this chapter.) Names are also used to identify functions, such as the following in our sample program:

```
sum      count      average
```

Generally, LISP variables are not declared; activation of a variable occurs dynamically, whenever the variable is first referenced during execution of the program. Moreover, the *type* of value stored for a variable may vary during execution. When a variable is used in an arithmetic context, therefore, the program must assure that its current value is numeric. Otherwise, a run-time error will occur.

The use of LISP primitive function names (Figure 9-1) for variable names should be avoided, even though they are not, strictly speaking, "reserved words." Program legibility suffers, for instance, when "and" and "or" are used as variable names in the following expression:

```
(and and or)
```

Because variables are not declared, they should not be assumed to have preassigned initial values. In some LISP systems, variables are all automatically initialized to "nil," but reliance on this is generally not good programming practice.

9-2.3 Arrays and Other Data Structures

A "list" is formally defined in LISP as follows:

(i) "nil" is a list, and can also be written as ().
(ii) If e_1, e_2, . . . , and e_n are lists or atoms, then so is (e_1 e_2 . . . e_n).

The first rule describes formation of the *empty* list, called "nil" or (). The second rule recursively defines how larger lists can be formed from simpler lists and atoms, using enclosing parentheses to delimit their beginning and end. Thus, the following are lists:

```
(2 3)
(+ 2 3)
nil
(* (+ (- 2 3) 4) (/ 5 6))
(cond ((null x) 0)((atom x) x)(t (+ (car x) (sum (cdr x)))))
```

These examples illustrate how a list can represent both data and program, using the same basic syntax. At least one blank must appear between adjacent atoms in any list. Lists like the last one above are usually written on several lines, using indentation and the "multiple closure" bracket,], for clarity and accuracy. That is, the last list above is more clearly written as follows:

```
(cond ((null x) 0)
      ((atom x) x)
      (t (+ (car x) (sum (cdr x)]
```

Thus defined, the list is the basic building block for all LISP data structures. To understand how lists are internally represented, it is necessary to introduce another formalism known as the "s-expression." This is a linear form of representing binary trees, and is defined as follows:

(i) "nil" is an s-expression.
(ii) Any atom is an s-expression.
(iii) If s and t are s-expressions, so is (s . t).

Here, the definition parallels that of lists, except for rule (iii). This rule allows s-expressions to be formed only out of *pairs* of simpler ones. Thus, the following are three s-expressions:

```
(2 . 3)
(2 . (3 . nil))
(cond . (((atom . (x . nil)) . (x . nil)) .
          (t . (+ . ((car . (x . nil)) .
               ((sum . (cdr . (x . nil))) . nil))))))
```

The first two of these correspond to the following binary trees:

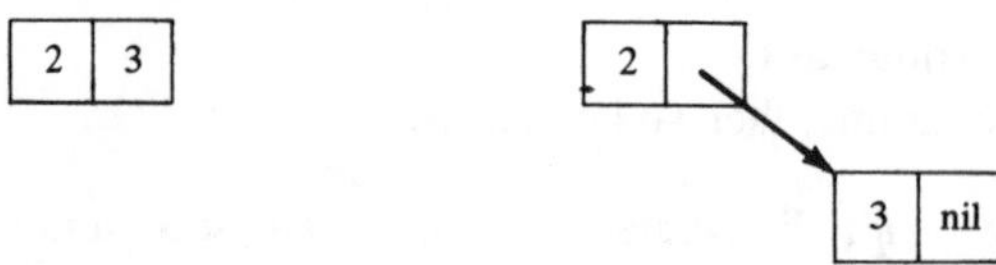

That is, whenever a parenthesized s-expression properly contains another parenthesized s-expression as its lefthand or righthand member, a corresponding left-branch or right branch is drawn from the corresponding node. Otherwise, the atom or "nil" is inserted directly into the corresponding node.

The association between lists and s-expressions is defined as follows:

(i) A list which is "nil" corresponds to the s-expression "nil."
(ii) An atom corresponds to the same s-expression.
(iii) A list of the form (e_1 e_2 . . . e_n) corresponds to the s-expression (e_1 . (e_2 . (. . . (e_n . nil) . . .))).

In this association, it should be clear that every list has a corresponding s-expression, but not every s-expression has a corresponding list.

Arrays An array may be declared explicitly in some dialects of LISP using the "array" function, which has the following form:

```
(array name t size)
```

Here, "name" identifies the array and "size" is a sequence of integers which identify the number of elements in each dimension. For instance, suppose A is a five-element array and B is a 5 × 4 array, as pictured in Figure 9-2. These can be declared as follows:

```
(array A t 5)
(array B t 5 4)
```

An array entry is referenced by a list containing the array's name and a series of subscripts, identifying the entry's position in the array. Rows and columns, for this purpose, are prenumbered from 0 (as in the C language), rather than from 1 (as in most other languages). Thus, the third entry in A is referenced by (A 2), and the entry in the fourth row and third column of B is referenced by (B 3 2).

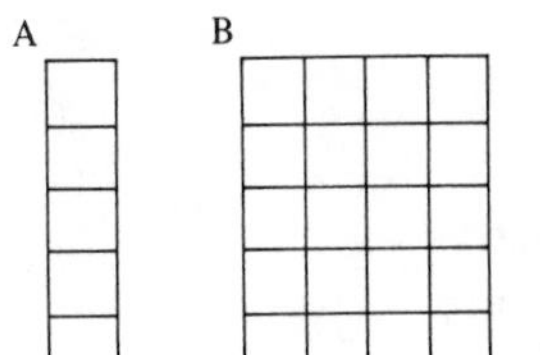

FIGURE 9-2

To assign a value to an array entry, the following function is used:

(store (name subscripts) value)

For example, to store the value 0 in the entry in the fourth row and third column of B, we write:

(store (B 3 2) 0)

In general, the value stored may specify any LISP expression, and each of the subscripts may also be any LISP expression whose value is an integer in the appropriate range. Thus, arrays in LISP are generally typeless, since each entry may be different in structure and type from the rest.

Property Lists A much more useful method of structuring data in a list is the so-called "property list." This is a list which has the following general form:

$(p_1\ v_1\ p_2\ v_2\ .\ .\ .\ p_n\ v_n)$

where the p's are atoms denoting properties, and the v's are values associated with those properties. To illustrate, suppose we have the information shown for an individual shown in Figure 9-3.

Here, there are four properties, a name, a social security number, a gross pay, and an address. We can define a property list, say PERSON, with these properties as follows:

```
(NAME (ALLEN B TUCKER)
SS# 275407437
GROSS_PAY 25400
ADDRESS ((1800 BULL RUN) ALEXANDRIA VA 22200)
)
```

The result is a tree-like structure shown in Figure 9-4.

FIGURE 9-3

ALLENƀB.ƀTUCKERƀƀƀƀƀƀƀƀƀ

275407437

25400.00

1800ƀBULLƀRUN,ƀALEXANDRIA,ƀVA.ƀ22200ƀƀƀƀ

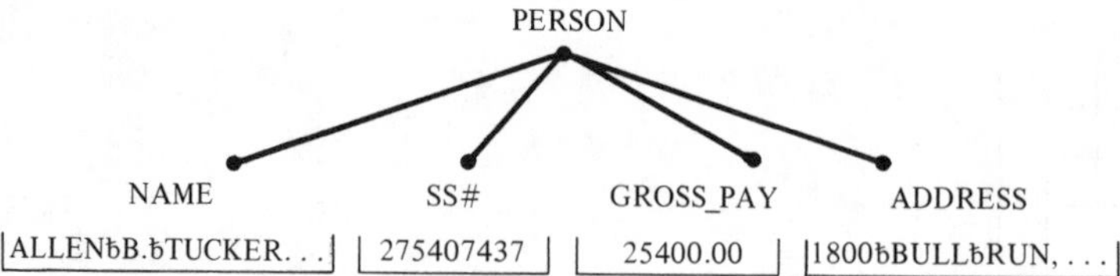

FIGURE 9-4

To retrieve information from a property list, we use the function "get" as follows:

(get name p)

Here, "name" identifies the list and p identifies the property whose value is desired. For instance, to retrieve a PERSON's SS#, we write

(get PERSON SS#)

and the value returned, for the above example, will be 275407437.

To replace information in a property list, the "put" function is used.

(put name p v)

Here, "name" identifies the list, p identifies the property whose property is to be replaced, and v is the new value. For example,

(put PERSON GROSS_PAY 30000)

alters the GROSS_PAY property of PERSON, so that its value becomes 30000 instead of 25400, as it had been in the present example.

Finally, the function "remprop" *removes* a property and its associated value from the list.

(remprop name p)

Here, "name" identifies the affected property list, and p identifies the property and value to be removed.

Property lists are very useful, therefore, in defining what are known in other languages as "records." A property list typically represents a node in a larger linked list of records, all of which have the same set of properties. This larger list is more commonly known as a "file" in other languages. For instance, the PERSON record discussed above may be a single node in a list which contains all the persons employed by a particular organization. Similarly, another specific property list can be defined for a single entry in a library card catalog, and the list of all such entries can represent the catalog itself.

9-2.4 Basic Statements

In describing the different statements of LISP, we need only to define and illustrate its functions themselves. In this section, we discuss LISP functions for performing arithmetic, assignment, and basic list manipulation.

In section 9-2.5, conditional expressions, the "program feature," and loops are introduced, together with their related functions. Section 9-2.6 introduces the functions for input and output, section 9-2.7 discusses programmer-defined functions in more detail, and section 9-2.8 introduces some important special functions. In summary, the following table classifies the functions according to the sections in which they appear:

Section	Functions
9-2.4	add1, append, car, cdr, cons, difference (−), length, list, plus (+), reverse, quote ('), quotient (/), reverse, rplaca, rplacd, set, setq, sub1, subst, times (*).
9-2.5	and, atom, cond, equal, fixp, floatp, go, greaterp, lessp, minusp, not, null, numberp, or, plusp, prog, zerop.
9-2.6	prin1, princ, print, read, readch, terpri.
9-2.7	abs, defun (de), expt, lambda, max, min, return.
9-2.8	apply, eval, macro (dm), macroexpansion (expand), mapcan, mapcar.

Several LISP functions remain untouched by this coverage, but those tend to be more specialized and less uniformly defined among different implementations. Some discussion of these appears in section 9-3.2.

Arithmetic Functions and Value Assignment The basic LISP arithmetic functions are "plus," "difference," "times," and "quotient," which are abbreviated on most systems by the familiar signs +, −, *, and /. All of these functions have zero or more operands, or arguments, and are written in prefix form like the other LISP functions. When combined to form the equivalent of arithmetic expressions, these functions are fully parenthesized, and thus there is no need in LISP to define any hierarchical precedence among them.

To illustrate, suppose H, I, N, and X are LISP variables. The algebraic expressions shown on the left below (as they would be written in other languages) are written in LISP as shown on the right.

Expression	LISP form
H + 2	(+ H 2)
H + 2 + I	(+ (+ H 2) I)
H + 2 * I	(+ H (* 2 I))
SUM(X)/N	(/ (SUM X) N)

Since the LISP forms are fully parenthesized, their order of evaluation is always explicit. The second example assumes left-to-right evaluation of operations with the same precedence, while the third assumes that "*" has precedence over "+," in the left-hand expressions. The fourth example illustrates the application of a programmer-defined function in the context of a larger expression.

Assignment of the value of an expression to another variable is accomplished by either the "setq" or the "set" function. These have two operands, as shown:

```
(setq variable expression)
(set 'variable expression)
```

In either of these, "variable" denotes the name of a variable which is the target of the assignment and "expression" denotes a list whose resulting value will be assigned. For example, the function

```
(setq I (+ I 1))
```

is equivalent to the familiar form I := I + 1 in Pascal. The expression on the right is first evaluated, and the result is assigned to the variable I. In general, this result may be an atom (a number or a symbol) or a list, as we shall see in later examples.

The unary functions "add1" and "sub1" are provided in LISP to simplify specification of the common operation of adding or subtracting 1 from a variable's value. This operation is ubiquitous in all programming applications, and is especially prevalent in *recursive* programming.

Quote (') and Evaluation The quotation mark ('), the letter q in setq, and the function "quote" are used in LISP to distinguish explicitly between evaluated and unevaluated expressions. This distinction is needed because of the dual nature of a LISP symbol in some contexts: its use as an item of data and its use as a variable name. If "E" denotes any LISP expression, then its appearance within a program usually implies that it be immediately evaluated, and the resulting value be used in subsequent execution. However, the expression

```
(quote E)
```

which is usually abbreviated by 'E, denotes that E stands for *itself,* and is *not* to be further evaluated.

For example, consider the following two expressions, where X is shown to be used as a variable (on the left) and as a literal value (on the right):

```
((setq X 1)        ((setq X 1)
 (setq Y X))        (setq Y 'X))
```

In the left-hand expression, variables X and Y are both assigned the value 1. In the right-hand expression, X is assigned the value 1 and Y is assigned the (literal) value X. The latter is, in effect, a character string of length 1, or a nonnumeric atom.

This helps explain the distinction between "set" and "setq" in the previous paragraph. "Setq" is just a convenient way of combining "set" with a quoted first argument. That is, the variable name on the left of an assignment should not be evaluated; it designates an address rather than a value. Thus, the following are equivalent:

```
(setq X 1)
(set 'X 1)
(set (quote X) 1)
```

The first form is usually preferred in practice; the third is the historical precedent of the other two.

List Manipulation Functions The main strength of LISP lies in its power for manipulating *symbolic expressions* rather than numeric ones. To illustrate, suppose we have a list L composed of the names of the languages in Chapters 2 to 5 of this book. That is,

L = (pascal, fortran, cobol, pli)

The value of L can be assigned by the following statement:

```
(setq L '(pascal fortran cobol pli))
```

Note here that the quote (') forces treatment of the list of languages as a literal, rather than a collection of variables named "pascal," "fortran," etc.

Recall that, in general, a list may be either nil, an atom, or a series of elements in parentheses (e_1 e_2 . . . e_n). In this latter case, the underlying s-expression is

$$(e_1 \;.\; (e_2 \;.\; (\;.\;.\;.\; (e_n \;.\; \text{nil}) \;.\;.\;.\;)))$$

which is a linearization of an underlying binary tree.

Two basic functions, called "car" and "cdr," are used to divide lists (i.e., their underlying representations) into two parts. "Car" defines the first element, e_1, in a list, and "cdr" defines the list comprising the remaining elements (e_2 . . . e_n). In the special case where n = 1, the cdr is defined as nil, in accordance with the underlying s-expression representation. When the original list is a single atom or nil itself, the car and cdr functions yield undefined values, and will raise a run-time error. (Some implementations take exception to this, defining the car and cdr as nil in this special case. This compromise sometimes simplifies programming in "boundary" situations, even though it sacrifices consistency and portability.)

To illustrate, assume we have L with the following value:

```
(pascal fortran cobol pli)
```

Then the following applications of car and cdr yield the results shown on the right:

Function	Result
(car L)	pascal
(cdr L)	(fortran cobol pli)
(car (cdr L))	fortran
(cdr (car L))	undefined
(cdr (cdr L))	(cobol pli)
(cdr (cdr (cdr L)))	(pli)
(cdr (cdr (cdr (cdr L))))	nil

Note the difference between a list which is an atom and one which contains a single atom in parentheses. That is, the list (pli) has as its s-expression (pli . nil), which is different from the atom pli.

Multiple applications of the car and cdr functions can be abbreviated in LISP with the following conventions:

Full form	Abbreviation
(car (cdr L))	(cadr L)
(cdr (car L))	(cdar L)
(car (car (. . . (car L) . . .)))	(caa . . . ar L)
(cdr (cdr (. . . (cdr L) . . .)))	(cdd . . . dr L)
etc.	

Some LISP implementations limit the degree of nesting that can be abbreviated in this way. However, three levels can be safely assumed for most implementations.

In contrast with taking a list apart into its constituents is the function of constructing a list out of other lists. This is supported in LISP by the following functions. In this description, e_1, e_2, . . . denote arbitrary lists.

Function	Meaning
(cons e_1 e_2)	Construct the s-expression (e_1 . e_2)
(list e_1 e_2 . . . e_n)	Construct a list of the form (e_1 e_2 . . . e_n)
(append e_1 e_2 . . . e_n)	Construct a list of the form (f_1 f_2 . . . f_n), where each f is the result of dropping the outermost parentheses from each e. The e's here cannot be atoms.

To illustrate the use of these functions, reconsider the list L whose value is (pascal fortran cobol pli). If we wish to construct a new list M, whose elements are the list L and the new list (snobol apl lisp), we can write the following:

```
(setq M (list L '(snobol apl lisp)))
```

The resulting value of M is:

```
((pascal fortran cobol pli) (snobol apl lisp))
```

which is a list of *two* elements, not seven. The structure of M is given by the following binary tree:

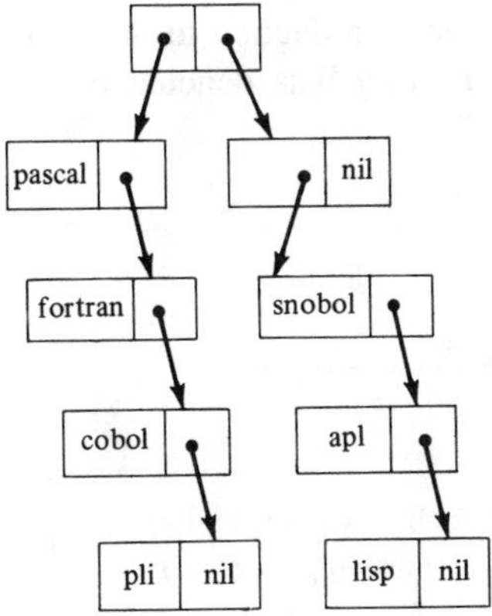

Its basic list structure is ((A) (B)), whose s-expression is

```
((A . nil) . ((B . nil) . nil))
```

which gives rise to the above tree structure.

"Cons," on the other hand, always has two arguments and constructs an s-expression from them. Thus,

```
(cons 'snobol (cons 'apl (cons 'lisp nil)))
```

constructs the s-expression

```
(snobol . (apl . (lisp . nil)))
```

which is equivalent to the list (snobol apl lisp). This list could therefore have been equivalently constructed by the following function:

```
(list 'snobol 'apl 'lisp)
```

"Append" is slightly different from "list," in the sense that it requires its arguments to be parenthesized lists, and it subsequently drops them in constructing the result. Thus,

(append L '(snobol apl lisp))

gives the seven-element list:

(pascal fortran cobol pli snobol apl lisp)

which is structurally distinct from the list M formed in the previous illustration.

Five additional list manipulation functions complete our introduction to the basic statements of LISP. These are described below, for arbitrary lists denoted by e_1, e_2, . . . , e_n.

Function	**Meaning**
(rplaca e_1 e_2)	Replace the car of e_1 by e_2.
(rplacd e_1 e_2)	Replace the cdr of e_1 by e_2.
(subst e_1 e_2 e_3)	Replace every instance of e_2 in e_3 by (the substitute) e_1.
(reverse (e_1 e_2 . . . e_n))	Reverse the elements of the list, forming (e_n . . . e_2 e_1).
(length (e_1 e_2 . . . e_n))	The number of elements in the list, n.

In the functions "rplaca" and "rplacd," the argument e_1 must denote a parenthesized list, in order that the corresponding car and cdr be well defined. Similarly, the argument e_3 in the function "subst" must also be a parenthesized list.

To illustrate these, assume again that we have the lists L and M, with respective values (pascal fortran cobol pli) and ((pascal fortran cobol pli) (snobol apl lisp)). The following expressions yield the values shown on the right:

Expression	**Result**
(rplaca L 'modula)	(modula fortran cobol pli)
(rplacd M 'prolog)	((pascal fortran cobol pli) prolog)
(reverse (cadr M))	(lisp apl snobol)
(subst 'ada 'pli L)	(pascal fortran cobol ada)
(length L)	4
(length M)	2

9-2.5 Control Structures

LISP functions can be evaluated serially, conditionally, iteratively, or recursively. Recursion is discussed in section 9-2.7, while conditional and iterative evaluation are discussed in this section.

Behind the notion of conditional evaluation is a collection of LISP functions which are classified as "predicates." A predicate is any function which, when evaluated, returns either the value t (meaning *true*) or "nil" (meaning *false*). In other languages, these basic predicates are usually defined via "relational" and "Boolean" operators. Below is a list of the principal predicates found in LISP, together with their meanings. Here, e, e_1, and e_2 denote lists, x, x_1, and x_2 denote *arithmetic* expressions, and p, p_1, p_2, . . . denote predicates.

Predicate	**Meaning**
(plusp x)	Returns t if $x > 0$, and nil otherwise.
(minusp x)	Returns t if $x < 0$, and nil otherwise.
(zerop x)	Returns t if $x = 0$, and nil otherwise.
(lessp x_1 x_2)	Returns t if $x_1 < x_2$, and nil otherwise.
(greaterp x_1 x_2)	Returns t if $x_1 > x_2$, and nil otherwise.
(and p_1 p_2 . . . p_n)	Returns t if *all* of $p_1, p_2, \ldots, p_n$ are t, and nil otherwise.
(or p_1 p_2 . . . p_n)	Returns t if any *one or more* of $p_1, p_2, \ldots, p_n$ is t, and nil otherwise.
(not p)	Returns t if p is nil, and nil otherwise.
(fixp x) (floatp x)	Returns t if x is integer or floating point, respectively, and nil otherwise.
(equal e_1 e_2)	Returns t if the value of e_1 is the same as the value of e_2, and nil otherwise.
(numberp e)	Returns t if e is a numeric atom, and nil otherwise.
(atom e)	Returns t if e is an atom, and nil otherwise.
(null e)	Returns t if e is nil, and nil otherwise.

To illustrate these functions, assume that the list SCORES has the value (87.5 89.5 91.5) and the list L again has the value (pascal fortran cobol pli). Most of the examples in the table at the top of page 334 use these values to illustrate the LISP predicates.

Some of these examples illustrate the "boundary" situations that arise in list processing, and the importance of applying functions to the right kind of arguments. For example, the predicates "zerop," "plusp," "minusp," "lessp," and "greaterp" apply principally to expressions which have numeric values.

Predicate	Result
(plusp (car SCORES))	t
(minusp 3)	nil
(zerop (car L))	undefined
(lessp (car SCORES) (cadr SCORES))	t
(greaterp (car SCORES) 90)	nil
(and (plusp (car SCORES)) (lessp (car SCORES) 90))	t
(equal (car L) 'lisp)	nil
(or (greaterp (car SCORES) 90) (greaterp (cadr SCORES) 90))	nil
(numberp (car L))	nil
(not (numberp (car L)))	t
(atom L)	nil
(atom (car L))	t
(atom (cdr L))	nil
(null nil)	t
(atom nil)	t

Conditional Expressions A conditional expression in LISP is equivalent to a series of nested **if** statements in Pascal-like languages. It has the following general form:

$$
\begin{aligned}
&(\text{cond } (p_1\ e_1)\\
&\qquad (p_2\ e_2)\\
&\qquad \vdots\\
&\qquad (p_n\ e_n))
\end{aligned}
$$

Here, each of $p_1, \ldots, p_n$ denotes a predicate and each of e_1, results in the evaluation and return of the *first* e in the sequence for which the corresponding p is true, and subsequent bypassing of the rest. (If none of the p's is true, the cond function returns nil.) In effect, therefore, it is the same as the following Pascal code:

if p_1 **then** e_1
else if p_2 **then** e_2
  else
   ⋮
   else if p_n **then** e_n

In the event that we want the *last* alternative e_n to be evaluated in "all other cases"—i.e., whenever all the p's are nil—then we set p_n to t in this conditional expression. For instance, suppose we want to compute a person's TAX as 25 percent of GROSS income whenever the latter exceeds $18000, and 22 percent of GROSS otherwise. The following conditional expression will accomplish this:

```
(cond ((greaterp GROSS 18000) (setq TAX (* 0.25 GROSS)))
      (t                      (setq TAX (* 0.22 GROSS))))
```

This is equivalent, then, to the Pascal expression:

if GROSS > 18000 **then** TAX := .25 * GROSS
  else TAX := .22 * GROSS

Some confusion may arise when we reach the end of a complex LISP expression like this, over how many right parentheses should appear at the end in order to maintain proper balance. This is a good situation for using the bracket,], to force multiple closure without having to tediously count matching left parentheses. Thus, we can write the above as:

```
(cond ((greaterp GROSS 18000) (setq TAX (* 0.25 GROSS)))
      (t                      (setq TAX (* 0.22 GROSS]
```

and all unmatched open parentheses will be closed backward to the beginning of the conditional expression.

Iteration Although *recursion* is LISP's primary form of expressing repetitive processes, some situations prefer the specification of "iterative" loops. To serve this need, LISP provides the "prog feature" which, combined with the "go" function (yes, that's the old **go to** statement!), allows a primitive kind of looping to be specified. Moreover, some LISP implementations provide other control structures comparable to the **while** or **for** statements found in Pascal-like languages.

The "prog feature" also provides a facility for defining "local variables" within a function definition. Unless so specified, all variables in a LISP program are (by default) global in scope. The general form of the program feature is as follows:

(prog (locals)
e_1 e_2 . . . e_n)

Here, "locals" denotes a list identifying the local variables for this function. Each of the e's here denotes an arbitrary LISP expression, and may optionally be preceded by a "label." The label may itself be any distinct symbol, and it serves to provide a branch point for a "go" function which appears elsewhere among these expressions.

The go function has the following general form:

(go label)

Here, "label" denotes the symbolic label which precedes some other expression within this list of expressions. For example, if we want to specify the repeated execution of an expression e 10 times, controlled by the (local) variable I, we can write the following program segment:

```
(prog (I)
      (setq I 1)
   loop
      (setq I (add1 I))
      (cond ((lessp I 11) (go loop)))
)
```

This is equivalent to the following Pascal-like loop:

```
   I := 1;
loop:
   I := I + 1;
   if I < 11 then goto loop
```

9-2.6 Input-Output Conventions

LISP is an interactive language, so that the input-output function is principally carried on at the terminal. Most implementations provide for secondary storage of files as well, but those provisions are quite implementation dependent. In this section, we shall discuss only the terminal oriented input-output functions.

The function ''read'' has no arguments, and calls for a list to be entered at the terminal. It has the following form:

```
(read)
```

When this is encountered, the program waits for the user to enter a list, and that becomes the value returned by this function. In order to assign that value to a variable in the program, read may be combined within a ''setq'' function, as follows:

```
(setq X (read))
```

In effect, this says ''assign to X the next input value.'' Thus, if we type 14 in response to the read function, 14 will become the value of X.

The most straightforward way to display output on the terminal screen is to use the ''print'' function, which has the following form:

```
(print e)
```

Here, e may be any LISP expression, and its value will be displayed on the screen as a result of this function's execution.

Three variations of "print" are also available in LISP, and these are called "terpri," "prin1," and "princ." The expression

```
(terpri)
```

is used to skip to the beginning of a new line. The expression

```
(prin1 e)
```

is like (print e), except that it does *not* start on a new line. The expression

```
(princ e)
```

is used to suppress vertical bars, which are used to enclose atoms which contain special characters (like "$" and "blank," which are not ordinarily allowed within an atom). For instance, if we want an atom to have the value HURRAH! we would have to enclose it within vertical bars, as shown:

```
|HURRAH!|
```

If it were displayed using print or prin1, the vertical bars would appear as well.

9-2.7 Subprograms, Functions, and Libraries

Each LISP implementation provides an extensive library of predefined functions for list and string processing. The following are examples found in most implementations. Here, x, x_1 . . . , x_n denote any numeric valued expressions.

Function	Meaning
(abs x)	The absolute value of x.
(max x_1 x_2 . . . x_n)	The largest (maximum) value among x_1, . . . , x_n.
(min x_1 x_2 . . . x_n)	The smallest (minimum) value among x_1, . . . , x_n.
(expt x)	The exponential function of x, e^x.

Moreover, LISP provides powerful facilities for the programmer to extend the language by defining additional functions. This feature has the following general form:

(defun name (parameters)
  e_1 e_2 . . . e_n)

Here, "name" identifies the function, "parameters" is a list of atomic symbols which denote the function's parameters, and e_1, . . . , e_n are the expressions which define the function. Three such functions, named "sum," "count," and "average," are defined in the sample program at the beginning of the chapter. The first two have the parameter x, while the third has *no* parameters, and serves as the main program.

Different LISP implementations require slightly different syntax for function definition. Among these are the following simple variations of the above:

```
(def name
   (lambda (parameters)
   e1 e2 . . . en))
(de name (parameters)
   e1 e2 . . . en)
name : (lambda (parameters)
   e1 e2 . . . en)
```

In these, the word "lambda" is a holdover from earlier versions of LISP, in which the syntax conformed more strictly with that of Church's lambda notation, from which LISP originated. Yet all of these versions serve the same purpose, and none is intrinsically superior to the others. We use the original form throughout this chapter, assuming that the reader will assimilate another variation if necessary.

At the heart of function definition is the idea of recursion. It is to LISP as the "DO statement" is to FORTRAN. Recursive function definition comes directly from mathematics, as illustrated in the following definition of the factorial function.

$$\text{factorial}(n) = 1 \quad \text{if } n \leqslant 1$$
$$= n \times \text{factorial}(n - 1) \quad \text{if } n > 1$$

As is evident, the definition of the factorial relies upon itself in order to be complete for any particular value of $n > 1$.

For instance, the factorial of 4 is dependent upon the prior calculation of the factorial of 3, and so forth. The process terminates when the factorial of 1 is reached, at which time each of the other calculations which were dependent upon it can now be completed. This function definition can be directly written in LISP, taking advantage of the fact that a function can invoke itself.

```
(defun fact (n)
   (cond ((lessp n 2) 1)
         (t (* n (fact (sub1 n)]
```

Here we have identified the parameter n, and defined "fact" via the conditional expression which is equivalent to the following Pascal-like expression:

if n < 2 **then** 1
else n * fact (n − 1)

In one case, the result returned will be 1, while in the other the result will be the calculation (* n (fact (sub1 n))), which reinvokes the function itself.

To invoke such a function, the same form is used as for LISP-provided functions:

```
(name arg1 arg2 . . . )
```

Here, ''name'' identifies the function and ''arg1 arg2 . . . '' is a series of expressions corresponding with the parameters in the function definition.

Thus, to compute the factorial of 4 we write ''(fact 4).'' The resulting evaluation will result in the subsequent expression

```
(* 4 (fact 3))
```

to be evaluated, which in turn will activate

```
(* 3 (fact 2))
```

and finally the following will be raised:

```
(* 2 (fact 1))
```

Now, four different invocations of ''fact'' are active, and the last one finally returns the value 1. This allows evaluation of the expression (* 2 1), and the result 2 is passed upward to the expression (* 3 2), and so forth until all activations are completed.

Two other simple recursive definitions appear in the sample program at the beginning of the chapter, one for the function ''sum'' and the other for the function ''count.'' Each one combines the list processing primitives ''car'' and ''cdr'' with numeric calculations to arrive at its intended result. Recursion is essential here because the *lengths* of the lists typically vary from one run to the next.

Reexamination of the function sum with the argument (87.5 89.5 91.5 93.5) shows that, since this argument is neither ''null'' nor an atom, the recursive invocation

```
(+ (car x) (sum (cdr x)))
```

is evaluated next. The complete series of invocations for this particular argument is summarized below:

Invocation	Argument (x)	(car x)	(cdr x)
1	(87.5 89.5 91.5 93.5)	87.5	(89.5 91.5 93.5)
2	(89.5 91.5 93.5)	89.5	(91.5 93.5)
3	(91.5 93.5)	91.5	(93.5)
4	(93.5)	93.5	nil
5	nil		

At this point, invocation 5 discovers that (null x) is true, so the result sent back to invocation 4 is 0. This chain continues in the following order:

Invocation	Result Returned	To invocation
5	0	4
4	(+ 93.5 0) = 93.5	3
3	(+ 91.5 93.5) = 185.0	2
2	(+ 89.5 185.0) = 274.5	1
1	(+ 87.5 274.5) = 362.0	original

Functions, Local Variables, and the Program Feature Although recursion is the primary device for defining LISP functions, some occasions require iteration and looping. Moreover, most functions require the use of local variables for temporary storage while carrying out their tasks. Either of these two requirements force the use of the "prog feature" within the function definition as follows:

```
(defun name (parameters)
  (prog (locals)
  e1 e2 . . . en
  ))
```

Here, the sequence of expressions e_1 . . . e_n may now include the go function, while "parameters" and "locals" have the same meaning as they did when originally introduced.

In many cases, the nature of the function definition forces *explicit* denotation of the result to be returned to the invocation. This is enabled by the "return" function, which has the following form within a function definition:

```
(return expression)
```

Here, "expression" denotes the value to be returned to the invoking expression and the return of control occurs immediately upon encountering this function. To illustrate, the following is an iterative rendition of the factorial function:

```
(defun fact (n)
(prog (i f)
  (setq f 1)
  (setq i 1)
loop (cond ((greaterp i n) (return f))
           (t ((setq f (* f i))
              (setq i (add1 i))
              (go loop))]
```

Here, we have locals f and i, both initialized to 1.The conditional statement labeled ''loop'' is repeated until i > n, at which time the resulting value of f is returned. Otherwise, the calculations

$$f := f * i$$
and $i := i + 1$

are made, and the test for i > n is repeated.

Although this example illustrates the use of the ''return'' function, the program feature, and iteration, it serves also to underscore the expressive superiority of recursion as a descriptive device in LISP.

9-2.8 Additional Features

Among the several additional features in LISP, the macro definition facility and the functions ''eval,'' ''mapcar,'' ''mapcan,'' and ''apply'' are perhaps the most important.

Macro Definition and Expansion The notion of a ''macro,'' in general, is one which allows a function to be automatically reinstantiated, or ''generated'' *in* line within the text of a program wherever it is needed. Macros have been an important tool of systems programmers for a long time, but their power has principally been utilized at the assembly language level.

In LISP, the macro provides an alternative to the function for the same purpose. A LISP macro definition has the following basic form:

(defun name macro (parameter)
  e_1 e_2 . . . e_n)

(Some implementations require a slightly different syntax than this, using ''dm'' for ''define macro'' instead of ''defun'' and ''macro.'' The reader should be able to assimilate these syntactic differences.) Here, ''name'' denotes the macro and ''parameter'' denotes a value that will be substituted into the expressions e_1, e_2, . . . , and e_n when the macro is expanded. The result of the expansion is then executed in line.

A macro is invoked just as if it were a function:

(name arguments)

But the action that takes place is not a transfer of control, as with a function, but instead is an in-line generation of program text, which is subsequently executed.

To illustrate, suppose we want to define a macro which simulates a **while** statement in another language; that is,

(while X Y)

should repeatedly execute Y until X becomes 0. The ''pattern'' of this loop will be as follows:

```
(prog ()
loop (cond ((greaterp X 0)
   (Y
   (setq X (sub1 X))
   (go loop)))))
```

That is, if X > 0 then Y is executed, X is decremented by 1, and the loop is repeated.

A macro named ''while'' can thus be defined with the above pattern as its body, and parameter P represents the whole macro invocation (while X Y), as follows:

```
(defun while macro (P)
   (subst (cadr P) 'X)
   (subst (caddr P) 'Y)
   '(prog ()
   loop (cond ((greaterp X 0)
      (Y
      (setq X (sub1 X))
      (go loop)))))
)
```

Here, the two ''subst'' functions replace the first and second arguments in the call for X and Y in the body of the macro definition, and then the body is executed. For instance, the following macro call repeats calculation of the factorial F of N, as long as the value of I is greater than 0.

```
(while I (setq F (* F I)))
```

The expansion of this macro invocation, which is executed, appears below.

```
(prog ()
loop (cond ((greaterp I 0)
   ((setq F (* F I))
   (setq I (sub1 I))
   (go loop)))))
```

Note that (cadr P) is I in this case and (caddr P) is (setq F (* F I)). This code thus compares with the iterative version of the factorial function presented in the previous section.

Eval, Mapcar, and Apply The macro facility is a device for temporarily suspending execution within a program while certain program statements are being automatically generated, or transformed. The same can be done in a more modest way using the ''eval'' function.

Eval is the opposite of "quote," in the following sense. If a variable X has the value (A B), then the expression

```
(list X 'C)
```

gives the result (A B C). However, the expression (list 'X 'C) forces X to be treated as an unevaluated literal, rather than a variable, so the result is (X C) instead.

When eval is applied to a quoted expression, it "undoes" the effect of the quote, and forces evaluation of the expression itself. Thus continuing with the above example,

```
(list (eval 'X) 'C)
```

again gives the result (A B C), since (eval 'X) is equivalent to the expression X in this context.

The function "mapcar" has the following general form:

```
(mapcar 'name 'args)
```

Here, "name" denotes the name of some function and "args" denotes a list of arguments to which the named function should be repeatedly applied, in turn. For example,

```
(mapcar 'sub1 '(1 2 3))
```

gives the resulting expression:

```
((sub1 1) (sub1 2) (sub1 3))
```

That is, the car is mapped, or copied, across the individual elements of the list, giving as a result a list of applications of the same function to different arguments.

The function "apply" is used to cause the repeated application of a function across a list of arguments, rather than just once to the number of arguments required by the function. Its general form is:

```
(apply function (arguments))
```

For example, suppose we want to compute the sum of the elements in the list (1 2 3). We can do this by writing

```
(apply '+ (1 2 3))
```

which is equivalent to the nested evaluation, (+ (+ 1 2) 3). Note that

```
(+ (1 2 3))
```

would not work, since "+" is strictly a function of numeric arguments.

9-3 APPLICATIONS OF LISP

Now that we have a thorough introduction to LISP, the next section evaluates its effectiveness in artificial intelligence (AI) programming. There, we apply LISP to Case Study 4—Missionaries and Cannibals, as described in Appendix D. Then we discuss several implementation-dependent features of LISP in section 9-3.2. Notably the overall differences between MACLISP and INTERLISP, the evolution of database tools for LISP, the LISP programming environment, and hardware which directly executes LISP programs, are discussed there. The chapter concludes with an overall evaluation of LISP in section 9-3.3.

9-3.1 LISP Case Study Implementation

The missionaries and cannibals problem was implemented on a VAX UNIX system in Franz Lisp, and on an IBM PC in IQLISP. The program was principally developed by Sergei Nirenburg for a course in AI at Colgate University.

The principal data structure for this problem is a queue of all paths from the starting state to the ending state. A ''state'' in this context is a record of the number of missionaries and cannibals on each bank, and a switch to tell whether the boat is on the left or the right bank. Each state is composed of two triples in a list as follows:

Left bank	Right bank
((M C B)	(M C B))

Here, M and C denote the number of missionaries and the number of cannibals on each bank, and B is 1 or 0 depending on whether or not the boat is on that particular bank. Thus, the original state of the game is

```
( (3 3 1) (0 0 0) )
```

with all the missionaries, cannibals, and the boat on the left bank. The desired final state is represented as

```
((0 0 0) (3 3 1))
```

As the game progresses, the queue grows each time a feasible state transition is found, and checks are made at each stage to see that no cannibalism takes place as a result of a state transition. The name of this queue in the program is q.

A single move, denoted by the variable ''onemove,'' is also given by a triple, which contains the number of missionaries in the boat, the number of cannibals in the boat, and the constant 1 denoting the boat itself. Thus, for instance, (1 1 1) denotes a move in which the boat contains 1 missionary and 1 cannibal.

The variable "history" contains a history of all states of the left bank which have already been tried earlier in the game. The variable "possibles" is a constant list containing all possible alternatives for "onemove"; that is, all possible combinations of missionaries and cannibals that can transit the river in one crossing.

The program consists of a principal function "mandc" and several auxiliary functions "eaten," "expand," "moveok," "move," and "display." Each of these is briefly documented in the text of the program, in Figure 9-5.

```
(defun mandc ()
 (prog (q history) ; initialize the queue and possible moves
     (setq possibles '((0 2 1)(0 1 1)(1 1 1)(1 0 1)(2 0 1)))
     (setq q (list (list (list '(3 3 1) '(0 0 0)))))

  repeat ; this loop is repeated until the left bank is empty
     (cond ((equal (caaar q) '(0 0 0))
            (return (display (reverse (car q)))))
          ; discard a path if either cannibalism occurs or
          ; the path represents a loop
            ((or (eaten (caar q)) (member (caaar q) history))
               (setq q (cdr q))
               (go repeat))
     )

     ; now add this state to the history and expand to the
     ; next state.
     (setq history (cons (caaar q) history))
     (setq q (append (expand (car q) possibles) (cdr q)))
     (go repeat)
]

(defun eaten (state)
     ; this function checks for cannibalism by looking at the
     ; left bank (car state).  There, if M is 1 or 2 and M ≠ C
     ; then there is cannibalism on one bank or the other.
     ; Otherwise, there is none.

     (and (or (equal (caar state) 1) (equal (caar state) 2))
          (not (equal (caar state) (cadar state))))
]

(defun expand (path possibles)
     ; this function develops all possible moves out of the
     ; current state.

     (cond ((null possibles) nil)
           ((moveok (car path) (car possibles))
              (cons (cons (move (car path) (car possibles)) path)
                    (expand path (cdr possibles))))
            (t (expand path (cdr possibles)))
]

(defun moveok (state onemove)
     ; here, we subtract the number of missionaries and
     ; cannibals in the boat from the number remaining on
     ; the current bank, to be sure that we don't take more
     ; than are there!

     (cond ((zerop (caddar state))   ; see if boat on right
              (subtractall (cadr state) onemove))
           (t  (subtractall (car state) onemove))
]
```

FIGURE 9-5

```
(defun subtractall (triple onemove)
     ; this function subtracts all three numbers in a
     ; single move of the boat from the contents of a bank,
     ; and returns nil if any one of the differences is < 0

     (not (minusp (apply 'min (mapcar '- triple onemove)
]

(defun move (state onemove)
     ; this function carries out a move by subtracting the
     ; numbers in a single move of the boat from one bank
     ; and adding them to the other.

     (cond ((zerop (caddar state))   ; check for boat on right
                (list (mapcar '+ (car state) onemove)
                      (mapcar '- (cadr state) onemove)))
           (t   (list (mapcar '- (car state) onemove)
                      (mapcar '+ (cadr state) onemove)))
]

(defun display (path)
     ; this function displays the resulting solution

     (cond ((null path) 'end)
           (t (print (car path))
              (terpri)
              (display (cdr path))
]
```

FIGURE 9-5 *(Continued)*

The program was run on the LISP implementations shown in Figure 9-6. The resulting performance is summarized in Figure 9-6.

FIGURE 9-6
EFFICIENCY OF LISP CASE STUDY 4 PROGRAM

Implementation	Compile speed	Execution speed
1 Digital VAX-750/UNIX Franz LISP	na	1.6 sec
2 IBM PC/DOS IQLISP	na	2.4 sec

9-3.2 Implementation-Dependent Extensions of LISP

Notable among the implementations of LISP are their different provisions of special functions, their handling of files and databases, and their different programming environments: debuggers, trace facilities, and editors. Here, we will briefly compare the features of INTERLISP and MACLISP in these respects, and then discuss the recent advent of "LISP machines."

INTERLISP and MACLISP The arithmetic and trigonometric functions and basic list construction and analysis functions are about the same between these two implementations. Yet, giving functions an incorrect number of arguments in INTERLISP does not raise an error; instead, missing arguments are filled in with nil and extra arguments are dropped in the evaluation. Thus, in INTERLISP,

```
(add1 x)
and (add1 x y z)
```

have the same effect, since the values of y and z will be ignored in the second function. MACLISP would raise an error for the second function.

Function definition has slightly different syntax in INTERLISP. There, the form is

```
(defineq ((name (parameters) expression)))
```

instead of the form used in MACLISP which we have used here:

```
(defun name (parameters) expression)
```

The predicates are about the same between MACLISP and INTERLISP as well. Minor differences appear in INTERLISP's restriction of "greaterp" and "lessp" to two arguments; MACLISP allows any number, in which case the maximum and minimum are obtained. Also, INTERLISP restricts "zerop" to numeric arguments, and the test for a *real* number zero must be given by the expression (equal number 0.0) rather than (zerop number).

In INTERLISP, "mapcar" reverses the order of function and arguments. Thus, (mapcar 'sub1 (1 2 3)) in MACLISP is written equivalently as (mapcar (1 2 3) 'sub1) in INTERLISP. A similar deviation occurs with the "putprop" function, while the MACLISP function "get" is written as "getprop" in INTERLISP.

INTERLISP only allows one-dimensional arrays to be defined by the "array" function, and the arguments here appear in a different order as well. MACLISP's "prin1" function is called "prin2" in INTERLISP. Macro definition and invocation facilities differ significantly between the two. Even comments are different with INTERLISP requiring comments to begin with "(*" and end with "*)."

Both implementations support run-time tracing, which is activated by the function "break" ("break1" in INTERLISP), but the ordering of the arguments here is also different between them. Both implementations also support string processing, but in completely different ways. The run-time environments for both systems are extensive, with interactive text editors, tracing, and program library facilities. Since LISP makes no differentiation between program and data, a program library can be managed in a manner similar to an on-line database.

As this brief comparison shows, the two major implementations of LISP—MACLISP and INTERLISP—differ so significantly that any effort to standardize the language would be very difficult. LISP programmers seem generally to be unconcerned about this, however, since one can always define the functions that are desired but are not provided by one's own implementation. However, this practice does not solve the problem of functions which share the same name in both implementations, but whose arguments and results are slightly different. To develop portability for these cases, an "intelligent" alteration of the program text itself, either by a person or by a program, is necessary.[9]

LISP Machines In the past few years, a significant development of hardware for AI research has occurred; this takes the form of so-called "LISP machines." These machines replace the traditional von Neumann type architecture with one which can directly evaluate LISP functions and programs. LISP primitives are directly executed, thus saving substantial time in execution. These machines are manufactured by several corporations, including Xerox and Symbolics, and provide powerful research tools for large AI experiments that are developed in LISP.

The power of the LISP machine is derived not only from its direct execution of LISP functions, but also from its provision of extensive tools for large database development (called "knowledge engineering"), graphics, text editing, and program libraries. In short, these machines have dispelled the old myth that "LISP is impractical because its programs run slowly and they are tedious to develop and debug."

9-3.3 Overall Evaluation of LISP

From our experience with LISP, we evaluate it in the artificial intelligence application area as follows:

1 Expressivity	Good
2 Well-definedness	Excellent
3 Data types and structures	Good
4 Modularity	Excellent
5 Input-output facilities	Poor
6 Portability	Fair
7 Efficiency	Good
8 Pedagogy	Fair
9 Generality	Poor

LISP's strength's appear to be its "well-definedness" and its "modularity." Its syntactic simplicity and nearly total reliance on recursion for its control structures leave a very "clean" semantic content. The absence of a dichotomy between "functions" and "procedures," which is distinct from other languages, seems to be an enhancement to modularity rather than a hindrance. Control of local and global variables is still in the programmer's hands, where it ought to be.

On the negative side, LISP's most serious weaknesses are its limited "input-output facilities" and its total lack of "generality." The former is undoubtedly compensated by the advent of LISP machine architectures with their strong support for database processing. The latter may not be viewed as a weakness, since LISP never pretended to be a general-purpose language. Mild weaknesses still persist for LISP in the areas of "pedagogy" (really good textbooks are just beginning to emerge, and the lack of a standard also encumbers teaching the language) and "portability." As long as AI programmers continue to use LISP strictly as a research tool, the problem of portability will not be a serious one. But the development of *production* systems in LISP is highly problematic unless some degree of standardization takes place.

EXERCISES

1 Let x, y, z, i, j, and k be variables with the following values:

```
x  =2.5       i = 1
y  = −10      j = −5
z = 8         k = 12
```

Compute the result delivered by evaluating each of the following expressions:

(a) (+ x (* y z))
(b) (* (+ x y) z)
(c) (− (/ (+ x y) z) 3)
(d) (+ x (/ y (− z 3)))
(e) (sub1 i)
(f) (greaterp i j)
(g) (* (/ i j) k)
(h) (cond ((equal i j) k) (t z))

2 Write a function named Max which will return the maximum value in a list, A, of numbers.

3 If your installation has a different LISP system than the ones used here, adapt our LISP Case Study 4 implementation to run under it. How difficult was that adaptation?

4 Implement Case Study 3—Text Formatter in LISP. Evaluate LISP as a text processing language from this experience.

5 Implement Case Study 0 (which you defined at the end of Chapter 1) in LISP. Evaluate LISP's performance and suitability for this application.

6 Consider implementing Case Study 1—Matrix Inversion in LISP. What are LISP's strengths for scientific applications such as this? What are its weaknesses?

7 Revise the averaging program given at the beginning of the chapter so that it averages only the *positive* numbers in the input, rather than all of them.

8 There is no dichotomy between a LISP program and its data. This facilitates the definition of the LISP interpreter itself, since a program can be considered as a special instance of a fully parenthesized list, in which the car of each sublist is a function name. On this basis try writing the eval function in LISP itself, assuming that programs are composed only of the primitive LISP functions car, cdr, cons, cond, atom, quote, and nil. Compare your result with that given in various LISP references and texts.

REFERENCES

1 John McCarthy, "Recursive Functions of Symbolic Expressions and their Computation by Machine: Part I," *Communications of the ACM* 3(4): 184–195 (1960).

2 Phyllis Fox, *LISP 1 Programmers Manual,* internal papers, MIT, Cambridge, Mass., 1960.

3 John McCarthy, et al., *LISP 1.5 Programmers Manual,* MIT Press, Cambridge, Mass., 1962.

4 David Moon, *MACLISP Reference Manual* (version 0), Laboratory for Computer Science, MIT, Cambridge, Mass., April 1974, revised 1978.

5 Warren Teitelman, *INTERLISP Manual,* Xerox PARC, Palo Alto, Calif. and BBN, Cambridge, Mass., 1974, revised 1978.

6 John K. Foderaro and Keith Sklower, *The Franz Lisp Manual: A Document in Four Movements,* University of California—Berkeley, April 1982.

7 Lars Ericson, "Translation of Programs from MACLISP to INTERLISP," MTR-3874, Mitre Corp., Bedford, Mass., November 1979.

8 J. B. Marti, et al., *Standard LISP Report,* University of Utah Symbolic Computation Group Report #60, Provo, Utah, 1978.

9 Ericson, op. cit.

CHAPTER **10**

LANGUAGE DESIGN: SEMANTICS

At the close of Chapter 6, the idea of a strong bond between language syntax and its run-time behavior, or ''semantics,'' was established. There, it was shown how the parse of an expression could be used to dictate the sequence of evaluation for its individual operations.

In this chapter, we take a more comprehensive view of programming language semantics, identifying major issues as well as their solutions in contemporary programming language implementations. The major categories of these issues are identified as follows:

- Types, binding, operators, and coercion
- Storage allocation
- Control structures
- Procedures and parameters
- Run-time environment

To motivate discussion of these issues, we begin the chapter by introducing a simple, yet representative model of computer organization, addressing, and instruction set. This, in turn, will be used throughout the remainder of the chapter to illustrate the implementation details related to the several semantic issues in programming language design.

10.1 A SIMPLE MACHINE AND NOTATIONAL MODEL

We assume that readers have had some experience with assembly language programming and computer organization, perhaps with a VAX, an IBM mainframe, or a microprocessor such as an 8086. The model and notation introduced here mirrors these types of machines but, for pedagogical reasons, is a simplification of the real machines.

In this model, we shall assume that main *memory* is composed of eight-bit bytes, addressed serially by decimal addresses. Moreover, we assume that there is a collection of 16 high-speed thirty-two-bit *registers* which are used primarily for addressing and arithmetic, and whose addresses are given by the symbols R0, R1, . . . and R15. We also assume the presence of a run-time stack, and the contents of its topmost bytes are addressed by STACK, STACK − 1, STACK − 2, and so forth. All this is pictured below.

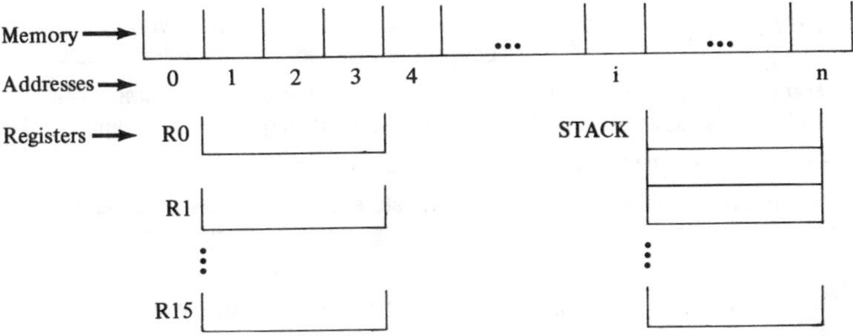

Adjacent bytes of memory are often grouped in twos, called "words," and fours, called "longwords." The following built-in data types are assumed for this machine model.

Type	Code	Memory (bytes)	Range of values
Binary integer	I	2	-2^{15} to $2^{15}-1$
Long integer	L	4	-2^{31} to $2^{31}-1$
Real (float)	E	4	$\pm 10^{75}$, six-digit precision
Double precision real	D	8	$\pm 10^{75}$, sixteen-digit precision
Address	A	4	0 to $2^{32}-1$
Boolean (logical)	B	1	**true, false**
Character (ASCII)	C	1	128-character ASCII set
Packed decimal	P	½ byte per decimal digit, plus ½ byte for sign, rounded to whole byte	

As shown, several of these elementary types require more than one byte, in which case they are referenced by the address of their leftmost byte. For pedagogical convenience, all memory addresses and their numeric contents will be shown in decimal notation, all characters will be written as they would be displayed, and all Boolean values will be written simply as **true** and **false**.

This machine's instruction set has the following two types of instructions:

(i) opcode operand
(ii) opcode operand1, operand2

Comments are designated by a leading semicolon (;) on the line. Otherwise, an instruction must have one of the above two forms. The ''opcodes'' for single-operand (type i) instructions are defined below.

Opcode	Meaning
B	Branch, or transfer to the address given by "operand."
CALL	Invoke the procedure whose first instruction is at the address given by "operand," and push the return address onto the top of the run-time stack.
RETURN	Transfer to the instruction whose address is at the top of the run-time stack, and pop that address from the stack into the location given by "operand."
PUSH	Push the value at the address "operand" onto the stack.
POP	Pop the value at the top of the stack and store it at the address "operand."

Opcodes of type ii, which have two operands, are summarized as follows:

Opcode	Meaning
ADD	Add the long integers at the addresses given by "operand1" and "operand2," storing the result at the longword addressed by "operand2."
SUB MUL DIV	Defined as for ADD.
MOV	Move the longword from "operand1" address to "operand2" address.
CMP	Compare the longword integers at "operand1" and "operand2" addresses, and set the STATUS byte (see next page) accordingly.
GETMAIN	Request from the operating system a block of main memory containing "operand1" contiguous bytes, and leave the address of its first byte in the longword addressed by "operand2."
FREEMAIN	Release to the operating system a block of storage defined by "operand1" and "operand2," as for GETMAIN.
CVTxy	Convert the value at address "operand1," of type x, to an equivalent value of type y, and store the result at address "operand2." Here, x and y may be any of the basic machine types summarized above (I, L, E, D, A, B, C, or P), as long as the conversion is a reasonable one. Conversion errors are noted in the STATUS byte, as described below. Conversion of variable length values (type C and P) is also described below.

The arithmetic instructions (ADD, SUB, MUL, DIV, CMP, MOV) also have variants for other types besides longword integers. These variants are specified by affixing the appropriate type code (I, E, D, B, or C) to the basic opcode. For example, we may specify sixteen-bit integer addition by ADDI, floating-point addition by ADDE, and so forth. In each case, the operand values taking part in the operation must *both* have the appropriate *type*.

The arithmetic and conversion instructions (CVTxy) sometimes apply to operand values which are of varying length (such as C and P type operands). In these cases, the internal representations are assumed to be preceded by a sixteen-bit integer value which gives the length of the operand in bytes. For example, the packed decimal representation of −21 occupies four bytes, and its "unpacked" representation as a character string occupies five bytes, two for the length and three for the value −21. This is assumed to be the direct result of a CVTPC operation, where "operand1" is the address of the packed decimal value and "operand2" is the address of the target character representation.

The STATUS byte is a special control location which is set by the system as certain instructions are executed, as summarized below.

Instruction	STATUS byte setting
ADD, SUB, MUL, DIV, CVT	0 = no exceptional conditions 1 = overflow (out of range for the given type) 2 = division by zero 3 = operand stored is not of the correct type
CMP	0 = operands equal 1 = operand1 < operand2 2 = operand1 > operand2 3 = operand stored is not of the correct type
PUSH, POP, GETMAIN, FREEMAIN	0 = no exceptional conditions 1 = stack overflow or underflow (PUSH or POP), or failure to complete GETMAIN or FREEMAIN

Concurrently, the following variants of the transfer (B) opcode are available, to realize conditional branching:

Opcode	Meaning
BOV	Transfer on overflow, stack overflow, GETMAIN or FREEMAIN error (STATUS = 1)
BZD	Transfer on zero divide (STATUS = 2)
BTY	Transfer on improper operand type (STATUS = 3)
BE, BZ	Transfer on equal or zero result (STATUS = 0)
BL	Transfer on less (STATUS = 1)
BG	Transfer on greater (STATUS = 2)
BLE	Transfer on less or equal (STATUS = 0 or 1)
BGE	Transfer on greater or equal (STATUS = 0 or 2)
BNE	Transfer on not equal (STATUS = 1 or 2)

"Operands" in this language are usually addressed by single symbols, each being a 1 to 8 letter sequence, such as A, B, LOOP, SUM, and so forth. Symbols are defined by their appearance in the left-hand margin of the program. A symbol may define a statement, for purposes of providing a branch point, by simply being placed in the left margin before the opcode of that statement. A symbol may define a storage area of a particular data type, possibly initialized by a particular value, in one of the following ways:

```
symbol   DS   nt
symbol   DC   ntv
```

Here, DS stands for "define storage without initializing its value," and DC stands for "define constant" (i.e., "define storage with initialization"). Also, n optionally denotes an integer repetition factor, t denotes the type, and v denotes the initial value to be stored. The value of t can be any of the built-in type codes described above, with the extra requirement that the length (in bytes) for character string (type C) and packed decimal storage (type P) must be affixed to t. The following examples illustrate these conventions:

Declaration	**Meaning**
X DS E	X is a real value.
A DS 5E	A is an array of five real values.
PI DC E3.14159	PI is a real constant with value 3.14159.
M DS C10	M is a character string of ten bytes.
M DC C'hello'	M is a five-byte character constant with value "hello."

Operands can also designate registers, using the special symbols R0 through R15, the run-time stack, using the special symbol STACK, and the following additional variations (where X may be any constant address number, symbol, register number, or STACK):

X = the contents of location X.

@X = the contents of the address given by location X (indirect addressing).

X+c (or X−c) = the contents of location displaced c bytes from location X, where c denotes an integer constant.

X(Ri) = the contents of location displaced from X by the contents of register Ri (i = 0, . . . , 15); that is, indexed addressing.

'string' = any literal character string.

#n = any literal integer value n.

No input-output provisions are included in this brief machine description; we assume that input-output provisions will be accomplished through an appropriate collection of macros, which will be introduced later in the chapter as needed. The basic machine language and underlying architecture are, in all other respects, reasonably complete. This will certainly be adequate to motivate the principles of programming language semantics in the remainder of this chapter.

10-2 TYPES, BINDING, OPERATORS, AND COERCION

The first semantic issue that arises when considering the implementation of programming languages is that of representation for the basic data types in the language. As we can see, our particular machine language directly supports most of the basic types in Pascal, FORTRAN, COBOL, and PL/I. This correspondence is, historically speaking, not accidental and is summarized in the table below.

Machine type	Corresponding type in . . . Pascal	FORTRAN	COBOL	PL/I
I—integer	**integer**	INTEGER*2	COMP	FIXED BIN (15)
L—long integer	na	INTEGER	COMP-1	FIXED BIN (31)
E—real	**real**	REAL	COMP-2	FLOAT DEC (6)
D—long real	na	DOUBLE PRECISION	na	FLOAT DEC (16)
A—address	reference	na	na	ADDR or POINTER
B—Boolean	**Boolean**	LOGICAL	na	BIT(1)
C—string	**array of char**	CHARACTER	PIC X	CHAR
P—packed decimal	na	na	COMP-3	FIXED DEC

Thus, the run-time storage requirements for languages in which variables are statically allocated can be determined using this type of correspondence as a basis. Moreover, since *all* variables in some languages (notably FORTRAN and COBOL) are statically allocated, run-time storage requirements and allocation can be completed at compile time. (Storage allocation for arrays, records, and list structures is treated separately in a later section.)

Storage Allocation for Character Strings and Decimal Numbers Since some convention must be adopted for representing the length of these varying length types, the language design must provide some way of specifying that length. Moreover, if the length of such a type is allowed to *vary* during execution, either a maximum length must be specifiable in the language or the implementation must be prepared to dynamically monitor storage allocation, fragmentation, and reclamation in a way which is transparent to the program. Explicit maximum length specification is supported in PL/I. SNOBOL, on the other hand, allows strings to vary completely, and thus assumes complete responsibility for dynamic storage management.

If a character string of maximum length n [as, for example, it is declared in PL/I as CHAR (n) VARYING] is needed, then our machine design requires a storage block of length n + 2 to be reserved. The first two bytes contain the string's current length, and the remaining bytes contain its current value. For instance, the string "HELLO THERE" would be stored as follows:

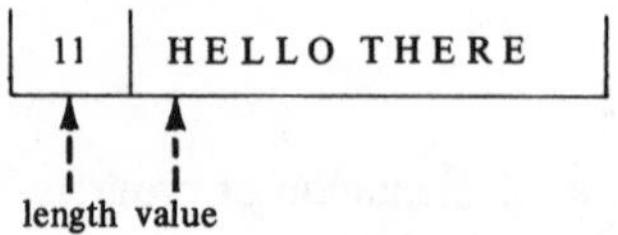

This requires a total of thirteen bytes. This type is supported directly in some extensions of Pascal (called **string**), FORTRAN, and COBOL, as well as in PL/I.

Strings can be allocated at run time in some languages, such as PL/I and SNOBOL. In this case, the compiler must have generated code to accomplish both of the following:

(i) Obtain an amount of storage which satisfies the variable's declared maximum length or initial value.

(ii) Initialize the value of that variable.

For example, suppose we write in PL/I the following code:

```
DCL S CHAR(25) VAR INIT ('HELLO');
```

At the time the procedure with this declaration is activated, the following machine code must be executed.

```
GETMAIN    #27,S            ; obtain 27 bytes for S
MOVI       #5,@S            ; initialize the length of S
MOVC       'HELLO',@S+2     ; initialize value of S
```

Thus, the following storage initialization for S will occur:

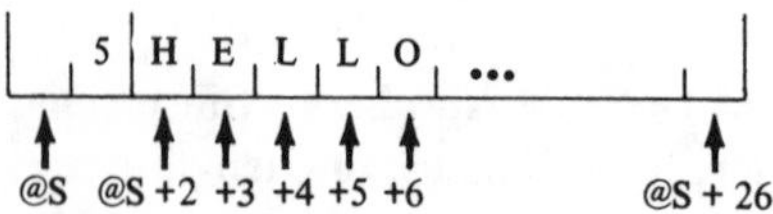

Now all subsequent references to this string will be made by the expression @S + 2, and all references to its length will be made by the expression @S.

Binding In its most general sense, the notion of "binding" suggests an act of associating a particular program element (such as a variable, a statement, or a procedure) with a particular semantic, or run-time property (such as a type, a block of storage, or a data value).

Some bindings take place when the program is written, such as the choice of a data type for a particular variable. Others take place when the program is compiled, such as the choice of machine instructions for a particular statement. Still others do not occur until run time, such as the allocation of storage for a local variable in a called procedure. Ultimately, we can view the time when the language is originally defined (usually taken for granted by the programmer) as perhaps the most significant binding time of all; at that time such elements as the set of all possible types, the set of statements and control structures, and so forth are selected and assigned exact syntactic representations and meanings.

For example, consider the particular binding of a variable, say I, to a storage location of *integer* type. In many languages (Pascal, FORTRAN, COBOL, PL/I) this is done when the program is written, either explicitly by declaration or implicitly by the ''I through N rule'' of FORTRAN. In SNOBOL, this binding doesn't take place until run time, since the type of a SNOBOL variable may vary as execution proceeds.

On the other hand, the binding of *integer* variable I to a particular location within the machine language program may take place either at compile time (as in PL/I's STATIC storage class, FORTRAN, and COBOL) or during execution (as in PL/I's other storage classes, Pascal's local variables, and all variables in the interpreted versions of SNOBOL, APL, and LISP). The former binding is commonly called ''static storage allocation,'' and languages which bind all variables in this way are called ''static languages.'' ''Dynamic storage allocation'' and ''dynamic languages'' are common designations for the latter binding method.

The binding of a variable to a value, of course, usually takes place at execution time, and typically occurs over and over again. However, initial values (as in PL/I's INIT attribute, FORTRAN's DATA specification, and COBOL's VALUE clause) are assigned at compile time.

One significant outcome of different binding times appears in Pascal's handling of the standard ''input'' file in batch and interactive environments. For batch input, the file is bound to the program at the *beginning* of execution, so that the presence of an empty file (flagged by the function ''eof'') is known at the outset of execution. For interactive input, the file is not bound until the first read statement is executed, so that an empty file cannot be detected until then. Thus, Pascal programming logic is significantly different when switching between batch and interactive input, and the reason is explained by the difference in binding times.

Operators and Coercion The first major divergence that takes place between a high-level language program and its machine implementation occurs in the semantics of arithmetic and value assignment. For example, the following Pascal assignment statement

```
A := B + 2 * C
```

will have several additional ''hidden'' operations beyond the addition, multiplication, and assignment which appear explicitly.

In the most straightforward interpretation of this statement, A, B, and C all denote

integer vaqriables, and its parse immediately suggests the following sequence of machine instructions:

```
MOVI #2,R1     ; R1 : = 2
MUL C,R1       ; R1 : = 2 * C
ADD B,R1       ; R1 := B + 2 * C
MOVI R1,A      ; A:= B + 2 * C
```

Here,the sequence of machine instructions is minimal, since all operands are the same type.

However, if we suppose even the slightest perturbation among the types of A, B, and C, the resulting machine code will grow in order to accommodate the necessary type conversions. That is, the compiler must insert appropriate CVTxy instructions and utilize temporary storage locations to meet the strict requirements of the machine arithmetic instructions. Moreover, it must insert appropriate run-time checks to assure that the inserted conversions take place without an intermediate error. All of this activity is known collectively as "coercion."

That is, "coercion" is the proper conversion of a data value of a particular type to an "equivalent" data value of another type, in order to satisfy the semantic constraints of the machine instruction set or the global context where that original value occurs. In the above assignment statement, the following kinds of coercions are possible:

Coercion	**Cause**
of B to **real**	B is **integer** and the value of 2 * C is **real**
of B + 2 * C to **real**	B + 2 * C is **integer** and A is **real**

These are the only two kinds of implicit coercion that can occur in Pascal, due to its *stringent constraints* on the types that an expression and left-hand variable can have. A language which imposes such constraints and their compile-time enforcement is called a "strongly typed" language.

To illustrate coercion for this Pascal example, assume that A and B are **real** variables, and C is an **integer** variable. Now the equivalent machine code appears as follows:

```
MOVI #2,R1        ; R1:= 2
MUL C,R1          ; R1:= 2 * C
CVTLE R1,R1       ; coerce 2 * C to real
ADDE B,R1         ; R1 := B + 2 * C
MOVE R1,A         ; A := B + 2 * C
```

The changes from the original version are underlined in this revision. As we can see, the **integer** product 2 * C must be converted to conform to the type of B, in order that the **real** addition (ADDE) and assignment (MOVE) instructions may be used in the next two steps. The fact that machine arithmetic operations require both operands to have the same type generally dictates the kind of coercions that are needed.

Automatic coercion does not take place only within arithmetic and assignment statements. Most languages perform it, for instance, whenever an input value is retrieved and its external type disagrees with that of the variable where it is to be stored. Typically, this is true of numbers which are entered in response to a read statement in Pascal. Thus,

```
read (X)
```

when executed will cause coercion of the character string of decimal digits, sign, and decimal point to an equivalent internal representation according to the type of X. If X is **real**, for instance, the following code will physically appear after the physical transfer of that character string from the keyboard to a BUFFER in memory:

```
CVTCE    BUFFER,X
BTY      ERROR
```

The first instruction converts the input BUFFER value to **real**, and the second checks to see that no error occurred in the process. Such an error will occur, for instance, when a character string is typed which does not properly represent a number, such as 22A.

Some languages such as PL/I take an *opposite* view from Pascal, and will permit type mismatches of all kinds within a program. These are called "weakly typed" languages, and experience shows that this philosophy tends to encourage questionable and potentially unreliable programming styles. In the PL/I rendition of the above assignment, for instance

```
A = B + 2 * C ;
```

we may have A declared as a character string, B as a bit string, and C as a **real** variable, in which case the following sequence of machine instructions is needed.

```
MOVE #2,R1      ; R1 := 2
MULE C,R1       ; R1 := 2 * C
CVTEB R1,R1     ; convert 2 * C to Boolean
BTY ERROR       ; check for success
OR B,R1         ; logical "or" of B with 2 * C
CVTBC R1,A      ; convert B + 2 * C to character
BTY ERROR       ; check for success
```

(Here, the underlined instruction was *not* defined for our machine, but is an entirely plausible candidate as an additional machine instruction.) The overall problem here, of course, is the inherent danger that weakly typed languages impose on the unsuspecting programmer. Errors tend to go unnoticed and unanticipated until run time, and then they are far more difficult to detect. The unrestricted use of such automatic coercion, therefore, increases programming "power" at the expense of explicitness and reliability in the language.

In the area of record input-output functions, *no* coercion takes place automatically. That is, when a record is transmitted to or from an external file, its constituent fields are retained in rigid form; any necessary coercion for subsequent processing must be given in a separate statement. The most prevalent example of this occurs in COBOL, as we recall from Chapter 4. There, the **DISPLAY** representation of a decimal numeric field in a file must be coerced explicitly to an equivalent internal representation, before it can subsequently participate in any arithmetic calculations. That coercion is usually done with a COBOL **MOVE** instruction.

10-3 STORAGE ALLOCATION

Allocation of storage for arrays, records, and linked lists is somewhat more complex than for scalar values, especially when it occurs at run time. In this section, we introduce the basic techniques and discuss the issues that are related to the allocation and addressing of values in such data structures.

Array Storage Allocation The problem of storage allocation for arrays is essentially one of mapping an n-dimensional structure to a one-dimensional contiguous sequence of memory locations, and thus defining the correspondence between a particular set of subscript values in the source language and its associated address in the machine language version.

In most languages, an array is an n-dimensional collection of values, all having the *same* type, and in each dimension an entry is referenced by an *integer* subscript within a predefined interval range. For example, the one-, two-, and three-dimensional arrays A, B, and C shown in Figure 10-1 may be declared in Pascal as follows:

```
var A: array [1..5] of integer;
    B: array [0..4, 0..3] of string[5];
    C: array [1..5, 1..4, 1..2] of real;
```

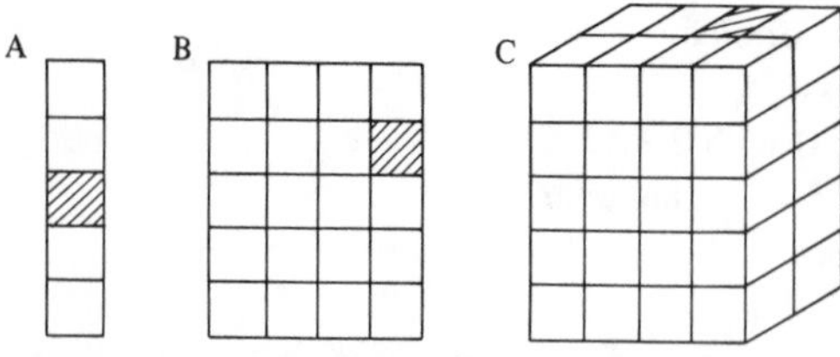

FIGURE 10-1

What varies from one of these arrays to the next?

Description of array	A	B	C
Its number of dimensions (n)	1	2	3
Its number of entries in each dimension ($k_1, k_2, \ldots, k_n$)	5	5, 4	5, 4, 2
Its subscript range in each dimension ($l_1 \ldots u_1, \ldots, l_n \ldots u_n$)	1 . . 5	0 . . 4, 0 . . 3	1 . . 5, 1 . . 4, 1 . . 2
Its type (number of bytes c in each entry)	**integer** (c = 2)	**string**[5] (c = 7)	**real** (c = 4)

These characteristics combine to *describe* an array in the form of its so-called "dope vector," or "array description record," whose general form is as follows:

<table>
<tr><td rowspan="2">address of
1st element</td><td rowspan="2">type</td><td rowspan="2">c</td><td rowspan="2">n</td><td rowspan="2">k1</td><td rowspan="2">•••</td><td rowspan="2">kn</td><td>l1</td><td rowspan="2">•••</td><td>ln</td></tr>
<tr><td>u1</td><td>un</td></tr>
</table>

This gives all the information needed to compute the address of an individual entry in any array. For instance, the dope vectors for the arrays A, B, and C declared above are given below.

<table>
<tr><td rowspan="2">address of
A[1]</td><td rowspan="2">integer</td><td rowspan="2">2</td><td rowspan="2">1</td><td rowspan="2">5</td><td>1</td></tr>
<tr><td>5</td></tr>
</table>

<table>
<tr><td rowspan="2">address of
B[0,0]</td><td rowspan="2">string[5]</td><td rowspan="2">7</td><td rowspan="2">2</td><td rowspan="2">5</td><td rowspan="2">4</td><td>0</td><td>0</td></tr>
<tr><td>4</td><td>3</td></tr>
</table>

<table>
<tr><td rowspan="2">address of
C[1, 1, 1]</td><td rowspan="2">real</td><td rowspan="2">4</td><td rowspan="2">3</td><td rowspan="2">5</td><td rowspan="2">4</td><td rowspan="2">2</td><td>1</td><td>1</td><td>1</td></tr>
<tr><td>5</td><td>4</td><td>2</td></tr>
</table>

The dope vector also contains sufficient information to determine, for a given set of subscript values, whether or not they are properly within the allowable range for the array as declared. This information is given by $l_i \ldots u_i$ for each dimension i.

Two pertinent issues govern the binding of an array's dope vector and the formula which is used to allocate the addresses to individual entries. In the first place, the binding of an array's dope vector cannot be done until its dimensionality is known. In some languages, like FORTRAN, Pascal, and COBOL, this is known at compile time; array declarations are required to have *constant* bounds. In others, like PL/I, SNOBOL, and

APL, an array's bounds are not known until run time. For example, PL/I permits the declaration

DCL A(N);

which, at run time, specifies an N-element array A, and N is a variable whose value is not known until just before this declaration is encountered. Thus, in this case, the dope vector for A must be dynamically assigned its values, and the array's storage must be dynamically allocated.

The second issue to be resolved before address calculation for an array entry becomes well defined is the choice of *ordering* for the array's entries in memory. For a one-dimensional array, this presents no problem; the entries are arranged, in increasing order of subscript values, in successive bytes of storage. For example, our array A declared above would be allocated, with two bytes per entry, as follows:

A[1]
A[2]
A[3]
A[4]
A[5]
addr(A[1]) + 0
+2
+4
+6
+8

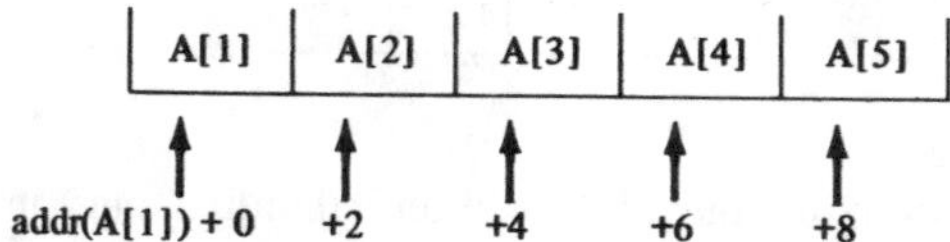

Note here that the *displacements* of successive entries in A occur in increments of two bytes, since each entry must accommodate an *integer* value.

For higher dimensional arrays, either of two alternative strategies for storage allocation is employed: "row-major" order or "column-major" order. Most languages use the former, but some (including FORTRAN) use the latter. Row-major order means simply that the array is stored so that each row occupies a contiguous block of storage. In column-major order, each column is stored contiguously instead.

To illustrate, the following diagram shows how B, declared above, would be stored in row-major order:

B[0, 0]
B[0, 1]
B[0, 2]
B[0, 3]
B[1, 0]
•••
B[4, 3]
addr (B[0,0]) + 0
+7
+14
+21
+28
+133

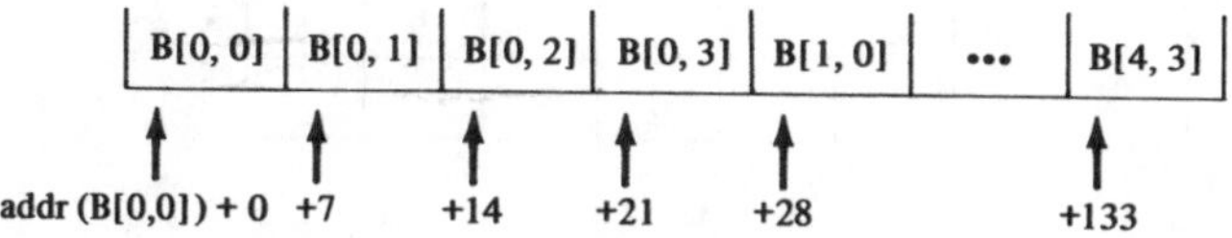

By contrast, the column-major allocation of B would result in the following:

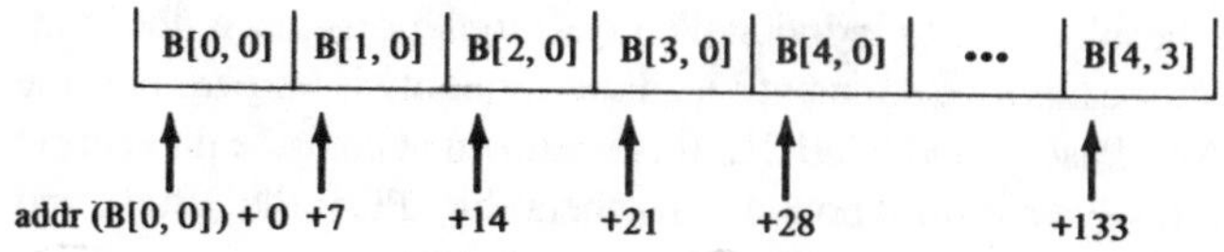

B[0, 0]
B[1, 0]
B[2, 0]
B[3, 0]
B[4, 0]
•••
B[4, 3]
addr (B[0, 0]) + 0
+7
+14
+21
+28
+133

The three-dimensional array C declared above would use a similar strategy. Below is its storage representation in row-major order.

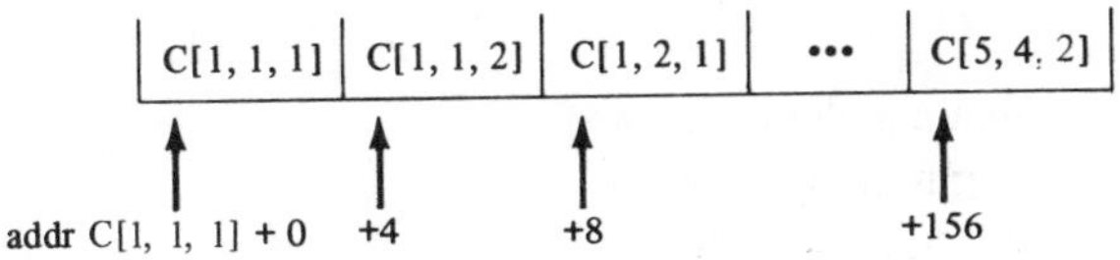

C[1, 1, 1]	C[1, 1, 2]	C[1, 2, 1]	•••	C[5, 4, 2]
addr C[1, 1, 1] + 0	+4	+8		+156

The pattern should now be clear. For a one-dimensional array, say a, the address of its ith element a_i is calculated as:

$$\text{addr}(a_i) = \text{addr}\,(a_{l_1}) + c(i - l_1)$$

Here, the meanings of l_1 and c are the same as in the dope vector, namely the lower bound of the subscript range and the number of bytes for each entry, respectively.

For two- and three-dimensional arrays, stored in row-major order, the calculations are as follows:

$$\text{addr}\,(a_{ij}) = \text{addr}(a_{l_1 l_2}) + c[(i - l_1)k_2 + (j - l_2)]$$
$$\text{addr}(a_{ijk}) = \text{addr}(a_{l_1 l_2 l_3}) + c[((i - l_1)k_2 + (j - l_2))k_3 + (k - l_3)]$$

For an n-dimensional array in row-major order, the address of $a_{i_1 i_2 \ldots i_n}$ is calculated in the following general way:

$$\text{addr}(a_{i_1 i_2 \ldots i_n}) = \text{addr}(a_{l_1 l_2 \ldots l_n}) + c[(\ldots((i_1 - l_1)\text{k}_2 + (i_2 - l_2))\text{k}_3 + \ldots + (i_n - l_n))]$$

For example, let us compute the particular addresses of entries A[4], B[4, 2], and C[2, 1, 1], for the arrays declared above, using these formulas:

$$\text{addr(A[4])} = \text{addr(A[1])} + 2(4 - 1) = \text{addr(A[1])} + 6$$
$$\text{addr(B[4, 2])} = \text{addr(B[0, 0])} + 7[(4 - 0)4 + (2 - 0)]$$
$$= \text{addr(B[0, 0])} + 126$$
$$\text{addr(C[2, 1, 1])} = \text{addr(C[1, 1, 1])} + 4[((2 - 1)4 + (1 - 1))2 + (1 - 1)]$$
$$= \text{addr(C[1, 1, 1])} + 32$$

The reader should check that these calculations yield the same displacements as shown for these particular entries in the foregoing diagrams for A, B, and C.

Implementation of an array therefore involves three separate steps: (1) allocation and assignment of values to the dope vector, (2) allocation of storage for the array itself, and (3) calculation of a displacement, or index value, for an array element when given a set of subscripts. Optionally, a fourth provision is advised; generation of a run-time check for subscripts out of range. In the worst case, all four of these steps must be deferred until run time. To illustrate, let us show the machine code needed for each of these four steps, considering the array B declared above.

1 Allocation and initialization of the dope vector for B.

```
GETMAIN #40,BDOPE     ; obtain a block of storage
MOV #7,@BDOPE+8       ; length of an entry (c)
MOV #2,@BDOPE+12      ; no of dimensions (n)
MOV #5,@BDOPE+16      ; no of rows (k1)
MOV #4,@BDOPE+20      ; no of columns (k2)
MOV #0,@BDOPE+24      ; lower bound (l1)
MOV #4,@BDOPE+28      ; upper bound (u1)
MOV #0,@BDOPE+32      ; lower bound (l2)
MOV #3,@BDOPE+36      ; upper bound (u2)
```

2 Allocation of storage for B itself, after calculating the amount of storage needed (c * k1 * k2).

```
MOV @BDOPE+16,R1
MUL @BDOPE+20,R1
MUL @BDOPE+8,R1
GETMAIN R1,BDOPE        ; addr(B[0,0]) -> BDOPE
```

3 Calculation of the address of B[I, J], given variables I and J, whose values are assumed to already exist.

```
MOVI I,R1
SUB @BDOPE+24,R1      ;I - l1
MUL @BDOPE+20,R1      ;(I - l1) * k2
MOVI J,R2             ;J - l2
SUB @BDOPE + 32,R2
ADD R1,R2             ;(I - l1) * k2 + (J - l2)
MUL @BDOPE+8,R2       ;c * [(I - l1) * k2 + (J - l2)]
ADD @BDOPE,R2         ;c * [(I - l1) * k2 + (J - l2)] + addr(B[0, 0])
```

Now the address of B[I, J] is in register R2, ready for use by whatever instruction referenced it.

4 Check that the subscripts I and J are within the bounds $l_1..u_1$ and $l_2..u_2$, respectively, and transfer to ERROR if not.

```
CMP  I,@BDOPE+24
BL   ERROR            ;I < l1
CMP  I,@BDOPE+28
```

```
BG     ERROR              ; I > u1
CMP    J,@BDOPE+32
BL     ERROR              ; J < l2
CMP    J,@BDOPE+36
BG     ERROR              ; J > u2
```

Step 3 is usually implemented in a more optimal form, recognizing that the address calculation formula can be rewritten using a smaller number of arithmetic operations at run time. This is critical to the efficiency of large mathematical programs which, typically, execute thousands of array references in a single run. For a two-dimensional array, the constant terms may be gathered and the address calculation rewritten as follows:

$$addr(a_{ij}) = addr(a_{l_1 l_2}) + c * (k_2 * i + j) - c * (k_2 * l_1 + l_2)$$

Now the first and third terms are constant, and their sum can be calculated and stored in the dope vector at the time that vector is developed. The remaining run-time calculations are thus reduced to *two* multiplications and *two* additions, which compares favorably with the above run-time code. More significant savings of this kind can be realized for higher dimensioned arrays.

Record Structures Storage allocation and addressing for a structure is somewhat different than for an array; the total amount of storage needed for a record is the *sum* of that required for each of its constituents, all of which typically have different types. The *order* in which storage is allocated to the elementary items in a structure is defined by the textual order of their appearance in the record declaration. The *displacement* of a particular element from the beginning of a structure is calculated as the sum of the respective lengths, in bytes, of all elements which precede it in the declaration. To illustrate, reconsider the structure discussed in the Pascal, COBOL, and PL/I chapters, as shown in Figure 10-2. This can be declared in PL/I as follows:

```
DCL 1 PERSON,
        2 NAME,
          3 FIRST CHAR(10),
          3 MIDDLE CHAR(5),
          3 LAST CHAR(10),
        2 SS# PIC '9(9)',
        2 GROSS FIXED DEC (7,2),
        2 ADDRESS,
          3 STREET CHAR(17),
          3 CITY CHAR(12),
          3 STATE CHAR(6),
          3 ZIP PIC '99999';
```

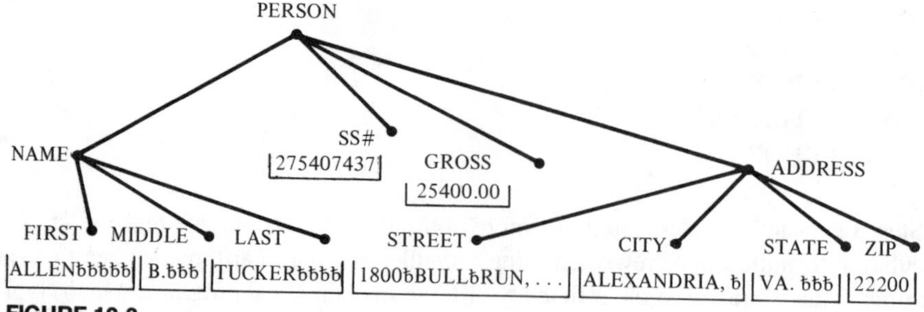

FIGURE 10-2

Storage allocation for this structure takes place as follows:

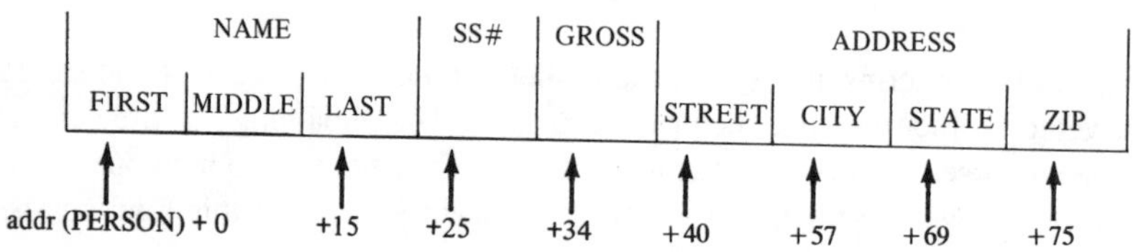

Thus, the total *record length* is eighty bytes, a number that is used to determine, for example, the buffer size for input-output transfer of such records to external files.

In some machines, storage allocation for records is complicated by *boundary alignment* requirements for certain types of fields. Integers and reals, for instance, may be required to be aligned on addresses which are even multiples of two and four bytes, respectively. To accomplish this, one or more "padding bytes" must sometimes be inserted before such fields in order to maintain proper alignment. Consider, for example, the following Pascal declaration for an airline flight record and variable F.

```
type flight = record
      airline: string[9];
      number: integer;
      price: real
   end;
var F: flight;
```

Storage allocation for F, with padding byte shaded, is shown below.

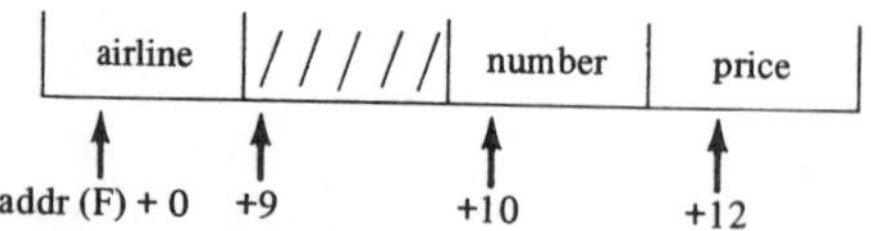

The total number of bytes for the record, therefore, is fifteen rather than the optimal fourteen, due to the extra padding byte inserted before the F.number field.

Such machine-dependent restrictions can encumber portability of programs, unless the programmer is circumspect enough to anticipate *all* future implementations (not a likely possibility) where the program will eventually run. It should be evident, in this case and others like it, that the automatic insertion of padding bytes can be completely avoided by systematic rearrangement of the record's fields, or else by explicit insertion of ''dummy'' fields within the record type declaration itself. The latter is usually a preferred solution, since the former usually results in a rearrangement which destroys, on an intuitive level, the best ordering among the fields.

Dynamic List Structures Dynamic list structures occur regularly in such languages as Pascal, PL/I, SNOBOL, LISP, and Ada. They are not included in FORTRAN or COBOL, since traditional scientific and data processing applications have limited use for dynamic lists.

The implementation of dynamic lists depends upon (1) a representation scheme for pointers, (2) a method for dynamically allocating and freeing blocks of storage for individual nodes in the list, and (3) a strategy for automatically reclaiming storage that has been released by the program when all other available storage is occupied. The latter strategy is called ''garbage collection,'' and is a common element of languages like SNOBOL and LISP, which provide no explicit storage management facilities to the program itself.

In this section, we shall concentrate on the run-time representations for (1) and (2) above, and illustrate the machine representation of some simple Pascal and PL/I list processing statements at run time. Recall, for this discussion, the program ''lister'' shown in section 2-2.8 (Pascal). The run-time representation for the list shown in Figure 2-11 can be described as follows:

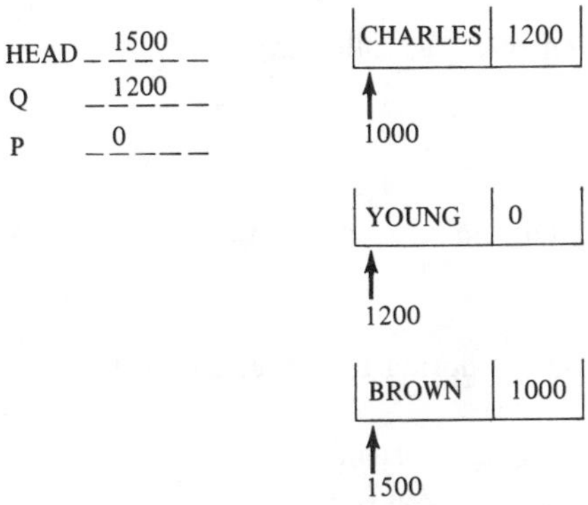

```
HEAD   1500          | CHARLES | 1200 |
Q      1200          ^
P      0             1000

                     | YOUNG   | 0    |
                     ^
                     1200

                     | BROWN   | 1000 |
                     ^
                     1500
```

Here, the pointers HEAD, Q, P, and FPTR (in all three nodes on the right) are actually implemented as *addresses,* and the individual nodes of the list are in noncontiguous, and randomly addressed blocks of storage. Each node is a 21-byte storage block obtained by a GETMAIN machine instruction. The addresses 1000, 1200, and 1500 are arbitrarily assigned addresses, assumed to be obtained from the three executions of GETMAIN. By convention, the **nil** pointer is represented by the distinct address 0.

Following these conventions, we can assimilate the implementation of individual list processing instructions. The two Pascal instructions,

```
new (P);
head := P
```

are implemented in the following machine language statements:

```
GETMAIN #21,P
MOV P,HEAD
```

Assignment to a field within the node addressed by P, such as the NAME field, with a value such as 'BROWN', is done with indirect addressing:

```
MOVC 'BROWN', @ P
```

Here, the correspondence between indirect addressing (@) and the notion which a Pascal pointer conveys is immediate. Finally, the link from a node to its successor in the list is done with the following sequence, with the corresponding Pascal statements shown on the right as comments:

```
MOV P,Q              ; q := p
GETMAIN #21,P        ; new (p)
MOV P,@Q+17          ; q ↑ . fptr := p
```

The freeing of a node is also immediately implemented, as follows:

```
FREEMAIN #21,P       ; dispose (p)
```

This brief illustration exposes two problems that can occur during development of a list processing program.

1 It's impossible to meaningfully trace variables during the execution of list processing programs.

2 A node or segment of a linked list can become "lost in space" (i.e., have no pointer which references it), even though it has not yet been freed.

The first problem occurs simply because a pointer is nothing more than an address, and that address has no intuitive meaning to the programmer, as would, for example, the value of an **integer** or **real** variable.

The second problem can occur as a result of any number of anomalies within the program logic, such as the following Pascal sequence:

new (p);
p := **nil**

The second statement "disconnects" pointer p from the node just allocated, leaving no way of subsequently referencing or disposing of it. Yet that node perpetually occupies a storage block, until either the program terminates or *all* available space becomes occupied.

In this last event, the next execution of a "new" statement will interrupt execution. Short of aborting the program, the system may be equipped to perform "garbage collection" at this point. That is, a systematic sweep of all allocated storage blocks is made, and those which are referenced by *no* pointer can be reclaimed. Thus, nodes in our list which had become "lost in space" are now freed, and program execution can resume normally.

Garbage collection is especially important in languages where the programmer has no direct control over the allocation and freeing of storage, such as LISP and SNOBOL. Other languages, like PL/I and Pascal, leave this responsibility to the programmer and typically provide no automatic garbage collection facility. Since this is a complex subject in general, readers are referred to other texts for a more thorough discussion of various garbage collection strategies and algorithms. Case Study 5—Job Scheduler includes a simple garbage collection scheme (see Appendix E), in the context of an operating systems programming problem.

10-4 CONTROL STRUCTURES

Since machine languages do not embody the control structures found in high-level languages, such as **if . . . then . . . else**, **while**, and **for**, these must be simulated using different combinations of the lower-level compare and branch instructions. Compilers typically generate a "template," or pattern of machine instructions corresponding to each of each of these control structures. For our machine, these templates are as follows:

Control structure		Template	
if [b] **then** [s]		CMP	[b], **true**
		BNE	$L0001
		[s]	
	$L0001		
if [b] **then** [s1]		CMP	[b], **true**
else [s2]		BNE	$L0001
		[s1]	
		B	$L0002
	$L0001	[s2]	
	$L0002		

Control structure	Template		
for i := e1 **to** e2		MOV	e1, i
do s	$L0001	CMP	i, e2
		BG	$L0002
		s	
		ADD	#1,i
		B	$L0001
	$L0002		
while b **do** s	$L0001	CMP	b,**true**
		BNE	$L0002
		s	
		B	$L0001
	$L0002		
case i **of**		CMP	i, v1
v1: s1;		BNE	$L0002
v2: s2;		s1	
:		B	$L000_{n+1}$
vn: sn	$L0002	CMP	i,v2
end		BNE	$L0003
		s2	
		B	$L000_{n+1}$
	$L000_n$	CMP	i,vn
		BNE	$L000_{n+1}$
		sn	
	$L000_{n+1}$		

In these templates, the boxed elements denote expressions or statements which need to be further expanded into machine code, and the labels $L0001, $L0002, etc., denote *compiler-generated* symbols which are needed as branch points for other instructions in the template. Thus, these templates are like ordinary assembly language macros, and each is "expanded" in line by the compiler as the corresponding control structure is encountered in the source language.

10-5 PROCEDURES AND PARAMETERS

Perhaps the primary control structure in programming language design is the "procedure invocation." It forms the basis for the subsequent development of modular programming and structured design concepts, and these are basic tools in any advanced software engineering project in all application areas. From a language design point of view, there are two major issues involved in procedure invocation.

1 Linkage of control
2 Linkage of parameters and arguments

We discuss these issues separately in the two sections that follow.

Linkage of Control between Procedures When a procedure is invoked, a link back to the point of invocation, or "return point," must be established. This corresponds to the "return address" in machine language parlance. In addition, all local variables declared within the procedure, if they are dynamic, must be allocated memory space and initialized as appropriate.

In order to implement these steps, a "run-time stack" is presumed; each time a procedure is invoked, or activated, a so-called "activation record" is pushed onto the stack. Concurrently, whenever the procedure returns control to the invoking procedure, the topmost activation record is popped off the stack. Thus, at any point during execution, a run-time image of the hierarchy of all active procedures is obtained by examining the series of activation records which comprise the run-time stack. In our machine language, a run-time stack is already provided. In others, the run-time stack may not be provided, and therefore must be simulated.

The contents of an activation record can be defined as follows:

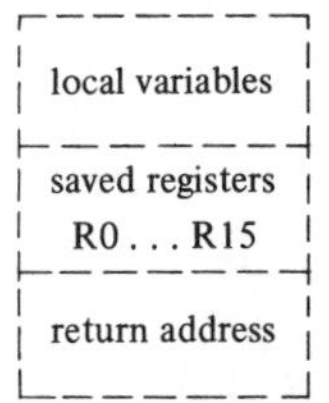

Here, we have added provisions for saving the contents of registers R0 . . . R15 so that the procedure may freely reuse them, as well as local variables. These values will be restored into the registers upon return from the procedure.

Thus, the procedure invocation can be implemented as

CALL name

where "name" is the symbolic address of the first executable instruction in the procedure. At the time this is executed, the return address is automatically pushed onto the run-time stack, thus initiating a new activation record. The remaining parts of the activation record are stored immediately by the first few instructions of the procedure itself. That is, the "entry sequence" in the procedure must:

1 Push the registers R0 . . . R15 onto the stack.
2 Push and initialize its local variables on the stack.

Following this sequence is the procedure body itself, and finally the "return sequence" systematically deletes its activation record from the stack and restores the register contents for the invoking program. Thus, the following steps:

1 Pop the local variables from the stack.
2 Restore the registers R0 . . . R15 from the stack.
3 RETURN to the invoking procedure (and simultaneously pop the return address from the stack).

To illustrate these conventions, consider the following Pascal program and procedures:

```
Address
------------------------------------------------
              program P;
                  var i,j: integer;
                  procedure Q;
                      var j,k: integer;
                      procedure R;
                          var i,k: integer;
                          begin
 1                            writeln('enter & exit R')
                          end;
                      begin
 2                        writeln('enter Q');
 3                        R;
 4                        writeln('exit Q')
                      end;
                  procedure S;
                      var i,j: integer
                      begin
 5                        writeln('enter S');
 6                        Q;
 7                        writeln('exit S')
                      end;
                  begin
 8                    writeln('enter P');
 9                    S;
10                    writeln('exit P')
                  end.
```

For simplicity, the addresses here are assigned to executable instructions in the order in which they appear, and we have temporarily ignored the fact that each of these Pascal instructions corresponds to a sequence of machine instructions which takes *several* bytes rather than just one. The principles of procedure linkage, however, are not affected by these simplifications.

The sequence of procedure activations for this program thus occurs chronologically as follows:

Address	Activated	Output	Run-time stack actions
8	P	enter P	PUSH locals (i,j)
9	S		CALL S (push 10)
			save registers from P
5		enter S	PUSH locals (i,j)
6	Q		CALL Q (push 7)
			save registers from S
2		enter Q	PUSH locals (j,k)
3	R		CALL R (push 4)
			save registers from Q
1		enter & exit R	PUSH locals (i,k)
			POP locals (i,k)
			restore registers for Q

Address	Activated	Output	Run-time stack actions
4	Q		RETURN
		exit Q	POP locals (j,k)
			restore registers for S
7	S		RETURN
		exit S	POP locals (i,j)
			restore registers for P
10	P		RETURN
		exit P	POP locals (i,j)

In the middle of this sequence of events, when procedure R is activated,the run-time stack contains the following activation records:

R's activation record	locals i, k registers from Q return address (4)
Q's activation record	locals j, k registers from S return address (7)
S's activation record	locals i, j registers from P return address (10)
P's activation record	locals i, j

It should be clear that this run-time organization accommodates two other language properties as well:

1 The notion of scope and block structure
2 Recursion

As we can see, the scope of all local variables declared within a procedure is automatically delimited. All references to i and k in procedure R, for instance, are resolved by looking at R's activation record. However, references to global variables are *not* always resolved by a straightforward search into the stack. For example, suppose that we want to reference global variable i from procedure Q. A direct search of the stack from the top will yield the variable i declared in S, before it will reach the variable i declared in P, which would be the correct choice.

The point here is that the *static* structure of nested procedures defines the scope of variables, while the *dynamic* structure is not always the same. How, then, can a global variable's scope be properly represented at run time? The solution lies in the syntactic analysis of the program, when the static structure of the program is actually present. At that time, each reference to a global variable can be qualified by an explicit denotation of the procedure in which it was declared. Thus, a reference to, say, i within Q will be tagged as a reference to i.P (i.e., that version of i declared in P) rather than i.S. Thus, at run time, a search of the stack will continue until we reach the activation record for P and thereby locate the correct instance of i.

The second advantage of the run-time stack lies in its support of recursion. We shall illustrate this in the next section, after introducing the implementation of parameter linkage.

Linkage of Parameters and Arguments When invoking a procedure or function, a number of arguments may be passed, and these correspond one for one with the parameters in the procedure's declaration. Parameters divide into three distinct classes, according to their use in the procedure.

- *Input parameters* supply values to the procedure or function.
- *Output parameters* deliver results from the procedure or function. In most languages, the function's name itself plays the role of ''distinguished output parameter.'' All other output parameters in a function are usually classified as side effects.
- *Input-output parameters* supply values to *and* deliver results from the procedure or function. Typically, an array parameter for a sort procedure has this characteristic.

Different languages support these alternatives in different ways. Some strictly enforce proper usage, in the sense that each argument corresponding to an input parameter not be altered within the body of the procedure, and each argument corresponding to an output parameter must be so altered. Other languages pass this responsibility completely to the programmer.

Moreover, particular implementation alternatives for these different classes of parameters exist, and are summarized below. Here, *p* denotes a particular parameter, *a* denotes its corresponding argument, and *f* denotes the procedure or function itself.

1 **Call by value.** At the time of the invocation, the argument *a* is evaluated, and that value is *copied* into a local storage area corresponding to the parameter *p*. That area is used by all references to *p* during the execution of *f*, and it is destroyed (along with all other local variables) when that invocation terminates.

2 **Call by reference.** At the time of invocation, the argument *a* becomes a *synonym* for the parameter *p*, and all references to *p* within *f* are effectively references to the storage area for *a* itself. Argument *a*, in this case, *must* be a simple variable, array, or structure name whose type agrees with that of *p*.

3 **Call by name.** Here, the expression *a* is *unevaluated* at the time of invocation, and instead it literally replaces all instances of *p* as a *textual portion* of the source program. The resulting text of *f* can then be (interpretively) executed.

4 **Call by value-result.** This is a kind of double-ended call by value, since the value of *a* is stored in a local storage area for *p* at the *beginning* of the invocation, and the final value of that area is copied back to the variable *a* at the *end* of the invocation.

Not all of these conventions can be illustrated in a single language, so we assume for the moment a pseudo-Pascal, in which all four choices can be specified. The reserved words **value**, **var**, **name**, and **value-result**, respectively will be used to designate these four linkage conventions.

Consider the following procedure Sigma, which computes the sum of all n elements of an array A:

```
procedure Sigma (value A: array; value n: integer; var Sum: real);
  var i: integer;
  begin
    Sum := 0;
    for i := 1 to n do
      Sum := Sum + A[i]
  end;
```

As a general rule, **value** corresponds to strictly input parameters and **var** corresponds to strictly output parameters. An exception usually occurs with input arrays, which are often declared as **var** parameters to avoid unnecessarily copying a large array into a temporary location; time and space are wasted.

Thus, the following invocation

Sigma (B,5,Bsum)

when B has the values

7	3	9	8	4

will result in the following parameter linkages.

(i) The values of B and 5 are copied into locals associated with parameters A and n.

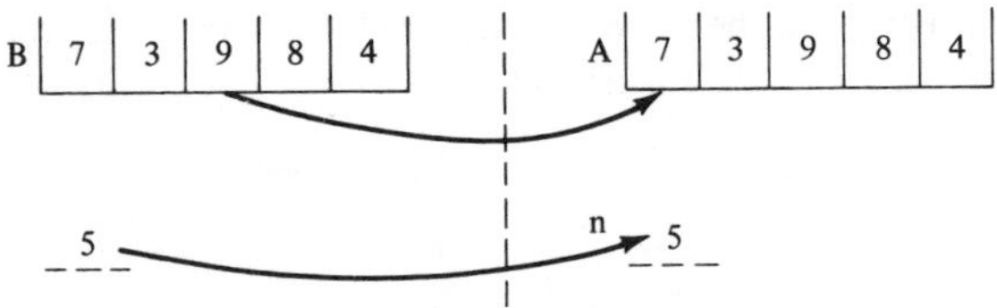

(ii) The parameter Sum is made synonymous with the argument Bsum.

Bsum ------ ←→ Sum

Now the procedure is executed, and all effects on the parameter Sum are actually taking place within the storage location for Bsum, its synonym.

Bsum ~~7~~ ~~10~~ ~~19~~ ~~27~~ 31 ⟷ Sum

Finally, all local variables, together with the storage areas created for A and n, are destroyed and control reverts to the invoking procedure with the result remaining in Bsum.

With this illustration, it is clear that any *output* parameter *must* be called by reference. If called by value, its computed result will be left in a local storage area, which is subsequently lost upon return from the procedure.

To illustrate call by name, consider the following *different* rendition of the Sigma procedure (this illustration is attributed to Jensen, and is often referred to as "Jensen's device"):

```
procedure Sigma (name A; var i: integer;
                    value n: integer; var Sum: real);
  begin
    Sum := 0;
    for i := 1 to n do
      Sum := Sum + A
  end;
```

Now, consider the following invocation, which is designed to have the same effect as the one above:

Sigma (B[i], i,5,Bsum)

Here, the dynamics of n and Sum are the same as before, but now we are passing a description of the "general element" B[i] and an "explicit argument" i to be used as the subscript. The critical change here is the designation of parameter A as "call by name." The effect for this invocation is to replace all instances of the name A in the *text* of the procedure by the expression B[i], and then execute the resulting text. Thus, for this call, we have the following associations and resulting text:

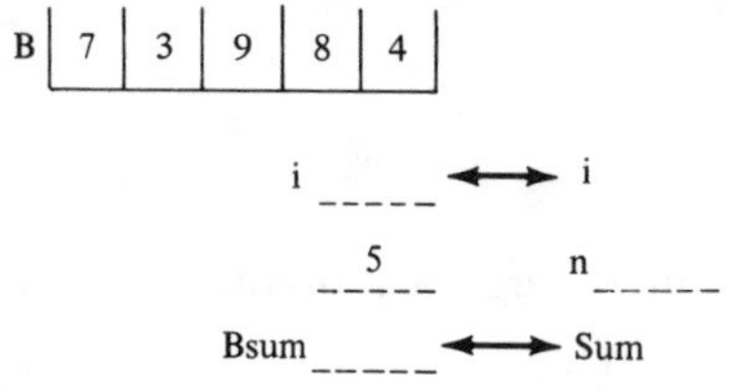


```
begin
    Sum:= 0;
    for i:= 1 to n do
        Sum := Sum+ B[i]
end
```

But the power of call by name is that it allows parameters to become "generic." That is, the above procedure Sigma can be used equally well to compute the "inner product" of two vectors:

$$\sum_{i=1}^{n} b_i c_i$$

by the following invocation:

```
Sigma (B[i] * C[i],i,5,Sum)
```

Here, the resulting text of the procedure body is as follows:

```
begin
   Sum := 0;
   for i := 1 to n do
      Sum := Sum + B[i] * C[i]
end
```

Call by value-result is perhaps less useful than the other parameter passing mechanisms. As we shall see in Chapter 13, Ada supports this by way of the designation **in-out**, which suggests a parameter which is used both for input and for output in a single invocation.

In general, different languages support one, two, or more of these four parameter linkage strategies. For instance, call by reference is by far the most commonly used, and is supported by Pascal, FORTRAN, COBOL, PL/I, SNOBOL, APL, LISP, C, and Ada. Call by value is not supported by FORTRAN, COBOL, SNOBOL, or APL. Call by name is a facility originating from Algol 60, but has not been significantly retained in more recent languages. PROLOG has its own method of parameter-argument linkage, which is distinct from all of these. We shall defer its discussion until Chapter 11.

It is also valuable to point out that some languages (notably PL/I) permit the choice between call by reference and call by value to be made by the *invocation* rather than in the procedure declaration. The PL/I convention for making this distinction is based on the nature of the argument a and the parameter p, in the following way:

1 If a and p have different type, then call by value is used.
2 If a is an expression with operators, then call by value is used.
3 If a is a constant, then call by value is used.

In all other cases (i.e., a is a variable with the same type as p), call by reference is used.

Type coercion is thus automatically performed in PL/I whenever the argument a is called by value. This is a departure from "strongly typed" languages like Pascal, where type coercion between an argument a and its parameter p is not allowed; a and p must always be of the same type, or else a syntax error is raised.

There are arguments on both sides of this question. Proponents of the PL/I strategy point out the enhanced generality of procedures which results. The Pascal strategy, on the other hand, tends to enhance program reliability by forcing more errors to be detectable at compile time. This is certainly an advantage for the novice programmer. More advanced programming efforts can be encumbered by the Pascal strategy, as we saw in Chapter 2 when we tried to deal with variable-sized arrays as parameters.

Implementation of Procedures and Parameters Linkage of call by reference and call by value parameters can be implemented in different ways, depending upon the underlying conventions which are used by the host machine. With our particular machine and activation record conventions, the following method is effective:

1 For each call by reference parameter *p*, a location P is added to the local variables in the activation record. In that location, the *address* of the corresponding argument is stored at the time of invocation, and all references to that parameter are indirect references (@P) which use that address.

2 For each call by value parameter *p*, a local variable P is established in the activation record, and a copy of the value of the corresponding argument is placed in that location. All references to P within the procedure body will thereby be references to that location, and its final value at the time of RETURN from the procedure will be lost because the entire activation record will be popped.

To illustrate these conventions, consider the following factorial procedure:

```
procedure factorial (n: integer; var f: integer);
  var i: integer;
  begin
    f := 1;
    for i := 2 to n do
      f := f * i
  end;
```

An "argument address list" is assumed to have been built by the invoking procedure, and the address of this list is assumed to be stored in register R1. Each of the addresses in this list contains the address of an argument in the invocation. For instance, the invocation

factorial (5, Fivefact)

leaves in R1 the address of the following list:

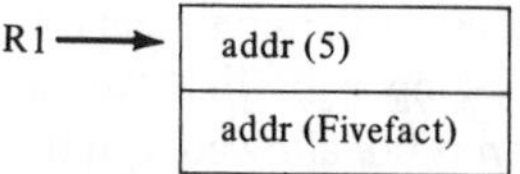

Thus, the *value* 5 is given by the double indirection @@R1, and the *address* of the variable Fivefact is given by the indirection @(R1 + 4). The annotated machine code for the procedure factorial is given below.

```
I DS L
FACT PUSHALL R0,R15                ; save registers from invocation
  PUSH I                           ; local variable
  PUSH @(R1 + 4)                   ; addr of var parameter f
  PUSH @@R1                        ; copy of parameter value n
; Now all references to parameter n below are given by
; STACK, all references to parameter f are given by
; @(STACK - 4), and all references to i by STACK - 8.
     MOV #1,@(STACK - 4)            ; f := 1
     MOV #2,STACK-8                 ; i := 1
$L0001 CMP STACK-8,STACK            ; if i > n
     BG $L0002                      ; then exit the loop
     MOV @(STACK-4),R2
     MUL R2,STACK-8
     MOV R2,@(STACK-4)              ; f := f * i
     MOV STACK-8,R3
     ADD #1,R3
     MOV R3,STACK-8                 ; i := i + 1
     B $L0001
; Now begin the return sequence
$L0002 POP                          ; destroy n
     POP                            ; destroy @f
     POP                            ; destroy local variable i
     POPALL R0,R15                  ; restore registers
     RETURN
```

(Here, we assume the existence of additional macros PUSHALL and POPALL, for the convenience of saving and restoring all the registers in a single line of code. Most assembly languages provide this kind of instruction in one form or another.)

The code given here reflects a direct copy of each statement in the original Pascal procedure, with no regard for the potential optimizations that could be achieved. This is the likely output of a nonoptimizing compiler. Of course, if the machine language coding were done directly by hand, or by an optimizing compiler, the redundant moving of i and f in and out of registers R2 and R3 would be eliminated. The interested reader is referred to any of several excellent texts on compilers for further discussion of these ideas.

Linkage for Recursive Procedures The above conventions are adequate to implement recursive procedures as well, since the value of each local variable *for each in-*

vocation is stored in a separate activation record on the run-time stack. To illustrate, consider the recursive version of the factorial function.

```
function factorial (n: integer): integer;
  begin
    if n <= 1 then factorial := 1
    else factorial := n * factorial (n - 1)
  end;
```

As a convention, we assume that the result returned by a function is left in register R0. Thus, *each* activation of factorial must leave the result in R0 immediately before exiting, and no activation can do anything else with the R0 in the meantime.

```
TEMP       DS L                    ; temporary value of n - 1
TEMPADDR   DS A                    ; address of TEMP
FACT       PUSHALL R1,R15          ; save all but R0
           PUSH @@R1               ; value of parameter n
           MOV #1,R0               ; assume result = 1 (n <= 1)
           CMP STACK,#1
           BLE $L0001
           MOV STACK,R2            ; n > 1, prepare for call
           SUB #1,R2               ; compute n - 1
           MOV R2,TEMP
           MOV @TEMP,TEMPADDR
           MOV @TEMPADDR,R1        ; argument linkage
           CALL FACT
           MUL STACK,R0            ; n * factorial (n - 1)
$L0001     POP                     ; return sequence
           POPALL R1,R15
           RETURN
```

Unlike R0, the contents of R1 and R2 are saved and restored at each level of recursion. Thus, each invocation need not be concerned about destroying another's values in these registers. The reader should trace execution of this code for, say, the factorial of 5 in order to see the dynamics of recursive invocation with the run-time stack.

EXERCISES

1. To become comfortable with the machine language introduced at the beginning of this chapter, write the familiar averaging program which appears at the beginning of each language chapter in this machine language.
2. Briefly compare this machine language with the one which you know best. Are there significant differences?
3. For your own implementation of Pascal, FORTRAN, COBOL, PL/I, SNOBOL, LISP, or APL, determine how its basic data types are represented in memory. What conventions are used for representing variable length types, such as character strings and decimal numbers?

4 For each of the following statements, discuss the possible coercions which can occur:
  (a) DO 10 I = 1,N (in FORTRAN)
  (b) READ EMPLOYEE-REC FROM EMPLOYEE-FILE (in COBOL)
  (c) X ← Y + 3 (in APL)
  (d) DO I = 1 TO N BY .5; (in PL/I)
  (e) X 'HI' = 'BYE' (in SNOBOL)
  (f) (setq X (car Y)) (in LISP)

5 Write machine code for part (c) of question 4, assuming
  (a) that X and Y are scalar real variables, and
  (b) that X and Y are one-dimensional arrays of real variables.

6 Do the same for part (e) of question 4, assuming that X is a character string with maximum length 100, stored using the conventions described in this chapter.

7 For arrays A, B, and C declared in section 10-3:
  (a) Use the formulas to calculate the addresses of A[3], B[2, 3], and C[5, 3, 2].
  (b) Give appropriate formulas for address calculation of A[i], B[i, j], and C[i, j, k] assuming instead that they are stored in column-major order, as in FORTRAN.
  (c) Implement in machine code the address calculation for B[i, j], assuming column-major order.

8 Prescribe a revision of the array dope vector which would take into account the efficiencies of address calculation which are obtained by gathering and computing all constant terms at the time the dope vector is filled, assuming a two-dimensional array. With this revision, write a machine code which will accomplish that calculation.

9 Write in Pascal a routine which will automatically allocate storage displacements for the elements of a structure, assuming that longword address alignment must be maintained for long integers, addresses, and reals, and word alignment must be maintained for integers. Assume that the record's elements can be any elementary data type which is defined for the machine.

10 For your own implementation of Case Study 0 in the language of your choice, develop our machine code for two or three of its control structures (**for**, DO, PERFORM, etc.). Then obtain an assembly language dump of those same control structures on your own computer. Compare the two; does your compiler appear to be optimizing the code?

11 Determine the procedure and parameter linkage conventions in use for your machine. Can you identify procedure activation records on a (simulation of the) run-time stack?

12 Show how Jensen's device can be used to facilitate matrix multiplication.

13 Find an example for which call by value-result is a preferred parameter linkage choice over the other three alternatives.

14 For the machine implementation given in the nonrecursive version of the factorial procedure, trace the contents of the run-time stack, the locals, and the arguments as the factorial of 5 is computed.

15 Write machine code which will properly invoke the factorial procedure, using 5 as an argument and the linkage conventions described in section 10-5.

16 Trace the execution of the recursive version of the factorial function with the argument 5, by showing the sequence of activation records, local variables, and contents of all pertinent registers.

CHAPTER **11**

PROLOG

11-1 INTRODUCTION TO PROLOG

The PROLOG (Programming in Logic) language represents a relatively new style of programming. Designed principally for artificial intelligence (AI) applications, PROLOG's style is based on the notion of defining objects and inferential relationships among classes of objects. It has strong theoretical foundations in the propositional calculus. Much recent attention has been paid to PROLOG because of its prominent role in Japan's "fifth generation" computer project. Moreover, PROLOG's design represents a dramatic departure from traditional ideas about program behavior, which are all based on the architecture of the von Neumann machine. It is safe to say that no other language discussed in this text presumes a run-time environment like that of PROLOG. We hope to capture the substance and spirit of these differences in this chapter.

11-1.1 Brief History of PROLOG

PROLOG was developed in the early 1970s by Philippe Roussel of the Artificial Intelligence Group at the University of Marseille.[1] Its first interpreter was implemented in 1972. Since the use of PROLOG has remained within the AI community—which has a relatively small programming constituency compared with that of, for example, the data processing community—the language has not yet become widely known. Moreover, for the same reason, PROLOG has not changed dramatically since its inception, nor has any effort been made to standardize the language. However, the resurgence of interest in AI programming in general has led to the development of many recent implementations. A comparison of PROLOG and LISP for AI programming was made by Warren and Pereira in 1977.[2]

11-1.2 Implementations and Variations of PROLOG

PROLOG is implemented interpretively on interactive systems, including the following:

Digital PDP-10, PDP-11, VAX
IBM PC
ICL 2980

The IBM PC version is an adaptation of the PDP-11 and VAX PROLOG interpreters. These have significant differences from the PDP-10 version (which is historically the original version), and those differences are summarized in section 11-3.2. In this chapter, we use the PDP-11/VAX/IBM PC versions of PROLOG as the basis for discussion, since it seems to represent the de facto version for the language at the present time.

11-1.3 Major Applications of PROLOG

Defined as an AI language, PROLOG has been used in the following kinds of applications:

- Theorem proving and problem solving
- Mathematical logic
- Natural language understanding
- Expert systems
- Knowledge representation

Because the style of logic programming is so distinct from that of other application domains, PROLOG has not enjoyed (and likely will not enjoy) widespread use in areas outside of AI. Its underlying execution structure, as we shall see, imposes a different programming style, and that style has not yet been shown to be effective in numerical programming, data processing, or systems programming applications.

11-2 WRITING PROLOG PROGRAMS

A PROLOG program is a series of "sentences," each terminated by a period (.), and each sentence has a "head" and an optional "body." The form of a sentence is written in one of the following two ways.

```
head.
head :- body.
```

The head and the body are each composed of so-called "goals" which semantically behave like procedure invocations in other languages. The symbol :− is read "if," and the body may contain a *series* of such goals separated by a comma (,), meaning "and," and |, meaning "or." Thus, for example, the sentence

```
P(X) :- Q(X),R(X).
```

is read as "compute P(X) *if* you can compute both Q(X) *and* R(X)."

The goals P, Q, and R here sometimes assume the role of predicates, and thus deliver Boolean results "true" and "fail" (for false). At other times they assume the role of ordinary functions, and thus deliver numerical, symbolic, or list-structured results. These two major classes are therefore not distinguished from each other in the syntax.

The following PROLOG program computes the integer average Av of a series of integers X, counting their number N as it proceeds. (Numerical problems are strictly *not* PROLOG's forte, but we shall continue with this example because it provides a simple theme for initial exposure and a common thread with the introductions to other languages in this text.)

```
% This program averages numbers X and displays the
% result.

average :- getinput (Sum, N),
           Av is Sum/N,
           print ('Average = ',Av).

getinput (Sum, N) :- ratom (X),
           not (eof),
           getinput (Sum1, N1),
           Sum is Sum1+X,
           N is N1+1.

getinput (0, 0) :- eof.
```

The first two lines are PROLOG comments; in general, any line which begins with "%" is a comment, and serves only as documentation for the program.

The program itself comprises two functions, named "average" and "getinput." The first function has three goals, separated by commas. The commas signify that all three goals must be simultaneous in order for the goal "average" itself to be satisfied. The three goals themselves are an invocation of "getinput," an assignment of the quotient (Sum/N) to the variable Av, and a display of the result as output (print).

The second function, "getinput," accumulates the sum (Sum) and count (N) of all input integers read [by "ratom(X)"], until end of file (eof) is reached. This function is recursively defined, and finally returns 0 as the resulting sum and count when the lowest level of recursion is reached at the end of the input. As long as eof is *not* reached, the recursion is continued by the three goals:

getinput (Sum1, N1),
Sum is Sum1 + X,
N is N1 + 1.

This says, in effect, to invoke getinput again (with its new result assigned to Sum1 and N1), add the current value (X) to the value of Sum1 thus returned, and add 1 to the value of N1 thus returned.

Variables and parameters in PROLOG are treated differently than in other languages. We shall see that the same variable (as Sum in this example) may have *several* "activations," each with a different value for a different invocation of the function in which it appears. Moreover, an assignment (via the "is" operator) can be made to an activation of a variable only *once* for a single invocation. Thus, we cannot write statements like

N is N + 1

in PROLOG and expect that an assignment will take place. This statement, in the event that N already has a value, now expresses the predicate, "is N equal to N + 1?", to which the answer is of course always false!

These fundamental differences force an entirely new programming style in PROLOG. In this chapter, we shall explore that style (known in AI as "logic programming"), and draw a useful basis for comparison with conventional styles.

11-2.1 Elementary Data Types and Values

The elementary data types in PROLOG are "integers" and "atoms." Integers are written in the usual way, as a sequence of decimal digits possibly preceded by a sign. For example,

0   −17   234

are three integers. (Note that there is *no* provision in PROLOG for decimal numbers. As a symbol manipulation language, PROLOG does not seem to need them. On the other hand, this limitation severely restricts the utility of PROLOG in other application areas outside of AI.)

An atom may be any sequence of symbols from the ASCII character set (see Figure 11-1), and it plays the role of an unevaluated constant, or simple character string value. The following are examples of PROLOG atoms:

alpha
noun
grandfather
−−>
integral

Further, atoms which contain special symbols, or which begin with an uppercase letter (A–Z) should be enclosed in apostrophes ('') whenever they would be confused with

FIGURE 11-1
PROLOG CHARACTER SET

```
A B C D E F G H I J K L M N O P Q R S T U V W X Y Z
a b c d e f g h i j k l m n o p q r s t u v w x y z
0 1 2 3 4 5 6 7 8 9
+ − * / \ ^ < > = ‘ ~ : . ? @ # $ &
! " % ( ) ' | { } [ ] _ ; ,
```

variable names or other punctuation marks that appear within a PROLOG program. Examples of these kinds of atoms are below.

'Alpha'
'john doe'
','

Principally, atoms are used to denote data values, and they are also used for function names and programmer-defined operators, as we shall later see. Some PROLOG atoms have predefined uses in the language, and as such should not generally be used for any other purpose. The principal ones are summarized in Figure 11-2.

11-2.2 Names, Variables, and Declarations

A PROLOG variable name may be any series of letters, digits, and underscores (_), provided that it begins with an uppercase letter (A–Z) or underscore. The following are examples of variable names:

X
Av
_result
_

FIGURE 11-2
THE MAJOR PREDEFINED ATOMS IN PROLOG

Atoms	Predefined use in PROLOG
:– , . ? ! ( ) repeat	Punctuation and program control
– \= < > <= >=	Relational operators
is	Assignment and comparison
+ – * / mod	Integer arithmetic
op	Operator definition
[ ]	Definition of lists
_	"Don't care," or throwaway variable
=.. | append member	List structure construction and interrogation
true fail	Boolean constants
var nonvar atom integer atomic	Classification of a value
listing trace load save spy retract retractall	Interactive debugging
get write skip display read see tell put seeing nl seen told tab	Input/output commands

The special variable name "_" has a unique use in PROLOG; it denotes an "anonymous variable" and as such may be used at any place in the program where we don't care *where* a particular value is stored, but only that it be stored *somewhere*. This is somewhat analogous to the generic name **FILLER** which is used in those portions of a COBOL record structure that we do not intend to reference, but nevertheless occupies space in the record (see Chapter 4).

PROLOG variables are not declared, and generally may take on different types of values during execution. A variable is activated each time the function in which it appears is invoked. At that time, the variable is said to be "uninstantiated," which means simply that it has no value. Satisfaction of the goals which appear within that function yields, as a byproduct, an assignment of values, or an "instantiation," of the variables therein.

To illustrate, consider the procedure "getinput" from the sample program, activated by the invocation

getinput (Sum, N)

within the procedure "average." This results in the following sequence of activations and instantiations of the variables Sum and N as getinput is recursively invoked, assuming the sequence 87, 89, 91, and 93 appears as the actual input. Superscripts which appear on Sum and N in the illustration below are used to indicate different activations; i.e., Sum^1 is the first activation, Sum^2 is the second, and so forth. The notation "—" here denotes "uninstantiated."

Invocation	Variables activated	Initial values	Final values	Returned from invocation
1	Sum^1	—	360	1
	N^1	—	4	1
	X^1	87		1
	$Sum1^1$	—	273	2
	$N1^1$	—	3	2
2	Sum^2	—	273	2
	N^2	—	3	2
	X^2	89		2
	$Sum1^2$	—	184	3
	$N1^2$	—	2	3
3	Sum^3	—	184	3
	N^3	—	2	3
	X^3	91		3
	$Sum1^3$	—	93	4
	$N1^3$	—	1	4
4	Sum^4	—	93	4
	N^4	—	1	4
	X^4	93		4
	$Sum1^4$	—	0	5
	$N1^4$	—	0	5
5	none			

Recalling the original definition of the goal "getinput," we see that it can be satisfied in one of two alternative ways. The second alternative returns the results 0,0 when the simple goal eof is true. This finally occurs with invocation 5 in the above table. The first alternative returns as a result the values of Sum and N whenever its five separate goals become *simultaneously* satisfied for a particular set of values for Sum, N, X, Sum1, and N1.

The table above shows the effects of recursion when the given four input values are used. Upon reaching eof, we see that these five variables take on the values 93, 1, 93, 0, and 0, respectively, coming out of the fourth invocation. Now, 93 and 1 become instantiations for Sum1 and N1 in the third invocation, from which Sum^3 and N^3 are instantiated to the values 184 and 2, in the process of satisfying *its* five goals simultaneously. Continuation of this process leads finally to satisfaction of the first invocation's five goals, and thus Sum^1 and N^1 receive their values 360 and 4 for return to the original invocation within "average."

In this example, the process of simultaneous goal satisfaction appears to be just another way of implementing recursion, and nothing more interesting than recursion in other languages. But we shall see in the next section that this process is much more general than recursion when it is used to define more complex relationships.

11-2.3 Arrays and Other Data Structures

Arrays are not directly supported in PROLOG, but *lists* and *structures* are. These are generalizations of the idea of an array, and are far more useful in the domain of AI programming.

A "list" is formally defined in PROLOG as either:

(i) [], which represents the empty list, or
(ii) [e1, e2, . . . , en] where each e is itself a list, a constant, a variable, or an expression.

The definition here is reminiscent in style and in utility to LISP, and we shall see that LISP's list processing primitives carry over to similar functions in PROLOG. The following are examples of this definition:

```
[2, 3]
[1, 2, 3]
[]
[tom, [Age, Occupation]]
```

The "head" of a list is its first element e1, while the "tail" is that list composed of the rest, or [e2, . . . , en]. For example, the head and tail of the list [1, 2, 3] are 1 and [2, 3] respectively.

PROLOG provides basic list manipulation functions in its syntax; the vertical bar (|) is used to associate the head and tail of a list with two variables, as follows:

```
[X | Y]
```

This denotes the list whose head is the value of X and whose tail is the value of Y. In some PROLOG implementations, this is written alternatively as [X , . . Y] with the same meaning. Readers should note that this is equivalent to LISP's "cons" function.

On the other hand, this same notation is also used to *separate* the head and tail of a list, as in the LISP "car" and "cdr" functions. For instance, the statement

```
[X | Y] = [a, b, c]
```

is satisfied by finding instantiations of X and Y which make the two sides equal, namely a and [b, c] respectively.

A "structure" is a compound term, having the following form:

```
functor (arguments)
```

Here, "functor" is any atom, and "argument" denotes any list of atoms, variables, or structures. In its simplest use, the structure can define a record structure of the usual kind. For example, suppose we have the record structure shown in Figure 11-3. This may be defined in PROLOG as follows:

```
person (name (first ('ALLEN'), middle ('B.'), last ('TUCKER')),
        ssnumber (275407437),
        grosspay (25400),
        address (street ('1800 BULL RUN,'), city ('ALEXANDRIA,'),
                 state ('VA.'), zip (22200))
        )
```

The extra apostrophes ('') here are needed to enclose atoms which contain special characters or begin with an uppercase letter.

Structures are also the basic building blocks from which PROLOG programs, as well as data values, are composed. For instance, the statement

```
getinput (Sum, N)
```

FIGURE 11-3

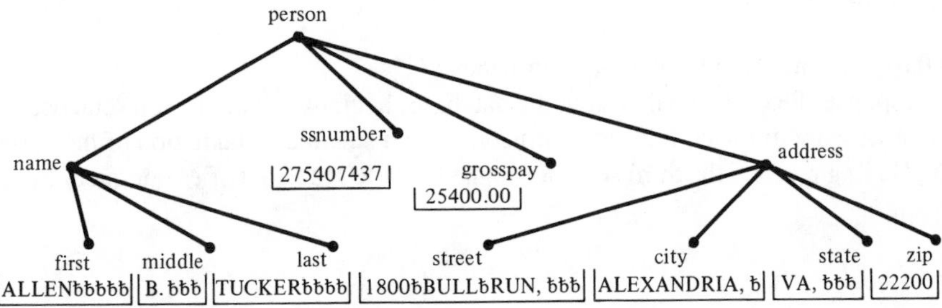

is syntactically a *structure,* as is

+ (N, 1)

which, for convenience, may be written in its usual form N + 1.

Writing a PROLOG program often requires integrating program statements and data structures as a single unit. For example, consider the following partial family tree:

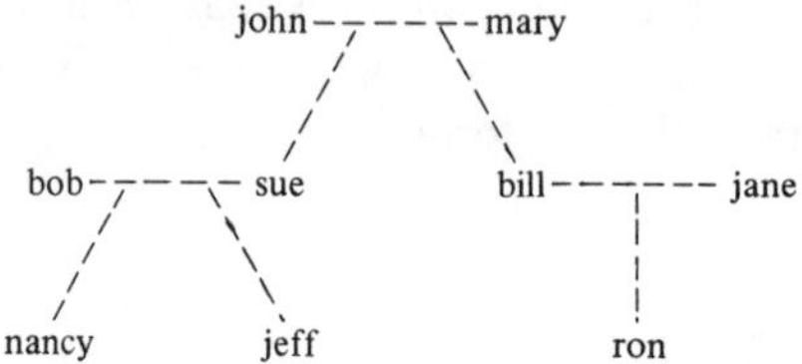

Here, john and mary are the parents of sue and bill, bob and sue are the parents of nancy and jeff, and bill and jane are parents of ron. This tree may be directly defined in PROLOG by the following set of structures.

```
father (sue, john).
father (bill, john).
father (nancy, bob).
father (jeff, bob).
father (ron, bill).
mother (sue, mary).
mother (bill, mary).
mother (nancy, sue).
mother (jeff, sue).
mother (ron, jane).
```

When written within a PROLOG program, each of these structures now becomes a fact, or unconditional assertion, in our "program database." We can ask questions of this database by inserting a variable, say X, in another structure whose functor matches one of those in the database (father or mother), and following it with a question mark. Thus,

```
father (nancy, X)?
```

asks the question, "Who is the father of nancy?"

In response, PROLOG will search the database, beginning with the top sentence, to find one which will match this entire structure, for a suitable instantiation of the variable X. Having reached the third sentence in the list, PROLOG satisfies our query by responding:

```
X = bob
```

A slight variation of this query, in the form

father (nancy, bob)?

asks the question "Is bob the father of nancy?", and now PROLOG will search for an exact match and answer "yes" or "no" accordingly.

Continuing with the program itself, we can add to our list of facts a definition of "parenthood" with the following sentence:

parent (A, B) :- father (A, B) | mother (A, B).

This says, "B is a parent of A if either B is the father of A or B is the mother of A." Thus, we may now form the following kinds of additional queries:

parent (nancy, X)?
parent (nancy, bob)?

The first asks to find *all* parents of nancy, while the second asks whether bob is a parent of nancy. Both of these queries use the newly added sentence in the program. We shall trace execution of the program for the first of these queries.

The first step is to search the program to find a structure whose functor matches the query's functor, "parent." Once the newly added sentence is so located, its variables A and B are simultaneously instantiated with the arguments "nancy" and X, respectively, and in all their instances in this sentence. The resulting sentence is thus:

parent (nancy, X) :- father (nancy, X) | mother (nancy, X).

Now the goal is to satisfy either of the two alternatives on the right-hand side, beginning with the first.

Thus, the database is searched again from the top, as if we had asked the question "father (nancy, X)?" Success is found when we reach the third statement, and thus the response

X = bob

is generated. However, the search doesn't stop here. Recall that the goal is to find all parents of nancy, so that the next alternative, "mother (nancy, X)?" must also be exhausted. This uncovers the second response:

X = sue

This example is our first illustration of PROLOG's departure from conventional execution environments. It actually has a built-in mechanism for "backtracking" which is used to answer any query for which there are possibly more than one answer. One of the important aspects of mastering PROLOG programming is the art of controlling this backtracking process so that it does not churn unnecessarily in cases where only a single response is desired.

We may add still another definition to this program, that of "grandparenthood," in the following way.

```
grandparent (C, D) :- parent (C, E), parent (E, D).
```

That is, to find a grandparent D of C, we must find an E which is both a parent of C and an offspring of D.

With this additional definition, we may ask questions like "Find all grandparents of nancy," and "Whose grandparent is john?" respectively as follows:

```
grandparent (nancy, X)?
grandparent (X, john)?
```

The response to the first query is:

```
X = john
X = mary
```

while the response to the second is:

```
X = ron
X = nancy
X = jeff
```

Finally, a more general query may be posed, "Find all grandparent-grandchild pairs," in the following way:

```
grandparent (X, Y)?
```

Its response, of course, gives all six pairs which are defined in the database. To retrieve all six pairs, the system automatically performs five separate backtracking steps after the first feasible pair is found.

11-2.4 Basic Statements

As shown in the foregoing examples, PROLOG's basic statement forms are:

(i) Structure.
(ii) Structure :- list of structures separated by "," or "|".

Form (i) is an unconditional assertion, which can be interpreted as a fact in the database. Form (ii) denotes an **if . . . then** arrangement, where the conditions to be satisfied are on the right of the operator :- and the conclusion is on the left. The separators "|" and "," ("|" is written ";" on some implementations) denote logical "or" and "and," respectively.

Moreover, execution of a PROLOG program is initiated by either of the following forms:

(i) A query, which is a structure followed by ?
(ii) An imperative, which is a structure followed by !

The query typically comes with one or more variables as arguments, since we are interested in finding all values in the database which satisfy the query. Such is the case, for instance, with the query "grandparent (X, Y)?" discussed above.

The imperative, on the other hand, typically initiates program execution of a more conventional sort, and its input and output are derived during execution via the "ratom" and "print" functions. This is used, for instance, to initiate execution of the averaging program given at the beginning of the chapter:

average!

Thus, we have introduced the entire syntax of PROLOG. The rest of the language is composed of functions and predicates which support particular kinds of symbol manipulation and arithmetic activities. In the remainder of this section we shall discuss the arithmetic and list processing functions. The rest are discussed in sections 11-2.5 through 11-2.8.

Arithmetic Functions and Value Assignment The basic PROLOG arithmetic functions are defined *only* for integers, and are as follows:

Function	Operation defined
+	integer addition
−	integer subtraction
*	integer multiplication
/	integer division
mod	integer remainder

Strictly speaking, these are written as prefix operators, in the style of structures, such as:

+ (N, 1)

Here, no priorities are needed, since multiple operations are fully nested.

However, PROLOG provides the "op" function which permits these (and others) to be redefined as ordinary infix, prefix, or postfix operators, with an assigned priority. The form of an op definition is as follows:

op (priority, type, name)!

Here, "priority" is an integer from 0 to 255 (the limit is implementation dependent), where 0 denotes the highest priority and 255 denotes the lowest. "Type" may be any of the following graphical descriptions of the operator (infix, postfix, or prefix):

```
xfx   xf   fx
xfy   yf   fy
yfx
yfy
```

The first column indicates the kinds of infix operators (f is the operator and x and y are the operands), the second indicates the postfix operators, and the third gives the prefix operators. The distinction between "x" and "y" here serves to separate an operand of lower priority (x) than f from an operand of higher priority than f. Thus, for instance, the type "yfx" denotes an infix operator whose left operand will take precedence and whose right operand will yield precedence to f. That is, it defines *left* associativity in cases where a series of operators with the same precedence occur in succession. For example,

```
op (30, yfx, -)!
```

defines subtraction as a priority 30 operator, with left associativity. We may therefore write

```
X - Y -Z
```

to imply the order which would be explicitly stated by:

```
- (- (X, Y), Z)
```

Parentheses may be used with infix operators to override the predefined order. For instance,

```
X - (Y - Z)
```

causes the evaluation of Y − Z before subtraction from X takes place.

A more complete list of the "standard" PROLOG operator definitions used in this chapter is given below:

```
op (255, xfx, ':-')!
op (255, xf, ?)!
op (255, xf, !)!
op (254, xfy, '|')!
op (60, fx, not)!
op (50, yf, '.')!
op (40, xfx, is)!
op (40, xfx, '=..')!
```

```
op (40, xfx, =)!
op (40, xfx, \=)!
op (40, xfx, <)!
op (40, xfx, <=)!
op (40, xfx, >)!
op (40, xfx, >=)!
op (40, xfx, ==)!
op (40, xfx, \==)!
op (30, yfx, +)!
op (30, yfx, -)!
op (20, yfx, *)!
op (20, yfx, /)!
op (10, yfx, mod)!
```

In addition to these operators, the programmer may define additional operators as well, according to the needs of the problem.

Since the arithmetic operators are defined only for integers, division (/) yields an integer quotient and "mod" yields an integer remainder. Real, or decimal arithmetic is not intrinsic to PROLOG; it must be simulated if it is needed.

Arithmetic assignment is accomplished by the (infix) operator "is," as we have seen. However, it only assigns a result if the left operand has not been instantiated. Otherwise, it acts as a comparison (=) operator, which gives a Boolean result instead. For example, suppose the variable Y has the value 4 and X has no value. Then the statement

```
X is 2 * Y + 1
```

evaluates the expression on the right, and assigns the result 9 to the variable X. Thus, X is said to become "instantiated."

However, if the value of X had been, say, 7 at the time this statement is reached, the Boolean result "fail" would occur instead, and the value of X would remain unchanged.

Assignment of nonarithmetic values—atoms and lists—must be accomplished by other means than "is," which is reserved exclusively for use with arithmetic values.

List and Structure Manipulation Functions The major functional strength of PROLOG lies in its capabilities for manipulating lists and structures. To illustrate, suppose we have the list variable L instantiated to the following value:

```
[pascal, fortran, cobol, pli]
```

This value could have been assigned, for instance, in satisfying the following goal:

```
L = [pascal, fortran, cobol, pli]
```

Here, "=" is a comparison operator, yielding the value 'true" or "fail," but in the process will instantiate L with the value on the right in order for the entire statement to succeed.

This value might alternatively have been assigned by an input loop, using the ''ratom'' function and the list construction function ''append'' defined as follows:

```
append ([], Z, Z).
append ([A|X], Y, [A|Z]) :- append (X, Y, Z).
```

The first rule here states that the result of appending the empty list to any other list Z is the list Z itself. The third argument defines, in effect, the result of the function.

The second rule states that the result of appending any list with head A, or [A|X], to any list Y is necessarily the list [A|Z], *provided* that the list Z is already known to be the result of appending X and Y. This is a recursive definition, although its style is somewhat unusual.

To illustrate how this works, suppose we have the command

```
append ([pascal, fortran], [cobol, pli] , Ans)?
```

in order to find out the result, ''Ans,'' of appending the two lists shown. The following sequence of goals will be tried in the process of reaching the solution:

```
[pascal, fortran, cobol, pli]
```

These are summarized below.

Goal	A	X	Y	Z
1	pascal	[fortran]	[cobol, pli]	[pascal|Z]
2	fortran	[ ]	[cobol, pli]	[fortran|Z]
3				[cobol, pli]

At the point goal 3 is reached, the first rule finally applies, since the first argument in the right-hand side of goal 2

```
append (X, Y, Z)
```

is instantiated for append ([], [cobol, pli], Z) and the result is to instantiate Z to [cobol, pli]. Now the value of Z for goal 2 is determined, and it is satisfied with Z instantiated as [fortran| [cobol, pli]], which is [fortran, cobol, pli]. Finally, the first goal is satisfied with Z as [pascal| [fortran, cobol, pli]], which is equivalent to the result shown above, and will become the instantiation of Ans.

Another useful list processing function is one named ''member,'' which can be used to determine whether a given argument A is a member of a list L.

member (A, [A|_]).
member (A, [_|X]) :– member (A, [X]).

Here, we are just saying that A is a member of *any* list whose head is A (expressed as [A|_]). Moreover, A is a member of any list if it is a member of that list's tail. Recall that the special variable _ is a "don't care" variable, so that the notation [_|X] means "any list with arbitrary head and tail X."

For example, suppose we want to ask whether prolog is a member of the list [pascal, fortran, cobol, pli]. Then, we would say,

member (prolog, [pascal, fortran, cobol, pli])?

and receive the response "no" after the following sequence of goals is tried:

Goal	A	[_ |X]
1	prolog	[_ | [fortran, cobol, pli]]
2	prolog	[_ | [cobol, pli]]
3	prolog	[_ | [pli]]
4	prolog	[_ | []]

At this point, goal 4 cannot be satisfied, so neither can any of the prior goals which depend upon it.

Although these two functions are not built into PROLOG, the following two functions are:

1 X =. . L builds the list L out of the structure X, making X's functor the head of the resulting list.

2 name (X, L) converts the atom X into the list L, where each element of L is a single character from X, and in the same order.

For example, if X has the value

father (nancy, bob)

then X =. . L will leave L with the value [father, nancy, bob]. Moreover, the function name (nancy, L) will build the list [n, a, n, c, y] out of the characters from the atom "nancy." Either of these functions can be used in the *reverse* sense, that is to convert a list into a structure or to convert a list of single characters into an atom. For instance,

X =. . [father, nancy, bob]

leaves X instantiated with the structure value

father (nancy, bob)

and

name (X, [n, a, n, c, y])

leaves X with the atomic value nancy.

There are two additional structure manipulation functions in PROLOG, ''functor'' and ''arg,'' which are defined as follows:

functor (S, F, N). Identifies within structure S its functor F and its number of arguments N.

arg (N, S, X). Instantiates X with the Nth argument of structure S.

For example, functor (+ (12,13),F,N) assigns + to F and 2 to N. Moreover, arg(2, + (12,13),X) assigns 13 to X.

11-2.5 Control Structures

PROLOG functions and predicates are normally defined recursively, as we have seen. Moreover, the backtracking mechanism allows several alternatives to be tried before success or failure is determined.

PROLOG has several built-in predicates, in addition to the functions discussed so far, and these deliver Boolean results ''true'' or ''fail'' when evaluated. The following logical operators are available for arithmetic values, and may be used as *infix* operators:

Logical operator (op)	Meaning of X op Y
=	X and Y are equal
<	X less than Y
>	X greater than Y
\=	X not equal Y
=< (or <=)	X less than or equal Y
>=	X greater than or equal Y
,	X and Y are true
| (or ;)	X or Y or both are true

The following additional predicates are also built in, and are defined as follows:

Predicate	Meaning
not	not(X) is true if X is not true.
eof	eof is true if the current input is at its end.
var	var(X) is true if X is a currently instantiated variable.
nonvar	nonvar(X) is true if X is instantiated to a nonvariable (structure).
atom	atom(X) is true if the value of X is an atom.
integer	integer(X) is true if X is an integer.
atomic	atomic(X) is true if X is either an atom or an integer.

Further predicates can be defined from these as well. For instance, if we want to compare two atoms to see if one is less (alphabetically) than the other, we can define the predicate ''alphaless'' as follows:

```
alphaless (A, B) :- name (A, LA),
                    name (B, LB),
                    listless (LA, LB).
listless ([], [_|_]).
listless ([C|_], [D|_]) :- C < D.
listless ([E|F], [G|H]) :- E = G,
                           listless (F, H).
```

The first line of this definition separates each of the atoms A and B into lists of single characters LA and LB. The ''listless'' predicate is then defined for such lists in three steps:

1 The empty list is less than *any* nonempty list.

2 A list whose first letter C is less than the first letter D of another list is less than that list.

3 For two lists whose first characters E and G are identical, their respective tails F and H are examined to decide which one is less (using the ''listless'' function recursively).

For example, the determination that ''program'' is less than ''prolog'' is done in the following steps:

1 Separate ''program'' into the list [p, r, o, g, r, a, m].
2 Separate ''prolog'' into the list [p, r, o, l, o, g].
3 Apply the predicate ''listless'' to these:
   (a) Since their first letters ''p'' are identical, apply ''listless'' again, to [r, o, g, r, a, m] and [r, o, l, o, g]. Continue in this way until two tails are obtained whose first letters are not identical, namely [g, r, a, m] and [l, o, g].
   (b) For these lists, compare the heads and determine that g < l is true. Thus, [g, r, a, m] < [l, o, g] is true and the result returned to each waiting activation is subsequently true.

The Cut Many times we need a function or predicate for which we would like to know whether or not it will succeed at least once, but we are not interested in *all* the instantiations of the variables for which it will succeed. For instance, recalling the foregoing definition of the predicate ''member,'' the query

```
member (b, [a, b, c, b])?
```

will succeed *twice,* once for the first instance of b in the list, and once for the second. Thus, the result will be:

```
yes
yes
```

even though our question is intended as, "Does b occur in this list?"

In short, we would like to have a device which can be inserted within a function definition which will terminate goal-seeking as soon as the goal has been satisfied *once*. Such a device is defined in PROLOG, and is called the "cut." It is represented by an exclamation mark (!) on the right side of a sentence. Basically, the cut terminates evaluation of that sentence as soon as it succeeds the first time. For example, suppose we redefine the predicate "member" as follows:

```
member (X, [X|_]) :- !.
member (X, [_|Y]) :- member (X, Y).
```

Here, the first rule forces termination of the predicate as soon as the first instance of X at the head of the list appears. Thus, for instance, the query

```
member (b, [a, b, c, b])?
```

will yield the single answer

```
yes
```

when the first occurrence of b in the list appears; the second occurrence will not be reached, because the cut will terminate execution. Thus, this redefined version of member accomplishes a more modest task than the original one, and at a substantial savings in execution time. For complex programs, the art of judiciously using the cut can result in substantial gains in efficiency.

Another illustration of the cut is shown in the following function "sum" which sums the integers from 1 to N:

```
sum (N, 1) :- N <= 1, !.
sum (N, S) :- N1 is N-1,
              sum (N1, S1),
              S is S1+N.
```

Here, if N <= 1 the sum is 1, and the process stops (!). Otherwise, the second definition applies, and we find the sum of the first N − 1 integers (recursively), and then add N to it. Without the cut, we would need to redundantly test the condition N <= 1 in both definitions, as shown below:

```
sum (N, 1) :- N <= 1.
sum (N, S) :- not (N <= 1),
              N1 is N-1,
              sum (N1, S1),
              S is S1+N.
```

Here the redundancy, in effect, makes the two definitions mutually exclusive.

Iteration Although recursion is usually preferred, PROLOG provides the "repeat" function to enable iterative control. When used, "repeat" causes indefinite repetition of the clauses which *follow* it within the right-hand side of the goal where it appears, until some condition arises which prevents successful fulfillment of all those clauses. To illustrate, consider the following loop:

```
loop :- print (a),
        repeat,
          ratom(X),
          print(b).
```

Here, indentation is used to identify the clauses which are being repeated. The effect of this program, when executed, is to display the letter a, and then repeatedly call for input [by "ratom(X)"] and display the letter b. Since there is no provision for exit, this loop is infinite, and program control must be terminated by external means.

The repeat statement has rare practical use in PROLOG, since most loops are better specified by recursion and there is no way to directly increment a "loop control" variable when iteration is used. This confounds conventional programming practices, and in fact encourages their abandonment in most cases.

11-2.6 Input-Output Conventions

The principal input-output medium for PROLOG programming is the terminal. Yet program and data may be transferred to and from other files as well, and we shall discuss these facilities in this section.

The principal input functions are "get0," "get," "ratom," and "read." We have already seen the use of "ratom" to input a single atomic value. The differences among these functions are summarized below.

Input function	Meaning
get0 (X)	Read the next single ASCII character and instantiate X with its value. ASCII value 26 designates eof.
get (X)	Like get0 (X), except that any ASCII character which is not a printing character (i.e., which has ASCII code <= 32) will be skipped.
ratom (X)	Read the next atom and instantiate X with its value.
read (X)	Read the next statement (ended by a period) and instantiate X with its value.

Thus, "get" is appropriate when we are reading text character by character, while "ratom" is useful when we read word by word. On the other hand, "read" is useful to dynamically add new statements to the program database itself.

For instance, the family tree relations established in an earlier example could have been entered as input in response to read statements, and thus merged with the father, mother, and grandparent functions, rather than being fixed among these functions themselves. That would have made the program more general, as it would be applicable to many different family trees besides the one that was originally entered.

The principal PROLOG output functions parallel the input functions, and are described as follows:

Output function	Meaning
put (X)	Display the integer X (from 0 to 127) in its equivalent ASCII character form.
write (X)	Display the value of X, which may be an atom, a variable, or a structure.
display (X)	Like write (X), except that operator declarations are ignored in the form of the output.
print (X1, X2, . . .)	Like write (X), except that several terms X1, X2, . . . are concatenated together on the same output line.
nl	Forces subsequent output to be displayed on a new line (rather than the current one).
tab (X)	Inserts X blank spaces on the current output line.

We have already illustrated the use of "print" in our prior examples. The distinction between "write"and "display" appears when a structure is shown. For instance, if X is instantiated to the expression

a + b + c

and normal operator definitions for + are assumed, then

write (X)

will produce the expression in its normal infix form, while

display (X)

will convert it to structural notation, and show it as follows:

+ (+ (a, b), c)

External Files Beyond the terminal screen, PROLOG supports transfer of data and programs to and from one or more external files, using the following functions:

Function	Meaning
see (F)	*Open* file named F for input; all subsequent "read" functions will bring data from file F, rather than from the terminal.
seen	*Close* the current input file, and revert all subsequent input to the terminal.
tell (F)	*Open* file named F for output; all subsequent "write" functions will send data to file F, rather than to the terminal.
told	*Close* the current output file, and revert all subsequent output to the terminal.
seeing (X)	Assign to variable X the name of the currently open input file.
telling (X)	Assign to variable X the name of the currently open output file.

By convention, the terminal is preassigned the (input and output) filename ''user'' by the system. Any other file to be established by the program can be assigned any atom as its filename, provided that the name chosen is unique among all files within the system.

To illustrate these functions, suppose we have a file named ''scores'' which contains test scores to be averaged by our original averaging program. The following revision of that program will compute and display the average of all scores in that file:

```
average :- see (scores),
           getinput (Sum, N),
           seen (scores),
           Av is Sum/N,
           print ('Average = ', Av).
getinput (Sum, N) :- ratom (X),
         not (eof),
         getinput (Sum1, N1),
         Sum is Sum1 + X,
         N is N1 + 1.
getinput (0, 0) :- eof.
```

As shown, the only change from the original program is the insertion of ''see'' and ''seen'' functions before and after the input values are summed. These redirect the getinput function to the scores file for the data, and then close that file when the input process is complete.

11-2.7 Subprograms, Functions, and Libraries

As we can see by now, a PROLOG program is nothing more than a collection of functions and data structures, coordinated for either reaching a Boolean conclusion or computing a result. Thus, there is no semantic distinction between the notion of "main program" and "subprograms" as we find in other languages; in fact, any program may be a subprogram of a larger task, and any function may be isolated and activated directly, without having to be "properly invoked" by a calling program.

Nearly all of PROLOG's built-in functions have already been described in previous sections. The following are also available, and are useful for maintaining the elements of a program-database library itself:

Function	Meaning
consult (F)	Append to the current workspace all PROLOG functions in file F. If there are functions in the current workspace with the same name, duplicate definitions are created.
reconsult (F)	Same as "consult," except that existing functions in the workspace with the same name are overridden by their counterparts in file F.
retract (X)	Remove all sentences in the current workspace which are identical with X.
retractall (X)	Remove all sentences in the current workspace whose heads are identical with X.

In these definitions, the notion of "workspace" means that place where the present program-database resides; it is temporary, in the sense that its contents disappear at the end of the session unless they are saved in a permanent file. Thus, PROLOG systems provide the following functions:

load F!—append to the current workspace the program stored in the permanent file F.

save F!—store the entire contents of the current workspace as the permanent file F.

Again, the current workspace is given the special file name "user", and thus the command

consult (user)

allows keyboard entry of additional statements to the program in the workspace. Moreover,

reconsult (user)

allows keyboard *replacement* of existing functions in the current workspace.

Thus, PROLOG has defined a complete program development environment *within* the realm of its own syntax. This is a distinguishing characteristic not found in most languages. PROLOG's symbiosis of program development, program, and database within a single conceptual framework tends to unify syntax and semantics of these notions, and marks a significant departure from conventional practices.

11-2.8 Additional Features

We discuss in this section those additional PROLOG functions that are provided for debugging. These are summarized below.

Function	Use in debugging
trace P	Traces all entries and exits from the sentence which has P as its head. Tracing several such sentences can be specified by "trace [P1, P2, . . .]".
untrace P	Disables tracing of sentence with head P.
assert (S)	Adds sentence S to the program database in the current workspace. The alternative form "asserta (S)" adds S to the *beginning* of all sentences whose head matches that of S. "Assertz (S)" adds S to the *end* of all such sentences.
pp P	Displays all sentences in the current workspace with head P.

In some PROLOG implementations, the ''trace'' and ''untrace'' functions are replaced by the following debugging functions, which are slightly different in their meaning:

Function	Use in debugging
trace	Traces entries and exits from *all* functions in the current workspace.
notrace	Disables all tracing.
spy P	Enables selective tracing for sentences with head P.
nospy P	Disables tracing for sentences with head P.
debugging	Displays all so-called "spy points" P that are currently set by "spy P" commands.
nodebug	Removes all such spy points.

To illustrate, if we precede the example averaging program by the command

```
trace [average, getinput]
```

the following output will be displayed:

```
C| > average
C|| > getinput(_1,_2)
> 87
```

```
C||| > getinput(_6,_4)
> 89
C|||| > getinput(_12,_10)
> 91
C||||| > getinput(_18,_16)
> 93
C|||||| > getinput(_24,_22)
> eof
R|||||| > getinput(0,0)
E|||||| < getinput(0,0)
E||||| < getinput(93,1)
E|||| < getinput(184,2)
E||| < getinput(273,3)
E|| < getinput(360,4)
Average = 90
E| < average
```

Here, the symbols > and < indicate entry and exit from a particular invocation of the procedure named and the number of vertical bars(|) indicates the level of recursion which is active. Variables beginning with "_" are system-generated instantiations of Sum and N, which are filled with different integer values as each level of recursion returns successfully. Thus, the trace gives a good picture of the structure of execution. It is particularly useful for coming to grips with the complexities of backtracking and the use of the cut.

11-3 APPLICATIONS OF PROLOG

As noted above, PROLOG is a language narrowly focused on applications of artificial intelligence. The extent of its utility has yet to be fully tested in this area, since it is not as widely used or understood as LISP. Yet it is safe to say that PROLOG will not seriously penetrate other application areas; it does not support common control structures found in those areas, nor does it seriously address the whole subject of decimal arithmetic, either from a scientific or from a data processing point of view. Thus, our case study implementation of PROLOG is focused on the missionaries and cannibals problem, as an illustration of its utility in AI programming.

11-3.1 PROLOG Case Study Implementation

The PROLOG program for Case Study 4—Missionaries and Cannibals comprises several functions. The data structure which is built to contain the solution is a *list* of the form

```
[sn, . . . , s2, s1]
```

where sn is the most recently developed *state* and s1 is the initial state. Each state has one of the following two forms:

left (M, C)
right (M, C)

where "left" and "right" denote the position of the boat, while M and C give the number of missionaries and the number of cannibals remaining on the *left* bank. The program completes, therefore, when it reaches the state

right (0,0)

which will become the leftmost entry sn in the list of states.

The pivotal function in this program is the "transit" function, which governs the passage of the boat from one side of the river to the other. The left-to-right transit goal is satisfied if all of the following are simultaneously true:

(i) We have M missionaries and C cannibals in the boat.
(ii) M and C are not greater than M1 and C1, the number that were available on the left bank.
(iii) The resulting numbers M2 and C2 on the left bank are M1 − M and C1 − C.
(iv) No devouring of missionaries by cannibals will occur as a result of this move.

These conditions are defined, in order, in the individual lines of the "transit" function. The right-to-left transit is done with similar considerations.

The function "developsolution" thus repeatedly invokes the transit function until a final state is reached; that is, the list has "right (0,0)" at its head. Otherwise, it takes the current list of moves

[This|Prior]

and repeatedly appends a Next move to it:

developsolution ([Next, This|Prior], Final)

The predicate

not (member (Next, Prior))

checks that a candidate next state is not among those already reached, thus avoiding a loop. The remainder of the program should be self-explanatory, and it is given in Figure 11-4.

This program was run on a VAX UNIX and an IBM PC implementation of PROLOG. The resulting execution speeds are shown in Figure 11-5.

```
mandc :-
        developsolution([left(3, 3)], Final),
        displayresult(Final).

transit(left(M1, C1), right(M2, C2)) :-
        inboat(M, C),
        M <= M1,
        C <= C1,
        M2 is M1 - M,
        C2 is C1 - C,
        nodevouring(M2, C2).
transit(right(M1, C1), left(M2, C2)) :-
        inboat(M, C),
        M2 is M1 + M,
        C2 is C1 + C,
        M2 <= 3,
        C2 <= 3,
        nodevouring(M2, C2).

displayresult([]) :- !.
displayresult([X, ..Y]) :-
        displayresult(Y),
        write(X),
        nl.

nodevouring(M, C) :- (M = C ; M = 3 ; M = 0).

developsolution([right(0, 0), ..Prior], [right(0, 0), ..Prior]) :- !.
developsolution([This, ..Prior], Final) :-
        transit(This, Next),
        not(member(Next, Prior)),
        developsolution([Next, This, ..Prior], Final).

member(State, [State]) :- !.
member(State, [State, .._]) :- !.
member(State, [_, ..X]) :- member(State, X).

inboat(2, 0).
inboat(1, 1).
inboat(1, 0).
inboat(0, 1).
inboat(0, 2).
```

FIGURE 11-4

FIGURE 11-5
EFFICIENCY OF PROLOG CASE STUDY 4 PROGRAM

Implementation	Compile speed	Execution speed
1 Digital VAX-750/UNIX PROLOG	na	3.1 sec
2 IBM PC/DOS PROLOG	na	3.8 sec

11-3.2 Implementation-Dependent Extensions of PROLOG

Since at this time there are not too many implementations of PROLOG in use, little has been done in the area of language extension. PROLOG has, until recently, been an experimental language, and thus has not had the kind of attention from hardware and software manufacturers as other languages.

The three principal implementations of PROLOG are similar in their overall design and functional capabilities. Those syntactic variations noted below mark differences from the presentation in this chapter.

PROLOG feature	Variation in other implementations
P :− Q, R.	P <− Q & R. + P − Q − R. (P Q R) P : Q ; R.
Variable begins with capital letter	Variable begins with lowercase letter
Atom begins with lowercase letter	Atom begins with capital letter
[X|Y]	[X, . . Y]
P?	?− P.
display	not always available (use "write" instead).
P :− Q	Q −> P
retract retractall	has different effects in other implementations.

Moreover, the debugging features and several built-in functions vary from one implementation to another. Some of these differences have been noted earlier in the chapter. A complete list is difficult to compile, especially in light of the dynamic pace of development for this language.

11-3.3 Overall Evaluation of PROLOG

On the basis of our experience with PROLOG in this chapter, we evaluate PROLOG as follows:

1 Expressivity	Good
2 Well-definedness	Excellent
3 Data types and structures	Good
4 Modularity	Good
5 Input-output facilities	Good
6 Portability	Poor
7 Efficiency	Fair
8 Pedagogy	Poor
9 Generality	Poor

PROLOG's exceptional "well-definedness" comes, of course, from its close ties with the propositional calculus and resulting formal properties. Its weak "efficiency" stems from the backtracking mechanism having a tendency to "overexecute" unless careful programming and judicious use of the cut are observed. Poor "pedagogy" stems from its relative obscurity and an almost total absence of good textbooks on logic programming. "Generality" is not expected to be very good, since PROLOG is unabashedly an AI language, and that's all. Finally, "portability" is handicapped by the lack of a widely accepted standard and the many syntactic variations that exist.

All in all, PROLOG is an interesting language in which innovative experimentation may uncover novel machine architectures in the future. However, it is not yet foreseeable how PROLOG can, in its present form, becomes a serious tool for production programming.

EXERCISES

1 Let I, J, K, X, Y, and Z be variables, and assume that they have the following values:

X = 2   I = 1
Y = −10   J = −5
Z = 8   K = 12

Compute the result delivered by evaluating each of the following expressions:

(a) X + Y * Z
(b) (X + Y) * Z
(c) (X + Y)/Z − 3
(d) X + Y/(Z − 3)
(e) I − 1
(f) I mod J * K
(g) I/J * K

2 What is the difference between the PROLOG "is" operator and the ordinary assignment operator found in other languages?

3 If your installation has a different PROLOG implementation than the ones used here, adapt our PROLOG Case Study 4 implementation to run under that system. How difficult was that adaptation?

4 Implement Case Study 3—Text Formatter in PROLOG. Evaluate PROLOG as a text processing language from this experience.

5 Implement Case Study 0 (which you defined at the end of Chapter 1) in PROLOG. Evaluate PROLOG's performance and suitability for this application.

6 Consider implementing Case Study 2—Employee File Maintenance in PROLOG. What are PROLOG's strengths for data processing applications such as this? What are its weaknesses?

7 For the family tree database given in section 11-2.3, trace execution of the queries "parent (X, mary)?" and "grandparent (X, Y)?" What questions do these queries characterize?

8 Given a "telephone directory" file whose records are structured as follows:

person (name, phone)

Write a function that will display all persons whose names begin with the letter A, together with their phone numbers.

9 Write a PROLOG function that will sort its three parameters into ascending sequence, assuming they are all integers.

10 Revise the averaging program given at the beginning of the chapter so that it averages only the *positive* numbers in the input, rather than all of them.

11 Write a function named ''zeros'' which counts the number of zero entries in an arbitrary list A of integers.

12 Write a PROLOG program that counts the number of words in a text that end with ''ing'' or ''ed'' and displays that count. Your program should also accommodate punctuation marks in a reasonable way. For example, if the text is as follows:

As the bells were ringing, we sped out of town.

your count should be 2.

13 Write a PROLOG function named ''substr'' which emulates the behavior of the PL/I function with the same name. That is, for a given string parameter S and integer parameters I and J, the function should return that substring in S, beginning at position I and having length J. If I and J do not define a proper substring of S, then the result returned should be the empty string.

REFERENCES

1 Pierre Roussel, *Prolog—Manuel de Reference et d'Utilisation,* Groupe d'Intelligence Artificielle, Universite d'Aix Marseille, 1975.

2 D. H. D. Warren and L. M. Pereira, ''PROLOG: the Language and its Implementation Compared to LISP,'' *Sigplan Notices* 12(8) (1977) and *Sigart Newsletter* 6(4) (1977).

CHAPTER **12**

C

12-1 INTRODUCTION TO C

The C programming language is designed to encourage economy of expression in a wide variety of applications. C's primary use is as a systems programming language, as it was used to produce over 90 percent of the code in the UNIX operating system. However, the C operators, data types, and function library are unusually rich and C is very portable, making its applications potentially widespread. Since C is the host language for UNIX, the current burgeoning use of UNIX in data processing and scientific programming will undoubtedly enhance the use of C in these areas as well.

12-1.1 Brief History of C

The historical development of C parallels that of UNIX itself. In 1969, Bell Laboratories sought an alternative to the Multics operating system for the PDP-7 computer. An original version of the UNIX operating system was thus written in assembler language. During the same period, an experimental language was being developed there by Kenneth Thompson. This language was named B,[1] and was designed after the earlier systems programming language BCPL.[2] In 1972, the language C was designed as an extension of B; the primary difference was that C had an extensive collection of standard types, while B was an essentially typeless language.

Soon thereafter, in 1973, UNIX itself was substantially extended and over 90 percent of this new version was rewritten in C. Because of this liberation from assembly language, UNIX (and hence C) became quite portable. It was quickly adapted to a variety of host systems, and soon gained widespread use. Moreover, the C language and its function library have since had a very stable life. All subsequent enhancements have been made to the library in such a way that preserved upward compatibility with existing programs.

In 1976–1977, UNIX was ported to the VAX system and a new version was independently developed at the University of California at Berkeley. The late 1970s and early 1980s have seen further proliferation of UNIX and C on diverse machines from mainframes to micros. Moreover, C has become independently supported outside the UNIX context, and compilers are available for many machines under their own operating systems. An excellent overview of the origins and characteristics of UNIX and C may be found in a series of articles in the *Bell Systems Technical Journal.*[3] The "standard" reference text for C is Kernighan and Ritchie,[4] and we shall use it as such throughout this chapter.

12-1.2 Implementations and Variations of C

Since its original implementation on the PDP-7, C has been implemented on a wide variety of computers, including the following:

Digital PDP-10, VAX
Honeywell 6000
IBM 370, 4341, PC, Series 1
Interdata 8/32
Various 68000-based micros

It is estimated that over 5000 UNIX sites had been established by 1982. Moreover, several UNIX imitators have emerged recently as well. Thus, UNIX (and hence C) promises to be widely implemented and utilized in the foreseeable future.

12-1.3 Major Applications of C

Although it was demonstrably designed as a systems programming language, C has spread in its popularity across several application areas. It is widely used in numerical, text processing, and database applications. Portability and the extensive function library permit diverse applications to be realized.

12-2 WRITING C PROGRAMS

A C program, in its simplest form, has a heading line; a left brace, {; a series of declarations (for variables, arrays, etc.); a series of statements; and a right brace,}. The left and right braces, { and }, play the role in C of **begin** and **end** in other languages, and thus delimit groups of statements which are to be treated as one. A prefix line, beginning with "#include" often appears as well, in order to append one or more libraries to the compilation process. C also has a small collection of reserved words, which are listed in section 12-2.2, and these appear in **boldface** throughout the chapter.

Below is a simple C program which computes and displays the average of an indeterminate number of input numbers. For instance, if the input were 85.5, 87.5, 89.5, and 91.5, the result displayed would be 88.5. The program uses the variable x to hold a single input number and the variable n to determine the number of input numbers in the process. The variables sum and av connote the numbers' sum and average, respectively.

```
#include <stdio.h>
main ()

/* This program averages n input numbers x */

{
        float x, sum, av;
        int n;

        n = 0;
        sum = 0;
        while(scanf("%f", &x) > 0) {
            ++n;
            sum += x;
        }
        av = sum / n;
        printf("%d numbers were given\n", n);
        printf("%f is their average\n", av);
}
```

The different types of statements in this program will be explained later. Generally, we see that the semicolon is used to terminate a statement and braces, {}, are used to group statements. Thus, the two statements following "**while** . . . " are treated as a group to be repeated until the end of the input occurs. Note also that the format of a C program is freely determined by the programmer.

The style of indenting shown here is a fairly conventional one that facilitates program readability. Comments in a C program may be inserted anywhere, provided that they are enclosed within the delimiters /* and */. Finally, we note that the full upper- and lowercase alphabet (A–Z and a–z) can be used in writing C programs. Additional details of this program will become clear as we introduce the various features of C throughout the chapter.

12-2.1 Elementary Data Types and Values

The basic C data types are numbers, which may be **int**, **float**, or **double**; or single ASCII characters, which are called **char**. Moreover, **int** numbers may be **short**, **long**, or **unsigned**.

Generally, an **int** number is a sequence of digits (0 . . . 9), which may be preceded by a sign (+ or −). **Long int** values are denoted by the character L (or l) appended as a suffix. Hexadecimal and octal integers can also be represented, by appending the prefix 0X (or 0x) and 0, respectively, to the number. Hexadecimal digits A through F (or a through f) are used along with 0 through 9 to represent hexadecimal numbers.

A **float** number is either an **int**, a decimal fraction, an exponent part, or some combination of these. The exponent part consists of the symbol E followed by an integer, denoting multiplication by that integer power of 10. Thus, for example, the **float** number −5.33E−4 consists of the integer −5, the decimal fraction .33, and the exponent part E−4, and is equivalent to the number −0.000533. Of course, the number −0.000533 is also a legitimate **float** and represents the same value as −5.33E−4. Additional examples of C number representations are given below:

	Representation				
Number	**int**	**long**	**octal**	**hexadecimal**	**float**
0	0	0L	00	0X0	0.0
25	25	25L	031	0X19	25.0
0.5					0.5
−1	−1	−1L	−01	−0X1	−1.0
22.55					22.55
					0.2255E2

Each number has, of course, several equivalent **float** representations. The range of valid **int** and **float** numbers depends upon the implementation. Moreover, most implementations support double precision **float** values, and C supports this by the **double** type. Typically single precision **float** values allow six significant digits, while double precision values allow sixteen.

The **char** data type provides the basis for string processing in C. A ''**char**'' data value is a single character (a letter, digit, or special character) enclosed in apostrophes, as in the following examples:

'A' '7' 'ƀ' '+' '$' 'a'

The set of characters available as **char** values depends on the implementation. Typically, this is the ASCII character set, except for some IBM implementations which prefer the EBCDIC set. Depending on its host representation (ASCII or EBCDIC), each character has an associated integer value. For instance, A has the integer value 65 in ASCII, 0 has the value 48, and so forth.

Moreover, some nongraphic characters have special representations using \ as an escape denotation. These are principally '\n' for newline, '\t' for tab, '\0' for null, '\b' for backspace, '\f' for form feed, '\r' for carriage return, '\\' for \, '\' for apostrophe, and '\ddd' for any three-digit decimal representation ddd of an ASCII (or EBCDIC) character.

A ''string constant'' in C is a series of characters enclosed in quotes, as shown in the following examples:

''SALES SUMMARY REPORT''
''5/15/83''
''May 15, 1983''

Strings are handled in C as arrays of characters terminated by a null byte, and a number of C library functions are provided to support string processing. We shall examine these later in the chapter.

The "symbolic constant" is a device that can be used at the top of a C program to identify a numerical value by name. It has the following form:

```
#define name value
```

For instance, if we wanted to define a very small number, say 10^{-5}, as "epsilon" in a mathematical computation, we could write:

```
#define epsilon 1.0E-5
```

This allows us to use the word "epsilon" as a synonym for 10^{-5} wherever it is needed throughout the program. The advantage of this occurs when we want to *change* the value of epsilon (to, for example, 10^{-8}) throughout the program. To accomplish that, we would need to change only the symbolic constant definition to:

```
#define epsilon 1.0E-8
```

and the change would be automatically effected.

12-2.2 Names, Variables, and Declarations

A C variable is a name which is associated with a value during execution of the program. The value of a variable may be changed by the program as execution proceeds. A variable name is called an "identifier," which formally is defined as follows:

> An *identifier* is a sequence of one or more letters (a–z, A–Z, or _) and/or digits (0–9), the first of which must be a letter.

However, only the first eight characters of an identifier are significant in distinguishing it from another one.

Each variable in a C program has an associated type and an associated storage class. The C storage classes are **auto** (default within functions), **extern** (default outside functions), **static**, and **register**. For the most part, variables used in a C program must be declared in a type declaration, which appears at the beginning of the program and has the following general form:

```
class type identifier list ;
```

Here, "type" may be one of **short**, **int**, **long**, **unsigned**, **float**, **double**, or **char**. "Class" denotes one of the four storage classes, and "identifier list" denotes a list of those variable names, separated by commas, whose values are to be of the designated type and storage class. For instance, the sample program has the following type declarations:

float x, sum, av;
int n;

which declare the three variables x, sum, and av to contain a **float** value, and the variable n to contain an **int** value. All four variables will have the **auto** storage class, which means that storage is dynamically allocated for them when the program or function in which they are declared begins execution, and is dynamically released when it terminates.

Initialization of C variables can be specified at the time they are declared, by simply appending an assignment symbol (=) and a value at the right of the variable name within the declaration. For instance, initialization of n's value at 0 can be specified as follows:

int n = 0;

and this will eliminate the need for explicitly assigning it the value 0 at the beginning of the program's executable part. Variables which have the external or static storage class are automatically initialized by the system to 0. However, it is not generally wise to rely on this convention, as program readability would suffer. Automatic and register variables are never initialized by the system.

As a final restriction, C variable names must not be identical with any of the language's *reserved words*. A full list of the C reserved words is given in Figure 12-1. Some implementations reserve the words **fortran** and **asm** as well as those listed in Figure 12-1.

There is an additional special use of variables in C that is very important in the context of data structures and parameter linkage. That is, a variable may be used to "point to" another storage location by containing that location's address as its value. When a variable, say PX, is used as a pointer in this way, it is declared with type **int** and prefixed with an asterisk as follows:

int *PX;

FIGURE 12-1
C RESERVED WORDS

auto	**do**	**for**	**return**	**switch**
break	**double**	**goto**	**short**	**typedef**
case	**else**	**if**	**sizeof**	**union**
char	**entry**	**int**	**static**	**unsigned**
continue	**extern**	**long**	**struct**	**while**
default	**float**	**register**		

Now PX may be assigned as its value the address of another variable, say X, using an ampersand prefix to denote "the address of" in the following way:

```
int X;
int *PX = &X;
```

Hence, every reference of the form *PX means "the contents of the address of X," and is thus equivalent to the reference X itself.

12-2.3 Arrays and Other Data Structures

The three internal data structures provided by C are "arrays," "structures," and "unions." For all of these, the aforementioned notions of "pointer" and "address" are essential.

An array is declared via an "array declaration," which has the following form:

```
type identifier [ size ] [ size ] . . . [ size ] ;
```

Here, "type" denotes the type of all values stored in the array, "identifier" names the array, and "size" gives the number of elements in each dimension of the array. However, the subscript range in each dimension goes from 0 to size − 1 (rather than from 1 to size!). Separation of subscript ranges with distinct pairs of brackets in this way emphasizes that an *n*-dimensional array is represented in storage as a one-dimensional array of (n − 1)-dimensional arrays. For example, suppose we want to define an array A of one dimension and five **int** entries, and an array B of two dimensions with five rows and four columns of **float** entries, as shown in Figure 12-2. Then we would declare A and B as follows:

```
int A[5];
float B[5][4];
```

Now, an array reference to any of the entries in A is written by giving the appropriate subscript (from 0 to 4) within brackets appended to the name A. Thus, the first element is A[0], the second is A[1], and so forth. Similarly, an entry of B is identified by giving a pair of bracketed subscripts, indicating respectively its row number and column number within B. Thus, the element in the first row, first column of B is referenced as B[0][0], the first row, second column as B[0][1], and so forth.

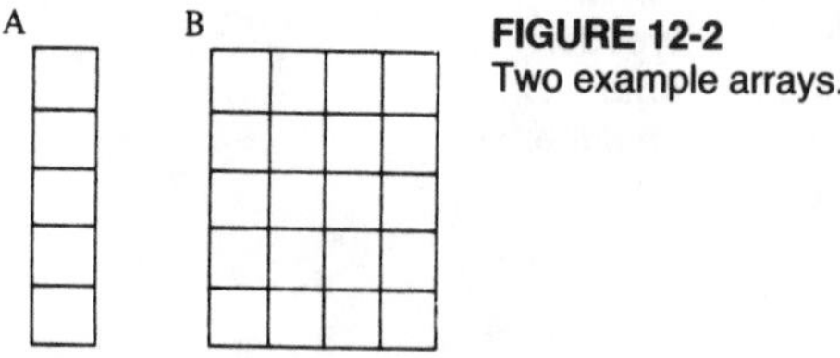

FIGURE 12-2
Two example arrays.

As mentioned above, a character string is represented in C as an array. Thus, a string variable is declared as a one-dimensional array of **char** values. For instance,

```
char name[20];
```

declares "name" as a fixed length twenty-character string variable. Individual characters within name may be accessed by using an appropriate reference, such as name[0], name [1], and so forth. We shall see in a later section that C provides powerful string manipulation functions, and versatile provisions for handling varying length strings.

The "structure" is C's vehicle for defining an entry in a file or a linked list. Such an entry is typically composed of different types of elements. An example structure is shown in Figure 12-3. Here, we see a structure composed of a name, a social security number, a gross pay amount, and an address. Each of these "fields" in the structure has a different type; the name is a twenty-five-character string, the social security number is an integer (which may alternately be defined as a ten-character string), the gross pay is a decimal number, and the address is a forty-character string. Note that each of the strings here is terminated by a null byte (\0). Alternately, a structure can be described as a tree to display its structure and name its nodes, as shown in Figure 12-4.

A structure in C is viewed as a new data type, and thus is defined by a structure declaration, as follows:

```
struct tag {
   type identifier;
   type identifier;
   :
   type identifier;
};
```

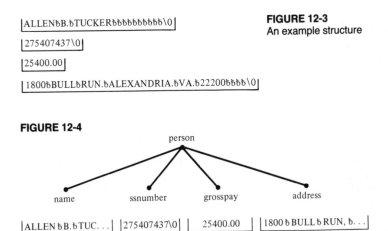

|ALLENƀB.ƀTUCKERƀƀƀƀƀƀƀƀƀƀ\0|

|275407437\0|

|25400.00|

|1800ƀBULLƀRUN.ƀALEXANDRIA.ƀVA.ƀ22200ƀƀƀƀ\0|

FIGURE 12-3
An example structure

FIGURE 12-4

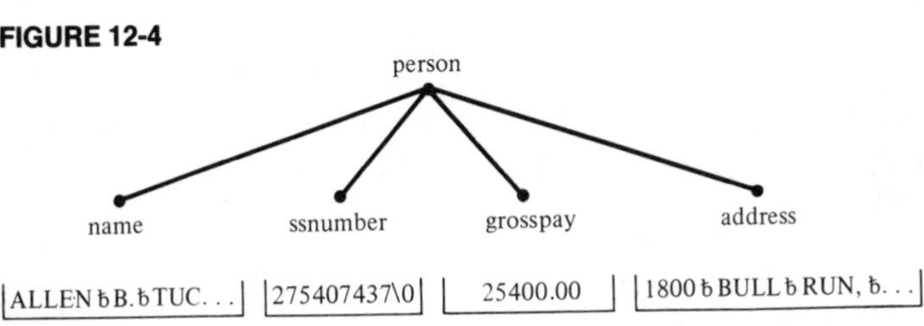

Here, the "tag" is an identifier which names the structure as a whole, while the other identifiers name and assign types to each of its constituent fields. Thus, the above example's structure can be characterized in the following type declaration:

```
struct person {
   char name[25];
   char ssnumber[10];
   float grosspay;
   char address[40];
};
```

Having defined the new type "person," we can proceed to declare variables with this type, as in the variable PER below:

```
struct person PER;
```

Alternately, we can give the **struct** description for the variable PER directly when we declare it as follows:

```
struct {
char name[25];
   ⋮
} PER;
```

Records, like trees, can have multiple levels of structure, as shown in the following refinement of our example (Figure 12-5). In this case, we embed an additional **struct** description in place of each elementary type in our structure where a nonleaf node appears. Thus, the type "person" is refined as follows:

```
struct person {
   struct name {
      char first[10];
      char middle[5];
      char last[10];
   };
   char ssnumber[10];
   float grosspay;
   struct address {
      char street[16];
      char city[12];
      char state[6];
      char zip[6];
   };
};
```

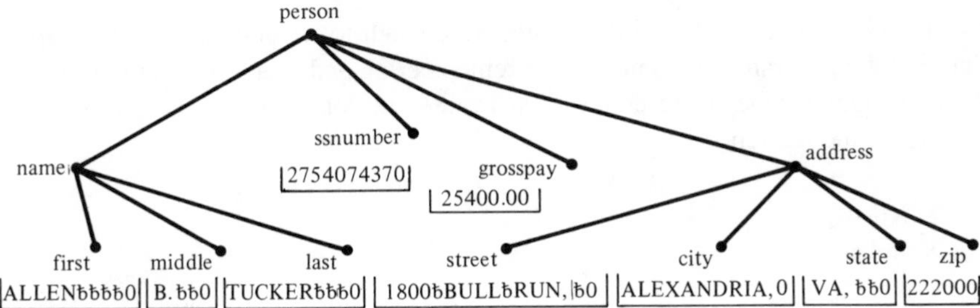

FIGURE 12-5

To reference an *entire structure* within a C program, only the name of a variable declared with that structure tag needs to be given. For example, the name PER references collectively all four fields of a "person" structure. On the other hand, to reference a *single field* of a structure, we "qualify" the variable by following it with a dot (.) and the corresponding field name. For example, to reference a "person" structure's name field we say

```
PER.name
```

and to reference the street address, we say

```
PER.address.street
```

and so forth.

A "union" is a characteristic of C which permits a single variable to have different types of values at different times during execution; that is, the variable's type is generic in the same sense as in SNOBOL. However, C requires the program to declare the alternatives explicitly, using the following type declaration:

```
union tag {
   type identifier;
   type identifier;
   ⋮
};
```

Here, "tag" identifies the particular union being defined, while the types and identifiers serve to specify the alternative types that will be permitted under this tag. For example, suppose we want to permit a variable X to be either **float** or **char** at different times during program execution. Then, the following declarations will be needed:

```
union floatchar {
   float Xfloat;
   char Xchar;
};
floatchar X;
```

Now the variable X will be allocated storage enough to accommodate either type of value, but the program is responsible for remembering and properly handling the most recently assigned value. To reference such a value, the dot notation is used, as for structures. Thus, the reference

X.Xfloat
or X.Xchar

properly refers to the **float** or the **char** value most recently stored in X.

Initialization of Arrays and Structures Initial values may be stored in any **static** or **extern** array or structure variable at the time it is declared. Automatic arrays and structures may not be so initialized. The general form of such an initialization is as follows:

= { list of values }

Here, "list of values" denotes any list of values which are to be taken in the order written and stored successively in the individual entries of the array or structure. In the case of a two-dimensioned or higher array, the list of values are stored in row-major order. If the list does not have a sufficient number of values to fill the array or structure, the remaining elements are automatically filled with zeros.

To illustrate, suppose that A is a five-element array of **int** values, which should be initialized with the particular values 3, 4, −7, 25, and 9 respectively. The following declaration can be used:

int A[5] = {3, 4, −7, 25, 9};

The initialization can be used to define automatically the number of entries in a one-dimensional array, by simply leaving out the size specification within the declaration's brackets. So the above array A could have equivalently been declared as follows:

int A[] = {3, 4, −7, 25, 9};

This is a particularly handy device for defining and initializing character string variables, since a list of characters within single quotes ('') can be abbreviated as a string within double quotes (""). For example, the string variable SALUTE can be declared and initialized with the string value "Hello!" in any of the following equivalent ways:

char SALUTE[7] = {'H', 'e', 'l', 'l', 'o', '!', '\0'};
char SALUTE[] = {'H', 'e', 'l', 'l', 'o', '!', '\0'};
char SALUTE[] = "Hello!";

The last is, of course, always preferred.

12-2.4 Basic Statements

The following is a list of the C statements and a general description of their purpose:

Statement	Purpose
Expression statement	To perform a series of arithmetic operations (addition, subtraction, etc.) or function calls, and possibly assign the result to a variable, array, or structure entry.
Compound statement	To unify a series of statements to be treated as a single statement.
Goto statement **Break** statement **Continue** statement **Return** statement	To alter the sequence of program statement execution by transferring control to a statement which does not immediately follow in the program text.
Conditional statement **Switch** statement	To select a statement for execution depending on whether or not a particular condition is true.
For statement **While** statement **Do...while** statement	To repeat execution of a sequence of statements.

The expression and compound statements will be discussed in this section. The function reference, together with the function definition and **return** statement, will be discussed in sections 12-2.6 and 12-2.7. The rest are control statements, and will be discussed in section 12-2.5.

The compound statement is C's device for grouping several statements so that they can be treated as one. This is especially valuable in the specification of loops, as we shall see. The form of the compound statement is

```
{S S . . . S}
```

where S denotes any other C statement. An example of the compound statement appears in the averaging program at the beginning of section 12-2.

The "expression statement" has the following basic form:

```
expression;
```

Here, "expression" denotes a calculation, function reference, or constant which will give a value. Examples of expression statements are given in the averaging program such as the following:

```
++n;
sum += x;
av = sum / n;
```

The third is an example of the familiar "assignment statement" from other languages. However, in C this is just a special case of an expression since "=" is a binary operator with low priority.

A C expression is generally a more comprehensive notion than in other languages, with few arbitrary restrictions on operand pairing and including provision for a broad range of operators and operand types. Central to this concept is the notion of "lvalue," which in C is any expression that can be resolved to a memory address. Lvalues include, therefore, variable names, array references, and structure references. They exclude constants.

At the highest priority are the following operators:

```
()    []    .    ->
```

These designate, in turn, the arguments in a function reference, the subscripts of an array, and two forms of referencing an element in a structure or union. They are evaluated from left to right.

At the next highest priority are the following unary prefix operators, which evaluate from right to left, and whose meaning is summarized below:

Operator	Meaning
*	pointer value
&	address
−	negation
!	logical negation
~	1's complement
++	increment (add 1)
−−	decrement (subtract 1)
sizeof	number of bytes required by the operand
(type-name)	conversion of the operand to type-name

Moreover, the operators ++ and −− can be used either in prefix position or postfix position. Both of these operators *require* their operand to be an lvalue, since the result must be assigned to a storage location.

Most of these operators have already been encountered. The sizeof operator illustrates the degree of control over storage allocation which the programmer can exercise. The last operator can be used to force explicit conversion of a value to a specific type. For instance, the expression (**float**)3 converts the value 3 to **float** representation.

At the next priority level are the binary operators, listed on the next page in decreasing order of priority among themselves. These all evaluate from left to right within the same level of priority. These are all fairly common as well, except for the bit-shift operators and the bitwise logical operators. Again, these additions emphasize the potential system-level control afforded by C.

Operator	Meaning
* / %	multiplication, division, remainder
+ −	addition, subtraction
>> <<	bit-shift right, bit-shift left
< > <= >=	less than, greater than, less than or equal to, greater than or equal to
== !=	equal, not equal
&	bitwise "and"
^	bitwise exclusive "or"
|	bitwise "or"
&&	logical "and"
||	logical "or"

Finally, the assignment operators share the lowest priority, are evaluated from right to left, and are summarized below:

Operator (op)	Meaning of a op b
=	ordinary assignment
+=	abbreviates a = a + b
−=	abbreviates a = a − b
*=	abbreviates a = a * b
/=	abbreviates a = a / b
%=	abbreviates a = a % b
>>=	abbreviates a = a>>b
<<=	abbreviates a = a<<b
&=	abbreviates a = a & b
^=	abbreviates a = a ^ b
|=	abbreviates a = a | b

Below all of these operators in priority is the comma (,), which is evaluated from left to right. Finally, there is one ternary operator ?:, which is an abbreviation for **if . . . then . . . else** in the following way. If x, y, and z are expressions then the expression

x ? y : z

means, "if expression x is true then evaluate y else evaluate z." Since this form can be embedded within a larger expression, the effect is to enable conditional expressions to occur within assignments, function calls, and so forth.

Parentheses may be used to override the order of evaluation defined for these operators, in the usual way. To illustrate these conventions, consider the following expression and the indicated order in which its operations are carried out:

```
3 + B * (C − D)
  ↑   ↑    ↑
 (3) (2)  (1)
```

Note that if we had not parenthesized "C − D" then the implied order would have been as follows:

```
3 + B * C − D
  ↑   ↑   ↑
 (2) (1) (3)
```

The result of evaluating such an expression is determined also on the basis of the coercions which are either expressed or implied by the type of its operands.

Coercion C permits a variety of different types to coexist within a single expression, wherever it makes sense to do so. Thus, C may be classified as a "weakly typed" language. Moreover, because the logical values "true" and "false" in C are represented by the integers 1 and 0, and the **char** values all have equivalent integer (ASCII or EBCDIC) internal representations, a variety of useful coercions can be assumed by the programmer.

Arithmetic coercions occur as expected. More precisely, for each arithmetic operator, the following coercions occur.

1 Each **char** or **short** is converted to **int**, and each **float** is converted to **double**.
2 If either operand is **double**, the other is converted to **double**.
3 If either operand is **long**, the other is converted to **long**.
4 If either operand is **unsigned**, the other is converted to **unsigned**.

The result of the arithmetic operation has as its type that of the operands after these rules have been applied.

Coercion also takes place across an assignment operation; the value on the right of the assignment operator is converted to the type of the operand on the left. This includes integer to character conversion, and vice versa, using the ASCII or EBCDIC integer codes for the characters. In the assignment of a **float** value to an **int**eger variable, the former is truncated in the conversion. However, assignment of a **double** value to a **float** variable causes *rounding* to take place in the conversion.

Automatic coercion also occurs in a function call, whenever the type of an argument is **char**, **short**, or **float**. The first two are converted to **int**, while the latter is converted to **double**.

Explicit coercion, as mentioned above, can be forced by a prefix type in parentheses before the expression to be coerced. Thus, for example, the expression

(**double**) (x + y) + z

converts the result of x + y to **double** precision before it is added to z.

12-2.5 Control Structures

In this section, the C statements that control the structure of program execution are presented and illustrated.

Goto Statements The basic form of the "**goto** statement" is the following:

```
goto label;
```

Here, "label" denotes the label of some other statement in the program, and can be any unreserved identifier followed by a colon (:). When executed, the **goto** statement serves to interrupt the normal (textual) sequence of statement execution by transferring control to the statement having the indicated label. For instance, the **goto** statement:

```
goto loop;
```

causes the statement labeled "loop" to be the next one executed, rather than the statement that follows sequentially.

Conditional Statements The form of the conditional statement may be one of the following:

(i) **if** (e) S_1
(ii) **if** (e) S_1 **else** S_2

Here, e denotes any expression, while S_1 and S_2 denote any statements. A conditional statement of form (i) is executed in two steps. First, the expression e is evaluated. Second, if the result is nonzero, the statement S_1 is executed. Otherwise, S_1 is not executed.

Form (ii) is executed also in two steps. As before, the expression is first evaluated. Second, either S_1 or S_2 is executed (and the other one is not executed) depending on whether the result of evaluating expression e is nonzero or zero, respectively.

Form (i) of the conditional statement is illustrated in the following example:

```
if (a < b) {
   a++;
   b--;
}
```

Here, the expression is "a < b", while the statement S_1 is a compound statement.

For a more practical example, consider writing a C program segment to solve for the real roots x of the quadratic equation

$$ax^2 + bx + c = 0 \qquad (\text{for } a \neq 0)$$

where a, b, and c are **float** and given.

The number of roots and their values can be determined by first computing the discriminant d from a, b, and c as follows:

$$d = b^2 - 4ac$$

If $d < 0$ then there are no real roots. If $d = 0$, then there is one real root x_1, given by the calculation $-b/(2a)$. If $d > 0$, then there are two roots, x_1 and x_2, given by the following calculations:

$$x_1 = \frac{-b + \sqrt{d}}{2a}$$

$$x_2 = \frac{-b - \sqrt{d}}{2a}$$

The C program segment to compute the number of roots, say NROOTS, and their values x1 and x2, given the coefficients a, b, and c, can be written as follows:

```
d = b * b-4 * a * c;
if (d < 0)
   NROOTS = 0;
else if (d == 0) {
   NROOTS = 1;
   x1 = -b/(2 * a);
   }
else {
   NROOTS = 2;
   x1 = (-b + sqrt(d))/(2 * a);
   x2 = (-b - sqrt(d))/(2 * a);
   }
```

Both conditional statements in this example are of form (ii). The notation sqrt(d) is a reference to a library function named "sqrt," which calculates the square root of d.

For Statements and Iterative Loops C provides several forms of the "**for** statement" as an aid to specifying iterative loops. Many such loops are "countercontrolled" loops, in which a control variable is initialized and tested and incremented each time the sequence of statements is executed. When the variable is incremented beyond a specific limit, the loop's execution terminates. This is pictured in two different forms in the flowcharts in Figure 12-6.

In the figure, "i" denotes the control variable and m_1, m_2, and m_3 denote arithmetic expressions which are the initial value, the limit, and the increment value for the control variable, respectively.

Flowchart (*b*) can be written equivalently as a C **for** statement as follows:

```
for (i = m1; i <= m2; i += m3) {
| Sequence of |
| Statements  |
}
```

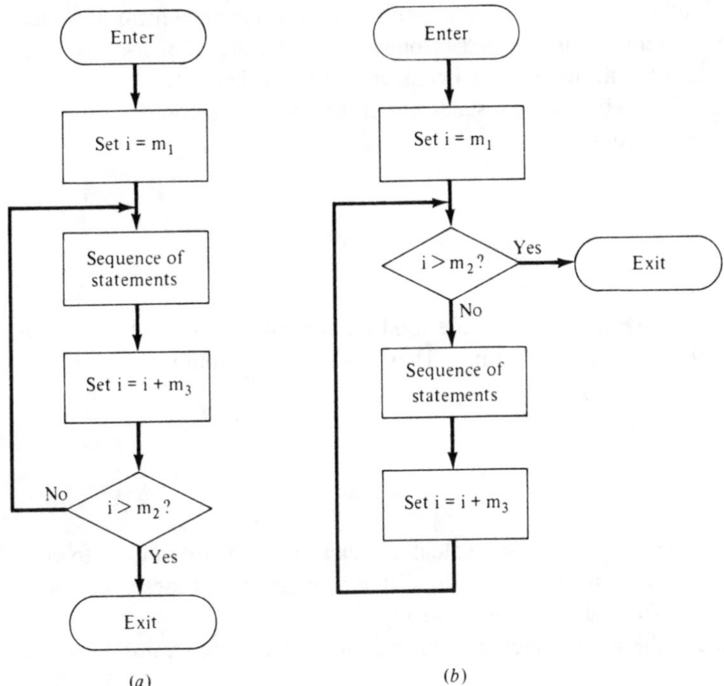

FIGURE 12-6
Two forms of iterative loops

In the event that the sequence of statements contains only one statement, the compound braces may be dropped. For example, the following **for** statement sums the integers from 1 to 10:

```
for (i = 1; i <= 10; i += 1)
    sum += i;
```

assuming that "sum" was originally set to zero.

The **for** statement is actually more general than the above common characterization suggests. That is, the following form can be used:

```
for (e1; e2; e3)
    statement
```

Here, e1, e2, and e3 denote *any* expressions, and the "statement" is repeated in the following way:

- The expression e1 is evaluated.
- The following sequence is repeated as long as e2 is nonzero (true): "statement" is executed, and e3 is evaluated.

Moreover, any or all of e1, e2, and e3 may be omitted from this general form. If e1 and e3 are omitted, the ''statement'' is repeated as long as e2 is nonzero. If e2 itself is omitted, the loop is potentially infinite (but see **break** and **continue** below).

For another example, the following restatement of the above loop computes the sum of ten integers in reverse order.

```
for (i = 10; i >= 1; i--)
   sum += i;
```

The **while** and **do. . .while** statements are used for controlling loops which are repeated for an unpredictable number of times. They have the following forms:

```
while (B) S
do S while (B);
```

Here, B denotes any expression, whose evaluation determines whether or not to continue repeating evaluation of statement S. The different semantics of these two forms are shown in Figures 12-7*a* and 12-7*b*, respectively.

One common use of the **while** statement occurs in the example program, where we see:

```
while (scanf("%f", &x) >0) {
   ⋮
}
```

FIGURE 12-7 (*a*) The **while** statement. **(*b*)** The **do while** statement.

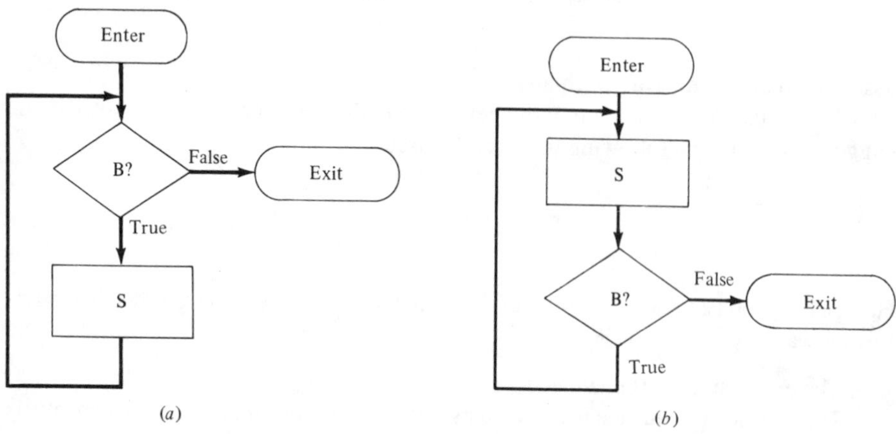

Here, the expression B combines the input function ''scanf'' (which stores a value in x) with a test to see whether or not ''end of file'' has occurred in the input. If so, the result returned by the scanf function will be negative, and repetition of the loop will terminate.

Another use for these forms occurs in numerical analysis, where a sequence of approximations is computed until a specific convergence condition is satisfied. For example, suppose we are developing an approximation to the square root of A by Newton's method. There the next approximation, Y, is computed from the previous one, X, by the formula:

$$Y = 0.5(X + A/X)$$

This is repeated until the absolute value of the difference between two successive approximations is sufficiently small, say less than 0.0001. The following loop will exit when that condition occurs:

```
Y = 0.5 * (X - A/X);
while (fabs(Y - X) >= 0.0001) {
   X = Y;
   Y = 0.5 * (X - A/X);
}
```

Here, fabs(Y − X) denotes a reference to the absolute value function. Alternatively, this loop can be specified by the **do**. . .**while** statement:

```
do {
   X = Y;
   Y = 0.5 * (X - A/X);
} while (fabs (Y - X) > = 0.0001);
```

Often a situation arises in which either a premature exit from a loop or a premature termination of a single iteration of a loop is desired. This, of course, can be done with a **goto** statement and an appropriately placed label. However, C provides the **break** and **continue** statements as preferable devices to accomplish these ends and keep the program relatively clean. Specifically, the ''**break** statement'' is written simply as

```
break;
```

and specifies premature discontinuation of the (innermost) **for**, **while**, or **do**. . .**while** loop in which it is embedded. The ''**continue** statement'' is written as

```
continue;
```

and designates that the *next* iteration of such a loop should immediately begin, abandoning the remaining statements in the current iteration.

This final example, which demonstrates matrix multiplication, illustrates how a loop may be nested within another loop.

```
for (i = 1; i <= m; i++)
   for j = 1; j<=p; j++){
      C[i][j] = 0;
      for (k = 1; k <= n; k++)
         C[i][j] = C[i][j] + A[i][k] * B[k][j];
   }
```

Here, the m × n matrix A and the n × p matrix B are multiplied, with their product being stored in the m × p matrix C. The ijth element of C is computed as follows:

$$C_{ij} = \sum_{k=1}^{n} A_{ik} B_{kj} \qquad \text{for } i = 1, \ldots, m \text{ and } j = 1, \ldots, p$$

Note that the "innermost" nested statement is executed n times for each one of the m × p entries in C, or m × n × p times altogether. Note also that the arrays A, B, and C would need to be declared with an *extra* element in each dimension, since their subscript ranges start at 0.

The Switch Statement The "**switch** statement" provides selection of one or more from a series of alternative statements, depending on the value of an expression. It has the following form:

```
switch (e) {
   case v1: S1
   case v2: S2
      ⋮
   case vn: Sn
   default: T
}
```

Here, e denotes an expression, v1, . . . , vn denote lists of possible values that e can have, and each of S1, . . . , Sn denotes the corresponding statement to be executed for each value. The "**default** alternative statement" T is executed in the event that expression e has *none* of the values v1, . . . , vn. Moreover, more than one of the statements S may be executed. That is, if the value of e satisfies vi (say), then all of Si through Sn are executed in order.

For example, suppose we want to take one of four different actions depending on whether the current wind direction DIR is 'N,' 'S,' 'E,' or 'W' respectively, or else a fifth action in the event that DIR is none of these. This can be specified in a **switch** statement as follows:

```
switch (DIR) {
   case 'N':/* action 1 */; break;
   case 'S':/* action 2 */; break;
   case 'E':/* action 3 */; break;
   case 'W':/* action 4 */; break;
   default:/* action 5 */;
}
```

Thus, the **switch** is a replacement for a series of conditional statements. The above example can be given equivalently as:

```
if (DIR = = 'N' /* action 1 */;
   else if (DIR = = 'S') /* action 2 */;
      else if (DIR = = 'E') /* action 3 */;
         else if (DIR = = 'W') /* action 4 */;
            else /* action 5 */;
```

Note that the break statement is used in the **switch** here to force exit of control after one action is complete.

12-2.6 Input-Output Conventions

A "file" is a sequence of data values which are external to the program. In C, there are three "standard files," called "stdin," "stdout," and "stderr." Normally, these are all assigned to the terminal, so that input is entered at the keyboard, and output and error messages are displayed on the terminal screen.

The special command at the head of a C program,

```
#include <stdio.h>
```

effectively links the program with the "standard" input-output functions which transfer data to and from these files. At the time a program begins execution, these three files are automatically opened and subsequent input and output statements can transfer data to them without any additional provisions. The principal input functions for this purpose are called "getchar" and "scanf," while the corresponding output functions are called "putchar" and "printf."

The functions getchar and putchar are the most primitive input-output functions in C, transferring only a single character to or from the program at one time. They have the following form:

```
c = getchar();
putchar(c);
```

Here, c denotes any **char** variable, into which a single input character may be stored from stdin, and from which a single output character may be displayed in stdout.

Along with getchar (and scanf, as well) comes a special provision for indicating end of file within the program. The definition

```
#define EOF -1
```

is provided within the standard input-output package stdio, and the result returned by getchar will be − 1 whenever end of file occurs. Thus, the expression

```
((c = getchar()) ! = EOF)
```

serves the dual purpose of obtaining from the input the next character and simultaneously checking for end of file. A similar form is used in the sample program at the beginning of the chapter, using the scanf function in place of getchar.

More useful in general are the scanf and printf functions for input and output. These provide for the usual transfer of numbers, character strings, and other data in a convenient and versatile way. Scanf and printf can be used for data which is either free-form or formatted, and have the following syntax:

```
scanf (control, p1, p2, . . . )
printf (control, e1, e2, . . . )
```

Here, "control" denotes a quoted string containing a series of format descriptions for the individual data items as they appear in the input or output file, p1, p2, . . . denote a series of pointers to addresses where the input values will be stored, and e1, e2, . . . denote a series of expressions whose values will be displayed as output.

Each format description in the "control" part of these functions can be one of the following, and carries a meaning described on the right:

Format description	Meaning
%d	A decimal integer
%o	An octal integer
%x	A hexadecimal integer
%c	A single character
%s	A character string
%f	A decimal (**float** or **double**) number
\n	Skip to a new line
\t	Horizontal tab
\b	Backspace
\"	Literal quote
\\	Literal backslash

The last five of these may be used only in the printf function for the purpose of horizontal and vertical spacing. The others are equally applicable to the scanf and the printf functions.

Two examples of these controls appear in the sample program at the beginning of the chapter, as follows:

scanf(''%f'', &x)

and

printf(''%f is their average\n'', av)

The scanf function literally says to scan forward in the input file (stdin) until the next value is located, interpret it as a decimal value, and store it in memory address x. The printf function here says to display both the decimal value of the variable av and the string value ''is their average,'' and then to skip to a new line. When no further format specifications are given, the system uses the values themselves to determine individual field widths in a conventional way.

The input and output values are otherwise taken as a continuous *stream* of values, and each successive scanf (or printf) function will proceed to the next available value (or position) in the stream. Still further control of spacing between adjacent values and/or the representation of a single value can be obtained by refining the format specifications according to the following options:

1 Following ''%'' may occur a minus sign (−) to designate left-adjustment of a value within the field where it appears.

2 Following this, an integer may occur to explicitly specify the field width.

3 A period and an integer number may follow, in order to designate an explicit number of decimal digits or string characters to be displayed.

Thus, for example, if the **int** variable SCORE has the value −14 and the **float** variable AV has the value 10.25, the statement

printf(''%5d %8.2f'', SCORE, AV)

will leave the following output:

```
1     6      13
↓     ↓      ↓
ƀƀ−14 ƀƀƀ10.25
```

Input and output can also be directed to other files besides the standard ones. A file may reside on disk, magnetic tape, or any other suitable medium. Data may be transferred to and from such a file by invoking additional file processing functions which are summarized below. The functions described here are only the most primitive ones. C programs running under UNIX (which is usually the case) have access to additional file processing functions, which are implementation dependent.

At the outset, a program which uses an external file must declare and open it in the following way:

```
FILE *fopen(), *fp;
fp = fopen(filename, mode);
```

Here, ''fp'' designates a pointer to the file named ''filename,'' and ''mode'' must be either r (for an input file), w (for an output file), or a (for a file to which additional data will be appended at its end).

Opening a file whose name does not exist in the system, with mode ''w'' or ''a'', effectively creates that file. Specifying mode r in this instance leads to an error, which returns the NULL pointer value to fp (the name NULL, like EOF, is predefined). Opening an existing file with mode r positions the program at the beginning of the file for reading data. Mode ''w'' with an existing file effectively leads to destructive replacement of all data in the file, while mode ''a'' allows for graceful addition of data to the end of the file.

Single characters may be read from or written to a file thus opened by way of the following extensions of the getc and putc functions introduced above:

```
c = getc(fp);
putc(c, fp);
```

Here, fp is identically the file pointer under which the file was opened, and c designates the **char** variable where the input or output character is stored.

Finally, the function ''fclose'' is used to disconnect the file from the program, after all input-output operations are concluded. It has the following form:

```
fclose(fp);
```

where ''fp'' designates the same file pointer with which the file was originally opened.

Individual lines of input or output may be transferred to or from a file using the following functions and conventions. To support these, the name MAXLINE is assumed here to denote the maximum line length for the implementation. To read or write a single line as a string of characters, the following functions are used:

```
fgets(string, MAXLINE, fp)
fputs(string, fp)
```

Here, ''string'' designates the string to be transferred (for fgets, it must of course be an lvalue), and ''fp'' again designates the file to and from which the line will be transferred.

Formatting and unformatting this string in memory, just before a "fputs" or just after a "fgets" respectively, so that individual data values in the line may be gathered from or spread to individual variables, is aided by the following variations of the printf and scanf functions which were introduced earlier:

```
sprintf(string, control, e1, e2, . . . )
sscanf(string, control, p1, p2, . . . )
```

Here, the meaning of "control," "e1, e2, . . . ", and "p1, p2, . . . " is the same as for scanf and printf. "String" designates an area in memory where the formatted value is stored. Thus, sprintf and sscanf perform formatting but use a string in memory rather than a line in an input or output file.

Now we can see how individual lines containing composite data values can be transferred to or from a file. For input, we can combine fgets and sscanf as follows:

```
fgets(string, MAXLINE, fp);
sscanf(string, control, p1, p2, . . . );
```

which results in a line of input being taken from a file into the storage buffer "string" and subsequently spread among the individual variables "p1," "p2," and so forth. Similarly, the pair sprintf and fputs can be combined for the opposite transfer as follows:

```
sprintf(string, control, e1, e2, . . . );
fputs(string, fp);
```

12-2.7 Subprograms, Functions, and Libraries

Most practical programming tasks are large enough to justify segmenting the program into a number of functional units, all linked together by a "main" program which controls the sequence in which these units will be executed. The other advantage of program segmentation is that it permits the reuse of code without rewriting and debugging it each time it is needed.

C is especially well suited for program segmentation in this way. The C main program is just a special case of a function, and generally several such functions are written to accomplish a specific task. Many functions, such as the input-output functions discussed in the preceding section, are so important that they are provided in a "standard function library" (such as stdio.h) and do not need to be redefined by the programmer when they are needed. Others are more specialized and can be selectively defined as an individual program needs them. The process of function definition and invocation in C is described and illustrated in this section.

In addition to the standard input-output library, most C implementations provide additional libraries of functions to suit the needs of different applications. For example, mathematical applications typically require the trigonometric and logarithmic functions, and these are provided in a library called "math.h". Specifically, this library contains the following functions:

Function	**Meaning**
sin	trigonometric sine
cos	cosine
tan	tangent
cotan	cotangent
asin	arc sine
acos	arc cosine
atan	arc tangent
log	natural logarithm
log10	log to the base 10
exp	exponential
sqrt	square root
pow	power
sinh	hyperbolic sine
cosh	hyperbolic cosine
tanh	hyperbolic tangent

Any function, whether it is a standard function or a programmer-defined function, is invoked by virtue of the appearance of a "function call" within a larger expression. A function call is written in the following way:

name (e1, e2, . . . , en)

Here, "name" denotes the function's name and e1, e2, . . . , en denote expressions whose respective values will be passed to the function at the time of invocation. For example, suppose we have **double** variables a, b, and c; the values of a and b are 2 and 3, respectively; and we want to compute c as follows:

$$c = \frac{a + b}{\sqrt{a^2 + b^2}}$$

Then we can use the standard function "sqrt" as follows:

```
c = (a + b)/sqrt(a*a + b*b);
```

Note that the expression "a*a + b*b" is first evaluated, then the result (13) is passed as the argument to the function "sqrt," and that result is (a close approximation to) the square root of 13, say 3.60555. This value then becomes the divisor for the remaining evaluation.

It is important also to note that the standard functions listed above are *not generic*, in the sense that they accept as an argument a **double** expression, and the result delivered is **double**.

Writing Functions When the C standard functions do not provide the kind of computation desired, the programmer may define a new function by way of a ''function definition.'' It can then be invoked using a function call, in the same way that the standard functions are invoked.

Because a (programmer-written) function is invoked in the context as a standard function, it must deliver no more than a single value as a result. The type (**float**, **int**, **char**, etc.) of that result is identified at the beginning of the declaration, whose general form is as follows:

```
type name (parameters)
  parameter declarations
  {
    local variables
    statements
  }
```

Here, ''type'' identifies the type of the result returned by the function, ''name'' denotes the function, ''parameters'' is a list (possibly empty) of the function's parameters, ''parameter declarations'' declares the types of the parameters, ''local variables'' declares variables (automatic and static) which will be used only locally within the body of the function, and ''statements'' defines the function body itself.

To illustrate, let's write a function which computes the factorial of an integer n, defined as follows:

$$\text{factorial}\ (n) = n \times (n - 1) \times \cdots \times 3 \times 2 \qquad \text{for } n > 1$$
$$= 1 \qquad \text{for } n = 1$$

The one parameter, n, is an **int**, and the result will also be an **int**. When writing the function body, we treat n as if it were an ordinary **int** variable whose factorial we are computing. The function declaration can thus be written as follows:

```
int factorial (n)
  int n;
{
  int i, f;
  f = 1;
  for (i = 2; i <= n; i++)
    f *= i;
  return(f);
}
```

The function's body generally contains a return statement, whose execution will cause a value to be returned to the invocation. This statement has one of the following two forms:

```
return (expression);
return;
```

The second form is used when no value is to be returned, and in this case the call must not rely upon such a result. In our example, the result returned is the computed factorial.

Invoking Functions As mentioned, a function may be invoked only by execution of a function call within an expression. The function call gives a list of expressions as arguments which match, one for one, with the parameters in the function's definition.

An invocation of the function involves the following steps. First, each parameter is assigned the current *value* of its corresponding actual parameter (i.e., all parameters are called by value). Second, the body is executed. Third, control is returned to the expression which contained the function call when a return statement is encountered. The result returned is the value of the expression in the return statement, if present, or undefined otherwise. To illustrate, suppose we want to compute the binomial coefficients

$$a_i = \frac{N!}{i!\,(N - i)!} \qquad \text{for } i = 0, 1, \ldots, N$$

for the familiar polynomial:

$$(x + y)^N = a_N x^N + a_{N-1} x^{N-1} y + \cdots + a_i x^i y^{N-i} + \cdots + a_0 y^N$$

We can write the following program which reads N and displays the desired sequence of coefficients a:

```
#include <stdio.h>
main()
{
   int N,a,i;
   scanf("%d", & N);
   for (i = 0; i <= N; i++){
      a = factorial(N) / (factorial(i) * factorial (N - i));
      printf("a[%2d]= %d", i, a);
   }
}
```

We will focus attention on the underlined expression statement which contains three different function calls for the function "factorial."

The first invocation occurs as ''factorial(N).'' Suppose that the actual value of N is 4. First, the parameter n is assigned the value 4 of N (its corresponding argument). Second, the body

```
{
    int i, f;
    f = 1;
    for (i = 2; i <= n; i++)
        f *= i;
    return(f);
}
```

is executed, leaving ''factorial'' with the correctly computed factorial of N, or 24. This is then returned to the expression, whose subsequent evaluation will be as follows.

```
a = 24/(factorial(i) * factorial (N - i))
```

The next call is ''factorial(i),'' which similarly returns the value 1, and the expression to be reduced as follows:

```
a = 24/(1 * factorial (N - i))
```

The third invocation will reduce the expression as follows;

```
a = 24/(1 * 6)
```

The expression's final result can now be computed.

Parameters Called by Reference Since all parameters are, by default, called by value in C, there is an explicit mechanism which allows an argument to be called by reference. Basically, this is done by passing the *address* of the argument, rather than its name, and writing the function definition appropriately. One uses this mechanism in cases where results are to be returned through the arguments themselves, rather than explicitly within a return statement.

For instance, if we want to invoke a function ''swap'' which switches the values of two variables, say x and y, then we would say

```
swap (&x, &y)
```

rather than

```
swap (x, y)
```

since the function swap requires the *addresses* of x and y, not their values. Correspondingly, the function definition declares the parameters for x and y as follows:

```
swap (px, py)
int *px, *py;
```

That is, parameters px and py designate pointers, or addresses, for x and y, and the values stored in those addresses should be interpreted as **int** values. Thus, every reference within the body of the function to the integer in location px must be written as *px rather than simply px.

To illustrate, let's rewrite the factorial function with an additional parameter pf which designates an address to hold the resulting factorial.

```
factorial (n, pf)
  int n, *pf;
{
  int i;
    *pf = 1;
  for (i = 2; i <= n; i++)
    *pf = *pf * i;
  return;
}
```

Now, to make use of this revision, the main program which computes the binomial coefficients can be rewritten as follows:

```
#include <stdio.h>
main()
{
  int N, Nfact, n1, n2, i, a;
  scanf("%d", & N);
  factorial (N, &Nfact);
  for (i = 0; i <= N; i++){
    factorial (i, &n1);
    factorial (N - i, &n2);
    a = Nfact / (n1 * n2);
    printf("a[%2d] = %d", i, a);
  }
}
```

Note here that new variables Nfact, n1, and n2, are used to hold intermediate results delivered by the parameters called by reference.

Recursion Functions in C can be defined recursively, in the usual way. Local variables have automatic storage class by default, so that each new call initiates new instances of its locals. We shall not otherwise belabor recursion here, except to encourage its use in the usual ways.

12-2.8 Additional Features

C has a number of additional features, the following of which are discussed in this section:

- Scope and externals
- Static storage class
- List processing

As may be evident by now, a complete C program is just a sequence of functions, one of which is called ''main,'' which are mutually external to each other. They are written separately, and may be individually compiled as well. However, no function may be syntactically embedded within another.

Within this framework, variables are generally local to that function in which they are declared. That is, they may not be referenced explicitly from outside their declaring function. There is one exception to this, and that is when a variable is declared syntactically outside of *any* function. In this case, the variable is said to be ''external'' and may potentially be referenced by *any* one or more functions within the entire program. To reference such a variable, the function must redeclare it as **extern** within its own body whenever that function is separately compiled.

For example, suppose we have the **int** variable x to be shared between the function main and the function f, as if it were a FORTRAN COMMON variable. The following structure is appropriate:

```
int x;
main()
{
   ⋮
}
f()
{
   extern int x;
   ⋮
}
```

Here, we assume that the **extern** variable x's declaration is compiled with the function main, and that the function f is separately compiled. If the two were compiled together, the explicit declaration within f of **extern int** x would not be necessary. Thus, external variables provide an alternative to parameters and arguments as a device for sharing a variable among several functions. We shall use this device specifically in our C solution to Case Study 3—Text Formatter.

Static variables may be internal or external. In either case, these variables are allocated storage once, at load time. Thus, a static variable within a function retains its value from one call to the next. This is necessary in some cases, such as random number generators. To declare that a variable have static storage class, the reserved word "**static**" is placed before the type specification in the variable's declaration.

C's list-processing facilities are provided through address variables, automatic storage class, and structures. Address variables themselves serve as pointers to structures which, in turn, are nodes on a dynamically linked list or tree structure. For instance, if we wish to create a linked list of fifteen-character names, a typical node would be defined as follows:

```
struct node {
   char name [16];
   struct node *fptr;
};
```

Here, the "node" has two parts, one for the "name" itself, and one for the pointer ("fptr") that will link this node to the next one in the list. Thus, the following picture

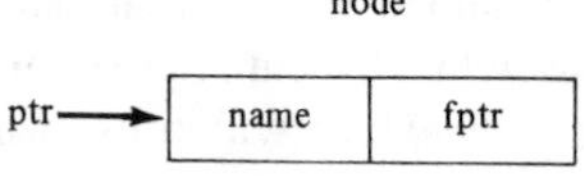

shows that a node in a linked list is identified by variables of type "ptr," and consists of two parts, a name and a fptr, which is an address and serves as a *link* to the next entry in the list. The special value NULL is the designation that a pointer points nowhere. Assuming the above declarations, we may declare variables "head," "p," and "q" to point to structures of type node as follows:

```
struct node *head, *p, *q;
```

Pointer manipulation in C is facilitated by the fact that an integer may be added to or subtracted from an address.Thus, displacements within a character string (or, for that matter, within any array) may be calculated directly. However, the particular method by which blocks of storage are dynamically procured and released by a C program depends upon the operating system and hardware environment.

12-3 APPLICATIONS OF C

Now that we have developed a working knowledge of C, we present and discuss a C solution to Case Study 3—Text Formatter. Following that we will introduce major implementation dependent extensions of C, especially those found in the UNIX environment. This chapter concludes with an overall evaluation of C, using this case study and the evaluation criteria discussed in Chapter 1.

12-3.1 C Case Study Implementation

Case Study 3—Text Formatter was implemented as a main program and four principal functions (''ctls,'' ''readtxt,'' ''movetxt,'' and ''justify''). These are shown in Figures 12-8 through 12-12. All functions use the auxiliary functions ''-index,'' ''-strmcmp,'' and ''-strcmp,'' which are also defined in the main program.

```
#include <stdio.h>          /* Case Study 3 -- Text Formatter in C  */
#define MAXWIDTH 120
#define MAXLINES 60
struct formatcontrols {
      int width;
      int lines;
      int tabs;
      char heading;
      int spacing;
      int breaksent;
} fctls;
int p1, p2, eofsw, error; char head[40];
char textin[(MAXWIDTH+1)*(MAXLINES+1)];
char textout[MAXLINES+1][MAXWIDTH+1];
FILE *fopen(), *text; char *strcpy();

main()
{     int i, j;

      p1=1; p2=0; eofsw=0; error=0;
      ctls();
      if (error>0) {
           fprintf(stderr, "*** format control error ***");
           return(-1);
      }
      text = fopen("case3.dat","r");
      strcpy(&head," "); strcpy(&textin," ");
      while (eofsw==0 && p1>=p2) {
           readtxt(); if (error) return(-1);   /* fill input buffer     */
           movetxt(); if (error) return(-1);   /* move to output buffer */
           justify(); if (error) return(-1);   /* right justify text    */
           for (i=1; i<=fctls.lines; i++)  {   /* display a page        */
               for (j=1; j<fctls.tabs && textout[i][j]=='\0'; j++)
                   textout[i][j] = ' ';         /* erase leading NULLs   */
               printf("%s\n",textout[i]+1);
           }
      }
      fclose(text);
      return(1);
}

int _index(s,t)              /* return the index of string t in string s */
char s[], t[];               /* or -1 if t does not occur in s */
{     int i, j, k;
      for (i=0; s[i] != '\0'; i++) {
          for (j=i, k=0; t[k]!='\0' && s[j]==t[k]; j++, k++) ;
          if (t[k]=='\0') return(i);
      }
      return(-1);
}
int _strncmp(s,t,n)        /* compare s and t for exactly n   */
char s[], t[];             /* characters, and return 0 only   */
int n;                     /* if they are identical.          */
{     int i;
      for (i=0; i<=n; i++)
          if (s[i]!=t[i]) return(-1);
      return(0);
}
```

FIGURE 12-8

```
int _strcmp(s,t)          /* compare strings s and t; if unequal   */
char s[], t[];        /* length return 0 if the tail of the      */
{                     /* longer one is all blanks and the rest   */
    int i, j;         /* is identical with the shorter one.      */
    for (i=0; s[i]==t[i] && s[i]!='\0' && t[i]!='\0'; i++) ;
    if (s[i]!=t[i]) return(s[i]-t[i]);
    if (s[i]=='\0') {       /* s is less or equal in length to t */
       if (t[i]=='\0') return(0);
       else {
          for (j=i+1; t[j]!='\0' && t[j]==' '; j++) ;
          if (t[j]=='\0') return(0);
          else return(-1);
       }
    }
    else {                  /* t is shorter than s */
       for (j=i+1; s[j]!='\0' && s[j]==' '; j++) ;
       if (s[j]=='\0') return(0);
       else return(-1);
    }
}
```

FIGURE 12-8 (*Continued*)

```
#include <stdio.h>
#define BUFSIZE 81
extern struct formatcontrols {
        int width;
        int lines;
        int tabs;
        char heading;
        int spacing;
        int breaksent;
} fctls;
extern int eofsw, error;
FILE *fopen(), *cntrols;
char ctlrec[BUFSIZE];

ctls()
{
static int dupecheck[6] = {0,0,0,0,0,0}, i;

fctls.width=80;        /* default format control values */
fctls.lines=60;
fctls.tabs=5;
fctls.heading='C';
fctls.spacing=1;
fctls.breaksent=0;
cntrols = fopen("controls","r");
while (fgets(ctlrec,BUFSIZE,cntrols) > 0 && error == 0) {
        if ((i=_index(ctlrec,"WIDTH=")) >= 0) {
                if (dupecheck[0]!=0) error=1;
                dupecheck[0]=1;
                i+=6;
                fctls.width=atoi(ctlrec+i);
                if (fctls.width<40 || fctls.width>120) error=1;
        }
        if ((i=_index(ctlrec,"LINES=")) >= 0) {
                if (dupecheck[1]!=0) error=1;
                dupecheck[1]=1;
                i+=6;
                fctls.lines=atoi(ctlrec+i);
                if (fctls.lines<20 || fctls.lines>60) error=1;
        }
```

FIGURE 12-9

```
        if ((i=_index(ctlrec,"TABS=")) >= 0) {
                if (dupecheck[2]!=0) error=1;
                dupecheck[2]=1;
                i+=5;
                fctls.tabs=atoi(ctlrec+i);
                if (fctls.tabs<1 || fctls.tabs>20) error=1;
        }
        if ((i=_index(ctlrec,"HEADING=")) >= 0) {
                if (dupecheck[3]!=0) error=1;
                dupecheck[3]=1;
                i+=8;
                if (ctlrec[i]=='L' || ctlrec[i]=='C' || ctlrec[i]=='R')
                        fctls.heading=ctlrec[i];
                else error=1;
        }
        if ((i=_index(ctlrec,"SPACING=")) >= 0) {
                if (dupecheck[4]!=0) error=1;
                dupecheck[4]=1;
                i+=8;
                if (ctlrec[i]=='1' || ctlrec[i]=='2' || ctlrec[i]=='3')
                        fctls.spacing=atoi(ctlrec+i);
                else error=1;
        }
        if ((i=_index(ctlrec,"BREAK=")) >= 0) {
                if (dupecheck[5]!=0) error=1;
                dupecheck[5]=1;
                i+=6;
                if (ctlrec[i]=='1' || ctlrec[i]=='2' || ctlrec[i]=='3')
                        fctls.breaksent=atoi(ctlrec+i);
                else error=1;
        }
      }
fclose(cntrols);
return;
}
```

FIGURE 12-9 *(Continued)*

These programs share the format controls stored in the external structure "fctls," the external buffers "textin" and "textout," and certain other control fields. The maximum sizes of the variables "fctls.width" and "fctls.lines" are used to define the sizes of these buffers.

The function ctls reads and sets all format controls, either as directed explicitly by the user or by default. It also edits those user-specified controls for validity and returns the "error" value -1 if one is invalid. The remainder of ctls is self-explanatory.

The function readtxt fills the buffer "textin" from the input file "text." When text becomes empty, readtxt sets the external switch "eofsw." Upon exit from readtxt, the pointers p1 and p2 indicate the extent of the currently available textin.

The function movetxt moves text from textin to textout according to the format controls. During this process, movetxt must prevent a single word from being split between two lines, properly handle headings and the beginning of new paragraphs, and prevent a sentence or paragraph from being split between two pages (as dictated by the "fctls.break" format control).

The main loop here is repeated once for each line of text moved to textout from

```
#include <stdio.h>
#define BUFSIZE 81
extern char textin[];
extern char head[];
extern struct formatcontrols {
     int width;
     int lines;
     int tabs;
     char heading;
     int spacing;
     int breaksent;
} fctls;
extern FILE *text;
extern int error, eofsw, p1, p2;

readtxt()         /* This function refills the buffer 'textin' */
{                 /* and sets 'eofsw' when end of file occurs   */
     static struct {
          char indata[71];
          char spare[10];
     } inrec;
     char *strcpy();
     int i, k, nsb;

     if (p1>1) {
        strcpy (&textin[1], &textin[p1]);   /* shift active text    */
        p2 = p2 - p1 + 1;                  /* forward in 'textin'  */
        p1 = 1;
     }
     while (p2+70<=fctls.width*fctls.lines
            && fgets(inrec.indata,BUFSIZE,text) >0) {
        if (_strcmp(inrec.indata," ")==0) continue;  /* skip blank lines */
        nsb = 0;                /* nsb is # of nonsignificant blanks */
        inrec.indata[70] = NULL;
        for (i=0; i<=68 && _strcmp(inrec.indata+i," ")!=0; i++)
            while (strncmp(inrec.indata+i,"  ",2)==0) {
               strcpy(&(inrec.indata[i]), &(inrec.indata[i+1]));
               nsb=nsb+1;
            }
        if (inrec.indata==' ')
           if (p2==0) k=1;
           else if (textin[p2]==' ') k=1;
                else k=0;
        else k=0;
        strcpy(&(textin[p2+1]),&(inrec.indata[k]));
        p2 += strlen(inrec.indata+k);
     }
     if (p2<=0) eofsw = 1;
     return;
}
```

FIGURE 12-10

textin. Once that loop completes, there is a final check that an impermissible break has not been made at the end of the page. If one has been made, then the beginning of the incorrectly unended sentence or paragraph is deleted from textout, and the pointer p1 is adjusted for textin accordingly.

The function justify performs right-justification of the page image in textout. Textout is then displayed as a complete page by the main program.

Note also the following two special tasks of the function readtxt. First, it deletes superfluous blanks from the input text as it reads. Second, it shifts the remainder of textin

```
#include <stdio.h>
#define MAXWIDTH 120
#define MAXLINES 60
extern struct formatcontrols {
       int width;
       int lines;
       int tabs;
       char heading;
       int spacing;
       int breaksent;
} fctls;
extern int error, eofsw, p1, p2;
extern char head[];
extern char textin[];
extern char textout[MAXLINES+1][MAXWIDTH+1];

movetxt()              /* this function moves text from 'textin' */
{                      /* to  a series of lines in 'textout', in */
     int ns, np = 0; /* accordance with formatting constraints */
     static int pno = 0;
     int i, j, k, kk, l, lp, lp1, lps, lpos;
     static char hold[MAXWIDTH+2] = " ";
     char *strcpy(),*sprintf(),*strncpy();

     for (i=0; i<=fctls.lines; i++)                /* initialization */
         strncpy(textout[i],"",fctls.width+1);
     pno++;
     if (strncmp(textin+p1,")H",2) == 0)  /* check for heading */
        if ((j=_index(textin+p1+2,")H")) < 0) return(error=1);
        else if (j>=40) return(error=1);
             else {
                  strncpy(head+1,textin+p1+2,j-1);
                  head[j]='\0';
                  p1 += j+3;
             }
     if (_strcmp(head+1,"")!=0)
       if (fctls.heading=='L')
         strcpy(&(textout[1][1]),&(head[1]));
       else if (fctls.heading=='C')
         strcpy(&(textout[1][(int)(fctls.width-strlen(head+1))/2]),&(head[1]));
         else strcpy(&(textout[1][fctls.width-strlen(head+1)+1]),&(head[1]));
     sprintf(&(textout[2][1]),"PAGE %3d",pno);

     /* now move the text itself to the output buffer 'textout' */
     if (fctls.spacing==2) kk=2; else kk=1;
     for (l=4; l<=fctls.lines && p2>=p1; l+=kk) {
         while (textin[p1]==' ' && p2>=p1) p1++; /* find 1st nonblank */
         if (p2<p1) break;                     /* exit if past end of text */
         if ((i=p2-p1+1) < fctls.width)
             {strncpy(hold+1,textin+p1,i); hold[i+1] = '\0';}
         else {
              strncpy(hold+1,textin+p1,fctls.width);
              hold[fctls.width+1] = '\0';
         }
         if ((i=_index(hold+1,")H")) >= 0) {
            strncpy(textout[l]+1,hold+1,i);
            p1+=i-1;
            return;
         }
         if ((i=_index(hold+1,")P")) < 0) {        /* no new paragraph */
             strcpy(&(textout[l][1]),&(hold[1]));
             p1 += strlen(hold+1);
         }
```

FIGURE 12-11

```
          else if (i==0) {                          /* new paragraph in pos 1 */
                  if (strlen(hold+1)<=fctls.width-fctls.tabs+3)
                       k = strlen(hold+1);
                  else k = strlen(hold+1)-fctls.tabs+4;
                  strcpy(&(textout[l][fctls.tabs]),&(hold[4]));
                  textout[l][fctls.width+1]='\0';
                  p1 += k;
               }
               else {  np++;                        /* new paragraph past pos 1 */
                  lp = l;
                  strncpy(textout[l]+1,hold+1,i-1);
                  p1 += i-1;
                  lp1 = p1-1;
                  if (fctls.spacing==3) l++;
               }
          /* adjust for possible word break at end of line */
          if (textout[l][fctls.width]!=' ' && p1<=p2 && textin[p1]!=' ') {
               for (i=fctls.width; textout[l][i]!=' ' && i>0; i--)
                  textout[l][i] = '\0';
               p1 = p1 - fctls.width + i;
          }
          /* count no of sentences 'ns' ended this line */
          for (i=1; i<=fctls.width-1; i++) {
               if (_strcmp(textout[l]+i,". ")==0 ||
                  _strcmp(textout[l]+i,"! ")==0 ||
                  _strcmp(textout[l]+i,"? ")==0) {
                 ns++; lps = l;             /* line no of sentence end */
                 lpos = i+1;                /* position on the line    */
               }
          }
     }
     /* now clean up possible illegal end of page break */
     if (fctls.breaksent==0 || fctls.breaksent>=1 && ns==0 ||
          fctls.breaksent==2 && np==0)   return(error=0);
     if (fctls.breaksent==2 && strncmp(textin+p1,")P",2)!=0 && eofsw==0) {
          p1 = lp1;             /* backtrack to beginning of paragraph */
          for (i=lp+kk; i<=fctls.lines; i+=kk) strcpy(&(textout[i])," ");
          return(error=0);
     }
     if (fctls.breaksent>=1 && strncmp(textin+p1-2,". ",2)!=0
        && strncmp(textin+p1-2,"! ",2)!=0
        && strncmp(textin+p1-2,"? ",2)!=0) {
          if (lpos<fctls.width) strcpy(&(textout[lps][lpos+1])," ");
          for (i=lps+kk; i<=fctls.lines; i++) strcpy(&(textout[i])," ");
          while (p1>=1 && strncmp(textin+p1,". ",2)!=0
                       && strncmp(textin+p1,"! ",2)!=0
                       && strncmp(textin+p1,"? ",2)!=0) p1--;
          if (p1>=1) { p1 += 2; return(error=0); }
          else return(error=1);
     }
}
```

FIGURE 12-11 *(Continued)*

(that was not moved to textout for the previous page) forward to the beginning of textin, and adjusts p1 and p2 accordingly.

The program was run on the computers and compilers shown in Figure 5-13. As input, a text of ninety-six records (partly shown in Appendix F) was used. The efficiency of C for this case study is shown in Figure 12-13.

```
#include <stdio.h>
#define MAXWIDTH 120
#define MAXLINES 60
extern struct formatcontrols {
        int width;
        int lines;
        int tabs;
        char heading;
        int spacing;
        int breaksent;
} fctls;
extern int error, eofsw, p1, p2;
extern char textout[MAXLINES+1][MAXWIDTH+1];
static char blanks[MAXWIDTH+1];

justify()                /* this function performs right margin  */
{                        /* justification of the text 'textout'  */
      int i, j, k, l, nw, ns;

      /* initialize comparison string to NULLs */
      for (i=0; i<=fctls.width; i++) blanks[i]='\0';

      for (l=4; l<=fctls.lines && lastline(l-1)==0; l++) {
          if (_strncmp(textout[l]+1,blanks,fctls.width)==0
              || lastline(l)>0 || endpar(l)>0) continue;
          nw = 0;        /* no of words on line          */
          ns = 0;        /* no of righthand spaces on line */
          for (i=fctls.width;
              i>=1 && _strncmp(textout[l]+1,blanks,i)!=0; i--)
              if (textout[l][i]=='\0' || textout[l][i]==' ')
                 if (nw==0) ns++;
                 else nw++;
              else if (nw==0) nw = 1;
          if (ns==0 || nw==1) continue;   /* cant justify this line */
          for (j=1; ns>0; j++)
              for (i=fctls.width-ns;
                   i>=1 && ns>0 && _strncmp(textout[l]+1,blanks,i)!=0; i--)
                  if (textout[l][i]==' ') {
                     for (k=fctls.width; k>=i+1; k--)
                         textout[l][k] = textout[l][k-1];
                     textout[l][i] = ' ';
                     ns--;
                  }
      }
}
lastline(l)         /* determine whether line l is the last */
int l;              /* nonblank line in 'textout'          */
{     int i;
      for (i=l+1; i<=fctls.lines
            && _strncmp(textout[i]+1,blanks,fctls.width)==0; i++) ;
      if (i>fctls.lines) return(1);
      else return(0);
}
endpar(l)           /* determine whether line l is the end  */
int l;              /* of a paragraph in 'textout'         */
{     int k;
      if (l==fctls.lines) return(0);
      else if (l==fctls.lines-1
              && (_strncmp(textout[l+1]+1,blanks,fctls.width)==0
                 || textout[l+1][1]=='\0')) return(0);
           else {
              if (_strncmp(textout[l+1]+1,blanks,fctls.width)==0) k=l+2;
              else k = l+1;
              if (_strncmp(textout[k]+1,blanks,fctls.width)==0
                  || textout[k][1]!='\0') return(0);
              else return(1);
           }
}
```

FIGURE 12-12

FIGURE 12-13
EFFICIENCY OF C CASE STUDY 5 PROGRAM

Implementation	Compile speed	Execution speed
1 Digital VAX750/UNIX C	48.7 sec	13.6 sec
2 IBM PC/DOS AZTEC C	242.8 sec	129.6 sec

12-3.2 Implementation Dependent Extensions of C

Since the principal implementation of C is within the UNIX operating system, its principal extensions are those provided under UNIX.

File I/O under UNIX provides a number of functions, including random access functions, for the programmer to retrieve and manipulate data in files. Moreover, since file *directories* are also files in UNIX, these may be accessed also from within a C program. Dynamic storage allocation is provided under UNIX by way of the function ''sbrk.'' Moreover, there is a way to pass command-line arguments to the main program at the outset of execution, as if the main program were itself a function with parameters.

12-3.3 Overall Evaluation of C

From our case study experience, we evaluate C using the nine criteria of Chapter 1 as follows:

1 Expressivity	Good
2 Well-definedness	Excellent
3 Data types and structures	Good
4 Modularity	Excellent
5 Input-output facilities	Good
6 Portability	Excellent
7 Efficiency	Excellent
8 Pedagogy	Fair
9 Generality	Good

C's excellent ''well-definedness,'' ''modularity,'' ''portability,'' and ''efficiency'' stem mainly from the simplicity of its design and the widespread use of its host operating system, UNIX. Modularity is strongly supported by independent compilation of functions, while efficiency is encouraged by its variety of ''low-level'' data types and operators. Weak typing also contributes to C's efficiency, but at the same time detracts from its ''pedagogy.''

We find at this writing a serious shortage of good texts on C programming, as well as on UNIX itself. C's pedagogy promises to improve, however, with its recent implementations on microcomputers and more widespread use in different areas of systems programming. The main reason for C's good generality is its availability of extensive library functions, in the areas of mathematical programming, file processing, and text processing, as well as in its native area of systems programming.

EXERCISES

1 Let x, y, and z be **float** variables, and let i, j, and k be **int** variables. Assume that they have the following values.

x = 2.5	i = 1
y = −10	j = −5
z = 8	k = 12

Compute the result delivered by evaluating each of the following expressionsz:

(a) x + y * z	**(e)** i − 1
(b) (x + y) * z	**(f)** i && j * k
(c) (x + y)/z − 3	**(g)** i/j * k
(d) x + y/(z − 3)	**(h)** 4 * i ? k : j

2 Suppose we have a 5 × 5 array A of **float** values. The "Trace" of A is defined as the sum of its diagonal elements.
(a) Write a declaration for A.
(b) Write an input statement which will store these values in A, assuming they are typed row by row as input lines.
(c) Write a **for** loop which will compute the Trace of A.
(d) Write another **for** loop which will leave the maximum value from A in the **float** variable named "Amaxim," and leave that value's row and column numbers in the **int** variables named "Arow" and "Acol."

3 Write a function "Trace" which will return the trace of any n × n **float** array A.

4 Rewrite the function of Exercise 3 so that the result is returned as a call by reference parameter.

5 If your installation has a different C compiler than the ones used here, adapt our C Case Study 3 implementation to run under that compiler. How difficult was that adaptation?

6 Implement Case Study 4—Missionaries and Cannibals in C. Evaluate C as an AI programming language from this experience.

7 Implement Case Study 0 (which you defined at the end of Chapter 1) in C. Evaluate C's performance and suitability for this application.

8 Consider implementing Case Study 2—Employee File Maintenance in C. What are C's strengths for data processing applications such as this? What are its weaknesses?

9 Consider implementing Case Study 5—Job Scheduler in C. Evaluate C as a systems programming language on this basis.

10 Write a C program that counts the number of words in a text that end with "ing" or "ed" and displays that count. Your program should also accommodate punctuation marks in a reasonable way. For example, if the text is as follows:

> As the bells were ringing, we sped out of town.

your count should be 2.

11 Write a C function named SUBSTR which emulates the behavior of the PL/I function with the same name. That is, for a given string parameter S and integer parameters I and J, the function should return that substring in S beginning at position I and having length J. If I and J do not define a proper substring of S, then the result returned should be the empty string.

12 The FORTRAN EQUIVALENCE statement allows two variables to share the same storage area at run time. How can this be accomplished in C?

REFERENCES

1 S. C. Johnson and B. W. Kernighan, *The Programming Language B,* Computer Science Tech. Rep. No. 8, Bell Laboratories, Murray Hill, N.J., January 1973.

2 M. Richards, ''BCPL: A Tool for Compiler Writing and Systems Programming,'' *Proc AFIPS SJCC* 34: 557–566 (1969).

3 D. M. Ritchie, et al., ''The C Programming Language,'' *Bell Systems Tech. J.* 57(6): 1991–2019 (August 1978).

4 B. W. Kernighan and D. M. Ritchie, *The C Programming Language,* Prentice-Hall, Englewood Cliffs, N.J., 1978.